Contents

II Key map Restricted motorway junctions

IV Route planner

MILES TO 45 ONE INCH

VI Legend Distance table

2 Road maps

MILES TO 4 ONE INCH

112 Orkney Isles and Shetland Isles at 7 miles to 1 inch

114 Town and city plans

MILE TO 1/5 ONE INCH

114 Aberdeen	116 Chester	118 Hull	150 Northampton	156 Stoke
124 Bath	116 Colchester	118 Ipswich	119 Norwich	120 Stratford-upon-Avon
122 Birmingham	128 Coventry	136 Leeds	130 Nottingham	148 Sunderland
114 Blackpool	116 Croydon	128 Leicester	119 Oxford	120 Swansea
115 Bournemouth	130 Derby	118 Lincoln	151 Plymouth	121 Torquay
136 Bradford	117 Dundee	138 Liverpool	154 Portsmouth	154 Winchester
115 Brighton	117 Durham	144 London streets	119 Reading	121 Windsor
124 Bristol	132 Edinburgh	146 Manchester	119 Salisbury	121 Worcester
115 Cambridge	117 Exeter	118 Middlesbrough	120 Scarborough	121 York
115 Canterbury	134 Glasgow	150 Milton Keynes	152 Sheffield	
126 Cardiff	117 Gloucester	148 Newcastle upon Tyne	154 Southampton	
116 Cheltenham	156 Hanley		120 Southend	

114 Keys to town plan and approach mapping symbols

122 Urban approach maps

MILES TO 2 ONE INCH

122 Birmingham	130 Derby Nottingham	136 Leeds Bradford	148 Newcastle Sunderland	152 Sheffield
124 Bristol / Bath	132 Edinburgh	138 Liverpool	150 Northampton Milton Keynes	154 Southampton Portsmouth Winchester
126 Cardiff	134 Glasgow	140 London	151 Plymouth	156 Stoke-on-Trent
128 Coventry Leicester		146 Manchester		

157 Road maps of Ireland – at 10 miles to 1 inch

164 Town and city plans – Ireland

164 Belfast	164 Derry / Londonderry	164 Cork	164 Dublin

165 Index to road maps of Ireland

167 Index to road maps of Britain

First published in 1997 by George Philip Ltd
an imprint of Reed Books
Michelin House, 81 Fulham Road, London SW3 6RB
and Auckland, Melbourne

First edition 1997
First impression 1997

Information for Tourist Attractions in England supplied by the British Tourist Authority / English Tourist Board.

Information for National Parks, Areas of Outstanding Natural Beauty, National Trails and Country Parks in Wales supplied by the Countryside Council for Wales.

Information for National Parks, Areas of Outstanding Natural Beauty, National Trails and Country Parks in England supplied by the Countryside Commission.

Data for Regional Parks, Long Distance Footpaths and Country Parks in Scotland provided by Scottish Natural Heritage.

Gaelic name forms used in the Western Isles provided by Comhairle nan Eilean.

Cartography by Philip's

Printed and bound in Italy

GW00514867

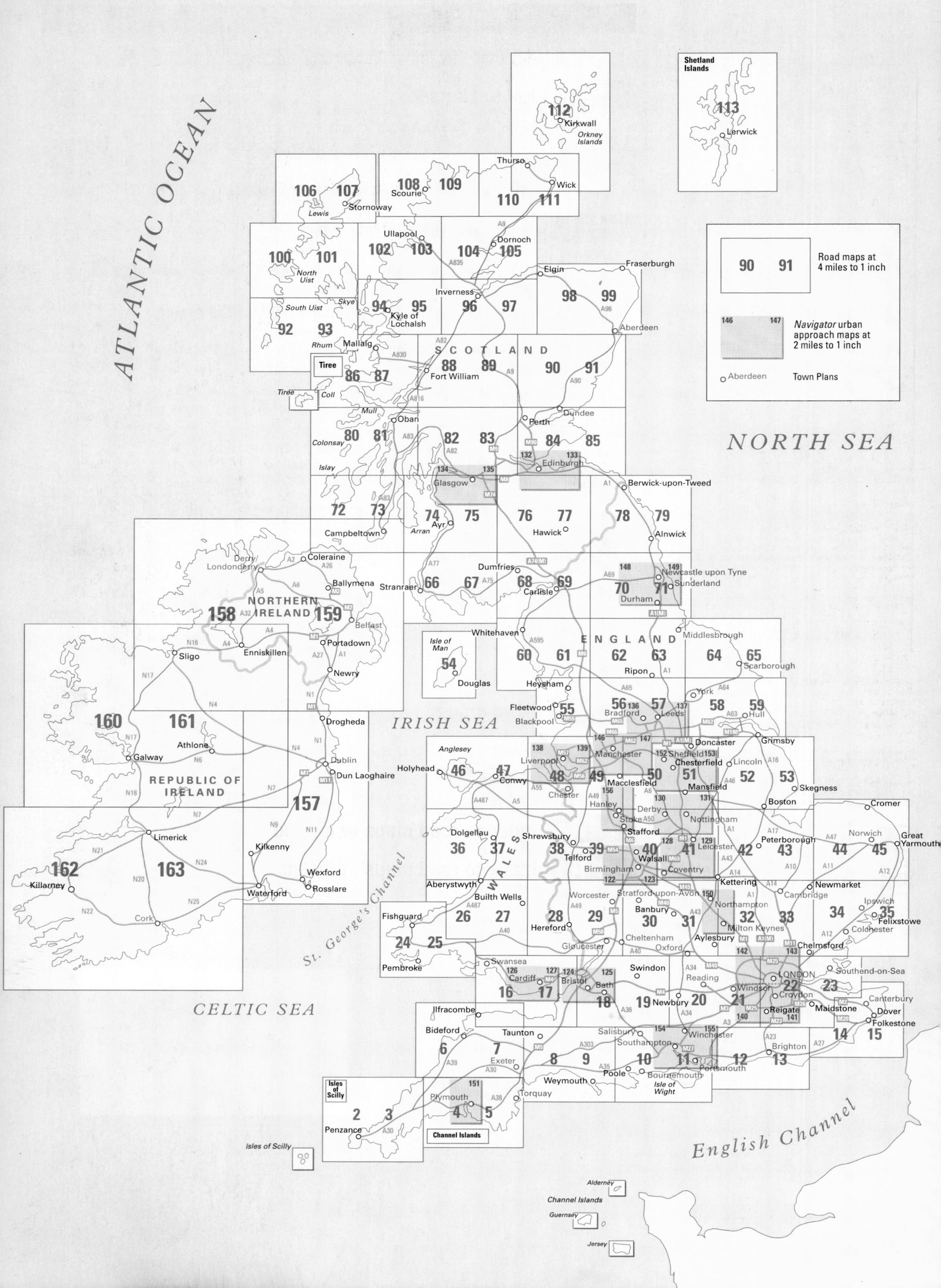
ATLANTIC OCEAN
NORTH SEA
IRISH SEA
CELTIC SEA
St. George's Channel
English Channel
SCOTLAND
ENGLAND
WALES
NORTHERN IRELAND
REPUBLIC OF IRELAND
Shetland Islands
Orkney Islands
Isle of Man
Isles of Scilly
Channel Islands
Road maps at 4 miles to 1 inch
Navigator urban approach maps at 2 miles to 1 inch
Aberdeen Town Plans
112 Kirkwall
113 Lerwick
Thurso
Wick
Stornoway
Scourie
Lewis
North Uist
South Uist
Skye
Rhum
Tiree
Coll
Mull
Colonsay
Islay
Arran
Ullapool
Dornoch
Elgin
Fraserburgh
Inverness
Kyle of Lochalsh
Aberdeen
Mallaig
Fort William
Oban
Perth
Dundee
Edinburgh
Glasgow
Ayr
Campbeltown
Berwick-upon-Tweed
Hawick
Alnwick
Dumfries
Stranraer
Carlisle
Newcastle upon Tyne
Sunderland
Durham
Middlesbrough
Whitehaven
Douglas
Heysham
Ripon
Scarborough
York
Fleetwood
Blackpool
Bradford
Leeds
Hull
Grimsby
Doncaster
Liverpool
Manchester
Sheffield
Chesterfield
Lincoln
Skegness
Anglesey
Holyhead
Conwy
Chester
Macclesfield
Mansfield
Hanley
Stoke
Derby
Nottingham
Boston
Cromer
Norwich
Great Yarmouth
Dolgellau
Shrewsbury
Telford
Stafford
Walsall
Leicester
Peterborough
Birmingham
Coventry
Kettering
Aberystwyth
Builth Wells
Worcester
Stratford-upon-Avon
Northampton
Cambridge
Newmarket
Ipswich
Felixstowe
Colchester
Fishguard
Hereford
Banbury
Milton Keynes
Cheltenham
Gloucester
Oxford
Aylesbury
Chelmsford
Pembroke
Swansea
Cardiff
Bristol
Bath
Swindon
Reading
Windsor
LONDON
Southend-on-Sea
Croydon
Canterbury
Newbury
Reigate
Maidstone
Dover
Folkestone
Ilfracombe
Bideford
Taunton
Salisbury
Southampton
Winchester
Brighton
Exeter
Weymouth
Poole
Bournemouth
Portsmouth
Isle of Wight
Torquay
Plymouth
Penzance
Alderney
Guernsey
Jersey
Derry/Londonderry
Coleraine
Ballymena
Belfast
Enniskillen
Portadown
Newry
Sligo
Drogheda
Athlone
Galway
Dublin
Dun Laoghaire
Limerick
Kilkenny
Wexford
Rosslare
Waterford
Killarney
Cork

M1

	Northbound	Southbound
2	No exit	No access
4	No exit	No access
6a	No exit	No access
	Access from M25 only	Exit to M25 only
7	No exit	No access
	Access from M10 only	Exit to M10 only
17	No access	No exit
	Exit to M45 only	Access from M45 only
19	No exit to A14	No access from A14
21a	No access	No exit
23a		Exit to A42 only
35a	No access	No exit
44	No exit	No access
45	No access	No exit
46		No access
47	No access	No exit or access

M2

	Eastbound	Westbound
1	Access from A2 eastbound only	Exit to A2 westbound only

M3

	Eastbound	Westbound
8	No exit	No access
10	No access	No exit
13		No access to M27 eastbound
14	No exit	No access

M4

	Eastbound	Westbound
1	Exit to A4 eastbound only	Access from A4 westbound only
2	Access to A4 eastbound only	Access to A4 westbound only
21	No exit	No access
23	No access	No exit
25	No exit	No access
25a	No exit	No access
29	No exit	No access
38		No access
39	No exit or access	No exit
41	No access	No exit
41a	No exit	No access
42		Exit to A483 only
46	No exit	No access

M5

	Northbound	Southbound
10	No exit	No access
11a	No access from A417 eastbound	No exit to A417 westbound
12	No access	No exit
29	No access	No exit

M6

	Northbound	Southbound
4a	No exit	No access
	Access from M42 southbnd only	Exit to M42 only
5	No access	No exit
10a	No access	No exit
	Exit to M54 only	Access from M54 only
20	No exit to M56 eastbound	No access from M56 westbound
24	No exit	No access
25	No access	No exit
30	No exit	No access
	Access from M61 nthbnd only	Exit to M61 southbound
31a	No access	No exit

M8

	Eastbound	Westbound
3	Exit to A899 southbound only	Exit to A899 southbound only
	Access from A899 nthbnd only	Access from A899 northbnd only
8	No exit to M73 northbound	No access from M73 southbound
9	No access	No exit
14	No access	No exit
16	No exit	No access
17	No exit	No access
18		No exit
19	Exit to A814 westbound only	Access from A814 eastbound only
20	No exit	No access
21	No access	No exit
22	No exit	No access
	Access from M77 only	Exit to M77 only
23	No exit	No access
25	Exit to A739 southbound only	Exit to A739 northbound only
	Access from A739 southbnd only	Access from A739 southbnd only
28	No exit	No access

M9

	Eastbound	Westbound
1	No exit	No access
2	No access	No exit
3	No exit	No access
6	No access	No exit
8	No exit	No access

M11

	Northbound	Southbound
4	No exit	No access
5	No access	No exit
9	No access	No exit
13	No access	No exit
14	No exit to A428 westbound	No exit
		Access from A14 westbound only

M20

	Eastbound	Westbound
2	No access	No exit
3	No exit	No access
	Access from M26 eastbound only	Exit to M26 westbound only
11a	No access	No exit

M23

	Northbound	Southbound
7	No exit to A23 southbound	No access from A23 northbound

M25

	Clockwise	Anticlockwise
5	No exit to M26 eastbound	No access from M26 westbound
19	No access	No exit
21	No exit to M1 southbound	No exit to M1 southbound
	Access from M1 southbound only	Access from M1 southbound only
31	No exit	No access

M27

	Eastbound	Westbound
10	No exit	No access
12	No access	No exit

M40

	Eastbound	Westbound
3	No exit	No access
7	No exit	No access
13	No exit	No access
14	No access	No exit
16	No access	No exit

M42

	Northbound	Southbound
1	No exit	No access
7	No access	No exit
	Exit to M6 northbound only	Access from M6 northbound only
7a	No access	No exit
	Exit to M6 only	Access from M6 northbound only
8	No exit	Exit to M6 northbound
	Access from M6 southbnd only	Access from M6 southbound only

M45

	Eastbound	Westbound
Junction with M1		
	Access to M1 southbound only	No access from M1 southbound
Junction with A45 (Dunchurch)		
	No access	No exit

M53

	Northbound	Southbound
11	Exit to M56 eastbound only	Exit to M56 eastbound only
	Access from M56 westbnd only	Access from M56 westbound only

M56

	Eastbound	Westbound
1	No exit to M63 westbound	No access from M63 eastbound
	No exit to A34 southbound	No access from A34 northbound
2	No exit	No access
4	No exit	No access
7		No access
8	No exit or access	No exit
9	No access from M6 northbound	No access to M6 southbound
15	No exit to M53	No access from M53 northbound

M57

	Northbound	Southbound
3	No exit	No access
5	No exit	No access

M58

	Eastbound	Westbound
1	No exit	No access

M61

	Northbound	Southbound
2	No access from A580 eastbound	No exit from A580 westbound
3	No access from A580 eastbound	No exit from A580 westbound
9	No access	No exit
Junction with M6 junction 30		
	No exit to M6 southbound	No access from M6 northbound

M62

	Eastbound	Westbound
14	No exit to A580	No exit to A580 eastbound
	No access from A580 westbound	No access from A580
15	No exit	No access
23	No access	No exit

M63

	Eastbound	Westbound
7	No exit (Exit from Junc 6 only)	No access (Access from Junc. 6 only)
9	No exit to A5103 northbound	No exit to A5103 southbound
	No access from A5103 northbnd	No access from A5103 southbound
10	No exit to M56 or A34 northbnd	No exit to A34 northbound
	No access from A34 southbound	No access from M56 or A34 sthbnd
11	No access	No exit
13	No access	No exit
14	No exit	No access
15		No exit or access

M65

	Eastbound	Westbound
9	No access	No exit
11	No exit	No access

M66

	Northbound	Southbound
1	No access	No exit
12	No exit	No access

M67

	Eastbound	Westbound
1	No access	No exit
2	No exit	No access

M69

	Northbound	Southbound
2	No exit	No access

M73

	Northbound	Southbound
2	No access from M8 or A89 estbnd	No exit to M8 or A89 westbound
	No exit to A89	No access from A89
3	Exit to A80 northbound only	Access from A80 southbnd only

M74

	Northbound	Southbound
2	No access	No exit
3	No exit	No access
7	No exit	No access
9	No exit or access	No access
10		No exit
11	No exit	No access
12	No access	No exit

M77

	Northbound	Southbound
4	No exit	No access
Junction with M8 junction 22		
	Exit to M8 eastbound only	Access from M8 westbound only

M80

	Northbound	Southbound
5	No access from M876	No exit to M876

M90

	Northbound	Southbound
7	No exit	No access
8	No access	No exit
10	No access from A912	No exit to A912

M180

	Eastbound	Westbound
1	No access	No exit

M876

	Northbound	Southbound
2	No access	No exit

A1(M)

	Northbound	Southbound
2	No access	No exit
3		No access
5	No exit	No access
57	No access	No exit
65	No access	No exit

A3(M)

	Northbound	Southbound
4	No access	No exit

A38(M)

	Northbound	Southbound
Junction with Victoria Road (Park Circus)		
	No exit	No access

A40(M)

	Eastbound	Westbound
Westway Junction at Royal Oak (A404)		
	No access	No exit
Junction at western end of Marylebone flyover (A404)		
	No exit	No access

A48(M)

	Northbound	Southbound
Junction with M4 Junction 29		
	Exit to M4 eastbound only	Access from M4 westbound only
29a	Access from A48 eastbound only	Exit to A48 westbound only

A57(M)

	Eastbound	Westbound
Junction with A5103		
	No access	No exit
Junction with A34		
	No access	No exit

A58(M)

	Southbound
Junction with Park Lane/Westgate	No access

A64(M)

	Eastbound	Westbound
Junction with A58 (Clay Pit Lane)		
	No access	No exit
Junction with Regent Street		
	No access	No access

A74(M)

	Northbound	Southbound
18	No access	No exit
19		No access
Junction with A75		
	No access from A75	No exit to A75 westbound

A102(M)

	Northbound
Blackwall Tunnel Southern approach Junction with A2203	
	No exit

A167(M)

	Northbound	Southbound
Newcastle Central Motorway Junction with Camden Street		
	No exit	No exit or access

A194(M)

	Northbound	Southbound
Junction with A1 and A1(M) Gateshead Western By-pass		
	Access from A1(M) northbound only	Exit to A1(M) southbound only

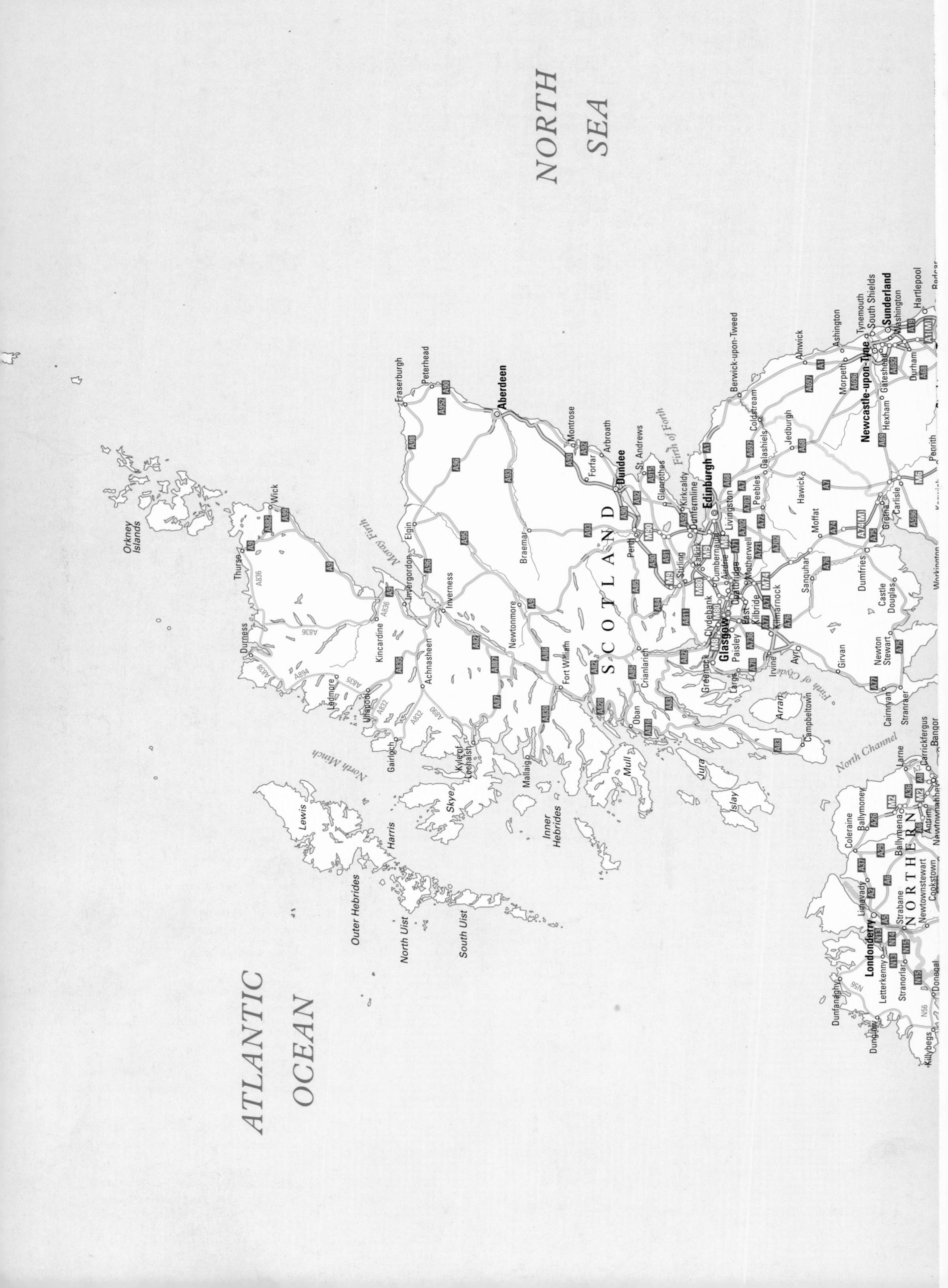
NORTH SEA
ATLANTIC OCEAN
SCOTLAND
NORTHERN
Orkney Islands
Outer Hebrides
Lewis
Harris
North Uist
South Uist
Skye
Inner Hebrides
Mull
Jura
Islay
Arran
North Minch
Moray Firth
Firth of Forth
Firth of Clyde
North Channel
Thurso
Wick
Durness
Kincardine
Ledmore
Ullapool
Gairloch
Achnasheen
Kyle of Lochalsh
Mallaig
Fort William
Invergordon
Inverness
Elgin
Newtonmore
Braemar
Fraserburgh
Peterhead
Aberdeen
Montrose
Arbroath
Forfar
Dundee
St. Andrews
Glenrothes
Kirkcaldy
Dunfermline
Perth
Stirling
Falkirk
Crianlarich
Oban
Edinburgh
Livingston
Cumbernauld
Airdrie
Coatbridge
Motherwell
Clydebank
Glasgow
Paisley
East Kilbride
Kilmarnock
Greenock
Largs
Irvine
Ayr
Campbeltown
Girvan
Cairnryan
Stranraer
Newton Stewart
Castle Douglas
Dumfries
Sanquhar
Moffat
Peebles
Galashiels
Jedburgh
Hawick
Coldstream
Berwick-upon-Tweed
Alnwick
Morpeth
Ashington
Tynemouth
South Shields
Newcastle-upon-Tyne
Gateshead
Sunderland
Washington
Durham
Hartlepool
Hexham
Carlisle
Gretna
Penrith
Workington
Larne
Carrickfergus
Bangor
Coleraine
Ballymoney
Ballymena
Antrim
Newtownabbey
Cookstown
Newtownstewart
Strabane
Limavady
Londonderry
Letterkenny
Stranorlar
Dunfanaghy
Dungloe
Donegal
Killybegs
A9
A836
A838
A894
A835
A832
A890
A882
A99
A96
A95
A98
A952
A90
A93
A92
A915
A82
A86
A87
A830
A85
A816
A83
A84
A811
M9
M90
M8
M80
M74
A71
A73
A77
A76
A78
A702
A703
A7
A68
A1
A697
A696
A692
A69
A19
A1(M)
A74(M)
A75
A701
M6
A595
A26
A29
A37
A2
A6
A5
M2
A8
A36
N13
N14
N15
N56

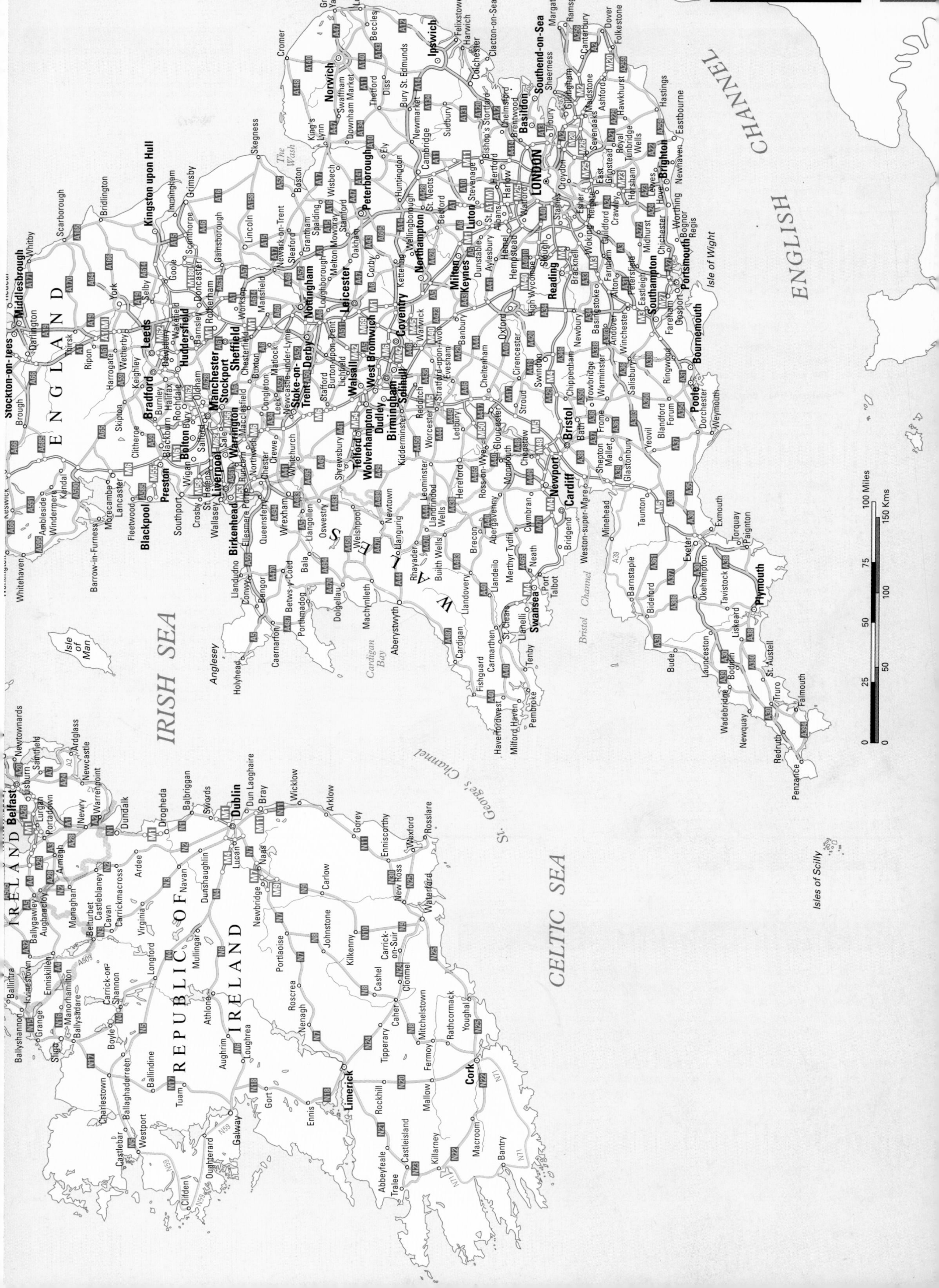
ENGLAND
WALES
REPUBLIC OF IRELAND
IRELAND
IRISH SEA
CELTIC SEA
ENGLISH CHANNEL
St. George's Channel
Bristol Channel
Cardigan Bay
The Wash
Isle of Man
Anglesey
Isle of Wight
Isles of Scilly
LONDON
Birmingham
Manchester
Liverpool
Leeds
Sheffield
Bristol
Cardiff
Swansea
Newport
Nottingham
Leicester
Coventry
Southampton
Portsmouth
Plymouth
Brighton
Norwich
Ipswich
Kingston upon Hull
Middlesbrough
Stockton-on-Tees
Dublin
Belfast
Cork
Limerick
Galway
Waterford
0 25 50 75 100 Miles
0 50 100 150 Kms

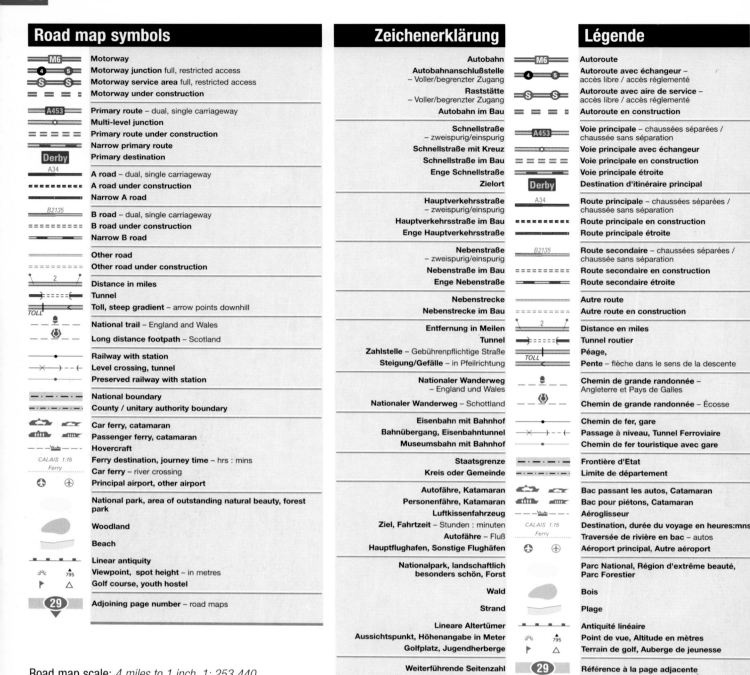

Road map symbols

- **Motorway**
- **Motorway junction** full, restricted access
- **Motorway service area** full, restricted access
- **Motorway under construction**

- **Primary route** – dual, single carriageway
- **Multi-level junction**
- **Primary route under construction**
- **Narrow primary route**
- **Primary destination**

- **A road** – dual, single carriageway
- **A road under construction**
- **Narrow A road**

- **B road** – dual, single carriageway
- **B road under construction**
- **Narrow B road**

- **Other road**
- **Other road under construction**

- **Distance in miles**
- **Tunnel**
- **Toll, steep gradient** – arrow points downhill

- **National trail** – England and Wales
- **Long distance footpath** – Scotland

- **Railway with station**
- **Level crossing, tunnel**
- **Preserved railway with station**

- **National boundary**
- **County / unitary authority boundary**

- **Car ferry, catamaran**
- **Passenger ferry, catamaran**
- **Hovercraft**
- **Ferry destination, journey time** – hrs : mins
- **Car ferry** – river crossing
- **Principal airport, other airport**

- **National park, area of outstanding natural beauty, forest park**
- **Woodland**
- **Beach**

- **Linear antiquity**
- **Viewpoint, spot height** – in metres
- **Golf course, youth hostel**

- **Adjoining page number** – road maps

Road map scale: *4 miles to 1 inch, 1: 253 440*

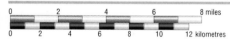

0 2 4 6 8 miles

0 2 4 6 8 10 12 kilometres

Zeichenerklärung

- **Autobahn**
- **Autobahnanschlußstelle** – Voller/begrenzter Zugang
- **Raststätte** – Voller/begrenzter Zugang
- **Autobahn im Bau**

- **Schnellstraße** – zweispurig/einspurig
- **Schnellstraße mit Kreuz**
- **Schnellstraße im Bau**
- **Enge Schnellstraße**
- **Zielort**

- **Hauptverkehrsstraße** – zweispurig/einspurig
- **Hauptverkehrsstraße im Bau**
- **Enge Hauptverkehrsstraße**

- **Nebenstraße** – zweispurig/einspurig
- **Nebenstraße im Bau**
- **Enge Nebenstraße**

- **Nebenstrecke**
- **Nebenstrecke im Bau**

- **Entfernung in Meilen**
- **Tunnel**
- **Zahlstelle** – Gebührenpflichtige Straße
- **Steigung/Gefälle** – in Pfeilrichtung

- **Nationaler Wanderweg** – England und Wales
- **Nationaler Wanderweg** – Schottland

- **Eisenbahn mit Bahnhof**
- **Bahnübergang, Eisenbahntunnel**
- **Museumsbahn mit Bahnhof**

- **Staatsgrenze**
- **Kreis oder Gemeinde**

- **Autofähre, Katamaran**
- **Personenfähre, Katamaran**
- **Luftkissenfahrzeug**
- **Ziel, Fahrtzeit** – Stunden : minuten
- **Autofähre** – Fluß
- **Hauptflughafen, Sonstige Flughäfen**

- **Nationalpark, landschaftlich besonders schön, Forst**
- **Wald**
- **Strand**

- **Lineare Altertümer**
- **Aussichtspunkt, Höhenangabe in Meter**
- **Golfplatz, Jugendherberge**

- **Weiterführende Seitenzahl**

Légende

- **Autoroute**
- **Autoroute avec échangeur** – accès libre / accès réglementé
- **Autoroute avec aire de service** – accès libre / accès réglementé
- **Autoroute en construction**

- **Voie principale** – chaussées séparées / chaussée sans séparation
- **Voie principale avec échangeur**
- **Voie principale en construction**
- **Voie principale étroite**
- **Destination d'itinéraire principal**

- **Route principale** – chaussées séparées / chaussée sans séparation
- **Route principale en construction**
- **Route principale étroite**

- **Route secondaire** – chaussées séparées / chaussée sans séparation
- **Route secondaire en construction**
- **Route secondaire étroite**

- **Autre route**
- **Autre route en construction**

- **Distance en miles**
- **Tunnel routier**
- **Péage,**
- **Pente** – flèche dans le sens de la descente

- **Chemin de grande randonnée** – Angleterre et Pays de Galles
- **Chemin de grande randonnée** – Écosse

- **Chemin de fer, gare**
- **Passage à niveau, Tunnel Ferroviaire**
- **Chemin de fer touristique avec gare**

- **Frontière d'Etat**
- **Limite de département**

- **Bac passant les autos, Catamaran**
- **Bac pour piétons, Catamaran**
- **Aéroglisseur**
- **Destination, durée du voyage en heures:mns**
- **Traversée de rivière en bac** – autos
- **Aéroport principal, Autre aéroport**

- **Parc National, Région d'extrême beauté, Parc Forestier**
- **Bois**
- **Plage**

- **Antiquité linéaire**
- **Point de vue, Altitude en mètres**
- **Terrain de golf, Auberge de jeunesse**

- **Référence à la page adjacente**

Route-finding system

This atlas incorporates a special route-finding system. The town names printed in yellow on a green background are those used on Britain's signposts to indicate primary destinations.

To find your route quickly and easily when driving, simply follow the signs to the primary destination immediately beyond the town or village you require.

Right Driving from Maidenhead to Marlow, follow the signposts to High Wycombe, the first primary destination beyond Marlow. These will indicate the most direct main route to the side turning for Marlow.

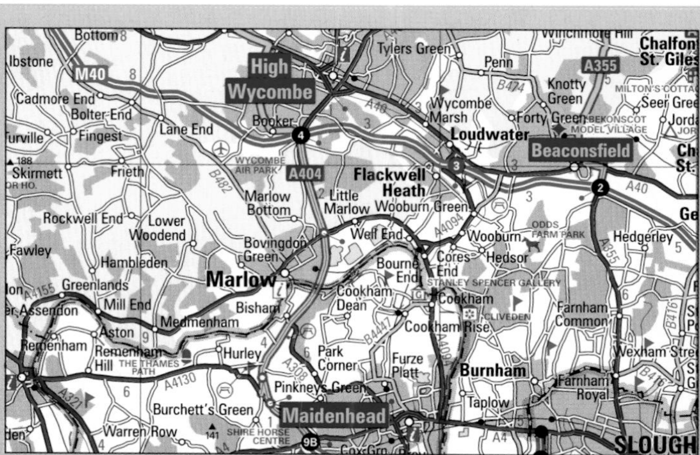

Tourist information

- **Abbey/Cathedral/Priory**
  Abbaye, Cathédrale, Prieuré
  Abtei, Kathedrale, Priorei
- **Ancient Monument**
  Monument historique
  Kulturdenkmal
- **Aquarium**
  Aquarium
  Aquarium
- **Art Gallery**
  Gallerie d'Art
  Kunstgalerie
- **Bird Collection/Aviary**
  Volière
  Vogelsammlung/Aviarium
- **Castle**
  Château
  Schloß, Burg
- **Church**
  Église
  Kirche
- **Country Park (England & Wales)**
  Parc de Loisirs (Angleterrre et Pays de Galles)
  Landschaftspark (England und Wales)
- **Country Park (Scotland)**
  Parc de Loisirs (Écosse)
  Landschaftspark (Schottland)
- **Farm Park**
  Parc d'Animaux Fermiers
  Landwirtschaftspark
- **Garden**
  Jardin
  Garten
- **House**
  Manoir, Palais
  Historisches Haus
- **House & Garden**
  Manoir, Palais avec jardin
  Historisches Haus mit Garten
- **Historic Ship**
  Bateau historique
  Historisches Schiff
- **Motor Racing Circuit**
  Circuit de Courses automobiles
  Autorennbahn
- **Museum**
  Musée
  Museum
- **Picnic Area**
  Emplacement de pique-nique
  Picknickplatz
- **Preserved Railway**
  Chemin de fer touristique
  Museumsbahn
- **Race Course**
  Hippodrome
  Pferderennbahn
- **Roman Antiquity**
  Antiquité romaine
  Römischer Altertümer
- **Safari Park**
  Parc animalier
  Wildpark
- **Theme Park**
  Parc à Thème
  Freizeitpark
- **Tourist Information Centre open all year**
  Office de tourisme: ouvert toute l'année
  Informationsbüro (Ganzjährij Geöffnet)
- **Tourist Information Centre open seasonally**
  Office de tourisme: ouvert en saison
  Informationsbüro (saisonal geöffnet)
- **Zoo**
  Zoo
  Tiergarten
- **Other Place of Interest**
  Autre curiosité
  Sonstige Sehenswürdigkeit

Distance table

How to use this table

Cambridge					*272* / 169
Cardiff				*813* / 505	*253* / 157
Carlisle			*465* / 289	*425* / 264	*446* / 277
Dover		*626* / 389	*383* / 238	*201* / 125	*325* / 202
Dundee	*842* / 523	*245* / 152	*710* / 441	*654* / 406	*692* / 430

Distances are shown in miles and, in *italics*, kilometres

Example:the distance between Cambridge and Dundee is 406 miles or 654 km

	Swansea	Stranraer	Southampton	Shrewsbury	Sheffield	Plymouth	Oxford	Oban	Norwich	Newcastle upon Tyne	Manchester	Liverpool	Lincoln	Leeds	Land's End	Kingston upon Hull	John o' Groats	Inverness	Holyhead	Harwich	Gloucester	Glasgow	Fort William	Fishguard	Edinburgh	Dundee	Dover	Carlisle	Cardiff	Cambridge	Bristol	Brighton	Bournemouth	Birmingham	Aberystwyth	Aberdeen	London
Aberdeen																																				*832* / 517
Aberystwyth																																			*716* / 445	*340* / 211
Birmingham																																		*183* / 114	*676* / 420	*188* / 117
Bournemouth																																	*237* / 147	*333* / 207	*908* / 564	*172* / 107
Brighton																																*148* / 92	*262* / 163	*407* / 253	*922* / 573	*84* / 52
Bristol																															*237* / 147	*132* / 82	*130* / 81	*201* / 125	*793* / 493	*196* / 122
Cambridge																														*272* / 169	*187* / 116	*248* / 154	*161* / 100	*344* / 214	*758* / 471	*87* / 54
Cardiff																													*306* / 190	*72* / 45	*293* / 182	*188* / 117	*166* / 103	*169* / 105	*813* / 505	*253* / 157
Carlisle																												*465* / 289	*425* / 264	*446* / 277	*596* / 370	*552* / 343	*315* / 196	*360* / 224	*356* / 221	*484* / 301
Dover																											*626* / 389	*383* / 238	*201* / 125	*325* / 202	*132* / 82	*280* / 174	*312* / 194	*478* / 292	*947* / 588	*114* / 71
Dundee																										*842* / 523	*245* / 152	*710* / 441	*654* / 406	*692* / 430	*832* / 517	*797* / 495	*562* / 349	*605* / 376	*108* / 67	*721* / 448
Edinburgh																									*90* / 56	*744* / 462	*154* / 96	*620* / 385	*555* / 345	*600* / 373	*734* / 456	*707* / 439	*470* / 292	*515* / 320	*201* / 125	*628* / 390
Fishguard																								*642* / 399	*740* / 460	*533* / 331	*478* / 297	*180* / 112	*435* / 270	*248* / 154	*468* / 291	*357* / 222	*274* / 170	*90* / 56	*811* / 504	*418* / 260
Fort William																							*782* / 486	*232* / 144	*204* / 127	*959* / 596	*332* / 206	*781* / 485	*771* / 479	*782* / 486	*926* / 575	*867* / 539	*631* / 392	*692* / 430	*240* / 149	*821* / 510
Glasgow																						*163* / 101	*605* / 376	*71* / 44	*134* / 83	*786* / 488	*154* / 96	*620* / 385	*599* / 372	*600* / 373	*753* / 468	*707* / 439	*470* / 292	*515* / 320	*233* / 145	*639* / 397
Gloucester																					*557* / 346	*731* / 454	*246* / 153	*562* / 349	*660* / 410	*307* / 191	*398* / 247	*90* / 56	*198* / 123	*56* / 35	*256* / 159	*159* / 99	*90* / 56	*164* / 102	*753* / 468	*175* / 109
Harwich																				*316* / 196	*695* / 432	*874* / 543	*542* / 337	*665* / 413	*755* / 469	*201* / 125	*541* / 336	*396* / 246	*108* / 67	*349* / 217	*206* / 128	*301* / 187	*269* / 167	*452* / 281	*861* / 535	*122* / 76
Holyhead																			*562* / 349	*307* / 191	*531* / 330	*705* / 438	*269* / 167	*536* / 333	*634* / 394	*580* / 360	*372* / 231	*348* / 216	*435* / 270	*332* / 206	*538* / 334	*463* / 288	*238* / 148	*179* / 111	*707* / 439	*433* / 269
Inverness																		*763* / 474	*916* / 569	*811* / 504	*267* / 166	*106* / 66	*872* / 542	*254* / 158	*212* / 132	*1001* / 622	*422* / 262	*884* / 549	*813* / 505	*867* / 539	*993* / 617	*961* / 597	*737* / 458	*782* / 486	*169* / 105	*885* / 550
John o' Groats																	*208* / 129	*970* / 603	*1116* / 693	*1011* / 628	*475* / 295	*314* / 195	*1080* / 671	*459* / 285	*417* / 259	*1201* / 747	*629* / 391	*1094* / 680	*1014* / 630	*1075* / 668	*1193* / 741	*1165* / 724	*924* / 574	*967* / 601	*373* / 232	*1067* / 663
Kingston upon Hull																*834* / 518	*634* / 394	*372* / 231	*316* / 196	*272* / 198	*409* / 254	*594* / 369	*451* / 280	*377* / 234	*475* / 295	*412* / 256	*254* / 158	*393* / 244	*224* / 139	*375* / 233	*394* / 245	*425* / 264	*216* / 134	*359* / 223	*586* / 364	*296* / 184
Land's End															*678* / 421	*1397* / 868	*1193* / 741	*652* / 405	*628* / 390	*378* / 235	*922* / 573	*1104* / 686	*568* / 353	*924* / 574	*1033* / 642	*613* / 381	*768* / 477	*394* / 245	*602* / 374	*322* / 200	*496* / 308	*330* / 205	*452* / 281	*504* / 313	*1114* / 692	*478* / 297
Leeds														*652* / 405	*89* / 55	*784* / 487	*579* / 360	*283* / 176	*359* / 223	*280* / 174	*346* / 215	*530* / 329	*381* / 237	*325* / 202	*415* / 258	*418* / 260	*192* / 119	*373* / 232	*233* / 145	*312* / 194	*419* / 260	*410* / 255	*182* / 113	*272* / 169	*526* / 327	*304* / 189
Lincoln													*109* / 68	*597* / 371	*71* / 44	*892* / 554	*687* / 427	*348* / 216	*249* / 155	*256* / 159	*468* / 291	*642* / 399	*438* / 272	*415* / 258	*505* / 314	*325* / 202	*307* / 191	*335* / 208	*137* / 85	*295* / 183	*317* / 197	*336* / 209	*145* / 90	*320* / 199	*616* / 383	*211* / 131
Liverpool												*208* / 129	*121* / 75	*581* / 361	*209* / 130	*822* / 511	*615* / 382	*164* / 102	*427* / 265	*225* / 140	*348* / 216	*530* / 329	*257* / 160	*348* / 216	*460* / 286	*481* / 299	*193* / 120	*272* / 165	*312* / 194	*259* / 161	*438* / 272	*377* / 234	*150* / 93	*167* / 104	*549* / 341	*325* / 202
Manchester											*56* / 35	*135* / 84	*64* / 40	*581* / 361	*153* / 95	*805* / 500	*600* / 373	*200* / 124	*367* / 228	*203* / 126	*346* / 215	*530* / 329	*317* / 197	*346* / 215	*459* / 285	*444* / 276	*192* / 119	*295* / 183	*266* / 165	*259* / 161	*414* / 257	*365* / 227	*129* / 80	*208* / 129	*547* / 340	*298* / 185
Newcastle upon Tyne										*212* / 132	*270* / 168	*256* / 159	*148* / 92	*802* / 498	*212* / 132	*636* / 395	*431* / 268	*438* / 272	*496* / 308	*428* / 266	*238* / 148	*407* / 253	*529* / 329	*177* / 110	*267* / 166	*576* / 358	*92* / 57	*523* / 325	*388* / 241	*481* / 299	*567* / 352	*558* / 347	*333* / 207	*414* / 257	*378* / 235	*460* / 286
Norwich									*425* / 264	*298* / 185	*354* / 220	*169* / 105	*283* / 176	*678* / 421	*240* / 149	*1053* / 654	*852* / 529	*501* / 311	*117* / 73	*328* / 204	*620* / 385	*811* / 504	*552* / 343	*589* / 366	*679* / 422	*280* / 174	*465* / 289	*422* / 262	*100* / 62	*406* / 252	*282* / 175	*344* / 214	*267* / 166	*444* / 276	*798* / 496	*183* / 114
Oban								*792* / 492	*375* / 233	*494* / 307	*496* / 308	*623* / 387	*494* / 307	*1070* / 665	*557* / 346	*393* / 244	*188* / 117	*687* / 427	*843* / 524	*710* / 441	*148* / 92	*79* / 49	*774* / 481	*108* / 123	*188* / 117	*942* / 585	*303* / 188	*768* / 477	*753* / 468	*748* / 465	*910* / 565	*853* / 530	*618* / 384	*663* / 412	*286* / 178	*803* / 499
Oxford							*744* / 462	*233* / 145	*418* / 260	*232* / 144	*277* / 172	*221* / 137	*270* / 168	*441* / 274	*309* / 192	*1056* / 656	*856* / 532	*383* / 238	*233* / 145	*84* / 52	*573* / 356	*760* / 472	*330* / 205	*599* / 372	*697* / 433	*227* / 141	*418* / 260	*174* / 108	*134* / 83	*119* / 74	*174* / 108	*145* / 90	*103* / 64	*248* / 154	*777* / 483	*92* / 57
Plymouth						*320* / 199	*945* / 587	*552* / 343	*660* / 410	*455* / 283	*455* / 283	*472* / 293	*509* / 316	*143* / 89	*571* / 355	*1271* / 790	*1069* / 664	*528* / 328	*497* / 309	*253* / 157	*797* / 495	*958* / 595	*425* / 264	*798* / 496	*888* / 552	*483* / 300	*642* / 399	*269* / 167	*472* / 293	*196* / 122	*361* / 224	*206* / 128	*327* / 203	*382* / 237	*990* / 615	*351* / 218
Sheffield					*455* / 283	*217* / 135	*546* / 339	*235* / 146	*201* / 125	*61* / 38	*116* / 72	*74* / 46	*53* / 33	*581* / 361	*105* / 65	*837* / 520	*632* / 393	*270* / 168	*301* / 187	*203* / 126	*399* / 248	*560* / 348	*346* / 215	*378* / 235	*468* / 291	*394* / 245	*245* / 152	*312* / 194	*193* / 120	*259* / 161	*364* / 226	*348* / 216	*122* / 76	*256* / 159	*579* / 360	*256* / 159
Shrewsbury				*132* / 82	*362* / 225	*171* / 106	*586* / 364	*330* / 205	*323* / 201	*111* / 69	*93* / 58	*214* / 133	*175* / 109	*488* / 303	*272* / 169	*912* / 567	*705* / 438	*182* / 113	*386* / 240	*124* / 77	*438* / 272	*615* / 382	*233* / 145	*441* / 274	*531* / 330	*404* / 251	*283* / 176	*179* / 111	*256* / 159	*166* / 103	*364* / 226	*298* / 185	*72* / 45	*124* / 77	*642* / 399	*258* / 160
Southampton			*298* / 185	*320* / 199	*243* / 151	*103* / 64	*853* / 530	*332* / 206	*521* / 324	*356* / 221	*385* / 239	*328* / 204	*373* / 232	*367* / 228	*412* / 256	*1164* / 723	*963* / 598	*472* / 293	*264* / 164	*169* / 105	*697* / 433	*871* / 541	*375* / 233	*705* / 438	*805* / 500	*230* / 143	*521* / 324	*195* / 121	*238* / 148	*122* / 76	*98* / 61	*50* / 31	*206* / 128	*323* / 201	*880* / 547	*124* / 77
Stranraer		*716* / 445	*446* / 277	*423* / 263	*805* / 500	*610* / 379	*238* / 148	*649* / 403	*254* / 158	*354* / 220	*356* / 221	*480* / 298	*354* / 220	*942* / 585	*417* / 259	*610* / 379	*422* / 262	*544* / 338	*660* / 435	*552* / 343	*135* / 84	*314* / 195	*631* / 392	*200* / 124	*269* / 167	*798* / 496	*163* / 101	*628* / 390	*610* / 379	*608* / 378	*765* / 475	*715* / 444	*478* / 297	*523* / 325	*367* / 228	*647* / 402
Swansea	*671* / 417	*259* / 161	*190* / 118	*349* / 217	*332* / 206	*227* / 141	*815* / 506	*485* / 301	*559* / 347	*301* / 187	*314* / 195	*375* / 233	*399* / 248	*459* / 285	*425* / 264	*1120* / 696	*921* / 572	*296* / 184	*430* / 267	*143* / 89	*658* / 409	*798* / 496	*108* / 67	*663* / 412	*761* / 473	*441* / 274	*497* / 309	*66* / 41	*365* / 227	*137* / 85	*357* / 222	*269* / 167	*192* / 119	*117* / 73	*816* / 507	*312* / 194
York	*438* / 272	*357* / 222	*415* / 258	*214* / 133	*84* / 52	*536* / 333	*291* / 181	*497* / 309	*291* / 181	*135* / 84	*103* / 64	*159* / 99	*121* / 75	*39* / 24	*661* / 411	*60* / 37	*771* / 479	*566* / 352	*328* / 204	*367* / 228	*304* / 189	*349* / 217	*531* / 330	*420* / 261	*312* / 194	*402* / 250	*454* / 282	*195* / 121	*393* / 244	*266* / 165	*357* / 222	*443* / 275	*433* / 269	*209* / 130	*314* / 195	*513* / 319	*333* / 207

Isles of Scilly
White Island
St. Helens
St. Martin's
Bryher
Cromwell's Castle
New Grimsby
Higher Town
Tresco
Tresco Abbey Gardens
Eastern Isles
Samson
North West Passage
The Road
Crow Sound
Newford
Maypole
Longstone Heritage Cen.
St. Mary's
Hugh Town
Old Town
St. Mary's
Crim Rocks
Broad Sound
Annet
Smith Sound
St. Mary's Sound
St. Agnes
Gugh
St. Agnes
Penzance 2:40 (Summer only)
Bishop Rock
St. Agnes Hd.
Porthtowan
Portreath
Illogan
Navax Pt.
Godrevy Island
Godrevy Pt.
Tehidy Woods
Cornish Engines
Mines Museum
Roscroggan
The Carracks
Clodgy Pt.
The Island
St. Ives Bay
Gwithian
Kehelland
Pool
Tuckingmill
Carnkie
Tate Gallery
Barbara Hepworth Museum
St. Ives
South West Coast Path
Carbis Bay
Phillack
Rosewarthy
CAMBORNE
Gurnard's Head
Zennor
Halsetown
Lelant
Connor Downs
Barripper
Shire Horse Farm
Troon
Towednack
Copperhouse
Porthmeor
Wayside Folk Museum
Cripplesease
Paradise Park
Hayle
Carnhell Green
Penhale
South West Coast Path
Morvah
Chysauster Ancient Village
Nancledra
Canonstown
Praze-an-Beeble
Bojewyan
Praze
Fraddam
Burras
Penmar
Geevor Tin Mine Museum
Pendeen
Higher Boscaswell
Newmill
St. Erth
Leedstown
Crowan
Trewellard
Carnyorth
Penzance Heliport
Drym
Releath
Botallack
Ludgvan
Crowlas
Townshend
Cape Cornwall
St. Just
Trengwainton
Madron
Gulval
Relubbus
Nancegollan
Poldark Mine
The Bisons
Ballowall Barrow
Land's End (St. Just)
Newbridge
Heamoor
Chyandour
St. Hilary
Godolphin House
Trescowe
Godolphin Cross
Wendron
Bosavern
Marazion
Goldsithney
Crowntown
Kelynack
Sancreed
Penzance
St. Michael's Mount
Perranuthnoe
Germoe
Ashton
Sithney
Carn Euny Village
Tredavoe
Trinity House National Lighthouse Centre
Breage
Trewenn
Land's End
Brane
Lower Drift
Newlyn
Newlyn Art Gallery
South West Coast Path
Praa Sands
Helston
Whitesand Bay
Crows-an-wra
Catchall
Paul
Cudden Pt.
Rinsey
Sennen Cove
Kerris
Mousehole
Village Theme Park
Longships
Sennen
St. Buryan
St. Clement's Island
Trewavas Hd.
Porthleven
The Loe
LAND'S END
Land's End
Trewoofe
South West Coast Path
Polgigga
Lamorna
Porthleven Sands
Garras
Porthcurno
Tregiffian Burial Chamber
Lamorna Cove
Berepper
Museum of Submarine Telegraphy
Treen
Boskenna
Gunwalloe
St. Levan
Cury
Gwennap Hd.
Runnel Stone
Mullion
Mullion Cove
Mullion Island
Mullion Cove
Predannack Wollas
Isles of Scilly 2:40 (Summer only)
Vellan Hd.
Kynance Cove
LIZARD POINT
CORNWALL
MOUNTS BAY
A30
A394
A3071
B3306
B3311
B3315
B3283
B3318
B3301
B3302
B3303
B3304
B3280
B3297
A3083
B3296
B3309

6
7
8
9
10
Bay
Port Isaac
Helstone
Pentire Pt.
Port Quin Bay
Port Quin
Port Gaverne
St. Teath
Rough Tor 400
High Moor
New Polzeath
Padstow Bay
Long Cross
Trelights
Pendoggett
Treveighan
420 Brown Willy
Gulland Rock
Polzeath
St. Endellion
Trelill
Michaelstow
Trebetherick
331 Garrow Tor
Codda
Gunver Hd.
St. Minver
Trewethern
St. Tudy
St. Breward
Jamaica Inn Museums
A30
Bolventor
Trevose Head
Crugmeer
Prideaux Place
Pityme
Chapel Amble
St. Kew
Row
Bodmin Moor
Trevone
Rock
St. Kew Highway
Bradford
Treyarnon Bay
Constantine Bay
Constantine
St. Merryn
Padstow
Camel
Wenfordbridge
Treyarnon
Shop
Bodieve
Blisland
Fernleys
Dozmary Pool
South West Coast Path
Little Petherick
Trevanson
Wadebridge
St. Mabyn
Temple
Porthcothan
Whitecross
Colliford Lake
Penrose
St. Issey
St. Breock
Egloshayle
Pencarrow House
Helland
Park Hd.
St. Ervan
Rumford
Tredinnick
A39
Burlawn
Maidenwell
Millpool
Rare Breeds Centre
St. Jidgey
Shire Horse Centre
St. Breock Downs Monolith
208
Washaway
Bodmin Forest
Warleggan
Trenance
Cardinham
St. Neot
Bodmin
Berryl's Pt.
Trevarrian
St. Mawgan
Ruthernbridge
Nanstallon
Mount
Museum
Carnglaze Slate Caves
Ley
Rosenannon
St. Lawrence
Watergate Bay
Talskiddy
Withiel
Bodmin and Wenford Railway
Fowey
Tregurrian
Newquay
St. Columb Major
St. Wenn
B3274
Tregonetha
4
Lanhydrock House
East Taphouse
West Taphouse
Towan Hd.
Newquay Bay
Porth
St. Columb Minor
A3059
Cornwall
227
Lanivet
Trebyan
Fistral Bay
Pentire
Trebudannon
Belowda
Victoria
Sweethouse
Restormel Castle
Braddock
Kelsey Hd.
Animal World
Colan
Miniature Pony Centre
Lockengate
Redmoor
Herodsfoot
Newquay
Mountjoy
Ruthvoes
West Pentire
Crantock
Sea Life Centre
Trevarren
Tregoss
Roche
Bilberry
Lostwithiel
Holywell Bay Fun Park
Lane
A392
Kestle Mill
Indian Queens
Tresayes
Bugle
Lanlivery
Couch's Mill
Penhale Pt.
The Fun Factory
St. Columb Road
Fraddon
Holywell
Carines
Dairy Land Farm World
Penhale
St. Dennis
Hensbarrow Downs
A391
Luxulyan
Milltown
Bocaddon
Ligger or Perran Bay
Cubert
Penhale Sands
Trerice
Newlyn East
Gummow's Shop
St. Enoder
Retew
Whitemoor
312
Stenalees
Lerryn
Mount
Rejerrah
Lappa Valley Steam Railway
Summercourt
Treviscoe
Nanpean
Penwithick
Penpillick
Lanreath
South West Coast Path
Rose
Newlyn Downs
Trethosa
Carthew
Wheal Martyn China Clay Heritage Centre
Trethurgy
St. Blazey
Golant
St. Veep
Perranporth
Goonhavern
World in Miniature
Mitchell
Brighton
Foxhole
Carclaze
Tywardreath
Penpoll
Automobilia
High Street
Boscoppa
Trenewan
Bolingey
Perranzabuloe
Carland Cross
St. Austell
Par
Lanteglos Highway
Trelassick
St. Stephen
Trewoon
Holmbush
Polkerris
Fowey
Bodinnick
Trevellas
Zelah
New Mills
Coombe
St. Mewan
Shipwreck & Heritage Centre
Menabilly
Mithian
St. Allen
Charlestown
Lansallos
Agnes
Callestick
Trispen
St. Erme
Ladock
Grampound Road
Polgooth
St. Austell Brewery
St. Catherine's Castle
Polruan
Callestock Cider Farm
Porthpean
St. Austell Bay
Goonbell
Marazanvose
Sticker
Hewas Water
South West Coast Path
Pencarrow Hd.
Gribbin Hd.
Allet
Trenarren
A390
Mount Hawke
A30
Probus
Grampound
Black Hd.
Shortlanesend
Probus Gdns
Trewithen
Pentewan
Three Burrows
Tresillian
Creed
The Lost Gardens of Heligan
Mevagissey Bay
Blackwater
Kenwyn
St. Ewe
Mawla
Truro
Tresawle
Polmassick
Kestle
World of Model Railways
Mevagissey
Cathedral
Merther
Tregony
Scorrier
Chacewater
Threemilestone
Royal Cornwall Mus.
Portmellon
St. Day
Baldhu
Kea
St. Clement
Trevarrick
Chapel Pt.
Twelve Heads
Ruan Lanihorne
St. Michael Caerhays
Gorran Churchtown
Redruth
Bissoe
Malpas
Old Kea
St. Michael Penkevil
Lamorran
Gorran Haven
Carharrack
Playing Place
Gwennap Pit
Carnon Downs
Portholland
Boswinger
Gwennap
Treworga
Penare
Lanner
Perranarworthal
Penpol
Trelissick
Philleigh
Veryan Bay
Portloe
Dodman Pt.
Lanes
Devoran
Feock
Veryan
South West Coast Path
Ponsanooth
Treworlas
Carne
Gerrans Bay
Stithians
Burnthouse
Mylor Bridge
Carrick Roads
St. Just in Roseland
Trewithian
Nare Hd.
Stithians Res.
Penryn
Gerrans
Portscatho
Flushing
Longdowns
Mabe Burnthouse
Falmouth
St. Mawes
Greeb Pt.
Rame
Art Gallery
Maritime Mus.
Bohortha
Budock Water
Pendennis Castle
181
Pendennis Pt.
Zone Pt.
Seworgan
Treverva
Penjerrick
Falmouth Bay
Constantine
Mawnan Smith
South West Coast Path
Porth Navas
Glendurgan
Rosemullion Hd.
Helford Passage
Trebah
Mawnan
Gweek
Seal Sanctuary
Helford River
Helford
St. Anthony
Manaccan
Nare Pt.
Mawgan
St. Martins
Trelowarren
Tregidden
Halliggye Fogou
Newtown
Porthallow
Porthoustock
Manacle Pt.
Cross Lanes
St. Keverne
The Manacles
Goonhilly Satellite Earth Station
113
Traboe
Lowland Pt.
Goonhilly Downs
Coverack
Trelan
Chynhalls Pt.
Gwenter
Kuggar
Black Hd.
St. Ruan
Ruan Minor
Cadgwith
South West Coast Path
Landewednock
Hot Pt.
Cornwall
D
E
F
G
H

CORNWALL
Cornwall
BODMIN MOOR
TAMAR VALLEY
Cambeak
Crackington Haven
Rosecare
Jacobstow
Wainhouse Corner
Tresparrett Posts
Fire Beacon Pt.
Beeny
Marshgate
Tresparrett
Boscastle Harbour
Boscastle
Trevalga
Otterham
Warbstow
Trelash
Castle
Tintagel Hd.
Old Post Office
Tintagel
Bossiney
Trewarmett
Treknow
Start Pt.
Trebarwith
Davidstow
Trewassa
Tremail
Hallworthy
Treneglos
Tremaine
Tresmeer
Tregeare
Cold Northcott
Davidstow Moor
Crowdy Res.
Camelford
Delabole
Treligga
South West Coast Path
Port Isaac Bay
Port Isaac
Port Gaverne
Pendoggett
Helstone
Valley Truckle
St. Teath
Treveighan
Michaelstow
St. Breward
Endellion
Trelill
St. Tudy
St. Kew
St. Kew Highway
Row
Wenfordbridge
Bradford
Blisland
Wadebridge
Egloshayle
St. Mabyn
Pencarrow House
Helland
Camel
Burlawn
Washaway
Bodmin Forest
Bodmin
Nanstallon
St. Lawrence
Museum
Bodmin and Wenford Railway
Lanivet
Lanhydrock House
Trebyan
Cardinham
Millpool
Temple
High Moor
Rough Tor
Brown Willy
Garrow Tor
Jamaica Inn Museums
Bolventor
Codda
Altarnun
Trewint
Fernleys
Dozmary Pool
Colliford Lake
Warleggan
Maidenwell
St. Neot
Mount
Carnglaze Slate Caverns
Dobwalls Adventure Park
Dobwalls
Ley
East Taphouse
West Taphouse
Doublebois
St. Pinnock
Liskeard
Fowey
Restormel Castle
Lostwithiel
Braddock
Sweethouse
Redmoor
Lockengate
Roche
Bilberry
Bugle
Lanlivery
Luxulyan
Stenalees
Penwithick
Carthew
Trethurgy
St. Blazey
Carclaze
Boscoppa
St. Austell
Par
Tywardreath
Holmbush
Shipwreck & Heritage Centre
Charlestown
St. Austell Brewery
Polgooth
Porthpean
St. Austell Bay
Polkerris
Menabilly
Fowey
Polruan
St. Catherine's Castle
Gribbin Hd.
Bodinnick
Lanteglos Highway
Lansallos
Pencarrow Hd.
Trenarren
Black Hd.
Pentewan
Mevagissey Bay
World of Model Railways
Mevagissey
Portmellon
Chapel Pt.
Gorran Churchtown
Gorran Haven
Penare
Dodman Pt.
Couch's Mill
Milltown
Golant
Lerryn
St. Veep
Penpoll
Lanreath
Bocaddon
Herodsfoot
Muchlarnick
Pelynt
Trenewan
Polperro
Talland Bay
Porthallow
West Looe
East Looe
Looe Bay
St. George's or Looe I.
St. Martin
Morval
Sandplace
Duloe
Trewidland
St. Keyne
Music Machines
Menheniot
Merrymeet
St. Cleer
Tremar
Trethevy Quoit
King Doniert's Stone
Darite
Commonmoor
Caradon Hill
Minions
The Hurlers Stone Circle
Siblyback Lake
Upton Cross
Henwood
Kilmar Tor
Rilla Mill
North Hill
Trebartha
Congdon's Shop
Lewannick
Polyphant
Trewen
Laneast
St. Clether
Piper's Pool
Trethorne Leisure Farm
Tregadillett
Daw's House
South Petherwin
Launceston
Launceston Steam Railway
Castle
Dutson
St. Stephen's
Egloskerry
Langore
Yeolmbridge
North Petherwin
Tamar Otter Sanctuary
Canworthy Water
Brazacott
Bennacott
Maxworthy
West Curry
South Wheatley
Boyton
Northcott
Chapmans Well
Luffincott
Tetcott
Lana
Langdon
Bridgetown
Werrington
St. Giles on the Heath
Ashwater
Henford
Virginstow
East Panson
Germansweek
Eworthy
Broadbury
Boasley Cross
Roadford Res.
Gnnacombe Moor
Bratton Clovelly
Gridley Corner
Broadwoodwidger
Cross Green
Liftondown
Lifton
Tinhay
Stowford
Dingle's Steam Village
Thrushelton
Lewdown
Portgate
Lewtrenchard
Lydford Castle
Coryton
North Brentor
Chillaton
Kelly
Bradstone
Lawhitton
Milton Abbot
Dunterton
Rezare
Trekenner
Lezant
Trebullett
Treburley
Coad's Green
Bray Shop
Stoke Climsland
Sydenham Damerel
Horsebridge
Lamerton
National Ambulance Heritage Centre
Wilminstone
Tavistock
Luckett
Latchley
Downgate
Linkinhorne
South Hill
Bathpool
Golberdon
Haye
Kelly Bray
Kit Hill
Callington
Harrowbarrow
Cotehele
Chilsworthy
Gunnislake
St. Ann's Chapel
Drakewalls
Gulworthy
Albaston
Morwellham Quay
Calstock
Higher Walreddon
Horrabridge
Buckland Monachorum
Buckland Abbey
St. Dominick
Bere Alston
Weirquay
Bere Ferrers
Tamerton Foliot
Lopwell
Pensilva
Trevigro
Gang
St. Ive
Newbridge
Pengover Green
Quethiock
St. Mellion
Pillaton
Blunts
Cargreen
Landulph
Hatt
Botusfleming
Tideford Cross
Landrake
Tideford
Trematon
Saltash
St. Budeaux
Mary Newman's Cottage
St. Stephens
Antony House
St. Germans
St. Erney
Hessenford
Trerule Foot
Widegates
Polbathic
Sheviock
Crafthole
Antony
Torpoint
Devonport
Plymouth
Merchant's House
Cremyll
Mount Edgcumbe
Drake's I.
The Sound
Seaton
Downderry
Portwrinkle
St. John
Millbrook
South West Coast Path
Freathy
Whitsand Bay
Kingsand
Cawsand
Rame
Rame Hd.
Penlee Pt.
Bovisand Bay
Heybrook Bay
Great Mew Stone
Roscoff 6:00
Santander 24:00 (Mar-Nov)
St. Malo 8:00 (Nov-Mar)
A30
A39
A38
A390
A388
A395
A391
A387
A374
A3082
1
2
3
4
5
A
B
C
D
E

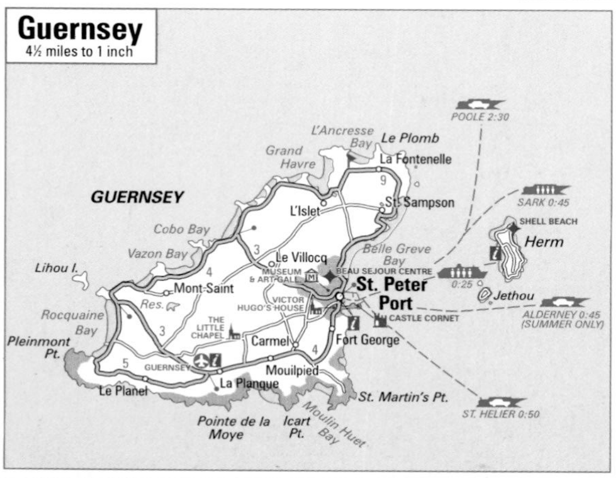
Guernsey
4½ miles to 1 inch
GUERNSEY
L'Ancresse Bay
Le Plomb
Grand Havre
La Fontenelle
St. Sampson
L'Islet
Cobo Bay
Vazon Bay
Le Villocq
Belle Greve Bay
St. Peter Port
Castle Cornet
Beau Sejour Centre
Lihou I.
Mont Saint
Victor Hugo's House
Rocquaine Bay
Pleinmont Pt.
The Little Chapel
Carmel
Fort George
Mouilpied
Le Planel
La Planque
Pointe de la Moye
Icart Pt.
Moulin Huet Bay
St. Martin's Pt.
Herm
Shell Beach
Jethou
Poole 2:30
Sark 0:45
Alderney 0:45 (Summer only)
St. Helier 0:50

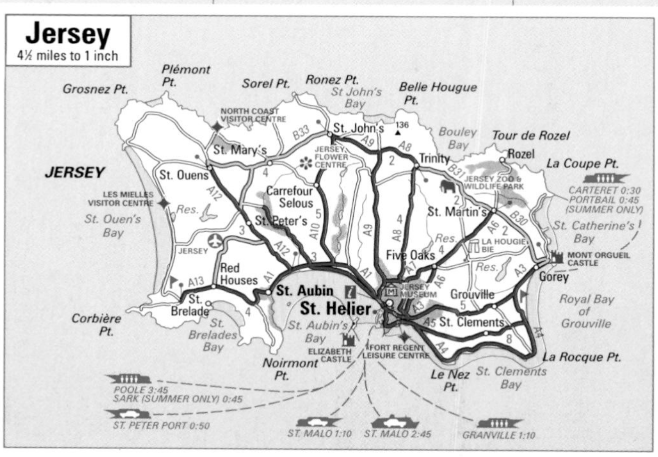
Jersey
4½ miles to 1 inch
JERSEY
Grosnez Pt.
Plémont Pt.
Sorel Pt.
Ronez Pt.
St John's Bay
Belle Hougue Pt.
North Coast Visitor Centre
St. Mary's
St. John's
Bouley Bay
Tour de Rozel
Rozel
La Coupe Pt.
Trinity
Jersey Zoo & Wildlife Park
St. Ouens
Les Mielles Visitor Centre
St. Ouen's Bay
Carrefour Selous
St. Peter's
Jersey Flower Centre
St. Martin's
St. Catherine's Bay
Mont Orgueil Castle
Gorey
La Hougue Bie
Five Oaks
Red Houses
St. Aubin
St. Helier
Jersey Museum
St. Brelade
Corbière Pt.
St. Brelades Bay
St. Aubin's Bay
Elizabeth Castle
Fort Regent Leisure Centre
Noirmont Pt.
Grouville
St. Clements
Royal Bay of Grouville
La Rocque Pt.
Le Nez Pt.
St. Clements Bay
Carteret 0:30
Portbail 0:45 (Summer only)
Poole 3:45
Sark (Summer only) 0:45
St. Peter Port 0:50
St. Malo 1:10
St. Malo 2:45
Granville 1:10

5
Okehampton
EXETER
Topsham
Exmouth
Dawlish
Teignmouth
DARTMOOR
DARTMOOR NATIONAL FOREST
DARTMOOR NATIONAL PARK
Devon
Moretonhampstead
Chagford
Bovey Tracey
Chudleigh
Kingsteignton
NEWTON ABBOT
Ashburton
Buckfastleigh
Princetown
Yelverton
Plympton
Ivybridge
Totnes
Paignton
Torquay
TORBAY
TOR BAY
BABBACOMBE BAY
Brixham
Berry Head
Dartmouth
Kingswear
Modbury
Kingsbridge
Salcombe
Slapton Sands
START BAY
START POINT
Bolt Tail
Bolt Hd.
Prawle Pt.
BIGBURY BAY
Burgh I.
Bigbury on Sea
Stoke Pt.
Newton Ferrers
SOUTH DEVON
Alderney
4½ miles to 1 inch
ALDERNEY
Braye
St. Anne
Quesnard Pt.
Longis Bay
Clonque Bay
Telegraph Bay
Brehou
ST. PETER PORT 0:45 (SUMMER ONLY)

LUNDY
North West Point
North East Point
South West Point
Surf Point
ILFRACOMBE 2:15
BIDEFORD 2:15
CLOVELLY 1:30
LUNDY 2:15
LUNDY 1:30
Ilfrac
Bull Pt.
Lee
Rockham Bay
Mortehoe
Morte Point
Whitestone
Woolacombe
MORTE BAY
Woolacombe Sand
SOUTH WEST COAST PATH
Pickwell
Baggy Pt.
Putsborough
North Buckland
Croyde Bay
Georgeham
Croyde
Darracott
Lobb
Saunton
ELLIOT GALLERY
Saunton Sands
Braunton Burrows
Wrafton
NORTH DEVON
BIDEFORD BAY
NORTH DEVON MARITIME MUSEUM
Appledore
Instow
Yelland
Westward Ho!
Northam
Westleigh
Orchard Hill
Eastleigh
Bideford
THE BIG SHEEP
Abbotsham
East-the-Water
HARTLAND POINT
Windbury Pt.
Titchberry
Hartland Quay
Stoke
Hartland
CLOVELLY VILLAGE
Clovelly
Dyke
Buck's Mills
Horns Cross
Fairy Cross
Handy Cross
Ford
Landcross
Woodtown
Milford
Philham
Eddistone
Buck's Cross
Goldsworthy
Littleham
Elmscott
Tosberry
Parkham
Buckland Brewer
Monkleigh
Woolfardisworthy
Hartland Forest
Alminstone Cross
Parkham Ash
Knaps Longpeak
South Hole
Welcombe
Meddon
Frithelstock
Frithelstock Stone
Taddiport
Ashmansworthy
Tythecott
Woolley
Gooseham
Eastcott
Youlstone
Morwenstow
East Putford
West Putford
Higher Sharpnose Pt.
Shop
Dinworthy
Langtree
Woodford
Bradworthy
Bulkworthy
Stibb Cross
Lower Sharpnose Pt.
Bradworthy Cross
Peters Marland
Coombe
Kilkhampton
Alfardisworthy
Sutcombe
Abbots Bickington
Newton St. Petrock
Woollaton
Stibb
Venn Green
Milton Damerel
Soldon Cross
Buckland Filleigh
BUDE BAY
Poughill
Hersham
Holsworthy Beacon
Thornbury
Shebbear
Flexbury
Grimscott
Woodacott
Bradford
Bude Haven
Stratton
Chilsworthy
Sheepwash
Bude
Launcells
Pancrasweek
Cookbury
Black Torrington
Upton
Holemoor
Marhamchurch
Derril
Derriton
Holsworthy
Brandis Corner
Bridgerule
Pyworthy
Chasty
Whimble
Hollacombe
Graddon Moor
Widemouth Bay
Budd's Titson
Chilla
Widemouth Sand
Halwill Junction
Coppathorne
Leworthy
Millook
Halwill
Beaworthy
Dizzard Pt.
Poundstock
Clawton
Tregole
Treskinnick Cross
Whitstone
Patchacott
St. Genny's
Trewint
Week St. Mary
North Tamerton
Quoditch
BROADBURY
Cambeak
Crackington Haven
Rosecare
Tetcott
Lana
Jacobstow
Ashwater
Wainhouse Corner
Luffincott
Henford
Eworthy
Trespparrett Posts
South Wheatley
West Curry
Chapmans Well
Virginstow
Germansweek
Boasley Cross
Fire Beacon Pt.
Beeny
Maxworthy
BOSCASTLE HARBOUR
Tresparrett
Marshgate
Bennacott
Northcott
East Panson
Grinacombe Moor
Roadford Res.
Bratton Clovelly
Boscastle
Lesnewth
Canworthy Water
Otterham
Brazacott
Boyton
St. Giles on the Hth.
Trevalga
Trelash
Warbstow
Langdon
Gridley Corner
CASTLE
Tintagel Hd.
OLD POST OFFICE
TINTAGEL
Bossiney
Tintagel
Tremaine
TAMAR OTTER SANCTUARY
North Petherwin
Bridgetown
Broadwoodwidger
Treknow
Trewarmett
Davidstow
Hallworthy
Treneglos
Werrington
Cross Green
Thrushelton
Tresmeer
Yeolmbridge
Stowford
Start Pt.
Trebarwith
Trewassa
Tremail
Egloskerry
Langore
Dutson
Liftondown
DINGLE'S STEAM VILLAGE
Lewdown
Tregeare
St. Stephen's
LAUNCESTON STEAM RAILWAY
Portgate
Lewtrenchard
Treligga
Cold Northcott
Piper's Pool
Launceston
Lifton
Tinhay
SOUTH WEST COAST PATH
Delabole
TRETHORNE LEISURE FARM
Tregadillett
LYDFORD CASTLE
Valley Truckle
Camelford
Crowdy
St. Clether
Laneast
Trewen
Coryton
Davidstow Moor

6
7
8
9
10
A
B
C
D
E
F
G
H
Foreland Pt.
Highveer Pt.
Woody Bay
Lynmouth Bay
Lynmouth
Lynton
Countisbury
Hurlstone Pt.
Porlock Bay
Porlock
Porlock Weir
Bossington
Allerford
Selworthy
Minehead
Alcombe
Dunster
Carhampton
Rillage Pt.
Combe Martin Bay
Combe Martin
Berrynarbor
Sterridge
Hele
Trentishoe
Martinhoe
Heale
Girt Down
Parracombe
Martinhoe Cross
Barbrook
Cheriton
Furzehill
Shallowford
East Ilkerton
Brendon
Malmsmead
Oare
Brendon Common
EXMOOR
EXMOOR FOREST
NATIONAL
PARK
Kentisbury
Kentisbury Ford
Blackmoor Gate
Patchole
Berry Down Cross
Berry Down
Cheglinch
West Down
Bittadon
East Down
Churchill
Arlington
Challacombe Common
Challacombe
Pinkworthy Pond
Exe Plain
Simonsbath
Edgcott
Exford
Luckwell Bridge
Cutcombe
Wheddon Cross
Luxborough
Kingsbridge
Timberscombe
Cowbridge
Withycombe
BRENDON FOREST
Wootton Courtenay
West Luccombe
Luccombe
Holnicote Estate
DUNKERY BEACON
Halsinger
Milltown
Muddiford
Loxhore
Knightacott
Shoulsbarrow Common
Leworthy
Marwood
Guineaford
Kingsheanton
Prixford
Pippacott
Heanton Punchardon
Shirwell
Shirwell Cross
Bratton Fleming
Stoke Rivers
Benton
Lydcott
Withypool
Withypool Common
Winsford
Winsford Hill
Horsen Hill
Exton
Bridgetown
Liscombe
Hawkridge
Brompton Regis
Withiel Florey
Ashford
Chivenor
Burridge
Barnstaple
Goodleigh
Gunn
Brayford
High Bray
North Radworthy
North Heasley
South Radworthy
Heasley Mill
Charles
Pilton
Westacott
Bickington
Newport
Bishops Tawton
Landkey
Swimbridge Newland
Swimbridge
West Buckland
East Buckland
Molland Common
Twitchen
Anstey Common
West Anstey
East Anstey
Molland
North Molton
Dulverton
Battleton
Wimbleball Lake
Haddon Hill
Upton
Skilgate
Bury
Tawstock
Newton Tracey
Filleigh
Cobbaton
Herner
Chapelton
Ensis
Hiscott
East Stowford
Chittlehampton
South Molton
Bish Mill
Newtown
Yeo Mill
Nightcott
Brushford
Morebath
Oldways End
Exebridge
Petton
Shillingford
Bampton
Fishleigh Barton
Yarnscombe
Atherington
Umberleigh
Clapworthy
Warkleigh
Satterleigh
George Nympton
Bishops Nympton
Alswear
Ash Mill
Knowstone
Roachill
Oakfordbridge
Oakford
Langridge Ford
Sherwood Green
High Bickington
Chittlehamholt
Mariansleigh
Rose Ash
High Bullen
St. Giles in the Wood
Great Torrington
Kingscott
Roborough
Romansleigh
King's Nympton
Meshaw
Creacombe
Stoodleigh Beacon
Stoodleigh
Huntsham
Cove
Rackenford
Burrington
Cadbury Barton
Elstone
Week
Lutworthy
Queen Dart
Loxbeare
Washfield
East Mere
Chevithorne
Uplowman
Beaford
Riddlecombe
Chulmleigh
Cheldon
West Worlington
East Worlington
Drayford
Witheridge
Templeton Bridge
Templeton
Calverleigh
Bolham
Chettiscombe
Halberton
Ashreigney
Thelbridge Barton
Washford Pyne
No Man's Land
Cruwys Morchard
Withleigh
Cotteylands
Cowleymoor
Tiverton
Merton
Huish
Dolton
Dowland
Hollocombe
Ashley
Wembworthy
Chawleigh
Filleigh
Black Dog
Pennymoor
Puddington
Way Village
Well Town
Petrockstow
Meeth
Iddesleigh
Winkleigh
Brushford
Coldridge
Nymet Rowland
Lapford
Eastington
Morchard Bishop
Woolfardisworthy
Poughill
Upham
Cadeleigh
Butterleigh
Bickleigh
Cullompton
Broadwood Kelly
Kennerleigh
Stockleigh English
Cheriton Fitzpaine
Oldborough
Monkokehampton
Hatherleigh
West Leigh
East Leigh
Zeal Monachorum
Down St. Mary
Ash Bullayne
East Village
Cadbury
Stockleigh Pomeroy
Bradninch
Silverton
Bondleigh
Honeychurch
Newbuildings
Copplestone
Sandford
Upton Hellions
Thorverton
Up Exe
Hele
Ellerhayes
Jacobstowe
Exbourne
North Tawton
Sampford Courtenay
Bow
Knowle
Coleford
Nymet Tracey
Crediton
Shobrooke
Efford Shute
Nether Exe
Rewe
Budlake
Westwood
Northlew
Inwardleigh
Oak Cross
Ashbury
Itton
Colebrooke
Hillerton
Yeoford
Uton
Hookway
Sweetham
Brampford Speke
Newton St. Cyres
Venny Tedburn
Stoke Canon
Upton Pyne
Broadclyst
Folly Gate
Taw Green
Spreyton
Okehampton
Hittisleigh
Tedburn St. Mary
Cowley
Poltimore
Dog Village
Pinhoe
Sticklepath
South Tawton
South Zeal
Belstone
Whiddon Down
Cheriton Bishop
Crockernwell
Whitestone
Exwick
EXETER
Whipton
Heavitree
Sowton
Clyst Honiton
Clyst St. Mary
Thorndon Cross
Meldon
Okehampton Camp
Okehampton Common
Drewsteignton
Longdown
Whiteley
St. Thomas
Countess Wear
Alphington
Sourton
Yes Tor
High Willhays
Cosdon Hill
Throwleigh
Wonson
Sandypark
Easton
Ide
Bridestowe and Sourton Common
Gidleigh
Murchington
Dunsford
Shillingford St. George
Topsham
Clyst St. George
Shortacombe
Okement Hill
Teigncombe
Chagford
Doccombe
Bridfordmills
Exminster
Ebford
Hangingstone Hill
Frenchbeer
Moretonhampstead
Bridford
Christow
Doddiscombsleigh
Kennford
Exton
Higher Ashton
Kenn
Powderham
Lympstone
Lettaford
North Bovey
Lower Ashton
Kenton
Tawstock
Teign
Exe
Taw
Torridge
Barle
Mole
Yeo
Bray
Dart
Little Dart
Dalch
Kenn
Culm
Clyst
Lew
West Lyn
Dane's Brook
EXE VALLEY
Devon

Bridgwater
QUANTOCK FOREST
Crowcombe
Elworthy
Somerset
Wiveliscombe
VALE OF TAUNTON DEANE
Taunton
Wellington
Bampton
Dulverton
Wimbleball Lake
Clatworthy Res.
BLACKDOWN HILLS
Tiverton
Cullompton
Devon
Chard
Ilminster
Honiton
Axminster
Ottery St. Mary
EAST DEVON
Exeter
Topsham
Sidmouth
Seaton
Beer
Lyme Regis
Charmouth
Budleigh Salterton
Exmouth
Dawlish
Teignmouth
Torquay
BABBACOMBE BAY
Seaton Bay
Charlton Bay
LYME
Straight Pt.
Danger Pt.
Hope's Nose
Beer Hd.
Ladram Bay
Yarcombe
Cullompton
Crediton
Silverton
Kentisbeare
Hemyock
Dunkeswell
Broadhembury
Feniton
Whimple
Woodbury
Colyton
Musbury
Kilmington

Street
Pedwell
Walton
Butleigh Wootton
Parbrook
Ham Street
Baltonsborough
Butleigh
Overleigh
Ditcheat
Lamyatt
Wraxall
Alhampton
Bruton
North Brewham
Brewham
Norton Ferris
Keysley Down
Chicklade
Hornblotton Green
Sutton
Ansford
Cole
Pitcombe
Hardway
Redlynch
Stourhead
Stourton
White Sheet Hill
King Alfred's Tower
King's Sedge Moor
Henley
Compton Dundon
Dundon
Barton St. David
Southwood
West Lydford
East Lydford
Alford
Lovington
Castle Cary
Stoney Stoke
Shepton Montague
Penselwood
Zeals
Queen Oak
Mere
West Knoyle
The Green
Fonthill
High Ham
Stembridge Tower Mill
Littleton
Kingweston
Keinton Mandeville
Lydford-on-Fosse
Galhampton
Hadspen Garden
Bratton Seymour
Wincanton
Charlton Musgrove
Leigh Common
Bourton
Barrow Street
East Knoyle
Aller
Low Ham
Somerton
Charlton Adam
Babcary
North Barrow
Yarlington
Bayford
Huntingford
Pitney
Haynes Motor Museum
Stoke Trister
Milton on Stour
Sedgehill
Newtown
Langport
Charlton Mackerell
Lytes Cary Manor
Cary Fitzpaine
South Barrow
North Cadbury
Cucklington
Gillingham
Coppleridge
Huish Episcopi
Long Sutton
Kingsdon
Sparkford
Holton
Maperton
Lattiford
Wyke
Ham Common
Semley
Drayton
Muchelney
Podimore
West Camel
Queen Camel
South Cadbury
Compton Pauncefoot
Blackford
North Cheriton
South Cheriton
Buckhorn Weston
Motcombe
Donhead St. Mary
Isle
Yeo
Northover
Fleet Air Arm Mus.
Bridgehampton
Sutton Montis
Corton Denham
Charlton Horethorne
Horsington
Abbas Combe
Kington Magna
West Stour
Knap Corner
Long Load
Ilchester
Yeovilton
Limington
Chilton Cantelo
Marston Magna
Rimpton
Sandford Orcas Manor House
Stowell
Temple Combe
East Stour
Shaftesbury
Ivy Cross
Kingsbury Episcopi
Stapleton
Ash
Ashington
Adber
Sandford Orcas
Milborne Wick
Henstridge Ash
Yenston
Fifehead Magdalen
Stour Provost
Stour Row
Guy's Marsh
Cann
Cann Common
East Lambrook
Martock
Coat
Tintinhull
Tintinhull House Garden
Chilthorne Domer
Yeovil Marsh
Mudford
Poyntington
Henstridge
Henstridge Marsh
Pillwell
Todber
Melbury Abbas
Melbury Down
East Lambrook Manor
Barrington Ct. Gdn. & Court House
Hurst
Bower Hinton
South Petherton
Stoke sub Hamdon
Montacute House
Trent
Nether Compton
Oborne
Milborne Port
Sherborne Old Castle
Goathill
Purse Caundle
Purse Caundle Manor
Stalbridge
Marnhull
Margaret Marsh
Bedchester
Compton Abbas
Ashmore
Stoke-sub-Hamden Priory
Montacute
Preston Plucknett
Yeovil
Over Compton
Sherborne
Sherborne Castle
Stalbridge Weston
Hinton St. Mary
East Orchard
West Orchard
Fontmell Magna
Norton sub Hamdon
Odcombe
Ham Hill
Brympton
Conservation Worldwide and Lullingstone Silk
North Wootton
Haydon
Stourton Caundle
Manston
Sutton Waldron
Seavington St. Michael
Over Stratton
Chiselborough
Alweston
Bishop's Caundle
Lydlinch
Sturminster Newton
Mill
Hammoon
Iwerne Courtney or Shroton
Iwerne Minster
Cranborne Chase
Lopen
West Chinnock
West Coker
Barwick
Stoford
Bradford Abbas
Thornford
Folke
Fiddleford
Dinnington
Merriott
East Chinnock
North Coker
East Coker
Lillington
Longburton
Holwell
Newton
Broad Oak
Child Okeford
Hinton St. George
Haselbury Plucknett
Hardington Mandeville
Ryme Intrinseca
Beer Hackett
Blackmoor Vale
Woodbridge
King's Stag
Fifehead Neville
Shillingstone
Crewkerne
North Perrott
Pendomer
Closworth
Yetminster
Crouch Hill
Okeford Fitzpaine
Stourpaine
Pimperne
Hardington Marsh
Holnest
Kingston
Hewish
Misterton
Leigh
Glanvilles Wootton
Pulham
Hazelbury Bryan
Ibberton
Durweston
South Perrott
Halstock
Melbury Osmond
Chetnole
Hermitage
Middlemarsh
Woolland
Turnworth
Clapton
Seaborough
Mosterton
Chedington
Corscombe
West Chelborough
Melbury Sampford
Melbury Bubb
Hilfield
Lyon's Gate
Duntish
Westfields
Mappowder
Stoke Wake
Bryanston
Blandford Forum
Blandford St. Mary
Drimpton
Evershot
Buckland Newton
Minterne Magna
Minterne Gardens
Higher Ansty
Winterborne Houghton
Winterborne Stickland
Charlton Marshall
Burstock
The Craft and Design Centre
Broadwindsor
Holywell
Batcombe
Frome St. Quintin
Up Cerne
Alton Pancras
Melcombe Bingham
Hilton
Milton Abbey
Winterborne Clenston
Thorncombe
Rampisham
Beaminster
Parnham
Up Sydling
Abbey Pottery
Cerne Abbas
Plush
Whatcombe
Milton Abbas
Spetisbury
Charlton Down
Bettiscombe
Stoke Abbott
Netherbury
Wraxall
Cattistock
Chilfrome
Sydling St. Nicholas
Piddletrenthide
Cheselbourne
Winterborne Whitechurch
Dorset
Pilsdon
Mapperton
Hooke
Toller Porcorum
Maiden Newton
Nether Cerne
White Lackington
Dewlish
Winterborne Kingston
Winterborne Zelston
Melplash
North Poorton
Broad Oak
Salway Ash
West Milton
Powerstock
Toller Fratrum
Godmanston
Piddlehinton
Milborne St. Andrew
Anderson
Whitchurch Canonicorum
Ryall
Dottery
Nettlecombe
Wynford Eagle
Forston
Athelhampton
Martyrs Museum
Morcombelake
Bradpole
Loders
Eggardon Down
West Compton
Frampton
Grimstone
Puddletown
Tolpuddle
Bere Regis
Symondsbury
Bridport
Uploders
Askerswell
Muckleford
Stratton
Charminster
Burleston
Affpuddle
Turners Puddle
Chideock
Walditch
Bothenhampton
Compton Valence
Kingston Russell
Bradford Peverell
Dorchester
Hardy's Cottage Garden
Stinsford
Tincleton
Briants Puddle
Lane End
Wareham Forest
Eype
South West Coast Path
West Bay
Shipton Gorge
Chilcombe
Litton Cheney
Long Bredy
Winterborne Abbas
The Tutankhamun Exhibition
Kingston Maurward
West Stafford
Woodsford
T.E. Lawrences House
Military Museum
The Dinosaur Museum
Moreton
Bovington Camp
Trigon Hill
Burton Bradstock
Littlebredy
Winterborne Steepleton
Martinstown
Maiden Castle
Winterborne Monkton
Whitcombe
Crossways
Monkey World
Tank Museum
Bay
Swyre
Puncknowle
Black Down
Winterborne Herringston
West Knighton
Frome
Mill House Cider Museum
East Burton
Stokeford
North
West Bexington
Portesham
Broadmayne
Warmwell
Wool
East Stoke
Stoborough
Abbotsbury
Tithe Barn Country Museum
Sub Tropical Gardens
Swannery
Rodden
Upwey
Bincombe
Poxwell
Owermoigne
East Knighton
Winfrith Newburgh
Coombe Keynes
West Holme
Grange Heath
Broadwey
Preston
Upton
Holworth
Chaldon Herring or East Chaldon
Langton Herring
Nottington
Overcombe
Jordan Hill Roman Temple
Osmington
Toll
Chaldon Down
Osmington Mills
Ringstead Bay
West Lulworth
East Lulworth
Lulworth Cove
Purbeck
Chesil Beach
Chickerell
Radipole
Water Gardens
Weymouth Sea Life Park
Melcombe Regis
Durdle Door
Westham
Weymouth
Nothe Fort
Brewer's Quay and Timewalk
Charlestown
Weymouth Bay
Lulworth Cove
Worbarrow Bay
Tyneham
Kimmeridge Bay
Rodwell
Wyke Regis
Portland Harbour
Portland Castle
Fortuneswell
West Bay
Grove
Isle of Portland
Easton
Weston
Museum
Southwell
Lighthouse
Bill of Portland
A37
A303
A3088
A30
A356
A35
A354
A352
A357
A350
A31
A371
A359
A372
A3030
B3151
B3153
B3145
B3148
B3081
B3092
B3091
B3143
B3142
B3146
B3157
B3159
B3162
B3163
B3164
B3165
B3390
B3070
B3071
18
10
6
7
8
9
10
G
H

Wiltshire
Dorset
Cranborne Chase
West Wiltshire Downs
Vale of Wardour
Salisbury
Wilton
Mere
Gillingham
Shaftesbury
Blandford Forum
Wimborne Minster
Ferndown
Verwood
Fordingbridge
Ringwood
Bournemouth
Boscombe
Christchurch
Highcliffe
New Milton
Barton on Sea
Milford on Sea
Brockenhurst
Poole
Hamworthy
Upton
Wareham
Swanage
Studland
Sandbanks
Corfe Castle
Langton Matravers
Worth Matravers
Kimmeridge
Wool
West Lulworth
Bere Regis
Tisbury
Fovant
Dinton
Broad Chalke
Bowerchalke
Sixpenny Handley
Cranborne
Alderholt
Downton
Redlynch
Burley
Sway
Lymington
Purbeck Hills
Isle of Purbeck
Poole Harbour
Brownsea Island
Poole Bay
Christchurch Bay
Hengistbury Head
Swanage Bay
Durlston Head
Peveril Pt.
St. Alban's Head
Kimmeridge Bay
Worbarrow Bay
Lulworth Cove
The Foreland
The Needles
Studland Bay
Wareham Forest
Ringwood Forest
New Forest
Jersey 3:45
Guernsey 2:30
Jersey 3:45
Cherbourg 4:15
A303
A30
A36
A338
A354
A350
A31
A35
A348
A351
A352
A337
A3094
19
9

Hampshire
Isle of Wight
EAST HAMPSHIRE
Winchester
Kings Worthy
New Alresford
Stockbridge
Nether Wallop
Crawley
Worthy Down
Little Somborne
Upper Somborne
King's Somborne
Broughton
Houghton
Horsebridge
Ashley
Sparsholt
Farley Mount
Littleton
Headbourne Worthy
Martyr Worthy
Itchen Abbas
Itchen Stoke
Easton
Avington
Ovington
Alresford
The Grange
Northington
Bighton
Gundleton
North Street
Bishops Sutton
Soldridge
Ropley
Ropley Dean
Four Marks
Kitwood
Monkwood
Lower Farringdon
Upper Farringdon
Chawton
Oakhanger
Selborne
Gilbert White's House
Newton Valence
Whitehill
Blackmoor
East Tisted
Greatham
Colemore
Empshott
Longmoor
Hawkley
Liss Forest
West Liss
East Liss
Liss
Tichborne
Cheriton
West Tisted
Bramdean
New Cheriton
Hinton Ampner
Beauworth
Kilmeston
Privett
High Cross
Steep
Steep Marsh
Stoner Hill
Froxfield Green
Stroud
Sheet
Petersfield
Rother
Langrish
West Meon
East End
Warnford
Brockwood
Longwood Warren
Morestead
Lane End
Owslebury
Baybridge
Upham
Twyford
Shawford
Otterbourne
Colden Common
Marwell Zoological Park
Compton
Oliver's Battery
Stanmore
Chilcomb
Standon
Hursley
Pucknall
Hillier Gardens and Arboretum
Michelmersh
Mottisfont
Brook
Braishfield
Timsbury
Awbridge
Abbotswood
Ampfield
Upper Ratley
Romsey
Cupernham
Whitenap
East Wellow
West Wellow
North Baddesley
Chandler's Ford
EASTLEIGH
Chilworth
Bishopstoke
Fair Oak
Fisher's Pond
Lower Upham
Ashton
Dean
Droxford
Exton
Corhampton
Meonstoke
Brockbridge
Soberton
Swanmore
Hoe
Chidden
Clanfield
Hambledon
East Meon
Ramsdean
Weston
Butser Hill
Combe
Buriton
Nursted
War Down
Queen Elizabeth
South Harting
Uppark
Chalton
North Marden
Compton
Up Marden
West Marden
Finchdean
Forestside
Stoughton
Rowland's Castle
Stansted Park
Walderton
Horndean
Blendworth
Catherington
Lovedean
Denmead
Anthill Common
Hoe Gate
Soberton Heath
Newtown
Hundred Acres
North Boarhunt
Cowplain
Forest of Bere
Waterlooville
Southwick
Purbrook
Leigh Park
Stockheath
Westbourne
Funtington
Woodmancote
HAVANT
Warblington
Bedhampton
Hermitage
Emsworth
Southbourne
Hambrook
Nutbourne
Broadbridge
Chidham
Thorney
Chichester Harbour
West Thorney
Northney
North Hayling
Stoke
Langstone
Langstone Harbour
Hayling Island
Fleet
West Town
Eastoke
South Hayling
West Wittering
East Wittering
Wintershill
Newtown
Bishops Waltham
Horton Heath
Durley
Long Common
Waltham Chase
Shirrell Heath
Curdridge
Shedfield
Botley
Hedge End
Thornhill
West End
Southampton
SOUTHAMPTON
Swaythling
Bassett
Rownhams
Nursling
Lee
Upton
Toothill
Ridge
Wigley
Ower
Calmore
Testwood
Totton
Copythorne
Winsor
Netley Marsh
Bartley
Woodlands
Ashurst
Pooksgreen
Marchwood
Lyndhurst
Shirley
Portswood
Bitterne
Northam
Sholing
Woolston
Itchen
Millbrook
Eling
Old Netley
Lowford
Bursledon
Burridge
Hamble
Netley
Hound
Swanwick
Lower Swanwick
Park Gate
Locks Heath
Warsash
Hamble-le-Rice
Titchfield
Newtown
Wickham
Funtley
Boarhunt
Fort Nelson
Ports Down
Wallington
Fareham
Portchester
Wymering
Cosham
Drayton
Hilsea
Portsmouth
PORTSMOUTH
North End
Fratton
Milton
Eastney
Southsea
Portsea
Whale I.
Brockhurst
Hardway
Fleetlands
Bridgemary
Peel Common
Stubbington
Hill Head
Lee on the Solent
GOSPORT
Alverstoke
Gilkicker Pt.
Stokes Bay
Spithead
The Solent
Southampton Water
Hythe
Dibden
Dibden Purlieu
Buttsash
Hardley
Holbury
Fawley
Ashlett
Calshot
Blackfield
Langley
Denny Lodge
Denny Lodge Walk
Beaulieu Heath
Hill Top
Beaulieu
Palace Ho.
National Motor Mus
Balmerlawn
Clayhill
Hatchet Gate
East Boldre
Setley
Beaulieu Heath
Battramsley
Boldre
Bull Hill
Pilley
Norleywood
Portmore
East End
Bucklers Hard
Exbury
Lepe
Stone Pt.
Needs Ore Pt.
Walhampton
Waterford
Woodside
Lower Pennington
Keyhaven
Hurst Castle
Sconce Pt.
Colwell Bay
Totland
Norton
Norton Green
Yarmouth
Freshwater
Freshwater Bay
Afton
Thorley Street
Wellow
Cranmore
Hamstead
Shalfleet
Ningwood
Newbridge
Calbourne
Shalcombe
Brighstone Forest
Mottistone
Hulverstone
Brook
The Needles Old Battery
The Undercliff
Brighstone
Moortown
Limerstone
Yafford
Thorncross
Brighstone Bay
Atherfield Pt.
Little Atherfield
Pyle
Chale Green
Chale
Chale Bay
Blackgang
Blackgang Chine
Niton
St. Catherine's Point
Whitwell
St. Lawrence
The Undercliff
Ventnor
Bonchurch
Dunnose
Luccombe Village
Luccombe Chine
Wroxall
Stenbury Down
Shanklin
Sandown
Sandown Bay
Lake
Apse Heath
Whiteley Bank
Winford
Branstone
Sandford
Godshill
Roud
Kingston
Shorwell
Gatcombe
Chillerton
Rookley
Merstone
Horringford
Arreton
Newchurch
Alverstone
Brading
Yaverland
Culver Cliff
Whitecliff Bay
Hillway
Lane End
Foreland
Bembridge
St. Helens
Steyne Cross
Newport
NEWPORT
Carisbrooke
Clatterford
Shide
Blackwater
Bowcombe
Gunville
Hunny Hill
Staplers
Downend
Havenstreet
Wootton Bridge
Wootton Common
Binstead
RYDE
Elmfield
Seaview
Nettlestone
Nettlestone Pt.
Fishbourne
Whippingham
Parkhurst
Parkhurst Forest
Porchfield
Newtown
Northwood
Rew Street
Gurnard
Gurnard Bay
Thorness Bay
Cowes
East Cowes
Osborne House
Osborne Bay
Barton Manor
Medina
Isle of Wight Steam Railway
BILBAO 30:00
SANTANDER 30:00
(Nov - Mar)
ST. MALO 6:00
CHERBOURG 5:00
LE HAVRE 5:30
ST. MALO 8:45
M3
M27
M271
M275
A3(M)
A3
A27
A31
A32
A35
A272
A3054
A3055
A3020
20
12
6
7
8
9
10
A
B
C
D
E
F
G
H

Alton
Petersfield
Midhurst
Chichester
Bognor Regis
Worthing
HAVANT
LITTLEHAMPTON
Godalming
Milford
Elstead
Haslemere
Hindhead
Grayshott
Liphook
Bordon
Cranleigh
Billingshurst
Petworth
Pulborough
Storrington
Arundel
Rustington
Angmering
Ferring
Steyning
Horndean
Emsworth
Southbourne
Bosham
Selsey
SELSEY BILL
East Wittering
South Hayling
HAYLING ISLAND
CHICHESTER HARBOUR
Middleton on Sea
West Sussex
Sussex
SURREY
SOUTH DOWNS
Hurt Wood
Compton
The Sands
Farnham
Shackleford
Hurtmore
Farncombe
Bramley
Wonersh
Peper Harow
Eashing
Frensham
Churt
Thursley
Witley
Hambledon
Hascombe
Dunsfold
Alfold
Loxwood
Plaistow
Northchapel
Fernhurst
Lurgashall
Lodsworth
Easebourne
Cocking
Singleton
West Dean
East Dean
Goodwood
Halnaker
Boxgrove
Fontwell
Slindon
Walberton
Yapton
Felpham
Pagham
Sidlesham
Selsey
Rogate
Liss
Steep
Buriton
Chalton
Compton
Stoughton
Funtington
Westbourne
Fishbourne
Apuldram
Sutton
Bignor
Amberley
Houghton
Burpham
Findon
Washington
Sompting
Lancing
Broadwater
Durrington
Goring by Sea
West Worthing
Slinfold
Rudgwick
Ewhurst
Ockley
Capel
Horsham
Warnham
Holmwood
Coldharbour
Leith Hill

Salfords
Horley
GATWICK AIRPORT
Crawley
Three Bridges
East Grinstead
Lingfield
Edenbridge
Dormansland
Felbridge
TONBRIDGE
Southborough
ROYAL TUNBRIDGE WELLS
Pembury
Paddock Wood
Lamberhurst
Groombridge
Forest Row
Hartfield
Withyham
Crowborough
Rotherfield
Mayfield
Wadhurst
Ticehurst
Stonegate
ASHDOWN FOREST
Nutley
Wych Cross
Chelwood Gate
Danehill
Horsted Keynes
Sharpthorne
West Hoathly
Turners Hill
Balcombe
Handcross
Staplefield
Slaugham
Cuckfield
Haywards Heath
Lindfield
Ardingly
Fletching
Maresfield
Buxted
Uckfield
Framfield
Heathfield
Burwash
Etchingham
Burgess Hill
Hurstpierpoint
Hassocks
Keymer
Ditchling
Plumpton
Chailey
Newick
Isfield
Barcombe
Ringmer
Lewes
Glynde
Laughton
Chiddingly
Hailsham
Herstmonceux
Hellingly
Polegate
Pevensey
Pevensey Bay
Westham
Willingdon
Eastbourne
BEACHY HEAD
Birling Gap
East Dean
Friston
Seaford
Bishopstone
Newhaven
Peacehaven
Telscombe Cliffs
Rottingdean
Woodingdean
Falmer
Kingston near Lewes
Brighton and Hove
BRIGHTON
HOVE
Southwick
Portslade
SHOREHAM BY SEA
Kemp Town
Patcham
Pyecombe
Clayton
Poynings
Fulking
Edburton
Alfriston
Berwick
Wilmington
Selmeston
Arlington
West Firle
Beddingham
Rodmell
Southease
East Sussex
HIGH WEALD
SOUTH DOWNS
DIEPPE 2:15
DIEPPE 4:00
6
7
8
9
10
A
B
C
D
E
F
G
H

Tilbury
East Tilbury
Cliffe
St. Mary's Hoo
Allhallows
Lower Stoke
Isle of Grain
Grain
Sheerness
NORTHFLEET
GRAVESEND
High Halstow
Church Street
Lower Higham
Cliffe Woods
Chalk
Perry Street
Singlewell
Shorne
Higham
Wainscott
Chattenden
Hoo
Stoke
North Street
Medway
West Minster
Halfway Houses
Minster
Warden Pt.
Warden
Queenborough
Rushenden
Eastchurch
Leysdown on Sea
Chetney Marshes
ISLE OF SHEPPEY
Thong
Strood
Frindsbury
Upnor
ROCHESTER
Gillingham
Brompton
Grange
Ham Green
Lower Halstow
Iwade
Upchurch
Shell Ness
Isle of Harty
WHITSTA
Longfield
New Barn
Sole Street
Cobham
Hartley
Meopham Station
Meopham
Luddesdown
Hook Green
Cuxton
North Halling
CHATHAM
Luton
Rainham
Breach
Kemsley
The Swale
Milton Regis
SITTINGBOURNE
Conyer
Uplees
Seasalter
New Ash Green
Upper Halling
Halling
Wouldham
Wayfield
Hempstead
Walderslade
Moor Street
Wigmore
Newington
Hartlip
Bobbing
Borden
Bapchild
Barrow Green
Teynham
Oare
Graveney
Goodnestone
Faversham
Dargate
Culverstone Green
Stansted
Fairseat
Vigo Village
Snodland
Birling
Burham
Bluebell Hill
Eccles
Bredhurst
Stockbury
Oad Street
Tunstall
Highsted
Rodmersham
Lynsted
Ospringe
Preston
Hernhill
Boughton Street
Dunkirk
Trottiscliffe
Ryarsh
New Hythe
Aylesford
Boxley
South Green
Bredgar
Bicknor
Swanton Street
Milstead
Doddington
Newnham
North Street
South Street
Wrotham
Wrotham Heath
Addington
Leybourne
West Malling
Ditton
Sandling
British Legion Village
East Malling
Detling
Thurnham
Hucking
Broad Street
Wormshill
Frinsted
Wichling
Eastling
Sheldwich
Selling
Oversland
Chartham Hatch
Platt
Offham
Crouch
Claygate
Maidstone
Roseacre
Hollingbourne
Eyhorne Street
Bearsted
Throwley
Old Wives Lees
Plaxtol
Mereworth
Kent Street
East Barming
Teston
Tovil
Shepway
Otham
West Street
Stalisfield Green
Leaveland
Badlesmere
Shottenden
Chilham
Dunk's Green
West Peckham
Wateringbury
West Farleigh
East Farleigh
Loose
Boughton Monchelsea
Langley
Leeds
Broomfield
Harrietsham
Lenham
Warren Street
Sandway
Molash
Shipbourne
Nettlestead
Nettlestead Green
Coxheath
Langley Heath
Warmlake
Kingswood
Lenham Heath
Godmersham
Pittswood
Hadlow
Yalding
Hunton
Chart Corner
Sutton Valence
Grafty Green
Boughton Malherbe
Charing
Challock Lees
Sole St
Higham Wood
Hale Street
Benover
Linton
Chart Sutton
Ulcombe
Charing Heath
Westwell Leacon
Westwell
Boughton Aluph
Crundale
East Peckham
Golden Green
Barnes Street
Beltring
Laddingford
Chainhurst
Egerton
Boughton Lees
Hassell Street
TONBRIDGE
Whetsted
Five Oak Green
Queen Street
Collier Street
Rabbit's Cross
Cross-at-Hand
Southernden
Little Chart
Ram Lane
Egerton Forstal
Goat Lees
Wye
Tudeley
Paddock Wood
Claygate
Milebush
Marden
Hawkenbury
Headcorn
Pluckley
Pluckley Thorne
Hothfield
Kennington
Brook
Hastingleigh
High Brooms
Castle Hill
Marden Beech
Marden Thorn
Staplehurst
Sinkhurst Green
Smarden Bell
Smarden
Maltman's Hill
Great Chart
Ashford
Willesborough
Hinxhill
Willesborough Lees
Brabourne
Matfield
Pembury
Brenchley
Winchet Hill
Knox Bridge
Frittenden
Lashenden
Haffenden Quarter
Wissenden
Sevington
Petteridge
Horsmonden
Curtisden Green
Standen
Bethersden
Stubbs Cross
Kingsnorth
Mersham
Smeeth
ROYAL TUNBRIDGE WELLS
Hazel Street
Collier's Green
Cranbrook Common
Three Chimneys
Biddenden
Tanden
Shadoxhurst
Cheeseman's Green
Hawkenbury
Lamberhurst Quarter
Goudhurst
Iden Green
Wilsley Pound
Sissinghurst
High Halden
Bromley Green
Aldington Frith
Clap Hill
Aldington
Bells Yew Green
Lamberhurst
Henghurst
Bonnington
Court-at-Street
Frant
Hook Green
Kilndown
Cranbrook
East End
St. Michael's
Shirkoak
Orlestone
Cousley Wood
Bartley Mill
Hartley
Parkgate
Woodchurch
Ruckinge
Bilsington
Wood's Green
Bewl Bridge Reservoir
Bedgebury Forest
Benenden
Tenterden
Brook Street
Kenardington
Hamstreet
Durgates
Wadhurst
Three Leg Cross
Gill's Green
Leigh Green
Warehorne
Royal Military Canal
Burm
Bestbeech Hill
Flimwell
High Street
Iden Green
Dingleden
Rolvenden
Appledore Heath
Newchurch
Riseden
Union Street
Hawkhurst
Small Hythe
Reading Street
Snave
Tidebrook
Shover's Green
Wallcrouch
Ticehurst
Horns Corner
Four Throws
Rolvenden Layne
ISLE OF OXNEY
Appledore
ROMNEY MARSH
St. Mary in the Marsh
Stonegate
Swiftsden
The Moor
Sandhurst
Linkhill
Peening Quarter
Snargate
Coggins Mill
Hurst Green
Sandhurst Cross
Newenden
Wittersham
Stone
Brenzett
Ivychurch
St.
Witherenden Hill
Etchingham
Bodiam
Ham Green
The Stocks
Rother
Rother Levels
Brookland
Old Romney
Littlest
Burwash Common
Burwash
Northbridge Street
Northiam
Ewhurst Green
Beckley
Four Oaks
Iden
New Romney
Romney Sands
Salehurst
Robertsbridge
Millcorner
Clayhill
Peasmarsh
Houghton Green
Walland Marsh
Greatstone
Burwash Weald
Oxley's Green
Staple Cross
Horns Cross
Rye Foreign
Playden
East Guldeford
Cade Street
Brightling
John's Cross
Cripp's Corner
Rye
Lydd
Punnett's Town
Three Cups Corner
Mountfield
Vinehall Street
Tillingham
Denge Marsh
Old Heathfield
Darwell Hole
Broad Oak
Broadland Row
Udimore
Camber
Rushlake Green
Dallington
Netherfield
Whatlington
Sedlescombe
Rye Harbour
Warbleton
Canadia
Sedlescombe Street
Brede
Winchelsea
Rye Bay
Denge Beach
Penhurst
Battle
Guestling Thorn
Winchelsea Beach
Foul Mile
Ponts Green
Three Oaks
Icklesham
Kent Street
Westfield
Bodle Street Green
Catsfield
Telham
Pett
Cowbeech
Baldslow
Guestling Green
Cliff End
Herstmonceux
Windmill Hill
Henley's Down
Crowhurst
Ninfield
Hollington
St. Helen's
Ore
Fairlight
Fairlight Cove
Magham Down
Boreham Street
Lunsford's Cross
Hooe Common
Hooe
Silverhill
Hailsham
Wartling
Sidley
St. Leonards
Hastings
Little Common
Bulverhythe
West Marina
Pevensey Levels
Cooden
BEXHILL
Hankham
Norman's Bay
Pevensey
Westham
Pevensey Bay
Stone Cross
Friday Street
Kent
East Sussex
KENT DOWNS
HIGH WEALD

THE SHELL GROTTO
Margate
Cliftonville
Foreness Pt.
Kingsgate
NORTH FORELAND
Westgate on Sea
RECULVER TOWERS AND ROMAN FORT
Minnis Bay
Reculver
Birchington
Northdown
St. Peter's
BROADSTAIRS
BLEAK HOUSE
DICKENS HOUSE MUSEUM
HERNE BAY
Hillborough
QUEX PARK
Isle of Thanet
SPITFIRE AND HURRICANE MEM.
Tankerton
Swalecliffe
Beltinge
St. Nicholas at Wade
Acol
Northwood
Greenhill
Herne
Broomfield
Boyden Gate
Sarre
MANSTON
Manston
Newington
Dumpton
Chestfield
Way
Ramsgate
MARITIME MUSEUM
South Street
BRAMBLES WILDLIFE PARK
Hoath
Chislet
Monkton
Minster
Cliffsend
Pegwell
MOTOR MUSEUM
Pegwell Bay
Calcott
Upstreet
Stour
West Stourmouth
DUNKIRK 2:30
OSTEND 4:00
Honey Hill
Hersden
East Stourmouth
Broadoak
Grove
Westmarsh
Tyler Hill
Preston
RICHBOROUGH CASTLE
DUNKIRK 1:30
OSTEND 1:50
Blean
Sturry
Westbere
Ware
Hales Place
Stodmarsh
Elmstone
Hoaden
Rough Common
Fordwich
Great Stonar
Canterbury
Wickhambreux
WINGHAM BIRD PARK
Sandwich Bay
Ickham
Guilton
Ash
Sandwich
Harbledown
ST. AUGUSTINE'S ABBEY
Littlebourne
Wingham
Marshborough
TOLL
ROYAL ST. GEORGE'S
CANTERBURY TALES
ROMAN MUS.
Stone Cross
Thanington
HOWLETTS WILD ANIMAL PARK
Bramling
Staple
Woodnesborough
Worth
Bekesbourne
Gore
Chartham
Patrixbourne
Goodnestone
Ham
Nackington
Adisham
GOODNESTONE PARK
Eastry
Finglesham
Bridge
Knowlton
Street End
Lower Hardres
Chillenden
NORTH DOWNS WAY
Betteshanger
Sholden
MARITIME AND LOCAL HISTORY MUSEUM
DEAL
THE DOWNS
Bishopsbourne
Aylesham
Easole Street
Nonington
Northbourne
DEAL CASTLE
Petham
Kingston
Upper Hardres Court
Snowdown
Tilmanstone
Great Mongeham
Walmer
WALMER CASTLE AND GARDENS
Elvington
Womenswold
Barham
Barfreston
Ripple
Waltham
Bossingham
Derringstone
EAST KENT RLY.
East Studdal
Sutton
Woolage Green
Eythorne
West Langdon
Ringwould
Kingsdown
Stelling Minnis
Shepherdswell
Coxhill
Martin
Coldred
East Langdon
Denton
LYDDEN
Martin Mill
Wingmore
Bodsham
Wootton
Whitfield
Elmsted
Lyminge Forest
Lydden
Guston
St. Margaret's at Cliffe
Selsted
THE BAY MUSEUM
Elham
West Cliffe
St. Margaret's Bay
Ewell Minnis
Temple Ewell
Swingfield St.
BUTTERFLY CENTRE
THE PINES GARDEN
Lymbridge Green
CRABBLE CORN MILL
SOUTH FORELAND
Rhodes Minnis
Swingfield Minnis
Buckland
Ottinge
Alkham
ROMAN PAINTED HOUSE
DOVER CASTLE & HELLFIRE CORNER
Stowting Lees
Densole
Drellingore
Maxton
KENT BATTLE OF BRITAIN MUSEUM
Lyminge
Farthingloe
West Hougham
Paddlesworth
Hawkinge
DOVER
Etchinghill
Postling
CHANNEL TUNNEL
Capel le Ferne
Aycliff
CALAIS 1:15
CALAIS 0:35
CALAIS 0:45
Sellindge
Lees
Beachborough
Stanford
Newington
East Wear Bay
BROCKHILL
Pedlinge
Cheriton
Folkestone
ROTUNDA
Lympne
LYMPNE CASTLE
Saltwood
Sandgate
Hythe
Palmarsh
ROMNEY, HYTHE AND DYMCHURCH MUSEUM
Dymchurch
CHANNEL TUNNEL
BOULOGNE 0:55
ENGLISH CHANNEL
Sangatte
Wissant
Cap Griz-Nez
FRANCE
Wimereux
M20
A2
A20
A28
A253
A256
A257
A258
A259
A260
A261
A290
A291
A299
B2068
6
7
8
9
10
A
B
C
D
E
F
G
H

Pontardulais
Pontardawe
Clydach
Gorseinon
Swansea
Neath
Port Talbot
Rhondda
Cynon
Taff
Merthyr Tydfil
ABERDARE
MOUNTAIN ASH
Treharris
Abercynon
Porth
Tonypandy
Treorchy
RHONDDA
Ferndale
Maerdy
Treherbert
Tynewydd
Glyncorrwg
Cymer
Blaengarw
Pontycymmer
MAESTEG
Bridgend
PONTYPRIDD
Tonyrefail
Beddau
Llantrisant
Pencoed
Pyle
Porthcawl
Cowbridge
Vale of Glamorgan
Llantwit Major
Rhoose
Aberavon
Margam
Baglan
Skewen
Morriston
Llansamlet
Mumbles
The Mumbles
West Cross
Black Pill
Killay
Sketty
Dunvant
Mayals
Newton
SWANSEA BAY
Mumbles Hd.
CORK 10:00
VALE OF NEATH
Rheola Forest
Kenfig
Kenfig Burrows
Tusker Rock
Nash Pt.
Breaksea Pt.
Southerndown
Ogmore by Sea
St. Brides Major
Wick
Broughton
Monknash
Marcross
St. Donat's
Boverton
St. Athan
Gileston
Porthkerry
Aberthin
Penllyn
Llanblethian
Llandough
St. Hilary
Llantrithyd
Bonvilston
Walterston
Flemingston
Llancarfan
Penmark
Moulton
Talygarn
Llanharry
Llanharan
Talbot Green
Miskin
Groes faen
M4
A48
BRISTOL CHANNEL
Foreland Pt.
Lynmouth Bay
Highveer Pt.
Woody Bay
Lynmouth
Lynton
Countisbury
Trentishoe
Martinhoe
Heale
Barbrook
Brendon
Malmsmead
Oare
Porlock
Porlock Weir
Porlock Bay
Hurlstone Pt.
Bossington
Selworthy
Allerford
Minehead
Alcombe
Dunster
Blue Anchor Bay
Blue Anchor
Carhampton
Old Cleeve
Watchet
Williton
Washford
EXMOOR
EXMOOR FOREST
EXMOOR NATIONAL PARK
Brendon Common
Holnicote Estate
Dunkery Beacon
Exford
Simonsbath
Withypool
Withypool Common
Winsford
Exton
Wheddon Cross
Cutcombe
Luxborough
Brendon Forest
BRENDON HILLS
Parracombe
Kentisbury
Blackmoor Gate
Challacombe
Challacombe Common
Shoulsbarrow Common
Exe Plain
Pinkworthy Pond
Lydcott
Brayford
North Radworthy
North Heasley
Arlington
Loxhore
Shirwell
Goodleigh
Gunn
Westacott
Elworthy
Monksilver
Sampford Brett
Stogumber

Torfaen
Monmouthshire
Caerphilly
Newport
Cardiff
North Somerset
Bristol
Somerset
MOUTH OF THE SEVERN
BRIDGWATER BAY
MENDIP HILLS
QUANTOCK FOREST
POLDEN HILLS
Caldicot Level
New Tredegar
Abertillery
Abersychan
PONTYPOOL
Usk
Bargoed
Oakdale
Crumlin
Blackwood
Gelligaer
Hengoed
Lanfach
Abercarn
Crosskeys
Risca
Cwmbran
Pontnewydd
Caerleon
Chepstow
Caldicot
Magor
Bedwas
Machen
CAERPHILLY
Newport
Llanedeyrn
Rumney
Whitchurch
CARDIFF
PENARTH
BARRY
Barry Island
Sully Island
Flat Holme
Steep Holme
Brean Down
Avonmouth
FILTON
Patchway
Portishead
Redcliff Bay
Clevedon
Nailsea
Long Ashton
Yatton
Wrington
Weston super Mare
Banwell
Cheddar
Burnham on Sea
Highbridge
Wedmore
Wells
Shepton Mallet
Glastonbury
Street
Bridgwater
Hereford
Tintern Parva
Severn Beach
STERT FLATS
BERROW FLATS
Gore Sands
King's Sedge Moor
M4
M5
M48
M49
A38
A39
A48
A370
A371
18
28
8
9

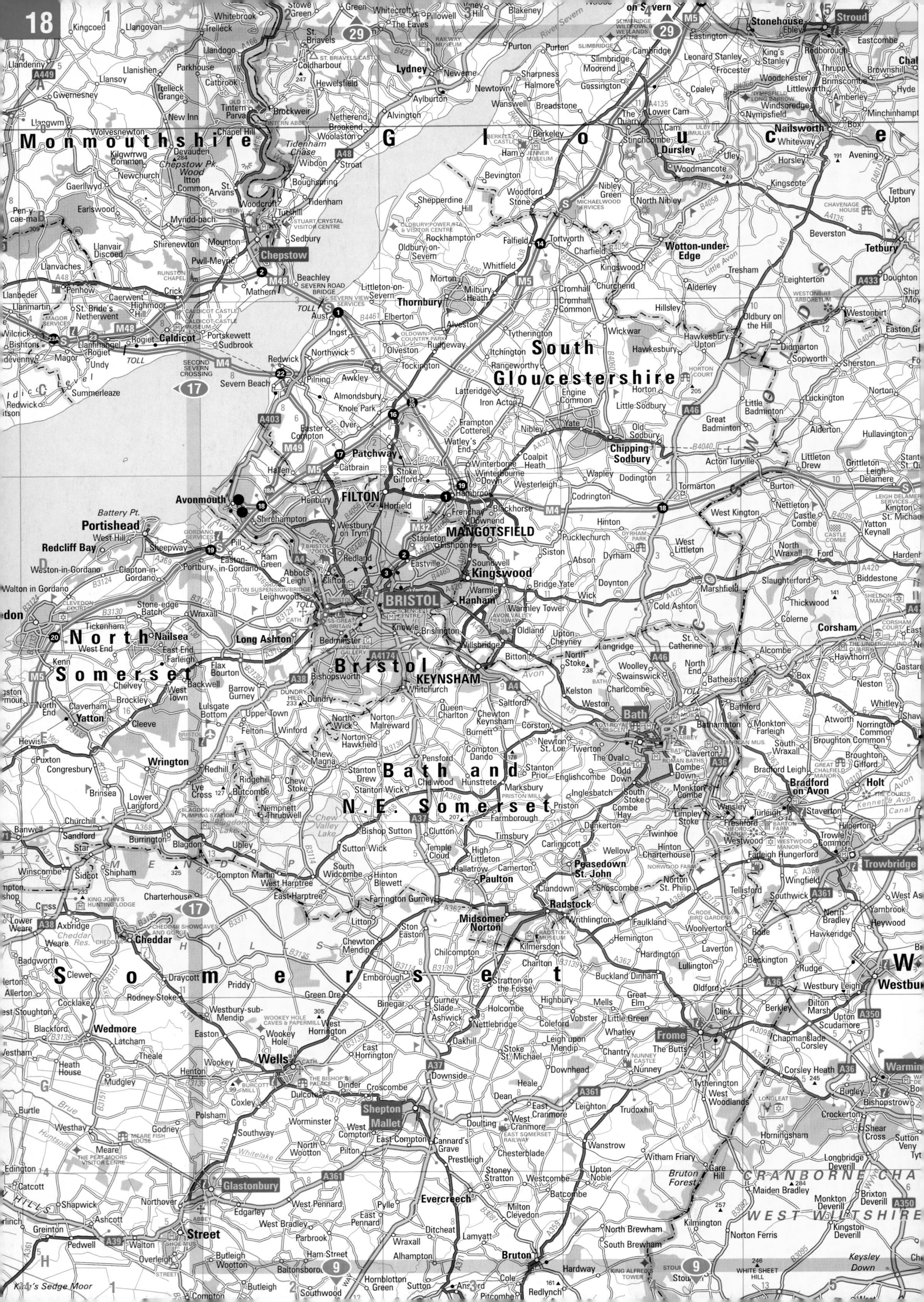

Monmouthshire
Gloucestershire
South Gloucestershire
North Somerset
Bristol
Bath and N.E. Somerset
Somerset
WEST WILTSHIRE
CRANBORNE CHASE
Chepstow
Stroud
Stonehouse
Lydney
Nailsworth
Dursley
Wotton-under-Edge
Tetbury
Thornbury
Portishead
Avonmouth
Filton
Patchway
Mangotsfield
Kingswood
BRISTOL
KEYNSHAM
Chipping Sodbury
Yate
Nailsea
Clevedon
Yatton
Long Ashton
Bath
Corsham
Bradford on Avon
Trowbridge
Frome
Radstock
Midsomer Norton
Paulton
Peasedown St. John
Wells
Shepton Mallet
Glastonbury
Street
Cheddar
Wedmore
Evercreech
Bruton
Caldicot
Magor
Severn Beach
Marshfield
Holt
Westbury
Warminster
Wrington
Blagdon
Chew Magna
Saltford
M4
M5
M48
M49
M32
A38
A46
A36
A37
A39
A361
A350
29
17
9

Cirencester
Fairford
Lechlade
South Cerney
Cricklade
Faringdon
Highworth
Swindon
Thamesdown
Stratton St. Margaret
Wootton Bassett
Purton
Chippenham
Calne
Marlborough
Hungerford
Devizes
Pewsey
Melksham
North Tidworth
Durrington
Amesbury
Andover
Ludgershall
Stockbridge
Carterton
Malmesbury
Wiltshire
SALISBURY PLAIN
VALE OF WHITE HORSE
NORTH WESSEX DOWNS
VALE OF PEWSEY
MARLBOROUGH DOWNS
LAMBOURN DOWNS
Savernake Forest
Collingbourne Forest
Harewood Forest
Great Ridge
VALE OF WARDOUR
Wylye Valley
Grovely Wood
Oakley Wood
Kingston Warren
Pewsey Down
Littleton Down
Black Heath
Compton Down
Enford Down
West Lavington Down
West Down
Orcheston Down
Knighton Down
Haxton Down
Doles Wood
Stonehenge
Avebury
Lambourn
Ramsbury
Aldbourne
Tilshead
Shrewton
Wylye
Ogbourne St. George
Upavon
Burbage
Bulford
Larkhill
Lyneham
M4
A419
A420
A346
A338
A303
A36
A350
A4

Oxfordshire
Berkshire
Hampshire
NORTH WESSEX DOWNS
LAMBOURN DOWNS
VALE OF WHITE HORSE
Oxford
Cowley
Wheatley
Thame
Chinnor
ABINGDON
Didcot
Wallingford
Wantage
Henley on Thames
Reading
Caversham
Woodley
Earley
Tilehurst
Whitley
Hungerford
Newbury
Thatcham
Tadley
Basingstoke
Hook
Andover
Whitchurch
Overton
Alton
Stockbridge
Kings Worthy
New Alresford
Goring
Pangbourne
Lambourn
Kingsclere
Micheldever Forest
Harewood Forest
Bramshill Forest
Thames or Isis
Kennet
Stoke Row
Nettlebed
Watlington
Benson
Cholsey
Blewbury
Harwell
Steventon
Faringdon
Bampton
Marcham
Sutton Courtenay
Dorchester
Chalgrove
Burghclere
Highclere
Hurstbourne Tarrant
Ludgershall
Silchester
Mortimer
Theale
Bradfield
Compton
Chieveley
Shinfield
Arborfield
Eversley
Odiham
Winchfield
Old Basing
Oakley
Overton
Dummer
Preston Candover
Medstead
Four Marks
Chawton

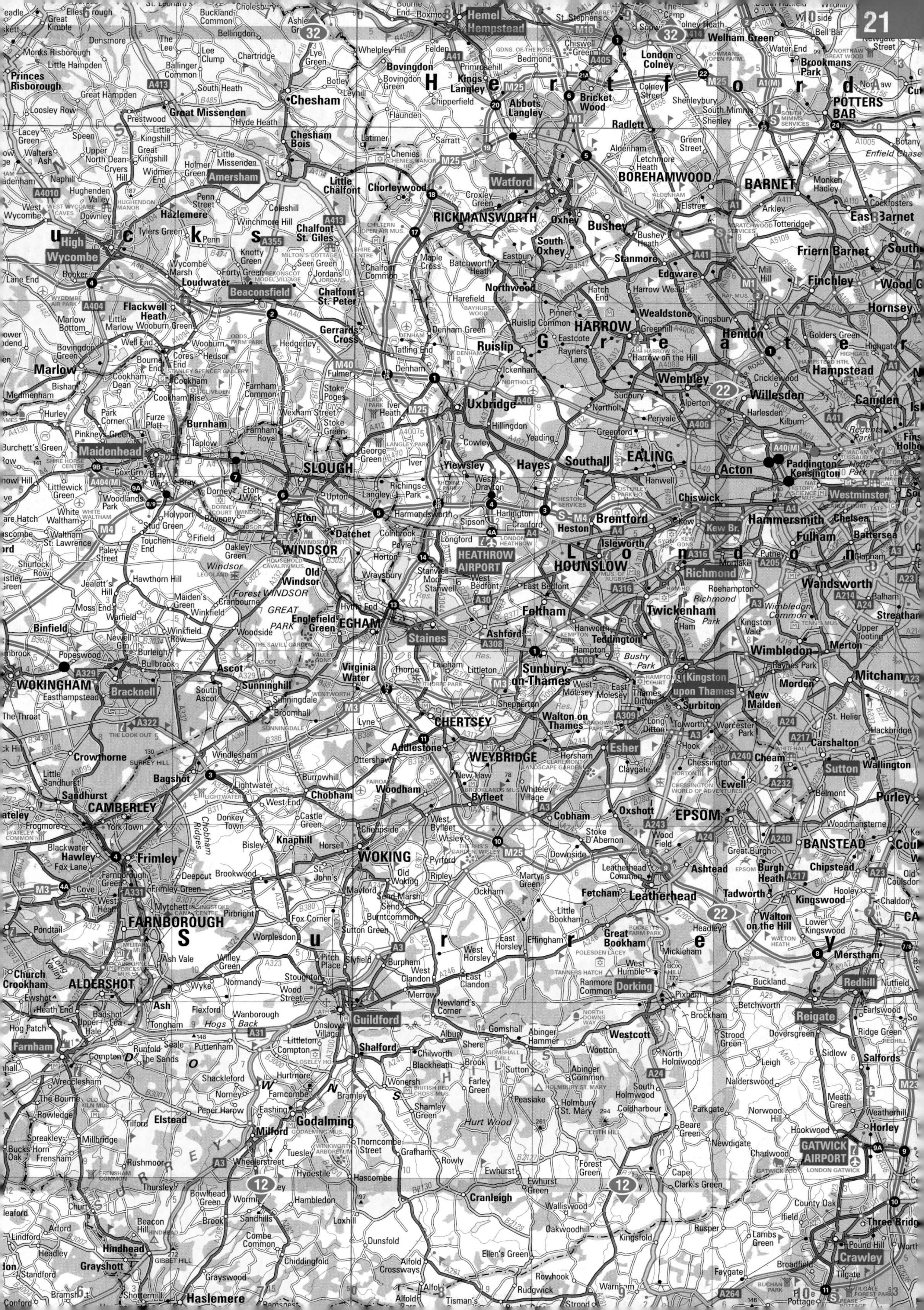
Hemel Hempstead
Welham Green
Princes Risborough
Chesham
Bovingdon
Kings Langley
Abbots Langley
Radlett
POTTERS BAR
Great Missenden
Chesham Bois
Amersham
Watford
BOREHAMWOOD
BARNET
High Wycombe
Hazlemere
RICKMANSWORTH
Chorleywood
Bushey
East Barnet
Beaconsfield
Chalfont St. Giles
Chalfont St. Peter
Northwood
Stanmore
Edgware
Finchley
Marlow
Gerrards Cross
Ruislip
HARROW
Hendon
Hornsey
Hampstead
Wembley
Willesden
Camden
Maidenhead
Uxbridge
SLOUGH
Hayes
Southall
EALING
Acton
Paddington
Kensington
Westminster
Burnham
WINDSOR
Eton
Datchet
HEATHROW AIRPORT
HOUNSLOW
Brentford
Chiswick
Hammersmith
Chelsea
Fulham
Battersea
Kew Br.
Richmond
Wandsworth
Staines
EGHAM
Feltham
Twickenham
Wimbledon
WOKINGHAM
Bracknell
Ascot
Sunninghill
Virginia Water
Sunbury-on-Thames
Kingston upon Thames
Surbiton
Mitcham
Morden
New Malden
CHERTSEY
Addlestone
WEYBRIDGE
Walton on Thames
Esher
Sutton
Crowthorne
CAMBERLEY
Bagshot
Chobham
Byfleet
Cobham
EPSOM
Purley
BANSTEAD
Frimley
WOKING
Leatherhead
Ashtead
FARNBOROUGH
ALDERSHOT
Guildford
Dorking
Reigate
Redhill
Farnham
Godalming
Milford
Shalford
GATWICK AIRPORT
Horley
Cranleigh
Hindhead
Haslemere
Crawley
Grayshott
M25
M4
M3
M40
M1
A40
A4
A3
A30
A31
A24
A23
A217
A316
A308
A404

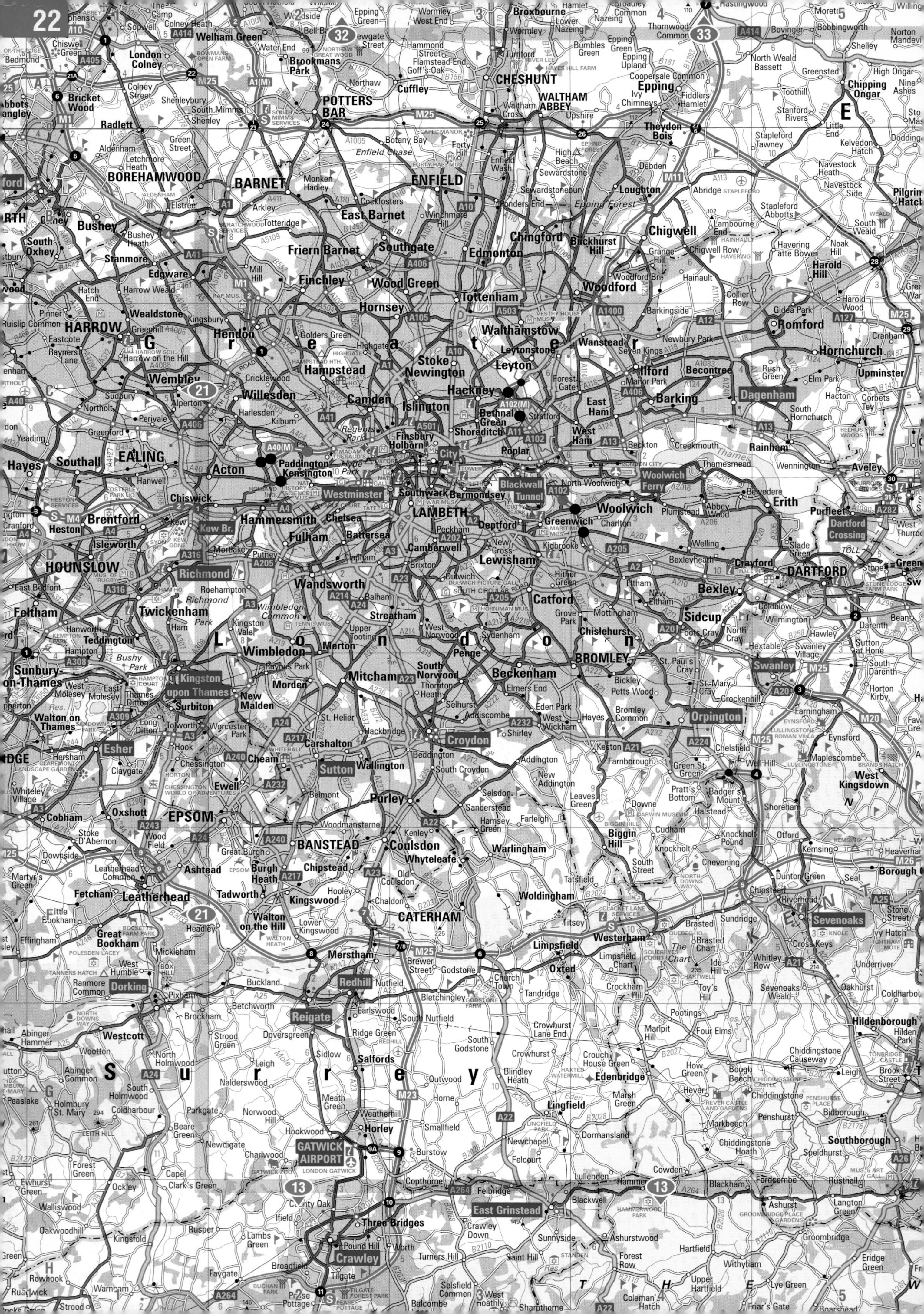
Greater London
Surrey
Kent
Essex
Herts
POTTERS BAR
ENFIELD
BARNET
BOREHAMWOOD
CHESHUNT
WALTHAM ABBEY
Epping
Loughton
Chigwell
Chingford
Edmonton
Tottenham
Walthamstow
Leyton
Hackney
Islington
Camden
Hampstead
Wembley
Willesden
HARROW
Hendon
Finchley
Wood Green
Hornsey
Stoke Newington
Ilford
Barking
Dagenham
Romford
Hornchurch
Upminster
Woodford
Wanstead
Stratford
West Ham
Poplar
City
Westminster
Paddington
Kensington
Acton
EALING
Southall
Hayes
HOUNSLOW
Brentford
Chiswick
Hammersmith
Fulham
Chelsea
Battersea
LAMBETH
Southwark
Bermondsey
Deptford
Greenwich
Woolwich
Blackwall Tunnel
Lewisham
Camberwell
Brixton
Wandsworth
Richmond
Twickenham
Wimbledon
Merton
Mitcham
Streatham
Catford
Bexley
Sidcup
Erith
DARTFORD
Dartford Crossing
BROMLEY
Beckenham
Croydon
Sutton
Kingston upon Thames
Surbiton
Esher
EPSOM
Purley
Coulsdon
BANSTEAD
CATERHAM
Orpington
Swanley
Sevenoaks
Westerham
Oxted
Redhill
Reigate
Leatherhead
Dorking
Horley
GATWICK AIRPORT
Crawley
East Grinstead
Edenbridge
Lingfield
Tonbridge
Southborough
M25
M1
M4
M11
M20
M23
M26
A1
A10
A12
A13
A2
A3
A4
A40
A406
A20
A21
A22
A23
A24
A25
A264
21
32
33
13

Chelmsford
Great Baddow
Galleyend
Sandon
Danbury
Maldon
Heybridge Basin
Northey I.
Osea I.
Bradwell on Sea
Ramsey Island
St. Lawrence
Tillingham
Steeple
Mundon
Lower Mayland
Asheldham
Dengie
Mayland
Latchingdon
Cold Norton
Purleigh
Rudley Green
Cock Clarks
Bicknacre
Woodham Mortimer
Runsell Green
Howe Green
Galleywood
Margaretting
Mill Green
Blackmore
Fryerning
Ingatestone
Stock
West Hanningfield
East Hanningfield
Woodham Ferrers
Stow Maries
Althorne
Southminster
Ray Sand
Essex
Reservoir
Swallows Cross
Heybridge
Coalhill
South Hanningfield
Rettendon
South Woodham Ferrers
North Fambridge
Bridgemans Island
Ostend
Stoneyhills
Burnham on Crouch
Montsale
Deal Hall
Foulness Sand
Foulness Pt.
Crouch
Hutton
Shenfield
BRENTWOOD
Billericay
Ramsden Heath
Runwell
Downham
Ramsden Bellhouse
Wickford
Rettendon Place
Hullbridge
Battlesbridge
South Fambridge
Canewdon
Rawreth
Hockley
Ashingdon
Paglesham Churchend
Paglesham Eastend
Courtsend
Churchend
South Green
Shotgate
Little Burstead
Great Burstead
Crays Hill
Nevendon
Ingrave
Herongate
Dunton Wayletts
Little Warley
Hawkwell
Great Stambridge
Ballards Gore
Potton Island
FOULNESS ISLAND
RAYLEIGH
Stroud Green
Rochford
Basildon
North Benfleet
Bowers Gifford
Thundersley
Eastwood
Barling
Little Wakering
Havengore Island
MAPLIN SANDS
Laindon
West Horndon
Langdon Hills
Pitsea
Vange
Daws Heath
Hadleigh
Hope's Grn.
South Benfleet
Prittlewell
Southchurch
Great Wakering
Bournes Green
North Shoebury
Leigh on Sea
Westcliffe on Sea
Southend on Sea
Thorpe Bay
Shoeburyness
Cambridge Town
Bulphan
Horndon on the Hill
Fobbing
Corringham
CANVEY ISLAND
Canvey Island
Coryton
Leigh Beck
Stanford le Hope
Orsett
Baker Street
Mucking
Thames Haven
THAMES ESTUARY
Chadwell St. Mary
Linford
West Tilbury
East Tilbury
Little Thurrock
Grays
Tilbury
Halstow Marshes
St. Mary's Marshes
St. Mary's Hoo
Allhallows-on-Sea
Allhallows
Lower Stoke
Isle of Grain
Grain
Cliffe
Cooling
High Halstow
Stoke
NORTHFLEET
GRAVESEND
Church Street
Lower Higham
Cliffe Woods
North Street
Sheerness
West Minster
Halfway Houses
Minster
Medway
Queenborough
Rushenden
Chetney Marshes
Eastchurch
Warden Pt.
Warden
Leysdown on Sea
ISLE OF SHEPPEY
Chalk
Perry Street
Southfleet
Singlewell
Shorne
Higham
Wainscott
Chattenden
Hoo
Upnor
Thong
Strood
Frindsbury
Brompton
Grange
ROCHESTER
Gillingham
CHATHAM
Ham Green
Lower Halstow
Upchurch
Iwade
Shell Ness
Isle of Harty
The Swale
WHITSTABLE
Seasalter
Istead Rise
New Barn
Sole Street
Cobham
Meopham Station
Hook Green
Luddesdown
Meopham
Cuxton
North Halling
Luton
Wayfield
Rainham
Breach
Bobbing
Kemsley
Milton Regis
SITTINGBOURNE
Conyer
Uplees
New Ash Green
Upper Halling
Halling
Wouldham
Walderslade
Hempstead
Moor Street
Wigmore
Newington
Hartlip
Borden
Bapchild
Barrow Green
Teynham
Oare
Graveney
Faversham
Goodnestone
Dargate
Yorkletts
Culverstone Green
Stansted
Snodland
Burham
Bluebell Hill
Bredhurst
Stockbury
Oad Street
Rodmersham
Tunstall
Highsted
Lynsted
Ospringe
Preston
Hernhill
Boughton Street
Dunkirk
Fairseat
Vigo Village
Birling
Trottiscliffe
Ryarsh
New Hythe
Aylesford
Eccles
Boxley
South Green
Bredgar
Bicknor
Swanton Street
Milstead
Doddington
Newnham
Eastling
Sheldwich
North Street
South Street
Oversland
Chartham Hatch
Addington
Leybourne
Wrotham Heath
West Malling
Ditton
Sandling
Detling
Thurnham
Hucking
Wormshill
Frinsted
Wichling
Throwley
Selling
Badlesmere
Old Wives Lees
Platt
Offham
East Malling
British Legion Village
Broad Street
Maidstone
Roseacre
Bearsted
Hollingbourne
Eyhorne Street
West Street
Stalisfield Green
Leaveland
Shottenden
Chilham
Crouch
Claygate Cross
Kent
Kent Street
Mereworth
East Barming
Tovil
Shepway
Otham
Leeds
Broomfield
Harrietsham
Lenham
Sandway
Warren Street
Molash
Shalmsford Street
Garlinge Green
Teston
Wateringbury
West Farleigh
East Farleigh
Loose
Boughton Monchelsea
Langley
Langley Heath
Kingswood
Lenham Heath
Charing
Charing Heath
Challock Lees
Godmersham
Sole Street
West Peckham
Nettlestead Green
Coxheath
Chart Corner
Warmlake
Sutton Valence
Chart Sutton
Ulcombe
Grafty Green
Boughton Malherbe
Westwell Leacon
Westwell
Boughton Aluph
Bilting
Crundale
Hadlow
Hale Street
Yalding
Hunton
Linton
Benover
East Peckham
Golden Green
Barnes Street
Beltring
Laddingford
Chainhurst
Rabbit's Cross
Egerton
Egerton Forstal
Boughton Lees
Hassell Street
Wye
Whetsted
Five Oak Green
Queen Street
Collier Street
Cross-at-Hand
Milebush
Southernden
Little Chart
Ram Lane
Hothfield
Goat Lees
Kennington
Brook
Hastingleigh
Paddock Wood
Claygate
Marden
Hawkenbury
Headcorn
Pluckley
Pluckley Thorne
Castle Hill
Marden Beech
Marden Thorn
Staplehurst
Sinkhurst Green
Smarden
Smarden Bell
Maltman's Hill
Great Chart
Ashford
Willesborough
Hinxhill
Willesborough Lees
Brabourne
Matfield
Pembury
Brenchley
Horsmonden
Winchet Hill
Knox Bridge
Frittenden
Lashenden
Haffenden Quarter
Wissenden
Sevington
Brabourne Lees
Petteridge
Curtisden Green
Bethersden
Kingsnorth
Mersham
Smeeth
TUNBRIDGE WELLS
Hazel Street
Collier's Green
Cranbrook Common
Three Chimneys
Standen
Stubbs Cross
Cheeseman's Green
Sellindge
Lamberhurst Quarter
Goudhurst
Biddenden
Tenden
Shadoxhurst
Bells Yew Green
Lamberhurst
Iden Green
Wisley Pound
Sissinghurst
High Halden
Bromley Green
Aldington Frith
Clap Hill
Aldington
Henghurst
Bonnington
Kilndown
Cranbrook
East End
Shirkoak
Court-at-Street
Hook Green
Cousley Wood
Hartley
St. Michael's
Woodchurch
Orlestone
Bilsington
Wood's Green
Bewl Bridge
Bedgebury
Benenden
Parkgate
Tenterden
Brook Street
Kenardington
Ruckinge
Hamstreet

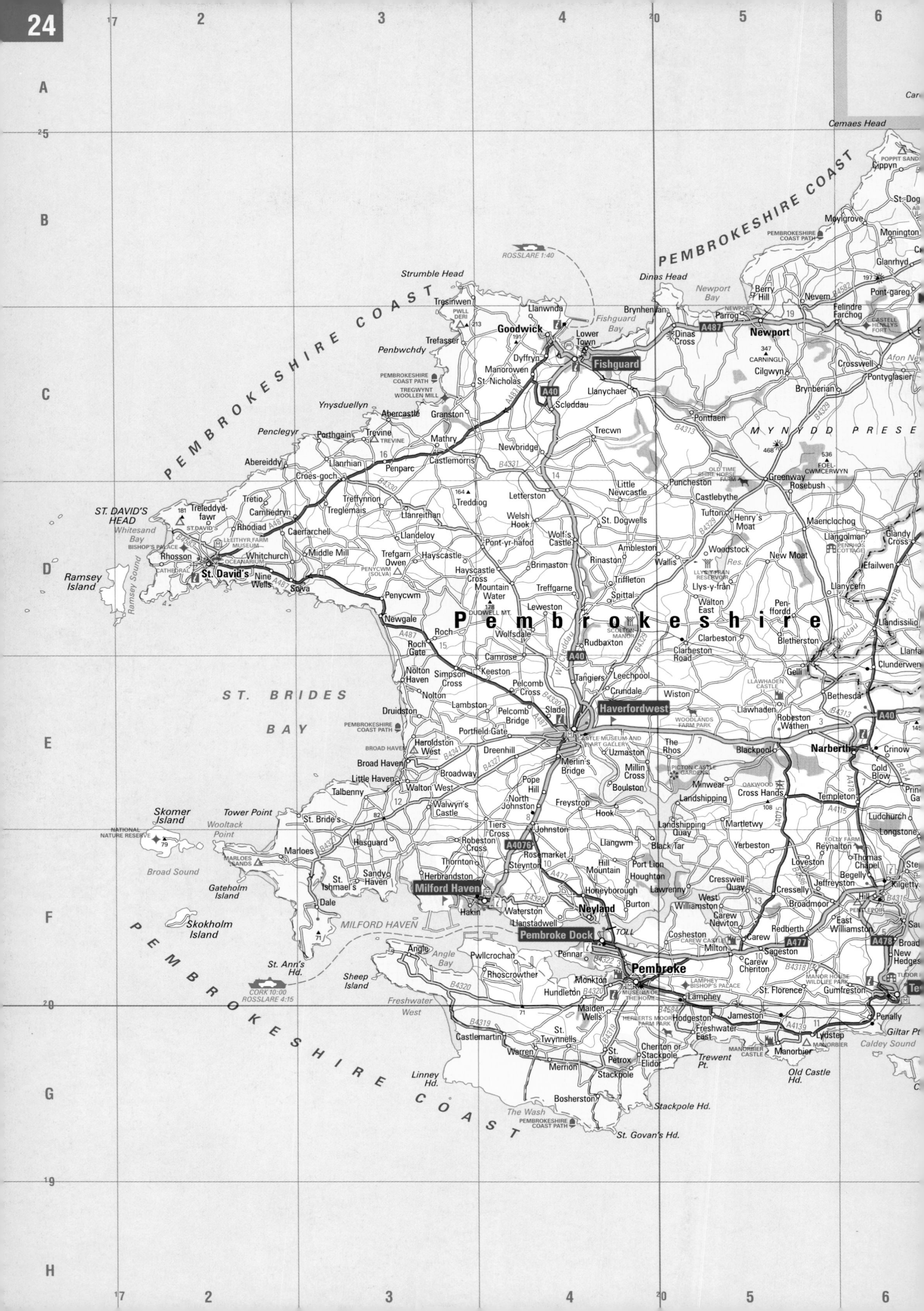
Pembrokeshire
PEMBROKESHIRE COAST
ST. BRIDES BAY
MILFORD HAVEN
Ramsey Island
Ramsey Sound
Skomer Island
Skokholm Island
Gateholm Island
Broad Sound
Wooltack Point
Tower Point
St. Ann's Hd.
Sheep Island
Freshwater West
Linney Hd.
The Wash
St. Govan's Hd.
Stackpole Hd.
Trewent Pt.
Old Castle Hd.
Caldey Sound
Giltar Pt
Strumble Head
Dinas Head
Cemaes Head
ST. DAVID'S HEAD
Whitesand Bay
Penbwchdy
Ynysduellyn
Penclegyr
Newport Bay
Fishguard Bay
MYNYDD PRESE
ROSSLARE 1:40
CORK 10:00
ROSSLARE 4:15
St. David's
Fishguard
Goodwick
Haverfordwest
Milford Haven
Pembroke Dock
Pembroke
Neyland
Narberth
Newport
Solva
Nine Wells
Whitchurch
Rhosson
Middle Mill
Caerfarchell
Rhodiad
Treleddyd-fawr
Tretio
Carnhedryn
Croes-goch
Llanrhian
Abereiddy
Porthgain
Trevine
Abercastle
Granston
Mathry
Castlemorris
Penparc
Treffynnon
Treglemais
Llanreithan
Llandeloy
Trefgarn Owen
Hayscastle
Hayscastle Cross
Mountain Water
Penycwm
Newgale
Roch
Roch Gate
Nolton Haven
Nolton
Simpson Cross
Druidston
Keeston
Camrose
Wolfsdale
Pelcomb Cross
Pelcomb Bridge
Lambston
Portfield Gate
Slade
Haroldston West
Broad Haven
Little Haven
Talbenny
Walton West
Broadway
Dreenhill
Walwyn's Castle
St. Bride's
Marloes
Hasguard
Dale
St. Ishmael's
Sandy Haven
Herbrandston
Thornton
Robeston Cross
Tiers Cross
Hakin
Waterston
Llanstadwell
Steynton
Rosemarket
Johnston
North Johnston
Pope Hill
Freystrop
Merlin's Bridge
Uzmaston
Hook
Llangwm
Honeyborough
Hill Mountain
Burton
Houghton
Port Lion
Black Tar
Millin Cross
Boulston
The Rhos
Minwear
Landshipping
Landshipping Quay
Martletwy
Yerbeston
Lawrenny
Cresswell Quay
West Williamston
Carew Newton
Carew
Cosheston
Milton
Sageston
Carew Cheriton
Redberth
East Williamston
Pennar
Angle
Pwllcrochan
Rhoscrowther
Monkton
Hundleton
Lamphey
Maiden Wells
Hodgeston
Freshwater East
Jameston
Manorbier
Lydstep
Penally
St. Florence
Gumfreston
Castlemartin
Warren
St. Twynnells
Merrion
St. Petrox
Cheriton or Stackpole Elidor
Stackpole
Bosherston
Tresinwen
Trefasser
Llanwnda
Dyffryn
Manorowen
St. Nicholas
Lower Town
Scleddau
Llanychaer
Trecwn
Newbridge
Letterston
Treddiog
Welsh Hook
Pont-yr-hafod
Wolf's Castle
Brimaston
Treffgarne
Leweston
Rudbaxton
Tangiers
Crundale
Leechpool
St. Dogwells
Little Newcastle
Ambleston
Rinaston
Wallis
Triffleton
Spittal
Puncheston
Castlebythe
Tufton
Henry's Moat
Woodstock
Llys-y-frân
Walton East
Clarbeston
Clarbeston Road
Wiston
Llawhaden
Robeston Wathen
Blackpool
Bethesda
Gelli
Bletherston
Pen-ffordd
New Moat
Maenclochog
Llangolman
Glandy Cross
Efailwen
Llanycefn
Llandissilio
Clunderwen
Crinow
Cold Blow
Templeton
Cross Hands
Ludchurch
Longstone
Reynalton
Loveston
Thomas Chapel
Begelly
Jeffreyston
Cresselly
Broadmoor
Kilgetty
Hill
New Hedges
Bryn-henllan
Dinas Cross
Parrog
Berry Hill
Nevern
Felindre Farchog
Pont-gareg
Moylgrove
Monington
St. Dogmaels
Glanrhyd
Cippyn
Cilgwyn
Crosswell
Pontyglasier
Brynberian
Pontfaen
Greenway
Rosebush
A40
A487
A477
A478
A4076
A4075
B4313
B4329
B4330
B4331
B4320
B4319
B4584
B4585
B4318
B4327
B4341
OCEANARIUM
BISHOP'S PALACE
CATHEDRAL
PEMBROKESHIRE COAST PATH
TREGWYNT WOOLLEN MILL
PENYCWM (SOLVA)
DUDWELL MT.
SCOLTON MANOR
CASTLE MUSEUM AND ART GALLERY
PICTON CASTLE GARDENS
WOODLANDS FARM PARK
LLAWHADEN CASTLE
OAKWOOD
CAREW CASTLE
LAMPHEY BISHOP'S PALACE
MANOR HOUSE WILDLIFE PARK
MANORBIER CASTLE
HERBERTS MOOR FARM PARK
MUSEUM OF THE HOME
NATIONAL NATURE RESERVE
MARLOES SANDS
LLYS-Y-FRAN RESERVOIR
OLD TIME SHIRE HORSE FARM
FOEL-CWMCERWYN
CARNINGLI
CASTELL HENLLYS FORT
PENRHOS COTTAGE
FOLLY FARM
TOLL

Carmarthenshire
Swansea
CARMARTHEN
BAY
PEMBROKESHIRE COAST
Brechfa Forest
GOWER
Cardigan
Newcastle Emlyn
Lampeter
Carmarthen
St. Clears
Llandeilo
Ammanford
Llanelli
Burry Port
Kidwelly
Pontardulais
Gorseinon
Swansea
The Mumbles
Llandysul
Llanybydder
Whitland
Laugharne
Pendine
Pendine Sands
East Marsh
Pembrey Forest
Pembrey
Whiteford Pt.
Llanrhidian Sands
Burry Holms
Rhossili Bay
Rhossili
Worms Head
Port Eynon
Port Eynon Pt.
Port Eynon Bay
Oxwich Bay
Pwlldu Hd.
Mumbles Hd.
Ynys-Lochtyn
Llangrannog
Aberporth
Synod Inn
Tresaith
Gwbert
Crymych
Cynwyl Elfed
Abergwili
Llansteffan
Ferryside
Pontyberem
Cross Hands
Tumble
Llandybie
Talley
Brechfa
Edwinsford
Horeb
Loughor
Penclawdd
Dunvant
Killay
Sketty
Mumbles
Oystermouth Castle
Mynydd Pencarreg
Afon Tywi
Afon Teifi
Afon Taf
Afon Cothi
Afon Duad
Gwendraeth Fach
Lliedi Resrs.
A40
A48
A484
A485
A486
A475
A476
A477
A478
A483
A487
A4138
M4

36
25
C A R D I G A N
B A Y
Cardigan I.
Cemaes Head
Ynys-Lochtyn
Cwmtudu
Chancery
Blaenplwyf
A487
Llanddeiniol
Llanrhystud
Llansantffraed
Llanon
Rhyd-Rosser
Rhydfudr
Nebo
SEA AQUARIUM
Aberarth
Aberaeron
Cross Inn
Pennant
Monachty
Bethania
Crynfe
Ffos-y-ffin
New Quay
Cilcennin
Cei-bach
Newbridge
Llwyncelyn
Bwlch-Llan
Maen-y-groes
Gilfachrheda
Oakford
Ciliau Aeron
Afon Aeron
Cross Inn
Llanarth
Trefilan
Llundain-fach
Nanternis
Ystrad Aeron
Tal-sarn
Gartheli
Caerwedros
Dihewid
Abermeurig
Blaencelyn
Llwyndafydd
Mydroilyn
Felinfach
Felindre
Llangrannog
Synod Inn
Temple Bar
Pontgarreg
Caledrhydiau
Ffynnon-oer
Penbryn
Plwmp
Penmorfa
Pentregat
Cribyn
Silian
Parcllyn
Tresaith
Brynhoffnant
Gorsgoch
Felinwynt
Aberporth
Sarnau
Talgarreg
Maestir
Olwen
Gwbert
Tan-y-groes
Capel Cynon
Bwlch-y-fadfa
Aber
Cwrt-newydd
Lampeter
Ferwig
Blaenannerch
Glynarthen
Castell-Howell
POPPIT SANDS
Tremain
Blaenporth
Rhydlewis
Ffostrasol
Cippyn
Penparc
Bettws Ifan
Hawen
Llanwnnen
Pentre-bach
Cardigan
CASTLE
Beulah
Maesymeillion
Pont-siân
Cwmsychpant
St. Dogmaels
ABBEY
Bridgend
Pantgwyn
Penrhiw-pâl
Coed-y-bryn
Llanwenog
Dre-fach
Alltyblaca
Llangoedmor
Ponthirwaun
Tregroes
Rhydowen
Pencarreg
Parc-y-rhôs
Moylgrove
Bryngwyn
Brongest
Troedyraur
Maesllyn
Llanybydder
Monington
Llechryd
Llandygwydd
Capel Tygwydd
Croes-lan
Prengwyn
Brynteg
Croft
Pen-y-bryn
CILGERRAN CASTLE
FELIN GERI FLOUR MILL
Horeb
Capel Dewi
Rhuddlan
Glan-Duar
Ty Mawr
Glanrhyd
Bridell
Cilgerran
Carreg-wen
Cwm-cou
Llandyfriog
Aber-banc
Penrhiw-llan
ROCK MILL WOOLLEN MILL
Maesycrugiau
Mynydd Pencarreg
Llantood
CORACLE CENTRE & FLOUR MILL
Cenarth
TEIFI VALLEY RAILWAY
Llandysul
Pont-gareg
Rhos-hill
Abercych
Newcastle Emlyn
Pentrecagal
Henllan
Llanfihangel-ar-Arth
Aber-Giâr
A487
Newchapel
Felindre Farchog
CASTELL HENLLYS FORT
Penrherber
Aber-Arad
WOOLLEN MILL
Llangeler
Drefach
Llanllwni
Eglwyswrw
Cilwendeg
Felindre
Pentre-cwrt
Bancyffordd
Boncath
Drefelin
Saron
Llanfair-Nant-Gwyn
Cwmhiraeth
Llidiad Nenog
Blaenffos
Cwmpengraig
New Inn
Crosswell
Afon Nevern
Bwlchygroes
Cwmcych
Capel Iwan
Pencader
Pontyglasier
Eglwyswen
Rhôs
MOELFRE
Penygroes
Star
Clydey
Gwyddgrug
Cwmorgan
Tanglwst
Dolgran
Gwernogle
Abergorlech
MYNYDD PRESELI
Crymych
Tegryn
MYNYDD RHOS-WEN
FOEL-CWMCERWYN
Pentre-galar
Brechfa Forest
Nant-y-ffin
Pen-y-garn
Hermon
Hen-feddau fawr
Cwmduad
Alltwalis
Mynachlog-ddu
Llanfyrnach
Trelech
Hermon
Dinas
Afon Taf
Llanpumsaint
Llanllawddog
Brechfa
Glandwr
Carmarthenshire
Maenclochog
Hebron
Blaen-waun
Blaen-y-coed
Pen-y-bont
Cynwyl Elfed
Pontarsais
Horeb
Llanfynydd
Capel Isaac
Llangolman
Glandy Cross
Llanglydwen
Plâs
PENRHOS COTTAGE
Pant-y-Caws
Cefn-y-pant
Cwmbach
Llanwinio
Rhydargaeau
Pant-glas
Efailwen
Talog
Afon Duad
GWILI RAILWAY
Pant-teg
Felingwm uchaf
Pant-gwyn
Llanycefn
Maesgwynne
Cross-hands
Cwmfelin Mynach
Ty-hen
Bwlchnewydd
Felingwm isaf
Login
Llanboidy
Gellywen
Abernant
Newchurch
Bronwydd Arms
Peniel
Llanfihangel-uwch-Gwili
Pentrefelin
Capel Gwyn
Court Henry
Broad Oak
Llandissilio
Dyffryn
Ffynnon ddrain
White Mill
Pont-ar-gothi
Hiraeth
Tre-vaughan
Tanerdy
Abergwili
Nantgaredig
Felindre
Henllan Amgoed
LOVESPOON GALLERY
Llanegwad
Dryslwyn
Llanfallteg
Meidrim
Merthyr
Carmarthen
CARMARTHEN
Capel Dewi
Llanarthney
Afon Tywi
Clunderwen
Cwmfelin Boeth
Llangynin
Sarnau
Llanllwch
Johnstown
Llangunnor
Pensarn
Nantycaws
Bethesda
Bancyfelin
Penrhiw-goch
Temple Bar
Pwll-trap
A40
A48
Whitland
Llangynog
Cwmffrwd
Llanddarog
Maesybont
Llanddewi Velfrey
Backe
St. Clears
Trevaughan
Llangain
Croesyceiliog
Cwmisfael
Porthyrhyd
Narberth
Lampeter Velfrey
Llwyn-y-brain
Afon Taf
Idole
Bancycapel
Crinow
Llanddowror
Gwendraeth Fach
Foel-gastell
Cefneithin
Corslas
Cold Blow
Afon Cywyn
Llangendeirne
Tavernspite
Morfa Bach
Afon Tywi
Drefach
Cwm-y-glo
Templeton
Princes Gate
A477
WHISPERING WATER VALLEY
Halfpenny Furze
Pontantwn
Crwbin
Cwm-mawr
Cross Hands
Tumble
Llanybri
Bancffosfelen
Red Roses
Llandyfaelog
Ludchurch
Llanteg
Llandawke
DYLAN THOMAS BOATHOUSE
Llansteffan
Pontyberem
Longstone
Laugharne
CASTLE
Meinciau
Pentre
Cwmgwili
FOLLY FARM
Reynalton
Llansadurnen
Brook
Broadway
Ferryside
Pont-Henri
Thomas Chapel
Stepaside
COLBY WOODLAND GARDEN
Marros
East Marsh
Broadlay
KIDWELLY INDUSTRIAL MUSEUM
Four Roads
Mynyddygarreg
Pontyates
Llannon
Llwyn-teg
Begelly
Kilgetty
Pendine
Llansaint
Cynheidre
Sylen
PONT ABRAHAM SERVICES
Jeffreyston
Pendine Sands
Kidwelly
Hill
Amroth
PEMBROKESHIRE COAST
Carway
Five Roads
Trimsaran
Horeb
Lliedi Resrs.
Saundersfoot
East Williamston
PENTLEPOIR
Broadfield
New
Pembrey Forest
PEMBREY
Pinged
Waun-y-clyn
Hendy
Allt
Fforest
49
48
A478
A484
A485
A486
A475
A482
A4115
B4313
B4314
B4316
B4317
B4308
B4309
B4306
B4310
B4297
B4300
B4301
B4298
B4299
B4312
B4328
B4329
B4332
B4333
B4334
B4336
B4337
B4338
B4339
B4342
B4459
B4476
B4546
B4548
B4570
B4577
B4582
1
2
3
4
5
A
B
C
D
E
F
G

New Cross
Llanfihangel-y-Creuddyn
Mynydd Bach
Trisant
Devil's Bridge
PEN Y GARN
Blaenycwm
Nantgwyn
Pant-y-dwr
RED LION HILL
37
Llanilar
Pentre-llyn
Cnwch-coch
Abermagwr
New Row
Cwmystwyth
Bwlch-y-sarnau
St. Harmon
Rhos-y-garth
Crosswood
Llanafan
Pont-rhyd-y-groes
GEIFAS
Wenallt
Mynydd Bach
Ysbyty Ystwyth
Abbeycwmhir
MOEL HYWEL
Llangwyryfon
Lledrod
Tynygraig
Tanyrhydiau
TRAWSALLT
Craig-goch Res.
Llandewi Ystradenny
Trefenter
Bronnant
Ystradmeurig
Penygarreg Res.
Rhayader
Gaufron
Swydd-ffynnon
Ffair-Rhos
Pontrhydfendigaid
Llansantffraed Cwmdeuddwr
Nantmel
Bontnewydd
STRATA FLORIDA ABBEY
Claerwen Reservoir
Elan Village
Garreg-ddu Res.
Fron
Gwystre
Crossgates
Ceredigion
DIBYN DU
Nant-glas
Blaenpennal
Tyncelyn
Llanwrthwl
Argoed Mill
Llanyre
Caban-coch Res.
Afon Claerwen
Llandrindod Wells
Ty'n-yr-eithin
BLAENCARON
Ridgebourne
WELSH GOLD CENTRE
Tregaron
DRUM-DDU
Newbridge on Wye
Capel Betws Lleucu
Y DRUM
BRYN CRWN
DRYGARN FAWR
Disserth
Howey
Crossway
Commins Capel Betws
DOLGOCH
Tywi Forest
ESGAIR CERRIG
Llanafan-fawr
Llanddewi-Brefi
Pentre-rhew
TYNCORNEL
Pentre-llwyn-llwyd
Cwmbach
Builth Road
28
Llansantffraed-in-Elvel
Olmarch
Troed rhiwdalar
Llanelwedd
Llyn Brianne Res.
Abergwesyn
BRYN BRAWD
Llanfair Clydogau
Beulah
Cilmery
Oaklands
Llanfaredd
Builth Wells
Llanfechan
Garth
Mynydd Trawsnant
Cwm Irfon
Tyn-y-graig
Pentrefelin
Llanwrtyd
CAMBRIAN WOOLLEN MILL
Maesmynis
Llanddewi'r Cwm
Aberedw
Ystradffin
Llanwrtyd Wells
Llangammarch Wells
Alltmawr
Llanycrwys
Ffarmers
Mynydd Mallaen
Nant-y-Bai
BRYN POETH UCHAF
Cefn-gorwydd
DRUM-DDU
Llandeilo Graban
Ffaldybrenin
Cwrt-y-cadno
Rhandirmwyn
Mynydd Eppynt
Pentre Dolau-Honddu
Gwenddwr
Erwood
Harford
Crickadarn
Llandre
ESGAIR FERCHON
Caeo Forest
Cynghordy
Crychan Forest
Tirabad
BRYN DU
Upper Chapel
Pumsaint
DOLAUCOTHI GOLD MINES
Cilycwm
Llanfair-ar-y-bryn
Caio
Crugybar
Porthyrhyd
Divlyn
Siloh
Llaneglwys
Llansawel
Blaendyryn
Merthyr Cynog
Lower Chapel
Llandefalle
Pentre-ty-gwyn
Babel
Mynydd Bwlch-y-groes
Llandovery
Powys
Llandeilo'r Fan
Llanfihangel Nant Bran
Pont-faen
Edwinsford
TALLEY ABBEY
Talley
Garthbrengy
Pwllgloyw
Talachddu
CYNROS
Cwm-byr
Cwmdwr
Halfway
Pentre-bach
Sarnau
Felinfach
Waunclunda
Llandefaelog Fach
Llansadwrn
Llanwrda
Myrtle Hill
Llanddew
Cwmdu
Halfway
Llywel
Pentre'r-felin
Battle
Felindre
Cilgwyn
Myddfai
Usk Reservoir
Trecastle
Trallong
Aberyscir
BRECON GAER ROMAN FORT
Brecon
Llanywern
Llechfaen
Soar
Ashfield
Hermon
Llangadog
Cwmwysg
Pont ar Hydfer
Sennybridge
Defynnog
Penpont
Llanspyddid
Llanfaes
SOUTH WALES BORDERERS
Felindre
Manordeilo
WELSH WHISKY VISITORS CENTRE
Salem
Cwmifor
Talsarn
Mynydd Illtyd
MOUNTAIN CENTRE
Tai'r-Bull
Libanus
Llanfrynach
Rhosmaen
Bethlehem
Dyffryn Ceidrych
Twynllanan
Llanddeusant
Glas Fynydd Forest
Crai
Felin-Crai
Heol Senni
Pencelli
Vale of Tywi
Llandeilo
Pontbren Araeth
Pont-ar-llechau
LLANDDEUSANT
Cross Oak
Capel Gwynfe
TRICHRUG
Pont Aber
LLWYN-Y-CELYN
Glyn Tarell
Brecon Beacons
Talybont-on-Usk
Ffairfach
Neuadd
FAN BRYCHEINIOG
Cray Res.
A470
BRECON BEACONS
Aber-Village
Black Mountain
FAN FAWR
Beacons Res.
Talybont Res.
Neuadd Reservoirs
Trapp
CARREG CENNEN CASTLE
FAN GIHIRYCH
Fforest Fawr
Llandyfan
FOEL FRAITH
Ystradfellte Res.
Abercynafon
Dre-fach
Glyntawe
Afon Twrch
Cantref Res.
Llandybie
CRAIG-Y-NOS
Nant-ddu
Craig-y-nos
Penwyllt
Twynmynydd
Brynamman
Rhosaman
Pen-y-cae
Pontsticill Reservoir
Tir-y-dail
Glanaman
Cwmllynfell
Ystradfellte
Llwyn-on Res.
BRECON MOUNTAIN RAILWAY
Ammanford
Pontamman
Garnant
Gwaun-Leision
Tairgwaith
Ystradowen
Abercraf
Betws
Gwaun-Cae-Gurwen
Upper Cwm-twrch
Cwmgiedd
Caehopkin
Coelbren
Pontsticill
Pantyffynnon
Cwmgors
Lower Cwm-twrch
Penrhos
Vaynor
Princetown
Tycroes
Ystradgynlais
Onllwyn
Dyffryn Cellwen
Gurnos
Garnswllt
Ystalyfera
Seven Sisters
Penderyn
Cefn-coed-y-cymmer
Dowlais
Mynydd y Gwair
Swansea Valley
Nant-y-cafn
Pontneddfechan
Glyn-Neath
Pontbren Llwyd
CASTLE MUSEUM & ART GALLERY
Godre'r-graig
Morfa Glas
Pen-yr-Heolgerrig
Gellideg
Climaen gwyn
Rheola Forest
Rhigos
Hirwaun
GRAIG FAWR
Merthyr Tydfil
Fochriw
Pentrebach
Rhyd-y-fro
Ynys-meudwy
Blaengwrach
Cwm-hwnt
YNYSFACH IRON HERITAGE CENTRE
Pontardawe
Cilybebyll
Crynant
Cwmgwrach
DAN-YR-OGOF SHOWCAVES
Penywaun
Tre-Gibbon
Trecynon
Abercanaid
Pentrebach
16
Cwm-Dulais
Rhyd-y-gwin
Craig-cefn-parc
Trebanos
Gellinudd
Rhôs
CEFNCOED COLLIERY MUSEUM
Vale of Neath
RESOLVEN
Cwmdare
Aber-nant
Aberdare
Troedyrhiw

Powys
Herefordshire
Worcestershire
Monmouthshire
Merthyr Tydfil
RADNOR FOREST
BLACK MOUNTAINS
BRECON BEACONS
Mynydd Llangynidr
Mynydd Llangattock
Mynydd Troed
Golden Valley
Llangorse Lake
Neuadd Reservoirs
Talybont Res.
Pontsticill Reservoir
Wye
Lugg
Teme
Arrow
Monnow
Usk
Afon Honddu
Knighton
Presteigne
Kington
Llandrindod Wells
Builth Wells
Hay on Wye
Brecon
Abergavenny
Tredegar
EBBW VALE
Rhymney
Blaenau Gwent
Brynmawr
Nantyglo
Blaina
Blaenavon
Abertillery
Abersychan
New Tredegar
Merthyr Tydfil
Crickhowell
Talgarth
Llyswen
Glasbury
Three Cocks
Bronllys
Painscastle
Clyro
Cusop
Dorstone
Peterchurch
Longtown
Pandy
Llanvihangel Crucorney
Llanthony
Pontrilas
Grosmont
Skenfrith
Raglan
Kingcoed
Llangattock-Vibon-Avel
Dingestow
Llanarth
Bryngwyn
Llanover
Gilwern
Govilon
Clydach
Llanfoist
Llanelly Hill
Beaufort
Sirhowy
Dukestown
Trefil
Rassau
Garnlydan
Blackrock
Talybont-on-Usk
Llangynidr
Bwlch
Llangorse
Llansantffraed
Pencelli
Libanus
Llanfaes
Llanfrynach
Scethrog
Tretower
Cwmdu
Cwmrhos
Pengenffordd
Llanelieu
Talachddu
Felinfach
Garthbrengy
Llandefaelog Fach
Llanddew
Erwood
Llanstephan
Rhydnest
Boughrood
Llowes
Cwmbach
Crickadarn
Gwenddwr
Upper Chapel
Llaneglwys
Lower Chapel
Aberedw
Alltmawr
Llanbedr
Llandeilo Graban
Llanbadarn-y-Garreg
Rhulen
Bryngwyn
Rhosgoch
Newchurch
Michaelchurch-on-Arrow
Hengoed
Huntington
Gladestry
Colva
Glascwm
Cregrina
Hundred House
Llansantffraed-in-Elvel
Frank's Bridge
Llanfihangel-nant-Melan
Llanelwedd
Cilmery
Llanfaredd
Newbridge on Wye
Disserth
Howey
Crossway
Ridgebourne
Llanyre
Argoed Mill
Nantmel
Gwystre
Crossgates
Penybont
Llandegley
Dolau
Llanfihangel Rhydithon
Bleddfa
Monaughty
Pilleth
Whitton
Cascob
Maes-Treylow
Beggar's Bush
Kinnerton
Evenjobb
New Radnor
Old Radnor
Walton
Yardro
Dolyhir
Burlingjobb
Llandewi Ystradenny
Llanbister
Abbeycwmhir
Gaufron
Bwlch-y-sarnau
St. Harmon
Crug
Llangunllo
Rhyd-moel-ddu
Llanvair Waterdine
Skyborry Green
Knucklas
Stowe
Bucknell
Bedstone
Buckton
Brampton Bryan
Milebrook
Walford
Leintwardine
Kinton
Downton on the Rock
Burrington
Adforton
Wigmore
Leinthall Starkes
Richards Castle
Lingen
Limebrook
Stapleton
Kinsham
Combe
Byton
Combe Moor
Rodd
Nash
Knill
Titley
Staunton on Arrow
Shobdon
Kingsland
Eardisland
Pembridge
Lyonshall
Headbrook
Marston
Bearwood
Holme Marsh
Almeley
Woonton
Sarnesfield
Weobley
Kinnersley
Eardisley
Willersley
Whitney
Winforton
Clifford
Letton
Staunton on Wye
Bredwardine
Moccas
Preston on Wye
Madley
Kingstone
Allensmore
Thruxton
Kilpeck
St. Devereux
Wormbridge
Kentchurch
Garway
Broad Oak
St. Maughans
Newcastle
Llanvetherine
Llantilio Crossenny
Llanvapley
Llanddewi Rhydderch
Llangattock nigh Usk
Mardy
Llantilio Pertholey
Pen-y-clawdd
Mitcheltroy Common
Wonastow
Tre-wyn
Clodock
Walterstone
Oldcastle
Cwmyoy
Stanton
Craswall
Michaelchurch Escley
Urishay Common
Vowchurch
Turnastone
Bacton
Abbey Dore
Ewyas Harold
Rowlstone
Kerry's Gate
Didley
Cockyard
Credenhill
Kenchester
Bishopstone
Byford
Mansell Lacy
Mansell Gamage
Yazor
Tillington
Wellington
Canon Pyon
King's Pyon
Westhope
Ledgemoor
Dilwyn
Sollers Dilwyn
Monkland
Ivington
Barons Cross
Cholstrey
Lawton
Lucton
Mortimer Cross
Aymestrey
Yatton
Leinthall Earls
Bircher
Yarpole
Eyton
Cobnash
Aston
Elton
Penderyn
Vaynor
Pontsticill
Cefn-coed-y-cymmer
Dowlais
Gellideg
Pen-yr-Heolgerrig
Trefechan
Abercanaid
Pentrebach
Troedyrhiw
Fochriw
Pontlottyn
Abertysswg
Princetown
Tafarnau-bach
Llechryd
Garn-yr-erw
Coalbrookvale
Briery Hill
Waunlwyd
Cwm
Cwmtillery
Varteg
Cwmavon
Garndiffaith
Pen-groes-oped
Goetre
Penperlleni
Nant-y-derry
Kemeys Commander
Little Mill
Llandenny
Llanishen
Twyn-y-Sheriff
Bettws Newydd
Rhyd-y-meirch
Llanellen
Forge Side
Llangenny
Cwrt-y-gollen
Glangrwyney
Llwyn-du
Blaenawey
Llanbedr
Coed-yr-ynys
Ffawyddog
Llangattock
Abercynafon
Aber-Village
Cross Oak
Penderyn
Nant-ddu

Kidderminster
Bewdley
Stourport on Severn
Bromsgrove
Tenbury Wells
Droitwich
Leominster
Worcester
Bromyard
Broadwas
Great Malvern
Malvern Link
West Malvern
Pershore
Upton upon Severn
Hereford
Ledbury
Tewkesbury
Bishop's Cleeve
Newent
Ross-on-Wye
Cheltenham
Charlton Kings
Gloucester
Churchdown
Hucclecote
Cinderford
Frampton on Severn
Stonehouse
Stroud
Lydney
Chalford
COTSWOLDS
FOREST OF DEAN
MALVERN HILLS
Wyre Forest
River Severn
The Noose
Hereford
Worcester
Gloucester

40
Bromsgrove
Catshill
Aston Fields
Redditch
Studley
Alcester
Dorridge
Kenilworth
Henley in Arden
Warwick
Royal Leamington Spa
Stratford-upon-Avon
W a r w i c k
Evesham
Pershore
V A L E O F E V E S H A M
Shipston on Stour
Moreton-in-Marsh
Chipping Campden
Broadway
Winchcombe
Bishop's Cleeve
Cheltenham
Charlton Kings
Stow on the Wold
Chipping Norton
Charlbury
Burford
Witney
G l o u c e s t e r
C O T S W O L D S
O x f
29
19
Tewkesbury
Upton Snodsbury
Inkberrow
Wellesbourne
Kineton
Halford
Bidford on Avon
Mickleton
Blockley
Bourton-on-the-Water
Northleach
Bibury
Fairford
Carterton
Lechlade
Andoversford
Naunton
Lower Slaughter
Upper Slaughter
Kingham
Shipton-under-Wychwood
Milton-under-Wychwood
Long Compton
Hook Norton
Brailes
Chesterton
Gaydon
Edge Hill
Wootton Wawen
Claverdon
Hampton-in-Arden
Tanworth-in-Arden
Lapworth
Hockley Heath
Earlswood
Hopwood
Alvechurch
Feckenham
Droitwich
Coughton
Wickhamford
Badsey
Honeybourne
Aston Subedge
Willersey
Snowshill
Stanton
Temple Guiting
Guiting Power
Ford
Condicote
Longborough
Donnington
Broadwell
Oddington
Adlestrop
Daylesford
Evenlode
Batsford
Bourton on the Hill
Sezincote
Ilmington
Admington
Newbold on Stour
Tredington
Ettington
Alderminster
Pillerton Priors
Oxhill
Tysoe
Shenington
Little Rissington
Great Rissington
Great Barrington
Little Barrington
Taynton
Fulbrook
Asthall
Minster Lovell
Finstock
Ramsden
Leafield
Ascott-under-Wychwood
Chadlington
Spelsbury
Enstone
Salford
Over Norton
Little Compton
Great Wolford
Little Wolford
Todenham
Barcheston
Willington
Burmington
Cherington
Stourton
Whichford
Ascott
Sibford Gower
Sibford Ferris
Swalcliffe
Wigginton
Swerford
Great Rollright
Heythrop
Little Tew
Church Enstone
Lidstone
Tackley
Shilton
Bradwell Grove
Holwell
Westwell
Signet
Brize Norton
Alvescot
Black Bourton
Clanfield
Filkins
Broughton Poggs
Kencot
Southrop
Eastleach Turville
Eastleach Martin
Hatherop
Coln St. Aldwyn's
Quenington
Barnsley
Ampney
Bagendon
Daglingworth
Baunton
North Cerney
Rendcomb
Calmsden
Coln Rogers
Winson
Ablington
Arlington
Fossebridge
Coln St. Dennis
Chedworth
Yanworth
Cassey Compton
Compton Abdale
Hampnett
Turkdean
Hazleton
Salperton
Notgrove
Cold Aston
Sevenhampton
Whittington
Syreford
Brockhampton
Hawling
Charlton Abbots
Sudeley Castle
Cleeve Hill
Woodmancote
Prestbury
Southam
Swindon
Uckington
Golden Valley
Leckhampton
Shurdington
Up Hatherley
Badgeworth
Dowdeswell
Shipton Solers
Withington
Colesbourne
Elkstone
Cowley
Coberley
Birdlip
Brimpsfield
Syde
Winstone
Miserden
Duntisbourne Abbots
Duntisbourne Leer
Duntisbourne Rouse
Sapperton
Oakley Wood
Chalford
Oakridge
Edgeworth
Bisley
Sudgrove
The Camp
Whiteway
Great Witcombe
Bentham
Ullenwood
Crickley Hill
Elmstone Hardwicke
Stoke Orchard
Gotherington
Gretton
Greet
Hailes
Didbrook
Stanway
Toddington
Alderton
Dumbleton
Great Washbourne
Teddington
Aston Cross
Ashchurch
Northway
Kemerton
Overbury
Conderton
Beckford
Kinsham
Bredon
Bredon's Norton
Ashton under Hill
Kersoe
Hinton on the Green
Sedgeberrow
Aston Somerville
Childswickham
Wormington
Laverton
Buckland
Elmley Castle
Great Comberton
Little Comberton
Netherton
Bricklehampton
Birlingham
Defford
Eckington
Strensham
Besford
Wick
Cropthorne
Charlton
Fladbury
Lower Moor
Wyre Piddle
Throckmorton
Harvington
Norton
Lenchwick
Offenham
Aldington
Bengeworth
Hampton
Fairfield
Bretforton
South Littleton
Middle Littleton
North Littleton
Cleeve Prior
Pebworth
Broad Marston
Dorsington
Long Marston
Lower Quinton
Upper Quinton
Meon Hill
Hidcote Boyce
Hidcote Manor Garden
Kiftsgate Court Garden
Weston Subedge
Saintbury
Ebrington
Charingworth
Paxford
Broad Campden
Stretton on Fosse
Draycott
Aston Magna
Lower Lemington
Barton on the Heath
Welford on Avon
Luddington
Binton
Temple Grafton
Ardens Grafton
Exhall
Wixford
Broom
Barton
Marlcliff
Salford Priors
Abbots Salford
Iron Cross
Dunnington
Weethley Gate
Arrow
Ragley Hall
Oversley Green
Haselor
Walcote
Billesley
Aston Cantlow
Great Alne
Little Alne
Shelfield
Wilmcote
Bishopton
Shottery
Clifford Chambers
Atherstone on Stour
Preston on Stour
Wimpstone
Ailstone
Loxley
Charlecote
Hampton Lucy
Alveston
Tiddington
Ingon
Snitterfield
Bearley
Langley
Edstone
Wolverton
Norton Lindsey
Sherbourne
Barford
Wasperton
Newbold Pacey
Ashorne
Moreton Morrell
Bishop's Tachbrook
Harbury
Whitnash
Radford Semele
Offchurch
Longbridge
Budbrooke
Hatton
Haseley
Shrewley Common
Rowington
Kingswood
Baddesley Clinton
Chadwick End
Wroxall
Honiley
Beausale
Leek Wootton
Old Milverton
Milverton
Lillington
Cubbington
Stoneleigh
Ashow
Stareton
Bubbenhall
Weston under Wetherley
Hunningham
Eathorpe
Princethorpe
Wappenbury
Baginton
Ryton on Dunsmore
Burton Green
Crackley
Balsall Common
Temple Balsall
Fen End
Meer End
Catchems Corner
Knowle
Bentley Heath
Stivichall
Willenhall
Tollbar End
Umberslade Children's Farm
Kemps Green
Lowsonford
Preston Bagot
Oldberrow
Ullenhall
Gorcott Hill
Mappleborough Green
Morton Bagot
Ipsley
Headless Cross
Crabbs Cross
Hunt End
Astwood Bank
Sambourne
New End
King's Coughton
Cookhill
Abbots Morton
Rous Lench
Ab Lench
Church Lench
Atch Lench
Harvington Cross
Bishampton
Abberton
Flyford Flavell
North Piddle
Naunton Beauchamp
Peopleton
Pinvin
Drake's Broughton
Stoulton
White Ladies Aston
Churchill
Egdon
Broughton Hackett
Upton Snodsbury
Grafton Flyford
Kington
Dormston
Stock Green
Stock Wood
Holberrow Green
Himbleton
Huddington
Crowle
Tibberton
Sale Green
Oddingley
Shernal Green
Hadzor
Witton
Woolmere Green
Hanbury
Ham Green
Bradley Green
Bentley
Webheath
Woodgate
Stoke Prior
Upton Warren
Wychbold
Elmbridge
Rock Hill
Finstall
Tardebigge
Tutnall
Sidemoor
Lickey End
Blackwell
Barnt Green
Marlbrook
Lickey
Cofton Hackett
Rubery
Fairfield
Wildmoor
Bournheath
Dodford
Bluntington
Chaddesley Corbett
Portway
Rowney Green
Branson's Cross
Wood End
Holt End
Beoley
Wythall
Drake's Cross
Whitlock's End
Monkspath
Shirley
Dickens Heath

Northampton
Milton Keynes
Buckingham
Oxford
Rugby
Daventry
Northampton
Wellingborough
Banbury
Brackley
Towcester
Buckingham
Bicester
Woodstock
Kidlington
Oxford
Aylesbury
Thame
Haddenham
Wendover
Winslow
Bletchley
Newport Pagnell
Olney
Stony Stratford
Wolverton
Middleton Cheney
Headington
Cowley
Wheatley
Dunchurch
Hillmorton
Crick
West Haddon
Long Buckby
Weedon Bec
Kislingbury
Duston
Stoke Bruerne
Silverstone
Whittlebury
Whittlewood Forest
Salcey Forest
Yardley Chase
Deanshanger
Passenham
Calverton
Fenny Stratford
Far Bletchley
Newton Longville
Great Horwood
Little Horwood
Padbury
Steeple Claydon
Middle Claydon
East Claydon
Botolph Claydon
Marsh Gibbon
Quainton
Waddesdon
Westcott
Brill
Boarstall
Long Crendon
Chearsley
Cuddington
Stone
Dinton
Weston Turville
Aston Clinton
Stoke Mandeville
Princes Risborough
Monks Risborough
Kingsey
Towersey
Tiddington
Great Milton
Cuddesdon
Horspath
Iffley
Kennington
Botley
Cumnor
Wytham
Eynsham
Yarnton
Begbroke
Bladon
Tackley
Kirtlington
Weston-on-the-Green
Bletchingdon
Islip
Charlton on Otmoor
Ambrosden
Launton
Chesterton
Ardley
Fewcott
Fritwell
Souldern
Aynho
Croughton
Evenley
Turweston
Westbury
Finmere
Tingewick
Gawcott
Biddlesden
Syresham
Helmdon
Sulgrave
Culworth
Thorpe Mandeville
Chacombe
Wardington
Cropredy
Claydon
Fenny Compton
Byfield
Woodford Halse
Eydon
Moreton Pinkney
Canons Ashby
Adstone
Blakesley
Greens Norton
Bugbrooke
Nether Heyford
Flore
Weedon
Dodford
Badby
Newnham
Charwelton
Hellidon
Staverton
Braunston
Barby
Kilsby
Watford
Ashby St. Ledgers
Guilsborough
Ravensthorpe
Holdenby
East Haddon
Brixworth
Spratton
Pitsford Reservoir
Moulton
Boughton
Kingsthorpe
Weston Favell
Great Billing
Little Billing
Ecton
Earls Barton
Mears Ashby
Sywell
Overstone
Wilby
Grendon
Whiston
Cogenhoe
Castle Ashby
Denton
Yardley Hastings
Hackleton
Piddington
Horton
Quinton
Roade
Courteenhall
Blisworth
Milton Malsor
Collingtree
Wootton
Hardingstone
Great Houghton
Hartwell
Ashton
Hanslope
Castlethorpe
Haversham
Cosgrove
Potterspury
Yardley Gobion
Paulerspury
Pury End
Alderton
Grafton Regis
Leckhampstead
Akeley
Maids Moreton
Thornborough
Nash
Whaddon
Mursley
Swanbourne
Drayton Parslow
Stewkley
Soulbury
Hoggeston
Dunton
Granborough
North Marston
Oving
Pitchcott
Whitchurch
Cublington
Aston Abbotts
Wingrave
Rowsham
Hulcott
Bierton
Weedon
Hardwick
Buckland
Halton
Ellesborough
Great Kimble
Little Kimble
Owlswick
Meadle
Askett
Longwick
Ilmer
Kimble Wick
Ford
Aston Sandford
Cuddington
Upper Winchendon
Lower Winchendon
Ashendon
Chilton
Dorton
Oakley
Worminghall
Ickford
Shabbington
Waterperry
Waterstock
Holton
Forest Hill
Stanton St. John
Beckley
Horton-cum-Studley
Noke
Oddington
Murcott
Merton
Piddington
Ludgershall
Kingswood
Grendon Underwood
Edgcott
Poundon
Twyford
Charndon
Calvert
Hillesden
Preston Bissett
Chetwode
Barton Hartshorn
Newton Purcell
Mixbury
Cottisford
Hardwick
Hethe
Stoke Lyne
Fringford
Stratton Audley
Bucknell
Caversfield
Middleton Stoney
Lower Heyford
Upper Heyford
Steeple Aston
Middle Aston
North Aston
Somerton
Deddington
Clifton
Hempton
Barford St. John
Barford St. Michael
Bloxham
Milton
Adderbury
King's Sutton
Charlton
Newbottle
Astrop
Warkworth
Overthorpe
Thenford
Marston St. Lawrence
Greatworth
Farthinghoe
Halse
Radstone
Whitfield
Hanwell
Drayton
Wroxton
Horley
Great Bourton
Williamscot
Mollington
Shotteswell
Warmington
Farnborough
Avon Dassett
Burton Dassett
Wormleighton
Priors Hardwick
Priors Marston
Marston Doles
Ladbroke
Napton on the Hill
Southam
Stockton
Long Itchington
Leamington Hastings
Birdingbury
Frankton
Marton
Bourton on Dunsmore
Stretton on Dunsmore
Thurlaston
Draycote Water
New Bilton
Bilton
Clifton upon Dunsmore
Yelvertoft
Lamport
Draughton
Maidwell
Haselbech
Cold Ashby
Thornby
Winwick
Cottesbrooke
Creaton
Hollowell
Teeton
Coton
Scaldwell
Old
Walgrave
Hannington
Holcot
Broughton
Pytchley
Isham
Orlingbury
Little Harrowden
Great Harrowden
Hardwick
Great Doddington
Strixton
Easton Maudit
Warrington
Emberton
Filgrave
Tyringham
Gayhurst
Lathbury
Sherington
Great Linford
New Bradwell
Bradwell
Loughton
Woughton on the Green
Shenley Church End
Shenley Brook End
Simpson
Walton
Woolstone
Broughton
Milton Keynes Village
Stoke Hammond
South End
North End
Linslade
Burcott
Wing
Mentmore
Puttenham
Wilstone
Long Marston
Drayton Beauchamp
St. Leonard's
Dunsmore
The Lee
Little Hampden
Pitch Green
Emmington
Moreton
Chinnor
Easington
Tetsworth
Thame
Kidlington
Shipton on Cherwell
Thrupp
Hampton Poyle
Wolvercote
Summertown
Marston
Elsfield
Barton
New Hinksey
North Hinksey
South Hinksey
Chawley
Wootton
Farmoor Reservoir
Swinford
Stanton Harcourt
Sutton
Long Hanborough
Church Hanborough
Cassington
Barnard Gate
Glympton
Kiddington
M1
M40
M45
A5
A43
A45
A508
A509
A421
A413
A418
A41
A34
A40
A44
A4260
A361
A423
A422
A428
A4146
A4010
S
20
32
41

Northampton
Milton Keynes
Bedford
Cam
Hertf
Buckingham
Wellingborough
Burton Latimer
Irthlingborough
Higham Ferrers
Rushden
Raunds
Finedon
Isham
Pytchley
Broughton
Orlingbury
Great Harrowden
Little Harrowden
Hardwick
Sywell
Mears Ashby
Wilby
Overstone
Earls Barton
Great Doddington
Wollaston
Strixton
Grendon
Whiston
Cogenhoe
Castle Ashby
Easton Maudit
Bozeat
Yardley Hastings
Denton
Yardley Chase
Horton
Piddington
Hackleton
Lavendon
Warrington
Cold Brayfield
Turvey
Olney
Clifton Reynes
Newton Blossomville
Weston Underwood
Emberton
Ravenstone
Stoke Goldington
Filgrave
Tyringham
Sherington
Chicheley
Hardmead
Astwood
North Crawley
Gayhurst
Lathbury
Newport Pagnell
Great Linford
Haversham
Wolverton
New Bradwell
Bradwell
Milton Keynes
Broughton
Milton Keynes Village
Moulsoe
Cranfield
Salford
Woolstone
Loughton
Shenley Church End
Shenley Brook End
Woughton on the Green
Simpson
Walton
Woburn Sands
Bow Brickhill
Wavendon
Aspley Guise
Aspley Heath
Bletchley
Fenny Stratford
Far Bletchley
Newton Longville
Whaddon
Little Brickhill
Great Brickhill
Woburn
Husborne Crawley
Ridgmont
Brogborough
Lidlington
Millbrook
Eversholt
Church End
Steppingley
Tingrith
Milton Bryan
Potsgrove
Battlesden
Toddington
Stoke Hammond
Drayton Parslow
Mursley
Swanbourne
Soulbury
Heath and Reach
Leighton Buzzard
Linslade
Hockliffe
Tebworth
Eggington
Stanbridge
Tilsworth
Wingfield
Chalton
Billington
Burcott
Stewkley
Wing
Ledburn
Cublington
Slapton
Whitchurch
Aston Abbotts
Hardwick
Weedon
Wingrave
Rowsham
Hulcott
Mentmore
Cheddington
Long Marston
Marsworth
Ivinghoe
Ivinghoe Aston
Edlesborough
Eaton Bray
Totternhoe
Dunstable
Houghton Regis
Whipsnade
Studham
Dagnall
Pitstone
Pitstone Green
Ringshall
Little Gaddesden
Aldbury
Tring
Wigginton
Aylesbury
Bierton
Puttenham
Wilstone
Buckland
Drayton Beauchamp
Aston Clinton
Weston Turville
Stoke Mandeville
Halton
Wendover
Hastoe
Northchurch
Berkhamsted
Great Gaddesden
Nettleden
Potten End
Water End
Gadebridge
Hemel Hempstead
Boxmoor
Bourne End
Bovingdon
Felden
Chesham
Cholesbury
Ashley Green
Bellingdon
Lee Clump
The Lee
Chartridge
Ballinger Common
Dunsmore
Butler's Cross
Ellesborough
Great Kimble
Little Kimble
Askett
Meadle
Monks Risborough
Little Hampden
Princes Risborough
Kimble Wick
Terrick
Nash Lee
North Lee
St. Leonard's
Buckland Common
Bishopstone
Southcourt
Kempston
Stagsden
Bromham
Biddenham
Queen's Park
Box End
Oakley
Clapham
Stevington
West End
Pavenham
Carlton
Chellington
Harrold
Odell
Felmersham
Radwell
Sharnbrook
Milton Ernest
Bletsoe
Souldrop
Santa Pod
Podington
Hinwick
Farndish
Wymington
Irchester
Little Irchester
Knuston
Newton Bromshold
Chelveston
Caldecott
Stanwick
Hargrave
Shelton
Yielden
Melchbourne
Swineshead
Pertenhall
Riseley
Knotting
Knotting Green
Covington
Tilbrook
Lower Dean
Upper Dean
Kimbolton
Stonely
Catworth
Bythorn
Keyston
Molesworth
Brington
Leighton Bromswold
Buckworth
Barham
Woolley
Spaldwick
Easton
Stow Longa
Ellington
Grafham
Grafham Water
Brampton
Huntingdon
Hartford
Godmanchester
Wyton
Houghton
Hemingford Abbots
Little Stukeley
Great Stukeley
Alconbury
Sapley
Offord Cluny
Offord Darcy
Buckden
West Perry
East Perry
Dillington
Staughton Green
Staughton Highway
Great Staughton
Little Staughton
Southoe
Diddington
Great Paxton
Little Paxton
Papworth St. Agnes
Graveley
Toseland
Yelling
Hilton
Hail Weston
St. Neots
Eynesbury
Eaton Socon
Duloe
Staploe
Croxton
Eltisley
Wyboston
Little Barford
Abbotsley
Great Gransden
Little Gransden
Waresley
Tempsford
Gamlingay
Hatley St. George
Everton
Potton
Cockayne Hatley
East Hatley
Tadlow
Wrestlingworth
Eyeworth
Dunton
Sutton
Biggleswade
Upper Caldecote
Northill
Ickwell Green
Old Warden
Southill
Broom
Stanford
Langford
Edworth
Hinxworth
Ashwell
Astwick
Henlow
Arlesey
Church End
Stotfold
Caldecote
Newnham
Bygrave
Radwell
Norton
Baldock
Wallington
Clothall
Letchworth
Ickleford
William
Weston
Walsworth
Hitchin
Great Wymondley
Little Wymondley
Graveley
Hall's Green
Cromer
St. Ippolitts
Gosmore
Charlton
Preston
Great Offley
Lilley
Stevenage
Aston End
Shephall
Aston
Langley
Broadwater
Bragbury End
Knebworth
Old Knebworth
Datchworth
Woolmer Green
Oaklands
Burnham Green
Bull's Green
Codicote
Kimpton
Ayot St. Lawrence
Ayot St. Peter
Welwyn
Harmer Green
Digswell Park
Welwyn Garden City
Tewin
Panshanger
Woodhall
Hatfield Hyde
Cole Green
Letty Green
Hatfield
Stanborough
Essendon
The Ryde
Little Berkhamsted
Wildhill
South Hatfield
Woodside
Welham Green
Bell Bar
Water End
Brookmans Park
Newgate Street
Colney Heath
The Camp
Fleetville
Marshalswick
Jersey Farm
St. Albans
St. Stephens
Chiswell Green
Bedmond
Sopwell
London Colney
Sandridge
Childwick Green
Townsend
Redbourn
Harpenden
Hatching Green
Wheathampstead
Marshall's Heath
Batford
Blackmore End
Peter's Green
East Hyde
Kinsbourne Green
Markyate
Flamstead
Trowley Bottom
Jockey End
Kensworth
Kensworth Common
Caddington
Slip End
Luton
Farley Hill
Leagrave
Biscot
Limbury
Sundon Park
Stopsley
Hart Hill
Cockernhoe Green
King's Walden
St. Paul's Walden
Breachwood Green
Whitwell
Lower Sundon
Upper Sundon
Streatley
Sharpenhoe
Barton-le-Clay
Hexton
Pegsdon
Pirton
Holwell
Higham Gobion
Apsley End
Shillington
Harlington
Westoning
Pulloxhill
Flitwick
Greenfield
Flitton
Silsoe
Maulden
Clophill
Ampthill
Houghton Conquest
Haynes
Haynes Church End
Wilstead
Stewartby
Marston Moretaine
Lower Shelton
Upper Shelton
Broad Green
Bourne End
Wootton
Keeley Green
Kempston Hardwick
Elstow
Harrowden
Shortstown
Cardington
Cotton End
Littleworth
Fenlake
Goldington
Cople
Mogerhanger
Willington
Sandy
Beeston
Girtford
Hatch
Thorncote Green
Blunham
Great Barford
Renhold
Salph End
Ravensden
Wilden
Green End
Roxton
Colesden
Chawston
Duck's Cross
Rootham's Green
Colmworth
Thurleigh
Bolnhurst
Keysoe
Keysoe Row
Brook End
Beadlow
Shefford
Campton
Clifton
Meppershall
Upper Gravenhurst
Upper Stondon
Great Addington
Little Addington
Ringstead
Denford
Woodford
Barton Seagrave
Wellingborough
Salcey Forest
Eakley Lanes
Tathall End
Castlethorpe
Calverton
Little Horwood
Newton Longville
Dunton
Colney Heath

Oldhurst
Colne
Bluntisham
Earith
Hill Row
Doles
43
A1123
Witcham Toll
Haddenham
Wilburton
Little Thetford
Barway
Stretham
Soham Cotes
Soham
Soham Mere
Broad Hill
Isleham Fen
Isleham
Thistley Green
West Row
Beck Row
Mildenhall
Worlington
Barton Mills
Icklingham
St. Ives
Needingworth
Holywell
Aldreth
Great Ouse
Over
Willingham
Smithey Fen
Chittering
Wicken
Down Field Windmill
Fordham
Freckenham
Tuddenham
Lackford
Fenstanton
Fen Drayton
Swavesey
Rampton
Cottenham
Denny Abbey and Farmland Mus.
Upware
River Bank
New River
Adventures Fen
Chippenham
Red Lodge
Herringswell
Cavenham
Flempton
Boxworth End
Longstanton
Westwick
Landwade
Burwell
Snailwell
Kennett
Kentford
Risby
Conington
Boxworth
Oakington
Landbeach
Waterbeach
Reach
Exning
Higham
Little Saxham
Elsworth
Lolworth
Bar Hill
Dry Drayton
Histon
Impington
Milton
Commercial End
Swaffham Prior
Newmarket Heath
Newmarket
Moulton
Gazeley
Barrow
Great Saxham
Knapwell
Girton
Anglesey Abbey
Lode
Horningsea
Stow cum Quy
Swaffham Bulbeck
Newmarket National Stud
National Horseracing Museum
Cheveley
Ashley
Dalham
Denham
Madingley
Kings Hedges
Chesterton
Fen Ditton
Bottisham
Dunstall Green
Hargrave
Chevington
Highfields
Hardwick
Coton
Newnham
Cambridge
Fitzwilliam Mus.
Romsey Town
Teversham
Little Wilbraham
Stetchworth
Woodditton
Saxon Street
Ousden
Caxton
Great Wilbraham
Dullingham
Ditton Green
Kirtling
Upend
Lidgate
Depden Green
Chedburgh
Caldecote
Toft
Bourn
Comberton
Botanic Garden
Grantchester
Cherry Hinton
Fulbourn
Six Mile Bottom
Westley Waterless
Burrough Green
Kirtling Green
Depden
Kingston
Barton
Trumpington
Brinkley
Thorns
Cowlinge
Ambrook
Clopton Green
Longstowe
Great Eversden
Little Eversden
Wimpole Hall and Home Farm
Haslingfield
Hauxton
Great Shelford
Stapleford
Weston Colville
Weston Green
Carlton
Great Bradley
Little Bradley
Wickham Street
Denston
Stradishall
Stansfield
Harlton
Harston
Little Shelford
Babraham
Little Abington
West Wratting
Balsham
Little Thurlow
Great Thurlow
Arrington
Orwell
Barrington
New Wimpole
Newton
Sawston
Great Abington
Hildersham
West Wickham
Barnardiston
Hundon
Poslingford
Croydon
Willers Mill Wild Animal Sanctuary
Foxton
Whittlesford
Duxford Chapel
Pampisford
Streetly End
Horseheath
Great Wratting
Withersfield
Little Wratting
Shepreth
Wendy
Meldreth
Thriplow
Fowlmere
Duxford
Linton
Linton Zoo
Bartlow
Haverhill
Kedington
Chilton Street
Cavendish
Sue Ryder Foundation Mus.
Whaddon
Chiswick End
Kneesworth
Melbourne
Duxford Airfield (Imperial War Museum)
Hinxton
Ickleton
Stump Cross
Great Chesterford
Hadstock
Shudy Camps
Castle Camps
Sturmer
Boyton End
Clare
Stoke-by-Clare
Wixoe
Baythorn End
Abington Piggotts
Bassingbourn
Litlington
Little Chesterford
Ashdon
Church End
Helions Bumpstead
Birdbrook
Steeple Bumpstead
Ashen
Ovington
Belchamp St. Paul
Belchamp Otten
Royston & District Mus.
Royston
Heydon
Strethall
Elmdon
Littlebury
Little Walden
Saffron Walden
Ridgewell
Tilbury Juxta Clare
Little Yeldham
Great Chishill
Chrishall
Barley
Audley End House
Sewards End
Radwinter
Hempstead
Stambourne
Stambourne Green
Great Yeldham
Therfield
Little Chishill
Duddenhoe End
Littlebury Green
Wendens Ambo
Wimbish
Bridge Green
Cornish Hall End
Toppesfield
Colne Valley Railway
Audley End
Kelshall
Reed
Barkway
Nuthampstead
Tye Green
Great Sampford
Gainsford End
Castle Hedingham
Highstreet Green
Sible Hedingham
Sandon
Langley Lower Green
Langley Upper Green
Arkesden
Newport
Wimbish Green
Little Sampford
Howe Street
Finchingfield
Morris Green
Buckland
Howlett End
Debden
Roe Green
Mill End
Anstey
Meesden
Clavering
Wicken Bonhunt
Priors Hall Barn
Widdington
Mole Hall Wildlife Park
Debden Cross
Chipping
Wyddial
Brent Pelham
Starlings Green
Rickling
Thaxted
Little Bardfield
Wethersfield
Rushden
Throcking
Hare Street
Berden
Quendon
Hamperden End
Cutlers Green
Great Bardfield
Blackmore End
Buntingford
Great Hormead
Stocking Pelham
Ugley
Henham
Glendale Forge
Monk Street
Shalford
Beazley End
Gosfield
Cottered
Aspenden
Furneaux Pelham
East End
Ugley Green
Broxted
Lindsell
Church End
Shalford Green
Ardeley
Westmill
Hay Street
Patmore Heath
Manuden
House on the Hill Toy Mus.
Duton Hill
Great Easton
Bardfield Saling
Jasper's Green
Bocking Churchstreet
High Garrett
Wood End
Braughing
Clapgate
Farnham Green
Farnham
Elsenham
Brick End
Bran End
Great Saling
Great Munden
Nasty
Albury
Albury End
Stansted Mountfitchet
Molehill Green
Butcher's Pasture
Stebbing
Panfield
Bocking Windmill
Bocking
Braintree
Haultwick
Levens Green
Puckeridge
Little Hadham
London Stansted
Stansted Airport
Bambers Green
Little Easton
Stebbing Green
Churchend
Elitch Way
Rayne
Working Silk Mus.
Bradwell
Dane End
Standon
Wellpond Green
Birchanger
Takeley
Great Dunmow
Little Dunmow
Bannister Green
Tye Green
Whempstead
Collier's End
Hadham Ford
Bury Green
Bishop's Stortford
Birchanger Services
Takeley Street
Smith's Green
Hope End Green
Felsted
Row Green
Black Notley
Young's End
Cressing
Latchford
Much Hadham
Thorley Street
Hatfield Forest
Gt. Hallingbury
Barnston
Willows Grn.
Watton at Stone
Sacombe
Barwick
High Cross
Hadham Cross
Perry Green
Thorley
Spellbrook
Lit. Hallingbury
Bacon End
Bishop's Green
Hounslow Grn.
North End
Hartford End
White Notley
Tonwell
Wadesmill
Allens Green
Great Canfield
High Roding
Faulkbourne
Great Leighs
Thundridge
Baker's End
Sawbridgeworth
Hatfield Broad Oak
Ford End
Little Leighs
Fairstead
Chapmore End
Wareside
Widford
Hatfield Heath
Aythorpe Roding
Fuller Street
Terling
Ware
High Wych
High Easter
Howe Street
Flack's Green
Hertford
Hunsdon
Sheering
The Rodings
Leaden Roding
Pleshey
Great Amwell
Pye Corner
White Roding
Good Easter
Great Waltham
Little Waltham
Hertingfordbury
St. Margarets
Stanstead Abbots
Eastwick
Churchgate Street
Matching Tye
Matching
Margaret Roding
Abbess Roding
Chignall Smealy
Hatfield Peverel
Hertford Heath
Hailey
Mark Hall Cycle Museum
Netteswell
Matching Green
Mashbury
Chignall St. James
Broomfield
Nounsley
Hoddesdon
Rye Park
Rye House Gatehouse
Roydon
Harlow
Gt. Parndon
Potter Street
Foster Street
High Laver
Beauchamp Roding
Boyton Cross
Parsonage Green
Springfield
Boreham
Chelmer and Blackwater Navigation
Little Laver
Shellow Bowells
Chelmer Village
Brickendon
Paradise Wildlife Park
Roydon Hamlet
Ada Cole Memorial Stables
Broadley Common
Tye Green
Latton Bush
Hastingwood
Magdalen Laver
Roxwell
Little Baddow
Wormley
Broxbourne
Nazeing
Lower Nazeing
Fyfield
Willingale
Great Oxney Green
Writtle
Chelmsford
Moulsham Mill
West End
Wormley
Thornwood Common
Moreton
Cooksmill Green
Danbury Park
Hammond Street
Epping Green
Bumbles Green
Bovinger
Bobbingworth
Norton Mandeville
Widford
Great Baddow
Sandon
Danbury
Russell Green
Flamstead End
Epping Upland
Turnford
River Lee
Hayes Hill Farm
North Weald Bassett
Shelley
Norton Heath
Loves Green
Galleyend
Goff's Oak
Cheshunt
Coopersale Common
Greensted
High Ongar
Galleywood
Cambridge
Suffolk
Essex
Hertford
M11
A10
A11
A14
A505
A120
A130
A131
A1307
A414
A12
A1114
22
23
34
33

The King's Forest
Icklingham
Tuddenham
West Stow
Lackford
Culford
Ingham
Herringswell
Cavenham
Flempton
Hengrave
Fornham All Saints
Fornham St. Martin
Kennett
Kentford
Risby
Higham
Gazeley
Little Saxham
Westley
Barrow
Great Saxham
Bury St. Edmunds
Horringer
Ickworth House
Dalham
Denham
Ashley
Dunstall Green
Hargrave
Ousden
Chevington
Lidgate
Depden Green
Chedburgh
Depden
Rede
Thorns
Wickhambrook
Clopton Green
Wickham Street
Cowlinge
Denston
Stansfield
Hawkedon
Stradishall
Bradley
Barnardiston
Hundon
Poslingford
Kedington
Chilton Street
Clare
Cavendish
Pentlow
Boyton End
Stoke-by-Clare
Wixoe
Baythorn End
Ashen
Ovington
Belchamp St. Paul
Ridgewell
Tilbury Juxta Clare
Belchamp Otten
Belchamp Walter
Little Yeldham
Great Yeldham
Stambourne
Stambourne Green
Toppesfield
Gestingthorpe
Audley End
Castle Hedingham
Sible Hedingham
Hedingham
Great Maplestead
Little Maplestead
Wickham St. Paul
Twinstead
Lamarsh
Pebmarsh
Halstead
Gosfield
Colne Engaine
Earl's Colne
Wakes Colne
Chappel
Greenstead Green
High Garrett
Bocking Churchstreet
Braintree
Bocking
Stisted
Pattiswick Green
Bradwell
Coggeshall
Coggeshall Hamlet
Cressing
Silver End
Black Notley
Rayne
Kelvedon
Feering
Messing
Inworth
Tiptree
Rivenhall End
White Notley
Faulkbourne
Fairstead
Terling
Witham
Great Braxted
Chipping Hill
Hatfield Peverel
Wickham Bishops
Great Totham
Little Totham
Tolleshunt D'Arcy
Tolleshunt Major
Tollesbury
Langford
Heybridge
Heybridge Basin
Maldon
Woodham Walter
Danbury
Chelmsford
Springfield
Great Baddow
Galleyend
Boreham
Little Baddow
Nounsley
Goldhanger
Osea I.
Northey I.
Ramsey Island
St. Lawrence
Steeple
Tillingham
Bradwell Waterside
Bradwell on Sea
Blackwater
Mersea Island
West Mersea
East Mersea
Peldon
Great Wigborough
Salcott
Layer Marney
Layer Breton
Birch
Birch Green
Abberton Reservoir
Abberton
Langenhoe
Fingringhoe
Rowhedge
Wivenhoe
Alresford
Thorrington
Brightlingsea
St. Osyth
Point Clear
Great Clacton
Jaywick
Colne Pt.
Colchester
Lexden
Stanway
Marks Tey
Copford Green
Eight Ash Green
Fordham
West Bergholt
Aldham
Great Tey
Fordstreet
Mile End
Horkesley Heath
Great Horkesley
Boxted
Boxted Cross
Langham
Dedham
Dedham Heath
Lawford
Manningtree
Mistley
Bradfield
Wrabness
Ardleigh
Great Bromley
Little Bromley
Elmstead Market
Frating Green
Great Bentley
Weeley
Weeley Heath
Tendring
Thorpe-le-Soken
Little Clacton
Nayland
Stoke-by-Nayland
Bures
Mount Bures
Wormingford
Little Horkesley
Sudbury
Long Melford
Great Cornard
Little Cornard
Assington
Newton
Boxford
Hadleigh
Kersey
Lavenham
Brent Eleigh
Monks Eleigh
Chelsworth
Bildeston
Lindsey
Milden
Acton
Great Waldingfield
Little Waldingfield
Edwardstone
Groton
Polstead
Layham
Raydon
Shelley
Capel St. Mary
East Bergholt
Holton St. Mary
Stratford St. Mary
Higham
Brantham
Cattawade
Holbrook
Stutton
Tattingstone
Bentley
Freston
Wherstead
Belstead
Ipswich
Whitton
Westbourne
Chantry
Maidenhall
Sproughton
Bramford
Burstall
Hintlesham
Chattisham
Copdock
Elmsett
Aldham
Whatfield
Semer
Ash Street
Nedging Tye
Naughton
Offton
Somersham
Flowton
Needham Market
Barking
Stowmarket
Combs
Great Finborough
Buxhall
Onehouse
Rattlesden
Felsham
Gedding
Hitcham
Wattisham
Ringshall
Battisford
Creeting St. Mary
Stonham Aspal
Earl Stonham
Pettaugh
Helmingham
Crowfield
Coddenham
Ashbocking
Henley
Claydon
Akenham
Barham
Great Blakenham
Little Blakenham
Debenham
Mickfield
Winston
Wetherup Street
Mendlesham
Cotton
Bacton
Wyverstone
Westhorpe
Finningham
Gislingham
Thornham Magna
Eye
Yaxley
Mellis
Burgate
Botesdale
Rickinghall
Hinderclay
Wattisfield
Walsham-le-Willows
Stanton
Hepworth
Barningham
Sapiston
Honington
Bardwell
Ixworth Thorpe
Ixworth
Troston
Great Livermere
Ampton
Timworth Green
Great Barton
Pakenham
Stowlangtoft
Badwell Ash
Hunston
Langham
Norton
Thurston
Elmswell
Tostock
Woolpit
Drinkstone
Haughley
Wetherden
Beyton
Rougham
Rushbrooke
Hessett
Bradfield St. George
Bradfield Combust
Little Whelnetham
Great Whelnetham
Sicklesmere
Hawstead
Whepstead
Lawshall
Cockfield
Thorpe Morieux
Brettenham
Preston
Kettlebaston
Alpheton
Shimpling
Hartest
Stanstead
Glemsford
Boxted
Foxearth
Borley
Ballingdon
Bulmer
Middleton
Henny Street
Alphamstone
Castle Hedingham
Wethersfield
Shalford
Gainsford End
Sudbury
Stour
Colne
Dedham Vale

Southwold
Southwold Museum
Walberswick
Blythburgh
Wenhaston
Blackheath
Thorington
Bramfield
Walpole
Cookley
Huntingfield
Cratfield
Silverley's Green
Chippenhall Green
Wingfield
Battlesea Green
Pixey Green
Stradbroke
Swan Green
Ashfield Green
Banyard's Green
Wootton Green
Russel's Green
Wilby
Laxfield
Heveningham
Sibton Green
Ubbeston Green
Foals Green
Athelington
Brundish Street
Crown Corner
Stanway Green
Brundish
Owl's Green
Peasenhall
Sibton
Hemp Green
High Street
Darsham
Dunwich
Dunwich Forest
Dunwich Underwater Exploration Exhibition
Westleton
Yoxford
Middleton Moor
Middleton
Worlingworth
Tannington
Badingham
Rotten End
Bedfield
Maypole Green
Dennington
Bruisyard
North Green
Theberton
Eastbridge
Saxtead
Monk Soham
Saxtead Green Post Mill
Brabling Green
Cransford
Curlew Green
Kelsale
Rendham
Carlton
Leiston Abbey
Saxtead Green
Framlingham
Sweffling
Saxmundham
Leiston
Sizewell Visitors Centre
Sizewell
Earl Soham
Great Glemham
Knodishall
Lampardbrook
Cole's Green
Benhall Street
Sternfield
Aldringham
Brandeston
Stratford St. Andrew
Benhall Green
Coldfair Green
Cretingham
Kettleburgh
Parham
Friston
Thorpeness
Hacheston
Farnham
Gromford
Monewden
Easton
Marlesford
Easton Farm Park
Little Glemham
Snape Maltings Riverside Centre
Snape
Letheringham
Akenfield
Blaxhall
Aldeburgh
Charsfield
Lower Hacheston
Otley Hall
Otley
Wickham Market
Campsey Ash
Iken
Clopton Corner
Dallinghoo
Debach
Pettistree
Tunstall
High Street
Aldeburgh Bay
Tunstall Forest
Rendlesham
Sudbourne
Clopton
Bredfield
Ufford
Chillesford
Burgh
Eyke
Hasketon
Bromeswell
Butley
Melton
Orford Castle
Orford
Orford Ness
Woodbridge
Rendlesham Forest
Boot Street
Great Bealings
Butley High Corner
Sutton Hoo Archaeological Site
Playford
Maidensgrave
Capel St. Andrew
Little Bealings
Boyton
Martlesham
Sutton
Waldringfield Heath
Stores Corner
Kesgrave
Waldringfield
Shottisham
Duck Corner
Hollesley Bay
Hollesley
Brightwell
Warren Heath
Newbourne
Shingle Street
Bucklesham
Hemley
Alderton
Bawdsey
Nacton
Kirton
Levington
Falkenham
Pinmill
Thorpe Common
Trimley St. Martin
Chelmondiston
Orwell
Trimley Lower Street
Felixstoweferry
Trimley St. Mary
Shotley
Old Felixstowe
Walton
Shotley Gate
Shop Corner
FELIXSTOWE
Charles Manning's Amusement Park
Stour
HARWICH
Harwich Redoubt
Parkeston
Upper Dovercourt
Dovercourt
Little Oakley
Esbjerg 20:00
Gothenburg 24:00
Hamburg 20:00
Hook of Holland 3:40
Horsey Island
The Naze
Kirby le Soken
Walton on the Naze
Kirby Cross
Frinton on Sea
Great Holland
Holland on Sea
A12
A14
A144
A1120
A1094
A1152
A1214
A1156
B1117
B1116
B1120
B1119
B1121
B1122
B1125
B1069
B1353
B1078
B1084
B1083
B1438
B1387
B1123
B1456
B1033
B1032
B1034
B1079
B1078
Blyth
Alde
45
6
7
8
9
10
A
B
C
D
E
F
G
H

Morfa Nefyn
Nefyn
Pwllheli
Criccieth
Porthmadog
Abersoch
Aberdaron
Bardsey Island
Tywyn
Aberystwyth
L L E Y N
C A R D I G A N
B A Y
TREMADOG BAY
BARMOUTH BAY
Porth Dinllaen
Porth Ysgadan
Porth Golmon
Penrhyn Mawr
Bardsey Sound
Porth Neigwl or Hell's Mouth
St. Tudwal's Road
St. Tudwal's Island East
St. Tudwal's Island West
Trwyn Cilan
Trwyn Llanbedrog
Carreg yr Imbill
Carreg Ddu
Aberdovey Bar
Llanaelhaearn
Llithfaen
Pistyll
Edern
Tudweiliog
Rhos-y-llan
Pen-y-graig
Llangwnnadl
Ty-hen
Methlem
Rhydlios
Capel Carmel
Uwchmynydd
Bodermid
Pen-y-cil
Rhoshirwaun
Rhiw
Llanfaelrhys
Llanengan
Sarn Bach
Bwlchtocyn
Marchroes
Cilan Uchaf
Llangian
Llanbedrog
Mynytho
Nanhoron
Botwnnog
Bryncroes
Sarn Meyllteyrn
Llaniestyn
Garnfadryn
Dinas
Glanrhyd
Tan-y-graig
Boduan
Llannor
Efailnewydd
Rhyd-y-clafdy
Penrhos
Denio
South Beach
Fron
Rhos-fawr
Llanarmon
Chwilog
Abererch
Llanystumdwy
Pentrefelin
Tremadog
Penmorfa
Golan
Dolbenmaen
Garndolbenmaen
Bryncir
Llecheiddior
Glan-Dwyfach
Cenin
Pen-sarn
Pencaenewydd
Llangybi
Llwyndyrys
Rhoslan
Trefor
Llanfihangel-y-pennant
Prenteg
Morfa Bychan
Borth-y-Gest
Harlech
Llandanwg
Llanenddwyn
Llanddwywe
Llangelynin
Rhoslefain
Llanfendigaid
Tonfanau
Trefechan
Penparcau
Rhydyfelin
Chancery
Blaenplwyf
Upper Borth
Llandegwning
Llawr Dref
Bryn-mawr
Pen-y-groeslon
Morfa Dyffryn
Llanfihangel-y-traethau
Morfa Harlech
Traeth Bach
Dafarn Faig
Tyddyn-mawr
A487
A497
A499
A493
B4417
B4354
B4415
B4413
B4411
B4573
B4572
522 GYRN DDU
564 YR EIFL
552 MOEL-DDU
782 MOEL HEBOG
304 MYNYDD RHIW
191
167
LLEYN HISTORICAL MARITIME MUSEUM
BODVEL HALL ADVENTURE PARK
PENARTH FAWR MEDIEVAL HOUSE
STARCOAST WORLD
LLOYD GEORGE MEMORIAL MUSEUM
MARITIME MUSEUM
PORTMEIRION VILLAGE
WELSH HIGHLAND POTTERY
BRYNKIR WOOLLEN MILL
PLAS-YN-RHIW
MAES ARTRO TOURIST VILLAGE
RNLI LIFEBOAT MUSEUM
FAIRBOURNE & BARMOUTH STEAM RAILWAY
ARTS CENTRE
NATIONAL LIBRARY
CLIFF RAILWAY
CASTLE
46
26

Blaenau Ffestiniog
Bethania
Tanygrisiau
Congl-y-wal
Croesor
MOELWYN MAWR
FFESTINIOG POWER STATION
Tan-lan
Rhyd
Rhyd-y-sarn
Ffestiniog
Llanfrothen
Tan-y-bwlch
Bont Newydd
Maentwrog
Gellilydan
Penrhyndeudraeth
TRAWSFYNYDD NUCLEAR POWER STATION
Cilfor
Caerwych
Llyn Trawsfynydd
Pont Dolydd Prysor
Cwm Prysor
Trawsfynydd
Talsarnau
Glan-y-wern
Eisingrug
Glyn-cywarch
MOEL YSGYFARNOGOD
S N O W D O N I A
Pont yr Afon-Gam
Migneint
CARNEDD Y FILIAST
ARENIG FACH
Llyn Celyn
GRAIG WEN
Llyn Arenig fawr
ARENIG FAWR
MOEL LLYFRANT
Ty Mawr Cwm
Pen-y-gop
Ciltalgarth
Glan-yr-afon
Frongoch
Llidiardau
Rhyd-uchaf
Llanycil
Parc
Bala
Llanfor
Llyn Tegid or Bala Lake
Rhos-y-gwaliau
BALA
Bettws Gwerfil Goch
Ty-nant
Dinmael
Maerdy
Llangwm
Tai-mawr
Glan-yr-afon
Druid
Corwen
Cynwyd Forest
Cynwyd
FOEL GOCH
Wenallt
Sarnau
Bethel
Cefn-ddwysarn
Rhiwlas
Llandderfel
Pale
Landrillo
Cefn Coch
Pennant
Aber Hirnant
Blaen-y-Cwm
Pont Cwm Pydew
MOEL SYCH
Tyn-y-fedwen
Aberhirnant Forest
Llangower
BALA LAKE
Dolhendre
Llanuwchllyn
Buarthmeini
Mynydd Bryn-llech
Mynydd Bach
Bronaber
Afon Eden
G w y n e d d
Bed-y-coedwr
Cwm-hesgen
Pont Aber-Geirw
Pont-Rhyd-sarn
RHINOG FAWR
MAESGYM VISITOR CENTRE
Coed y Brenin Forest
Pen-y-bont
Gwynfryn
N A T I O N A L
Capel Hermon
RHOBELL FAWR
Pont Fronwydd
Y LLETHR
DIFFWYS
Ganllwyd
Talardd
Ty-nant
FOEL Y GEIFR
Cwm Cynllwyd
Tan-y-pistyll
Pencraig
Llangynog
Cefn Coch
Pennant Melangell
Alltforgan
Penybontfawr
Penygarnedd
Hirnant
Lake Vyrnwy
Ty-uchaf
Blaen-y-cwm
Llanwddyn
Abertridwr
Ddôl-Cownwy
Dyfnant Forest
Mynydd y Gadfa
Llanfihangel-yn-Ngwynfa
Pont Llogel
Afon Vyrnwy
Dolanog
Hen Gerrig
Aber-Rhiwlech
Pont y Pennant
ARAN FAWDDWY
Llanfachreth
Rhydymain
Afon Wnion
Blaen-y-cwm
Nannau
P A R K
Llanelltyd
CYMMER ABBEY
Pen-y-bryn
Bontddu
Caerdeon
Plas-canol
Llanaber
Cutiau
Penmaenpool
PENMAENPOOL CENTRE
Abergwynant
KINGS (DOLGELLAU)
Dolgellau
Rhyd-wen
Bont Newydd
Brithdir
Torrent Walk
Cywarch
Llanymawddwy
Y Gribin
Bryn Sion
Afon Cerist
TIR RHIWIOG
Moel y Llyn
Dinas-Mawddwy
Aber Cowarch
Minllyn
MEIRION MILL
Cwm-Cewydd
Mallwyd
WAUN-OER
Arthog
Ynysgyfflog
Friog
CADER IDRIS
Mynydd Ceiswyn
Mynydd Dolgoed
Dovey Forest
Wern
Foel
Llangadfan
Ffridd Goch
Minffordd
Corris Uchaf
CORRIS
Aberllefenni
Aberangell
Pen Coed
Llanerfyl
Four Crosses
Llanfihangel-y-pennant
Tal-y-llyn
Afon Dysynni
CRAFT CENTRE
Corris
CORRIS RAILWAY MUSEUM
Esgairgeiliog
Cwm-Llinau
Mynydd y Cemaes
Clegyrnant
Dolwen
Sychtyn
Neinthirion
Melin-y-grug
Melin-y-ddol
Abergynolwyn
Peniarth
Dol-fôr
Cemmaes
Pentre-Celyn
Pandy
Cwmderwen
Mynydd Waun Fawr
Bryn-y-Garth
Plas Llwyngwern
CENTRE FOR ALTERNATIVE TECHNOLOGY
Pantperthog
TARRENHENDRE
Pandy
Llanwrin
VALLEY
Cemmaes Road
Waun
Llanbrynmair
Dolfach
Commins Coch
Tafolwern
Abercegir
Darowen
Llanllugan
Llanwyddelan
Adfa
Rhyd-yr-onen
Pen-y-bont
SENEDD-DY-OWAIN GLYNDWR
Machynlleth
Penegoes
FELIN CREWI WATER MILL
Cwrt
Pennal
DOVEY
Tal-y-wern
Llan
Bont-Dolgadfan
Talerddig
Rhyd
Tregynon
Forge
Caethle
Derwenlas
Glaspwll
Melin-byrhedyn
Pant-glâs
MOELFRE
Pennant
Carno
Aberhosan
Aberdovey
Glandyfi
YNYS HIR RESERVE
Eglwys Fach
DYFI FURNACE
Fochno
P o w y s
Glaslyn
Dylife
Clatter
Bwlch-y-ffridd
Llanwnog
Llancynfelyn
Tre'r-ddôl
Tre-Taliesin
BORTH
MOEL-Y-LLYN
Staylittle
Llawryglyn
Gleiniant
Caersws
Milford
Trefeglwys
Source of R. Severn
Nant-y-Moch Reservoir
Tal-y-bont
Dôl-y-Bont
Llyn Clywedog
FAN HILL
Van
Oakley Park
Little London
Mochdre
Llandinam
Llandre
Pen-y-garn
Bont-goch
PLYNLIMON
Source of R. Wye
Pentre
Bow Street
Salem
Clarach
Penrhyn-coch
Pen-bont-Rhydybeddau
Plas Gogerddan
Tan Hinon
Old Hall
Glan-y-nant
Llanidloes
Hafren Forest
Comins Coch
Capel Dewi
Llanbadarn Fawr
LLYWERNOG SILVER LEAD MINE
Dyffryn Castell
Glynbrochan
Newchapel
Capel Bangor
Dollwen
Goginan
Pant Mawr
Llanifyny
Cwmbelan
Glanrafon
Cwmbrwyno
Ponterwyd
VALE OF RHEIDOL
Afon Rheidol
RHEIDOL HYDRO ELECTRIC STATION
Llangurig
Tylwch
Llaithddu
Moriah
Capel Seion
NANTEOS MANSION
Aberffrwd
Ystumtuen
YSTUMTUEN
Ysbyty-Cynfyn
David's Well
Gors
Pisgah
New Cross
Llanfihangel-y-Creuddyn
Mynydd Bach
Devil's Bridge
PEN Y GARN
Nantgwyn
Pant-y-dwr
RED LION HILL
Trisant
Cnwch-coch
Blaenycwm
Llanilar
Abermagwr
New Row
Cwmystwyth
Bwlch-y-sarnau
St Harmon

Llangollen
Corwen
Ruabon
Cefn-mawr
Overton
Chirk
Ellesmere
Oswestry
Whittington
Llanfyllin
Welshpool
Llanfair Caereinion
Montgomery
Newtown
Bishop's Castle
Clun
Church Stretton
Baschurch
Llanrhaeadr-ym-Mochnant
Llansantffraid-ym-Mechain
Llanymynech
Four Crosses
Middletown
Westbury
Pontesbury
Minsterley
Chirbury
Kerry
Clun Forest
Black Mountain
Corndon Hill
The Long Mynd
Stiperstones
Wenlock
P O W Y S
B E R W Y N
Cynwyd Forest
Llantysilio Mountain
Ruabon Mountain
Afon Tanat
Afon Vyrnwy
Severn
A5
A483
A495
A458
A490
A489
A488
A49
A470
A494
A539
A528
A525
A4113
48
37
28

Stafford
Shropshire
Newcastle-under-Lyme
Stoke-on-Trent
Whitchurch
Audlem
Madeley
Market Drayton
Stone
Eccleshall
Stafford
Newport
Gnosall
Penkridge
Wellington
Hadley
Donnington
Oakengates
Telford
Dawley
Shifnal
Albrighton
Brewood
Codsall
Tettenhall
Wolverhampton
Wednesfield
Willenhall
Bilston
Darlaston
Sedgley
Coseley
Tipton
Dudley
Oldbury
Rowley Regis
Brierley Hill
Wordsley
Stourbridge
HALESOWEN
Kidderminster
Bewdley
Bridgnorth
Much Wenlock
Madeley
Broseley
Shawbury
Wombourne
Kinver
Cheslyn Hay
Cannock
Longton
Fenton
Wem
Shrewsbury
Cleobury Mortimer
Catshill
Longbridge
Hodnet
Cheadle
M6
M54
M5
A5
A41
A442
A458
A449
A518
A53
A34
A51
A529
A4117
49
40
29

50
39
30
D e r b y
Derby City
Derby
S t a f f o r d
W e s t M i d l a n d s
W a r w
Stoke
Longton
Fenton
Cheadle
Alton
Rocester
Uttoxeter
Stone
Stafford
Rugeley
Abbots Bromley
NEEDWOOD FOREST
Tutbury
Burton-upon-Trent
Swadlincote
Ashby-de-la-Zouch
Measham
Mickleover
Normanton
Chellaston
Allestree
Duffield
Willington
Repton
Melbourne
CANNOCK CHASE
Cannock
Hednesford
Lichfield
Burntwood
Brownhills
Tamworth
Atherstone
Nuneaton
Bedworth
Coventry
Wednesfield
Willenhall
Walsall
Bilston
Darlaston
Wednesbury
West Bromwich
SUTTON COLDFIELD
Erdington
SMETHWICK
BIRMINGHAM
HALESOWEN
Dudley
Sedgley
Tipton
Oldbury
Rowley Regis
Solihull
Shirley
Coleshill
Castle Bromwich
Dorridge
Catshill
Kidderminster
M6
M42
M5
A38
A5
A50
A51
A34
A446
A452

Nottingham
Leicester
Northampton
Rutland
Nottingham
ARNOLD
Eastwood
Kimberley
ILKESTON
Carlton
Bingham
Radcliffe on Trent
Bottesford
Sedgebrook
Grantham
BEESTON
Stapleford
Sandiacre
WEST BRIDGFORD
LONG EATON
Clifton
Ruddington
Cotgrave
Keyworth
VALE OF BELVOIR
Belvoir
Castle Donington
Kegworth
East Leake
Loughborough
Shepshed
Melton Mowbray
Waltham on the Wolds
Wymondham
Whitwick
Charnwood Forest
Barrow upon Soar
Sileby
Mountsorrel
Syston
Birstall
Anstey
Thurmaston
Leicester City
Oakham
Oadby
Wigston Magna
Earl Shilton
Hinckley
Burbage
Uppingham
Market Harborough
Corby
Lutterworth
Desborough
Rothwell
Kettering
Rugby
Naseby Field
Sulby Reservoir
Eyebrook Reservoir
M1
M6
M69
A46
A52
A6
A47
A14
A606
A607
A5
A50

Lincolnshire
Rutland
Northampton
Cam
Grantham
Sleaford
Heckington
Helpringham
Swineshead
Donington
Gosberton
Pinchbeck
Spalding
Bourne
Rippingale
Morton
Folkingham
Billingborough
Horbling
Colsterworth
Great Ponton
Barkston
Great Gonerby
Sedgebrook
Bottesford
Long Bennington
Waltham on the Wolds
Wymondham
Oakham
Uppingham
Empingham
Stamford
Market Deeping
Deeping St. James
Crowland
Peterborough
Whittlesey
Yaxley
Sawtry
Ramsey
Oundle
Corby
Kettering
Thrapston
Burton Latimer
Rothwell
Huntingdon
Rutland Water
Deeping Fen
Holland Fen
Rockingham Forest
A1 BEING UPGRADED TO A1(M)

THE WASH
LYNN DEEPS
NORFOLK COAST
Lynn Channel
Brancaster Bay
Boston
Halltoft End
Benington
Butterwick
Freiston
Skirbeck
Skirbeck Quarter
Fishtoft
Scrane End
The Haven
Frampton
Sandholme
Skeldyke
Seadyke
Bucklegate
Algarkirk
Fosdyke
Holbeach St. Matthew
Holbeach St. Marks
Dawsmere
HOLBEACH MARSH
Gedney Marsh
Gedney Drove End
Moulton Seas End
Saracen's Head
Holbeach Hurn
Holbeach Bank
Holbeach Clough
Halesgate
Gedney Dyke
Lutton
Guy's Head
Whaplode
Holbeach
Fleet Hargate
Chapelgate
Little London
BUTTERFLY AND FALCONRY PARK
Gedney
Fleet
Gedney Broadgate
Long Sutton
Sutton Bridge
Terrington Marsh
Ongar Hill
Sutton Crosses
Whaplode St. Catherine
Tydd St. Mary
Holbeach St. Johns
Sutton St. James
Tydd Gote
Four Gotes
Tydd St. Giles
Newton
Tydd St. Giles Fen
Whaplode Drove
Sutton St. Edmund
Fitton End
Holbeach Drove
Gedney Hill
Gorefield
Leverington
Throckenholt
Church End
Parson Drove
PECKOVER HOUSE
Wisbech
WISBECH & FENLAND MUS
Walsoken
FENLAND AVIATION MUS
New Walsoken
Wisbech St. Mary
Murrow
Tholomas Drove
Rogue's Alley
Thorney Toll
Guyhirn Gull
Guyhirn
Ring's End
Waldersey
Coldham
Friday Bridge
Elm
Emneth
Emneth Hungate
Holly End
Outwell
Upwell
Laddus Fens
Chainbridge
STAGS HOLT FARM PARK
Three Holes
Eldernell
West Fen
Westry
Norwoodside
March
Turves
Binnimoor Fen
Euximoor Fen
Euximoor Drove
South District
Christchurch
Lakesend
Tipsend
Upwell Fen
Upwell Fen
Welney
Town End
Ranson Moor
BEDFORD LEVEL (MIDDLE)
Flood's Ferry
Wimblington
White Fen
Doddington
Benwick
ISLE OF ELY
Manea
Wimblington Fen
Purls Bridge
Ramsey Forty Foot
Forty Foot Drain
Vermuden's Drain
Sixteen Foot Drain
Horseway
Welches Dam
Chatteris
Ramsey Hollow
Langwood Fen
Tick Fen
Ferry Hill
GRAYS HONEY FARM
Horseley Fen
Chapel Head
Pidley Fen
Fenton
Pidley
Chatteris Fen
Mepal
Sutton
Witcham
Wardy Hill
Coveney
Wentworth
Witchford
Somersham
Colne
Bluntisham
Earith
Hill Row Doles
North Hill
Haddenham
Wilburton
Stretham
Aldreth
Ely
OLIVER CROMWELL'S HOUSE
CATHEDRAL AND MUS.
Little Thetford
Barway
Soham Cotes
Soham
Soham Mere
Stuntney
Middle Fen
Great Fen
Broad Hill
Isleham Fen
Isleham
Queen Adelaide
Prickwillow
Chettisham
West Fen
Little Downham
Pymore
Littleport
BEDFORD LEVEL (SOUTH)
Burnt Fen
Mare Fen
Fodder Fen
Apes Hall
Gold Hill
Shippea Hill Sta.
New Bedford River
Old Bedford River
Great Ouse
Nene (Old Course)
Orange Row
Clenchwarton
Walpole Cross Keys
Terrington St. Clement
Walpole St. Andrew
Walpole Marsh
Walpole St. Peter
Hay Green
Tilney High End
Tilney All Saints
Ingleborough
St. John's Highway
Terrington St. John
Tilney St. Lawrence
West Walton
West Walton Highway
Walpole Highway
Marshland
St. John's Fen End
Wiggenhall St. Mary Magdalen
Marshland St. James
Marshland Fen
Stowbridge
West Head
Stow Bardolph Fen
Nordelph
Barroway Drove
Saddle Bow
Wiggenhall St. Germans
Wiggenhall St. Mary the Virgin
Kings's Lynn
West Lynn
Gaywood
Fairstead
Hardwick
Watlington
Tottenhill Row
Tottenhill
Runcton Holme
South Runcton
Wimbotsham
Downham Market
Stow Bardolph
Broomhill
Denver
Fordham
Hilgay
Ten Mile Bank
Hilgay Fen
Southery
Southery Fens
Brandon Creek
Brandon Bank
West Winch
North Runcton
Setchey
Blackborough End
Middleton
Tower End
Fair Green
Wormegay
Shouldham
Shouldham Thorpe
Marham
Crimplesham
Bexwell
Wereham
West Dereham
Stradsett
Fincham
Barton Bendish
Boughton
Oxborough
OXBURGH HALL
Gooderstone
Eastmoor
Beachamwell
Beachamwell Warren
Shingham
Cockley Cley
Stoke Ferry
Wretton
Whitington
Foulden
Northwold
Brookville
Methwold Hythe
Methwold
Methwold Fens
Queen's Ground
Feltwell
Feltwell Fens
Hockwold cum Wilton
Hockwold Fens
Weeting
GRIMES GRAVES
Brandon
BRANDON PARK
Little Ouse
Lakenheath
Wangford Warren
Lakenheath Warren
Kenny Hill
Mildenhall Fen
Eriswell
Holywell Row
Beck Row
Thistley Green
West Row
Mildenhall
Barton Mills
Icklingham
Croxton
Hunstanton
SEA LIFE CENTRE
Old Hunstanton
Holme next the Sea
Thornham
Titchwell
Brancaster Staithe
Brancaster
Burnham
Ringstead
Heacham
NORFOLK LAVENDER
PEDDARS WAY & NORFOLK COAST PATH
Summerfield
Docking
Sedgeford
Snettisham
PARK FARM
Fring
Bircham Newton
Ingoldisthorpe
Shepherd's Port
Shernborne
Great Bircham
Bircham Tofts
BIRCHAM MILL
Dersingham
WOLFERTON STATION MUSEUM
SANDRINGHAM
Sandringham
Wolferton
Anmer
West Newton
Flitcham
New Houghton
Babingley
Castle Rising
Hillington
North Wootton
South Wootton
Congham
CONGHAM HALL HERB GARDEN
Roydon
Grimston
Pott Row
Massingham Heath
Gayton
Leziate
Ashwicken
Gayton Thorpe
East Winch
East Walton
West Bilney
Pentney
West Acre
Castle Acre
South Acre
Narborough
Harpley
Little Massingham
Great Massingham
Norfolk
Suffolk
Cambridge

Holkham Bay
Brancaster Bay
Blakeney Point
Holme next the Sea
Titchwell
Brancaster Staithe
Burnham Deepdale
Brancaster
Burnham Norton
Burnham Overy Staithe
Holkham
Wells-next-the-Sea
Stiffkey
Morston
Blakeney
Cley next the Sea
Wiveton
Newgate
Salthouse
Kelling
Weybourne
Sheringham
Upper Sheringham
Beeston Regis
West Runton
East Runton
Thornham
Burnham Market
Burnham Overy Town
Burnham Thorpe
Ringstead
Warham
Cockthorpe
Langham
Glandford
N O R F O L K
High Kelling
Bodham
East Beckham
West Beckham
Aylmerton
New Holkham
Wighton
Westgate
Binham
Saxlingham
Letheringsett
Holt
Field Dalling
Copy's Green
Summerfield
Docking
North Creake
Lower Green
Gresham
Sedgeford
Stanhoe
South Creake
Waterden
Great Walsingham
Little Walsingham
Bale
Sharrington
Hindringham
Hempstead
Baconsthorpe
Sustead
Snettisham
Fring
Bircham Newton
North Barsham
Houghton St. Giles
Brinton
Thornage
Hunworth
Bessingham
Stody
Edgefield
Matlaske
Thurgarton
Ingoldisthorpe
Barmer
West Barsham
Great Bircham
Syderstone
East Barsham
Great Snoring
Thursford
Gunthorpe
Briningham
Plumstead
Aldborough
Shernborne
Bircham Tofts
Little Snoring
Melton Constable
Edgefield Street
Little Barningham
Wickmere
Bagthorpe
Barney
Swanton Novers
Briston
Calthorpe
Erpingham
Dersingham
Sculthorpe
Kettlestone
Fulmodestone
Itteringham
Saxthorpe
Corpusty
Anmer
Tattersett
Dunton
Shereford
Hempton
Fakenham
Ingworth
Sandringham
West Rudham
Coxford
Tatterford
Little Ryburgh
Stibbard
Hindolveston
Thurning
Oulton
Blickling
West Newton
New Houghton
East Rudham
Toftrees
Wood Norton
Norton Corner
Silvergate
Flitcham
Great Ryburgh
Guestwick
Heydon
Oulton Street
Aylsham
Colkirk
Guestwick Green
Wood Dalling
Hillington
Harpley
Helhoughton
Oxwick
Guist
West Raynham
East Raynham
Salle
Southgate
Fengate
Congham
Little Massingham
Hamrow
Twyford
Foulsham
Themelthorpe
Little London
Roydon
South Raynham
Gateley
Broom Green
Bintree
Reepham
Cawston
Great Massingham
Weasenham St. Peter
Whissonsett
Horningtoft
Booton
Eastgate
Grimston
Weasenham All Saints
Wellingham
Tittleshall
Brisley
North Elmham
Foxley
Whitwell Street
Brandiston
The Heath
Pott Row
Massingham Heath
Stanfield
Billingford
Bawdeswell
Haveringland
Hevingham
Gayton
Rougham
East Bilney
Worthing
Sparham
Ashwicken
Mileham
Alderford
Swannington
Gayton Thorpe
West Lexham
Litcham
Bittering
Beetley
Mill Street
Lenwade
Upgate
Felthorpe
East Walton
East Lexham
Swanton Morley
Lyng
Elsing
Morton
Attlebridge
East Winch
Castle Acre
Gressenhall
Hoe
Woodgate
Primrose Green
Weston Longville
West Acre
Newton
Beeston
Longham
Bilney
Pentney
South Acre
Great Dunham
Drury Square
Sparrow Green
Etling Green
North Tuddenham
Weston Green
Ringland
Taverham
Drayton
Narborough
Little Dunham
Crane's Corner
East Dereham
Hockering
Great Fransham
Wendling
Honingham
Costessey
Great Palgrave
Sporle
Little Fransham
Scarning
Toftwood
Mattishall Burgh
Clint Green
Mattishall
East Tuddenham
Marham
Daffy Green
Yaxham
New Costessey
Easton
Bowthorpe
Swaffham
Necton
West End
Bradenham
Westfield
Whinburgh
Welborne
Colton
Marlingford
Earlham
Beachamwell Warren
North Pickenham
Holme Hale
Shipdham
Garvestone
Thuxton
Runhall
Brandon Parva
Barford
Bawburgh
N o r f o l k
Fincham
Barton Bendish
Crowshill
Letton Green
Barnham Broom
Great Melton
Little Melton
Colney
Cringleford
Beachamwell
Reymerston
Danemoor Green
Wramplingham
High Green
Shingham
Cockley Cley
Ashill
Cranworth
Southburgh
Carleton Forehoe
Hethersett
South Pickenham
Saham Hills
Hardingham
Kimberley
Eastmoor
Saham Toney
Woodrising
Crownthorpe
Ketteringham
Boughton
Ovington
Carbrooke
Wicklewood
Hackford
Wymondham
East Carleton
Oxborough
Gooderstone
Great Cressingham
Hingham
Caudlesprings
Oxburgh Hall
Hilborough
Deopham
Morley St. Botolph
Mulbarton
Stoke Ferry
Whitington
Foulden
Little Cressingham
Watton
Scoulton
Silfield
Griston
Little Ellingham
Suton
Bodney
Merton
Northacre
Deopham Green
Wreningham
Northwold
The Arms
Rockland St. Peter
Ashwellthorpe
Newton Flotman
Brookville
Caston
Great Ellingham
Spooner Row
Fundenhall
Hapton
Stow Bedon
Rockland All Saints
Fundenhall Street
Thompson
Besthorpe
Cranwich
Attleborough
Methwold Hythe
Methwold
Ickburgh
Lower Stow Bedon
Tacolneston
Forncett St. Mary
Mundford
Shropham
Bunwell
Forncett End
West Tofts
Puddledock
Carleton Rode
Forncett St. Peter
Old Buckenham
Great Hockham
B R E C K L A N D
Feltwell
Church Green
Hargate
Wacton
Eccles Road
Wilby
Aslacton
Wretham
New Buckenham
Tibenham
Great Moulton
Hockwold cum Wilton
Weeting
Larling
Hunt's Corner
Pristow Green
Sneath Common
Hockwold Fens
Santon Downham
Quidenham
Banham
Croxton
Goose Green
Tivetshall St. Margaret
Tivetshall St. Mary
Brandon
Kenninghall
Bridgham
East Harling
Winfarthing
Dam Green
Gissing
Kenninghall Heath
Mill Green
Lakenheath
Thetford
Brettenham
Shadwell
Thetford Warren
North Lopham
Shelfanger
Wangford Warren
Fersfield
Burston
Shimpling
Dickleburgh
Rushall
Rushford
South Lopham
Lakenheath Warren
Gasthorpe
Garboldisham
Bressingham
Roydon
Diss
Thelveton
Knettishall
Blo' Norton
Elveden
Euston
Hopton
Magpie Green
Palgrave
Scole
Thorpe Abbotts
Eriswell
Barnham
Coney Weston
Market Weston
Thelnetham
Redgrave
Holywell Row
Little Fakenham
Stuston
Oakley
Hoxne
Wortham
Barningham
Hinderclay
Thrandeston
Brome
Brome Street
Cross Street
S u f f o l k
West Row
Sapiston
Hepworth
Botesdale
Rickinghall
Burgate
Langton Green
Mildenhall
Honington
Mellis
Yaxley
Eye
The King's Forest
Barton Mills
Icklingham
Bardwell
Wattisfield
Thornham
Ixworth
Stanton
Cranley

6
7
8
9
10
A
B
C
D
E
F
G
H
CROMER MUSEUM
Cromer
Overstrand
Sidestrand
Felbrigg
Northrepps
Crossdale Street
Trimingham
COAST
Frogshail
Mundesley
Southrepps
Gimingham
STOW MILL
Thorpe Market
Lower Street
Trunch
Paston
Knapton
Bacton
Keswick
Walcott
Antingham
Bradfield
Edingthorpe
Broomholm
Suffield
Swafield
ALBY GARDENS
Colby
Edingthorpe Green
Witton Bridge
Ridlington
Happisburgh
North Walsham
Spa Common
Crostwight
Whimpwell Green
Eccles on Sea
Banningham
Happisburgh Common
Felmingham
Lessingham
Hempstead
Honing
Tuttington
East Ruston
Ingham Corner
Sea Palling
Westwick
Bengate
Waxham
Burgh next Aylsham
Skeyton
Worstead
Ingham
Swanton Abbot
Sloley
Dilham
Stalham
Smallburgh
Stalham Green
Brampton
BURE VALLEY RAILWAY
Hickling
Scottow
Sutton
Hickling Green
Lamas
Pennygate
Barton Turf
Buxton
Little Hautbois
Tunstead
Wood Street
Hickling Heath
Horsey
Hickling Broad
HORSEY WINDMILL
Sco Ruston
WROXHAM BARNS
Neatishead
Barton Broad
Catfield
Stratton Strawless
Coltishall
Ashmanhaugh
Irstead
Sharp Street
Potter Heigham
West Somerton
East Somerton
Winterton-on-Sea
Waterloo
Horstead
WILLOW FARM FLOWERS
Threehammer Common
Hainford
Belaugh
Hoveton
Thurne
Martham
Frettenham
Wroxham
Lower Street
Ludham
Bastwick
Newport
REDWINGS HORSE SANCTUARY
Upper Street
Horning
Upper Street
Repps
Rollesby
Hemsby
Newton St. Faith
Wroxham Broad
Thurne
Ormesby St. Michael
Scratby
California
Crostwick
Woodbastwick
Ranworth
Clippesby
THE VILLAGE
Filby Broad
Ormesby St. Margaret
Horsham St. Faith
Spixworth
Rackheath
Salhouse
FAIRHAVEN GARDEN TRUST
NORWICH
Panxworth
South Walsham
Billockby
Burgh St. Margaret
Filby
CAISTER ROMAN TOWN
Caister-on-Sea
New Rackheath
Mauthy
West Caister
Old Catton
Little Plumstead
Upton
THE CANDLEMAKER WORKSHOP
Thrigby
THRIGBY HALL WILDLIFE GARDENS
Sprowston
Hemblington
Runham
West End
YARMOUTH
Thorpe End
Blofield Heath
North Burlingham
Acle
Stokesby
NORTH DENES
Upper Hellesdon
Thorpe St. Andrew
Great Plumstead
Bure
New Catton
Damgate
Blofield
Lingwood
GREAT YARMOUTH
Great Yarmouth
NORWICH
Brundall
Beighton
Tunstall
THE
Halvergate Marshes
WAX WORKS
SEA LIFE CENTRE
CASTLE MUSEUM
Postwick
Moulton St. Mary
Lakenham
Trowse Newton
Strumpshaw
South Burlingham
Halvergate
Breydon Water
Cobholm Island
MARITIME, ELIZABETHAN HOUSE AND TOLHOUSE MUSEUMS
EXHIBITION GALLERIES
Eaton
Kirby Bedon
Surlingham
Buckenham
Hassingham
Freethorpe
BROADS
Burgh Castle
Southtown
Wickhampton
BERNEY ARMS AND MILL
Arminghall
Bramerton
Southwood
Caistor St. Edmund
Framingham Pigot
Rockland St. Mary
Cantley
Limpenhoe
Bradwell
Gorleston on Sea
Claxton
Framingham Earl
Hellington
Yare
Dunston
Ashby St. Mary
Langley Street
Reedham
Belton
Poringland
Stoke Holy Cross
Yelverton
Bergh Apton
Hardley Street
Ferry
Thurton
ST OLAVES PRIORY
Fritton
Hopton on Sea
Howe
Chedgrave
Lower Thurlton
Hawes Green
Shotesham
Brooke
Sisland
Chet
The Dell
Lound
SOMERLEYTON HALL
Stubb's Green
Loddon
Thurlton
Thorpe
Seething
Blundeston
Saxlingham Thorpe
Saxlingham Nethergate
Kirstead Green
Mundham
Stubbs Green
Hales
Herringfleet
Corton
Raveningham
Somerleyton
PLEASUREWOOD HILLS FAMILY THEME PARK
Saxlingham Green
RAVENINGHAM GARDENS
Haddiscoe
Maypole Green
Thwaite St. Mary
Hempnall
Toft Monks
Oulton
LOWESTOFT AND EAST SUFFOLK MARITIME MUSEUM
Road Green
Woodton
Kirby Cane
Stockton
Wheatacre
Normanstone
Stratton St. Michael
Hedenham
Burgh St. Peter
HERITAGE/VISITOR CENTRE
Hempnall Green
Fritton
Topcroft
Aldeby
Oulton Broad
Morningthorpe
Cobbler's Green
Ellingham
Kirby Row
LOWESTOFT MUSEUM
Lowestoft
Topcroft Street
Ditchingham
Broome
Geldeston
Gillingham
Kirkley
Shelton Green
Waveney
Shipmeadow
Beccles
Barnby
Hardwick
Mettingham
Worlingham
Carlton Colville
Pakefield
Great Green
Earsham
Bungay
Barsham
North Cove
Denton
OTTER TRUST
Ringsfield
Mutford
Gisleham
North Green
Ilketshall St. Andrew
Ringsfield Corner
Bush Green
Hulver Street
Rushmere
Alburgh
Flixton
Kessingland
Ilketshall St. Margaret
Ellough
Pulham St. Mary
Homersfield
NORFOLK AND SUFFOLK AVIATION MUSEUM
Henstead
Kessingland Beach
SUFFOLK WILDLIFE PARK
Starston
St. Cross South Elmham
St. Michael South Elmham
Ilketshall St. Lawrence
Redisham
Sotterley
Benacre
Harleston
Redenhall
Wortwell
Mendham
St. Margaret South Elmham
Stone Street
Shadingfield
West End
All Saints South Elmham
Cox Common
Wrentham
Needham
Brampton
Stoven
Clay Common
Frostenden
Covehithe
Withersdale Street
Mill Common
St. James South Elmham
Rumburgh
South Cove
Weybread
Metfield
Spexhall
Uggeshall
Westhall
Cove Bottom
Brockdish
Wissett
Broadway
Wangford
Linstead Parva
Chediston
Reydon Smear
Syleham
Fressingfield
WINGFIELD OLD COLLEGE
Little Whittingham Green
Halesworth
Holton
Blyford
Reydon
Wingfield
SOUTHWOLD MUSEUM
Southwold
Chippenhall Green
Silverley's Green
Battlesea Green
Cratfield
Cookley
Wenhaston
Blyth
Blythburgh
Pixey Green
Swan Green
Linstead
Blackheath
Thorington
Walberswick
Stradbroke
Ashfield Green
Banyard's Green
Walpole
Bramfield
Wootton
35
35

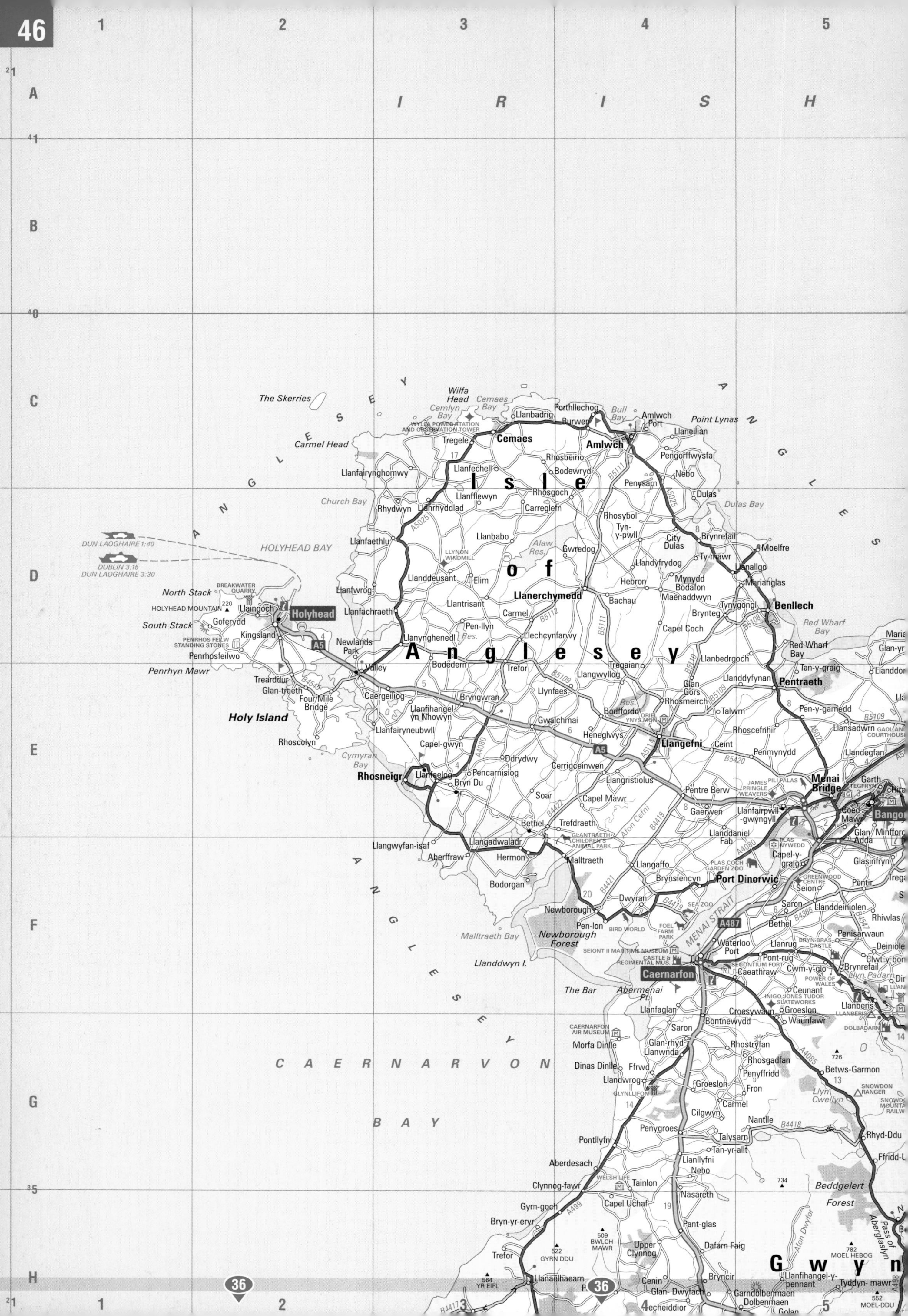
I R I S H
The Skerries
Wilfa Head
Cemaes Bay
Cemlyn Bay
WYLFA POWER STATION AND OBSERVATION TOWER
Llanbadrig
Porthllechog
Bull Bay
Amlwch Port
Point Lynas
Burwen
Cemaes
Amlwch
Llaneilian
Tregele
Carmel Head
Rhosbeirio
Pengorffwysfa
Llanfechell
Bodewryd
Nebo
Llanfairynghornwy
Isle
Penysarn
Rhosgoch
Llanfflewyn
Dulas
Church Bay
Dulas Bay
Rhydwyn
Llanrhyddlad
Carreglefn
Rhosybol
Tyn-y-pwll
City Dulas
Brynrefail
Moelfre
Llanfaethlu
Llanbabo
Alaw Res.
Gwredog
Ty-mawr
HOLYHEAD BAY
DUN LAOGHAIRE 1:40
DUBLIN 3:15
DUN LAOGHAIRE 3:30
LLYNON WINDMILL
of
Llandyfrydog
Lligwy
Llanallgo
Llanddeusant
Elim
Hebron
Mynydd Bodafon
Marianglas
North Stack
BREAKWATER QUARRY
Llanfwrog
Llanerchymedd
Maenaddwyn
Bachau
Tynygongl
Benllech
HOLYHEAD MOUNTAIN
220
Llaingoch
Holyhead
Llanfachraeth
Llantrisant
Carmel
Brynteg
South Stack
Goferydd
Pen-llyn
Res.
Red Wharf Bay
Kingsland
Capel Coch
PENRHOS FELW STANDING STONES
Newlands Park
Llanynghenedl
Llechcynfarwy
Red Wharf Bay
Penrhosfeilwo
A5
Anglesey
Llanbedrgoch
Tan-y-graig
Penrhyn Mawr
Valley
Bodedern
Trefor
Tregaian
Llangwyllog
Llanddyfnan
Pentraeth
Trearddur
Glan-traeth
Four Mile Bridge
Caergeiliog
Llynfaes
Glan Gors
Rhosmeirch
Bryngwran
Llanfihangel yn Nhowyn
Res.
Bodffordd
ORIEL YNYS MON
Talwrn
Pen-y-garnedd
Holy Island
Gwalchmai
Heneglwys
Rhoscefnhir
Llansadwrn
Llanfairyneubwll
Llangefni
Ceint
Rhoscolyn
Capel-gwyn
A5
Penmynydd
Cymyran Bay
Ddrydwy
Cerrigceinwen
Llandegfan
Rhosneigr
Llanfaelog
Pencarnisiog
Llangristiolus
JAMES PRINGLE WEAVERS
PILI PALAS
Menai Bridge
Bryn Du
Pentre Berw
Soar
Capel Mawr
Gaerwen
Llanfairpwll -gwyngyll
Bangor
Bethel
Trefdraeth
GLANTRAETH CHILDREN'S ANIMAL PARK
Afon Cefni
Llanddaniel Fab
PLAS NEWYDD
Glan Adda
Llangwyfan-isaf
Llangadwaladr
Capel-y-graig
Aberffraw
Hermon
Malltraeth
Llangaffo
PLAS COCH GARDEN ZOO
Glasinfryn
Bodorgan
Brynsiencyn
Port Dinorwic
GREENWOOD CENTRE
Seion
Pentir
Dwyran
SEA ZOO
Saron
Llanddeiniolen
Newborough
Rhiwlas
Pen-lon
BIRD WORLD
FOEL FARM PARK
Bethel
MENAI STRAIT
A487
Malltraeth Bay
Newborough Forest
Penisarwaun
SEIONT II MARITIME MUSEUM
Waterloo Port
Llanrug
BRYN-BRAS CASTLE
Deiniolen
Llanddwyn I.
CASTLE & REGIMENTAL MUS.
SEGONTIUM FORT
Pont-rug
Brynrefail
Caernarfon
Caeathraw
Cwm-y-glo
Llyn Padarn
POWER OF WALES
The Bar
Abermenai Pt.
Ceunant
INIGO JONES TUDOR SLATEWORKS
Llanberis
Llanfaglan
Croesywaun
Groeslon
Waunfawr
Bontnewydd
CAERNARFON AIR MUSEUM
Saron
DOLBADARN
Morfa Dinlle
Glan-rhyd
Llanwnda
Rhostryfan
Rhosgadfan
726
CAERNARVON
Dinas Dinlle
Ffrwd
Penyffridd
Betws-Garmon
Llandwrog
Groeslon
Fron
SNOWDON RANGER
GLYNLLIFON
Carmel
Llyn Cwellyn
BAY
Cilgwyn
Nantlle
B4418
Penygroes
Talysarn
Rhyd-Ddu
Pontllyfni
Tan-yr-allt
Llanllyfni
Aberdesach
Nebo
WELSH LIFE
734
Beddgelert Forest
Clynnog-fawr
Tainlon
Nasareth
Gyrn-goch
Capel Uchaf
Pass of Aberglaslyn
Bryn-yr-eryr
Pant-glas
509 BWLCH MAWR
Afon Dwyfor
Upper Clynnog
Dafarn Faig
782 MOEL HEBOG
522 GYRN DDU
Trefor
Gwyn
564 YR EIFL
Llanaelhaearn
Cenin
Bryncir
Llanfihangel-y-pennant
Tyddyn- mawr
Glan- Dwyfach
Garndolbenmaen
552 MOEL-DDU
Dolbenmaen
Golan
36
36

S E A
Great Ormes Head
Puffin Island
CONWY BAY
Llandudno
Penrhynside
Penrhyn Bay
Craig-y-don
Llandrillo-yn-Rhos
Rhos-on-Sea
COLWYN BAY
Llanrhos
Deganwy
Llandudno Junction
Mochdre
Old Colwyn
Llanddulas
Llysfaen
Abergele
Abergele Roads
Pensarn
Towyn
Kinmel Bay
RHYL
Rhuddlan
Y-Ffrith
Gronant
Prestatyn
Meliden
Gwaenysgor
Dyserth
Trelawnyd
St. Asaph
Rhuallt
Bodelwyddan
St. George
Conwy
Gyffin
Dwygyfylchi
Penmaenmawr
Penmaenan
Capelulo
Llanfairfechan
Nant-y-pandy
Beaumaris
Lavan Sands
Penmon
Llangoed
Abergwyngregyn
Aber Falls
Rowen
Ty'n-y-groes
Tal-y-cafn
Bodnant
Graig
Pontwgan
Llanbedr-y-cennin
Tal-y-bont
Eglwysbach
Glan-Conwy
Pentrefelin
Henryd
Bryn-y-maen
Llanelian-yn-Rhos
Rhyd-y-foel
Dolwen
Dawn
Betws-yn-Rhos
Hafod-lom
Llanfair Talhaiarn
Llannefydd
Glascoed
Groesffordd Marli
Plas-yn-Cefn
Trefnant
Bont-newydd
Cefn Berain
Henllan
Denbigh
Bryn Rhyd-yr-Arian
Llansannan
Bryn-nantllech
Pentre-Isaf
Llangernyw
Gell
Cefn-coch
Pentre'r Felin
Hendre-ddu
Bryn-glas
Dolgarrog
Bethesda
Gerlan
Braichmelyn
Rachub
Llanllechid
Ty'n-y-maes
Llyn Eigiau
Llyn Cowlyd
Llyn Crafnant
Trefriw
Tan-lan
Llanddoged
Pandy Tudur
Tŷ'r-felin-isaf
Pentre-tafarn-y-fedw
Llanrwst
Gwydyr Uchaf
Tai
Melin-y-coed
Gwytherin
Tan-y-fron
Clwt-grugoer
Bylchau
Waen
Nantglyn
Groes
Peniel
Llanrhaeadr
Prion
Saron
Meifod
Cyffylliog
Bontuchel
Tai-Ucha
Nant Uchaf
Nilig
Pennant
Clocaenog
Clocaenog Forest
Clawdd-newydd
Efenechtyd
Derwen
Bryn Saith Marchog
Melin-y-wig
Gwyddelwern
Bettws Gwerfil Goch
Corwen
Maerdy
Dinmael
Ty-nant
Llangwm
Pen-y-gop
Cerrigydrudion
Ty Mawr Cwm
Llanfihangel Glyn Myfyr
Pentre-llyn cymmer
Cefn-brith
Glasfryn
Pentrefoelas
Rhydlydan
Hafod-Dinbych
Glan-Conwy
Padog
Ysbyty Ifan
Nebo
Capel Garmon
Fairy Glen
Betws-y-coed
Conwy Falls
Penmachno
Gwydyr Forest
Cwm Penmachno
Carrog
Swallow Falls
Capel Curig
Pont Cyfyng
Pont-y-pant
Dolwyddelan
Pentre-bont
Garnedd
Mynydd Cribau
Blaenau Ffestiniog
Rhiwbryfdir
Tanygrisiau
Bethania
Congl-y-wal
Croesor
Tan-lan
Pen-y-Gwryd Hotel
Nant Peris
Pass of Llanberis
Pont Pen-y-benglog
Pont Rhyd-goch
Cornel
Llyn Ogwen
Marchlyn Mawr Res.
Llyn Llydaw
Llyn Gwynant
Llyn Dinas
Llyn Aled
Llyn Alwen
Alwen Reservoir
Brenig Res.
Mynydd Hiraethog
Mwdwl-eithin
Llyn Conwy
Conwy
VALE OF CONWY
VALE OF CLWYD
SNOWDONIA NATIONAL PARK
Denbighshire
Ty-draw
MOEL SEISIOG
Welsh Channel
A55
A470
A5
A543
A548
A547
A525
A494
A4086
A498
B5106
B5113
B5381
B5382
B5383
B4501
B4407
B5105
B5428
B5429
B5437
48
37
6
7
8
9
10
A
B
C
D
E
F
G
H

Lancashire
Merseyside
Flintshire
Denbighshire
Wrexham
LIVERPOOL BAY
Southport
Ainsdale
Formby
Crosby
LITHERLAND
Bootle
LIVERPOOL
Wallasey
Birkenhead
HOYLAKE
West Kirby
BEBINGTON
Heswall
Neston
Ellesmere Port
Chester
Huyton
Prescot
Garston
Speke
Liverpool Airport
Knowsley
ORMSKIRK
Burscough
Maghull
Kirkby
RHYL
Prestatyn
Rhuddlan
Dyserth
St. Asaph
Denbigh
Holywell
Flint
Connah's Quay
Shotton
Queensferry
Mold
Buckley
Hawarden
Ruthin
Hope
Caergwrle
Llay
Gresford
Wrexham
Rhostyllen
Ruabon
Corwen
Farndon
Holt
Malpas
Clocaenog Forest
Point of Ayr
West Hoyle Bank
Hilbre I.
Dawpool Bank
Welsh Channel
Crosby Channel
Formby Pt.
BELFAST 11:00
DOUGLAS 4:00
DOUGLAS 2:30
DUBLIN 3:30
VALE OF CLWYD
CLWYDIAN RANGE
M53
M57
M58
M56
A55
A41
A59
A565
A5117
A494
A483
55
47
38
39

Greater Manchester
Cheshire
MANCHESTER
SALFORD
Bolton
Bury
Rochdale
Wigan
Oldham
Stockport
Warrington
Widnes
Northwich
Macclesfield
Congleton
Crewe
Nantwich
Leigh
Trafford Park
Manchester Airport
Stoke-on-Trent
Newcastle-under-Lyme
Leek
WILMSLOW
Knutsford
WINSFORD
Sandbach
Middlewich
Alsager
Kidsgrove
Biddulph
Tunstall
Burslem
Hanley
Fenton
Altrincham
SALE
URMSTON
Stretford
Eccles
Cheadle
GATLEY
HAZEL GROVE
Bramhall
Poynton
Bollington
Hyde
Denton
Dukinfield
STALYBRIDGE
Ashton-under-Lyne
Middleton
Chadderton
ROYTON
HEYWOOD
Radcliffe
FARNWORTH
PRESTWICH
Swinton
Worsley
ATHERTON
WESTHOUGHTON
Horwich
Standish
ASHTON-IN-MAKERFIELD
Newton-le-Willows
Golborne
Lymm
Frodsham
Weaverham
Tarporley
Audlem
Madeley
Delamere Forest
M6
M56
M60
M62
M61
M66
M63
M67
M58
M602
M6 M1

Littleborough
Rochdale
Milnrow
Marsden
Meltham
Huddersfield
Slaithwaite
Holmfirth
Skelmanthorpe
Denby Dale
Clayton West
Darton
Royston
Barnsley
Shaw
ROYTON
Oldham
Mossley
Stalybridge
Ashton-under-Lyne
Dukinfield
Hyde
Denton
Glossop
Stockport
Marple
Romiley
HAZEL GROVE
New Mills
Low Leighton
Whaley Bridge
Chapel-en-le-Frith
Buxton
Bollington
Macclesfield
Penistone
Stocksbridge
Chapeltown
Sheffield
Hathersage
Tideswell
Bakewell
Baslow
Ashford in the Water
Dronfield
Chesterfield
Matlock
Cromford
Wirksworth
Youlgreave
Leek
Cheddleton
Ashbourne
Belper
Stoke-on-Trent
Cheadle
Longton
Biddulph
PEAK DISTRICT NATIONAL PARK
HIGH PEAK
HOPE FOREST
Y o r k
D e r b
S t a f f o r d
Saddleworth Moor
Wessenden Moor
Howden Moors
Midhope Moors
Broomhead Moor
Bradfield Moors
Shelf Moor
Kinder Scout
Edale
Castleton
Hope
Ladybower Res.
Derwent Res.
Howden Res.
Dove Dale
Axe Edge
Weaver Hills
East Moor
A6
A57
A623
A515
A628
A616
A61
A619
A635
A523
A53
A54
A537
A52
A50
M1
M60
M62
M67
49
56
57
40

Hemsworth
South Elmsall
South Kirkby
Adwick le Street
Carcroft
Skellow
Askern
Campsall
Norton
Smeaton
Stubbs
Sykehouse
Fenwick
Moss
Fosterhouses
Fishlake
Thorne
Moorends
Thorne Waste or Moors
Crowle
Eastoft
Luddington
Amcotts
Flixborough
Scunthorpe
Gunness
Keadby
Stainforth
Hatfield
Hatfield Chase
Hatfield Moors
Hatfield Woodhouse
Dunscroft
Sandtoft
Woodhouse
Westgate
Belton
Epworth
ISLE OF AXHOLME
Epworth Turbary
Haxey
Owston Ferry
East Ferry
Wildsworth
Laughton
Laughton Forest
Scotter
Yaddlethorpe
Bottesford
Messingham
Bentley
Doncaster
Armthorpe
Cantley
Bessacarr
Balby
Warmsworth
Mexborough
Conisbrough
Denaby Main
Old Denaby
Swinton
Wath upon Dearne
Bolton upon Dearne
Goldthorpe
Wombwell
Rawmarsh
Thrybergh
Rotherham
Dalton
Bramley
Wickersley
Maltby
Tickhill
Harworth
Bircotes
Bawtry
Austerfield
Misson
Finningley
Rossington
New Rossington
Loversall
New Edlington
Edlington
Sprotbrough
Cusworth
Wadworth
Stainton
Hellaby
Misterton
West Stockwith
East Stockwith
Walkeringham
Gringley on the Hill
Beckingham
Gainsborough
Morton
Everton
Scaftworth
Scrooby
Mattersey
Mattersey Thorpe
Wiseton
Clayworth
Saundby
Serlby
Styrrup
Oldcotes
Langold
Blyth
Carlton in Lindrick
Dinnington
North Anston
South Anston
Kiveton Park
Todwick
Whiston
Thurcroft
Brampton en le Morthen
Laughton en le Morthen
Aston
Aughton
Handsworth
Woodhouse
Beighton
Swallownest
Torworth
Ranskill
Lound
Barnby Moor
Sutton
North Wheatley
South Wheatley
Hayton
Clarborough
North Leverton with Habblesthorpe
Sturton le Steeple
Bole
Knaith Park
Knaith
Upton
Lea
Gate Burton
Marton
Stow
Sturton by Stow
Brampton
Torksey
Retford
West Retford
Babworth
Ordsall
Grove
Eaton
Ranby
Scofton
Gateford
Wigthorpe
Shireoaks
Rhodesia
Worksop
Kilton
Manton
Darfoulds
Netherthorpe
Thorpe Salvin
Harthill
Wales
Norwood
Killamarsh
Renishaw
Spinkhill
Eckington
Mastin Moor
Staveley
Barlborough
Clowne
Whitwell
Hodthorpe
Creswell
Elmton
Holbeck
Holbeck Woodhouse
Stanfree
Shuttlewood
Bolsover
Whaley
Whaley Thorns
Nether Langwith
Langwith
Langwith Junction
Cuckney
Norton
Carburton
Budby
Meden Vale
Warsop
Church Warsop
Shirebrook
Palterton
Scarcliffe
Glapwell
New Houghton
Pleasley
Mansfield Woodhouse
Mansfield
Clipstone
Old Clipstone
Edwinstowe
Ollerton
New Ollerton
Boughton
Wellow
Ompton
Kneesall
Walesby
Bevercotes
West Markham
Tuxford
East Markham
Markham Moor
Gamston
Headon
Upton
Askham
Elkesley
West Drayton
Milton
Haughton
Bothamsall
Hardwick
Perlethorpe
Kirton
Egmanton
Laxton
Moorhouse
Ossington
Norwell
Norwell Woodhouse
Cromwell
Carlton on Trent
Sutton on Trent
Grassthorpe
Weston
Normanton on Trent
Low Marnham
High Marnham
Fledborough
Ragnall
Darlton
Dunham
East Drayton
Laneham
Church Laneham
Rampton
Treswell
Woodbeck
Stokeham
Cottam
South Leverton
Littleborough
Coates
Fenton
Kettlethorpe
Newton on Trent
Laughterton
Saxilby
Thorney
North Clifton
South Clifton
Spalford
Wigsley
Harby
Doddington
Eagle
Eagle Moor
North Scarle
South Scarle
Girton
Besthorpe
Collingham
Swinderby
Thurlby
Norton Disney
Brough
Stapleford
Langford
Holme
North Muskham
South Muskham
Little Carlton
Bathley
Caunton
Maplebeck
Eakring
Bilsthorpe
Bilsthorpe Moor
Kersall
Knapthorpe
Winkburn
Kirklington
Hockerton
Farnsfield
Edingley
Halam
Southwell
Normanton
Upton
Kelham
Averham
Staythorpe
Rolleston
Farndon
Newark-on-Trent
Balderton
Hawton
Coddington
Beckingham
Barnby in the Willows
Claypole
Stubton
Dry Doddington
Long Bennington
Staunton in the Vale
Westborough
Marston
Fiskerton
Morton
Thorpe
East Stoke
Elston
Syerston
Flintham
Sibthorpe
Shelton
Hawksworth
Flawborough
Kneeton
Hoveringham
Gonalston
Thurgarton
Bleasby
Caythorpe
Gunthorpe
East Bridgford
Halloughton
Easthorpe
Park Hill
Oxton
Epperstone
Lowdham
Lambley
Burton Joyce
Woodborough
Calverton
Arnold
Bestwood
Bestwood Village
Hucknall
Papplewick
Linby
Newstead
Annesley
Annesley Woodhouse
Ravenshead
Blidworth
Haywood Oaks
White Post
Rainworth
Forest Town
Sutton in Ashfield
Kirkby in Ashfield
Huthwaite
Skegby
Stanton Hill
Teversal
Tibshelf
Pilsley
Stainsby
North Wingfield
Holmewood
Heath
Doe Lea
Sutton Scarsdale
Arkwright Town
Duckmanton
Poolsbrook
Brimington
Woodthorpe
Alfreton
South Normanton
Pinxton
Somercotes
Selston
Jacksdale
Underwood
Brinsley
New Brinsley
Codnor
Heanor
Eastwood
Moorgreen
Westville
Watnall
Kimberley
Nuthall
Bulwell
Awsworth
Cotgrave
Swingate
Selston
Ironville
Mapperley
Shipley
Smalley
Langley Mill
Aldercar
Ilkeston
Sherwood Forest
Cresswell Crags Visitor Centre
Rufford
Clumber Park
Nottingham
South Yorkshire Aircraft Mus
Doncaster
Worksop
Retford
Gainsborough
Scunthorpe
Mansfield
Newark-on-Trent
Rotherham

North Lincolnshire
North East Lincolnshire
Lincolnshire
Lincoln
Scunthorpe
Immingham
Gainsborough
Newark-on-Trent
Sleaford
Market Rasen
Horncastle
Brigg
Caistor
Grimsby
Healing
Keelby
Laceby
Waltham
Binbrook
Wragby
Woodhall Spa
Coningsby
Billinghay
Metheringham
Navenby
Leadenham
Ruskington
Leasingham
Heckington
Caythorpe
Claypole
Balderton
Collingham
Saxilby
Nettleham
Washingborough
Bardney
Boultham
North Hykeham
Waddington
Bassingham
Faldingworth
Kirton in Lindsey
Hibaldstow
Broughton
Messingham
Scotter
Sutton on Trent
Humberside
Laughton Forest
Wildmore Fen
South Kyme Fen
Holland Fen
A15
A18
A46
A57
A158
A631
M180
M181
51
58
59
42

Kilnsea
SPURN HEAD
59
CLEETHORPES
MOUTH OF THE HUMBER
CLEETHORPES COAST LIGHT RAILWAY
PLEASURE ISLAND THEME PARK
Humberston
Tetney Lock
North Coates
Tetney
Marshchapel
Donna Nook
Eskham
Wragholme
Grainthorpe
Fulstow
North Somercotes
Skidbrooke North End
Covenham St. Bartholomew
Conisholme
South Somercotes
Saltfleet
Covenham St. Mary
Utterby
Yarburgh
Skidbrooke
Fotherby
Little Grimsby
ALVINGHAM POTTERY AND CRAFTS
Alvingham
North Cockerington
Saltfleetby St. Clements
Great Eau
Saltfleetby All Saints
Theddlethorpe St. Helen
South Cockerington
Saltfleetby St. Peter
Keddington
Louth
Grimoldby
B1200
Theddlethorpe All Saints
Stewton
Manby
KIDS KINGDOM
ANIMAL GARDENS
Little Carlton
Great Carlton
Meers Bridge
Mablethorpe
Legbourne
RAILWAY MUS.
Little Cawthorpe
South Reston
Gayton le Marsh
Trusthorpe
North Reston
Tathwell
Strubby
Sutton on Sea
Haugham
Muckton
Tothill
Withern
Thorpe
Maltby le Marsh
Sandilands
Authorpe
Beesby
Maidenwell
Burwell
Woodthorpe
Hannah
WOODY'S TOP
Belleau
CLAYTHORPE WATER MILL AND WILDFOWL GARDENS
Saleby
Markby
Farforth
Ruckland
White Pit
Aby
Asserby
Swaby
ALFORD WINDMILL
Ketsby
South Thoresby
ALFORD MANOR HOUSE
Bilsby
Huttoft
Anderby
South Ormsby
Haugh
Rigsby
Alford
WOLDS
Calceby
Tetford
Farlesthorpe
Mumby
Authorpe Row
Brinkhill
Driby
Well
Cumberworth
Salmonby
Somersby
Helsey
Chapel St. Leonards
Sutterby
Ulceby
Bonthorpe
Hogsthorpe
Ashby Puerorum
Bag Enderby
Harrington
Claxby
Willoughby
LAKESIDE LEISURE
Greetham
Langton
Aswardby
Skendleby
Sloothby
HARDY'S ANIMAL FARM
Hagworthingham
Sausthorpe
Partney
Addlethorpe
Ingoldmells
SNIPE DALES
Lusby
FANTASY ISLAND CHILDREN'S PLAYDROME
Hameringham
Mavis Enderby
Raithby
Scremby
Welton le Marsh
FUNCOAST WORLD
Asgarby
Candlesby
Orby
Orby Marsh
Old Bolingbroke
Hundleby
Spilsby
Ashby by Partney
Burgh le Marsh
Winthorpe
Seathorne
Hareby
NORTHCOTE HEAVY HORSE CENTRE
Great Steeping
Bratoft
BOLINGBROKE
Halton Holegate
BURGH LE MARSH WINDMILL
NATURELAND SEAL SANCTUARY
West Keal
Toynton All Saints
Irby in the Marsh
CHURCH FARM MUS.
Skegness
East Keal
Toynton St. Peter
THE LIFEBOAT STATION
East Kirkby
Toynton Fen Side
Little Steeping
Firsby
LINCOLNSHIRE AVIATION HERITAGE CENTRE
Keal Cotes
Thorpe Culvert
Thorpe St. Peter
Croft
Seacroft
Revesby Bridge
Thorpe Fendykes
Wainfleet All Saints
Croft Marsh
Stickford
New Bolingbroke
Wainfleet Bank
Steeping
Fen Side
New Leake
Wainfleet Tofts
Wainfleet St. Mary
Midville
Stickney
Eastville
Friskney Eaudike
Wainfleet Sand
East Fen
Carrington
Friskney
Lade Bank
Wrangle Bank
Northlands
Friskney Tofts
SIBSEY TRADER MILL
Leake Commonside
Friskney Flats
Sibsey
Frithville
Old Leake
Wrangle Lowgate
Wrangle
Hurn's End
Hill Dyke
Boston Long Hedges
Leverton Outgate
Frith Bank
Leverton
Leverton Highgate
Cowbridge
Leverton Lucasgate
Benington
THE WASH
BOSTON DEEPS
LYNN DEEPS
Boston
Halltoft End
Butterwick
Freiston
Skirbeck
43
44
BRANCASTER
Brancaster Bay
Holme next the Sea
Titchwell
Brancaster Staithe
Brancaster
Thornham
Old
A16
A158
A1028
A52
A1031
A1104
A111
A157
B1449
B1196
B1195
B1184
B1183
A155
A149

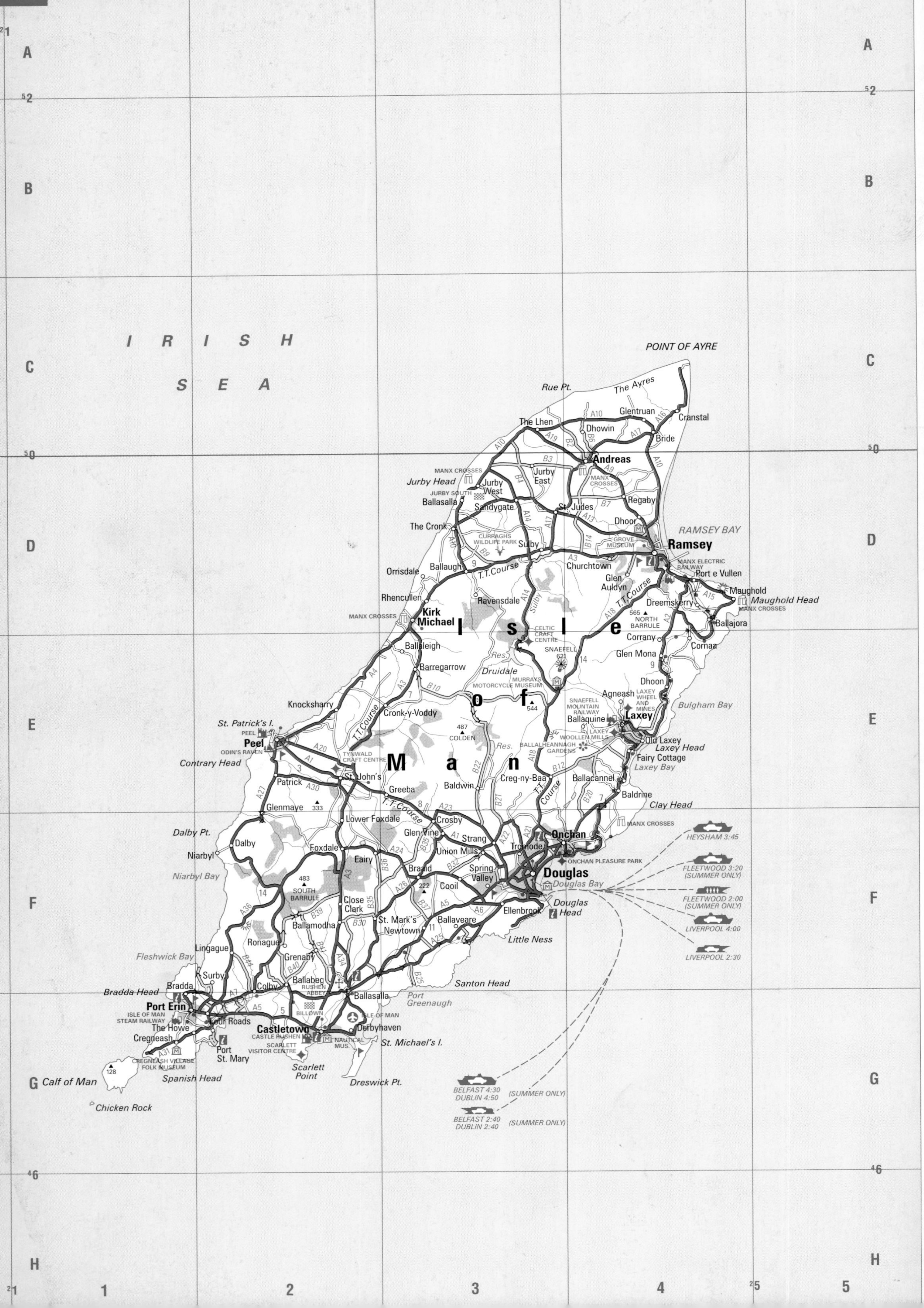
IRISH SEA
POINT OF AYRE
Rue Pt.
The Ayres
Glentruan
Cranstal
The Lhen
Dhowin
Bride
Andreas
MANX CROSSES
Jurby Head
Jurby West
Jurby East
JURBY SOUTH
Ballasalla
Sandygate
St. Judes
Regaby
Dhoor
The Cronk
CURRAGHS WILDLIFE PARK
Sulby
GROVE MUSEUM
RAMSEY BAY
Ramsey
MANX ELECTRIC RAILWAY
Port e Vullen
Orrisdale
Ballaugh
T.T. Course
Churchtown
Glen Auldyn
Maughold
Maughold Head
Rhencullen
Ravensdale
Dreemskerry
Kirk Michael
565 NORTH BARRULE
Ballajora
Isle of Man
CELTIC CRAFT CENTRE
Corrany
Cornaa
Ballaleigh
SNAEFELL 621
Glen Mona
Barregarrow
Res.
Druidale
MURRAYS MOTORCYCLE MUSEUM
Dhoon
Agneash
LAXEY WHEEL AND MINES
Knocksharry
544
SNAEFELL MOUNTAIN RAILWAY
Bulgham Bay
Cronk-y-Voddy
Laxey
St. Patrick's I.
PEEL
487 COLDEN
Ballaquine
Peel
ODIN'S RAVEN
LAXEY WOOLLEN MILLS
Old Laxey
Laxey Head
Contrary Head
TYNWALD CRAFT CENTRE
BALLALHEANNAGH GARDENS
Fairy Cottage
Laxey Bay
St. John's
Creg-ny-Baa
Ballacannel
Patrick
Greeba
Baldwin
Baldrine
Clay Head
Glenmaye
333
Lower Foxdale
Crosby
MANX CROSSES
Dalby Pt.
Glen Vine
Strang
Onchan
HEYSHAM 3:45
Dalby
Foxdale
Union Mills
Tromode
Niarbyl
Eairy
ONCHAN PLEASURE PARK
Braaid
Spring Valley
Douglas
FLEETWOOD 3:20 (SUMMER ONLY)
Niarbyl Bay
483 SOUTH BARRULE
222
Cooil
Douglas Bay
FLEETWOOD 2:00 (SUMMER ONLY)
Close Clark
Ellenbrook
Douglas Head
St. Mark's
Ballaveare
LIVERPOOL 4:00
Ballamodha
Newtown
Little Ness
Ronague
LIVERPOOL 2:30
Fleshwick Bay
Lingague
Grenaby
Surby
Ballabeg
RUSHEN ABBEY
Santon Head
Bradda Head
Bradda
Colby
Ballasalla
Port Greenaugh
Port Erin
BILLOWN
ISLE OF MAN
ISLE OF MAN STEAM RAILWAY
Four Roads
Castletown
Derbyhaven
The Howe
CASTLE RUSHEN
NAUTICAL MUS.
St. Michael's I.
Cregneash
Port St. Mary
SCARLETT VISITOR CENTRE
CREGNEASH VILLAGE FOLK MUSEUM
Scarlett Point
128
Calf of Man
Spanish Head
Dreswick Pt.
BELFAST 4:30
DUBLIN 4:50
(SUMMER ONLY)
Chicken Rock
BELFAST 2:40
DUBLIN 2:40
(SUMMER ONLY)

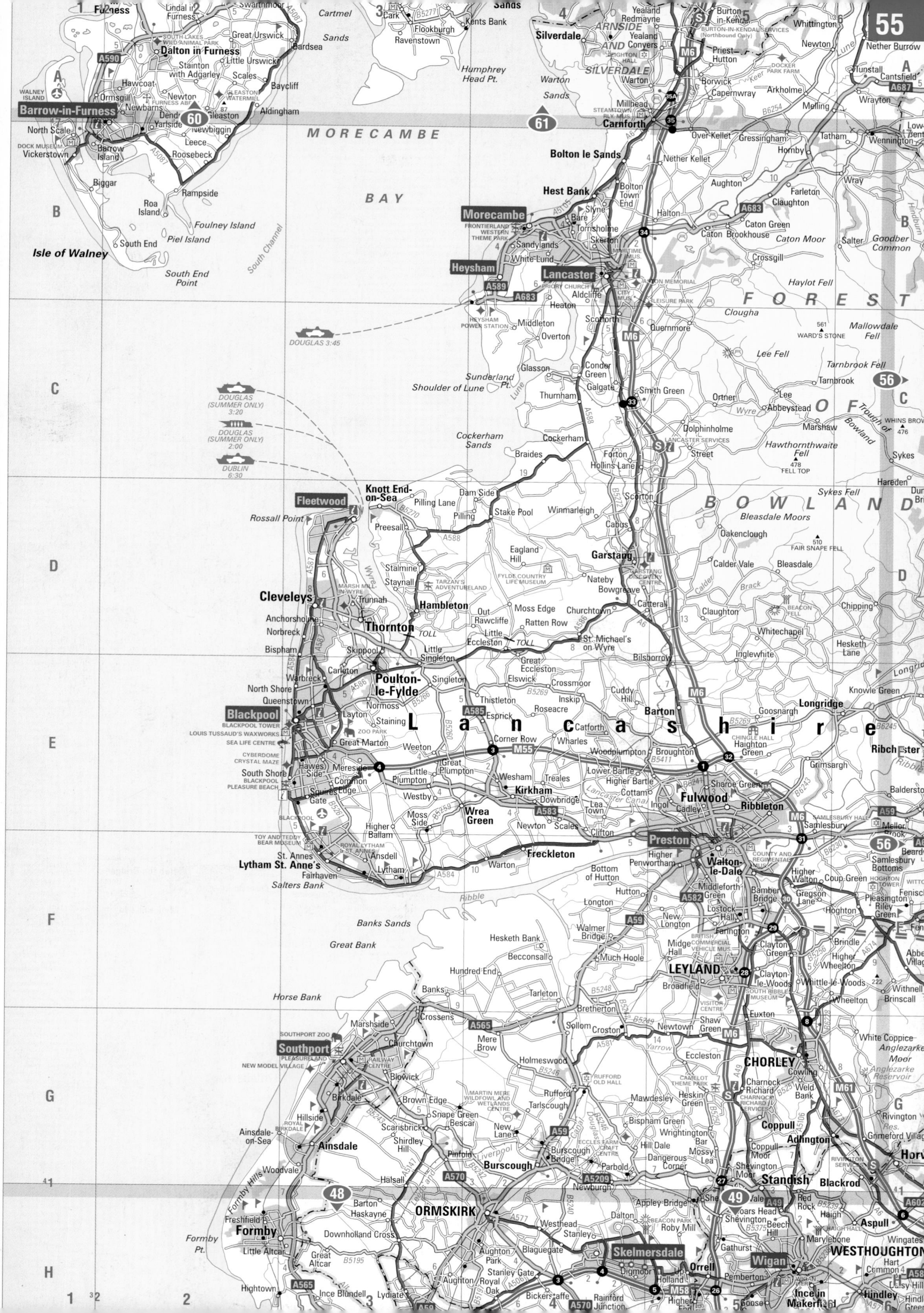

Barrow-in-Furness
Dalton in Furness
Lindal in Furness
Great Urswick
Little Urswick
Bardsea
Stainton with Adgarley
Scales
Baycliff
Hawcoat
Ormsgill
Newbarns
Newton
Gleaston
Aldingham
Dendron
Yarlside
Newbiggin
Leece
Roosebeck
Rampside
North Scale
Vickerstown
Barrow Island
Biggar
Roa Island
Foulney Island
Piel Island
South End
Isle of Walney
South End Point
South Channel
Cartmel
Sands
Cark
Flookburgh
Ravenstown
Kents Bank
Humphrey Head Pt.
Silverdale
Arnside and Silverdale
Yealand Redmayne
Yealand Conyers
Warton Sands
Warton
Burton-in-Kendal
Whittington
Newton
Nether Burrow
Priest Hutton
Borwick
Capernwray
Arkholme
Tunstall
Cantsfield
Melling
Wrayton
Millhead
Carnforth
Over Kellet
Gressingham
Tatham
Wennington
Hornby
Nether Kellet
Bolton le Sands
MORECAMBE BAY
Hest Bank
Bolton Town End
Aughton
Wray
Farleton
Claughton
Halton
Caton Green
Caton
Brookhouse
Caton Moor
Salter
Goodber Common
Morecambe
Slyne
Bare
Torrisholme
Skerton
Heysham
Sandylands
White Lund
Lancaster
Aldcliffe
Heaton
Middleton
Overton
Scotforth
Quernmore
Crossgill
Haylot Fell
FOREST OF BOWLAND
Clougha
Mallowdale Fell
Ward's Stone
Lee Fell
Tarnbrook Fell
Tarnbrook
DOUGLAS 3:45
DOUGLAS (SUMMER ONLY) 3:20
DOUGLAS (SUMMER ONLY) 2:00
DUBLIN 6:30
Glasson
Conder Green
Galgate
Sunderland Pt.
Shoulder of Lune
Thurnham
Smith Green
Ortner
Lee
Abbeystead
Trough of Bowland
Marshaw
Dolphinholme
Hawthornthwaite Fell
Cockerham Sands
Cockerham
Braides
Forton
Hollins Lane
Street
Sykes
Hareden
Knott End-on-Sea
Fleetwood
Rossall Point
Pilling Lane
Pilling
Dam Side
Stake Pool
Winmarleigh
Scorton
Sykes Fell
Preesall
Cabus
Bleasdale Moors
Oakenclough
Eagland Hill
Garstang
Fair Snape Fell
Stalmine
Staynall
Calder Vale
Bleasdale
Nateby
Bowgreave
Cleveleys
Trunnah
Hambleton
Out Rawcliffe
Moss Edge
Ratten Row
Churchtown
Catterall
Claughton
Chipping
Anchorsholme
Norbreck
Thornton
Little Eccleston
St. Michael's on Wyre
Whitechapel
Bispham
Skippool
Little Singleton
Great Eccleston
Bilsborrow
Inglewhite
Hesketh Lane
Carleton
Poulton-le-Fylde
Singleton
Elswick
Crossmoor
Cuddy Hill
Knowle Green
North Shore
Queenstown
Thistleton
Inskip
Blackpool
Normoss
Layton
Staining
Esprick
Roseacre
Barton
Goosnargh
Longridge
Lancashire
Catforth
Great Marton
Corner Row
Wharles
Haighton Green
Ribchester
Weeton
Woodplumpton
Broughton
Grimsargh
Hawes Side
Mereside
Great Plumpton
South Shore
Little Plumpton
Wesham
Treales
Lower Bartle
Higher Bartle
Sharoe Green
Balderstone
Squires Gate
Kirkham
Cottam
Westby
Dowbridge
Ingol
Fulwood
Ribbleton
Moss Side
Wrea Green
Lea Town
Cadley
Samlesbury
Mellor Brook
Higher Ballam
Newton
Scales
Clifton
Preston
St. Annes
Ansdell
Freckleton
Higher Penwortham
Walton-le-Dale
Samlesbury Bottoms
Lytham St. Anne's
Fairhaven
Lytham
Warton
Bottom of Hutton
Higher Walton
Coup Green
Salters Bank
Hutton
Middleforth Green
Bamber Bridge
Gregson Lane
Ribble
Longton
Lostock Hall
Pleasington
Riley Green
Banks Sands
New Longton
Hoghton
Walmer Bridge
Farington
Great Bank
Hesketh Bank
Midge Hall
Clayton Green
Brindle
Becconsall
Much Hoole
Higher Wheelton
Hundred End
LEYLAND
Clayton-le-Woods
Whittle-le-Woods
Withnell
Broadfield
Brinscall
Horse Bank
Banks
Tarleton
Wheelton
Bretherton
Euxton
Crossens
Marshside
Sollom
Croston
Newtown
Shaw Green
White Coppice
Anglezarke Moor
Southport
Churchtown
Mere Brow
Eccleston
CHORLEY
Anglezarke Reservoir
Holmeswood
Blowick
Rufford
Mawdesley
Charnock Richard
Cowling
Heskin Green
Weld Bank
Birkdale
Brown Edge
Tarlscough
Bispham Green
Coppull
Hillside
Snape Green
Bescar
New Lane
Rivington
Scarisbrick
Wrightington Bar
Adlington
Grimeford Village
Ainsdale-on-Sea
Ainsdale
Shirdley Hill
Burscough Bridge
Hill Dale
Mossy Lea
Coppull Moor
Pinfold
Burscough
Parbold
Dangerous Corner
Shevington Moor
Standish
Blackrod
Horwich
Woodvale
Formby Hills
Halsall
Newburgh
Barton
Haskayne
ORMSKIRK
Appley Bridge
Shevington Vale
Red Rock
Haigh
Aspull
Freshfield
Formby
Downholland Cross
Westhead
Dalton
Roby Mill
Shevington
Beech Hill
Formby Pt.
Little Altcar
Great Altcar
Aughton Park
Stanley
Blaguegate
Skelmersdale
Gathurst
Marylebone
Wigan
Westhoughton
Hart Common
Hightown
Ince Blundell
Lydiate
Stanley Gate
Aughton
Royal Oak
Digmoor
Orrell
Pemberton
Bickerstaffe
Holland
Rainford Junction
Ince in Makerfield
Hindley

YORKSHIRE DALES NATIONAL PARK
North Yorkshire
FOREST OF BOWLAND
Lancashire
Greater Manchester
Ingleton
High Bentham
Settle
Giggleswick
Grassington
Skipton
Gargrave
Hellifield
Long Preston
Gisburn
Barnoldswick
Earby
Colne
Nelson
Trawden
Foulridge
Clitheroe
Chatburn
Whalley
Great Harwood
Clayton-le-Moors
Padiham
Burnley
Brierfield
Accrington
Oswaldtwistle
Blackburn
Darwen
Haslingden
Rawtenstall
Bacup
Todmorden
Hebden Bridge
Mytholmroyd
Sowerby Bridge
Keighley
Haworth
Silsden
Glusburn
Ramsbottom
Edgworth
Horwich
Bolton
Bury
Heywood
Rochdale
Littleborough
Milnrow
Royton
Oldham
Middleton
Radcliffe
Farnworth
Westhoughton
Whitworth
Wardle
Slaithwaite
Marsden
Queensbury
Illingworth
THE FOREST OF PENDLE
THE FOREST OF TRAWDEN
Forest of Rossendale
Gisburn Forest
Ribblesdale

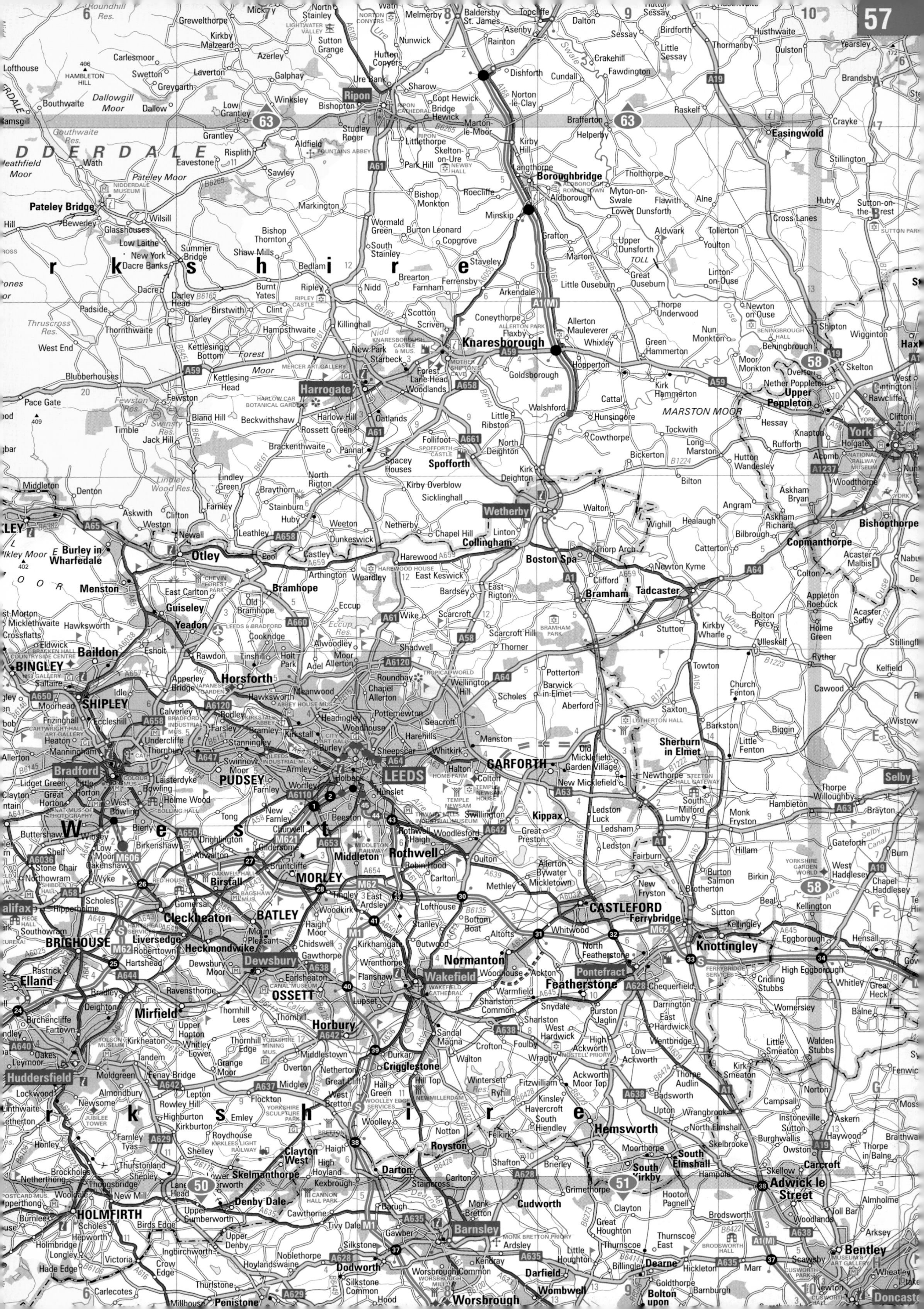

Ripon
Harrogate
Knaresborough
Boroughbridge
Wetherby
Otley
Tadcaster
Selby
York
Easingwold
Pateley Bridge
Ilkley
Burley in Wharfedale
Menston
Guiseley
Yeadon
Baildon
BINGLEY
SHIPLEY
Bradford
Horsforth
PUDSEY
LEEDS
GARFORTH
Sherburn in Elmet
MORLEY
BATLEY
Cleckheaton
BRIGHOUSE
Elland
Halifax
Heckmondwike
Dewsbury
Mirfield
OSSETT
Wakefield
Normanton
Rothwell
Middleton
CASTLEFORD
Ferrybridge
Knottingley
Pontefract
Featherstone
Huddersfield
HOLMFIRTH
Skelmanthorpe
Denby Dale
Penistone
Darton
Royston
Barnsley
Cudworth
Hemsworth
South Elmsall
South Kirkby
Adwick le Street
Bentley
Doncaster
Worsbrough
Wombwell
Darfield
Dodworth
Bolton upon Dearne
Crigglestone
Horbury
Kippax
Spofforth
Collingham
Boston Spa
Bramham
Bramhope
Copmanthorpe
Bishopthorpe
Upper Poppleton
Pannal
Rawdon
Birstall
Liversedge
Tingley
Ardsley
Stanley
Sandal Magna
Great Preston
Allerton Bywater
Upton
Carcroft
Askern
Marston Moor
Nidderdale
West Yorkshire
North Yorkshire
A1(M)
A1
M1
M62
M621
M606
A59
A61
A64
A65
A658
A660
A63
A19
A168
A639
A628
A635
A629
A642
A638
63
58
51
50

HOWARDIAN HILLS
North Yorkshire
City of York
The East Riding of Yorkshire
North Lincolnshire
Gilling East
Cawton
Hovingham
Little Habton
Great Habton
Ryton
Scampston
West Knapton
East Knapton
Potter Brompton
Thormanby
Husthwaite
Oulston
Yearsley
Coulton
Wath
Fryton
Slingsby
Barton-le-Street
Eden Farm Insight
Eden Camp Museum
Wykeham
Rillington
West Heslerton
Brandsby
Scackleton
Appleton-le-Street
Amotherby
Swinton
Broughton
Thorpe Bassett
Wintringham
Malton
Old Malton
Norton
Scagglethorpe
Place Newton
Butterwick
Stearsby
Dalby
Terrington
Skewsby
Conneysthorpe
Ganthorpe
Castle Howard
Crayke
Easingwold
Whenby
Whitewall Corner
Helperthorpe
Weaverthorpe
East Lutton
West Lutton
Stillington
Farlington
Bulmer
Welburn
High Hutton
Low Hutton
North Grimston
Duggleby
Kirby Grindalythe
Sheriff Hutton
Sheriff Hutton Park
Whitwell-on-the-Hill
Firby
Langton
Huby
Sutton-on-the-Forest
West Lilling
Thornton-le-Clay
Kirkham
Kirkham Priory
Kennythorpe
Birdsall
Wharram-le-Street
Sledmere
Cottam
Cross Lanes
Foston
Crambe
Westow
Burythorpe
Wharram Percy Medieval Village
Tollerton
Sutton Park
Barton-le-Willows
Howsham
Leavening
Youlton
Harton
Acklam
Linton-on-Ouse
Flaxton
Strensall
Bossall
Leppington
Thixendale
Fimber
Oak Rabbit Crafts
Garton-on-the-Wolds
Newton on Ouse
Claxton
Scrayingham
Towthorpe
Sand Hutton
Kirby Underdale
Fridaythorpe
Wetwang
Beningbrough Hall
Shipton
Nun Monkton
Wigginton
Painsthorpe
Elmswell
Beningbrough
Haxby
Earswick
Upper Helmsley
Buttercrambe
Skirpenbeck
Bugthorpe
Moor Monkton
Overton
Skelton
Moor End
Stockton on the Forest
Gate Helmsley
Wolds Way
Kelleythorpe
Nether Poppleton
Huntington
New Earswick
Stamford Bridge
Youlthorpe
Tibthorpe
Upper Poppleton
Rawcliffe
Warthill
Full Sutton
Bishop Wilton
Huggate
Kirkburn
Holtby
Low Catton
Gowthorpe
Great Givendale
Clifton
York Minster
Jorvik Centre
High Catton
Fangfoss
Hessay
Heworth
Murton
Dunnington
Yorkshire Museum of Farming
Knapton
York
Holgate
Osbaldwick
Bolton
Meltonby
Millington
North Dalton
Bainton
Rufforth
National Railway Museum
Castle Museum
Grimston
Wilberfoss
Yapham
Kilnwick Percy
Warter
Acomb
Nunthorpe
Heslington
Kexby
Middleton-on-the-Wolds
Hutton Wandesley
Woodthorpe
Fulford
Barmby Moor
Kilnwick
Askham Bryan
Newton upon Derwent
Pocklington
Lund
Angram
Askham Richard
Bishopthorpe
Crockey Hill
Yorkshire Air Museum
Elvington
Allerthorpe
Burnby Hall Gardens
Nunburnholme
Burnby
Holme on the Wolds
Lockington
Bilbrough
Copmanthorpe
Sutton upon Derwent
Acaster Malbis
Naburn
Wheldrake
Thornton
Hayton
Londesborough
South Dalton
Scorborough
Colton
Deighton
Storwood
Melbourne
Bielby
Thorpe le Street
Market Weighton
Goodmanham
Etton
Shiptonthorpe
Everingham
Gardham
Cherry Burton
Appleton Roebuck
Escrick
Thorganby
East Cottingwith
Seaton Ross
Acaster Selby
Bolton Percy
Kirkby Wharfe
Holme Green
Harswell
Ulleskelf
Stillingfleet
Laytham
Sancton
Bishop Burton
Ryther
Ellerton
Water End
Holme-on-Spalding-Moor
Northern Shire Horse Centre
Church Fenton
Kelfield
Aughton
Moor End
Skipwith
North Duffield
Harlthorpe
Foggathorpe
Sand Hole
North Cliffe
North Newbald
Walkington
Cawood
Riccall
Bubwith
Highfield
Rascal Moor
South Newbald
Barkston
Wistow
Gunby
The Real Aeroplane Museum
Willitoft
Gribthorpe
South Cliffe
Biggin
Barlby
Osgodby
Menthorpe
Spaldington
Hotham
High Hunsley
Little Fenton
Selby Abbey
Breighton
Bursea
Little Weighton
Selby
Lund
Cliffe
South Duffield
Foulness
North Cave
Rowley
Thorpe Willoughby
Wressle
North Howden
Everthorpe
Hambleton
East Common
Brind
Portington
Hive
South Cave
Riplingham
Monk Fryston
Brayton
Hemingbrough
Cavil
Sandholme
West End
Newsholme
Eastrington
Scalby
Newport
Howden Minster
Brantingham
Gateforth
Barlow
Barmby on the Marsh
Gilberdyke
Staddlethorpe
Ellerker
Hillam
Long Drax
Howden
Balkholme
Market Weighton Canal
Elloughton
Swanland
Burton Salmon
West Haddlesey
Burn
Asselby
Knedlington
Kilpin Pike
Kilpin
Broomfleet
Welton
Birkin
Chapel Haddlesey
Drax
Boothferry
South Farm Craft Gallery
Brough
Temple Hirst
Camblesforth
Newland
Laxton
North Ferriby
Beal
Kellington
Hirst Courtney
Hook
Skelton
Blacktoft
Faxfleet
Whitton
Sutton
Kellingley
Eggborough
Hensall
Carlton
Airmyn
Saltmarshe
Yokefleet
Redcliff Channel
Knottingley
Sobriety Waterways Adventure Centre
Goole
Reedness
Ousefleet
Read's Island
Snaith
East Cowick
Rawcliffe
Whitgift
Winteringham
Ferrybridge Services
High Eggborough
Gowdall
West Cowick
Rawcliffe Bridge
Swinefleet
Little Reedness
Julian's Bower
Alkborough
Cridling Stubbs
Whitley
Great Heck
Old Goole
Dutch River
Adlingfleet
West Halton
Walcot
Southfield Reservoir
Pollington
Womersley
Balne
Aire and Calder Navigation
Goole Fields
Fockerby
Garthorpe
Coleby
Winterton
Burton Stather
Burton upon Stather
Thealby
Little Smeaton
Walden Stubbs
Goole Moors
Luddington
Normanby
Normanby Hall
Roxby
Sykehouse
Picheon Green
Normanby Park Farming Museum
Kirk Smeaton
Fenwick
Eastoft
Moorends
Thorne Waste or Moors
Flixborough
Norton
Appleby
Campsall
Fosterhouses
Amcotts
Flixborough Stather
Dragonby
Askern
Moss
Far Bank
Fishlake
Thorne
Crowle
Instoneville
Sutton
Haywood
Braithwaite
Canal Side
Wike Well End
Stainforth & Keadby Canal
Windsor
Crosby
Santon
Burghwallis
Owston
Thorpe in Balne
Kirk Bramwith
Stainforth
Ealand
Keadby
Gunness
Frodingham
Carcroft
Skellow
Hatfield
Hatfield Chase
Scunthorpe
Wressle
Hampole
Adwick le Street
Barnby Dun
Dunscroft
Burringham
Althorpe
Brumby
Broughton
Almholme
Kirk Sandall
Hatfield Woodhouse
Sandtoft
Woodhouse
Sandtoft Transport Centre
Westgate
Derrythorpe
Ashby
Brodsworth
Toll Bar
Dunsville
West End
Grey Green
Yaddlethorpe
Woodlands
Arksey
Edenthorpe
Belton
Beltoft
East Butterwick
West Butterwick
Bottesford
Brodsworth Hall
Bentley
Armthorpe
Hatfield Moors
Church Town
Mill Place
Scawby
Scawsby
Museum & Art Gallery
Cusworth Park
Wheatley
Isle of Epworth
Messingham
Marr
Intake
Nutwell
Epworth
Old Rectory
Sturton
Newton
Cusworth
Doncaster
Wroot
Epworth Turbary
Axholme
Manton
Barnburgh
Hensall
Kirkby

Fordon
Wold Newton
Foxholes
Burton Fleming
Reighton
Speeton
Reighton Sands
Reighton Gap
Buckton
Bempton
Grindale
Flamborough
FLAMBOROUGH HEAD
Thwing
Octon
Octon Cross Roads
Langtoft
Rudston
Boynton
SEWERBY HALL AND GARDENS
Sewerby
BONDVILLE MINIATURE VILLAGE
BAYLE MUSEUM
PRIORY
Bridlington
West Hill
Hilderthorpe
Bessingby
Carnaby
Haisthorpe
Thornholme
BURTON AGNES HALL
Kilham
BURTON AGNES MANOR HOUSE
PARK ROSE POTTERY AND LEISURE PARK
Burton Agnes
BRIDLINGTON BAY
Ruston Parva
Harpham
Fraisthorpe
Lowthorpe
Gransmoor
Nafferton
Barmston
Great Kelk
Lissett
Driffield
Gembling
Ulrome
Foston on the Wolds
Wansford
Skerne
SKIPSEA CASTLE
Skipsea
CRUCKLEY ANIMAL FARM
Church End
Beeford
Skipsea Brough
Brigham
North Frodingham
Hutton
Hutton Cranswick
Rotsea
Dunnington
Hempholme
Watton
Watton Beck
Atwick
Bewholme
North Cliff
Hornsea
Burshill
Brandesburton
HORNSEA MUSEUM
Baswick Steer
Seaton
Hornsea Bridge
HORNSEA FREEPORT
Hornsea Mere
Sigglesthorne
Rolston
Aike
Leven Canal
Leven
Catwick
Goxhill
Arram
Mappleton
Little Hatfield
Leconfield
Eske
Great Cowden
Great Hatfield
Routh
Long Riston
Rise
Tickton
Arnold
THE GUILDHALL
Withernwick
Molescroft
BEVERLEY
Beverley
Weel
Meaux
Skirlaugh
New Ellerby
Marton
West Newton
Aldbrough
BEVERLEY FRIARY
MINSTER
Woodmansey
East Newton
Old Ellerby
BURTON CONSTABLE HALL
Flinton
Wawne
Bentley
Thearne
Garton
Swine
Coniston
Dunswell
Grimston
Skidby
Bransholme
Thirtleby
Sproatley
Humbleton
Fitling
Hilston
Cottingham
Kingston-upon-Hull
Sutton on Hull
Ganstead
SKIDBY WINDMILL
Inglemire
Bilton
Lelley
Owstwick
Tunstall
Sutton Ings
Elstronwick
Newland
Stoneferry
Burton Pidsea
Roos
North End
Willerby
Sculcoates
Summergangs
Preston
YORKSHIRE WATER MUSEUM
East Ella
WILBERFORCE HOUSE
Marfleet
West End
Waxholme
West Ella
Owthorne
Anlaby
STREETLIFE
Salt End
Hedon
Rimswell
Withernsea
Haven Side
Burstwick
Halsham
KINGSTON UPON HULL
Northfield
Camerton
East End
Hessle
FERENS ART GALLERY
Paull
Thorngumbald
Ryehill
Keyingham
HUMBER
Ottringham
Hollym
Goxhill Haven
Humber Bridge
Barton Waterside
New Holland
Little Humber
Winestead
ST. PETER'S CHURCH
Barrow Haven
Thorney Crofts
Holmpton
Patrington
Cherry Cob Sands
Out Newton
Goxhill
BAYSGARTH HO. MUS.
Barrow upon Humber
Welwick
Weeton
South End
East Halton
Kingsforth
Sunk Island
Skeffling
Easington
Thornton Curtis
North Killingholme
Burnham
Wootton
Kilnsea
Immingham
South Killingholme
Ulceby
Ulceby Skitter
MUSEUM
Habrough
Croxton
Kirmington
Elsham
Melton Ross
Brocklesby
Stallingborough
North
Pyewipe
Grimsby
ROTTERDAM 13:30
ZEEBRUGGE 13:45
SPURN HEAD
New Barnetby
HUMBERSIDE
Healing
West Marsh
Barnetby le Wold
Keelby
Great Coates
CLEETHORPES
Wrawby
East
NATIONAL FISHING HERITAGE CENTRE
Old Clee
Brigg
Great Limber
Riby Cross Roads
Aylesby
CLEETHORPES COAST LIGHT RAILWAY
PLEASURE ISLAND THEME PARK
Bigby
Riby
Laceby
Nunsthorpe
Somerby
Bradley
Scartho
CLEETHORPES
Searby
Owmby
Lincolnshire
Humberston
Howsham
Grasby
Clixby
Irby upon Humber
Barnoldby le Beck
Waltham
WALTHAM WINDMILL
New Waltham
Holton le Clay
Cadney
Swallow
Yorkshire Wolds
East Riding of Yorkshire
A165
A614
A1035
A164
A1079
A1033
A1174
A63
A1077
A15
A160
A180
A18
A1084
A1173
A16
A1098
A46
M180
B1249
B1229
B1255
B1259
B1253
B1242
B1244
B1243
B1238
B1239
B1240
B1362
B1445
B1231
B1233
B1206
B1218
B1211
B1210
B1434
B1219
65
52
53
6
7
8
9
10
A
B
C
D
E
F
G
H

Maryport
Maritime Museum
Dearham
Tallentire
High Ireby
Sunderland
Binsey
Over Water
Bewaldeth
Blindcrake
Bridekirk
Flimby
Broughton Moor
Standingstone
Dovenby
Orthwaite
Siddick
Camerton
Great Broughton
Little Broughton
Papcastle
Cockermouth
Wordsworth House
Embleton
Bassenthwaite
Seaton
Great Clifton
Brigham
Cockermouth Castle
Wythop Mill
Skiddaw Forest
Skiddaw
Skiddaw House
North Side
Workington Hall
Workington
Stainburn
Bridgefoot
Greysouthen
Little Clifton
Helena Thompson Mus.
Eaglesfield
Lorton Vale
Thornthwaite Forest
Mirehouse
Westfield
Mossbay
Deanscales
Harrington
High Harrington
Winscales
Marron
Dean
Low Lorton
High Lorton
Mosser
Thornthwaite
Thornthwaite Galleries
Whinlatter Pass
Cumberland Pencil Museum
Millbeck
Applethwaite
Cars of the Stars Motor Museum
Distington
Branthwaite
Ullock
Pardshaw
Mockerkin
Thackthwaite
Heritage/Visitor Centre
Braithwaite
Portinscale
Keswick
Lowca
Pica
Grisedale Pike
Lingholm Gardens
Beatrix Potter's Lake District
Moresby
Asby
Lamplugh
Loweswater
Brackenthwaite Fell
Stair
Derwent Water
Parton
Bransty
Moresby Parks
Arlecdon
Loweswater Fell
Little Town
Rowrah
Crummock Water
Rannerdale
Derwent Fells
Grange
High Seat
Whitehaven
Frizington
Kirkland
Croasdale
Buttermere
Thirlmere
19-20 Irish Street
Saltom Bay
Hensingham
Great Borne
Buttermere Fell
Watendlath
Mirehouse
Cleator Moor
Ennerdale Bridge
Ennerdale Water
Ennerdale Forest
Borrowdale (Longthwaite)
Rosthwaite
St. Bees Head
Sandwith
Moor Row
Ennerdale
High Stile
Borrowdale
Wath Brow
Seatoller
Stonethwaite
Rottington
Cleator
Ennerdale Fell
Honister House
Black Sail
Seathwaite
Ullscarf
St. Bees
Pillar
Egremont
Wilton
Lake
Great Gable
High White Stones
Coulderton
Thornhill
Seatallan
Wasdale Head
National
Middletown
Haile
Copeland Forest
Cumbrian Mountains
Nethertown
Calder
Bleng
Sca Fell
Langdale Pikes
Beckermet
Calder Bridge
Bow Fell
Braystones
Wast Water
Burnmoor Tarn
Sellafield Visitors Centre
Calder Hall
Wellington
Wastwater
Nether Wasdale
The Screes
Sellafield Station
Gosforth
Hard Knott Pass
Wrynose Pass
Brathay
Seascale
Santon Bridge
Eskdale Green
Beckfoot
Boot
Eskdale
Cockley Beck
Holmrook
Irt
Furness Fells
Drigg
Harter Fell
Seathwaite Tarn
Coniston Coppermines
Coniston (Holly How)
Mite
Esk
Birker Fell
The Old Man of Coniston
Saltcoats
Ravenglass and Eskdale Railway & Mus.
Ravenglass
Devoke Water
Muncaster Castle
Woodend
Hall Dunnerdale
Seathwaite
Bowmanstead
Ulpha Fell
Broad Oak
Duddon
Caw
Torver
Newbiggin
Lane End
Whitfell
Ulpha
Hoses
Corney Fell
Broughton Mills
Stub Place
Corney
Hycemoor
Selker Bay
Duddon Bridge
Lower Hawthwaite
Water Yeat
Blawith
Bootle
Broughton in Furness
Lowick Bridge
Black Combe
Hallthwaites
Lowick Green
Grizebeck
Foxfield
Whitbeck
The Green
Gawthwaite
Irish Sea
The Hill
Kirkby-in-Furness
Beck Side
Penny Bridge
Broughton Beck
Silecroft
Whicham
Soutergate
Kirksanton
Millom
Millom Folk Museum
Mansriggs
Laurel & Hardy Mus.
Haverigg
Duddon Sands
Ulverston
Askam in Furness
Ireleth
Pennington
Swarthmoor
Lindal in Furness
Great Urswick
South Lakes Wild Animal Park
Dalton in Furness
Little Urswick
Stainton with Adgarley
Scales
Walney Island
Hawcoat
Ormsgill
Newton
Furness Abbey
Gleaston Watermill
Newbarns
Dendron
Barrow-in-Furness
Gleaston
Aldingham
Yarlside
North Scale
Newbiggin
The Dock Museum
Barrow Island
Leece
Vickerstown
Roosebeck
Biggar
Rampside
Isle of Walney
Roa Island
Foulney Island
Piel Island
South End
A595
A596
A66
A5086
A590
A5092
A593
A5093
A591
B5292
B5289
B5294
B5345
B5344
68
55

Penrith
Kendal
Windermere
Morecambe
Kirkby Lonsdale
Ambleside
Bowness-on-Windermere
Appleby-in-Westmorland
Kirkby Stephen
Sedbergh
Ingleton
High Bentham
Carnforth
Milnthorpe
Staveley
Tebay
Shap
Coniston
Hawkshead
Grange over Sands
Arnside
Silverdale
Bolton le Sands
Hest Bank
Lancashire
NORTH PENNINES
YORKSHIRE DALES NATIONAL PARK
LAKE DISTRICT NATIONAL PARK
GRIZEDALE
FURNESS FELLS
MORECAMBE BAY
ULLSWATER
Haweswater Reservoir
Shap Fells
Ralfland Forest
Langdale Fell
Ravenstonedale Common
Baugh Fell
Ingleborough Common
Crosby Ravensworth Fell
Lambrigg Fell
Brant Fell
Milburn Forest
Dufton Fell
Murton Fell
Warcop Fell
Martindale Common
Bampton Common
Plumpton
Brockleymoor
Little Salkeld
Langwathby
Edenhall
Great Blencow
Newton Reigny
Carleton
Eamont Bridge
Clifton
Stainton
Dacre
Pooley Bridge
Askham
Lowther
Hackthorpe
Bampton
Bampton Grange
Rosgill
Great Strickland
Little Strickland
Morland
Bolton
Kirkby Thore
Temple Sowerby
Culgaith
Milburn
Dufton
Long Marton
Brampton
Crackenthorpe
Great Asby
Orton
Raisbeck
Gaisgill
Kelleth
Newbiggin on Lune
Ravenstonedale
Warcop
Brough
Soulby
Crosby Garrett
Smardale
Waitby
Nateby
Hartley
Garsdale Head
Garsdale
Dent
Cowgill
Deepdale
Gawthrop
Millthrop
Killington
Middleton
Barbon
Casterton
Mansergh
Kearstwick
Leck
Cowan Bridge
Ireby
Masongill
Westhouse
Burton in Lonsdale
Wennington
Wray
Hornby
Tatham
Melling
Arkholme
Whittington
Newton
Tunstall
Cantsfield
Wrayton
Clapham
Austwick
Lawkland
Keasden
Chapel-le-Dale
Ribble Head
Lowgill
Caton
Halton
Slyne
Bare
Torrisholme
Nether Kellet
Over Kellet
Gressingham
Borwick
Capernwray
Warton
Yealand Redmayne
Yealand Conyers
Burton-in-Kendal
Priest Hutton
Clawthorpe
Hutton Roof
Holme
Beetham
Storth
Farleton
Crooklands
Endmoor
Gatebeck
Stainton
Sedgwick
Levens
Heversham
Leasgill
Hincaster
Natland
Oxenholme
Old Hutton
Middleshaw
Barrows Green
Brigsteer
Underbarrow
Crosthwaite
Gregg Hall
Burneside
Crook
Winster
Storrs
Bowston
Garnett Bridge
Patton Bridge
Grayrigg
Lowgill
Beck Foot
Selside
Forest Hall
Lowbridge House
Kentmere
Sadgill
Troutbeck
Troutbeck Bridge
Ings
Skelwith Bridge
Elterwater
Little Langdale
Clappersgate
Waterhead
Rydal
Grasmere
Chapel Stile
Near Sawrey
Far Sawrey
Grizedale
Satterthwaite
Force Mills
Rusland
Finsthwaite
Lake Side
Newby Bridge
Staveley
Backbarrow
Haverthwaite
Ayside
High Newton
Low Newton
Lindale
Cartmel
Allithwaite
Flookburgh
Kents Bank
Cark
Holker
Ravenstown
Witherslack
Meathop
Field Broughton
Sampool Bridge
Patterdale
Glenridding
Bridgend
Hartsop
Kirkstone Pass
Wythburn
Thirlmere
Stanah
Fisher Place
Dockray
Matterdale End
Watermillock
Sandwick
Howtown
Threlkeld
Scales
Mungrisdale
Troutbeck
Penruddock
Motherby
Berrier
Hutton Roof
Mosedale
Johnby
Greystoke
Newbiggin
Sockbridge
Tirril
Yanwath
Melkinthorpe
Cliburn
Newby
King's Meaburn
Colby
Burrells
Hoff
Great Ormside
Sandford
Drybeck
Reagill
Sleagill
Maulds Meaburn
Crosby Ravensworth
Oddendale
Keld
Helton
Whale
Bretherdale Head
Greenholme
Bowderdale
Weasdale
Coldbeck
Little Asby
Little Musgrave
Great Musgrave
Bleatarn
Winton
Hillbeck
Knock
Newbiggin
Lowmoor Row
Blencarn
Skirwith
Kirkland
Ousby
Hunsonby
Winskill
Melmerby
Unthank
Skelton
Lamonby
Ellonby
Laithes
Catterlen
Little Blencow
Fair Hill
Hutton
Wreay
Longthwaite
Knotts
Aira Force
Dowthwaitehead
Brothers Water
Angle Tarn
Dale Head
Helvellyn
High Street
Harter Fell
Sizergh
Levens Hall
Leighton Hall
Docker Park Farm
Kirkby Lonsdale
Humphrey Head Pt.
Warton Sands
Cartmel Sands
Scales Moor
Blea Moor
Gayle Moor
Wold Fell
Mallerstang
Ingleborough Show Cave
White Scar Caves
Bentham Pottery

NORTH PENNINES
MILBURN FOREST
Ousby
Skirwith
Kirkland
Blencarn
Gulgaith
Milburn
Newbiggin
Temple Sowerby
Knock
Lowmoor Row
Kirkby Thore
Dufton
Long Marton
Brampton
Morland
Bolton
HIGHGATE FARM ANIMAL TRAIL
Crackenthorpe
Newby
King's Meaburn
Colby
APPLEBY CASTLE
Appleby-in-Westmorland
Burrells
Hoff
Great Ormside
Maulds Meaburn
Sandford
Warcop
Drybeck
Crosby Ravensworth
Oddendale
Great Asby
Crosby Ravensworth Fell
Orton
Raisbeck
Gaisgill
Kelleth
Tebay
Bowderdale
Weasdale
Newbiggin on Lune
Coldbeck
Ravenstonedale
Ash Fell
Langdale Fell
Ravenstonedale Common
Lowgill
Beck Foot
THE CALF
Brant Fell
Cautley
Sedbergh
Millthrop
KILLINGTON SERVICES (Southbound Only)
Killington
Baugh Fell
Garsdale Head
Garsdale
RISE HILL
Gawthrop
Dent
Dentdale
Cowgill
Stone House
DENTDALE
Middleton
CALF TOP
Deepdale
Old Town
Barbon
Mansergh
CRAG HILL
Whernside
Casterton
Kirkby Lonsdale
LECK FELL
Scales Moor
Chapel-le-Dale
Leck
Cowan Bridge
Ireby
Masongill
Nether Burrow
Westhouse
Ingleton
Tunstall
Cantsfield
Wrayton
Burton in Lonsdale
Ingleborough Common
INGLEBOROUGH SHOW CAVE
WHITE SCAR CAVES
SIMON FELL
Low Bentham
BENTHAM POTTERY
Newby
Tatham
Wennington
High Bentham
Wray
Mewith Head
Keasden
Wenning
Lowgill
Hindburn
Goodber Common
Salter
Tatham Fells
Burn Moor
Eldroth
YORKSHIRE DALES FALCONRY AND CONSERVATION CENTRE
Lawkland
Feizor
Austwick
Wharfe
Clapham
Helwith Bridge
Little Stainforth
Stainforth
Stackhouse
WATERSHED MILL VISITOR CENTRE
Langcliffe
Giggleswick
Settle
KIRKBY FELL
MALHAM
Malham Tarn
ROUND HILL
CROSS FELL
BURNHOPE SEAT
Ireshope Moor
Harwood
Harwood Beck
VIEWING HILL
Langdon Common
CHAPELFELL TOP
Langdon Beck
LANGDON BECK
Forest
Widdybank Fell
Cow Green Reservoir
Dufton Fell
PENNINE WAY
Maize Beck
Cronkley Fell
Ettersgill
BOWLEES VISITOR CENTRE
Newbiggin
Westerhope Moor
Newbiggin Common
Bollihope Common
Middleton Common
Holwick
TEESDALE
Middleton in Teesdale
Murton Fell
Mickle Fell
LUNE FOREST
Lune Moor
Bowbank
Thringarth
Mickleton
EGGLESTON HALL
Eggleston
Hill Top
Romaldkirk
Grassholme Reservoir
Grassholme
Hunderthwaite
Selset Reservoir
Hunderthwaite Moor
Hury
Hury Reservoir
Murton
Hilton
Warcop Fell
DOW CRAG
Stainmore Common
Balderhead Reservoir
Clove Lodge
BALDERSDALE
Cotherstone Moor
Cotherstone
Lartington
North Stainmore
Hillbeck
BROUGH CASTLE
Brough
South Stainmore
Deep Dale
Deepdale Beck
Bowes
BOWES CASTLE
Gilmonby
Bleatarn
Little Musgrave
Great Musgrave
Brough Sowerby
Kaber
Barras
Moudy Mea
Soulby
Winton
Heggerscales
Bowes Moor
STAINMORE FOREST
Sleightholme
Crosby Garrett
Little Asby
Hartley
KIRKBY STEPHEN
Kirkby Stephen
Nateby
Smardale
Waitby
Winton Fell
Sleightholme Moor
Scargill High Moor
CLEASBY HILL
Arkengarthdale Moor
Stonesdale Moor
Whaw
Raven Seat
Birkdale Common
ROGAN'S SEAT
West Stonesdale
Keld
KELD
GREAT PINSEAT
Melbecks Moor
Langthwaite
Arkle Town
Arkengarthdale
Hurst
Washfold
Outhgill
YORKSHIRE
Angram
Angram Common
Thwaite
Muker
Gunnerside
Satron
Feetham
Low Row
SWALE DALE
Healaugh
Reeth
Kearton
SWALEDALE FOLK MUSEUM
Fremington
Grinton
GRINTON LODGE
Marrick
Skelton
Mallerstang Common
GREAT SHUNNER FELL
Crackpot
Abbotside Common
North Yorkshire
Cotterdale
Askrigg Common
East Bolton Moor
Redmire Moor
DALES
High Shaw
Hardrow
Sedbusk
Askrigg
Newbiggin
Castle Bolton
BOLTON CASTLE
Preston-under-Scar
Redmire
Mossdale Moor
Appersett
Hawes
DALES COUNTRYSIDE MUSEUM
Bainbridge
Worton
Woodhall
Carperby
Ure
Wensley
WENSLEYDALE POTTERY
Gayle
Burtersett
WENSLEYDALE CREAMERY
Countersett
Cubeck
Thornton Rust
AYSGARTH FALLS
Aysgarth
YORKSHIRE MUSEUM OF CARRIAGES
Swinithwaite
West Witton
PENHILL
Widdale Fell
Semer Water
Wether Fell
Marsett
Carpley Green
Thoralby
West Burton
Agglethorpe
Stalling Busk
Dodd Fell
Newbiggin
Bishopdale Beck
Melmerby
Carlton
Wold Fell
NATIONAL
Cragdale Moor
Carlton Moor
Gammersgill
West Scrafton
Walden
Gayle Moor
Blea Moor
Oughtershaw
MIDDLE TONGUE
Kidstones
Horsehouse
Coverdale
Cam Fell
Walden Head
Braidley
Hindlethwaite Moor
LANGSTROTHDALE CHASE
Ribble Head
Yockenthwaite
Cray
BUCKDEN PIKE
Woodale
GREAT HAW
Hubberholme
PARK
Buckden
LITTLE WHERNSIDE
Cam Beck
High Birkwith
Foxup
Halton Gill
Scar House Res.
Angram Res.
Horton Moor
PEN-Y-GHENT
New Houses
Horton-in-Ribblesdale
Skirfare
Litton
Wharfe
Starbotton
GREAT WHERNSIDE
Middlesmoor
Littondale
Darnbrook Fell
KETTLEWELL
Stean
Riggs Moor
Kettlewell
FOUNTAINS FELL
Arncliffe
Hawkswick
Conistone Moor
Stean Moor
Kilnsey
KILNSEY PARK
Conistone
Hebden Moor
Grimwith Res.
Bordley
Grassington
UPPER WHARFEDALE MUSEUM
Threshfield
Hebden
Greenhow
Frosterley
Hill End
Wear
Pikeston Fell
PAWLAW PIKE
Redford
TOLL
Hamsterley Forest
Woodland
Woodland Fell
Howle
Copley
Kinninvie
Stainton
BARNARD CASTLE
THE JOSEPHINE & JOHN BOWES MUSEUM
Startforth
Barnard Castle
Westwick
Boldron
EGGLESTONE ABBEY
ROKEBY PARK
Greta
Brignall
Scargill
Barningham
The Stang Forest
Cumbria
A66
A67
A685
A683
A684
A65
A687
M6
B6276
B6277
B6278
B6279
B6282
B6281
B6277
B6260
B6259
B6270
B6255
B6479
B6160
B6265
B6480
B6542
B6412
B6261
B6257
56
61
70

Crook
Willington
Oakenshaw
Page Bank
Tudhoe
Spennymoor
Croxdale
Hett
Coxhoe
Kelloe
Trimdon Grange
Trimdon Colliery
Trimdon
Deaf Hill
Station Town
Hutton Henry
Sheraton
Hart Station
Hart
HEADLAND MUSEUM
SAINT HILDA'S PARISH CHURCH
H.M.S. TRINCOMALEE, P.S.S. WINGFIELD CASTLE
Hartlepool Bay
Hartlepool
High Throston
Elwick
West Park
Dalton Piercy
Rift House
Seaton Carew
Fir Tree
Helmington Row
Howden-le-Wear
Hunwick
High Grange
Witton-le-Wear
Bedburn
Byers Green
Newfield
Middlestone Moor
Binchester Blocks
BINCHESTER FORT
Kirk Merrington
Ferryhill
Ferryhill Station
Cornforth
Mainsforth
Chilton Lane
Bishop Middleham
Fishburn
Hamsterley
Witton Park
ESCOMB CHURCH
Escomb
Toronto
Low Etherley
High Etherley
Bishop Auckland
Coundon
Leasingthorne
Chilton
Middlestone
Rushyford
Sedgefield
HARDWICK HALL
SEDGEFIELD
Butterwick
Tees Bay
ENERGY INFORMATION CENTRE
Greatham
Graythorp
Toft Hill
Morley
Coundon Grange
Eldon
Old Eldon
Shildon
Middridge
Bradbury
Mordon
NEWTON AYCLIFFE
West Auckland
Evenwood
St. Helen Auckland
Bildershaw
Royal Oak
Evenwood Gate
Cockfield
Redworth
Aycliffe
Heighington
Thorpe Larches
Foxton
Stillington
Newton Bewley
Wolviston
Cowpen Bewley
BILLINGHAM ART GALLERY
BILLINGHAM
Coatham
Dormanstown
REDCAR
Saltburn
Burnt Houses
RABY CASTLE
Wackerfield
Bolam
Hilton
Ingleton
Houghton-le-Side
Walworth Gate
Killerby
Staindrop
Langton
Durham
Great Stainton
Elstob
Bishopton
Brafferton
Coatham Mundeville
Little Stainton
Whitton
Redmarshall
Thorpe Thewles
Carlton
Stockton-on-Tees
Norton
Roseworth
Haverton Hill
Port Clarence
South Bank
Grangetown
Kirkleatham
KIRKLEATHAM OLD HALL MUSEUM
North Ormesby
Lazenby
Wilton
Eston
Middlesbrough
DORMAN MUSEUM
Normanby
Ormesby
Park End
Guisborough
Little Cleatlam
Headlam
Summer house
Denton
Walworth
Skerne
Beaumont Hill
Barmpton
Sadberge
Fairfield
Hartburn
Thornaby on Tees
Acklam
NATURES WORLD
Marton
ORMESBY HALL
Nunthorpe
Gainford
Winston
Whorlton
Piercebridge
High Coniscliffe
Harrowgate Hill
Great Burdon
Darlington
DARLINGTON RAILWAY CENTRE
Haughton Le Skerne
Low Coniscliffe
Elton
Longnewton
Urlay Nook
Egglescliffe
Eaglescliffe
Ingleby Barwick
PRESTON HALL MUSEUM
Stainton
CAPTAIN COOK BIRTHPLACE
Hemlington
Thornton
Maltby
Hutton Village
Newton under Roseberry
Ovington
Caldwell
Eppleby
Forcett
Hutton Magna
Manfield
Cleasby
Carlton
Middleton St. George
TEESSIDE
Middleton One Row
Aislaby
Yarm
High Leven
Newby
Tanton
Great Ayton
Little Ayton
STANWICK IRON AGE FORTIFICATIONS
Lane Head
Stanwick-St-John
Aldbrough St. John
Blackwell
Stapleton
Low Dinsdale
Neasham
Low Worsall
Hilton
Seamer
Kirklevington
Middleton-on-Leven
Stokesley
Easby
West Layton
East Layton
Newsham
Newton Morrell
Croft-on-Tees
Hurworth Place
Eryholme
Dalton-on-Tees
CROFT
Sockburn
Girsby
Picton
Crathorne
Tame Bridge
Rudby
Hutton Rudby
Enterpen
Kirkby
Great Broughton
Great Busby
Ingleby Greenhow
Ravensworth
Gayles
Kirby Hill
Melsonby
Barton
Hartforth
Whashton
Gilling West
Middleton Tyas
Scotch Corner
Moulton
Hornby
Appleton Wiske
Great Smeaton
West Rounton
East Rounton
Welbury
Potto
Carlton in Cleveland
Faceby
Whorlton
Swainby
Urra
North Cowton
Atley Hill
East Cowton
Birkby
Deighton
Richmond
Easby
EASBY ABBEY
RICHMOND CASTLE
Skeeby
Uckerby
Scorton
Ingleby Arncliffe
Seave Green
Marske
Hudswell
Colburn
Brompton-on-Swale
CATTERICK
Bolton-on-Swale
Whitwell
Streetlam
Danby Wiske
Lovesome Hill
East Harlsey
MOUNT GRACE PRIORY
OSMOTHERLEY
Osmotherley
Whorlton Moor
Chop Gate
COCKAYNE RIDGE
Downholme
Hipswell
Catterick Bridge
Walkerville
Catterick
Catterick Garrison
Hipswell Moor
Scotton
Tunstall
Great Langton
Kirkby Fleetham
Brompton
Winton
Ellerbeck
Kirby Sigston
Yafforth
CLEVELAND HILLS
Snilesworth Moor
Bilsdale West Moor
Bilsdale East Moor
Yorkshire
East Appleton
Great Fencote
Little Fencote
Thrintoft
Ainderby Steeple
Romanby
Northallerton
Bullamoor
Thimbleby
CLEVELAND WAY
Over Silton
Nether Silton
Arden Great Moor
Fangdale Beck
East Moors
Barden
Garriston
East Hauxwell
Hunton
Hornby
Hackforth
Arrathorne
Constable Burton
SWINESIDE CERAMICS
Patrick Brompton
Little Crakehall
CRAKEHALL WATER MILL
Langthorne
Scruton
Morton-on-Swale
Warlaby
Leyburn
Harmby
Spennithorne
Finghall
Newton-le-Willows
Great Crakehall
Leeming Bar
Leeming
North Otterington
Thornton-le-Moor
Thornton-le-Beans
Borrowby
Leake
Kepwick
Cowesby
Hawnby
Helmsley Moor
Rievaulx Moor
Middleham
MIDDLEHAM CASTLE
Coverham
Thornton Steward
JERVAULX ABBEY
Cowling
Bedale
Aiskew
Gatenby
Londonderry
Sowber Gate
Newby Wiske
South Otterington
Knayton
Upsall
Kirby Knowle
Boltby
Old Byland
East Witton
Burrill
Exelby
Firby
Maunby
Thornton-le-Street
North Kilvington
Felixkirk
Thirlby
Rievaulx
CLEVELAND WAY
Cold Kirby
Scawton
Helmsley
Rye Dale
Thirn
Thornton Watlass
Theakston
THORP PERROW ARBORETUM
Burneston
Snape
Carthorpe
Kirby Wiske
Newsham
SION HILL HALL & BIRDS OF PREY CENTRE
Pickhill
South Kilvington
Thirsk
Old Thirsk
BOB HUNTER - HOME OF THE WREN
SUTTON BANK VISITOR CENTRE
HAMBLETON HILLS
Ellingstring
ELLINGSTRING
High Ellington
Low Ellington
Holme
Sandhutton
THE TRESKE SHOP
THIRSK
Sowerby
Sutton-under-Whitestonecliffe
Colsterdale
UREDALE GLASS
Fearby
Healey
THEAKSTON BREWERY VISITOR CENTRE
Masham
Low Burton
Well
Kirklington
Nosterfield
Binsoe
Ainderby Quernhow
Carlton Miniott
Bagby
Balk
Kilburn
Oldstead
Great Thirkleby
Little Thirkleby
MOUSEMAN VISITORS CENTRE
High Kilburn
Wass
Ampleforth
BYLAND ABBEY
Leighton
Warthermarske
Swinton
Thornborough
Howe
Skipton-on-Swale
Baldersby
Catton
Carlton Husthwaite
Coxwold
Gilling East
Leighton Res.
Ilton
West Tanfield
MARMION TOWER
Sutton Howgrave
Middleton Quernham
Roundhill Res.
Mickley
North Stainley
LIGHTWATER VALLEY
NORTON CONYERS
Wath
Melmerby
Baldersby St. James
Topcliffe
Asenby
Dalton
Hutton Sessay
Sessay
Birdforth
Little Sessay
Husthwaite
Thormanby
Oulston
Yearsley
Grewelthorpe
Kirkby Malzeard
Sutton Grange
Nunwick
Rainton
Hutton Conyers
Crakehill
Fawdington
Brandsby
Carlesmoor
HAMBLETON HILL
Lofthouse
Swetton
Laverton
Azerley
Galphay
Greygarth
Ure Bank
Dishforth
Cundall
Dallowgill Moor
Bouthwaite
Dallow
Winksley
Ripon
RIPON CATHEDRAL
Bishopton
Sharow
Copt Hewick
Bridge Hewick
Norton-le-Clay
Raskelf
Easingwold
Crayke
Ramsgill
Gouthwaite Res.
Low Grantley
Grantley
Studley Roger
Aldfield
FOUNTAINS ABBEY
Littlethorpe
Marton-le-Moor
Kirby Hill
Brafferton
Helperby
Stillington
NIDDERDALE
Heathfield Moor
Wath
Eavestone
Risplith
Sawley
Skelton-on-Ure
NEWBY HALL
Langthorpe
Boroughbridge
ALDBOROUGH ROMAN TOWN
Aldborough
Tholthorpe
Myton-on-Swale
Flawith
Alne
Huby
Pateley Moor
NIDDERDALE MUSEUM
Pateley Bridge
Bewerley
Wilsill
Glasshouses
Low Laithe
Markington
Bishop Monkton
Roecliffe
Minskip
Lower Dunsforth
Cross Lanes
Sutton-on-the-Forest
Bishop Thornton
Wormald Green
Burton Leonard
Staveley
Grafton
Upper Dunsforth
Aldwark
Tollerton
Youlton
South
Hill
SUTTON PARK

Durham
Hartlepool
Stockton-on-Tees
Middlesbrough
Redcar and Cleveland
North York Moors National Park
North Yorkshire
Cleveland Hills
Hambleton Hills
Howardian Hills
Coxhoe
Trimdon
Trimdon Colliery
Ferryhill
Sedgefield
Seaton Carew
Tees Bay
Salt Scar
REDCAR
Marske-by-the-Sea
Saltburn-by-the-Sea
Skinningrove
Loftus
Staithes
Brotton
Skelton
Guisborough
Billingham
Thornaby on Tees
Eaglescliffe
Egglescliffe
Darlington
Yarm
Nunthorpe
Great Ayton
Stokesley
Northallerton
Thirsk
Sowerby
Helmsley
Kirkbymoorside
Pickering
Malton
Easingwold
Ripon
Boroughbridge
Topcliffe
Hovingham
Osmotherley
Whorlton
Danby
Castleton
Lealholm
Glaisdale
Rosedale Abbey
Hutton-le-Hole
Ampleforth
Coxwold
Kilburn
Sutton-under-Whitestonecliffe
Commondale Moor
Danby Low Moor
Westerdale Moor
Glaisdale Moor
Egton High Moor
Farndale Moor
Rosedale Moor
Spaunton Moor
Bilsdale East Moor
Bilsdale West Moor
Snilesworth Moor
Whorlton Moor
Arden Great Moor
Helmsley Moor
Rievaulx Moor
Skiplam Moor
East Moors
Cropton Forest
Hartlepool Bay
Stockton-on-Tees
Middlesbrough
Hartlepool
Darlington
Thirsk
Ripon
71
63
58

6
7
8
9
10
A
B
C
D
E
F
G
H
Port Mulgrave
Runswick Bay
Runswick Bay
Kettleness
Goldsborough
A174
Lythe
Sandsend
Sandsend Wyke
SUTCLIFFE GALLERY
East Barnby
West Barnby
East Row
Dunsley
Whitby
Saltwick Bay
WHITBY ABBEY
WHITBY
Newholm
CAPTAIN COOK MEMORIAL MUSEUM
Ruswarp
B1410
Stainsacre
Aislaby
Sleights
Briggswath
High Hawsker
Sneaton
Ugglebarnby
B1447
Egton
Grosmont
Sneatonthorpe
B1416
Raw
Ness Pt.
CLEVELAND WAY
Robin Hood's Bay
Fylingthorpe
BOGGLE HOLE
Robin Hood's Bay
Esk Valley
Littlebeck
A169
A171
Old Peak
Beck Hole
Goathland
Ravenscar
Flask Inn
Fylingdales Moor
WHEELDALE
299
MOORS
20
Staintondale
STAINTONDALE SHIRE HORSE FARM
Harwood Dale Forest
CLEVELAND WAY
Goathland Moor
Saltergate
20
Harwood Dale
Pickering Forest
PARK
Langdale Forest
Derwent
Broxa Forest
Cloughton Newlands
Cloughton Wyke
Cloughton
A171
Burniston
Cromer Pt.
A165
A169
h
Newton Dale
TOLL
Langdale End
Broxa
Silpho
Suffield
Scalby
SCARBOROUGH
Scalby Ness Rocks
SEA LIFE CENTRE
KINDERLAND
North Bay
Levisham
LOCKTON
Lockton
Hackness
Staindale Forest
248
Trouts Dale
Wrench Green
Everley
Barrowcliff
Newby
WATERSPLASH WORLD
SCARBOROUGH CASTLE
ROTUNDA MUSEUM
Wykeham Forest
Scarborough
South Bay
Low Dalby
Dalby Forest
Falsgrave
NORTH YORKSHIRE MOORS RAILWAY
East Ayton
THE HONEY FARM
West Ayton
7
Osgodby
Cayton Bay
PICKERING CASTLE
MILEBUSH OPEN FARM
Sawdon
WORDSWORTH GALLERY
Hutton Buscel
A170
Irton
6
Eastfield
Yons Nab
CLEVELAND WAY
Ellerburn
Ruston
Seamer
B1261
A64
A165
Cayton
WOLDS WAY
A170
Thornton Dale
Wilton
Allerston
Ebberston
B1415
Snainton
Wykeham
Lebberston
Gristhorpe
A1039
Filey Brigg
17
Brompton
B1261
Filey
h
i
r
e
THE CARRS
Willerby
Flixton
Folkton
A1039
5
Muston
Filey Bay
Staxton
A169
Yedingham
Primrose Valley
High Marishes
Derwent
B1258
East Heslerton
Sherburn
Ganton
WOLDS WAY
Hunmanby Moor
Reighton Sands
Hunmanby
8
Low Marishes
West Knapton
East Knapton
16
Potter Brompton
Reighton Gap
Scampston
A64
West Heslerton
B1249
Fordon
Wykeham
Rillington
Reighton
Speeton
Wold Newton
Thorpe Bassett
Wintringham
10
B1229
Buckton
Bempton
Foxholes
Burton Fleming
Scagglethorpe
Place Newton
Butterwick
Grindale
A165
B1255
FLAMBOROUGH HEAD
Norton
Flamborough
Settrington
Helperthorpe
Weaverthorpe
15
Octon
Thwing
B1259
B1248
199
East Lutton
58
59
SEWERBY HALL AND GARDENS
B1255
Sewerby
West Lutton
Octon Cross Roads
Boynton
BONDVILLE MINIATURE VILLAGE
North Grimston
Rudston
B1253
BAYLE MUSEUM
PRIORY
Kirby Grindalythe
Bridlington
Duggleby
B1253
Langtoft
Bessingby
West Hill
Carnaby
Birdsall
Wharram-le-Street
162
Haisthorpe
A614
Hilderthorpe
Sledmere
Cottam
BURTON AGNES HALL
Thornholme
WHARRAM PERCY MEDIEVAL VILLAGE
Kilham
PARK ROSE POTTERY AND LEISURE PARK
BRIDLINGTON BAY
BURTON AGNES MANOR HOUSE

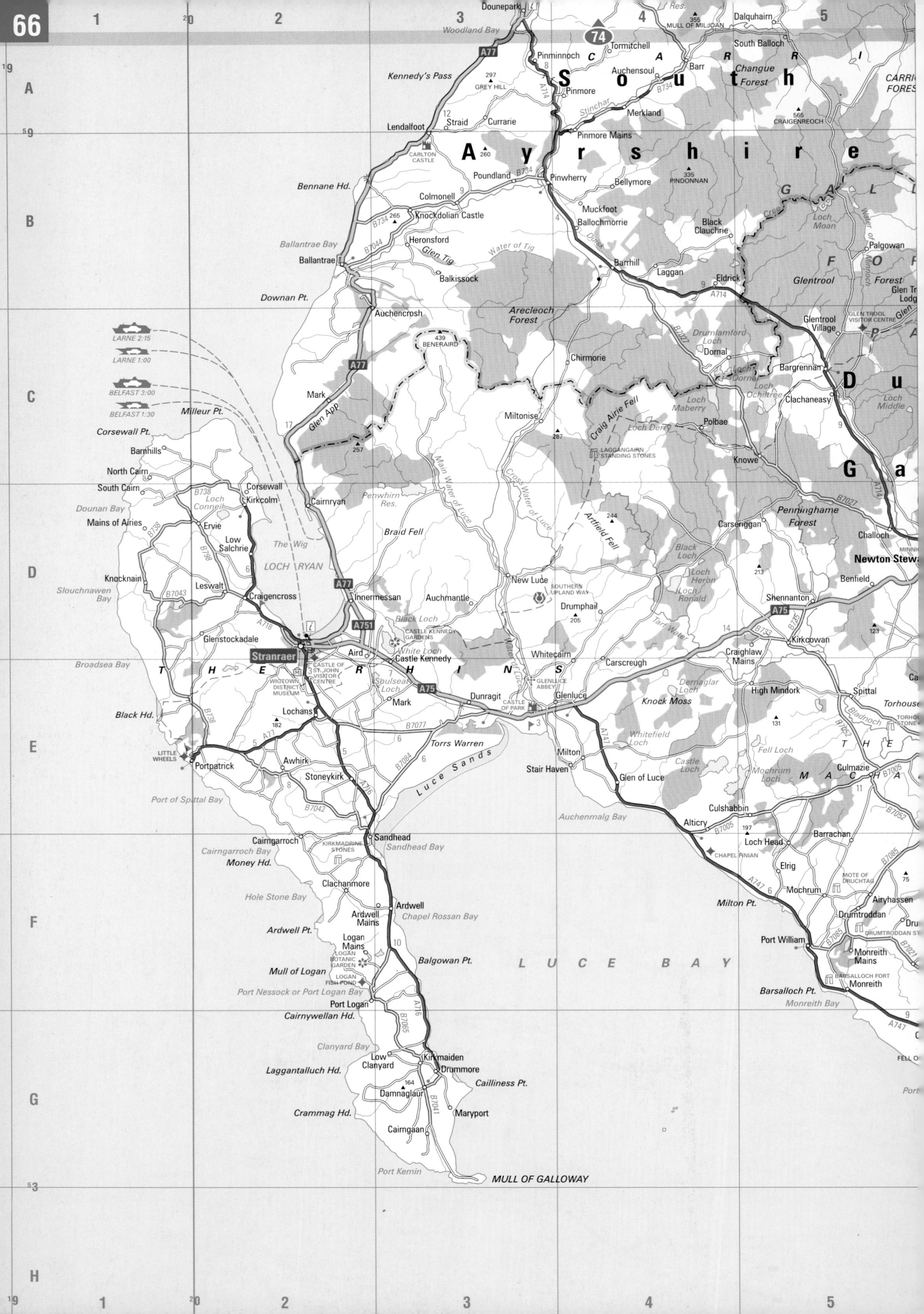

South Ayrshire
CARRICK
Dumfries and Galloway
GALLOWAY FOREST PARK
THE RHINS
THE MACHARS
LUCE BAY
LOCH RYAN
LARNE 2:15
LARNE 1:00
BELFAST 3:00
BELFAST 1:30
A77
A714
A751
A75
A747
A716
A718
A77
B734
B7044
B7027
B738
B798
B7043
B7077
B7084
B7042
B7065
B7041
B733
B735
B7052
B7005
B7085
B7021
Douneparl
Woodland Bay
Kennedy's Pass
297 GREY HILL
Pinminnoch
Tormitchell
355 MULL OF MILJOAN
Dalquhairn
South Balloch
Barr
Auchensoul
Changue Forest
Pinmore
Stinchar
Merkland
565 CRAIGENREOCH
CARRICK FOREST
Lendalfoot
Straid
Currarie
Pinmore Mains
CARLTON CASTLE
260
335 PINDONNAN
Poundland
Pinwherry
Bellymore
Bennane Hd.
Colmonell
Knockdolian Castle
Muckfoot
Ballochmorrie
Duisk
Black Clauchrie
Loch Moan
Water of Minnoch
Palgowan
Ballantrae Bay
Heronsford
Glen Tig
Water of Tig
Ballantrae
Balkissock
Barrhill
Laggan
Eldrick
Glentrool
Glen Trool Lodge
Downan Pt.
Auchencrosh
Arecleoch Forest
Drumlamford Loch
Dornal
Glentrool Village
GLEN TROOL VISITOR CENTRE
439 BENERAIRD
Chirmorie
Bargrennan
Loch Dornal
Loch Ochiltree
Clachaneasy
Loch Middle
Mark
Glen App
Milleur Pt.
Corsewall Pt.
Miltonise
Craig Airie Fell
Loch Maberry
Polbae
Loch Derry
287
257
LAGGANGAIRN STANDING STONES
Barnhills
North Cairn
Knowe
South Cairn
Corsewall
Kirkcolm
Loch Connell
Dounan Bay
Mains of Airies
Ervie
Cairnryan
Penwhirn Res.
Main Water of Luce
Cross Water of Luce
Artfield Fell
244
Penninghame Forest
Carseriggan
Challoch
Newton Stewart
Low Salchrie
The Wig
Braid Fell
Black Loch
Knocknain
Slouchnawen Bay
Leswalt
Craigencross
Innermessan
Auchmantle
New Luce
SOUTHERN UPLAND WAY
Loch Heron
Loch Ronald
213
Benfield
Shennanton
Drumphail
205
Tarf Water
Black Loch
CASTLE KENNEDY GARDENS
White Loch
Glenstockadale
Stranraer
Aird
Castle Kennedy
Whitecairn
Carscreugh
Craighlaw Mains
Kirkcowan
123
Broadsea Bay
CASTLE OF ST. JOHN VISITOR CENTRE
WIGTOWN DISTRICT MUSEUM
Soulseat Loch
Water of Luce
GLENLUCE ABBEY
Dernaglar Loch
Knock Moss
High Mindork
Spittal
Torhouse
Black Hd.
Lochans
Mark
Dunragit
CASTLE OF PARK
Glenluce
Bladnoch
182
131
Whitefield Loch
Torrs Warren
LITTLE WHEELS
Portpatrick
Awhirk
Milton
Stair Haven
Fell Loch
Stoneykirk
Luce Sands
Glen of Luce
Castle Loch
Mochrum Loch
Culmazie
Port of Spittal Bay
Auchenmalg Bay
Culshabbin
Alticry
197
Barrachan
Loch Head
CHAPEL FINIAN
Cairngarroch
Sandhead
KIRKMADRINE STONES
Sandhead Bay
Cairngarroch Bay
Money Hd.
Elrig
MOTE OF DRUCHTAG
75
Clachanmore
Mochrum
Airyhassen
Hole Stone Bay
Ardwell
Milton Pt.
Ardwell Mains
Chapel Rossan Bay
Drumtroddan
DRUMTRODDAN STONES
Ardwell Pt.
Logan Mains
LOGAN BOTANIC GARDEN
Balgowan Pt.
Port William
Monreith Mains
Mull of Logan
LOGAN FISH POND
Port Nessock or Port Logan Bay
BARSALLOCH FORT
Monreith
Barsalloch Pt.
Port Logan
Monreith Bay
Cairnywellan Hd.
Clanyard Bay
Low Clanyard
Kirkmaiden
Drummore
Laggantalluch Hd.
164
Cailliness Pt.
Damnaglaur
Crammag Hd.
Maryport
Cairngaan
Port Kemin
MULL OF GALLOWAY
1
2
3
4
5
A
B
C
D
E
F
G
H

75
75
68
68
Loch Bradan
DOON
LOCH DOON CASTLE
Craigmalloch
Lamloch
Brochloch
CAIRNSMORE OF CARSPHAIRN
580 BENBRACK
Benbuie
Auchenbrack
Auchenbainzie
Burnhead
Penpont
Thornhill
Garryhorn
Carsphairn
CAIRN AVEL
Bardennoch
Dundeugh Forest
SOUTHERN UPLAND WAY
Water of Ken
Shinnel W.
Scar Water
Dalwhat Water
Tynron
Keir Mill
Closeburn
Loch Riecawr
Loch Macaterick
THE GLENKENS
Knowehead
Kendoon Loch
Craigdarroch
Moniaive
Kirkland
MAXWELTON HOUSE
Glencrosh
Castlemaddy
695 MEAUL
768
Gala Lane
CORSERINE 814
KENDOON
Glenhoul
Black Water
385 WETHER HILL
Castlefairn
Dalmacallan Forest
Straith
Wallaceton
Glenmidge
Nith
Loch Harrow
Forrest Lodge
Carsfad Loch
692 MULLWHARCHAR
843 MERRICK
Loch Enoch
Loch Dungeon
RHINNS OF KELLS
Holmhead
Lochinvar
Lochurr
432 BOGRIE HILL
Loch Urr
Sundaywell
Milton
Dunscore
Loch Neldricken
Millquarter
Earlstoun Loch
746
Loch Valley
Drumbuie
St. John's Town of Dalry
Bogue
Corriedoo Forest
417
373
Cairn Water
240
Newtonairds
Trool
Loch Trool
Garroch
Glenlee
Blackcraig
Knocklearn
Drumpark
Glenkiln Res.
381
Clatteringshaws Loch
Loch Dee
New Galloway
Balmaclellan
Gibbshill
Glenkiln
398 Glen
Terregles
716 LAMACHAN HILL
BRUCE'S STONE
CLATTERINGSHAWS FOREST WILDLIFE CENTRE
BLOWPLAIN OPEN FARM
Ironmacannie
317 Craig
Corsock
Shawhead
Dumfries and Galloway
RAIDERS ROAD FOREST DRIVE
Merkland
Urr Water
Brooklands
Crocketford or Ninemile Bar
Brae
Lochfoot
353
WILD GOAT PARK
Loch Grannoch
470 FELL OF FLEET
Cairn Edward Hill
Dee
Loch Ken
Drumrash
Mossdale
Parton
Auchenreoch Loch
Milton Loch
Kirkpatrick Durham
Springholm
Milton
Beeswing
Penkiln Burn
Palnure Burn
Stroan Loch
Loch Skerrow
Woodhall Loch
Old Bridge of Urr
DRUMCOLTRAN TOWER
Minnigaff
Creebridge
711 CAIRNSMORE OF FLEET
Craig
Crossmichael
Haugh of Urr
Kirkgunzeon
Clarebrand
Lochenbreck Loch
Townhead of Greenlaw
MOTE OF URR
Clints of Dromore
Laurieston
Palnure
Laurieston Forest
343
Big Water of Fleet
Loch Glentoo
THREAVE CASTLE
Castle Douglas
Barhill
182
Dalbeattie
383 LONG FELL
Baltersan
Cree
Loch Whinyeon
Loch Mannoch
Loch Bargatton
Carlingwark Loch
Causeway End
GEM ROCK MUSEUM
Creetown
366 BENGRAY
Glengap Forest
Miefield
Bridge of Dee
THREAVE GARDENS
Rhonehouse or Kelton Hill
Gelston
Dalbeattie Forest
Drumstinchall
Glen
Ringford
Airieland
Palnackie
Barnbarroch
Wigtown Sands
Anwoth
MILL ON THE FLEET
Gatehouse of Fleet
CARDONESS CASTLE
Wigtown
456 CAIRNHARROW
Carsluith
CARSLUITH CASTLE
CAIRNHOLY CAIRNS
Girthon
Twynholm
TONGLAND POWER STATION
Tongland
391 BENGAIRN
ORCHARDTON TOWER
Kippford or Scaur
MOTE OF MARK
Rockcliffe
Colvend
Sandyhills
Portling
Bladnoch
Baldoon Sands
Sandgreen
Barharrow
Whinnieliggate
ROUGH ISLAND
Rough I.
Castlehill Pt.
Braehead
Kirkinner
Ravenshall Pt.
Ringdoo Pt.
Fleet Bay
STEWARTRY MUSEUM
Kirkcudbright
Auchencairn
Auchencairn Bay
Hestan I.
Whauphill
Islands of Fleet
Knockbrex
80
Borgue
St. Mary's Isle
Mutehill
Kirkcarswell
135
Dundrennan
Rascarrel
Balcary Pt.
Kirkandrews
Rascarrel Bay
Orroland
Sorbie
WIGTOWN BAY
Eggerness Pt.
Garlieston
GALLOWAY HOUSE GARDENS
Townhead
DUNDRENNAN ABBEY
Kirkcudbright Bay
Borness
Ross
Balmae
Netherlaw
Port Mary
Borness Pt.
108
Abbey Hd.
Little Ross
Cults
Port Allen
Bishopton
PRIORY AND MUSEUM
Whithorn
THE WHITHORN DIG
Portyerrock Bay
Cairn Hd.
ST. NINIAN'S CHAPEL
ST. NINIAN'S CAVE
Isle of Whithorn
Cutcloy
BURROW HEAD
A713
A702
A762
A712
A75
A713
A711
A714
A746
A745
A755
A76
B729
B7000
B7075
B794
B795
B796
B727
B736
B793
B7004
B7052
B7063
B733
B7005
B7085
6
7
8
9
10
A
B
C
D
E
F
G
H

Dumfries and Gal
SOLWAY FIRTH
SOLWAY COAST
76
67
60
Locherben
Auchenbainzie
Burnhead
Penpont
Thornhill
Gatelawbridge
Loch Ettrick
Forest of Ae
Lochwood
Newton
Black Esk Reservoir
Waterhead
Sandyford
Castle O'er Forest
Castle O'er
Tynron
Keir Mill
Closeburn
Park
St. Ann's
Johnstonebridge
Chapelhill
Blackacre
ANNANDALE WATER SERVICES
Dinwoodie Mains
Boreland
Kirkland
MAXWELTON HOUSE
Courance
Ae Village
Parkgate
Nethermill
Sibbaldbie
HART FELL
CALKIN RIG
Straith
Wallaceton
Dalmacallan Forest
Glenmidge
Auldgirth
Templand
Corrie Common
Dalswinton
Auchencairn
Millhousebridge
Sundaywell
Milton
Dunscore
ELLISLAND FARM
Duncow
Amisfield Town
Marjoriebanks
Lochmaben
Lockerbie
Paddockhole
Gallaberry
Kirkton
Tinwald
Bankshill
Newtonairds
Holywood
Locharbriggs
LOCHMABEN CASTLE
Castle Loch
Kirtleton
Drumpark
Heathhall
DUMFRIES AND GALLOWAY AVIATION MUS
Heck
Hightae
Burnswark
BURNSWARK FORT
Glenkiln Res.
Newbridge
LINCLUDEN COLLEGE
The Grove
Torthorwald
Birkshaw Forest
Castlemilk
Waterbeck
Glenkiln
Lincluden
Terregles Banks
GRACEFIELD ARTS CENTRE
Greystone
Kettleholm
Glen
Shawhead
Maxwelltown
Dumfries
Collin
Middleshaw
Middlebie
KIRKCONNEL CHURCHYARD
BURNS HOUSE
Greenlea
BIRRENS FORT
Springkell
Brooklands
Cargenbridge
Ecclefechan
THOMAS CARLYLE'S BIRTHPLACE
Eaglesfield
Brae
Lochfoot
Lochrutton Loch
Racks
Cleughbrae
Dalton
Hoddom Castle
Hoddomcross
Chapelknowe
Crocketford or Ninemile Bar
Milton Loch
Islesteps
Kingholm Quay
Mouswald
Kirtlebridge
MERKLAND CROSS
Auchenreoch Loch
Mabie Forest
Mabie
Kelton
Lochar Moss
Carrutherstown
Kirkpatrick-Fleming
Milton
Lochaber Loch
Brydekirk
Creca
Newton
Springholm
Beeswing
Loch Arthur
DRUMCOLTRAN TOWER
Glencaple
Bankend
Clarencefield
Charlesfield
Hollee
Kirkconnell
SHAMBELLIE HOUSE COSTUME MUSEUM
River Nith
Ruthwell
DUNCAN SAVINGS BANK MUSEUM
Gretna
Haugh of Urr
Kirkgunzeon
New Abbey
New Abbey Pow
SWEETHEART ABBEY
NEW ABBEY CORN MILL
Shearington
CAERLAVEROCK CASTLE
Bowhouse
Blackshaw
Cummertrees
Powfoot
Welldale
Annan
Shawhill
Dornock
Eastriggs
Rigg
Browhouses
MOTE OF URR
LONG FELL
Loch Kindar
Overton
Blackshaw Bank
Bowness-on-Solway
Port Carlisle
Barhill
Drumburn
CRIFFELL
Dalbeattie
Carsethorn
Glasson
Bowness Common
Drumburgh
Cardurnock
Easton
Anthorn
Dalbeattie Forest
Drumstinchall
Kirkbean
ARBIGLAND GARDENS
Whitrigg
Fingland
Palnackie
Barnbarroch
Caulkerbush
Prestonmill
Mainsriddle
JOHN PAUL JONES BIRTHPLACE MUSEUM
Skinburness
Newton Arlosh
Kirkbride
ORCHARDTON TOWER
Sandyhills
Colvend
Kippford or Scaur
MOTE OF MARK
Rockcliffe
Portling
Southerness
Southerness Pt.
Little Bampton
Wedholme Flow
Aikton
Calvo
Seaville
Silloth
Greenrow
Causewayhead
ROUGH ISLAND
Rough I.
Castlehill Pt.
Mersehead Sands
Kingside Hill
Wampool
Blitterlees
Abbeytown
Waver
Oulton
Kelsick
Lessonhall
Auchencairn
Auchencairn Bay
Hestan I.
Highlaws
Beckfoot
Pelutho
Dundraw
Waverbridge
Balcary Pt.
Newtown
Blencogo
Wigton
Rascarrel Bay
Bromfield
Waverton
Holme St. Cuthbert
Mawbray
Langrigg
Waterside
Red Dial
Dubmill Pt.
Edderside
New Cowper
Westward
Westnewton
Bolton Low Houses
Allonby
Watchhill
Fletchertown
Brocklebank
Aspatria
Hayton
Ellen
Allonby Bay
Prospect
Blennerhasset
Mealsgate
Boltongate
Oughterside
Sandale
Torpenhow
Allerby
Threapland
Crosscanonby
Crosby Villa
Parsonby
Plumbland
Bothel
Whitrigg
Ireby
Crosby
Bullgill
Gilcrux
MARYPORT MARITIME MUSEUM
Uldale
High Ireby
Maryport
Dearham
Tallentire
BINSEY
Over Water
Blindcrake
Sunderland
Flimby
Dovenby
Bridekirk
Bewaldeth
Orthwaite
Broughton Moor
Standingstone
Derwent
Siddick
Great Broughton
Little Broughton
Papcastle
WORDSWORTH HO.
Bassenthwaite
Camerton
Cockermouth
CASTLEGATE HO.
Embleton
GREAT CALVA
Seaton
Great Clifton
Brigham
North Side
WORKINGTON HALL
Bridgefoot
WYTHOP MILL
Wythop Mill
SKIDDAW FOREST
Workington
Stainburn
HELENA THOMPSON MUS
Little Clifton
Greysouthen
MIREHOUSE
SKIDDAW
SKIDDAW HOUSE
Westfield
Eaglesfield
Thornthwaite Forest
Bassenthwaite Lake
Mossbay
Deanscales
Marron
Lorton Vale
Millbeck
Applethwaite
Winscales
Low Lorton
Thornthwaite
THORNTHWAITE GALLERIES
Harrington
High Harrington
Dean
Mosser
High Lorton
Whinlatter Pass
CUMBERLAND PENCIL MUSEUM
CARS OF THE STARS MOTOR MUSEUM
Branthwaite
Pardshaw
HERITAGE VISITOR CENTRE
Distington
Ullock
Mockerkin
Thackthwaite
Braithwaite
Portinscale
Keswick
NITHSDALE
ANNANDALE
Cumbria

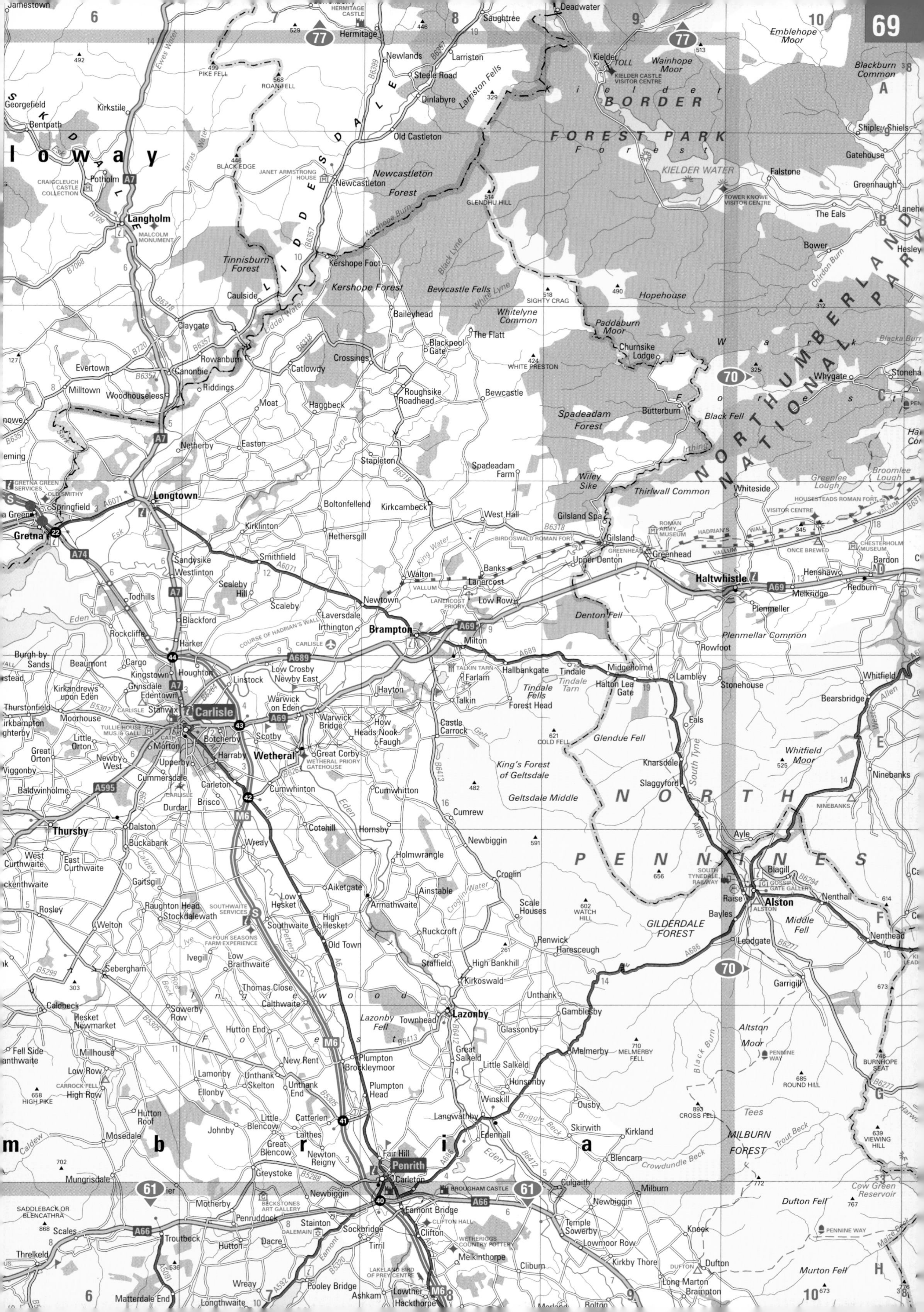

Jamestown
Hermitage Castle
Hermitage
77
Deadwater
Saughtree
Emblehope Moor
Blackburn Common
529
446
492
499 PIKE FELL
568 ROAN FELL
Newlands
Larriston
Steele Road
Kielder
TOLL
Wainhope Moor
KIELDER CASTLE VISITOR CENTRE
513
Larriston Fells
329
Dinlabyre
K i e l d e r
BORDER
FOREST PARK
F o r e s t
KIELDER WATER
Georgefield
Kirkstile
Bentpath
E S K D A L E
L I D D E S D A L E
Old Castleton
Shipley Shiels
Gatehouse
Falstone
l o w a y
Potholm
448 BLACK EDGE
JANET ARMSTRONG HOUSE
Newcastleton
Newcastleton Forest
CRAIGCLEUCH CASTLE COLLECTION
Langholm
MALCOLM MONUMENT
514 GLENDHU HILL
TOWER KNOWE VISITOR CENTRE
Greenhaugh
The Eals
Lanehead
Bower
Hesleyside
Chirdon Burn
Tinnisburn Forest
Kershope Burn
Kershope Foot
Black Lyne
Kershope Forest
Bewcastle Fells
White Lyne
518 SIGHTY CRAG
490
Hopehouse
312
Caulside
Liddel Water
Baileyhead
Whitelyne Common
Claygate
The Flatt
Paddaburn Moor
Churnsike Lodge
W a r k
F o r e s t
Blacka Burn
NORTHUMBERLAND NATIONAL PARK
127
Evertown
Rowanburn
Canonbie
Crossings
Catlowdy
Blackpool Gate
424 WHITE PRESTON
70
325
Whygate
Stonehaugh
Milltown
Woodhouselees
Riddings
Roughsike Roadhead
Bewcastle
Moat
Haggbeck
Spadeadam Forest
Butterburn
Black Fell
Netherby
Easton
Stapleton
Spadeadam Farm
Irthing
Wiley Sike
Thirlwall Common
Whiteside
Greenlee Lough
Broomlee Lough
GRETNA GREEN SERVICES
OLD SMITHY
Springfield
Gretna Green
Gretna
Longtown
Boltonfellend
Kirkcambeck
West Hall
Gilsland Spa
HOUSESTEADS ROMAN FORT
VISITOR CENTRE
Kirklinton
Hethersgill
BIRDOSWALD ROMAN FORT
Gilsland
ROMAN ARMY MUSEUM
HADRIAN'S WALL
345
CHESTERHOLM MUSEUM
Sandysike
Westlinton
Smithfield
King Water
Banks
Upper Denton
Greenhead
ONCE BREWED
Bardon Mill
Todhills
Scaleby Hill
Scaleby
Walton
VALLUM
Lanercost
Newtown
Low Row
LANERCOST PRIORY
Haltwhistle
Henshaw
Melkridge
Redburn
Plenmeller
Eden
Blackford
Rockcliffe
Laversdale
Irthington
Brampton
Milton
Denton Fell
Plenmellar Common
Harker
COURSE OF HADRIAN'S WALL
CARLISLE
Rowfoot
Burgh by Sands
Beaumont
Cargo
Houghton
Low Crosby
Newby East
TALKIN TARN
Farlam
Hallbankgate
Tindale
Tindale Tarn
Midgeholme
Halton Lea Gate
Lambley
Stonehouse
Whitfield
Kingstown
Kirkandrews upon Eden
Grinsdale
Edentown
Linstock
Stanwix
Carlisle
Warwick on Eden
Hayton
Talkin
Tindale Fells
Forest Head
Bearsbridge
Thurstonfield
Moorhouse
TULLIE HOUSE MUS. & GALL.
Warwick Bridge
How
Heads Nook
Faugh
Castle Carrock
Gelt
Eals
Kirkbampton
Oughterby
Little Orton
Great Orton
Botcherby
Morton
Scotby
Wetheral
Great Corby
WETHERAL PRIORY GATEHOUSE
621 COLD FELL
Glendue Fell
Whitfield Moor
525
Newby West
Upperby
Harraby
Knarsdale
King's Forest of Geltsdale
South Tyne
Viggonby
Cummersdale
Carleton
Cumwhinton
Cumwhitton
Slaggyford
Ninebanks
Baldwinholme
Brisco
482
Geltsdale Middle
N O R T H
P E N N I N E S
Durdar
Cumrew
NINEBANKS
Thursby
Dalston
Cotehill
Hornsby
Newbiggin
591
Ayle
Buckabank
Wreay
Holmwrangle
West Curthwaite
East Curthwaite
Caldew
Croglin
656
SOUTH TYNEDALE RAILWAY
Blagill
GOSSIPGATE GALLERY
Gaitsgill
Aiketgate
Ainstable
Croglin Water
Alston
Raise
Nenthall
Rosley
Raughton Head
Stockdalewath
SOUTHWAITE SERVICES
Low Hesket
Armathwaite
Scale Houses
602 WATCH HILL
Bayles
Middle Fell
Welton
Southwaite
High Hesket
Ruckcroft
GILDERDALE FOREST
Leadgate
Nenthead
FOUR SEASONS FARM EXPERIENCE
Old Town
Renwick
Haresceugh
Ivegill
Low Braithwaite
Petteril
261
Staffield
High Bankhill
Sebergham
303
Roe Beck
Thomas Close
Kirkoswald
Garrigill
Calthwaite
I n g l e w o o d
F o r e s t
Unthank
Caldbeck
Hesket Newmarket
Sowerby Row
Lazonby Fell
Townhead
Lazonby
Gamblesby
Hutton End
Glassonby
Alston Moor
Fell Side
Branthwaite
Millhouse
New Rent
Plumpton
Brockleymoor
Great Salkeld
Little Salkeld
710 MELMERBY FELL
Melmerby
Black Burn
PENNINE WAY
746 BURNHOPE SEAT
Low Row
CARROCK FELL
High Row
658 HIGH PIKE
Lamonby
Unthank
Skelton
Unthank End
Ellonby
Plumpton Head
Hunsonby
685 ROUND HILL
Hutton Roof
Little Blencow
Catterlen
Winskill
Langwathby
Ousby
893 CROSS FELL
Tees
Johnby
Mosedale
Laithes
Great Blencow
Newton Reigny
Fair Hill
Penrith
Edenhall
Briggle Beck
Skirwith
Kirkland
MILBURN FOREST
Trout Beck
639 VIEWING HILL
Harwood
702
Mungrisdale
Greystoke
Carleton
Blencarn
Crowdundle Beck
772
61
Newbiggin
BROUGHAM CASTLE
Culgaith
Milburn
Cow Green Reservoir
SADDLEBACK OR BLENCATHRA
868
Motherby
BECKSTONES ART GALLERY
Penruddock
Eamont Bridge
Newbiggin
Dufton Fell
767
Scales
Troutbeck
Stainton
DALEMAIN
Sockbridge
CLIFTON HALL
Clifton
Temple Sowerby
Knock
PENNINE WAY
Maize Beck
Threlkeld
Hutton
Dacre
Tirril
WETHERIGGS COUNTRY POTTERY
Lowmoor Row
Melkinthorpe
Cliburn
Kirkby Thore
Dufton
536
LAKELAND BIRD OF PREY CENTRE
Murton Fell
Wreay
Pooley Bridge
Lowther
Long Marton
Brampton
Matterdale End
Longthwaite
Askham
Hackthorpe
Morland
Bolton
673
A7
A74
A6071
A689
A69
A595
M6
A6
A66
A686
A5091
A592
B6318
B6357
B720
B709
B7068
B6399
B6357
B6413
B6412
B5305
B5299
B5288
B5320
B6277
B6294
B6263
6
7
8
9
10
A
B
C
D
E
F
G
H

Kielder
TOLL
KIELDER CASTLE VISITOR CENTRE
Wainhope Moor
Kielder
BORDER
FOREST PARK
Forest
KIELDER WATER
Emblehope Moor
78
PENNINE WAY
Blackburn Common
Blakehope Fell
PADON HILL
Troughend Common
Shipley Shiels
Gatehouse
Falstone
TOWER KNOWE VISITOR CENTRE
Greenhaugh
Lanehead
Charlton
The Eals
Bower
Hesleyside
Bellingham
BELLINGHAM
Redesmouth
Hareshaw Head
West Woodburn
East Woodburn
Elishaw
Otterburn Camp
Otterburn
REDESDALE CHEESE FARM
Elsdon
Raylees
Old Town
Northumberland
NORTHUMBERLAND NATIONAL PARK
Harwood Forest
Fontburn Res.
Fallowlees Burn
Fontburn Gate
Nunnykirk
Ewesley
Rothley Shield East
Netherwitton
Longwitton
Rothley
Hart Burn
A696
Knowesgate
Cambo
Scots' Gap
Kirkwhelpington
Middleton
Wansbeck
WALLINGTON
BOLAM LAKE
Ridsdale
A68
Rede
Sweethope Loughs
Great Bavington
Thockrington
Kirkharle
Capheaton
Harnham
Little Bavington
Kirkheaton
BELSAY HALL
Hopehouse
Paddaburn Moor
Chirdon Burn
Blacka Burn
Warks Burn
Churnsike Lodge
Wark Forest
69
Whygate
Stonehaugh
Wark
North Tyne
Birtley
Colt Crag Reservoir
Hallington Reservoir
Hallington
Great Swinburne
Colwell
Black Heddon
Ingoe
Ryal
Gunnerton
Barrasford
Park End
Simonburn
PENNINE WAY
Spadeadam Forest
Butterburn
Black Fell
Irthing
Haughton Common
Haughton Castle
Chollerton
Humshaugh
Chollerford
Bingfield
Fenwick
Matfen
Stamfordham
Heugh
Wiley Sike
Thirlwall Common
Whiteside
Greenlee Lough
Broomlee Lough
COURSE OF HADRIAN'S WALL
Walwick
Low Brunton
BRUNTON TURRET
CHESTERS ROMAN FORT
Great Whittington
Ouston
Gilsland Spa
HOUSESTEADS ROMAN FORT
VISITOR CENTRE
HADRIAN'S WALL
VALLUM
ROMAN ARMY MUSEUM
Gilsland
Greenhead
Upper Denton
ONCE BREWED
CHESTERHOLM MUSEUM
Wall
Hill Head
Fourstones
Newbrough
Warden
Acomb
ACOMB
Sandhoe
Halton
AYDON CASTLE
Aydon
Harlow Hill
Horsley
Newton Hall
STEPHENSON'S WYLAM RAILWAY
Newton
Ovingham
Ovington
Haltwhistle
A69
Melkridge
Henshaw
Bardon Mill
Redburn
Chesterwood
Haydon Bridge
South Tyne
Low Gate
MOOTHALL
THE GREEN
ABBEY
Corbridge
Hexham
BORDER HISTORY MUS.
Dilston
Riding Mill
Broomhaugh
Stocksfield
Mickley Square
High Mickley
CHERRYBURN
Branch End
Painshawfield
Denton Fell
Plenmeller
Plenmellar Common
LANGLEY CASTLE
Langley
HEXHAM
Rowfoot
Tindale
Tindale Tarn
Midgeholme
Halton Lea Gate
Lambley
Stonehouse
Whitfield
West Allen
Bearsbridge
Catton
Dye House
Dalton
Whitley Chapel
Slaley
Bromley
New Ridley
Hedley on the Hill
Healey
Whittonstall
Eals
Glendue Fell
COLD FELL
Knarsdale
Slaggyford
South Tyne
Whitfield Moor
Allendale Town
Hexhamshire Common
Broadwell House
Devil's Water
Slaley Forest
Kiln Pit Hill
Newlands
Ebchester
Shotleyfield
DERWENT RES.
Blanchland Moor
Ninebanks
NINEBANKS
East Allen
Sinderhope
Allendale Common
Blanchland
POW HILL
Carterway Heads
Bridgehill
Consett
Edmundbyers
EDMUNDBYERS
Muggleswick
Castleside
Allensford
A692
Ayle
Spartylea
Hunstanworth
NOOKTON FELL
Muggleswick Common
Horsleyhope
SOUTH TYNEDALE RAILWAY
Blagill
GOSSIPGATE GALLERY
Carrshield
Raise
Alston
ALSTON
Nenthall
Coalcleugh
Dirt Pot
Allenheads
BOLT'S LAW
Waskerley
Res.
WATCH HILL
GILDERDALE FOREST
Bayles
Middle Fell
Renwick
Haresceugh
Leadgate
Nenthead
A689
KILLHOPE LEADMINING CENTRE
Rookhope
ROOKHOPE NURSERIES
Stanhope Common
Middlehope Moor
Lanehead
COLLIER LAW
Tunstall Res.
Garrigill
NORTH
Unthank
Gamblesby
Cowshill
Wearhead
WEARDALE
Crawleyside
DURHAM DALES CENTRE
Wolsingham Park Moor
Stanhope
Eastgate
Westgate
Burnhope Reservoir
Altston Moor
PENNINE WAY
Ireshopeburn
St. John's Chapel
Daddry Shield
Durham
Wolsingham
Wear
Frosterley
Hill End
Melmerby
MELMERBY FELL
Black Burn
BURNHOPE SEAT
Ireshope Moor
ROUND HILL
PENNINES
Ousby
CROSS FELL
Tees
Harwood
Harwood Beck
Westernhope Moor
Bollihope Common
Pikeston Fell
Skirwith
Kirkland
MILBURN FOREST
Trout Beck
VIEWING HILL
Langdon Common
CHAPELFELL TOP
Newbiggin Common
Middleton Common
PAWLAW PIKE
TOLL
Redford
Blencarn
Crowdundle Beck
Langdon Beck
LANGDON BECK
Forest
Ettersgill
Widdybank Fell
Hamsterley Forest
Culgaith
Milburn
62
Dufton Fell
Cow Green Reservoir
BOWLEES VISITOR CENTRE
Newbiggin
Newbiggin
Temple Sowerby
Lowmoor Row
Knock
PENNINE WAY
Maize Beck
Cronkley Fell
TEESDALE
Holwick
Middleton in Teesdale
Woodland Fell
Woodland
Howle
Kirkby Thore
DUFTON
Dufton
Long Marton
Brampton
A66
Murton Fell
Mickle Fell
Lune Moor
Bowbank
Hill Top
Eggleston
EGGLESTON HALL
Mickleton
Thringarth
Copley
LUNE FOREST
Bolton

6
8
9
10
A
B
C
D
E
F
G
79
63
West Chevington
Druridge Bay
Helm
Widdrington
Vingates
Longhorsley
Causey Park Bridge
Stobswood
Widdrington Station
The Scars
Cresswell
Ellington
Lynemouth
Fenrother
Tritlington
Ulgham
Linton
A1
A697
A1068
A189
Stanton
Colliery Museum
Beacon Pt.
Woodhorn
Church Museum
Hebron
Longhirst
Ashington
Newbiggin-by-the-Sea
Pigdon
Pegswood
Northumbria Craft Centre
Wansbeck
Hirst
Mitford
Bothal
North Seaton
Throphill
Morpeth
Stakeford
Guide Post
Scotland Gate
West Sleekburn
Choppington
Cambois
Molesden
Meldon
Tranwell
Hepscott
Clifton
Bedlington
Bedlington Station
East Sleekburn
Cowpen
Whalton
BLYTH
Nedderton
Shilvington
Bebside
Saltwick
East Hartford
New Delaval
Newsham
Stannington
Plessey Woods
Ogle
Shankhouse
Nelson Village
New Hartley
Seaton
Seaton Sluice
Berwick Hill
Cramlington
Seaton Delaval Hall
Higham Dykes
Southfield
East Cramlington
Seaton Delaval
Hartley
St. Mary's Lighthouse
St. Mary's or Bait I.
Brenkley
Seaton Burn
Seghill
Holywell
Ponteland
Dinnington
Annitsford
Dudley
Wide Open
Earsdon
WHITLEY BAY
Spanish City
Brunswick Village
Burradon
Backworth
Prestwick
Camperdown
Monkseaton
Cullercoats
Sea Life Centre
Tynemouth Castle & Priory
Hazlerigg
Killingworth
Shiremoor
Darras Hall
High Callerton
Newcastle
Medburn
Marden
Woolsington
Black Callerton
Kenton Bankfoot
Longbenton
Stephenson Railway Museum
Tynemouth
AMSTERDAM 14:00
BERGEN 27:00
STAVANGER 20:45
GOTHENBERG 22:00
HAMBURG 23:00
SUMMER ONLY
Gosforth
North Walbottle
Westerhope
Wallsend
Willington
North Shields
Arbeia Roman Fort and Museum
South Shields
South Shields Museum
Jesmond
Kenton
Military Vehicle Mus.
Heddon-on-the-Wall
Throckley
Walbottle
NEWCASTLE UPON TYNE
Heaton
Tyne Tunnel
Toll
Bede's World St. Paul's Ch.
Westoe
The Leas and Marsden Rock
Marsden Bay
Jarrow
Harton
Marsden
Newburn
Byker
Clara Vale
Ryton
Scotswood
Walker
Hebburn
Souter Point Lighthouse
Castle Keep
Gateshead
Newcastle Discovery Mus.
Metroland
Crawcrook
West Wylam
Dunston
Hedworth
Boldon Colliery
Whiteleas
Cleadon
Whitburn Colliery
BLAYDON
Bensham
Pelaw
Whitburn
Greenside
Winlaton
Thorns Centre
Whickham
Felling
Shipley Art Gallery
Carr Hill
Boldon
Coalburns
Barlow
High Spen
High Fell
Downhill
Fulwell
Roker
Highfield
Sunniside
Street Gate
Chowdene
N.E. Aircraft Mus.
Hylton Castle
Southwick
Monkwearmouth
Chopwell
Rowland's Gill
Gibside
Byermoor
Wrekenton
Castletown
Station Mus.
Saint Peter's Church
Blackhall Mill
Derwentcote Steel Furnace
Leazes
Marley Hill
Lamesley
Springwell
Usworth
South Hylton
Pallion
Sunderland
Derwent Walk
Burnopfield
Blackfell
Hobson
Kibblesworth
Birtley
WASHINGTON
High Barnes
Hendon
Washington Birtley Services
Penshaw Monument
Pennywell
Lambton
The Wildfowl & Wetlands Trust
High Westwood
Tanfield
Beamish
Ouston
Grindon Mus.
Medomsley
Tantobie
Urpeth
Fatfield
Penshaw
East Herrington
New Silksworth
Dipton
Tanfield Lea
Beamish
Perkinsville
Barley Mow
Rickleton
Tunstall
Ryhope
STANLEY
Pelton
Shiney Row
New Herrington
Doxford Park
Ryhope Engines Mus.
Leadgate
Catchgate
West Pelton
Grange Villa
The Middles
CHESTER LE STREET
Bournmoor
Burdon
Annfield Plain
Newbottle
Seaton
Northlea
Craghead
The Ankers House
Fence Houses
SEAHAM
Templetown
Iveston
Waldridge
Chester Moor
Great Lumley
HOUGHTON-LE-SPRING
West Lea
Maiden Law
Colliery Row
Dalton-le-Dale
Delves
Burnhope
Edmondsley
Waldridge Fell
East Rainton
Hetton-le-Hole
Nettlesworth
Plawsworth
Cold Hesledon
Lanchester
West Rainton
Sacriston
Murton
Kimblesworth
Finchale Priory
Leamside
Hawthorn
Witton Gilbert
Easington Lane
Low Moorsley
Pity Me
South Hetton
East Butsfield
Framwellgate Moor
Beacon Pt.
Pittington
Easington Colliery
Langley Park
Durham Light Infantry Mus.
Carrville
Cornsay
Littletown
Hall Hill Farm
Esh
Bearpark
Haswell
Easington
Cornsay Colliery
Quebec
Sherburn
Durham
Sherburn Hill
Haswell Plough
Ushaw Moor
Durham Cathedral
Shotton Colliery
Horden
Broompark
Durham Univ. Oriental Mus.
Ludworth
Esh Winning
New Brancepeth
High Stoop
Waterhouses
Shadforth
PETERLEE
Shincliffe
Thornley
Blackhall Colliery
East Hedleyhope
Old Cassop
Shotton
Castle Eden Walkway
Brandon
Wheatley Hill
Blackhall Rocks
Cassop
Tow Law
Castle Eden
Sunniside
Old Quarrington
Hesleden
High Hesleden
Brancepeth
Bowburn
Durham Services
Billy Row
Sunderland Bridge
Croxdale
Quarrington Hill
Wingate
Deaf Hill
Station Town
Oakenshaw
Page Bank
Hett
Kelloe
Hart Station
Crook
Helmington Row
Willington
Tudhoe
Trimdon Grange
Trimdon Colliery
Hutton Henry
Sheraton
Hart
Coxhoe
Headland Museum
Fir Tree
Byers Green
Spennymoor
Cornforth
Trimdon
High Throston
Saint Hilda's Parish Church
Howden-le-Wear
Newfield
Ferryhill
H.M.S. Trincomalee, P.S.S. Wingfield Castle
Middlestone Moor
Ferryhill Station
Hartlepool Bay
Hunwick
Elwick
West Park
Fishburn
Hartlepool
Witton-le-Wear
High Grange
Binchester Blocks
Kirk Merrington
Binchester Fort
Westerton
Mainsforth
Bishop Middleham
Dalton Piercy
Rift House
Seaton Carew
Hamsterley
Witton Park
Toronto
Auckland Castle
Middlestone
Chilton Lane
Butterwick
Escomb Church
Escomb
Coundon
Leasingthorne
Chilton
Hardwick Hall
Low Etherley
Bishop Auckland
Sedgefield
High Etherley
Rushyford
Teesbay
Energy Information Centre
Toft Hill
Coundon Grange
Eldon
Bradbury
Greatham
Old Eldon
Sedgefield
Morley
Shildon
Middridge
Graythorp
Westerknowle
West Auckland
St. Helen Auckland
NEWTON AYCLIFFE
Mordon
Thorpe Larches
Newton Bewley
High Lands
Evenwood
Wolviston
Cowpen Bewley
Bildershaw
Foxton
Billingham Art Gallery
Coatham
Cockfield
Evenwood Gate
Royal Oak
Redworth
Aycliffe
Stillington
Thorpe Thewles
BILLINGHAM
Dormanstown
Kirkleatham Old
Salt
A19
A1(M)
A167
A689
A179
A178
A1018
A183
A1300
A184
A194
A194(M)
A1231
A690
A693
A691
A692
A696
A695
A69
A6085
A1058
A186
A191
A1056
A1147
A192
A1061
A193
A196
A197
A1172
A68
A688
A6072
A1086
A181
A177
A182
A1290
A1185

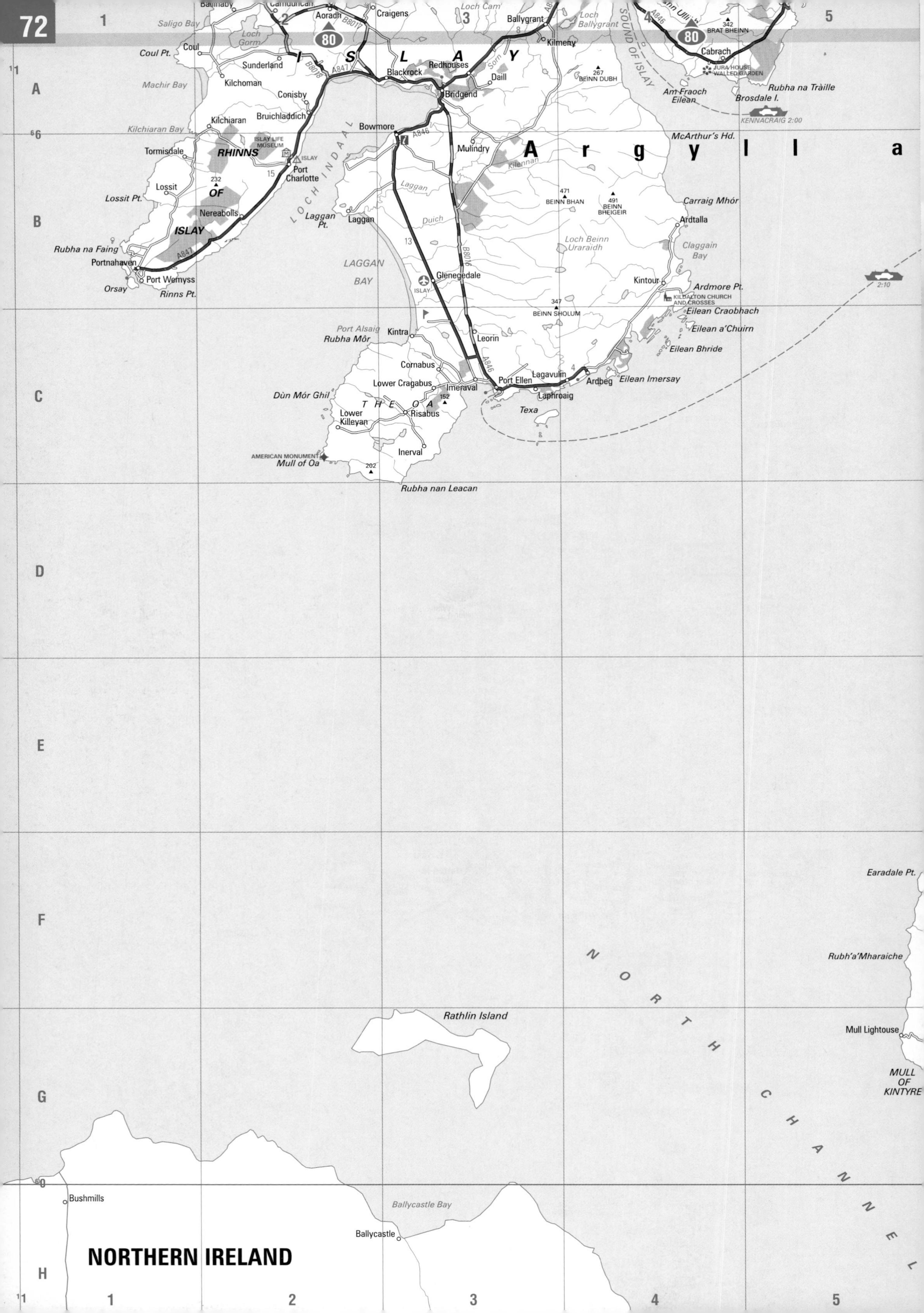
ISLAY
RHINNS OF ISLAY
THE OA
Argyll a
Saligo Bay
Loch Gorm
Coul Pt.
Coul
Sunderland
Kilchoman
Machir Bay
Conisby
Bruichladdich
Kilchiaran
Kilchiaran Bay
Tormisdale
ISLAY LIFE MUSEUM
Port Charlotte
Lossit
Lossit Pt.
Nereabolls
Rubha na Faing
Portnahaven
Port Wemyss
Orsay
Rinns Pt.
Aoradh
Craigens
Loch Cam
Ballygrant
Loch Ballygrant
Kilmeny
Blackrock
Redhouses
Daill
Bridgend
Bowmore
Mulindry
LOCH INDAAL
Laggan
Laggan Pt.
LAGGAN BAY
Glenegedale
Port Alsaig
Rubha Môr
Kintra
Leorin
Cornabus
Lower Cragabus
Imeraval
Port Ellen
Lagavulin
Laphroaig
Ardbeg
Texa
Dùn Mór Ghil
Lower Killeyan
Risabus
Inerval
AMERICAN MONUMENT
Mull of Oa
Rubha nan Leacan
BEINN DUBH
BEINN BHAN
BEINN BHEIGEIR
Loch Beinn Uraraidh
BEINN SHOLUM
SOUND OF ISLAY
BRAT BHEINN
Cabrach
JURA HOUSE WALLED GARDEN
Am Fraoch Eilean
Brosdale I.
Rubha na Tràille
KENNACRAIG 2:00
McArthur's Hd.
Carraig Mhór
Ardtalla
Claggain Bay
Kintour
Ardmore Pt.
KILDALTON CHURCH AND CROSSES
Eilean Craobhach
Eilean a'Chuirn
Eilean Bhride
Eilean Imersay
2:10
A846
A847
B8016
B8017
B8018
80
Earadale Pt.
Rubh'a'Mharaiche
Mull Lightouse
MULL OF KINTYRE
NORTH CHANNEL
Rathlin Island
Bushmills
Ballycastle Bay
Ballycastle
NORTHERN IRELAND
1
2
3
4
5
A
B
C
D
E
F
G
H

Argyll and Bute
North Ayrshire
ISLE OF ARRAN
KINTYRE
Kilberry Hd.
Kilberry
Sculptured Stones
Coulaghailtro
Cruach Lagain 264
Rhu
Corranbuie
Kennacraig
Redhouse
Cnoc a'Bhaileshios 422
Carse Ho.
Dunmore
Kilchamaig
Whitehouse
West Loch Tarbert
Loch Stornoway
Ardpatrick
Ardpatrick Ho.
Gartnagrenach
Portachoillan
Ardpatrick Pt.
Eilean Traighe
Port Askaig 2:00
Ronachan Pt.
Clachan
Loch Ciaran
Cruach nam Fiadh 269
Glenreasdell Mains
Skipness
Skipness Castle
Skipness Pt.
Skipness Bay
Claonaig
Claonaig Bay
Tarbert 0:30 (Winter only)
Eilean Garbh
West Tarbert Bay
East Tarbert Bay
Tarbert
Gigha Island
Druimyeon More
Ardminish
Ardminish Bay
Achamore Gardens
Gigalum Island
Cara Island
Sound of Gigha
Ballochroy
Crossaig Glen
Crossaig
Loch Garasdale
Cruach Mhic Gougan 248
Rhunahaorine
Tayinloan
Beinn Bhreac 241
Cour
Cour Bay
Cnoc nan Craobh 322
Cruach nan Gabhar 354
Carradale Water
Grogport
Killean
Beachmenach
Clachaig Water
Muasdale
Brackley
Amod
Beinn Bhreac 426
Carradale
Port Righ
Glenacardoch Pt.
Belloch
Barr Water
Glenbarr
Clan Macalister Centre
Bridgend
Torrisdale Square
Beinn an Tuirc 454
Carradale Pt.
Carradale Bay
Cleongart
Saddell Glen
Bellochantuy Bay
Bellochantuy
Killocraw
Saddell
Saddell Abbey
A'Chruach 341
Saddell Bay
Lussa Loch
Sgreadan Hill 397
Ugadale
Tangy Loch
Skeroblingarry
Black Bay
Westport
Kilchenzie
Glenlussa Water
Peninver
Ardnacross Bay
West Darlochan
Kilmichael
Low Smerby
Machrihanish Bay
Campbeltown
Campbeltown Heritage Centre
Campbeltown Loch
Machrihanish
Trodigal
Island Davaar
Davaar Island Cave Painting
Drumlemble
Stewarton
Kilkerran
Kildalloig
Knocknaha
Beinn Ghuilean 352
Achinhoan Hd.
The Slate 385
Cnoc Moy 446
Woodbank
Feochaig
Cnoc Odhar 277
Johnston's Pt.
Glen Breackerie
Conie Glen
North Carrine
Keprigan
Strone Glen
Macharioch
Polliwilline Bay
Southend
Carskiey
Cove Pt.
Brunerican Bay
Port Mean
Rubha Chlachan
Sheep I.
Sanda Island 123
Asgog Bay
Kilbride Bay
Ardlam
Ardlamont Pt.
Rubha Leathan
Ettrick Bay
Rothesay
Straad
Loch Fad
Inchmarnock
Scalpsie
Loch Quien
Ardscalpsie Pt.
Scalpsie Bay
Stravanan Bay
Kingarth
Kilchattan
St. Blane's Chapel
Garroch Hd.
Sound of Bute
Kilbrannan Sound
Cock of Arran
Loch Ranza
Lochranza
Lochranza Castle
Isle of Arran Distillery
Millstone Pt.
Catacol Bay
Catacol
North Sannox Farm Park
Meall nan Damh 570
Thundergay
Sannox
Sannox Bay
Glen Sannox
Pirnmill
Loch Tanna
Corrie
Whitefarland
Beinn Bharrain 721
Cir Mhòr 798
Beinn Tarsuinn 825
Goat Fell 874
Rothesay 2:05 (Summer only)
Imachar
Ardrossan 0:55
Glen Iorsa
Glen Rosa
Brodick Castle
Dougarie
Brodick Bay
Isle of Arran Heritage Museum
Brodick
Strathwhillan
Machrie Water
Auchagallon
Glenloig
Machrie Bay
A'Chruach 512
Glen Cloy
Clauchlands Pt.
Tormore
Machrie Moor Standing Stones
Margnaheglish
King's Cave
Ballymichael
Lamlash
Lamlash Bay
Holy Island
Cordon
Torbeg
Shiskine
Drumadoon Pt.
Blackwaterfoot
Drumadoon Bay
Kilpatrick
Tighvein 458
Auchencairn
Kingscross Pt.
Kingscross
Knockenkelly
Whiting Bay
Sliddery Water
North Kiscadale
South Kiscadale
Glenree
Glenashdale Falls
Largymore
Brown Hd.
Corriecravie
Kilmory Water
Largybeg
Dippen
Sliddery
Lagg
Levencorroch
Dippin Head
Torrylinn Cairn
Kilmory
Bennan
South Bank Farm Park
Kildonan
Bennan Hd.
Sound of Pladda
Pladda
Ailsa Craig 338

Port Bannatyne
Rothesay
Craigmore
Montford
Ascog
Kerrycroy
Scoulag
Scalpsie
Kingarth
Kilchattan Bay
ISLE OF BUTE
Ardlamont Pt.
Rubha Leathan
Inchmarnock
Skipness Pt.
SOUND OF BUTE
Cock of Arran
Lochranza
Catacol
Millstone Pt.
Sannox
Corrie
Brodick
Strathwhillan
Glenloig
Lamlash
Cordon
Holy Island
Kingscross
Whiting Bay
Largymore
Dippen
Kildonan
Pladda
Bennan
Kilmory
Lagg
Sliddery
Kilpatrick
Shiskine
Ballymichael
ISLE OF ARRAN
North Ayrshire
FIRTH OF CLYDE
Great Cumbrae Island
Millport
Little Cumbrae Island
Largs
Fairlie
West Kilbride
Seamill
Portencross
Ardrossan
Saltcoats
Stevenston
Kilwinning
Irvine
Dreghorn
Dalry
Kilbirnie
Beith
Lochwinnoch
Bridge of Weir
Renfrews
CLYDE-MUIRSHIEL REGIONAL PARK
Dundonald
Barassie
Troon
Lady Isle
Monkton
Prestwick
Ayr
Heads of Ayr
Dunure
Alloway
Dalrymple
Culzean Bay
Maybole
Maidens
Turnberry
Kirkoswald
Crosshill
Dailly
Girvan
Ailsa Craig
Pinminnoch
Barr
South Ayrshire
Kennedy's Pass
82
73
66

GLASGOW
COATBRIDGE
JOHNSTONE
Paisley
Rutherglen
Uddingston
Cambuslang
Bellshill
Bothwell
MOTHERWELL
HAMILTON
WISHAW
East Kilbride
Barrhead
Neilston
Newton Mearns
Eaglesham
Larkhall
Carluke
Stonehouse
Strathaven
Blackwood
Kirkmuirhill
Lanark
Lesmahagow
Coalburn
Douglas
Stewarton
Kilmarnock
Galston
Newmilns
Darvel
Mauchline
Catrine
Muirkirk
Auchinleck
Cumnock
Drongan
Tarbolton
New Cumnock
Kirkconnel
Sanquhar
Wanlockhead
Dalmellington
Patna
Carsphairn
Thornhill
East Renfrewshire
South Lanarkshire
East Ayrshire
Dumfries and Galloway
Lowther Hills
Carsphairn Forest
Tairlaw Forest
Loch Doon
Glengavel Reservoir
Afton Reservoir
Flow Moss
Airds Moss
Rough Moss
Kype Muir
Middle Muir
Kingshill Plantation
Glenmuirshaw
Cairn Table
Blackcraig Hill
Cairnsmore of Carsphairn
Mennock Pass
Southern Upland Way
M8
M73
M74
M77
A70
A71
A76
A77
A713
83
76
67

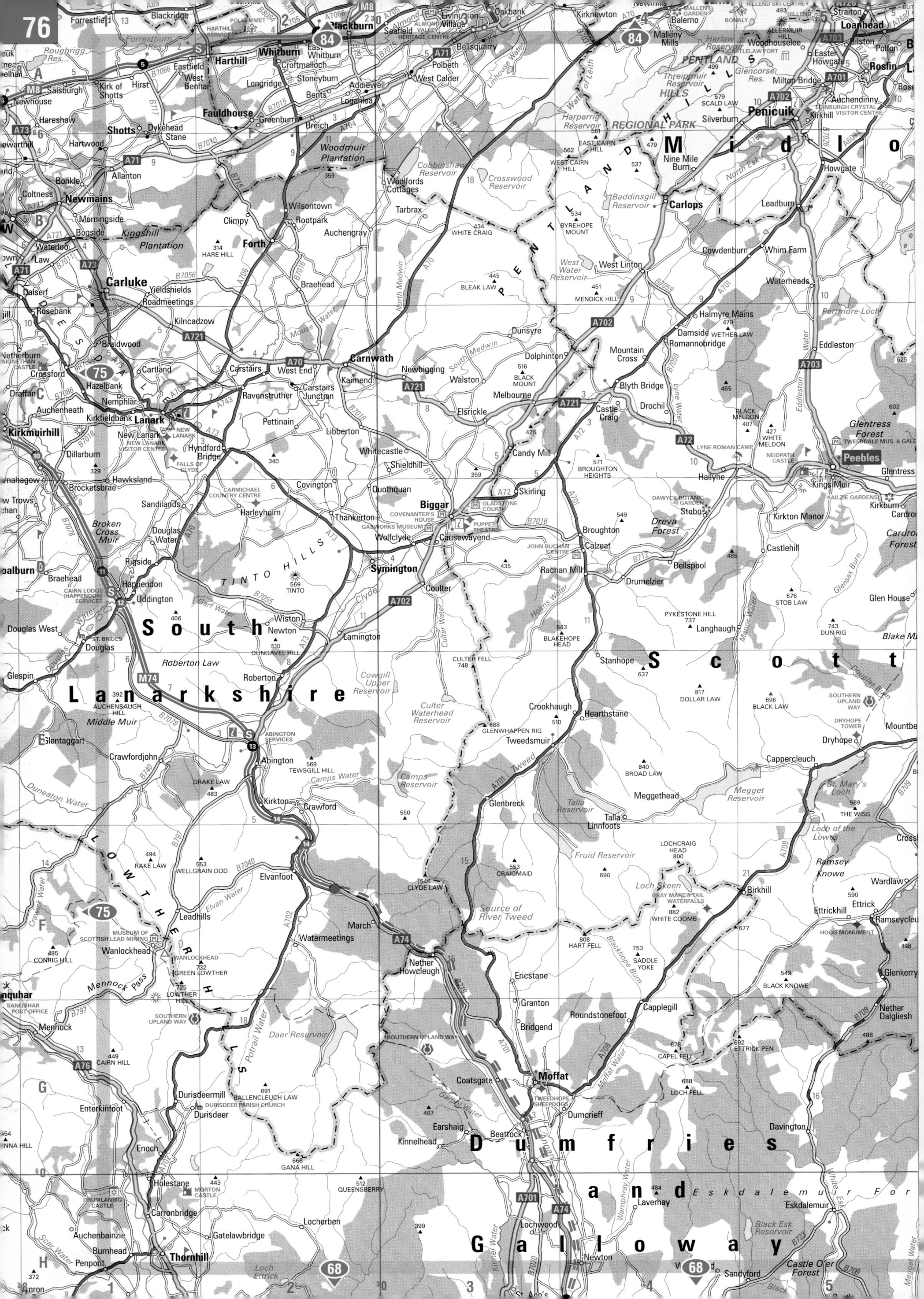
Forrestfield
Blackridge
Blackburn
Livingston Village
Oakbank
Kirknewton
Balerno
Straiton
Loanhead
Harthill
Whitburn
East Whitburn
Bellsquarry
Malleny Mills
Woodhouselee
Bilston
Polton
Roslin
Eastfield
West Benhar
Croftmalloch
Stoneyburn
Polbeth
West Calder
Easter Howgate
Salsburgh
Kirk of Shotts
Hirst
Longridge
Addiewell
Loganlea
Bents
Milton Bridge
Auchendinny
Newhouse
Fauldhouse
Greenburn
Breich
PENTLAND HILLS REGIONAL PARK
Penicuik
Kirkhill
Hareshaw
Shotts
Dykehead
Stane
Silverburn
Hartwood
Woodmuir Plantation
Allanton
Nine Mile Burn
Howgate
Cobbinshaw Reservoir
Crosswood Reservoir
Woolfords Cottages
Bonkle
Coltness
Newmains
Wilsontown
Carlops
Tarbrax
Baddinsgill Reservoir
Leadburn
Morningside
Climpy
Rootpark
Auchengray
Bogside
Kingshill Plantation
WHITE CRAIG
BYREHOPE MOUNT
Waterloo
Law
HARE HILL
Forth
Cowdenburn
Whim Farm
Carluke
Yieldshields
Roadmeetings
Braehead
West Water Reservoir
West Linton
Waterheads
BLEAK LAW
MENDICK HILL
Dalserf
Rosebank
Kilncadzow
Dunsyre
Halmyre Mains
Portmore Loch
Damside
WETHER LAW
Romannobridge
Eddleston
Braidwood
Carnwath
Netherburn
Crossford
Cartland
Carstairs
West End
Newbigging
Walston
Dolphinton
Mountain Cross
Hazelbank
Nemphlar
Kaimend
Carstairs Junction
BLACK MOUNT
Melbourne
Blyth Bridge
Draffan
Auchenheath
Ravenstruther
Elsrickle
Castle Craig
Drochil
Kirkfieldbank
Lanark
Pettinain
Libberton
Glentress Forest
Kirkmuirhill
New Lanark
Hyndford Bridge
Whitecastle
Candy Mill
BLACK MELDON
WHITE MELDON
Peebles
Dillarburn
Shieldhill
BROUGHTON HEIGHTS
Hallyne
Glentress
Hawksland
Brocketsbrae
Covington
Quothquan
Skirling
Kings Muir
Sandilands
Harleyholm
Biggar
Dawyck Botanic Garden
Stobo
Kirkburn
Thankerton
Broughton
Dreva Forest
Kirkton Manor
Broken Cross Muir
Douglas Water
Wolfclyde
Causewayend
Calzeat
Castlehill
Rigside
TINTO HILLS
Symington
Rachan Mill
Bellspool
Drumelzier
Braehead
Happendon
TINTO
Coulter
Uddington
STOB LAW
Glen House
South Lanarkshire
Wiston
Newton
Lamington
PYKESTONE HILL
Langhaugh
Douglas West
DUNGAVEL HILL
BLAKEHOPE HEAD
DUN RIG
Douglas
Roberton Law
CULTER FELL
Stanhope
Glespin
Roberton
Cowgill Upper Reservoir
Scott
AUCHENSAUGH HILL
Lanarkshire
DOLLAR LAW
BLACK LAW
Middle Muir
Culter Waterhead Reservoir
Crookhaugh
Hearthstane
GLENWHAPPEN RIG
Tweedsmuir
Glentaggart
Abington
Dryhope
Mountbenger
Crawfordjohn
TEWSGILL HILL
Cappercleuch
Camps Reservoir
BROAD LAW
DRAKE LAW
Meggethead
Megget Reservoir
St. Mary's Loch
Duneaton Water
Kirkton
Crawford
Glenbreck
Talla Reservoir
THE WISS
Talla Linnfoots
LOCHCRAIG HEAD
Loch of the Lowes
LOWTHER HILLS
RAKE LAW
WELLGRAIN DOD
CRAIGMAID
Fruid Reservoir
Ramsey Knowe
Elvanfoot
Loch Skeen
Birkhill
Wardlaw
CLYDE LAW
Source of River Tweed
Ettrick
Ettrickhill
Ramseycleuch
Leadhills
WHITE COOMB
March
Watermeetings
HART FELL
SADDLE YOKE
Wanlockhead
CONRIG HILL
Nether Howcleugh
Ericstane
Glenkerry
BLACK KNOWE
Sanquhar
Mennock Pass
LOWTHER HILL
Granton
Roundstonefoot
Capplegill
Nether Dalgliesh
Mennock
Daer Reservoir
Bridgend
ETTRICK PEN
CAIRN HILL
CAPEL FELL
Moffat
Coatsgate
LOCH FELL
BALLENCLEUCH LAW
Durisdeermill
Enterkinfoot
Durisdeer
Dumcrieff
Earshaig
Beattock
Davington
Kinnelhead
Dumfries and Galloway
Enoch
GANA HILL
Holestane
QUEENSBERRY
Morton Castle
Laverhay
Eskdalemuir Forest
Eskdalemuir
Drumlanrig Castle
Carronbridge
Lochwood
Locherben
Black Esk Reservoir
Auchenbainzie
Gatelawbridge
Burnhead
Penpont
Thornhill
Loch Ettrick
Newton
Sandyford
Castle O'er Forest

LAMMERMUIR HILLS
MOORFOOT HILLS
Scottish Borders
Lothian
Eskbank
Bonnyrigg and Lasswade
Newtongrange
Newbattle
Easthouses
Mayfield
Gorebridge
Arniston Engine
Pathhead
Crichton
Fala
Fala Dam
Fala Moor
Soutra Mains
Tynehead
North Middleton
Middleton
Temple
Humbie
Stobshiel
Blegbie
West Saltoun
Long Newton
Longyester
Quarryford
Whiteadder Reservoir
Hopes Reservoir
Cranshaws
Abbey St. Bathans
Ellemford
Nether Monynut
Longformacus
Watch Water Reservoir
Dye Water
Duns
Buxley
Cheeklaw
Clockmill
Choicelee
Gavinton
Polwarth
Fogo
Fogorig
Bogend
Sisterpath
Swintonmill
Leitholm
Orange Lane
Greenlaw
Wedderlie
Westruther
Halliburton
Thornydykes
Whiteburn
Blythe
Thirlestane
Houndslow
Lauder
Thirlestane Castle
Oxton
Addinston
Hillhouse
Kirktonhill
Gilston
Heriot
Carcant
Falahill
Fountainhall
Torquhan
Stow
Killochyett
Bow
Caitha Bowland
Langshaw
Buckholm
Galashiels
Clovenfords
Caddonfoot
Walkerburn
Innerleithen
Traquair
Kirkhouse
Elibank and Traquair Forest
Minch Moor
Yair Hill Forest
Gattonside
Melrose
Newstead
Darnick
Boleside
Abbotsford House
Eildon Hills
Earlston
Redpath
Brotherstone
Smailholm
Dryburgh
Bemersyde
Clintmains
Newtown St. Boswells
St. Boswells
Bowden
Lindean
Ovenscloss
Broadmeadows
Selkirk
Philiphaugh
Bowhill
Yarrow
Yarrow Feus
Sundhope
Ettrickbridge
Kirkhope
Ettrick Forest
Midlem
Longnewton
Maxton
Rutherford
Roxburgh
Kelso
Maxwellheugh
Heiton
Ednam
Stichill
Nenthorn
Hume
Eccles
Birgham
Hadden
Sprouston
Kerchesters
Lempitlaw
Hoselaw
Blakelaw
Frogden
Kalemouth
Eckford
Crookhouse
Linton
Morebattle
Cessford
Crailing
Crailinghall
Nisbet
Ancrum
Bonjedward
Jedburgh
Lanton
Newton
Bedrule
Hundalee
Ferniehirst Castle
Belses
Bloomfield
Greenhouse
Chesters
Lilliesleaf
Clerklands
Ashkirk
Woll
Hassendean
Minto
Horsleyhill
Clarilaw
Appletreehall
Denholm
Ashybank
Burnfoot
Wilton
Hawick
Cauldmill
Kirkton
Bonchester Bridge
Hobkirk
Cleuch Head
Southdean
Camptown
Mervinslaw
Oxnam
Mossburnford
Swinside Hall
Chatto
Whitton
Hownam
Falla
Leithope Forest
Redeside
Catcleugh
Byrness
Featherwood
Redesdale Forest
Catcleugh Reservoir
Kielder Forest
Kielderhead Moor
Kielder
Deadwater
Saughtree
Wauchope Forest
Langburnshiels
Singdean
Shankend
Priesthaugh
Dodburn
Northhouse
Broadhaugh
Newmill
Branxholme
Branxholm Park
Burnfoot
Borthwickbrae
Roberton
Borthwickshiels
Deanburnhaugh
Buccleuch
Craik Forest
Craik
Howpasley
Teviothead
Castleweary
Hermitage
Gorrenberry
Newlands
Larriston
Steele Road
Emblehope Moor
Blackburn Common
Redfordgreen
Tushielaw
Newburgh
Gilmanscleuch
Todrig
Akermoor Loch
Shaws Under Loch
Hellmoor Loch
Dewar
Colquhar
Blackhaugh
Windlestraw Law
Whitehope Law
Blackhope Scar
Rosebery Reservoir
Gladhouse Reservoir
Torfichen Hill
Hogs Law
Hunt Law
Collie Law
Meikle Says Law
Lammer Law
Dirrington Great Law
Smasha Hill
Rubers Law
Fanna Hill
Knox Knowe
Peel Fell
Wool Meath
Pike Fell
Tudhope Hill
Wisp Hill
Caldcleuch Head
Redcleuch Edge
Pike Hill
Hungry Law
Brownhart Law
Wooden Law
Nether Hindhope
Beefstand Hill
Hownam Law
Cliftoncote
Windywalls
A7
A68
A72
A697
A698
A699
A6091
A6105
A6088
A708
A6089
85
78
69

Scottish Borders
Northumberland
NORTHUMBERLAND NATIONAL PARK
THE CHEVIOT HILLS
LAMMERMUIR
MERSE
REDESDALE
ROTHBURY FOREST
Eyemouth
Berwick-upon-Tweed
Coldstream
Kelso
Jedburgh
Wooler
Rothbury
Duns
Chirnside
Coldingham
St. Abb's Haven
Grantshouse
Cranshaws
Abbey St. Bathans
Ellemford
Longformacus
Westruther
Greenlaw
Gordon
Polwarth
Swinton
Norham
Cornhill-on-Tweed
Wark
Ford
Etal
Lowick
Yetholm
Town Yetholm
Kirk Yetholm
Morebattle
Hownam
Camptown
Byrness
Catcleugh
Otterburn
Elsdon
Elishaw
Rochester
Horsley
Kielder
Deadwater
Alwinton
Harbottle
Holystone
Thropton
Whittingham
Chillingham
Belford
Fenwick
Kyloe Hills
Kidland Forest
Harwood Forest
Wauchope Forest
Redesdale Forest
Leithope Forest
Whiteadder Reservoir
Watch Water Reservoir
Catcleugh Reservoir
Fontburn Res.
The Cheviot
Kielderhead Moor
Craik Moor
Shill Moor
A1
A68
A697
A698
A699
A6105
A6112
A6088
A6089
85
77
70

6
7
8
9
10
A
B
C
D
E
F
G
H
NORTHUMBERLAND COAST
Emmanuel Hd.
Holy Island (Lindisfarne)
LINDISFARNE CASTLE
Holy Island
Castle Pt.
LINDISFARNE PRIORY
Guile Pt.
Farne Islands
Staple Sound
Inner Sound
Elwick
Ross
Budle Bay
Budle
BAMBURGH CASTLE
Bamburgh
Easington
B1342
Waren Mill
B1340
Spindlestone
Glororum
Burton
Mousen
Bradford
B1341
Seahouses
Bellshill
Adderstone
Elford
North Sunderland
Lucker
Newham Hall
Beadnell
Warenford
Swinhoe
Benthall
A1
Newham
Fleetham
Beadnell Bay
Newstead
Chathill
Rosebrough
Ellingham
Preston
B1340
High Newton-by-the-Sea
PRESTON TOWER
Brunton
Brockdam
Low Newton-by-the-Sea
Brownyside
Embleton Bay
North Charlton
Doxford
Christon Bank
B6347
Embleton
West Ditchburn
B1339
Dunstan Steads
Castle Point
DUNSTANBURGH CASTLE
South Charlton
Rock
Dunstan
Craster
B6347
169
Rennington
101
Littlemill
Howick
B6346
B6341
Littlehoughton
Howick Haven
Shipley
HULNE ABBEY
B1340
Longhoughton
Titlington
ALNWICK ABBEY
250
Denwick
B1339
Boulmer
Boulmer Haven
Abberwick
Alnwick
Broome Park
Hawkhill
Lemmington Hall
HOUSE OF HARDY MUS.
Lesbury
Bilton
EDLINGHAM CASTLE
A1
Alnmouth
JOHN SMITH OF ALNWICK
Alnmouth Bay
250
B6341
High Buston
Edlingham
Shilbottle
A1068
179
Low Buston
Birling
Eastfield Hall
Warkworth
Newton-on-the-Moor
Coquet
Coquet I.
188
Gloster Hill
Amble
A697
Hazon
Guyzance
Hauxley
Swarland Estate
Brainshaugh
North Togston
Swarland
Acklington
Togston
Radcliffe
B6345
Broomhill
DRURIDGE BAY
VISITOR CENTRE
Felton
South Broomhill
B6344
West Thirston
East Thirston
Red Row
Weldon
Hesleyhurst
Eshott
A1068
Druridge Bay
West Chevington
Helm
Widdrington
Wingates
71
Longhorsley
Causey Park Bridge
Stobswood
Widdrington Station
Cresswell
The Scars
A1

86
86
Little Colonsay
Staffa
FINGAL'S CAVE
Inch Kenneth
MACKINNON'S CAVE
Erisgeir
Balnahard
Derryguaig
B8035
591 BEINN A'GHRAIG
ISLAND OF MULL
966 BEN MORE
561
704 CORRA-BHEINN
519 BEINN NA SREINE
Glen Seilisdeir
ARDMEANACH
Killiemore House
Aird of Kinloch
Kilfinichen Bay
THE BURG
LOCH SCRIDAIN
Pennycross
Loch Fuaron
Torrans
503 BEINN NA CROISE
Leidle
BROLASS
Carsaig
376
Carsaig Bay
Rubha Dubh
Loch B
CARSAIG ARCHES
Malcolm's Pt.
Eilean Annraidh
Rubha nan Cearc
IONA ABBEY AND CATHEDRAL
100
Iona
Baile Mor
Kintra
Aridhglas
Loch na Lathaich
Eorabus
Stac an Aoineidh
Sound of Iona
Fionnphort
A849
Fidden
Tiraghoil
Bunessan
Lee
18
376 CRUACHAN MIN
Loch Assapol
Erraid
ROSS OF MULL
Soa I.
Ardalanish
Uisken
Ardchiavaig
Scoor
Rubha nam Braithrean
Eilean a'Chalmain
125
Rubh Ardalanish
Torran Rocks
2:10
Dubh Artach
Rubh'a'Geadha
Balnahard
Kiloran Bay
KILORAN GARDENS
Kiloran
Kilchattan
B8086
B8087
136
COLONSAY
Scalasaig
Loch Staosnaig
Garvard
B8085
Rubha Dubh
PRIORY
Dubh Eilean
Oronsay
Eilean nan Ron
Glendel
Corpach Bay
BEINN B
Shian Bay
453 RAINBERG MOR
Shian
Loch Righ Mòr
318
Rubh'an t-Sàilein
SUMMER ONLY 1:10
Loch Tarbert
Rubha Lang-aoinidh
Rubha a'Mhail
Rubha Bholsa
Lagg
439
Loch an Aircil
Loch Lesgamaill
364 SGARBH BREAC
Nave Island
Ardnave Pt.
785
755
PAPS OF JURA
JURA
Loch a Chnuic Bhric
15
Gortantaoid
Bunnahabhain
JURA FOREST
Corran
A846
An Dùn
Carraig Bhan
Ardnave
316
Knockrome
Leargybreck
Lowlandman's Bay
An Clachan
Killinallan
Gleann Astaile
SOUND OF ISLAY
Sanaigmore
ISLAY
Ruadh-phort Mor
561
Loch na Mile
Loch Gruinart
Leckgruinart
Port Askaig
Feolin Ferry
Braigo
B8018
FINLAGGAN CENTRE
Keills
Keils
LOCH GRUINART NATURE RESERVE VISITORS CENTRE
Loch Finlaggan
Gleann Ullibh
Small Isles
Ballinaby
Carnduncan
Craighouse
Aoradh
B8017
Craigens
Loch Cam
Saligo Bay
Loch Gorm
Ballygrant
Loch Ballygrant
342 BRAT BHEINN
Coul
Kilmeny
Coul Pt.
72
72
Cabrach
Sunderland
B8018
A847
Blackrock
Redhouse
Sorn
Daill
267 BEINN DUBH
JURA HOUSE WALLED GARDEN
Machir Bay
Kilchoman

Argyll and Bute
Firth of Lorn
Sound of Jura
Loch Fyne
Loch Awe
Craignure
Duart Castle
Torosay Castle
Lochdon
Glen More
Strathcoil
Croggan
Kinlochspelve
Barachandroman
Loch Uisg
Laggan Deer Forest
Frank Lockwood's Island
Kerrera
Oban
Dunbeg
Connel
Black Crofts
Dunstaffnage Castle
Ganavan
Dunollie
Altnacraig
Ballimore
Ardmore
Gallanach
Kilbride
Kilmore
Barran
Am Buth
Glen Feochan
Glen Lonan
Glenamachrie
Achnacloich
Fearnoch Forest
Taynuilt
Brochroy
Bonawe
Pass of Brander
Cruachan Reservoir
Falls of Cruachan
Loch Nant
Kilchrenan
Annat
North Port
Portsonachan
South Port
Cladich
Ardanaiseig
Innis Chonnell
Musdale
Kilninver
Barochreal
Glen Euchar
Bragleenmore
Loch Scamadale
Braes of Lorn
Blarann
Clachan-Seil
Clachan
Seil
Easdale
Balvicar
Cuan
Torsa
Luing
Cullipool
Achafolla
Toberonochy
Shuna
Lunga
Scarba
Garvellachs
Garbh Eileach
Eileach an Naoimh
Eilean Dubh Mor
Gulf of Corryvreckan
Dubh-fheith
Kilchoan
Ardanstur
Melfort
Loch Melfort
Kilmelford
Glenmore
Lagalochan
Arduaine
Kames
Garraron
Barravullin
Lunga
Kintraw
Ardfern
Aird
Craignish Pt.
Island Macaskin
Eilean Righ
Carnassarie Castle
Kilmartin
Slockavullin
Poltalloch
Crinan
Loch Crinan
Kilmahumaig
Bellanoch
Mòine Mhòr
Bridgend
Kilmichael Glassary
Cairnbaan
Lochgilphead
Ardrishaig
Loch Gilp
Achnamara
Kilmichael of Inverlussa
Tayvallich
Barrahormid
Taynish
Keillmore
New Ulva
Castle Sween
Island of Danna
Achahoish
Lochead
Ellary
Kilmory
Eilean Mòr
Clachbreck
Baile Boidheach
Ormsary
Pt. of Knap
Druimdrishaig
Cretshengan
Coulaghailtro
Kilberry
Kilberry Hd.
Tarbert
West Tarbert
Corranbuie
Barfad
East Loch Tarbert
Rhu
Inverneill
Auchbraad
Dunrostan
Erines
Barmore I.
Knapdale
Kinuachdrachd
Lealt
Ardlussa
Inverlussa
Lussagiven
Tarbert
Jura
Lochavich
Loch Avich
Kilmun
Dalavich
Inverinan
Ballimeanoch
Blargnour
Portinnisherrich
Inverliever Forest
Eredine
Durran
Kilmaha
Arichamish
Torran
Ford
Ederline
Fincharn
Eredine Forest
Loch Gaineamhach
Auchindrain
Furnace
Crarae
Minard
Tullochgorm
Lachlan Bay
Garbhallt
Lachlan Castle
Strathlachlan Forest
Lephinmore
Lephinchapel
Asknish
Lochgair
Carrick
Port Ann
Largiemore
Achnaba
Otter Ferry
Castleton
Eilean Mòr
Ballimore
Auchnaha
Kilfinan
Drum
Melldalloch
Tighnabruaich
Port Driseach
Auchenlochan
Kames
Millhouse
Portavadie
Blair's Ferry
Ardlamont Ho.
Ardlamont Pt.
Inveraray
Inveraray Castle
Dalchenna
Tullich
Glen Aray
Creggans
Strachur
Glensluain
Newton
Glenbranter
Dunans
Conchra
Glendaruel Forest
Clachan of Glendaruel
Balliemore
Craigendive
Glen Lean
Auchenbreck
Glenstriven
Loch Striven
Ardentraive
Colintraive
Algaltraig
Kyles of Bute
Isle of Bute
Port Lamont
Ardyne Pt.
Port Bannatyne
St. Colmac
Ettrick Bay
Rothesay
Rothesay Castle
Kilbride Bay
Asgog Bay
Glenan Bay
Auchalick Bay
Ardmarnock Bay
Kilfinan Bay
Lochranza 0:30 (Winter only)
Craignure 0:40 Tobermory 1:45 Castlebay 5:00 Coll 2:45
Achnacroish 0:50

Argyll and Bute
Stirling
West Dunbartonshire
Inverclyde
Renfrewshire
88
81
74
Bonawe
Brochroy
BONAWE IRON FURNACE
Taynuilt
Ichrachan
Glen Nant
Pass of Brander
Glen Liver
Glen Kinglass
Glen Noe
BEN CRUACHAN 1126
BEINN EUNAICH 989
Glen Strae
796 BEINN MHIC MHONAIDH
GLEN ORCHY
Arichastlich
840 BEINN UDLAIDH
Glen Lochy
A85
Arrivain
B8074
Cruachan Reservoir
Falls of Cruachan
897
KILCHURN CASTLE
Lochawe
B8077
Stronmilchan
Strath of Orchy
Achnafalnich
Inverlochy
Dalmally
CRUACHAN DAM VISITOR CENTRE
Loch Tromlee
MCINTYRE MONUMENT
Teatle Water
Loch Nant
277
B845
ARDANAISEIG GARDENS
Ardanaiseig
Innis Chonain
INISHAIL CHAPEL
Inishail
A819
Kilchrenan
Annat
North Port
Cladich
Portsonachan
South Port
Coillaig
Allt Fearna
Cladich
DORAIN
A82
901 BEINN ODHAR
Clifton
Tyndrum
880
Cononish
Strath Fillan
1130 BEN LUI
Eas a' Ghaill
978 BEINN DUBHCHRAIG
Inverherive
Crianlarich
CRIANLARICH
Loch Dochart
Loch Iubhair
739 MEALL NAN TIGHEARN
WEST HIGHLAND WAY
Dubh Eas
Glen Falloch
Falls of Falloch
Kenknock
1047 MEALL GLAS MHOR
Breadalbane
937 BEINN CHEATHAICH
1025 BEN CHALLUM
Allt Ribhain
Auchlyne West Burn
Lochdochart House
GLEN DOCHART
Benmore
1174 BEN MORE
1165 STOB BINNEIN
Braes of Balquhidder
Monachylemore
Craigruie
Loch Doine
Inverlochlarig
940 BEINN A'CHROIN
865 STOB A'CHOIN
771
687 BEINN BHREAC
Lochan Shira
Loch Stron Mor
948 BEINN BHUIDHE
Glen Fyne
Allt na Lairige
550 BEINN GHLAS
Brannie Burn
645 MAOL BREAC
Glenfyne Lodge
Glen Shira
Kilblaan Burn
Ballimeanoch
Tullich
Glen Aray
Allt Beochlich
589 CRUACH MHOR
Blargnour
ARDCHONNELL CASTLE
Innisherrich
Dubh Loch
Clachan
Drishaig
A83
Cairndow
ARDKINGLAS WOODLAND GARDEN
811
BELL TOWER
INVERARAY CASTLE
INVERARAY JAIL
Inveraray
ARTIC PENGUIN
Ardno
Glen Kinglas
Rest and Be Thankful
B828
901 BEINN AN LOCHAIN
St. Catherine's
Hell's Glen
B839
Monevechadan
565 CRUACH NAN CAPULL
514 AN SUIDHE
Douglas Water
Dalchenna
ARGYLL WILDFOWL PARK
482 BEINN DEARG
Auchindrain
AUCHINDRAIN OLD HIGHLAND TOWNSHIP
Creggans
Strachur
Strachur Bay
Furnace
LOCH FYNE
733 TROISGEACH
Inverarnan
Ben Glas Burn
Ardlui
Loch Sloy
941 BEN VORLICH
770
ROB ROY'S CAVE
Inveruglas
916
1011 BEINN IME
849
881
Glen Croe
847 BEN DONICH
Succoth
Tarbet
Ardgartan
Ardgartan Forest
Arrochar
Stuckgowan
Ardmay
Drimsynie
EUROPEAN SHEEP AND WOOL CENTRE
Lochgoilhead
Corrow
703 BEINN LOCHAIN
CNOC COINNICH
Craig Rostan
974 BEN LOMOND
Ptarmigan Lodge
Strath Gartney
Stronachlachar
LOCH KATRINE
Loch Arklet
Inversnaid Hotel
Loch Ard Forest
Frenich
SS SIR WALTER SCOTT
BEN VENUE 727
Loch Chon
B829
598
Kinlochard
Altskeith
Loch Ard
QUEEN ELIZABETH FOREST PARK
Glensluain
Newton
A886
B8000
Garbhallt
LACHLAN CASTLE
Strathlachlan Forest
493
Glenbranter
Glenbranter Forest
Invernoaden
779 BEINN BHEULA
ARGYLL FOREST PARK
Blairlomond
Loch Goil
Ardgoil Forest
ARDGARTAN
519 THE SADDLE
Carrick Castle
CARRICK CASTLE
618 BEINN BHEAG
Loch Eck
Whistlefield
Caol Ghleann
Dunans
741 BEINN MHOR
Bernice
659 CREACHAN MOR
BEINN RUADH 664
Glen Finart
GLENFINART DEER FARM
Glenfinart Forest
Ardentinny
Glendaruel Forest
Conchra
Glenmassan
Glen Massan
681 SGORACH MOR
Loch Tarsan
432 CRUACH NAN CUILEAN
Ballimore
Craigendive
YOUNGER BOTANIC GARDEN
Benmore
Uig
Ardbeg
Invereck
Dalinlongart
B836
Glen Lean
KILMUN ARBORETUM
Blairmore
Kilmun
Strone
Strone Pt.
Holy Loch
Auchenbreck
405
Loch Riddon
Clachaig
Glen Kin
Sandbank
Ardnadam
Hunter's Quay
578 CRUACH NAN CAPULL
Glenstriven
458 CRUACH CAORACH
LOCH STRIVEN
506 BEINN BHREAC
522 BLACK CRAIG
Kirn
Dunoon
Inverchaolain
Bullwood
Cloch Pt.
Ardentraive
Colintraive
Kyles of Bute
Algaltraig
Port Driseach
418 CORLARACH HILL
Glen Fyne
Corlarach Forest
Dunan
Lunderston Bay
ISLAND OF BUTE
278 WINDY HILL
Glen More
Port Lamont
Innellan
Ardyne Pt.
Kames B.
Toward
Toward Pt.
St. Colmac
A844
B875
Port Bannatyne
ROTHESAY CASTLE
Rothesay Bay
Craigmore
Ettrick Bay
Rothesay
ARDENCRAIG GARDENS
Montford
Glen Douglas
Inverbeg
Glenmallan
A814
DOUNE HILL 734
LOCH LOMOND
Rowardennan
596 BEINN UIRD
Rowardennan Forest
Loch Ard Forest
Duchray Water
577 BEINN BHREAC
Kelty Water
BEINN EICH 702
Edentaggart
Glen Luss
THISTLE BAGPIPE WORKS
Luss
Inchlonaig
461
Milarrochy
Moor Park
Portincaple
Whistlefield
713 BEINN CHAORACH
Garelochhead
593 BEINN RUISG
Aldochlay
Inchfad
Balmaha
Milton of Buchanan
Garadhban Forest
Inchcailloch
LOMOND
Inchmurrin
B837
Drymen
Glen Fruin
Faslane Port
GARE LOCH
B833
Coulport
Rahane
Shandon
Duchlage
Blairglas
Gartocharn
Croftamie
A809
Ardpeaton
GLENARN GARDEN
THE HILL HOUSE
B832
Bannachra Muir
Arden
A811
BALLOCH CASTLE
LOCH LOMOND
Craighat
Clynder
Rosneath
COVE CONSERVATION PARK
202
Rhu
Helensburgh
Craigendoran
Balloch
Jamestown
Auchincarroch
Stockiemuir
Cove Bay
Cove
Portkil
Kilcreggan
Rosneath Pt.
Colgrain
ALEXANDRIA
Bonhill
Dumbarton Muir
Geilston
Renton
401 DUNCOLM
KILPATRICK HILLS
Gourock
Ashton
Greenock West
Greenock
MCLEAN MUS. & ART GALL.
Midton
Levan
Larkfield
Braeside
Ravenscraig
Central
A770
A8
A78
Cardross
PORT GLASGOW
Castlehill
Townend
DUMBARTON
Brucehill
FINLAYSTONE HOUSE & GARDENS
DUMBARTON CASTLE
Milton
Bowling
Old Kilpatrick
Strone
Woodhall
Devol
Mid Auchinlech
Bardrainney
Langbank
Clyde
Erskine Bridge
M8
M898
Erskine
Bishopton
Rossland
CLYDEBANK
Dalmuir
Inchinnan
Loch Thom
Gryfe Resrs.
303
Inverkip
Shielhill
Garvock
Strathgryfe
A761
B789
Kilmacolm
CLYDE-MUIRSHIEL REGIONAL PARK
441 CREUCH HILL
Innellan
Wemyss Bay
Upper Skelmorlie
Skelmorlie
Duchal Moor
Quarrier's Homes
B786
B790
Houston
RENFREW
Bridge of Weir
Crosslee
Craigends
Ranfurly
Brookfield
Linwood
JOHNSTONE
Kilbarchan
Millarston
Queenside Muir
MUIRSHIEL
522
Noddsdale Water
TOLL
A82
A813
A814
A815
A880
A885
A886
A8003
B866
B883

Perth and Kinross
Stirling
Clackmannanshire
Falkirk
East Dunbartonshire
North Lanarkshire
Glasgow
89
84
75
Killin
Finlarig
Morenish
Milton Morenish
Ardeonaig
Boreland
Achmore
Auchlyne
Ardchyle
Ledcharrie
Glen Ogle
Lochearnhead
Dalveich
Edinample
Ardvorlich
Loch Earn
St. Fillans
Ardtrostan
Balquhidder
Auchtubh
Strathyre Forest
Strathyre
Ballimore
Ben Vorlich
Beinn Each
Ardchullarie More
Loch Lubnaig
Benvane
Ben Ledi
Anie
Pass of Leny
Leny Ho.
Kilmahog
Bochastle
Callander
Trossachs Hotel
Brig O'Turk
Coilantogle
Duncraggan
Lendrick
Loch Venachar
Loch Drunkie
Menteith Hills
Port of Menteith
Lake of Menteith
Inchmahome Priory
Malling
Ruskie
Thornhill
Cobleland
Gartmore
Dykehead
Flanders Moss
Kippen
Arnprior
Buchlyvie
Balfron
Balfron Station
Killearn
Fintry
Fintry Hills
Culcreuch Castle
Loch Walton
Earl's Seat
Dumgoyne
Blairquhosh
Strathblane Hills
Campsie Fells
Carron Valley Forest
Carron Valley Res.
Kilsyth Hills
Kilsyth
Lennoxtown
Milngavie
Bearsden
Bishopbriggs
Kirkintilloch
Cumbernauld
Coatbridge
Airdrie
Stepps
Muirhead
Chryston
Glasgow
Amulree
Corrymuckloch
Meall nam Fuaran
Ben Chonzie
Loch Turret Reservoir
Glen Turret
Glen Almond
Sma' Glen
Newton
Buchanty
Logiealmond Lodge
Harrietfield
Little Glenshee
Invergeldie
Funtullich
Glen Lednock
Loch Lednock Reservoir
Dunira
Melville Monument
Comrie
Tullybannocher
Ross
Dalginross
Lawers
Quoig
Ochtertyre
Falls of Turret
Monzie
Monzie Castle
Hosh
Gilmerton
Fowlis Wester
Crieff
Lochlane
Balloch
Madderty
Keillour Forest
Forest of Glenartney
Glen Artney
Dalchruin
Auchnashelloch
Culloch
Tighnablair
Torlum Wood
Drummond Castle Gardens
Muthill
Strathearn
Kinkell Bridge
Kirkton
St. David's
Aberuthven
Tullibardine
Auchterarder
Gleneagles Hotel
Gleneagles House
Glen Eagles
Blackford
Braco
Greenloaning
Strathallan
Ochtermuthill
Langside
Glenlichorn
Garrick
Ardoch Roman Camp
Ben Clach
Uamh Bheag
Braes of Doune
Drumvaich
Burn of Cambus
Doune
Deanston
Kinbuck
Ashfield
Dunblane
Sheriff Muir
Balhaldie
Braes of Ogilvie
Glendevon Resvrs.
Glen Devon
Pool o' Muckhart
Blairdenon Hill
Ben Cleuch
Bridge of Allan
Blair Drummond
Easter Row
Blairdrummond Moss
Drip Moss
Causewayhead
Stirling
Raploch
Cambuskenneth
Menstrie
Alva
Tillicoultry
Dollar
Tullibody
Fishcross
Devonside
Coalsnaughton
Forest Mill
Cambus
Alloa
Clackmannan
Kennet
Kilbagie
Fallin
Throsk
South Alloa
Dunmore
Kincardine
Kincardine Bridge
Culross
Airth
Letham
Cowie
Bannockburn
St. Ninians
Torbrex
Cambusbarron
Gargunnock
Gargunnock Hills
Touch Hills
Cauldhame
Glentirranmuir
Carleatheran
Earlsburn Reservoirs
Craigend
Loch Coulter
Plean
Easter Cringate
Muirmill
Carron Bridge
Fankerton
Stoneywood
Dunipace
Denny
Head of Muir
Torwood
Larbert
Stenhousemuir
Antonshill
Skinflats
Carron
Bainsford
Grangemouth
Bo'ness
Bonnybridge
Dennyloanhead
Falkirk
Laurieston
Redding
Polmont
Brightons
Whitecross
Linlithgow Bridge
Reddingmuirhead
Glen Village
Shieldhill
Maddiston
California
High Bonnybridge
Longcroft
Greenhill
Banknock
Castlecary
Dullatur
Croy
Cumbernauld Village
Twechar
Balloch
Abronhill
Jawcraig
Slamannan
Avonbridge
Westfield
Torphichen
Standburn
Crossburn
Binniehill
Limerigg
Longriggend
Greengairs
Riggend
Wattston
Caldercruix
Plains
Glenboig
Glenmavis
Armadale
Bathgate
Whitburn
Blackburn
Harthill
Eastfield
Forrestfield
Blackridge
Westrigg
Windyknowe
Mayfield
Bathville
Whiteside
Boghall

90
Perth
and
Kinross
Fife
West
Lothian
Edinburgh
Dundee
Perth
Stanley
Methven
Almondbank
New Scone
Scone Palace
Bridge of Earn
Newburgh
Abernethy
Auchtermuchty
Strathmiglo
Falkland
Ladybank
Cupar
Newport-on-Tay
Tay Bridge
Invergowrie
Longforgan
Errol
Firth of Tay
Carse of Gowrie
Braes of the Carse
Glenfarg
Milnathort
Kinross
Loch Leven
St. Serf's Island
Lomond Hills Regional Park
Leslie
Glenrothes
Markinch
Kennoway
Leven
Methil
Buckhaven
East Wemyss
Largo Bay
Kirkcaldy
Cowdenbeath
Lochgelly
Kelty
Cardenden
Burntisland
Kinghorn
Aberdour
Dunfermline
Rosyth
Inverkeithing
Dalgety Bay
Forth Road Bridge
Queensferry
North Queensferry
Firth of Forth
Inchkeith
Inchcolm
Cramond I.
Grangemouth
Bo'ness
Linlithgow
Kirkliston
Winchburgh
Broxburn
Uphall
Bathgate
Livingston
Blackburn
Whitburn
Edinburgh
Leith
Granton
Musselburgh
Prestonpans
Cockenzie and Port Seton
Tranent
Dalkeith
Loanhead
Bonnyrigg and Lasswade
Newtongrange
Currie
Balerno
Dollar
Yetts o' Muckhart
Oakley
Culross
Kincardine
Dunning
Auchterarder
Ochil Hills
Cleish Hills
Pentland Hills
76
77
83

8
9
10
11
A
B
C
D
E
F
G
H
Muirdrum
East Haven
Drumsturdy
Newbigging
Kellas
Panbride
Carnoustie
Barry
Mains of Ardestie
Baldovie
A92
Monifieth
Barry Links
CARNOUSTIE
West Ferry
Barnhill
Broughty Ferry
BROUGHTY CASTLE MUSEUM
Buddon Ness
Tayport
Tentsmuir Forest
Leuchars
LEUCHARS NORMAN CHURCH
EARLSHALL CASTLE AND GARDENS
Eden Mouth
Guardbridge
ST. ANDREWS BAY
ST. ANDREWS SEA LIFE CENTRE
BRITISH GOLF MUS.
Newpark
St. Andrews
CATH. & ST RULE'S TOWER
Brownhills
Buddo Ness
ST. ANDREWS BOTANIC GARDEN
Balone
CRAIGTOUN
Denhead
A915
Boarhills
Babbet Ness
Prior Muir
B9131
A917
Kingsbarns
Cambo Ness
CAMBO GARDENS
Carr Brigs
Tullybothy Craigs
Cameron Res.
Cameron Burn
Stravithie
Dunino
Balcomie
Craighead
Fife Ness
Peat Inn
Radernie
B940
Kingsmuir
SCOTLAND'S SECRET BUNKER
Crail
CRAIL MUSEUM AND HERITAGE CENTRE
Lathones
Lochty
Largoward
Carnbee
Pitcorthie
Pitkierie
West Ness
KELLIE CASTLE AND GARDEN
Arncroach
Kilrenny
B9171
Anstruther Easter
SCOTTISH FISHERIES MUSEUM
Colinsburgh
B942
Abercrombie
Pittenweem
Anstruther Wester
Balchrystie
Kilconquhar
ST. FILLAN'S CAVE
ST. MONAN'S WINDMILL
Ardross
St. Monans
ST. MONAN'S CHURCH
Elie
Earlsferry
Chapel Ness
Sauchar Pt.
Isle of May
Fidra
Craigleith
Bass Rock
Eyebroughy
North Berwick
TANTALLON CASTLE
Auldhame
MUIRFIELD
DIRLETON CASTLE
Dirleton
Gullane Bay
Gullane
Scoughall
A198
B1347
Kingston
Whitekirk
West Fenton
Fenton Barns
B1345
St. Baldred's Cradle
Aberlady
Drem
Tyne Mouth
MYRETON MOTOR MUSEUM
B1377
THE CHESTERS FORT
MUSEUM OF FLIGHT
East Fortune
Tyninghame
JOHN MUIR
Dunbar
Belhaven
West Barns
JOHN MUIR HO.
GOSFORD HOUSE
Ballencrieff
Athelstaneford
Peffer Burn
Preston
Spittal
East Linton
Broxburn
Barns Ness
B1343
PRESTON MILL
East Barns
HOPETOUN MON.
Longniddry
Huntington
Elvington
A1
HAILES CASTLE
Traprain
Biel Water
Pitcox
Spott
Meikle Pinkerton
Skateraw
TORNESS NUCLEAR POWER STATION VISTOR CENTRE
Thorntonloch
Tyne
ST. MARY'S COLLEGIATE CH.
Haddington
B6370
Stenton
Luggate Burn
Dry Burn
Halls
Innerwick
LENNOXLOVE
Papple
COCKLAW HILL 319
DUNGLASS COLLEGIATE CHURCH
Cove
Reed Pt.
Cockburnspath
East Lothian
Samuelston
Garvald
Siccar Pt.
Wheat Stack
FAST CASTLE
Bolton
Oldhamstocks
Dunbar Common
397 BRANSLY HILL
Easter Pencaitland
398
Carfrae
A1107
Lumsdaine
St. Abb's Head
KITTIWAKE GALLERY
B6355
Gifford
Ecclaw
Coldingham Moor
Northfield
East Saltoun
West Saltoun
Danskine
St. Abb's
Coldingham Bay
St. Abb's Haven
Bothwell Water
SOUTHERN UPLAND WAY
391 HEART LAW
Grantshouse
Huxton
Coldingham
COLDINGHAM PRIORY
Gilmerton
Quarryford
Spartleton Edge
Monynut Water
Nether Monynut
Ale Water
Long Newton
Longyester
78
Houndwood
Whiteadder Reservoir
Eye Water
Cairncross
Eyemouth
Stobshiel

Canna
A'Chill
Canna Harbour
Sanday
Garrisdale Pt.
Sound of Canna
Guirdil Bay
Kilmory
Kilmory Glen
Rubha Shamhnan Insir
1:15
MALLAIG 2:45
Kinloch Glen
Rubha na Roinne
A'Bhrideanach
Kinloch
Loch Scresort
R Ù M
KINLOCH CASTLE
Rubha Port na Caranean
Schooner Pt.
571 ORVAL
388
Harris
Glen Harris
812 ASKIVAL
781 AINSHVAL
Rubha Sgorr an t-Snidhe
Oigh-sgeir
Rubha nam Meirleach
93
SOUND OF RÙM
Glen Meadal
Rubha Charn nan Cearc
280
Aird of Sleat
Point of Sleat
LOCHBOISDALE 3:30
CASTLEBAY 5:30
(SUMMER ONLY)
1:30
1:15
Bay of Laig
Cleadale
Rubha an Fhasaidh
Eigg
Kildonnan
393 AN SGURR
Galmisdale
Eilean Chathastail
(SUMMER ONLY) 1:30
Luinga
Luinga Mh
SOUND OF EIGG
Eilean nan Each
1:00
Muck
137
Port Mor
Tiree
COLL
Feall Bay
Calgary Pt.
Gunna
TIREE
Vaul Bay
Salum
Caolas
Rubha Dubh
Vaul
Balephetrish Bay
B8069
Ruaig
Balevullin
Kenovay
B8068
Gott Bay
Soa
R. Chraiginis
Kilkenneth
Scarinish
COLL 1:05
Moss
TIREE
B8065
Middleton
Heylipol
Heanish
Port Mor
Crossapol
Rubha Traigh an Duin
Loch a'Phuill
Barrapol
Hynish Bay
B8067
Balemartine
Rinn Thorbhais
Balephuil
141
Mannal
Balephuil Bay
Hynish
Port Snoig
Cairns of Coll
Rubha Mor
Eilean Mor
Sorisdale
Bousd
Cliad Bay
Arnabost
Gallanach
B8072
MALLAIG (SUMMER ONLY) 3:15
Grishipoll
B8071
73
COLL
OBAN 2:45
1:20
Ballyhaugh
104
Loch Cliad
Hogh Bay
Arinagour
B8070
Totronald
Feall Bay
Anleod
Acha
Eilean Ornsay
Loch Eatharna
Friesland
Crossapol Bay
Soa
Loch Breachacha
Rubha Dubh
TIREE 1:05
Sanna Point
Fascadale
Kilmory
Ockle
Ockle Pt.
Rubha Aird Druimnich
Sanna Bay
Sanna
Branault
357 BEINN BHREAC
Portuairk
Achnaha
401
Point of Ardnamurchan
Achosnich
ARDNAMURCHAN
Loch Mudle
B8007
Kilchoan
MINGARY CASTLE
ARDNAMURCHAN NATURAL HISTORY VISITOR CENTRE
Ormsaigmore
Ormsaigbeg
An Acairseid
Kilchoan Bay
528 BEN HIANT
19
Glenborrodale
Ardslignish
Eilean Mor
Maclean's Nose
(SUMMER ONLY) 0:35
Oronsay
Ardmore Bay
Ardmore Pt.
Bloody Bay
Auliston Pt.
Quinish Pt.
Glengorm Castle
MULL AND IONA FOLKLORE MUSEUM
TOBERMORY
Tobermory
Calve I.
Rubha an Aird
Quinish
Mishnish
TOBERMORY DISTILLERY
Caliach Pt.
Sunipol
S AIRDE BEINN 292
Drimnin
Bonnavoulin
Upper Druimfin
Mornish
MULL LITTLE THEATRE
Penmore Mill
Achnadrish
OBAN 1:45
Calgary
Dervaig
THE OLD BYRE
Calgary Bay
SPEINNE MOR 444
AROS
A848
Rhemore
Ardnacross
Killundine
Treshnish Pt.
Ensay
342 CARN MOR
Loch Frisa
Lettermore
SOUND OF
Haunn
Bellart
10
B8073
Achnacraig
Rubh a'Chaoil
Burg
Kilninian
Achleck
Aros
Aros Mains
Rubha Mor
23
Fanmore
390
Crannich
Treshnish Isles
Fladda
Ballygown
LOCH TUATH
424 BEINN NA DRISE
Salen
Eilean Dioghlum
B8035
Killiechronan
Killbeg
Lunga
Gometra
Bearnus
Laggan Bay
Lagganulva
Kellan
Gruline
313
Oskamull
B8073
412
Ulva
Ulva House
Killiemor
ISLE
Bac Mor
Sound of Ulva
Eorsa
Knock
LOCH NA KEAL
Loch Bà
591 BEINN A'GHRAIG
Little Colonsay
Staffa
FINGAL'S CAVE
80
Inch Kenneth
80
Balnahard
17
Derryguaig
Glen Cannel

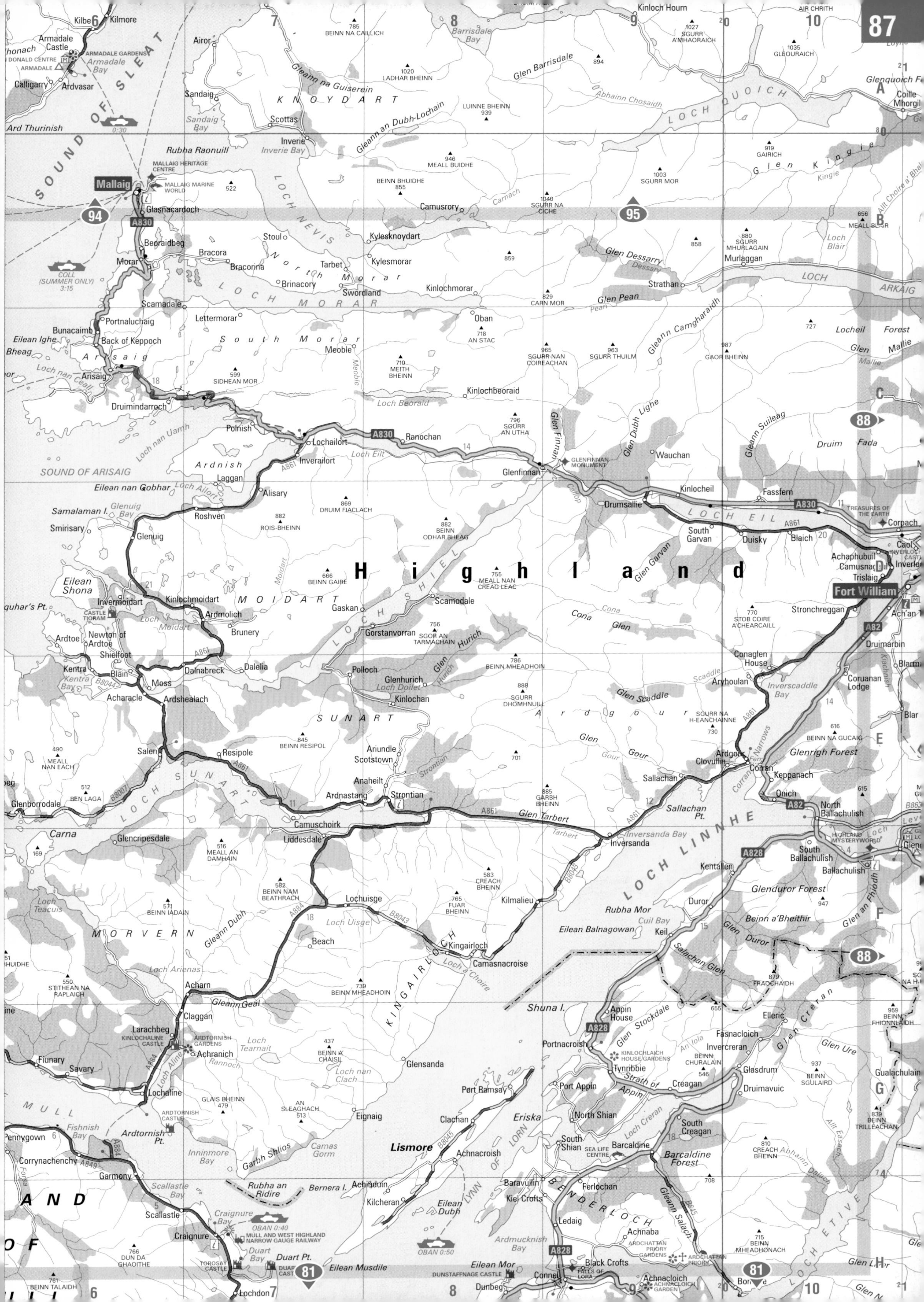

Kilbeg
Kilmore
Armadale Castle
Armadale Gardens
Armadale Bay
Clan Donald Centre
Armadale
Calligarry
Ardvasar
Ard Thurinish
Sound of Sleat
0:30
Airor
Sandaig
Sandaig Bay
Scottas
Inverie
Inverie Bay
Rubha Raonuill
Mallaig
Mallaig Heritage Centre
Mallaig Marine World
Glasnacardoch
A830
94
Beoraidbeg
Morar
Bracora
Bracorina
Coll (Summer only) 3:15
Scamadale
Portnaluchaig
Bunacaimb
Eilean Ighe
Bheag
Back of Keppoch
Arisaig
Loch nan Ceall
Druimindarroch
Loch nan Uamh
Sound of Arisaig
Polnish
Lochailort
Inverailort
Ardnish
Laggan
Eilean nan Gobhar
Loch Ailort
Alisary
Samalaman I.
Glenuig Bay
Roshven
Smirisary
Glenuig
Eilean Shona
Inversanda
Kinlochmoidart
Ardmolich
Moidart
Castle Tioram
Brunery
Ardtoe
Newton of Ardtoe
Shielfoot
Kentra
Kentra Bay
Blain
Moss
Dalnabreck
Dalelia
Acharacle
Ardshealach
Salen
Resipole
Loch Sunart
Glenborrodale
Ben Laga
Meall nan Each
Carna
Glencripesdale
Morvern
Loch Teacuis
Sithean na Raplaich
Loch Arienas
Acharn
Claggan
Larachbeg
Kinlochaline Castle
Ardtornish Gardens
Achranich
Loch Aline
Lochaline
Fiunary
Savary
Mull
Fishnish Bay
Ardtornish Pt.
Ardtornish Castle
Pennygown
Corrynachenchy
Garmony
Scallastle Bay
Scallastle
Craignure
Craignure Bay
Oban 0:40
Mull and West Highland Narrow Gauge Railway
Torosay Castle
Duart Bay
Duart Pt.
Duart Castle
Lochdon
Dun da Ghaoithe
Beinn Talaidh
Inninmore Bay
Garbh Shlios
Rubha an Ridire
Bernera I.
Eilean Musdile
81
Knoydart
Gleann na Guiserein
Beinn na Caillich
Ladhar Bheinn
Luinne Bheinn
Barrisdale Bay
Glen Barrisdale
Kinloch Hourn
Sgurr a'Mhaoraich
Air Chrith
Gleouraich
Loch Quoich
Abhainn Chosaidh
Glenquoich Forest
Coille Mhorgil
Gleann an Dubh-Lochain
Meall Buidhe
Beinn Bhuidhe
Loch Nevis
Camusrory
Sgurr na Ciche
95
Sgurr Mor
Gairich
Glen Kingie
Meall Blair
Loch Blair
Stoul
Kylesknoydart
Tarbet
Kylesmorar
Brinacory
North Morar
Swordland
Loch Morar
Kinlochmorar
Glen Dessarry
Sgurr Mhurlagain
Murlaggan
Strathan
Loch Arkaig
Glen Pean
Carn Mor
Lettermorar
Oban
An Stac
South Morar
Meoble
Meith Bheinn
Sidhean Mor
Sgurr nan Coireachan
Sgurr Thuilm
Gleann Camgharaidh
Gaor Bheinn
Locheil Forest
Glen Mallie
Loch Beoraid
Kinlochbeoraid
Sgurr an Utha
Glen Finnan
Glen Dubh Lighe
Gleann Suileag
Druim Fada
88
Ranochan
Loch Eilt
Glenfinnan
Glenfinnan Monument
Wauchan
Kinlocheil
Fassfern
Drumsallie
Loch Eil
South Garvan
Duisky
Blaich
Treasures of the Earth
Corpach
Caol
Inverlochy Castle
Achaphubuil
Camusnagaul
Trislaig
Fort William
Druim Fiaclach
Rois-Bheinn
Beinn Odhar Bheag
Highland
Loch Shiel
Beinn Gaire
Meall nan Creag Leac
Glen Garvan
Gaskan
Scamodale
Gorstanvorran
Sgor an Tarmachain
Glen Hurich
Cona Glen
Stob Coire a'Chearcaill
Stronchreggan
Ach'an
A82
Druimarbin
Polloch
Glenhurich
Loch Doilet
Kinlochan
Beinn Mheadhoin
Sgurr Dhomhnuill
Ardgour
Glen Scaddle
Conaglen House
Aryhoulan
Inverscaddle Bay
Coruanan Lodge
Sunart
Beinn Resipol
Ariundle
Scotstown
Anaheilt
Strontian
Ardnastang
Glen Gour
Garbh Bheinn
Sgurr na h-Eanchainne
Ardgour
Clovullin
Corran
Corran Narrows
Glenrigh Forest
Keppanach
Onich
North Ballachulish
Beinn na Gucaig
Sallachan
Sallachan Pt.
Glen Tarbert
A861
Camuschoirk
Liddesdale
Loch Linnhe
Highland Mysteryworld
South Ballachulish
Ballachulish
Meall an Damhain
Beinn nam Beathrach
Beinn Iadain
Gleann Dubh
Lochuisge
Loch Uisge
B8043
Creach Bheinn
Fuar Bheinn
Kilmalieu
Rubha Mor
Cuil Bay
Kentallen
A828
Glenduror Forest
Duror
Beinn a'Bheithir
Glen an Fhiodh
Eilean Balnagowan
Keil
Glen Duror
Salachan Glen
Beach
Kingairloch
Camasnacroise
Loch a'Choire
Beinn Mheadhoin
Gleann Geal
Shuna I.
Appin House
Glen Stockdale
Elleric
Glen Creran
Fraochaidh
Beinn Fhionnlaidh
Loch Tearnait
Beinn a'Chaisil
Glensanda
Loch nan Clach
Glais Bheinn
An Sleaghach
Eignaig
Port Ramsay
Clachan
Lismore
B8045
Achnacroish
Achinduin
Kilcheran
Eilean Dubh
Lynn of Lorn
Portnacroish
Kinlochlaich House Gardens
Tynribbie
Strath of Appin
Port Appin
North Shian
Eriska
South Shian
Sea Life Centre
Barcaldine
Loch Creran
Fasnacloich
Invercreran
Beinn Churalain
Glasdrum
Creagan
Druimavuic
South Creagan
Barcaldine Forest
Glen Ure
Beinn Sgulaird
Gualachulain
Beinn Trilleachan
Creach Bheinn
Baravullin
Kiel Crofts
Ferlochan
Benderloch
Ledaig
Achnaba
Ardchattan Priory
Ardchattan Priory Gardens
Glen Salach
Beinn Mheadhonach
Loch Etive
Ardmucknish Bay
Oban 0:50
Eilean Mor
Dunstaffnage Castle
Dunbeg
Connel
Falls of Lora
Black Crofts
Achnacloich
Achnacloich Garden
Bonawe
Glen Noe

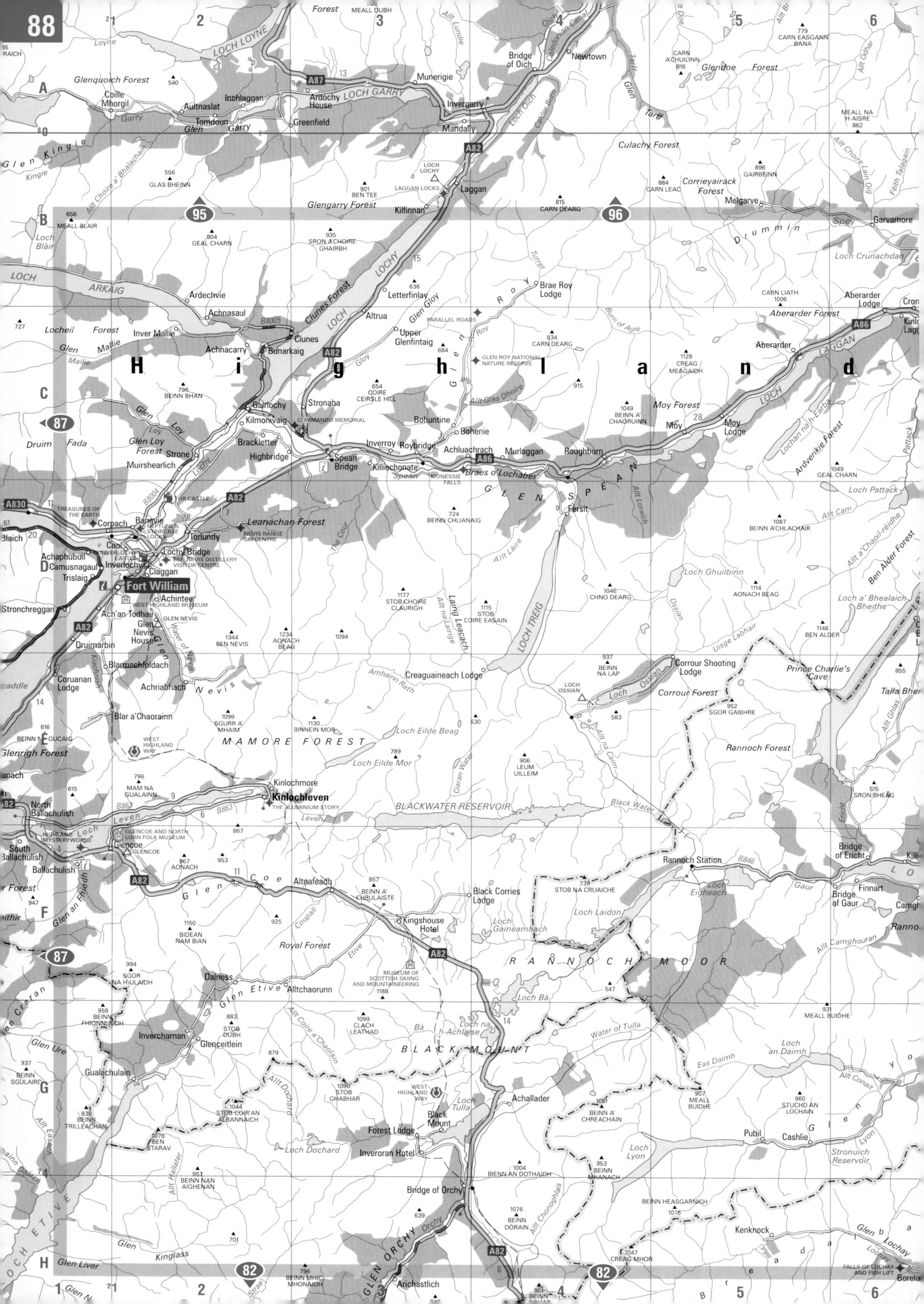

LOCH LOYNE
Glenquoich Forest
Coille Mhorgil
Aultnaslat
Inchlaggan
Ardochy House
LOCH GARRY
Tomdoun
Glen Garry
Greenfield
Munerigie
A87
Bridge of Oich
Newtown
Caledonian Canal
Invergarry
Mandally
Loch Oich
Glendoe Forest
CARN A'CHUILINN 816
779 CARN EASGANN BANA
MEALL NA H-AISRE 862
Culachy Forest
Glen Kingie
556 GLAS BHEINN
LOCH LOCHY
LAGGAN LOCKS
Laggan
901 BEN TEE
Glengarry Forest
Kilfinnan
A82
95
96
815 CARN DEARG
884 CARN LEAC
Corrieyairack Forest
896 GAIRBEINN
Melgarve
Garvamore
Spey
Drummin
Loch Crunachdan
656 MEALL BLAIR
Loch Blàir
804 GEAL CHARN
935 SRON A'CHOIRE GHAIRBH
LOCH ARKAIG
Ardechvie
Achnasaul
Clunes Forest
LOCH LOCHY
636 Letterfinlay
Altrua
Glen Gloy
Brae Roy Lodge
PARALLEL ROADS
Glen Roy
Burn of Agie
CARN LIATH 1006
Aberarder Lodge
Aberarder Forest
727
Locheil Forest
Glen Mallie
Inver Mallie
B8005
Clunes
Achnacarry
Bunarkaig
Upper Glenfintaig
684
834 CARN DEARG
GLEN ROY NATIONAL NATURE RESERVE
1128 CREAG MEAGAIDH
Aberarder
A86
LOCH LAGGAN
H i g h l a n d
796 BEINN BHAN
654 COIRE CEIRSLE HILL
915
87
Glen Loy
Gairlochy
Stronaba
Kilmonivaig
COMMANDO MEMORIAL
Bohuntine
Bohenie
Allt Glas Dhoire
1049 BEINN A' CHAORUINN
Moy Forest
Moy
Moy Lodge
Druim Fada
Glen Loy Forest
Strone
Brackletter
Highbridge
Spean Bridge
Inverroy
Roybridge
Achluachrach
Murlaggan
Roughburn
Braes o'Lochaber
Killiechonate
MONESSIE FALLS
GLEN SPEAN
Muirshearlich
Ardverikie Forest
1049 GEAL CHARN
Loch Pattack
A830
TREASURES OF THE EARTH
Corpach
Banavie
NEPTUNE'S STAIRCASE LOCKS
TOR CASTLE
B8004
Leanachan Forest
NEVIS RANGE SKI CENTRE
Torlundy
724 BEINN CHLIANAIG
Fersit
Allt Loraich
1087 BEINN A'CHLACHAIR
Caol
Achaphubuil
Camusnagaul
Trislaig
INVERLOCHY CASTLE
Lochy Bridge
BEN NEVIS DISTILLERY VISITOR CENTRE
Inverlochy
Claggan
Fort William
Achintee
WEST HIGHLAND MUSEUM
Stronchreggan
Ach'an Todhair
GLEN NEVIS
Glen Nevis House
Water of Nevis
Allt Laire
Loch Ghuilbinn
1046 CHNO DEARG
1114 AONACH BEAG
Ben Alder Forest
Loch a' Bhealaich Bheithe
1177 STOB CHOIRE CLAURIGH
Lairig Leacach
1115 STOB COIRE EASAIN
LOCH TREIG
Ossian
1148 BEN ALDER
Druimarbin
1344 BEN NEVIS
1234 AONACH BEAG
1094
Uisge Labhair
Blarmachfoldach
Coruanan Lodge
Achriabhach
Nevis
Amhainn Rath
Creaguaineach Lodge
937 BEINN NA LAP
Corrour Shooting Lodge
Prince Charlie's Cave
855
LOCH OSSIAN
Loch Ossian
Corrour Forest
952 SGOR GAIBHRE
Talla Bheith
Blar a'Chaorainn
1099 SGURR A' MHAIM
1130 BINNEIN MOR
630
583
Loch Eilde Beag
616 BEINN NA GUCAIG
Glenrigh Forest
WEST HIGHLAND WAY
MAMORE FOREST
789
Loch Eilde Mor
906 LEUM UILLEIM
Allt na Caim
Rannoch Forest
Caran Water
796 MAM NA GUALAINN
615
Kinlochmore
Kinlochleven
THE ALUMINIUM STORY
515 SRON BHEAG
North Ballachulish
B863
Loch Leven
BLACKWATER RESERVOIR
Black Water
HIGHLAND MYSTERYWORLD
GLENCOE AND NORTH LORN FOLK MUSEUM
867
South Ballachulish
Glencoe
GLENCOE
Ballachulish
967 AONACH
953
Glen Coe
Altnafeadh
857 BEINN A' CHRULAISTE
Rannoch Station
B846
Bridge of Ericht
Loch Eigheach
Gaur
Finnart
Bridge of Gaur
739 STOB NA CRUAICHE
Black Corries Lodge
947
Glen an Fhiodh
1150 BIDEAN NAM BIAN
925
Coupall
Kingshouse Hotel
Loch Laidon
Loch Gaineamhach
Allt Camghouran
Royal Forest
Etive
MUSEUM OF SCOTTISH SKIING AND MOUNTAINEERING
RANNOCH MOOR
994 SGOR NA H-ULAIDH
Dalness
Glen Etive
Alltchaorunn
1188
547
Glen Creran
959 BEINN FHIONNLAIDH
883 STOB DUBH
1099 CLACH LEATHAD
Loch Bà
Loch na h-Achlaise
931 MEALL BUIDHE
Water of Tulla
Inverchannan
Glenceitlein
Allt Coire a'Chaolain
BLACK MOUNT
Loch an Daimh
Glen Ure
879
Eas Daimh
937 BEINN SGULAIRD
Gualachulain
Allt Dochard
1090 STOB GHABHAR
Achallader
907 MEALL BUIDHE
Allt Conait
960 STUCHD AN LOCHAIN
Glen Lyon
1081 BEINN A' CHREACHAIN
839 BEINN TRILLEACHAN
1044 STOB COIR'AN ALBANNAICH
Black Mount
Loch Tulla
Forest Lodge
Pubil
Cashlie
Allt Easach
1078 BEN STARAV
Loch Dochard
Inveroran Hotel
Loch Lyon
Stronuich Reservoir
953 BEINN MHANACH
1004 BIENN AN DOTHAIDH
957 BEINN NAN AIGHENAN
Allt Hallater
Bridge of Orchy
LOCH ETIVE
BEINN HEASGARNICH 1076
639
1076 BEINN DORAIN
Allt Chonoghlais
Kenknock
Glen Lochay
Breadalbane
701
Glen Kinglass
GLEN ORCHY
1047 CREAG MHOR
Glen Liver
82
796 BEINN MHIC MHONAIDH
Arichastlich
FALLS OF LOCHAY AND FISH LIFT
Borelan

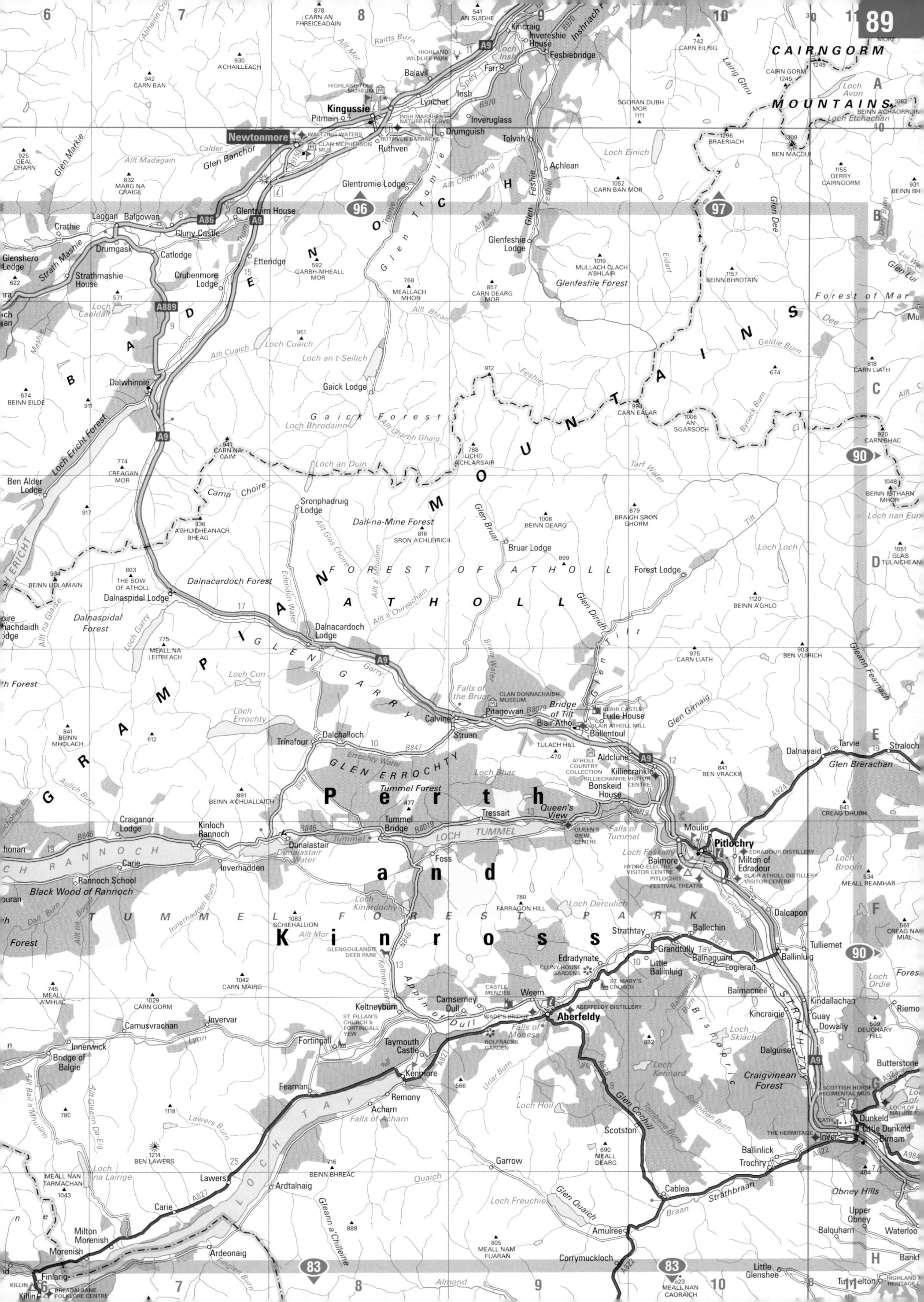
CAIRNGORM
MOUNTAINS
GRAMPIAN
MOUNTAINS
BADENOCH
FOREST OF ATHOLL
ATHOLL
GLEN GARRY
GLEN ERROCHTY
Perth and Kinross
TUMMEL FOREST PARK
LOCH TUMMEL
LOCH RANNOCH
LOCH TAY
STRATH TAY
Kincraig
Inshriach Forest
Invereshie House
Feshiebridge
Loch Insh
Balavil
Lynchat
Insh
Farr
Kingussie
Pitmain
Inverughlass
Drumguish
Tolvah
Newtonmore
Ruthven
Achlean
Glen Banchor
Glentromie Lodge
Glen Tromie
Glen Feshie
Glenfeshie Lodge
Glenfeshie Forest
Laggan
Balgowan
Crathie
Glentruim House
Cluny Castle
Drumgask
Catlodge
Glenshero Lodge
Strath Mashie
Strathmashie House
Crubenmore Lodge
Etteridge
Loch Cuaich
Loch an t-Seilich
Gaick Lodge
Gaick Forest
Loch Bhrodainn
Dalwhinnie
Loch Ericht Forest
Ben Alder Lodge
Loch an Duin
Cama Choire
Sronphadruig Lodge
Dail-na-Mine Forest
Glen Bruar
Bruar Lodge
Forest Lodge
Glen Tilt
Dalnacardoch Forest
Dalnaspidal Lodge
Dalnaspidal Forest
Dalnacardoch Lodge
Loch Con
Loch Errochty
Calvine
Pitagowan
Struan
Bridge of Tilt
Blair Atholl
Lude House
Ballentoul
Glen Girnaig
Dalchalloch
Trinafour
Aldclune
Killiecrankie
Bonskeid House
Tressait
Queen's View
Loch Bhac
Tummel Forest
Tummel Bridge
Dunalastair
Kinloch Rannoch
Craiganour Lodge
Carie
Rannoch School
Black Wood of Rannoch
Inverhadden
Foss
Moulin
Pitlochry
Balmore
Milton of Edradour
Dalnavaid
Tarvie
Straloch
Glen Brerachan
Dalcapon
Strathtay
Ballechin
Grandtully
Balnaguard
Logierait
Ballinluig
Tulliemet
Edradynate
Little Ballinluig
Weem
Camserney
Dull
Aberfeldy
Keltneyburn
Appin of Dull
Fortingall
Taymouth Castle
Kenmore
Fearnan
Remony
Acharn
Falls of Acharn
Camusvrachan
Invervar
Innerwick
Bridge of Balgie
Glen Lyon
Lawers
Ardtalnaig
Carie
Milton Morenish
Morenish
Ardeonaig
Finlarig
Killin
Glen Quaich
Loch Freuchie
Amulree
Corrymuckloch
Garrow
Glen Cochill
Scotston
Cablea
Strathbraan
Ballinlick
Trochry
Kindallachan
Kincraigie
Guay
Dowally
Dalguise
Craigvinean Forest
Dunkeld
Little Dunkeld
Birnam
Inver
Butterstone
Obney Hills
Upper Obney
Balquharn
Waterloo
Little Glenshee
Tullybelton
Bishopric
CAIRN GORM 1245
BEN MACDUI 1309
BRAERIACH 1296
BEN LAWERS 1214
SCHIEHALLION 1083
BEINN A'GHLO 1120
BEINN DEARG 1008
CARN NAN GABHAR
Forest of Mar
Dee
A9
A86
A889
A827
A826
A822
A823
A924
B846
B847
B8019
B8079
B970
B9150
96
97
90
83

CAIRNGORM MOUNTAINS
GRAMPIAN
BRAEMAR
GLEN AVON
Forest of Glenavon
THE BRUACH 715
BYNACK MORE 1090
Loch Avon
Loch Etchachan
BEINN A'CHAORRUINN 1082
BEN AVON 1171
Loch Builg
BROWN COW HILL 823
MORVEN 871
Migvie
Coynach
Dounesi
Logie Coldstone
Tarland
TOMNAVERIE STONE CIRCLE
Milton of Logie
Glendavan Ho
Ordie
SCAR HILL 299
Loch Davan
Loch Kinord
BURN O VAT
Dinnet
Muir of Dinnet
Glen Fenzie
Gairnshiel Lodge
Lary
Candacraig
GEALLAIG HILL 743
Glen Gairn
Coilacriech
Culsh
Bridge of Gairn
Milton of Tullich
Glascorrie
Ballater
Glen Tanar House
BRAELOIN INTERPRETIVE CENTRE
CARN EAS 1089
CULARDOCH 900
DERRY CAIRNGORM 1155
BEINN BHREAC 931
Derry Burn
Bush Crathie
CRATHIE CHURCH
Crathie
Littlemill
MCEWAN GALLERY
House of Glenmuick
BALMORAL CASTLE AND GARDENS
Inver
Easter Balmoral
CARN NA DROCHAIDE 818
BRAEMAR CASTLE
Invercauld House
Braemar
BRAEMAR HIGHLAND HERITAGE CENTRE
Allanaquoich
KINDROCHIT CASTLE
Mar Lodge
Glen Lui
Lui Water
Claybokie
Tomintoul
Forest of Mar
Ballochbuie Forest
Birkhall
Mill of Sterin
Glen Tanar
Water of Tanar
CLACHAN YELL 526
Forest of Glen Tanar
Aucholzie
Glen Gelder
LINN OF MUICK WATERFALL
Glen Muick
Muir
Linn of Dee
Inverey
Auchallater
BALMORAL FOREST
COCK CAIRN 727
HILL OF CAT 742
MOUNT KEEN 939
CARN LIATH 818
Glen Ey
Ey Burn
Allt Connie
Callater Burn
LOCHNAGAR 1150
CONACHCRAIG 850
GLENMUICK VISITOR CENTRE
Spittal of Glenmuick
FASHEILACH 721
Glen Mark
Water of Mark
Burn of Branny
Water of Tarf
Loch Callater
Glen Callater
Baddoch
Dubh Loch
Glas-allt Shiel
Loch Muick
CAIRN BANNOCH 1012
CARN BHAC 920
Glen Lee
Invermark Lodge
MONAWEE 696
Auchronie
Tarfside
BROAD CAIRN 998
AN SOCACH 939
Clunie Water
CARN AN TUIRC 1019
TOLMOUNT 958
Water of Unich
Loch Lee
Inchgrundle
BEINN IUTHARN MHOR 1048
Loch Vrotachan
Loch nan Eun
THE CAIRNWELL 933
LAIR OF ALDARARIE 832
Glen Effock
Glen Doll
Devil's Elbow
GLAS MAOL 1068
CAENLOCHAN NATIONAL NATURE RESERVE
GLENDOLL
Glendoll Lodge
Glendoll Forest
Braedownie
MUCKLE CAIRN 826
CRUYS 741
Caenlochan Forest
Loch Brandy
Water of Saughs
GLAS TULAICHEAN 1051
FINALTY HILL 905
Isla
WEST KNOCK 691
DRIESH 947
Clova
GLEN CLOVA
BEN GULABIN 806
758
WHITE HILL 778
Hunthill Lodge
Glenlochsie
MONAMEANACH 808
Wheen
Angus
Spittal of Glenshee
BEN VUIRICH 903
Gleann Fearnach
BEN EARB 801
Auchavan
Loch Beanie
Kilburn
Rottal
FINBRACKS 756
Glen Prosen
Glenprosen Lodge
BADENDUN HILL 740
Glen Shee
MEALL UAINE 794
DUCHRAY HILL 702
Balnaboth
Glenprosen Village
512
Clachnabrain
AULD DARKNEY 545
Dalnaglar Castle
Meikle Forter
Glenisla Forest
611
Glenmoy
Tarvie
Straloch
Dalnavaid
Glen Brerachan
Enochdhu
Cray
Folda
MOUNT BLAIR 744
Glenhead Farm
Backwater Res.
Easter Lednathie
Glenogil
Auchnacree
South Esk
Ashintully Castle
Brewlands Bridge
Kirkton of Glenisla
Glenquiech
Ogil
Fern
CREAG DHUBH 641
Kirkmichael
Blacklunans
STRATHARDLE
CAT LAW 668
Horniehaugh
Dykehead
Newmill of Inshewan
Bellaty
CREIGH HILL 497
Balintore
Pearsie
Cortachy
Memus
Tannadice
CAIRN GIBBS 520
Dykends
Balloch
Inverquharity
Murthill
Finavon
Perth and Kinross
MEALL REAMHAR 534
KNOCK OF BALMYLE 444
Black Water
Forest of Alyth
MILE HILL 409
Shielhill
Oathlaw
Ballintuim
Loch of Lintrathen
PEEL FARM TRAIL
Bridgend of Lintrathen
Kirkton of Kingoldrum
LOCH OF KINNORDY NATURE RESERVE
Kinnordy
Northmuir
Kirriemuir
BARRIE'S HOUSE
CREAG NAM MIAL 561
Ardle
BALDUFF HILL 425
REEKIE LINN WATERFALL
Bridge of Craigisla
Carse Gray
Tulliemet
Ballinluig
Netherton
Tullymurdoch
Westmuir
Mosside
Lunanhead
RESTENNETH PRIORY
Blackcraig Forest
Forest of Clunie
Loch Ordie
Bamff
Kirkton of Airlie
Mains of Ballindarg
Padanaram
FORFAR LOCH
Forfar
Bridge of Cally
Craigton
Leys of Cossans
ST ORLAND'S STONE
Drumgley
Kindallachan
Loch Benachally
Cochrage Muir
Shanzie
Ruthven
Dean Water
Teuchatcroft
Kingsmuir
Guay
Riemore
Tullyfergus
Alyth
Ruthven House
EASSIE SCULPTURED STONE
Caldhame
Lownie Moor
Dowally
DEUCHARY HILL 509
Lornty Burn
Middleton
New Alyth
GLAMIS CASTLE
Glamis
Douglastown
Craichie
Riechip
Lornty
Westfields of Rattray
Balhary
Castleton
Thornton
Kirkton
KEATHBANK MILL
Butterstone
Forneth
Achalader
Blairgowrie
Kinloch
Rattray
Leitfie
MEIGLE MUSEUM
Balkeerie
Eassie
Charleston
ANGUS FOLK MUSEUM
Foffarty
Whigstre
SCOTTISH HORSE REGIMENTAL MUS.
Loch of Lowes
LOCH OF LOWES NATURE RESERVE
Concraigie
Loch of Clunie
Loch of Drumellie
Kinloch
Meigle
Kirkinch
Gateside
Inverarity
Dunkeld
Clunie
Craigie
Muirton of Ardblair
Rosemount
River Ericht
Arthurstone
Wester Denoon
ARK HILL 340
Milton
Kirkbuddo
Little Dunkeld
Snaigow House
Kirkton of Lethendy
Ardler
New Bigging
Newtyle
Nether Handwick
Gallowfauld
Inver
Birnam
Spittalfield
Lunan Burn
Keillor
SIDLAW HILLS
Delvine
Caputh
Coupar Angus
Coldstream
Obney Hills
Gellyburn
Meikleour
BEECH HEDGE
Kinclaven
Isla
Kettins
Markethill
Campmuir
Hallyburton House
Long Loch
Bonnyton
Kirkton of Auchterhouse
Balkemback
Tealing
Kirkton
Newbigging
Monikie
Upper Obney
Murthly
Muir of Thorn
Ardoch
Woodside
Burrelton
Leys
Lundie
Auchterhouse
Leoch
East March
Wellbank
Balquharn
Waterloo
Cargill
Pitcur
Bucklerheads
Drumsturdy
Bankfoot
Airntully
Whitefield
Dronley
Bridgefoot
Burnside of Duntrune
Kellas
Ordie Burn
Tullybelton
HIGHLAND MOTOR HERITAGE CENTRE
Stanley
Wester Tofts
Wolfhill
Saucher
Collace
KING'S SEAT 377
Littleton
Muirhead
Birkhill
CLATTO
Fowlis
CAMPERDOWN
TEMPLETON WOODS
Liff
Downfield
Fintry
Douglas &
SOUTERRAIN ARDESTIE
Baldovie
89
97
98
84
A9
A93
A924
A923
A926
A94
A984
A90
A928
A932
A92
A939
B976
B9119
B955
B951
B950
B954
B957
B9127
B961
B9099
B978

Aberdeenshire
Aberdeen
Collmuir
Craskins
Tornaveen
Comers
Echt
Garlogie
Cairnie
Elrick
Westhill
Kingswells
Findrack Ho.
Drumlasie
Midmar Forest
South Kirkton
Culsh Souterrain
Lumphanan
Peel Ring of Lumphanan
Milton of Auchinhove
Auchlossan
Coull
Hill of Fare
Burn of Corrichie
Landerberry
Redhill
Benthoul
West Cullerlie
Hardgate
Torphins
Milton of Campfield
Slug of Dess Falls
Mid Beltie
Hirn
Drum Castle
Peterculter
Mains of Drum
Aboyne
Kincardine O'Neil
Tillydrine
Brathens
Backhill of Trustach
Bridge of Canny
East Mains
Upper Lochton
The Neuk
Myrebird
Drumoak
Crathes Castle and Gardens
Banchory Museum
Woodside of Arbeadie
Crathes
Birsemore
Birse
Dee
Marywell
Burn of Cattie
Arbeadie
Deebank
Banchory
Bridge of Feugh
Auchattie
Blackhall Forest
Tom's Cairn
Tillygarmond
Carnferg
Finzean
Percie
Strachan
Forest of Birse
Allochan
Water of Feugh
Kirkton of Durris
Crossroads
Durris Forest
Cairn Mon Earn
Lochton
Woodlands
Denside
Upper Burnhaugh
Borrowfield
Netherley
Muirskie
Garrol Hill
Mongour
Mount Shade
Kerloch
Glendye Lodge
Bridge of Dye
Water of Dye
Water of Aven
Burn of Sheeoch
Cowie Water
Fetteresso Forest
Mergie
Union Cottage
Rickarton
Raedykes Roman Camp
Blacktop
Contlaw
Milton of Murtle
Milltimber
Bieldside
Cults
Craigton
Easter Ord
Mannofield
Gordon Highlanders Museum
Ruthrieston
Garthdee
Banchory Devenick
Charlestown
Kincorth
Nigg
Torry
Ferryhill
Satrosphere
Marischal Museum
Duthie Park Winter Gardens
Nigg Bay
Greg Ness
Cove Bay
Hare Ness
Kirkton of Maryculter
Auchlunies
Marywell
Findon Ness
Hillside
Findon
Auchlee
Portlethen
Downies
Cammachmore Bay
Cammachmore
Newtonhill
Cookney
Bridge of Muchalls
Muchalls
Garron Pt.
Cowie
Kirktown of Fetteresso
Tewel
Stonehaven
Tolbooth Museum
Carmont
Castle Haven
Dunnottar Castle
Thornyhive Bay
Burn of Tennet
Mount Battock
Glen Dye
Tannachie
New Mill
Drumtochty Forest
Mains of Dellavaird
Burns Family Memorials
Glenfarquhar Lodge
Drumlithie
Glenbervie
Fiddes
Barras
Mill of Uras
Crawton
Fowlsheugh Nature Reserve
Crawton Bay
Meluncart
Cairn o' Mount
Drumtochty Castle
Pitforthie
Roadside of Catterline
Catterline
Braidon Bay
Todhead Point
Arncross
The Retreat Glen Esk Folk Mus.
Millden Lodge
Strath Finella
Clatterin Bridge
Glensaugh
Auchenblae
Monboddo House
Mondynes
Brownmuir
East Cairnbeg
Fordoun
Parkneuk
Arbuthnott
Roadside of Kinneff
Kinneff
Grassic Gibbon Centre
Arbuthnott Church
Arbuthnott House Gardens
Mains of Allardice
Little John's Haven
Inverbervie
Bervie Bay
North Esk
Auchmull
Mains of Balnakettle
Fasque House
Fasque
Thainston
Fettercairn Distillery Visitor Centre
Fettercairn
Howe of the Mearns
Scotston
Hill of Wirren
Dalbog
Meikle Strath
Mains of Thornton
Bent
Laurencekirk
Tulloch
Witton
Gannochy
Inch of Arnhall
Garvock
Garvock Hill
Redford
Damside Garden Herbs & Arboretum
Gourdon
Benholm
Edzell Castle and Gardens
Sauchieburn
Luthermuir
Luther Water
Dykelands
Bridgend
Balfield
Dunlappie
Edzell
West Water
Johnshaven
Lyarblet
Brown Caterthun
White Caterthun
North Water Bridge
Marykirk
Ecclesgreig
Kirkton of Menmuir
Tigerton
Inchbare
Newtonmill
Pert
Craigo
Lochside
Morphie
St. Cyrus
Milton Ness
Logie Pert
Logie
Belliehill
Mains of Balhall
Lochty
Little Brechin
Keithock
Muirton of Ballochy
Pathhead
West Muir
Trinity
Hillside
Brechin
House of Dun
Dun
Kirkhill
Careston
Cathedral & Round Tower
Caledonian Railway
South Esk
Montrose Basin Nature Reserve Visitor Centre
Montrose
Museum and Art Gallery
Scurdie Ness
William Lamb Memorial Studio
Aldbar Castle
Bridge of Dun
Montrose Basin
Netherton
Mains of Melgund
Middle Drums
Kinnaird Castle
Barnhead
Inchbraoch
Ferryden
Aberlemno Sculptured Stones
Aberlemno
Farnell
Bonnyton
Maryton
Kirkton of Craig
Montreathmont Forest
Carcary
Long Craig
Pitkennedy
Fishtown of Usan
Rossie Moor
Westerton
Dunninald
Montreathmont Moor
Boddin Pt.
Turin
Braehead of Lunan
Rescobie
Dubton
Bolshan
Lunan
Lunan Bay
Reswallie
Balgavies
Glasterlaw
Milldens
Guthrie
Kinnell
Redcastle
Letham
Pitmuies
House of Pitmuies Garden
Friockheim
Boysack
Inverkeilor
Lunan Water
Chapelton
Lang Craig
Idvies
Leysmill
Ethie Mains
Red Head
Cauldcots
Ethie Castle
Tulloes
Drunkendub
Letham Grange
Mosston
Colliston
Auchmithie
Greystone
Redford
Meg's Craig
St. Vigeans
Marywell
St Vigeans Museum
Hayshead
Cliffburn
The Deil's Heid
Hayhillock
Carmyllie
Denhead of Arbilot
Arbroath Abbey
Crombie
Arbirlot
Arbroath
Signal Tower Museum
Kirkton of Monikie
Balmirmer
Wormiehills
Craigton
Monikie Burn
Salmond's Muir
Carlungie Souterrain
Muirdrum
East Haven
Newbigging
Panbride
Barry Mill
Barry
Carnoustie
Mains of Ardestie
A90
A92
A93
A94
A930
A932
A933
A934
A935
A957
B9119
B9125
B977
B993
B976
B974
B979
B9077
B966
B967
B9120
B965
B961
B9113
B9134
B9127
B9128
B978
99
85

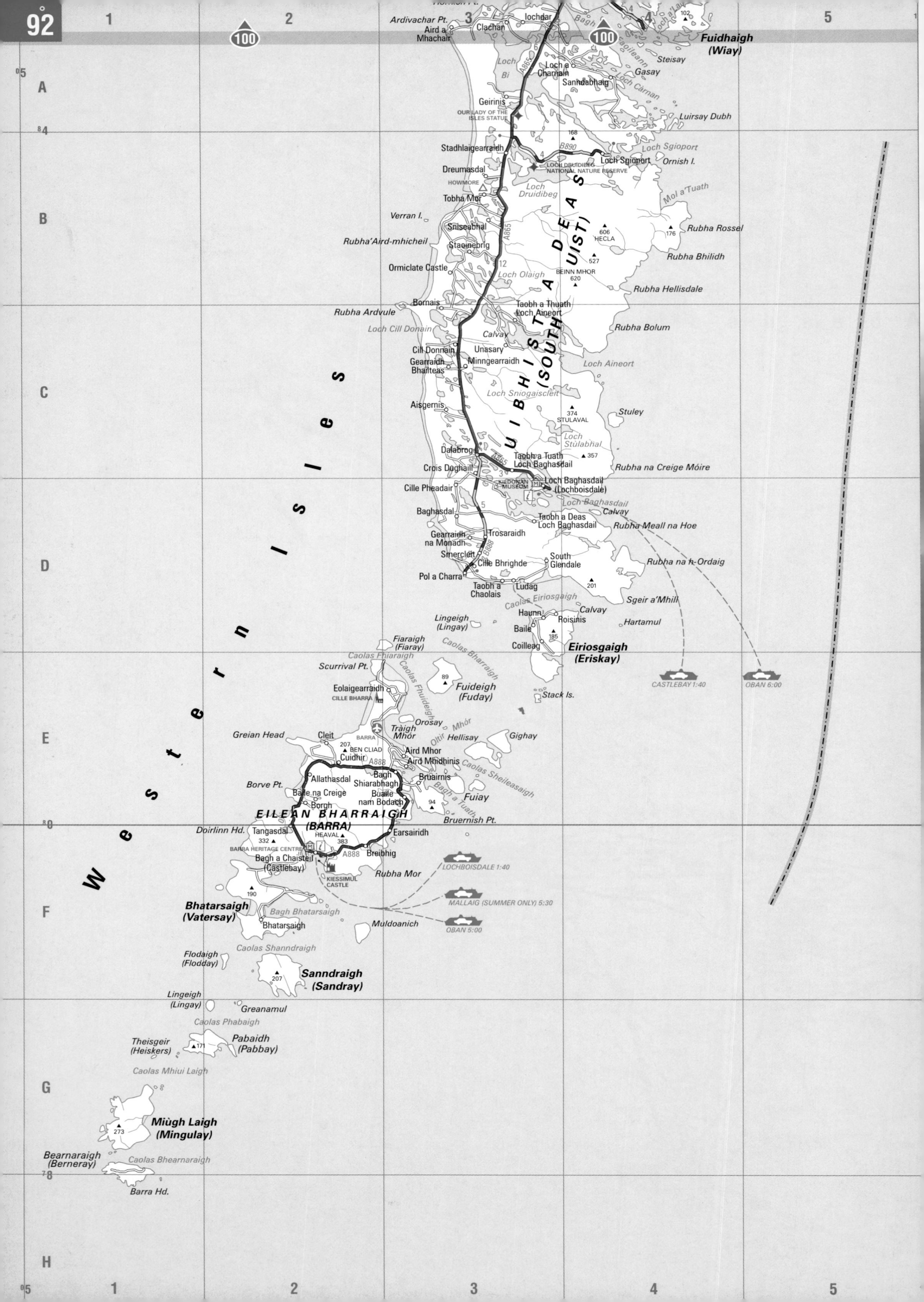

Western Isles
Uibhist a Deas (South Uist)
Fuidhaigh (Wiay)
Ardivachar Pt.
Aird a Mhachair
Clachan
Iochdar
Steisay
Gasay
Loch Càrnan
Loch a Charnain
Sanndabhaig
Loch Bì
Geirinis
Our Lady of the Isles Statue
Luirsay Dubh
Stadhlaigearraidh
Loch Sgioport
Ornish I.
Dreumasdal
Loch Druidibeg National Nature Reserve
Howmore
Loch Druidibeg
Tobha Mor
Mol a'Tuath
Verran I.
Sniseabhal
Rubha'Aird-mhicheil
Staoinebrig
606 Hecla
Rubha Rossel
Rubha Bhilidh
Ormiclate Castle
Loch Olaigh
Beinn Mhor 620
Rubha Hellisdale
Bornais
Rubha Ardvule
Taobh a Tuath Loch Aineort
Loch Cill Donain
Rubha Bolum
Calvay
Cill Donnain
Unasary
Gearraidh Bhailteas
Minngearraidh
Loch Aineort
Loch Sniogaiscleit
Aisgernis
374 Stulaval
Stuley
Loch Stùlabhal
Dalabrog
Taobh a Tuath Loch Baghasdail
Crois Dughaill
Rubha na Creige Móire
Kildonan Museum
Loch Baghasdail (Lochboisdale)
Cille Pheadair
Baghasdal
Taobh a Deas Loch Baghasdail
Rubha Meall na Hoe
Gearraidh na Monadh
Trosaraidh
Smercleit
Cille Bhrighde
South Glendale
Rubha na h-Ordaig
Pol a Charra
Taobh a Chaolais
Ludag
Caolas Eiriosgaigh
Sgeir a'Mhill
Lingeigh (Lingay)
Haunn
Roisinis
Hartamul
Baile
Coilleag
Eiriosgaigh (Eriskay)
Fiaraigh (Fiaray)
Caolas Fhiaraigh
Caolas Bharraigh
Scurrival Pt.
Fuideigh (Fuday)
Castlebay 1:40
Oban 6:00
Eolaigearraidh
Cille Bharra
Stack Is.
Caolas Fhuideigh
Orosay
Traigh Mhór
Oltir Mhór
Hellisay
Gighay
Greian Head
Cleit
Barra
Ben Cliad
Cuidhir
Aird Mhor
Aird Mhidhinis
Caolas Sheileasaigh
Allathasdal
Bagh Shiarabhagh
Bruairnis
Borve Pt.
Baile na Creige
Buaile nam Bodach
Fuiay
Borgh
Bagh a Tuath
Eilean Bharraigh (Barra)
Bruernish Pt.
Doirlinn Hd.
Tangasdal
Heaval 383
Earsairidh
Barra Heritage Centre
Bagh a Chaisteil (Castlebay)
Breibhig
Lochboisdale 1:40
Rubha Mor
Kiessimul Castle
Mallaig (summer only) 5:30
Bhatarsaigh (Vatersay)
Bagh Bhatarsaigh
Bhatarsaigh
Muldoanich
Oban 5:00
Flodaigh (Flodday)
Caolas Shanndraigh
Sanndraigh (Sandray)
Lingeigh (Lingay)
Greanamul
Caolas Phabaigh
Theisgeir (Heiskers)
Pabaidh (Pabbay)
Caolas Mhiui Laigh
Miùgh Laigh (Mingulay)
Bearnaraigh (Berneray)
Caolas Bhearnaraigh
Barra Hd.

6
7
8
9
10
101
Moonen Bay
Ramasaig
Lonmore
Roskhill
HEALABHAL MHOR 468
A'CHEARCAILL 266
Uigshader
Drumuie
Glengrasco
Achachork
Portree
Torvaig
Hoe Rape
Hoe Point
Macleod's Tables
488 HEALABHAL BHEAG
Roag
Vatten
Orbost
Harlosh
Balmore
Loch Varkasaig
Loch Caroy
Ose
A863
ISLAND OF SKYE
Loch Connan
B885
Snizort
Shulishaderbeg
SKYE HERITAGE CENTRE
Heatherfield
417
Penifiler
Glenmore
Mugeary
A87
Conordan
B883
Geodha Mor
Harlosh I.
Tarner I.
Ullinish
Bracadale
Struan
Coillore
Loch Duagrich
Tungadal
Loch Bracadale
Wiay
Idrigill Point
Oronsay
Portnalong
Fiskavaig
Rubha nan Clach
439 ROINEVAL
Glen Varragill
Varragill
Upper Ollach
Gedintailor
BATTLE OF BRAES MONUMENT
The Braes
444 BEN LEE
94
Loch Harport
B8009
Fernilea
ARNAVAL 369
TALISKER DISTILLERY
Carbost
Drynoch
Merkadale
Drynoch
A863
Gleann Oraid
Talisker Bay
Talisker
Sligachan Hotel
Eynort
Glen Brittle Forest
Grula
459
445 BEINN BHREAC
Eynort
Loch Eynort
SGURR NAN GILLEAN 964
Glen Sligachan
736 MARSCO
SGURR A'GHREADAIDH 973
Glen Brittle
Brittle
GLENBRITTLE
CUILLIN HILLS
Glenbrittle House
992 SGURR ALASDAIR
Loch Coruisk
Bualintur
Loch Brittle
924 SGURR NAN EAG
Camasunary
Rubh an Dunain
Soay Sound
Soay
Loch Scavaig
Mol-chlach
PRINCE CHARLES'S
Eilean h-Airigh
The Minch
Canna
A'Chill
Garrisdale Pt.
Canna Harbour
Sanday
Rubha Shamhnan Insir
Kilmory
Sound of Canna
Guirdil Bay
388
Kilmory Glen
1:15
MALLAIG 2:45
Kinloch Glen
Rubha na Roinne
A'Bhrideanach
571 ORVAL
RÙM
Kinloch
KINLOCH CASTLE
Loch Scresort
MALLAIG 1:30
Rubha Port na Caranean
Schooner Pt.
Oigh-sgeir
Harris
Glen Harris
812 ASKIVAL
781 AINSHVAL
Rubha Sgorr an t-Snidhe
1:15
1:15
SOUND OF RÙM
Rubha nam Meirleach
86
Bay of Laig
Cleadale
Rubha an Fhasaidh
Eigg
Kildonnan
393 AN SGURR
Galmisdale
Eilean Chathastail
SOUND OF EIGG
Eilean nan Each
1:00
Port Mor
137
Muck
A
B
C
D
E
F
G
H

TROTTERNISH
Romesdal
719 THE STORR
OLD MAN OF STORR
Eyre
The Aird
Kensaleyre
Bernisdale
Haultin
Tote
Borve
Skeabost
Carbost
Uigshader
Drumuie
Achachork
Glengrasco
Shulishaderbeg
SKYE HERITAGE CENTRE
Portree
Torvaig
Heatherfield
Penifiler
413 BEN TIANAVAIG
Glenmore
Mugeary
Camastianavaig
Tianavaig Bay
Conordan
Lower Ollach
Upper Ollach
Glen Varragill
Gedintailor
BATTLE OF THE BRAES MONUMENT
The Braes
444 BEN LEE
Peinchorran
439 ROINEVAL
Drynoch
Merkadale
A863
Sconser
775 GLAMAIG
Sligachan Hotel
Loch Sligachan
Glen Brittle Forest
Grula
964 SGURR NAN GILLEAN
736 MARSCO
Glen Sligachan
973 SGURR A'GHREADAIDH
GLENBRITTLE
CUILLIN HILLS
Bualintur
Glenbrittle House
992 SGURR ALASDAIR
Loch Coruisk
Loch Brittle
924 SGURR NAN EAG
Camasunary
Strathaird
Kirkibost
Kilmarie
346 BEN MEABOST
Soay Sound
Soay
Loch Scavaig
Mol-chlach
Elgol
Glasnakille
PRINCE CHARLES'S CAVE
Eilean na h-Airde
Rubha na h-Easgainne
928 BLA BHEINN
Loch na Crèitheach
570 GLAS BHEINN MHOR
OLD SKYE CROFTER'S HOUSE
Luib
Loch Ainort
Dunan
Scalpay
Scalpay Ho.
Caolas Scalpay
RED HILLS
Torrin
Kilbride
Loch Slapin
Strath Suardal
B8083
301
Heast
SKYE SERPENTARIUM
Corry
Broadford Bay
Broadford
Harrapool
SKYE ENVIRONMENTAL CENTRE
Lower Breakish
Upper Breakish
Skulamus
A851
Guillamon I.
Pabay
Longay
Kyle of Lochalsh
Kyleakin
CASTLE MOIL
Badicaul
Erbusaig
Black Is.
Drumbuie
Duirinish
Plockton
Port Cam
Balmacara Square
Balmacara
LOCHALSH WOODLAND GARDEN
Kirkton
Auchertyre
Nostie
Ardelve
Dornie
Totaig
Glas Eilean
LOCH ALSH
Ardintoul Pt.
739 SGURR NA COINNICH
Glen Arroch
Allt Mòr
Kyle Rhea
Kylerhea
Letterfearn
603 BEINN A'CHUIRN
Bernera
Galltair
Glenelg Bay
BERNERA BARRACKS
Glenelg
610 BEN ASLAK
Eilanreach
GLENELG BROCHS
Balvraid
Kinloch
Drumfearn
Loch Eishort
Rubha Suisnish
Ord
Isleornsay
Duisdalemore
Ornsay
Sandaig Is.
(SUMMER ONLY) 2:00
Upper Sandaig
742 BEINN A'CHAPAILL
974 BEINN SGRITHEALL
BEINN NAN CAORACH 774
Arnisdale
Glen Arnisdale
Corran
LOCH HOURN
DUNSGIATH CASTLE
Tokavaig
Tarskavaig
Tarskavaig Pt.
Achnacloich
Camuscross
Teangue
KNOCK CASTLE
Knock Bay
Ferrindonald
Kilbeg
Kilmore
Rubha Ard Slisneach
Inverguseran
785 BEINN NA CAILLICH
Barrisdale Bay
713 DRUIM FA
Armadale Castle
CLAN DONALD CENTRE
ARMADALE GARDENS
ARMADALE
Armadale Bay
Glen Meadhonach
Rubha Charn nan Cearc
280
Calligarry
Ardvasar
Aird of Sleat
Ard Thurinish
SLEAT
SOUND OF SLEAT
Airor
1020 LADHAR BHEINN
Glen Ba
Gleann na Guiserein
Sandaig
KNOYDART
Sandaig Bay
Scottas
LUINNE BHEINN 939
Gleann an Dubh-Lochain
Inverie
Inverie Bay
Rubha Raonuill
946 MEALL BUIDHE
MALLAIG HERITAGE CENTRE
Mallaig
MALLAIG MARINE WORLD
522
BEINN BHUIDHE 855
Glasnacardoch
Camusrory
A830
LOCH NEVIS
Stoul
Kylesknoydart
Beoraidbeg
Bracora
Bracorina
Brinacory
Morar
North Morar
Tarbet
Kylesmorar
Swordland
Kinlochmorar
859
LOCH MORAR
Scamadale
Lettermorar
Oban
718 AN STAC
Portnaluchaig
Bunacaimb
Back of Keppoch
South Morar
Meoble
Eilean Ighe
Luinga Bheag
Luinga Mhor
Arisaig
Loch nan Ceall
599 SIDHEAN MOR
710 MEITH BHEINN
Kinlochbeoraid
Loch Beoraid
Druimindarroch
Loch nan Uamh
Polnish
796 SGURR
Point of Sleat
LOCHBOISDALE 3:30
CASTLEBAY 5:30
(SUMMER ONLY)
1:30
COLL (SUMMER ONLY) 3:15
CANNA 1:15
Rubha na Roinne
Loch Scresort
KINLOCH CASTLE
RÙM
Rubha Port na Caranean
812 ASKIVAL
SOUND OF RÙM
MUCK 1:15
1:15
Bay of Laig
Cleadale
Rubha an Fhasaidh
Eigg
Kildonnan
393 AN SGURR
Galmisdale
Eilean Chathastail
(SUMMER ONLY) 1:30
0:30
Eilean Garbh
Island of Rona
Eilean Tigh
Caol Rona
Garbh Eilean
Loch a' Sguirr
An Caol
Holm I.
Bearreraig Bay
Loch Leathan
Loch Fada
Eilean Fladday
254
Torran
Manish Pt.
Loch Arnish
Arnish
PRINCE CHARLES'S CAVE
392
Rubha na h Airde Glaise
BROCHEL CASTLE
Brochel
ISLAND OF RAASAY
Glame
385
Balmeanach
Balachuirn
Holoman Bay
443 DUN CAAN
Oskaig
RAASAY
Clachan
Raasay Ho.
Rubha na'Leac
Narrows of Raasay
Inverarish
North Fearns
Eyre Point
SUMMER ONLY
Caol Mòr
SOUND OF RAASAY
INNER SOUND
Highland
ISLE OF SKYE
MINGINISH
Kenmore
Ardheslaig
Inveralligin
Torridon Ho.
Torridon VISITOR CENTRE
Loch Shieldaig
Upper Loch Torridon
Kalnakill
Abhainn Chuaig
Lonbain
Allt na h-Eirigh
Shieldaig
Balgy
A896
Loch Gaineamhach
493 CROIC-BHEINN
Ben-damph F
439 BEN SHIELDAIG
Loch Damh
902 BEINN DAM
626 BEINN A'CHLACHAIN
Loch nan Eun
Loch Lundie
Glenshieldaig Forest
513
Applecross Forest
CHAPEL OF ST. MAELRUBHA
Applecross Ho.
Applecross Bay
Applecross
896 BEINN BHAN
Loch Coultrie
Camusteel
Camusterrach
Culduie
710 MEALL GORM
Sanachan
Ardarroch
Achintraid
Slumbay
Eilean na Bà
Toscaig
Loch Kishorn
Kishorn I.
395
Stromemore
Ardnarff
Ardaneaskan
Stromeferry
LOCH CARRON
Crowlin Islands
Caolas Mòr
Uags
An Dubh-aird
Eilean Mór
Achmore
Gleann Udalain
Allt-nan-sùgh

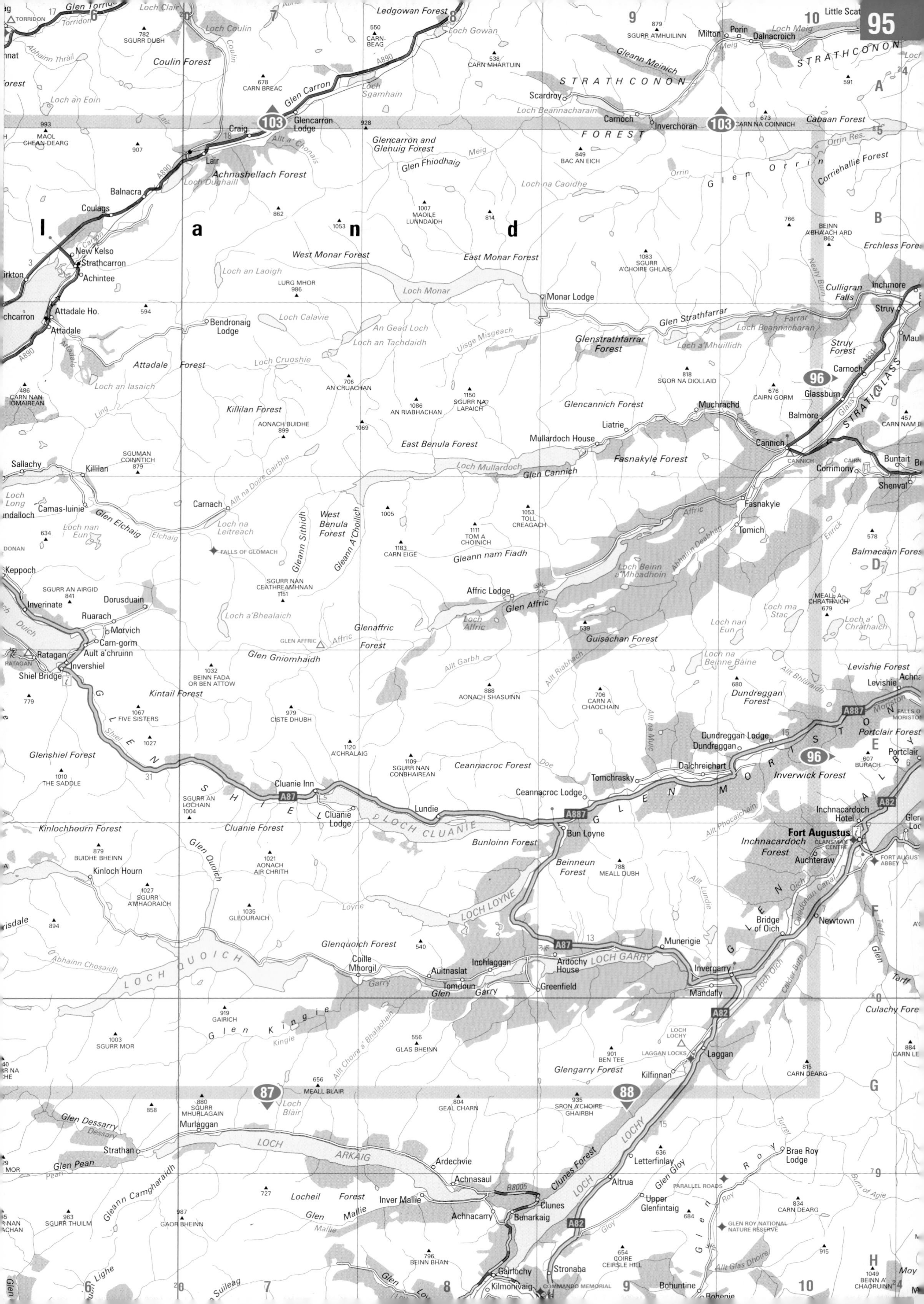
Glen Torridon
Torridon
Loch Clair
Ledgowan Forest
Little Scat
782
SGURR DUBH
550
CARN-BEAG
Loch Coulin
Loch Gowan
879
SGURR A'MHUILINN
Milton
Porin
Dalnacroich
Loch Meig
Meig
STRATHCONON
Abhainn Thràil
Coulin Forest
538
CARN MHARTUIN
Gleann Meinich
STRATHCONON
591
678
CARN BREAC
Glen Carron
Loch Sgamhain
Scardroy
Loch Beannacharain
Loch an Eoin
993
MAOL CHEAN-DEARG
Craig
Glencarron Lodge
928
Carnoch
Inverchoran
673
CARN NA COINNICH
Cabaan Forest
FOREST
Orrin Res.
Lair
Allt a' Chonais
907
Glencarron and Glenuig Forest
849
BAC AN EICH
Corriehallie Forest
Glen Fhiodhaig
Meig
Glen Orrin
Orrin
Achnashellach Forest
Loch Dughaill
Loch na Caoidhe
Balnacra
A890
Coulags
862
1007
MAOILE LUNNDAIDH
814
766
BEINN A'BHA'ACH ARD
862
l
a
n
d
1053
New Kelso
Strathcarron
Achintee
West Monar Forest
East Monar Forest
1083
SGURR A'CHOIRE GHLAIS
Erchless Forest
Loch an Laoigh
Loch Monar
LURG MHOR
986
Culligran Falls
Inchmore
Monar Lodge
Attadale Ho.
Attadale
594
Bendronaig Lodge
Loch Calavie
An Gead Loch
Loch an Tachdaidh
Uisge Misgeach
Glen Strathfarrar
Farrar
Loch Beannacharan
Struy
Glenstrathfarrar Forest
Loch a'Mhuillidh
Struy Forest
Attadale Forest
Loch Cruoshie
Carnoch
Loch an Iasaich
706
AN CRUACHAN
818
SGOR NA DIOLLAID
676
CAIRN GORM
Glassburn
486
CARN NAN IOMAIREAN
1086
AN RIABHACHAN
1150
SGURR NA LAPAICH
Glencannich Forest
Muchrachd
Balmore
STRATHGLASS
Killilan Forest
AONACH BUIDHE
899
1069
Liatrie
457
CARN NAM
East Benula Forest
Mullardoch House
Cannich
Fasnakyle Forest
SGUMAN COINNTICH
879
Sallachy
Killilan
Loch Mullardoch
Glen Cannich
CANNICH
CAIRN
Corrimony
Buntait
Shenval
Loch Long
Camas-luinie
Carnach
Allt na Doire Gairbhe
Glen Elchaig
Elchaig
Loch nan Eun
Loch na Leitreach
West Benula Forest
Gleann Sithidh
Gleann A'Chòilich
1005
1053
TOLL CREAGACH
Fasnakyle
Affric
Tomich
1111
TOM A CHOINICH
1183
CARN EIGE
Gleann nam Fiadh
634
DONAN
FALLS OF GLOMACH
578
Balmacaan Forest
Keppoch
SGURR AN AIRGID
841
SGURR NAN CEATHREAMHNAN
1151
Loch Beinn a'Mheadhoin
Abhainn Deabhag
Inverinate
Dorusduain
Affric Lodge
Glen Affric
MEALL A CHRATHAICH
679
Loch ma Stac
Ruarach
Morvich
Carn-gorm
Ault a'chruinn
Loch a'Bhealaich
Loch Affric
539
Loch nan Eun
Loch a' Chràthaich
Glenaffric Forest
GLEN AFFRIC
Guisachan Forest
Ratagan
Invershiel
Shiel Bridge
Glen Gniomhaidh
Allt Garbh
Allt Riabhach
Loch na Beinne Baine
Levishie Forest
Levishie
1032
BEINN FADA OR BEN ATTOW
Kintail Forest
888
AONACH SHASUINN
706
CARN A CHAOCHAIN
680
Dundreggan Forest
779
1067
FIVE SISTERS
979
CISTE DHUBH
Allt na Muic
A887
FALLS OF MORISTON
Portclair Forest
Dundreggan Lodge
Dundreggan
1027
1120
A'CHRALAIG
Glenshiel Forest
1109
SGURR NAN CONBHAIREAN
Ceannacroc Forest
Doe
Dalchreichart
Portclair
607
BURACH
GLEN SHIEL
Tomchrasky
GLEN MORISTON
Inverwick Forest
1010
THE SADDLE
SGURR AN LOCHAIN
1004
Cluanie Inn
A87
Cluanie Lodge
Lundie
Ceannacroc Lodge
Inchnacardoch Hotel
A82
Fort Augustus
Kinlochhourn Forest
Cluanie Forest
LOCH CLUANIE
A887
Bun Loyne
Allt Phocaichain
Inchnacardoch Forest
CLANSMAN CENTRE
Auchteraw
FORT AUGUSTUS ABBEY
Bunloinn Forest
Beinneun Forest
788
MEALL DUBH
879
BUIDHE BHEINN
Kinloch Hourn
Glen Quoich
1021
AONACH AIR CHRITH
Allt Lundie
1027
SGURR A'MHAORAICH
LOCH LOYNE
Caledonian Canal
GLEN OICH
1035
GLEOURAICH
Loyne
Bridge of Oich
Newtown
Glen Tarff
894
A87
Munerigie
LOCH GARRY
Glenquoich Forest
540
Abhainn Chosaidh
LOCH QUOICH
Coille Mhorgil
Aultnaslat
Inchlaggan
Ardochy House
Invergarry
Tarff
Garry
Tomdoun
Greenfield
Mandally
Loch Oich
Calder Burn
Glen Garry
Culachy Forest
919
GAIRICH
Glen Kingie
A82
Kingie
Allt Choire a' Bhalachain
1003
SGURR MOR
556
GLAS BHEINN
LOCH LOCHY
901
BEN TEE
LAGGAN LOCKS
Laggan
884
CARN LE
Glengarry Forest
Kilfinnan
815
CARN DEARG
656
MEALL BLAIR
880
SGURR MHURLAGAIN
858
804
GEAL CHARN
935
SRON A'CHOIRE GHAIRBH
Loch Blair
Glen Dessarry
Dessarry
Murlaggan
LOCH LOCHY
Turret
Strathan
LOCH ARKAIG
636
Letterfinlay
Brae Roy Lodge
Glen Pean
Pean
Ardechvie
Glen Roy
MOR
Gleann Camgharaidh
Achnasaul
Clunes Forest
Altrua
Glen Gloy
PARALLEL ROADS
Burn of Agie
727
Locheil Forest
Inver Mallie
B8005
Clunes
Upper Glenfintaig
834
CARN DEARG
963
SGURR THUILM
987
GAOR BHEINN
Glen Mallie
Mallie
Achnacarry
Bunarkaig
A82
684
Gloy
GLEN ROY NATIONAL NATURE RESERVE
796
BEINN BHAN
654
COIRE CEIRSLE HILL
Allt Glas Dhoire
915
Lighe
Suileag
Gairlochy
Stronaba
Bohuntine
1049
BEINN A' CHAORUINN
Moy
Kilmonivaig
COMMANDO MEMORIAL
Bohenie
103
96
87
88
A
B
D
E
F
G
H
6
7
8
9
10

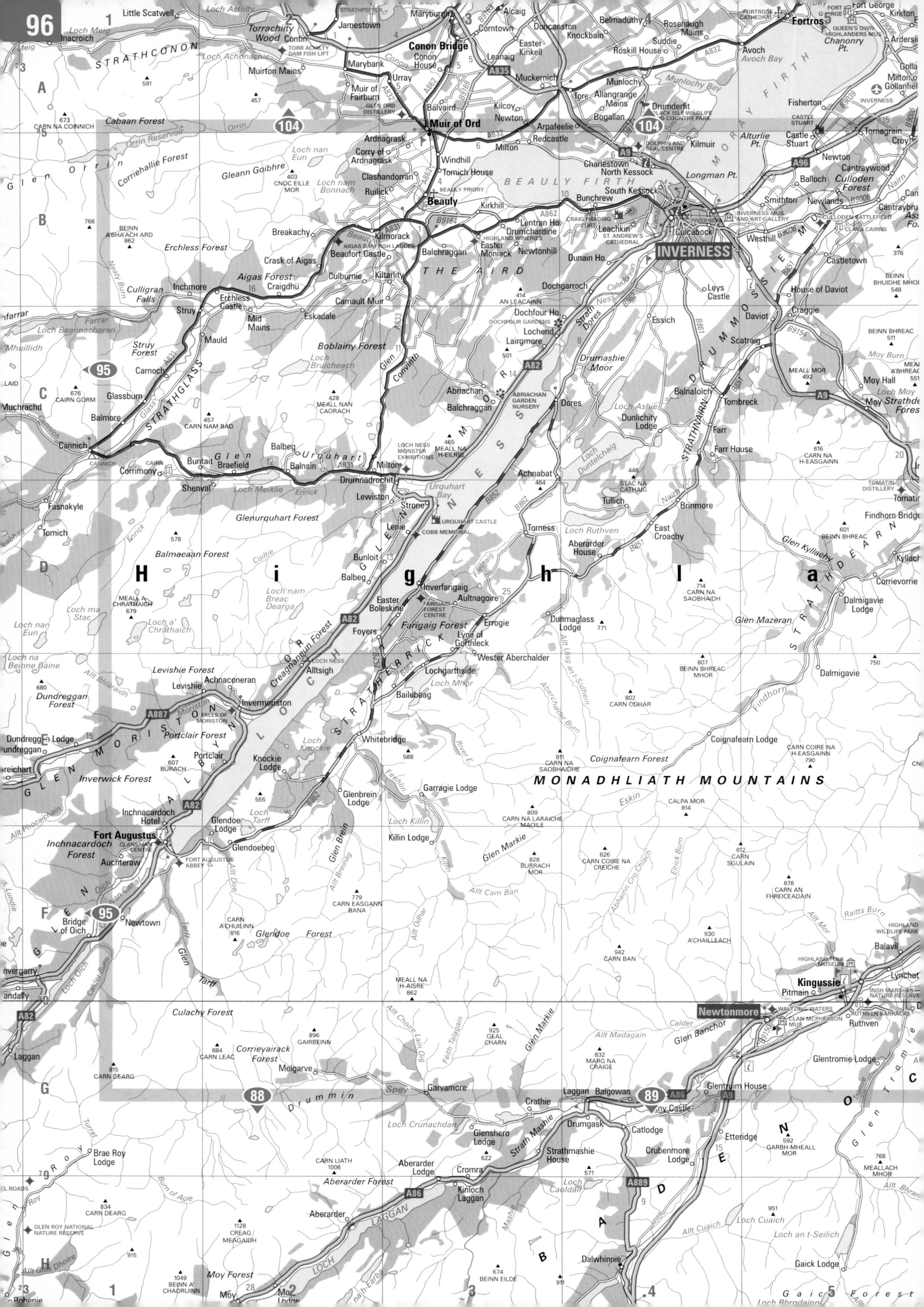
Little Scatwell
Inacroich
Loch Meig
STRATHCONON
Loch Achonachie
Torrachilty Wood
Contin
Jamestown
Maryburgh
Conon Bridge
Conon House
Marybank
Muirton Mains
Urray
Muir of Fairburn
Balvaird
Muir of Ord
Corntown
Duncanston
Alcaig
Belmaduthy
Knockbain
Easter Kinkell
Leanaig
Muckernich
Roskill House
Rosehaugh Mains
Suddie
Avoch
Avoch Bay
Fortrose
Chanonry Pt.
Fort George
Kirkton
Ardersier
MORAY FIRTH
Munlochy
Munlochy Bay
Tore
Allangrange Mains
Bogallan
Drumderfit
Kilcoy
Newton
Arpafeelie
Redcastle
Milton
Fisherton
Castle Stuart
Alturlie Pt.
Tornagrain
Croy
Kilmuir
Charlestown
North Kessock
Longman Pt.
Cabaan Forest
CARN NA COINNICH
Orrin Reservoir
Glen Orrin
Corriehallie Forest
Gleann Goibhre
CNOC EILLE MOR
Loch nan Eun
Loch nam Bonnach
Ardnagrask
Corry of Ardnagrask
Clashandorran
Ruilick
Windhill
Tomich House
BEAULY PRIORY
Beauly
BEAULY FIRTH
South Kessock
Bunchrew
Kirkhill
Lentran Ho.
Drumchardine
Newtonhill
Easter Moniack
Balchraggan
Kilmorack
Beaufort Castle
Breakachy
BEINN A'BHA'ACH ARD
Erchless Forest
Crask of Aigas
Aigas Forest
Craigdhu
Culburnie
Kiltarlity
THE AIRD
Culligran Falls
Inchmore
Erchless Castle
Struy
Mid Mains
Eskadale
Camault Muir
Farrar
Loch Beannacharan
Mauld
Strhy Forest
Carnoch
Glassburn
CAIRN GORM
Balmore
Cannich
Muchrachd
STRATHGLASS
Boblainy Forest
Loch Bruicheach
MEALL NAN CAORACH
CARN NAM BAD
Glen Convinth
Corrimony
Buntait
Braefield
Glen Urquhart
Balbeg
Balnain
Milton
Drumnadrochit
Shenval
Loch Meiklie
Fasnakyle
Tomich
Lewiston
Strone
Urquhart Bay
URQUHART CASTLE
Glenurquhart Forest
Balmacaan Forest
Bunloit
Balbeg
MEALL A' CHRATHAICH
Loch nam Breac Dearga
Loch ma Stac
Loch nan Eun
Loch a' Chrathaich
Loch na Beinne Baine
Levishie Forest
Levishie
Achnaconeran
Dundreggan Forest
Invermoriston
GLEN MORISTON
Portclair Forest
Portclair
BURACH
Inverwick Forest
Knockie Lodge
Loch Knockie
Inchnacardoch Hotel
Fort Augustus
Inchnacardoch Forest
Auchteraw
FORT AUGUSTUS ABBEY
Bridge of Oich
Newtown
Invergarry
Laggan
Glendoe Lodge
Glendoebeg
Glendoe Forest
CARN A'CHUILINN
Culachy Forest
Corrieyairack Forest
CARN LEAC
CARN DEARG
Melgarve
Drummin
Brae Roy Lodge
Glen Roy
GLEN ROY NATIONAL NATURE RESERVE
CREAG MEAGAIDH
BEINN A' CHAORUINN
Moy Forest
Moy
LOCH LAGGAN
Aberarder
Aberarder Lodge
Aberarder Forest
Kinloch Laggan
Cromra
CARN LIATH
Glenshero Lodge
Loch Crunachdan
Garvamore
Spey
Crathie
Laggan
Balgowan
Drumgask
Catlodge
Strath Mashie
Strathmashie House
Loch Caoldair
Crubenmore Lodge
Dalwhinnie
BEINN EILDE
Loch Cuaich
Loch an t-Seilich
Gaick Lodge
Gaick Forest
Etteridge
GARBH-MHEALL MOR
MEALLACH MHOR
Glentruim House
Newtonmore
Kingussie
Pitmain
Ruthven
Glentromie Lodge
Glen Tromie
Glen Banchor
MARG NA CRAIGE
GEAL CHARN
GAIRBEINN
MEALL NA H-AISRE
Glen Markie
CARN BAN
A'CHAILLEACH
CARN AN FHREICEADAIN
CARN SGULAIN
CARN COIRE NA CREICHE
BURRACH MOR
CARN EASGANN BANA
Killin Lodge
Loch Killin
Glenbrein Lodge
Garragie Lodge
Whitebridge
Bailebeag
Loch Mhor
Lochgarthside
Wester Aberchalder
Lyne of Gorthleck
Errogie
Farigaig Forest
Foyers
Easter Boleskine
Inverfarigaig
Aultnagoire
Dunmaglass Lodge
CARN ODHAR
CARN NA SAOBHAIDHE
Coignafearn Forest
Coignafearn Lodge
MONADHLIATH MOUNTAINS
CALPA MOR
CARN NA LARAICHE MAOILE
BEINN BHREAC MHOR
CARN NA SAOBHAIDH
Glen Mazeran
Dalmigavie
Dalmigavie Lodge
STRATHDEARN
Corrievorrie
Kyllachy
Glen Kyllachy
BEINN BHREAC
Findhorn Bridge
Tomatin
Aberarder House
Loch Ruthven
Torness
East Croachy
Brinmore
Tullich
STAC NA CATHAIG
Achnabat
Loch Duntelchaig
Dunlichity Lodge
Loch Ashie
Dores
Abriachan
Balchraggan
ABRIACHAN GARDEN NURSERY
Lairgmore
Lochend
Dochfour Ho.
AN LEACAINN
Dochgarroch
Dunain Ho.
Drumashie Moor
Strath Dores
Essich
Leys Castle
INVERNESS
Culcabock
Leachkin
Westhill
Smithton
Balloch
Culloden Forest
Newlands
Cantraywood
CULLODEN BATTLEFIELD
CLAVA CAIRNS
Castletown
House of Daviot
Daviot
Craggie
Scatraig
DRUMMOSSIE MUIR
Balnafoich
Tombreck
Farr
Farr House
STRATHNAIRN
CARN NA H-EASGAINN
MEALL MOR
Moy Hall
Loch Moy
Strathdearn Forest
Highland
LOCH NESS
Creag nan Eun Forest
Alltsigh
STRATHERRICK
GLEN ALBYN
BADENOCH
MONADHLIATH MOUNTAINS

Nairn
Tradespark
Moss-side
Auldearn
A96
B9092
B9090
B9101
Boath Dovecote
Darnaway Farm Visitor Centre
Earlsmill
Blackhills
Whitemire
Conicavel
Easter Milton
Wester Milton
Geddes House
Muir of the Clans
Rosefield
Regoul
Lalken Forest
Darnaway Forest
Clephanton
Cawdor
Piperhill
Culcharry
Kilravock Castle
Cawdor Castle and Gardens
Littlemill
Mid Urchany
Easter Galcantray
Achavraat
Kirkton of Barevan
Mains of Clunas
Redburn
Newlands of Fleenas Wood
Ardclach Tower
Ferness
Relugas
Glenernie
Beachans
Mount
Logie
Drumine Forest
Balmore
Glenferness House
Carn Sgumain 417
Dulsie
Aitnoch
Dallas Dhu Distillery
Rafford
Altyre Ho.
Altyre Woods
Newtyle Forest
Briach
Branchill
Dallas
Dallas Forest
Kellas
Glenlatterach
Craigroy
Mill Buie 371
Loch Dallas
Moray
Carn Uish 365
Thornshill
Whitewreath
A941
Glen of Rothes
Auchinroath
Newlands
Rothes
Glen Grant Distillery
Burn of Rothes
Elchies Forest
Carn na Cailliche 404
Whiteacen
Ladycroft Agricultural Museum
Dandaleith
Craigellachie
Speyside Cooperage Visitor Centre
Archiestown
Ringorm
Upper Knockando
Cardhu Distillery
Cardow
Knockando Ho.
Knockando
Carron
Speyview
Charlestown of Aberlour
Milltown of Edinvillie
Daugh of Kinermony
A95
Speyside Way
B9138
Marypark
Glenfarclas Distillery
Bellehiglash
Meikle Conval 569
Carn Kitty 521
Larig Hill 545
Hill of Aitnoch 406
Carn nan Tri-tighearnan 615
Daless
Findhorn
Lochindorb
Lochindorb Castle
Lochindorb Lodge
Carn-ruigh Charrach 484
Carn na Loine 549
Upper Derraid
Auchnagallin
Advie
Bridge of Avon
Dalchirach
Ben Rinnes 840
Favillar
Glen Rinnes
Kirkhill
Ruthven
Balvraid
Upper Coverbrough
Carn an t-Sean-liathanaich 635
Glaschoil
Lettoch
Camerory
Cottartown
Dellefure
Mains of Dalvey
Strathspey
Hills of Cromdale
Drumin
Glenlivet Distillery
Glenlivet
Shenval
Auchbreck
Carn a'Choire Mhoir 627
Carn Glas-choire 659
Glenbeg
Beinn Mhor 471
Achnahannet
Grantown-on-Spey
Cromdale
Auchroisk
Haughs of Cromdale
Ballcorach
Strath Avon
Tomnavoulin
Blackwater
Craggan
Speybridge
Congash
Dulnain Bridge
Carn Daimh 569
Carn an t-Suidhe 732
Slochd
Duthil
Skye of Curr
Lynemore
Creggan a'Chaise 722
Glenlivet Forest
Knockandhu
Ellan
Lochanhully
Carrbridge
Landmark Visitor Centre
Heather Heritage Centre
Sluggan
A9
A95
A938
B9153
Clashnoir
Braes of Glenlivet
Chapeltown
Dirdhu
Bridge of Brown
Wester Fodderletter
Dalnahaitnach
Drumuillie
Cullachie
Nethy Bridge
Birchfield
Dell Lodge
Lettoch
Chapelton
Boat of Garten
East Croftmore
Loch Garten
Loch Garten Nature Reserve
Abernethy Forest
Kinveachy
Eil
Avielochan
Strathspey Railway
Aundorach
Forest Lodge
Baddoch 568
Dorback Lodge
Tomintoul Museum
Tomintoul
Delnabo
Carn Meadhonach 588
Carn Mor 804
Ladder Hills
Carn Sleamhuinn 677
Auchgourish
Braes of Abernethy
Blairnamarrow
The Socach 718
Granish
Pityoulish
Aviemore
Craigellachie National Nature Reserve
Glen More Forest Park
Meall a'Bhuachaille 810
The Aviemore Ski Centre
Cairngorm Whisky Centre
Coylumbridge
Geal Charn Mor 824
Lecht Ski Centre
A939
Geal Charn 821
Carn Ealasaid 792
Inverdruie
The Queen's Forest
Cairngorm Reindeer Centre
Loch Morlich
Glenmore Lodge
Polchar
Rothiemurchus Estate Visitor Centre
Loch an Eilein Visitor Centre
Rothiemurchus
Loch an Eilein
Alvie
Loch Alvie
Big Garvoun 742
Glen Avon
Cock Bridge
Colnabaichin
Delnadamph Lodge
Corgarff Castle
Corgarff
An Suidhe 541
Kincraig
Invereshie House
Inshriach Forest
Feshiebridge
Carn Eilrig 742
Bynack More 1090
The Bruach 715
Forest of Glenavon
Brown Cow Hill 823
Loch Builg
Farr
Insh
Lairig Ghru
Cairngorm Mountains
Cairn Gorm 1245
Loch Avon
Beinn a'Chaorruinn 1082
Ben Avon 1171
Gairnshiel Lodge
Inveruglass
Sgoran Dubh Mor 1111
Braeriach 1296
Loch Etchachan
Ben Macdui 1309
Carn Eas 1089
Culardoch 900
Tolvah
Loch Einich
Achlean
Carn Ban Mor 1052
Derry Cairngorm 1155
Beinn Bhreac 931
Glen Dee
Bush Crathie
Crathie Church
Crathie
A93
Geallaig Hill 743
Glen Feshie
Glenfeshie Lodge
Carn na Drochaide 818
Braemar Castle
Braemar
Invercauld House
Inver
Balmoral Castle and Gardens
Easter Balmoral
Mullach Clach a'Bhlair 1019
Glenfeshie Forest
Beinn Bhrotain 1157
Glen Lui
Allanaquoich
Mar Lodge
Kindrochit Castle
Braemar Highland Heritage Centre
Ballochbuie Forest
Glen Gelder
Carn Dearg Mor 857
Forest of Mar
Claybokie
Inverey
Tomintoul
Muir
Linn of Dee
Auchallater
Balmoral Forest
Carn Liath 818
Glen Ey
Lochnagar 1150
Conachcraig 850
Loch Callater
Glen Callater
Carn Ealar 994
Baddoch
Glas-allt Shiel
105
98
90
89

Moray
Aberd
SPEY BAY
Halliman Skerries
Covesea Skerries
Lossiemouth
Branderburgh
Stotfield
Covesea
Duffus
Gordonstoun
Lossie Forest
Elgin
Bishopmill
New Elgin
Lhanbryde
Urquhart
Garmouth
Kingston
Spey Bay
Fochabers
Mosstodloch
Portgordon
Buckie
Buckpool
Findochty
Portknockie
Portessie
Gordonsburgh
Rathven
Cullen
Cullen Bay
Logie Hd.
Sandend
Sandend Bay
Portsoy
Seatown
Redhythe Pt.
Boyne Bay
Fordyce
Kirktown of Deskford
Shiel Muir
Speymouth Forest
Wood of Ordiequish
Teindland Forest
Rothes
Glen of Rothes
Keith
Mulben
Rosarie Forest
Balloch Wood
Glen of Coachford
Huntly
The Bin Forest
Clashindarroch Forest
Dufftown
Kirktown of Mortlach
Craigellachie
Charlestown of Aberlour
Elchies Forest
Glen Rinnes
Glen Fiddich
Glenfiddich Forest
Blackwater Forest
Glenlivet
Glenlivet Forest
Braes of Glenlivet
Tomintoul
Tomnavoulin
Knockandhu
Chapeltown
Ladder Hills
Cock Bridge
Corgarff
Strathdon
Glen Ernan
Candacraig Ho.
Tornashean Forest
Glenbuchat Lodge
Kildrummy
Rhynie
Lumsden
Correen Hills
Alford
Whitehaugh Forest
Insch
Strathbogie
Glens of Foudland
Tarland
Logie Coldstone
Aberchirder
Marnoch
Cornhill
Drumblade
Lessendrum
Kennethmont
Gartly
Cairnie
Grange Crossroads
Ballindalloch
Marypark
Knockando
Archiestown
Dandaleith
Carn Daimh
Ben Rinnes
Corrennie Forest
Lumphanan
Cromar

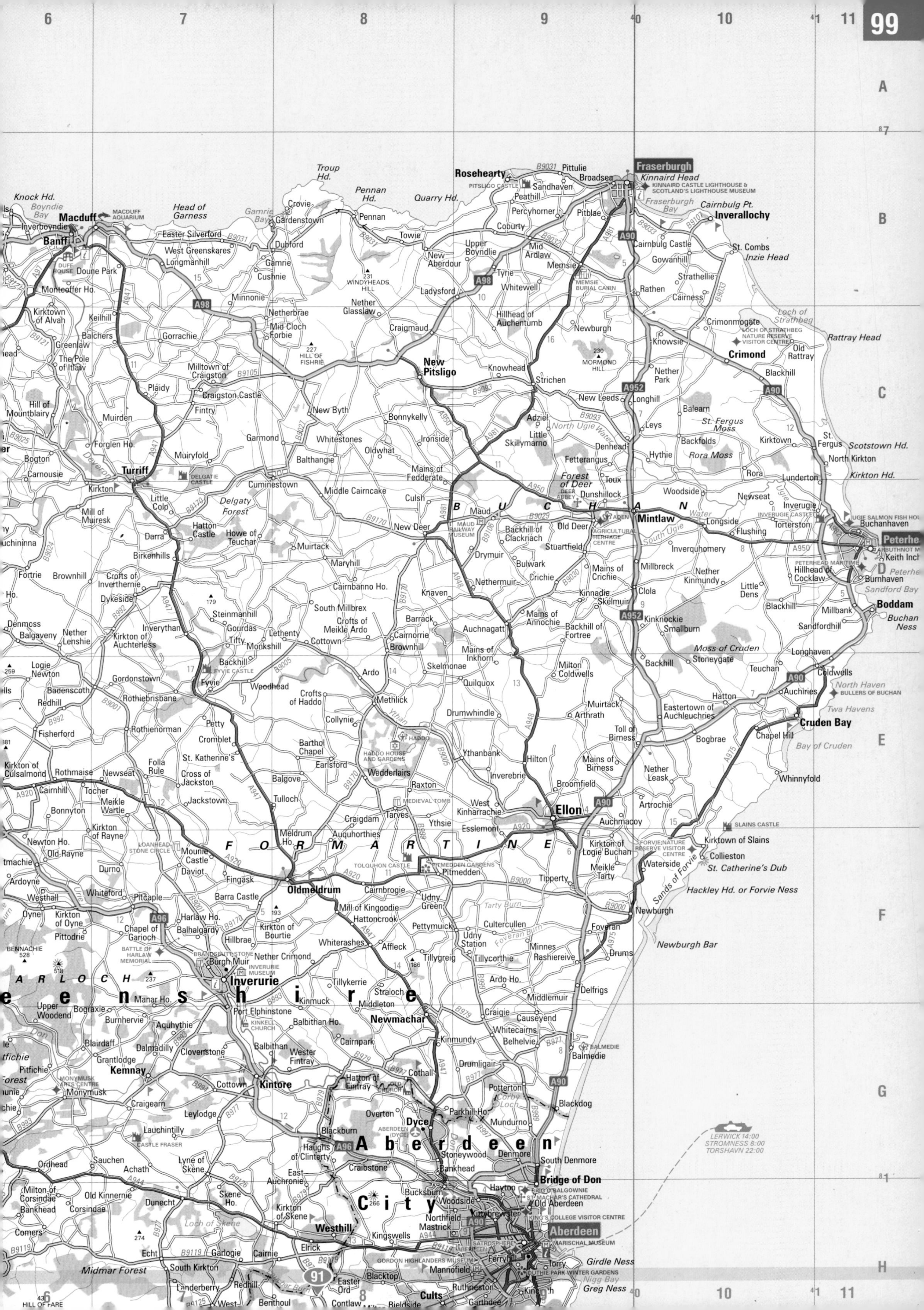

Fraserburgh
Kinnaird Head
Rosehearty
Pittulie
Broadsea
Sandhaven
Troup Hd.
Pennan Hd.
Quarry Hd.
Knock Hd.
Boyndie Bay
Macduff
Banff
Head of Garness
Gardenstown
Crovie
Pennan
Inverallochy
Cairnbulg Pt.
St. Combs
Inzie Head
Rattray Head
Crimond
Loch of Strathbeg
New Pitsligo
Strichen
Turriff
Cuminestown
New Deer
Maud
Mintlaw
Old Deer
Peterhead
Boddam
Buchan Ness
Longhaven
Cruden Bay
Bay of Cruden
Hatton
Ellon
Pitmedden
Oldmeldrum
Fyvie
Methlick
Tarves
Inverurie
Kintore
Kemnay
Newmachar
Dyce
Balmedie
Newburgh
Newburgh Bar
Collieston
Hackley Hd. or Forvie Ness
Sands of Forvie
Aberdeen
Bridge of Don
Old Aberdeen
Westhill
Girdle Ness
Greg Ness
Nigg Bay
Torry
Cults
Midmar Forest
B U C H A N
F O R M A R T I N E
Aberdeenshire
Aberdeen City
LERWICK 14:00
STROMNESS 8:00
TORSHAVN 22:00
A90
A98
A947
A948
A952
A920
A96
A950
A981
A975
A944
6
7
8
9
10
11
A
B
C
D
E
F
G
H

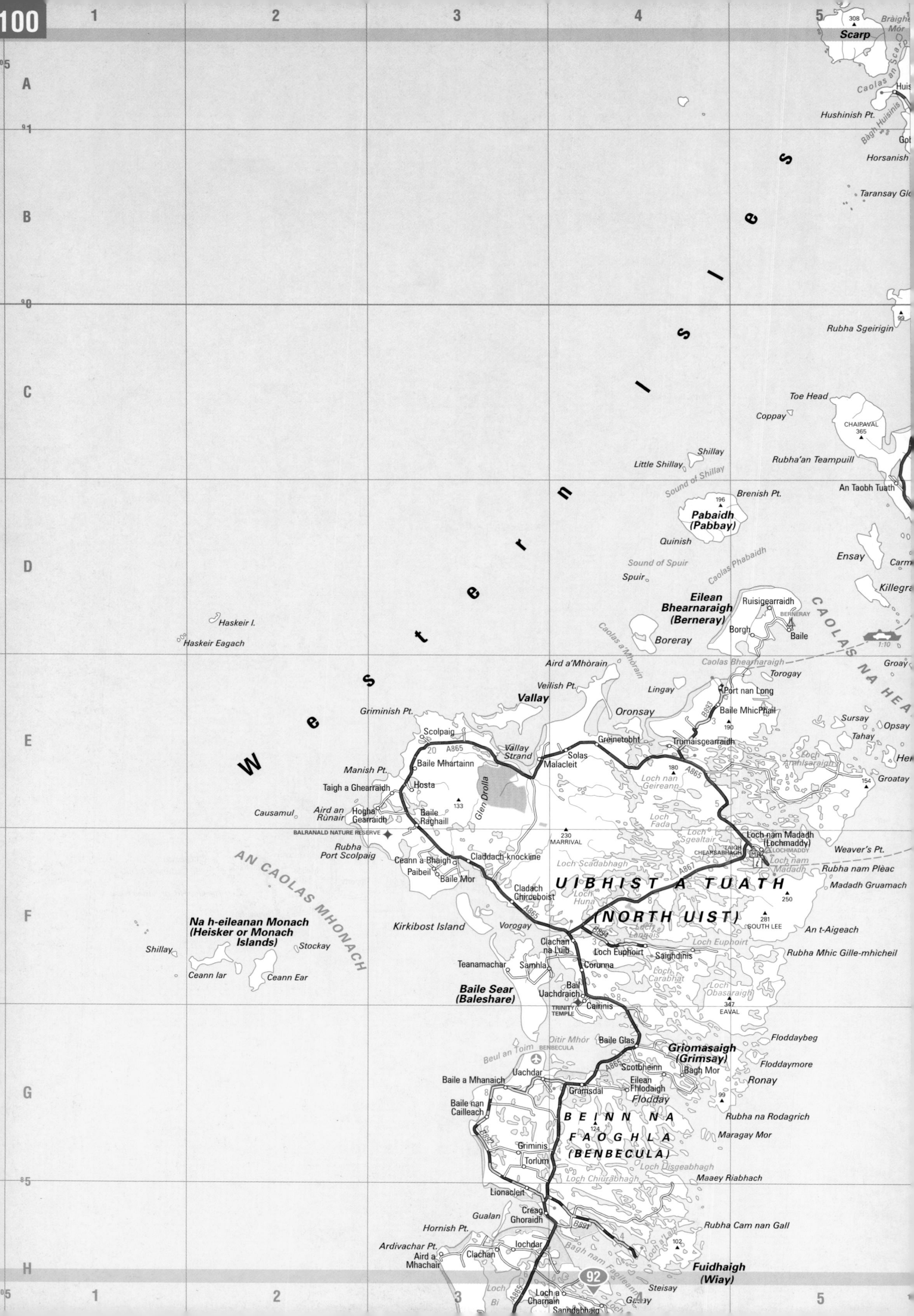
Western Isles
Scarp
Bràighe Mòr
Caolas an Scarp
Hushinish Pt.
Bàgh Huisinis
Horsanish
Taransay
Rubha Sgeirigin
Toe Head
Coppay
CHAIPAVAL
Rubha'an Teampuill
An Taobh Tuath
Little Shillay
Shillay
Sound of Shillay
Brenish Pt.
Pabaidh (Pabbay)
Quinish
Sound of Spuir
Caolas Phabaidh
Spuir
Ensay
Killegray
Eilean Bhearnaraigh (Berneray)
Ruisigearraidh
Borgh
Baile
Boreray
Caolas a'Mhorain
CAOLAS NA HEARADH
Haskeir I.
Haskeir Eagach
Aird a'Mhòrain
Caolas Bhearnaraigh
Torogay
Groay
Veilish Pt.
Lingay
Port nan Long
Vallay
Oronsay
Baile MhicPhail
Griminish Pt.
Sursay
Tahay
Opsay
Scolpaig
Greinetobht
Trumaisgearraidh
Vallay Strand
Solas
Malacleit
Baile Mhartainn
Loch Aonghais
Manish Pt.
Hosta
Taigh a Ghearraidh
Glen Drolla
Loch nan Geireann
Groatay
Causamul
Aird an Rùnair
Hogha Gearraidh
Baile Raghaill
Loch Fada
BALRANALD NATURE RESERVE
MARRIVAL
Loch Sgealtair
Loch nam Madadh (Lochmaddy)
Weaver's Pt.
Rubha Port Scolpaig
TAIGH CHEARSABHAGH
Ceann a Bhaigh
Claddach-knockline
Loch Scadabhagh
Rubha nam Plèac
Paibeil
Baile Mor
Madadh Gruamach
AN CAOLAS MHONACH
Cladach Chirceboist
UIBHIST A TUATH (NORTH UIST)
Loch Hunna
SOUTH LEE
An t-Aigeach
Na h-eileanan Monach (Heisker or Monach Islands)
Kirkibost Island
Vorogay
Loch Langais
Loch Euphoirt
Shillay
Stockay
Clachan na Luib
Saighdinis
Rubha Mhic Gille-mhicheil
Teanamachar
Samhla
Corunna
Loch Carabhat
Ceann Iar
Ceann Ear
Baile Sear (Baleshare)
Bail Uachdraich
Loch Obasaraigh
TRINITY TEMPLE
Cairinis
EAVAL
Oitir Mhór
Baile Glas
Floddaybeg
Beul an Toim
BENBECULA
Griomasaigh (Grimsay)
Uachdar
Scotbheinn
Bagh Mor
Floddaymore
Baile a Mhanaich
Eilean Fhlodaigh
Ronay
Gramsdal
Flodday
Baile nan Cailleach
BEINN NA FAOGHLA (BENBECULA)
Rubha na Rodagrich
Maragay Mor
Griminis
Torlum
Loch Uisgeabhagh
Loch Chiùrabhagh
Maaey Riabhach
Lionacleit
Gualan
Creag Ghoraidh
Rubha Cam nan Gall
Hornish Pt.
Ardivachar Pt.
Iochdar
Bagh nam Faoileann
Aird a Mhachair
Clachan
Fuidhaigh (Wiay)
Steisay
Loch a Charnain
Gasay
Sanndabhaig
92

Aird an Troim
Airidh a Bhruaich
Ceann Loch Shiphoirt
Loch Sgibacleit
Gleann Ghrabhair
Grabhair
Calbost
Loch Odhairn
Kebock Head
PARK OR PAIRC
Loch Shanndabhat
Orasaigh
Leumrabhagh
Eisgean
Loch Shell or Loch Sealg
Srianach
Eilean Iubhard
Loch a'Ghlinne
579 STULAVAL
679 TIRGA MOR
659 ULLAVAL
489
Aline Lodge
Seaforth I.
Aird a Mhulaidh
572 BEINN MHOR
Forest of Harris
Abhainn Suidhe
UISGNAVAL MORE 729
CLISHAM 799
Arda Mòra
CEANN A TUATH NA HEARADH
470 CRIONAIG
Soay Beag
Cliasmol
Soay Mór
Miabhag
Bun Abhainn Eadarra
Maraig
Loch Shiphoirt
Mol Truisg
LOCH A SIAR
Camus an t-suithean
559
449
Loch Claidh
Loch Bhrollum
Aird Asaig
REINIGEADAL (RENIGIDALE)
Reinigeadal
Gob Rubh'Uisenis
Rubha Bhrollum
Tarasaigh (Taransay)
Isay
Lochan Lacasdail
Tairbeart (Tarbert)
Loch Trollamarig
Rubha a'Bhaird
436 BEN LUSKENTYRE
Paible
Losgaintir
Urgha
467
Carragraich
CAOLAS NAN EILEAN
Garbh Eilean
Eilean Mhuire
Caolas Tharasaigh
LUSKENTYRE BEACH
South Harris Forest
Caolas Scalpaigh
Carnach
Na h-Eileanan Mòra (Shiant Islands)
Eilean an Tighe
Loch Ceann Dibig
Sgeotasaigh
Rudha Crago
Seilebost
Miabhag
Loch an Tairbeart
Eilean Scalpaigh (Scalpay)
102
Borve Lodge
Buirgh
NA HEARADH (HARRIS)
Drinisiadar
Kennacley
Plocropol Pt.
Aird Mhighe
Greosabhagh
Plocropol
Sgarasta Mhor
386
Leac a Li
Liceasto
STOCINIS (STOCKINISH)
Scadabhagh
398 BLEAVAL
Geocrab
Cluthar
Rubha Bhocaig
Loch Langabhat
Beicribhig
Caolas Stocinis
Loch Greosabhagh
Stockinish I.
Fleoideabhagh
Manais
Loch Steiseabhat
Aird Mhighe
Loch Fleoideabhagh
UIG 1:50
An t-Ob
459 ROINEABHAL
Fionnsbhagh
Cuidhtinis
Loch Fionnsbhagh
Lingreabhagh
Cairminis
Srannda
Lingarabay I.
ST. CLEMENT'S CHURCH
Roghadal
Vallay
Langay
Renish Pt.
Fladda-chùain
Gilsay
Lingay
Scaravay
Eilean Trodday
Rubha Hunish
Rubha na h-Aiseig
TARBERT 1:50
Balmacqueen
Duntulm
Kilmaluag
Lub Score
Hungladder
MUSEUM OF ISLAND LIFE
Eilean Flodigarry
Borneskeitaig
Flodigarry
MEALL NA SUIRAMACH 543
LOCHMADDY 1:50
Kilmuir
Digg
Staffin Bay
Staffin
Kilvaxter
THE QUIRAING
Glashvin
Balgown
Brogaig
Staffin
Stenscholl
UIG 1:50
Waternish Point
Linicro
Totscore
Kilbride Point
466 BIOD BUIDHE
Maligar
Ellishader
Loch Mealt
Ascrib Islands
Idrigill
Uig
Conon
Marishader
Garros
Uig Bay
Balnaknock
611 BEINN EDRA
Breckrey
Lealt
BEN GEARY 284
Geary
Ru Chorachan
Ard Beag
Trumpan
Knockbreck
Earlish
LOCH SNIZORT
WATERNISH
Gillen
Lower Halistra
Ardmore Pt.
Upper Halistra
Peinlich
Hallin
607 CREAG A'LAIN
Hinnisdal
Mingay
Lyndale Pt.
Greshornish Pt.
Dunvegan Head
Isay
Lusta
Stein
Loch Bay
Kingsburgh
Highland
Galtrigill
Lyndale Ho.
PIPING MUSEUM
Borreraig
Claigan
Greshornish
Loch Snizort Beag
Romesdal
719 THE STORR
OLD MAN OF STORR
Uig
Loch Greshornish
Treaslane
Flashader
Suladale
327 BEINN BHREAC
Bay River
Eyre
TROTTERNISH
LOCH DUNVEGAN
The Aird
An Ceannaich
Loch Poolteil
Feriniquarrie
Husabost Pier
Edinbane
Kensaleyre
Haultin
Lower Milovaig
Bernisdale
DUNVEGAN CASTLE
Glasphein
Totaig
Blackhill
Oisgill Bay
COLBOST FOLK MUSEUM
Tote
Upper Milovaig
Lephin
Colbost
Glen Bernisdale
Borve
Loch Fada
Holmisdal
Skeabost
Carbost
Neist
Glen Dale
Skinidin
Dunvegan
Kilmuir
Lonmore
CRUACHAN BEINN A'CHEARCAILL 266
Uigshader
Drumuie
Achachork
Moonen Bay
HEALABHAL MHOR 468
Roskhill
Glengrasco
Torvaig
Ramasaig
93
Roag
Vatten
Loch Connan
Shaderbeg
Portree
106
107
A B C D E F G H
6 7 8 9 10

Western Isles
Lacasaigh
Ceos
Eilean Chaluim Chille
Eilean Orasaid
Cromor
Eilean Thoraidh
Gearraidh Bhaird
Cearsiadar
Cabharstadh
Tabost
CEARSIADER (KERSHADER)
Marbhig
Calbost
Shiphoirt
Loch Sgibacleit
Gleann Ghrabhair
Grabhair
Loch Odhairn
Kebock Head
Loch Shanndabhat
PARK OR PAIRC
Orasaigh
Leumrabhagh
Eisgean
Loch Shell or Loch Sealg
Srianach
Eilean Iubhard
470 CRIONAIG
Mol Truisg
Loch Bhrollum
Gob Rubh'Uisenis
Rubha Bhrollum
Rubha a'Bhaird
CAOLAS NAN EILEAN
Garbh Eilean
Eilean Mhuire
Na h-Eileanan Mòra (Shiant Islands)
Eilean an Tighe
107
101
Fladda-chùain
Eilean Trodday
Rubha Hunish
Rubha na h-Aiseig
Balmacqueen
Duntulm
Kilmaluag
Lub Score
Eilean Flodigarry
Hungladder
MUSEUM OF ISLAND LIFE
Bornesketaig
Flodigarry
MEALL NA SUIRAMACH 543
Kilmuir
Staffin I.
Digg
Staffin Bay
Kilvaxter
Glashvin
THE QUIRAING
Balgown
Brogaig
Staffin
Stenscholl
TARBERT 1:50
LOCHMADDY 1:50
Linicro
Kilt Rock
KILT ROCK
Totscore
466 BIOD BUIDHE
Kilbride Point
Highland
Elishader
Maligar
Loch Mealt
Valtos
Idrigill
Uig
Conon
Marishader
Uig Bay
Garros
Rubha nam Brathairean
Balnaknock
611 BEINN EDRA
Ru Chorachan
Breckrey
Culnaknock
LOCH SNIZORT
Earlish
Lealt
Lower Tote
Upper Tote
A87
Peinlich
Hinnisdal
607 CREAG A'LAIN
Greshornish Pt.
Lyndale Pt.
Island of Rona
125
Eilean Garbh
Kingsburgh
Loch Snizort Beag
Romesdal
719 THE STORR
OLD MAN OF STORR
SOUND OF RAASAY
Greshornish
Lyndale Ho.
Loch Greshornish
Treaslane
Flashader
Suladale
Eyre
Bearreraig Bay
Eilean Tigh
Caol Rona
Garbh Eilean
Loch a' Sguirr
An Caol
TROTTERNISH
The Aird
Haultin
Holm I.
Kensaleyre
Bernisdale
Loch Leathan
Edinbane
Blackhill
Eilean Fladday
254
Torran
94
Tote
Glen Bernisdale
Borve
Loch Fada
PRINCE CHARLES'S
Manish Pt.
Loch Arnish
Arnish
Sròn a' Gheodha Dhuibh
Camas Mòr
Rubha Reidh
Loch an Draing
296 AN CUAIDH
Melvaig
Aultgrishan
Seana Chamas
Peterburn
B8021
Port Erradale
North Erradale
Rubha Bàn
Big Sand
Longa Island
Caolas Beag
CARN DEARG
Smithstown
LOCH GAIRLOCH
Port Henderson
B8056
Badachro
Opinan
Loch Clàir
South Erradale
Redpoint
Erradale
Craig
CRAIG
Rubha na Fearn
Fearnmore
Loch Torridon
Fearnbeg
Lower Diabaig
Arinacrinachd
Cuaig
Kenmore
Loch a' Chracaich
Ardheslaig
Abhainn Chuaig
Kalnakill
Allt na h-Eirigh
Lonbain
Loch Gaineamhach
493 CROIC-BHEINN
Abhainn Dubh
Loch nan Eun
626 BEINN A'CHLACHAIN
Loch Lund
A855
A850
B8036
B8060

6
7
8
9
10
A
B
C
D
E
F
G
2
3
5
108
104
95
Soyea I.
Loch Inver
Kirkaig Pt.
Lochinver
Lodge
540
Inchnadamph
A'Chleit
Inverkirkaig
Strathan
Loch Kirkaig
Glencanisp
Forest
Stronchrubie
Rubha na Breige
SUILVEN
731
846
CANISP
718
BREABAG
Rubha Coigeach
Eilean Mór
Kirkaig
Falls
Fionn Loch
Loch na Gainimh
Loanan
ENARD BAY
Camas Eilean Ghlais
Rubha Mor
Rubh'a' Choin
Inverpolly Lodge
Loch Veyatie
Loch Awe
Reiff
Brae of Achnahaird
Loch Sionascaig
INVERPOLLY NATIONAL NATURE RESERVE
Cam Loch
Ledbeg
Altandhu
Polly
Ledmore
Eilean Mullagrach
Loch Vatachan
Loch Osgaig
Aird of Coigach
Inverpolly Forest
849
CUL MOR
Elphin
Altnacealgach Hotel
Loch Ailsh
Isle Ristol
Drumrunie Forest
Polbain
613
Knockan
Glas-leac Mór
Loch Bad a'Ghaill
Loch an Doire Dhuibh
Loch Urigill
A837
Achiltibuie
HYDROPONICUM GARDENS
Badentarbat Bay
INVERPOLLY NATURE RESERVE KNOCKAN CLIFF VISITOR CENTRE
Tanera Beg
Polglass
769
CUL BEAG
Loch Lurgainn
CROMALT HILLS
A835
Cromalt
Summer Isles
Tanera Mór
ACHININVER
Horse Sound
17
Drumrunie
517
Glas-leac Beag
Horse I.
COIGACH
Culnacraig
743
BEINN MOR COIGACH
Achduart
Langwell Lodge
Eilean Dubh
Priest I.
Rappach
Strath Kanaird
Kanaird
Carn nan Sgeir
Strath nan Lon
578
MEALL AN FHUARAIN
Bottle I.
Runie
Strath
Kanaird
Camas Mór
Loch Kanaird
415
Greenstone Point
Isle Martin
Cailleach Hd.
Allt Beinn Donuill
Rappach W.
STORNOWAY 2:40
Ardmair
Rubha Beag
Annat Bay
Rhue
Rhidorroch Forest
Opinan
Rubha Mor
Stattic Pt.
Scoraig
Carnach
Mellon Udrigle
Morefield
Ullapool
ULLAPOOL MUSEUM
Rhidorroch Ho.
548
Loch an Daimh
LITTLE LOCH BROOM
Rireavach
ULLAPOOL
Eilean Furadh Mór
Gruinard I.
Badluarach
635
BEINN GHOBHLACH
Loch Achall
Glen Achall
Rhidorroch
Ullapool
LOCHBROOM MUSEUM
East Rhidorroch Lodge
Strath Mulzie
Mungasdale
Achgarve
Dumamuck
Allt na h-Airbhe
155
Gruinard Bay
Gruinard House
Badcaul
A835
558
BEINN EILIDEACH
LOCH BROOM
Mellon Charles
Laide
First Coast
Badrallach
LECKMELM SHRUBBERY AND ARBORETUM
Sand
Inchina
A832
Blarnalearoch
Ormiscaig
Second Coast
Leckmelm
642
677
MEALL NAM BRADHAN
Isle of Ewe
Tighnafiline
Little Gruinard
Gruinard
302
Ardessie
Rhiroy
MEALL DUBH
Aultbea
Camusnagaul
Strath
Ardcharnich
Drumchork
767
SAIL MHOR
29
Ardindrean
Douchary
Loch a'Bhaid-luachraich
Dundonnell Hotel
Eilean Darach
927
SEANA BHRAIGH
Dundonnell
Letters
Inverasdale
LOCH EWE
Midtown
Loch Fada
Little Gruinard
Beag
12
Inverlael Forest
Dundonnell House
Rubha 'Ard na Bà
14
Strathnasheallag Forest
AN TEALLACH
1062
Inverlael
LAEL FOREST GARDEN
Brae
Lael Forest
B8057
Naast
Tournaig
Loch na Sealga
Inverbroom
Lael
928
Aird Dubh
INVEREWE GARDENS
A832
Strath More
Loch Bad a'Chreamh
680
BEINN A'CHAISGEIN BEAG
Broom
Londubh
Dundonnell
Forest
Auchindrean
Poolewe
Fisherfield Forest
889
1084
BEINN DEARG
Strath na Sealga
908
BEINN DEARG MHOR
Braemore
Fain
954
Ewe
Loch Kernsary
Dundonnell
Strath
Loch Tollaidh
GAIRLOCH HERITAGE MUSEUM
FIONN LOCH
Abhainn Cuileig
MEALL LEACACHAIN
618
Gairloch
MEALL AN DOIREAN
420
Dubh Loch
914
BEINN A' CHLAIDHEIMH
A832
Braemore Forest
Abhainn Droma
Dirrie More
Charlestown
791
BEINN AIRIGH CHARR
807
Lochdrum
Loch Droma
A832
LOCH MAREE
Loch a'Bhraoin
Loch Glascarnoch
Kerrysdale
BEINN LAIR
860
Letterewe Forest
934
A835
1019
MULLACH COIRE MHIC FHEARCHAIR
Shieldaig
Eilean Subhainn
1110
SGURR MOR
BEINN LIATH MHOR A 'GHIUBHAIS LI
766
Kerry
Loch Bad an Sgalaig
Letterewe
Lochan Fada
748
GROBAN
999
A'CHAILLEACH
Talladale
Loch Garbhaig
Abhainn a' Gharbh Choire
Dubh Loch
19
980
SLIOCH
949
MEALL GORM
Kinlochluichart Forest
Abhainn Braigh-horrisdale
Abhainn a'Chadh'Bhuidhe
Fannich
Forest
Loch Gaineamhach
A832
Fannich Lodge
Flowerdale
Forest
Glen Grudie
BEINN NAN RAMH
711
875
BAOSBHEINN
Forest
Loch na h-Oidhche
692
Kinlochewe Forest
LOCH FANNICH
Grudie
Aultdearg
Shieldaig
Heights of Kinlochewe
Leckie
Strath Chrombuill
878
Lochrosque Forest
624
BEINN BHREAC
Loch a'Bhealaich
Taagan
Abhainn Bruachaig
558
AN CABAR
Kinlochewe Forest
Anancaun
BEINN EIGHE NATIONAL NATURE RESERVE
Incheril
Lochluichart
Kinlochewe
933
FIONN BHEINN
Achanalt
Grudie
1010
BEINN EIGHE
A832
985
BEINN ALLIGIN
Glen Docherty
Strath Bran
Loch Achanalt
WESTER ROSS
A'Ghairbhe
Badavanich
A832
Achnasheen
Bran
Torridon Forest
Alligin Shuas
1054
LIATHACH
A896
9
Loch a'Chroisg
Loch Gharnaich
Rechullin
Inveralligin
Torridon Ho.
Fasag
Glen Torridon
17
Abhainn Dubh
Ledgowan Forest
TORRIDON
Loch Clair
Upper Loch Torridon
Torridon VISITOR CENTRE
Torridon
Loch Coulin
Loch Gowan
879
SGURR A'MHUILINN
Milton
Porter
Meig
782
SGURR DUBH
550
CARN BEAG
Balgy
Abhainn Thrail
Coulin
538
CARN MHARTUIN
Glen Meinich
Annat
A896
Coulin Forest
A890
Ben-damph Forest
678
CARN BREAC
Loch Sgamhain
STRATHCONON
Shieldaig
Loch Damh
Glen Carron
Scardroy
Loch an Eoin
BEN SHIELDAIG
439
Loch Beannacharain
Lair
Glencarron Lodge
928
Carnoch
Inverchoran
Glenshieldaig Forest
902
BEINN DAMH
993
MAOL CHEAN-DEARG
Craig
18
Glencarron and Glenuig Forest
FOREST
Allt a' Chonais
Deargh
Lair
849
BAC AN EICH
Meig
Fhiodhaig

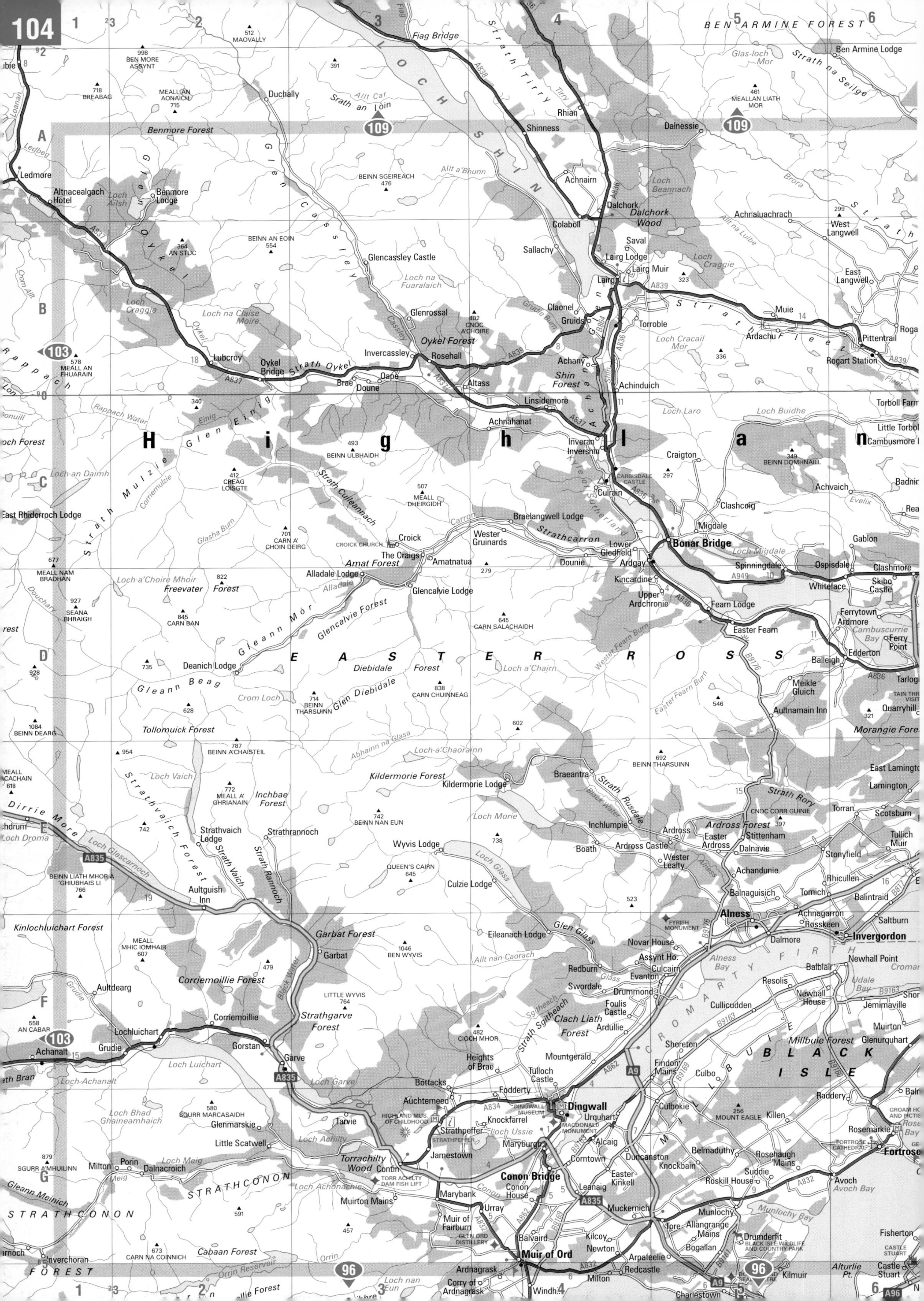
BEN ARMINE FOREST
Ben Armine Lodge
Strath na Seilge
Glas-loch Mor
461
MEALLAN LIATH MOR
Fiag Bridge
LOCH SHIN
Strath Tirry
Rhian
Shinness
Dalnessie
109
512
MAOVALLY
998
BEN MORE ASSYNT
391
718
BREABAG
MEALL AN AONAICH
715
Duchally
Allt Car
Strath an Loin
Benmore Forest
Glen Cassley
Ledmore
Altnacealgach Hotel
Loch Ailsh
Benmore Lodge
Glen Oykel
BEINN SGEIREACH
476
Allt a' Bhunn
Achnairn
Loch Beannach
Dalchork
Dalchork Wood
Colaboll
Achnaluachrach
299
West Langwell
A837
364
AN STUC
BEINN AN EOIN
554
Glencassley Castle
Sallachy
Saval
Lairg Lodge
Lairg Muir
Lairg
Loch Craggie
323
East Langwell
A839
Loch na Fuaralaich
Loch Craggie
Loch na Claise Moire
Glenrossal
402
CNOC A'CHOIRE
Claonel
Gruids
Torroble
Strath Fleet
Muie
Pittentrail
Rogart Station
103
578
MEALL AN FHUARAIN
Rappach
Lubcroy
Oykel Bridge
Strath Oykel
Invercassley
Rosehall
Oykel Forest
Achany
Shin Forest
Loch Cracail Mor
336
Ardachu
Brae
Doune
Oape
Altass
Achinduich
340
Rappach Water
Glen Einig
Linsidemore
Achnahanat
Loch Laro
Loch Buidhe
Torboll Farm
Little Torboll
Cambusmore Lodge
Highland
493
BEINN ULBHAIDH
Inveran
Invershin
Craigton
349
BEINN DOMHNAILL
Loch an Daimh
Strath Mulzie
412
CREAG LOISGTE
Strath Cuileannach
507
MEALL DHEIRGIDH
CARBISDALE CASTLE
Culrain
297
Achvaich
Badnin
East Rhidorroch Lodge
Kyle of Sutherland
Clashcoig
Braelangwell Lodge
Migdale
701
CARN A' CHOIN DEIRG
Glasha Burn
Croick
CROICK CHURCH
The Craigs
Wester Gruinards
Strathcarron
Lower Gledfield
Bonar Bridge
Gablon
Loch Migdale
677
MEALL NAM BRADHAN
Amat Forest
Amatnatua
279
Dounie
Ardgay
Spinningdale
Ospisdale
Clashmore
Loch a' Choire Mhoir
822
Freevater Forest
Alladale Lodge
Glencalvie Lodge
Kincardine
Upper Ardchronie
Whiteface
Skibo Castle
927
SEANA BHRAIGH
Douchary
845
CARN BAN
Gleann Mor
Glencalvie Forest
645
CARN SALACHAIDH
Fearn Lodge
Easter Fearn
Ferrytown
Ardmore
Cambuscurrie Bay
Ferry Point
Edderton
735
928
Deanich Lodge
EASTER ROSS
Diebidale Forest
Loch a'Chairn
Wester Fearn Burn
Balleigh
Gleann Beag
Crom Loch
714
BEINN THARSUINN
Glen Diebidale
838
CARN CHUINNEAG
Easter Fearn Burn
546
Meikle Gluich
Aultnamain Inn
321
Quarryhill
Tarlogie
628
602
Tollomuick Forest
Morangie Forest
1084
BEINN DEARG
954
787
BEINN A'CHAISTEIL
Abhainn na Glasa
Loch a'Chaorainn
692
BEINN THARSUINN
East Lamington
Lamington
MEALL ACACHAIN
618
Loch Vaich
772
MEALL A' GHRIANAIN
Inchbae Forest
Kildermorie Forest
Kildermorie Lodge
Braeantra
Strath Rusdale
Black Water
Strath Rory
CNOC CORR GUINIE
397
Torran
Scotsburn
Dirrie More
Strathvaich Forest
Strathvaich Lodge
Strathrannoch
742
BEINN NAN EUN
Loch Morie
Inchlumpie
Ardross
Ardross Forest
Easter Ardross
Stittenham
Dalnavie
Tullich Muir
Loch Droma
742
A835
Loch Glascarnoch
Strath Vaich
Strath Rannoch
Wyvis Lodge
738
Boath
Ardross Castle
Wester Lealty
Stonyfield
BEINN LIATH MHOR A' GHIUBHAIS LI
766
Aultguish Inn
QUEEN'S CAIRN
645
Loch Glass
Culzie Lodge
Achandunie
Rhicullen
Balnaguisich
Tomich
Balintraid
523
FYRISH MONUMENT
Alness
Achnagarron
Rosskeen
Invergordon
Saltburn
Kinlochluichart Forest
MEALL MHIC IOMHAIR
607
Garbat Forest
Garbat
1046
BEN WYVIS
Eileanach Lodge
Glen Glass
Novar House
Assynt Ho.
Dalmore
Alness Bay
Cromarty Firth
Newhall Point
Balblair
479
Corriemoillie Forest
Black Water
Allt nan Caorach
Redburn
Culcairn
Evanton
Swordale
Resolis
Udale Bay
Aultdearg
Grudie
LITTLE WYVIS
764
Strathgarve Forest
Drummond
Foulis Castle
Newhall House
Cullicudden
Jemimaville
558
AN CABAR
Corriemoillie
Lochluichart
Achanalt
Gorstan
482
CIOCH MHOR
Strath Sgitheach
Clach Liath Forest
Ardullie
Shoreton
Millbuie Forest
Glenurquhart
Muirton
Loch Luichart
Garve
Heights of Brae
Mountgerald
Findon Mains
BLACK ISLE
Loch Achanalt
A835
Loch Garve
Tulloch Castle
Bottacks
Fodderty
Dingwall
Culbo
Raddery
Culbokie
Loch Bhad Ghaineamhaich
580
SGURR MARCASAIDH
Glenmarskie
Tarvie
Auchterneed
HIGHLAND MUS. OF CHILDHOOD
DINGWALL MUSEUM
Knockfarrel
MACDONALD MONUMENT
Urquhart
Strathpeffer
Loch Ussie
256
MOUNT EAGLE
Killen
Rosemarkie
Little Scatwell
Loch Achilty
Maryburgh
Alcaig
FORTROSE CATHEDRAL
Fortrose
879
SGURR A' MHUILINN
Milton
Porin
Dalnacroich
Loch Meig
Torrachilty Wood
Contin
Jamestown
Corntown
Duncanston
Belmaduthy
Rosehaugh Mains
TORR ACHILTY DAM FISH LIFT
Conon Bridge
Easter Kinkell
Knockbain
Suddie
STRATHCONON
Loch Achonachie
Marybank
Conon House
Leanaig
A835
Roskill House
Avoch
Avoch Bay
Gleann Meinich
Muirton Mains
Urray
Muckernich
Munlochy
Munlochy Bay
591
457
Muir of Fairburn
Tore
Allangrange Mains
Drumderfit
BLACK ISLE WILDLIFE AND COUNTRY PARK
GLEN ORD DISTILLERY
Balvaird
Kilcoy
Newton
Bogallan
Fisherton
Inverchoran
673
CARN NA COINNICH
Cabaan Forest
Muir of Ord
Arpafeelie
CASTLE STUART
Orrin Reservoir
96
Ardnagrask
Redcastle
Alturlie Pt.
Castle Stuart
Corry of Ardnagrask
Milton
Kilmuir
Loch nan Eun
Windhill
Charlestown
A96
A9
A832
A862
A836
A949
B9176
B9163
B9169
B9161
B9160
A834

Kildonan Lodge
BAILE AN OR GOLDFISH SITE
BEINN DUBHAIN
414
Strath Skinsdale
Skinsdale
Tuarie Burn
Craggie
Craggie Burn
STRATH OF KILDONAN
Helmsdale
Torrish
Kilphedir
A897
ELDRABLE HILL
417
Marrel
West Helmsdale
HELMSDALE
Navidale
TIMESPAN
Helmsdale
Ord Point
Ousdale
A9
422
345
110
Black Water
628
BEINN DHORAIN
Glen Sletdale
Glen Loth
592
Gartymore
Portgower
Lothmore
Lothbeg
Lothbeg Pt.
Balnacoil
538
COL-BHEINN
Gordonbush
Brora
Loch Brora
Dalreavoch
Rhilochan
Farlary
BEN HORN
521
Loch Horn
Achrimsdale
East Clyne
West Clyne
Clynelish
Dalchalm
Brora
Doll
377
CAGAR FEOSAIG
Golspie Burn
466
BEINN LUNNDAIDH
Backies
Morvich
DUNROBIN CASTLE MUSEUM & GARDENS
Golspie
Culmaily
Kirkton
Lodge
Loch Fleet
Cambusavie Farm
Littleferry
Skelbo
SKELBO CASTLE
Fourpenny
Embo
Poles
Proncy
Embo Street
Pitgrudy
Evelix
WITCHES STONE
A949
B9168
DORNOCH CATHEDRAL
Dornoch
Lonemore
Dornoch Sands
DORNOCH FIRTH
Whiteness Sands
Tarbat Ness
Wilkhaven
Bindal
Portmahomack
Rockfield
GLENMORANGIE DISTILLERY
Tain
ST. DUTHUS'S CHAPEL
TAIN TOLBOOTH
Inver
Arboll
Balnagall
Tarrel
Lochslin
Aldie
Hilton
Loch Eye
Rhynie
B9165
Geanies House
Fearn Station
A9
Newfield
Hill of Fearn
Fearn
FEARN ABBEY
Loans of Tullich
Hilton of Cadboll
Logie Hill
Arabella
Balintore
Shandwick
Kildary
Milton
Tarbat Ho.
B9175
Ankerville
Chapelhill
Kilmuir
Nigg Bay
Pitcalnie
Port an Righ
Nigg
203
Sands of Nigg
Mount Canisp
King's Cave
Balnabruaich
Dunskeath Ness
Balnapaling
Castlecraig
Ferry
KIRKWALL 8:30
Cromarty
CROMARTY COURT HOUSE
HUGH MILLER'S COTTAGE
Sutors of Cromarty
Newton
A832
Upper Eathie
MORAY FIRTH
Halliman Skerries
Covesea Skerries
LOSSIEMOUTH FISHERIES & COMMUNITY MUSEUM
Covesea
Stotfield
Branderburgh
Lossiem
BURGHEAD MUSEUM
Burghead
Hopeman
B9040
Cummingstown
Duffus
Gordonstoun
Roseisle
DUFFUS CASTLE
Roseisle Forest
BURGHEAD BAY
PALACE OF SPYNIE
Spynie
98
Findhorn
Lower Hempriggs
Quarrywood
Newton
Bishopmill
Elgin
ELGIN MUSEUM
ELGIN CATHEDRAL
CASHMERE VISITOR CENTRE
OLD MILLS
New Elgin
A96
Findhorn Bay
Coltfield
Alves
Miltonhill
Kincorth Ho.
KINLOSS ABBEY
Kinloss
Grange Hall
Pittendreich
Miltonduff
Moss of Barmuckity
The Bar
Culbin Forest
Kintessack
Springfield
Moy Ho.
SUENO'S STONE
Mains of Burgie
Forres
FALCONER MUSEUM
Monaughty Forest
PLUSCARDEN PRIORY
Auchtertyre
Paddockhaugh
Longmorn
BIRNIE CHURCH
Blervie Castle
Califer
Barnhill
Foresterseat
Thornhill
Whitewre
NAIRN FISHERTOWN MUSEUM
NAIRN LITERARY INSTITUTE MUSEUM
BRODIE CASTLE
Dyke
DALLAS DHU DISTILLERY
Rafford
Whiteness Head
Nairn
BOATH DOVECOTE
DARNAWAY FARM VISITOR CENTRE
Earlsmill
Findhorn
FORT GEORGE
Fort George
Kirkton
Baddock
Tradespark
A96
QUEEN'S OWN HIGHLANDERS MUS
B9006
Ardersier
Chanonry Pt.
B9092
Moss-side
Auldearn
Blackhills
Whitemire
A940
Altyre Ho.
B9010
Black Burn
Briach
Dallas Forest
319
Kellas
Glenlatterach
A941
Glen of Rothes
338
Gollanfield
Milton of Gollanfield
Muir of the Clans
Geddes House
Lethen Forest
Conicavel
Easter Milton
Wester Milton
Darnaway Forest
Altyre Woods
Branchill
Newtyle Forest
Dallas
Moray
INVERNESS
Rosefield
Regoul
Clephanton
Cawdor
Piperhill
Logie
Drumine Forest
Craigroy
365
CAIRN UISH
Tomagrain
Croy
KILRAVOCK CASTLE
CAWDOR CASTLE AND GARDENS
97
Littlemill
Mid Urchany
A939
371
MILL BUIE
Burn of Rothes
Easter
A
B
C
D
E
F
G

Bàgh D
GEARRANNAN (GARENIN)
Gearrannan
Borghastan
Campay
Loch Chàrlabhaigh
DUN CARLOWAY BROCH
Floday
Little Bernera
Dun Charlabhaigh
Harsgeir
Crothair
An Galan Uigeach
AN CAOLAS
Tobson
Pabay Mor
Tolastadh a Ch
Aird Uig
Bhaltos
Vacsay
Breacleit
Great Bernera
Bàgh Fhiabhaig
205
Cliobh
Vuia Mòr
Circebost
Miabhig
Barraglom
Timsgearraidh
Riof
Tacleit
Cradhlastadh
Loch Ròg
B8011
Tobhtarol
Ard More Mangersta
Vuia Beag
Crulabhig
Cairisiadar
Floday
Mangurstadh
Eadar Dha Fhadhail
SUAINAVAL 429
Geisiadar
256
Aird Fenish
Loch Tungabhat
Loch Suainaval
Islibhig
Einacleit
Loch Ròg
Aird Brenish
Breanais
574 MEALISVAL
Loch Grunabhat
Giosla
B8011
Giosla
Loch Chaolartan
Loch Fuaroil
19
397 BEINN MHEADHONACH
Loch Morsgail
Mealasta Island
Caolas an Eilein
Loch Cro Criosdaig
Loch Coirigerod
Loch Tamanabhaigh
Loch Beiniseabhal
Morsgail Forest
Loch Tealasabhaigh
Loch Bodabhat
Kearstay
Loch Reasort
308
Bràighe Mòr
Loch Crabhadail
Scarp
Abhainn Bhearara
Ulladail
LOCH LANGAB
101
Loch a'Ghlinne

6
7
8
9
10
A
B
C
D
E
F
G
H
RUBHA ROBHANAIS
CHURCH OF ST. MOLVAG
Cunndal
Eoropaidh
Coig Peighinnean
B8013
B8014
Lional
Port Nis
Cross Sands
Suainebost
Cros
Tabost
B8015
Aird Dhail
Dail bho Dheas
Dail bho Thuath
Sgiogarstaigh
Glen Cross
Gabhsann bho Thuath
Gabhsann bho Dheas
A857
Mealabost
Baile Ard
Coig Peighinnean
Siadar
Siadar Iarach
Siadar Uarach
Baile an Truiseil
TRUSHAL STONE
Rubha Leathann
Aird Barvas
Cuiashader
Cellar Head
Gabhsann bho Dheas
Loch Langabhat
Borgh
Dail
Loch Mòr Shanndabhat
Abhainn Ghearadha
BLACK HOUSE MUSEUM
Barabhas Iarach
Barabhas Uarach
Barabhas
Labost
Arnol
Bru
Bragar
A858
Siabost bho Thuath
Siabost bho Dheas
Pairc Shiaboist
Dail Beag
Dail Mor
Carlabhagh
261 BEINN BRAGAR
Loch Urghag
Loch Breibhat
Gleann Mór Barvas
Gleann Bhruthadail
Glen Bragar
248 MUIRNEAG
Baile Ur
Tolastadh bho Thuath
Tolsta Head
B895
Loch Sgeireach Mor
Griais
Gleann Tholastaidh
Port Bun a'Ghlinne
Creag Fhraoch
Bac
Col
Col Uarach
Breibhig
Vatisker Pt.
Lacasdal
Loch Scarabhat Mhòr
Loch Mòr an Stàirr
292 BEINN MHOLACH
ISLE OF LEWIS (LEODHAIS)
Loch Lacsabhat Ard
Loch nan Stearnag
Lacasdail
Coll Sands
BROAD BAY OR LOCH A TUATH
Aird Thunga
Tunga
Sròn Ruadh
Rubha an t-Siumpain
Port Nan Giuran
Port Mholair
Fleisirin
Aird
Sulaisiadar
Seisiadar
Griánan
Newmarket
An Gleann Ur
Breascleit
Lacasdal
MUSEUM NAN EILEAN
STORNOWAY
Stornoway
Mealabost
Garrabost
EYE PENINSULA
Aiginis
Loch Urabhal
A858
Grioda
Sanndabhaig
AN LANNTAIR GALLERY
A866
Cnoc
Pabail Uarach
Pabail Iarach
Suardail
Bàgh Phabail
Tolm
Holm I.
A'Chearc
Gearraidh na h-Aibhne
Linsiadar
223 Loch a Ghainmhich
Acha Mor
A859
Arnish Moor
Loch Smùaiseabhal
B8011
Loch Orasaigh
Loch Tobhta Bridein
Loch nam Falcag
Griomsiadar
Ben Casgro
Liurbost
Ranais
Raerinish Pt.
Crosbost
ULLAPOOL 2:40
Soval Lodge
Loch Trealabhal
Laxay
Barkin Is.
Tabhaidh Mhor
Eilean Chaluim Chille
Ceos
Eilean Orasaidh
Lacasaigh
Cromor
Baile Ailein
Eireasort
Gearraidh Bhaird
Cabharstadh
Eilean Thoraidh
Loch Strandabhat
Sildinis
Cearsiadar
CEARSIADER (KERSHADER)
Tabost
B8060
Marbhig
Kintarvie
Airidh a Bhruaich
Ceann Loch Shiphoirt
Loch Sgibacleit
Loch nan Eilean
Calbost
Aird an Troim
Gleann Ghrabhair
Grabhair
Loch Odhairn
Kebock Head
101
Loch Shanndabhat
PARK

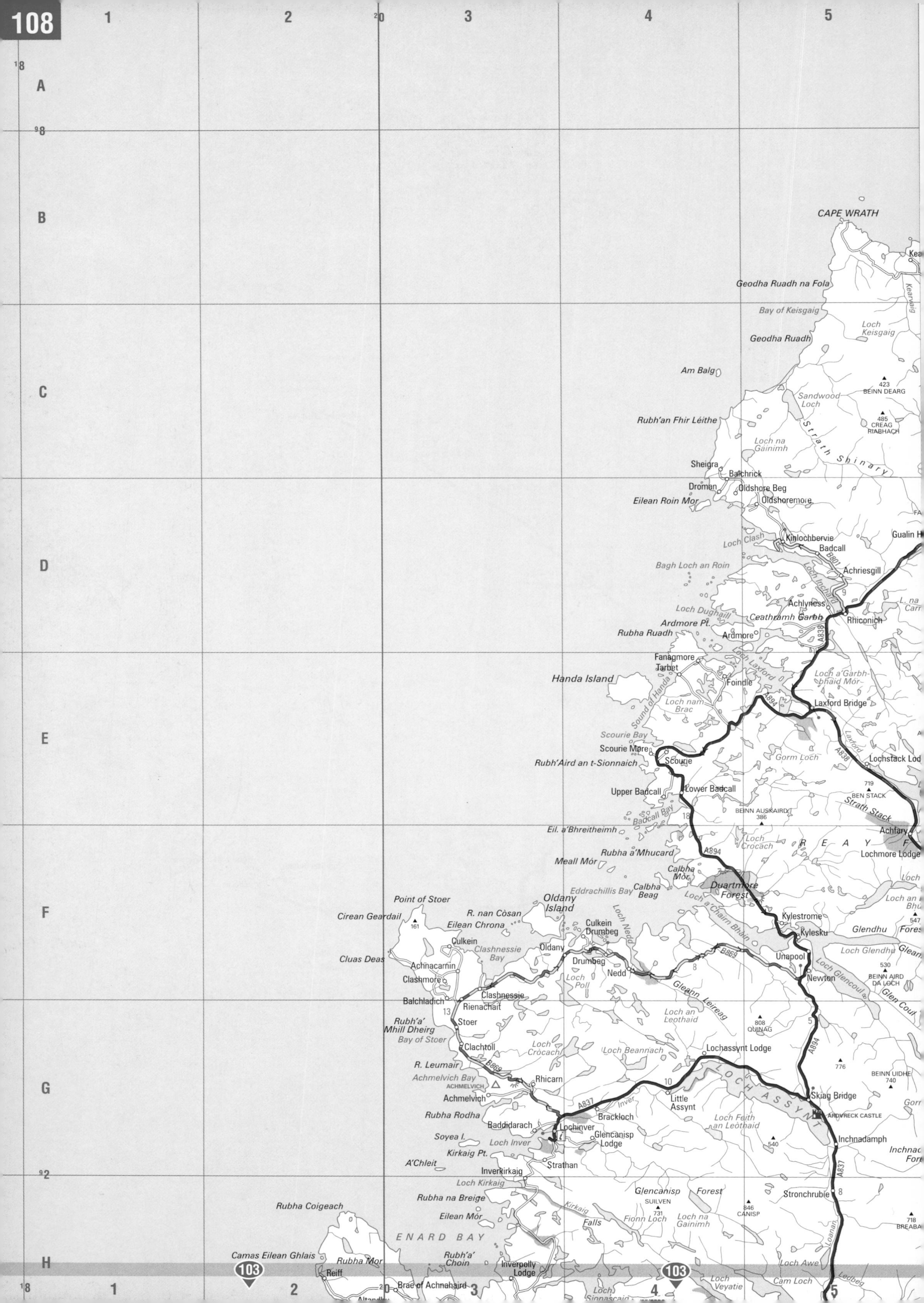

1
2
3
4
5
A
B
C
D
E
F
G
H
CAPE WRATH
Geodha Ruadh na Fola
Bay of Keisgaig
Loch Keisgaig
Kearvaig
Geodha Ruadh
Am Balg
423 BEINN DEARG
Sandwood Loch
485 CREAG RIABHACH
Rubh'an Fhir Léithe
Strath Shinary
Loch na Gainimh
Sheigra
Balchrick
Droman
Oldshore Beg
Eilean Roin Mor
Oldshoremore
Loch Clash
Kinlochbervie
Badcall
B801
Gualin H
Bagh Loch an Roin
Loch Inchard
Achriesgill
Achlyness
Loch Dughaill
Ceathramh Garbh
Rhiconich
Ardmore Pt.
Rubha Ruadh
Ardmore
A838
Fanagmore
Tarbet
Loch Laxford
Handa Island
Foindle
Loch a'Garbh-bhaid Mór
Sound of Handa
Loch nam Brac
A894
Laxford Bridge
Scourie Bay
Scourie More
Scourie
Gorm Loch
Laxford
Lochstack Lod
Rubh'Aird an t-Sionnaich
Upper Badcall
Lower Badcall
719 BEN STACK
Strath Stack
BEINN AUSKAIRD 386
Badcall Bay
Eil. a'Bhreitheimh
Achfary
Loch Crocach
REAY F
Lochmore Lodge
Rubha a'Mhucard
Meall Mór
Calbha Mór
Duartmore Forest
Eddrachillis Bay
Calbha Beag
Loch a'Chairn Bhain
Point of Stoer
Oldany Island
Kylestrome
Cirean Geardail
161
R. nan Còsan
Eilean Chrona
Culkein Drumbeg
Loch Nedd
Kylesku
Glendhu
Culkein
Clashnessie Bay
Oldany
Cluas Deas
Drumbeg
B869
Unapool
Loch Glendhu
530 BEINN AIRD DA LOCH
Achnacarnin
Clashmore
Nedd
Loch Poll
Gleann Leireag
Newton
Loch Glencoul
Glen Coul
Balchladich
Clashnessie
Rienachait
Loch an Leothaid
808 QUINAG
Rubh'a' Mhill Dheirg
Stoer
Bay of Stoer
Clachtoll
Loch Crocach
Loch Beannach
Lochassynt Lodge
R. Leumair
Achmelvich Bay
ACHMELVICH
Rhicarn
776
BEINN UIDHE 740
Achmelvich
A837
Little Assynt
LOCH ASSYNT
Skiag Bridge
Rubha Rodha
Inver
Brackloch
ARDVRECK CASTLE
Baddidarach
Lochinver
Loch Feith an Leòthaid
Soyea I.
Loch Inver
Glencanisp Lodge
540
Inchnadamph
Kirkaig Pt.
A'Chleit
Strathan
Inverkirkaig
Loch Kirkaig
Glencanisp Forest
Stronchrubie
Rubha na Breige
SUILVEN 731
846 CANISP
Rubha Coigeach
Eilean Mór
Kirkaig
Falls
Fionn Loch
Loch na Gainimh
718 BREABA
ENARD BAY
Camas Eilean Ghlais
Rubha Mor
Rubh'a' Choin
Inverpolly Lodge
Loch Awe
103
Reiff
Brae of Achnahaird
Loch Veyatie
Cam Loch
Ledbeg
Loanan

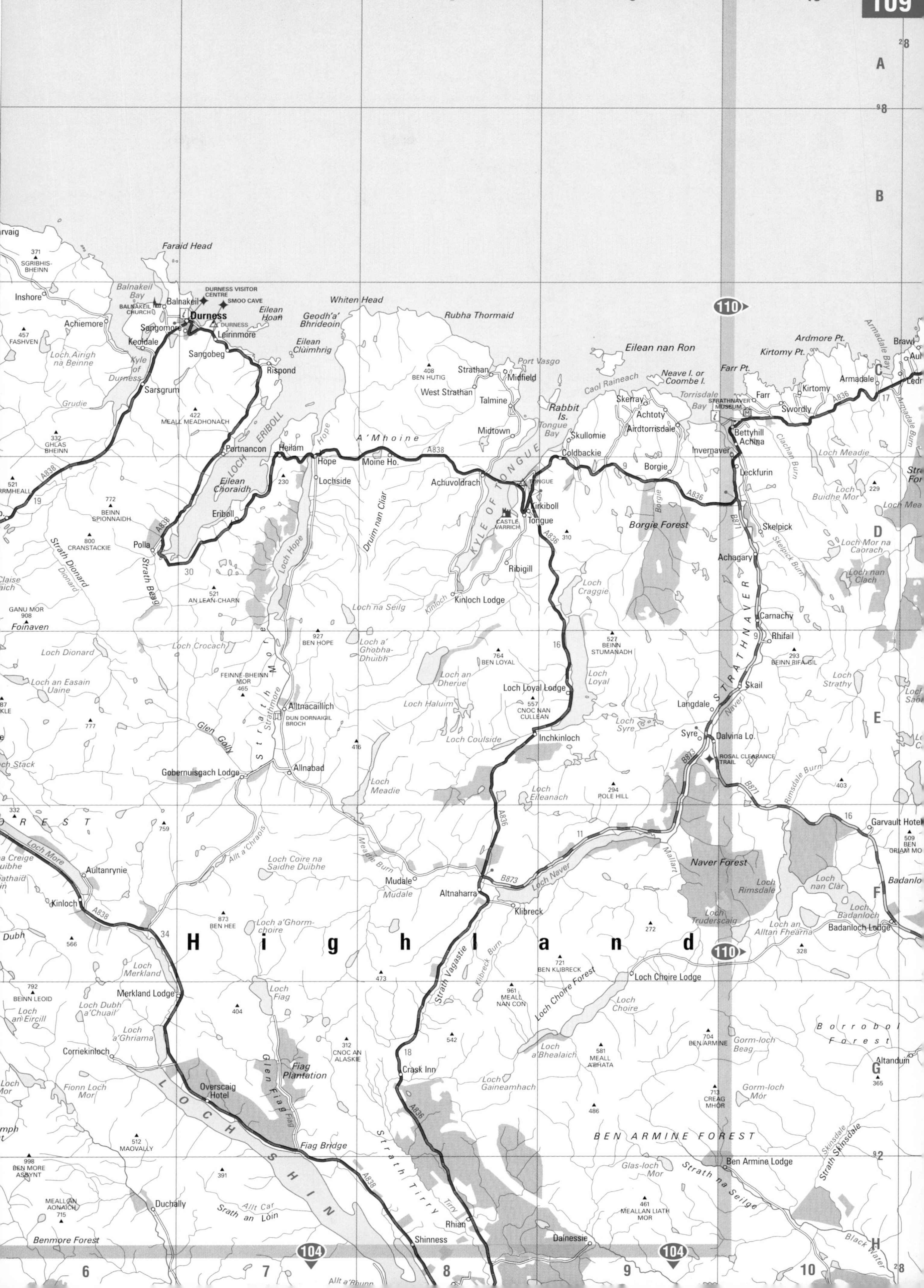

6
7
8
9
10
A
B
C
D
E
F
G
H
Faraid Head
371 SGRIBHIS-BHEINN
Balnakeil Bay
Balnakeil
BALNAKEIL CHURCH
DURNESS VISITOR CENTRE
SMOO CAVE
Durness
DURNESS
Inshore
Achiemore
Sangomore
Keoldale
Leirinmore
Eilean Hoan
Whiten Head
Geodh'a' Bhrideoin
Eilean Cluimhrig
Rubha Thormaid
110
457 FASHVEN
Loch Airigh na Beinne
Kyle of Durness
Sangobeg
Rispond
Sarsgrum
Grudie
422 MEALL MEADHONACH
LOCH ERIBOLL
332 GHLAS BHEINN
Portnancon
Heilam
Hope
A'Mhoine
A838
Moine Ho.
Lochside
230
521 RMHEALL
19
772 BEINN SPIONNAIDH
Eilean Choraidh
Eriboll
800 CRANSTACKIE
Strath Dionard
Dionard
Polla
Strath Beag
30
521 AN LEAN-CHARN
Loch Hope
Druim nan Cliar
GANU MOR 908
Foinaven
Loch Crocach
Loch Dionard
Loch an Easain Uaine
927 BEN HOPE
Loch na Seilg
Loch a' Ghobha-Dhuibh
FEINNE-BHEINN MOR 465
Strath More
Strathmore
Alltnacaillich
DUN DORNAIGIL BROCH
777
Glen Golly
416
Gobernuisgach Lodge
Allnabad
Loch Meadie
332
FOREST
759
Loch More
Allt a'Chraois
Loch Coire na Saidhe Duibhe
Meadie Burn
Mudale
Aultanrynie
Kinloch
A838
873 BEN HEE
Loch a'Ghorm-choire
566
34
Highland
Loch Merkland
473
792 BEINN LEOID
Merkland Lodge
Loch Fiag
404
Loch Dubh a'Chuail
Loch an Eircill
Loch a'Ghriama
312 CNOC AN ALASKIE
Glen Fiag
Fiag Plantation
Corriekinloch
Fionn Loch Mor
Overscaig Hotel
LOCH SHIN
Fiag Bridge
512 MAOVALLY
998 BEN MORE ASSYNT
391
MEALLAN AONAICH 715
Duchally
Srath an Loin
Allt Car
Benmore Forest
104
Allt a'Bhunn
Strath Tirry
Tirry
Rhian
Shinness
Crask Inn
18
A836
Strath Vagastie
Klibreck Burn
Altnaharra
Klibreck
Mudale
B873
Loch Naver
11
542
961 MEALL NAN CON
Loch Choire Forest
Loch a'Bhealaich
Loch Gaineamhach
581 MEALL A'BHATA
486
Dalnessie
408 BEN HUTIG
Strathan
West Strathan
Midfield
Port Vasgo
Talmine
Midtown
Achuvoldrach
KYLE OF TONGUE
TONGUE
Kirkiboll
CASTLE VARRICH
Tongue
Rabbit Is.
Tongue Bay
Skullomie
Coldbackie
Ribigill
Kinloch
Kinloch Lodge
310
Loch Craggie
16
764 BEN LOYAL
Loch an Dherue
Loch Haluim
Loch Loyal Lodge
557 CNOC NAN CULLEAN
Loch Loyal
Loch Coulside
Inchkinloch
Loch Eileanach
A836
Eilean nan Ron
Caol Raineach
Neave I. or Coombe I.
Skerray
Achtoty
Airdtorrisdale
Torrisdale Bay
Borgie
Borgie Forest
527 BEINN STUMANADH
Loch Syre
Syre
294 POLE HILL
Langdale
272
721 BEN KLIBRECK
Loch Choire Lodge
Loch Choire
704 BEN ARMINE
BEN ARMINE FOREST
Glas-loch Mor
461 MEALLAN LIATH MOR
Farr Pt.
Farr
STRATHNAVER MUSEUM
Invernaver
Bettyhill
Achina
Leckfurin
A836
B871
Skelpick
Achagary
STRATHNAVER
Carnachy
Rhifail
Skail
Naver
Dalvina Lo.
ROSAL CLEARANCE TRAIL
Mallart
Naver Forest
Loch Rimsdale
Loch Truderscaig
713 CREAG MHOR
Strath na Seilge
Ben Armine Lodge
Kirtomy Pt.
Ardmore Pt.
Kirtomy
Swordly
Armadale
Armadale Bay
Armadale Burn
17
Clachan Burn
Loch Meadie
229
Loch Buidhe Mor
Loch Mor na Caorach
Loch nan Clach
Skelpick Burn
293 BEINN RIFA-GIL
Loch Strathy
403
Rimsdale Burn
Garvault Hotel
509 BEN GRIAM MO
Loch nan Clàr
Loch Badanloch
Badanloch Lodge
Loch an Alltan Fhearna
328
Borrobol Forest
Gorm-loch Beag
Gorm-loch Mor
Altanduin
365
Strath Skinsdale
Skinsdale
Black Water
Brawl

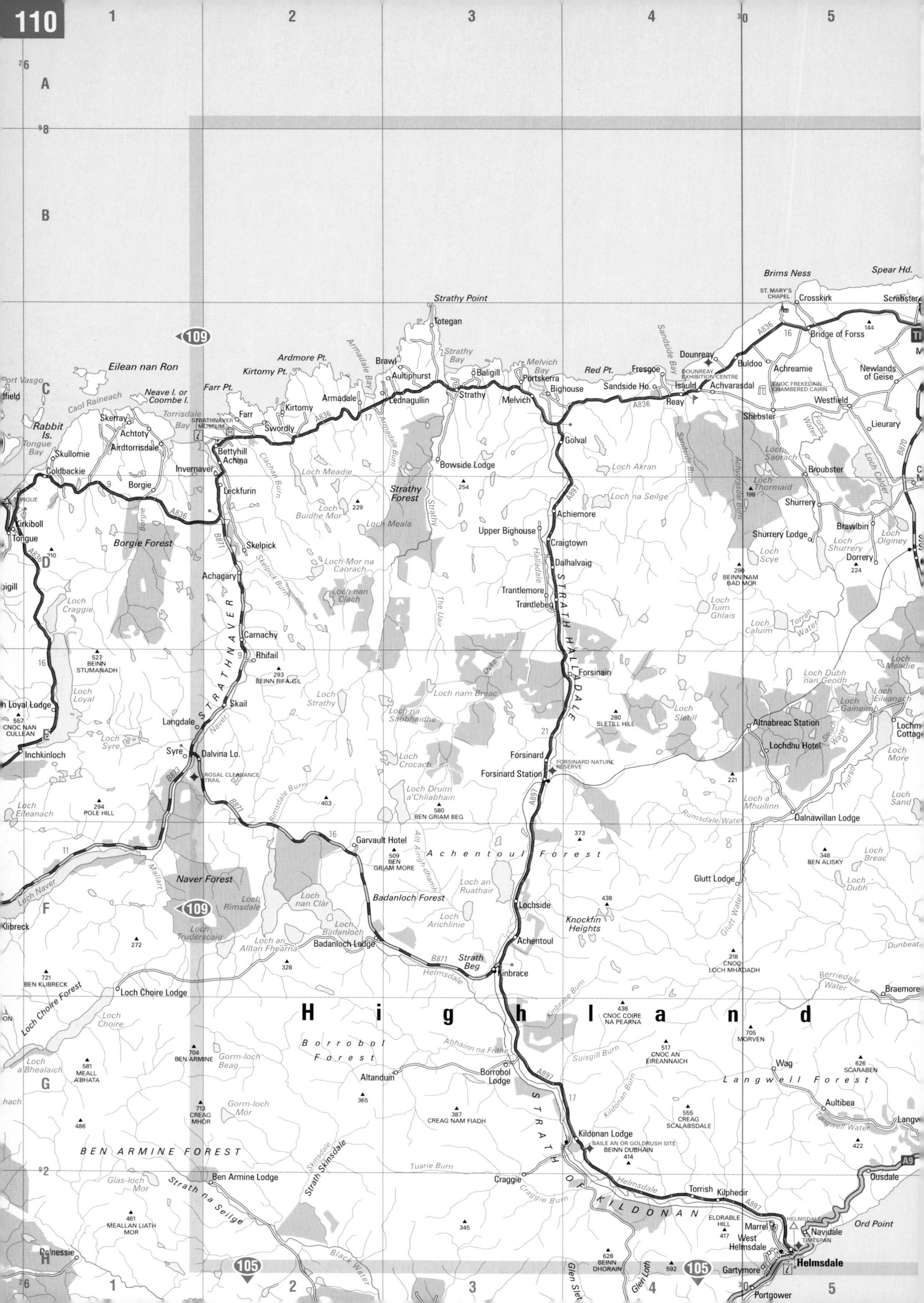
1
2
3
4
5
A
B
C
D
E
F
G
H
109
105
Brims Ness
Spear Hd.
Strathy Point
St. Mary's Chapel
Crosskirk
Scrabster
Totegan
Bridge of Forss
Strathy Bay
Dounreay
Buldoo
Achreamie
Newlands of Geise
Eilean nan Ron
Ardmore Pt.
Armadale Bay
Brawl
Aultiphurst
Baligill
Melvich Bay
Portskerra
Red Pt.
Fresgoe
Sandside Bay
Dounreay Exhibition Centre
Cnoc Freiceadain Chambered Cairn
Port Vasgo
Kirtomy Pt.
Farr Pt.
Neave I. or Coombe I.
Caol Raineach
Torrisdale Bay
Armadale
Lednagullin
Strathy
Melvich
Bighouse
Sandside Ho.
Isauld
Reay
Achvarasdal
Westfield
Rabbit Is.
Skerray
Achtoty
Farr
Kirtomy
Swordly
Strathnaver Museum
Shebster
Forss Water
Lieurary
Tongue Bay
Skullomie
Airdtorrisdale
Bettyhill
Achina
Golval
Bowside Lodge
Loch Akran
Loch Saorach
Coldbackie
Invernaver
Borgie
Clachan Burn
Loch Meadie
Strathy Forest
Loch Thormaid
Broubster
Loch Calder
Tongue
Kirkiboll
Leckfurin
Loch Buidhe Mor
Loch Meala
Loch na Seilge
Achiemore
Sandside Burn
Achvarasdal Burn
Shurrery
Brawlbin
Borgie Forest
Skelpick
Upper Bighouse
Craigtown
Shurrery Lodge
Loch Shurrery
Loch Olginey
Loch Scye
Dorrery
Achagary
Loch Mor na Caorach
Skelpick Burn
Halladale
Dalhalvaig
Beinn nam Bad Mor
Loch Craggie
Loch nan Clach
Trantlemore
Trantlebeg
Strath Halladale
Strathnaver
The Uair
Loch Tuim Ghlais
Carnachy
Loch Caluim
Torran Water
Beinn Stumanadh
Rhifail
Beinn Rifa-gil
Forsinain
Loch Dubh nan Geodh
Loch Meadie
Loch Loyal
Loch Strathy
Loch nam Breac
Loch Eileanach
Loch Gaineimh
Loyal Lodge
Skail
Loch na Saobhaidhe
Loch Sletill
Sletill Hill
Altnabreac Station
Cnoc nan Cullean
Langdale
Naver
Loch Syre
Lochdhu Hotel
Sleach Water
Lochmore Cottage
Inchkinloch
Syre
Dalvina Lo.
Loch Crocach
Forsinard
Forsinard Nature Reserve
Forsinard Station
Loch More
Rosal Clearance Trail
Loch Druim a' Chliabhain
Thurso
Loch Eileanach
Pole Hill
Rimsdale Burn
Ben Griam Beg
Loch a' Mhuilinn
Loch Sand
Rumsdale Water
Dalnawillan Lodge
Garvault Hotel
Ben Griam More
Allt Airigh-dhamh
Achentoul Forest
Ben Alisky
Loch Breac
Mallart
Naver Forest
Glutt Lodge
Loch Dubh
Loch Naver
Loch an Ruathair
Loch Rimsdale
Loch nan Clàr
Badanloch Forest
Lochside
Glutt Water
Klibreck
Loch Arichlinie
Knockfin Heights
Loch Badanloch
Loch Truderscaig
Loch an Alltan Fhearna
Badanloch Lodge
Achentoul
Dunbeath
Strath Beg
Cnoc Loch Mhadadh
Ben Klibreck
Helmsdale
Kinbrace
Berriedale Water
Loch Choire Lodge
Braemore
Loch Choire Forest
Kinbrace Burn
Highland
Loch Choire
Cnoc Coire na Pearnna
Morven
Borrobol Forest
Abhainn na Frithe
Loch a'Bhealaich
Ben Armine
Gorm-loch Beag
Suisgill Burn
Cnoc an Eireannaich
Scaraben
Meall a'Bhata
Wag
Altanduin
Borrobol Lodge
Langwell Forest
Kildonan Burn
Creag Mhor
Gorm-loch Mòr
Creag nam Fiadh
Creag Scalabsdale
Aultibea
Langwell Water
Langwell
Kildonan Lodge
Baile an Or Goldrush Site
Beinn Dubhain
Ben Armine Forest
Skinsdale
Tuarie Burn
Strath Skinsdale
Ben Armine Lodge
Craggie
Craggie Burn
Strath of Kildonan
Torrish
Kilphedir
Ousdale
Glas-loch Mor
Strath na Seilge
Meallan Liath Mor
Eldrable Hill
Marrel
Helmsdale Timespan
Navidale
Ord Point
West Helmsdale
Dalnessie
Black Water
Beinn Dhorain
Glen Loth
Glen Sletdale
Gartymore
Helmsdale
Portgower
A836
A897
B871
B873
B870
A9
A838
16
17
9
11
21
144
254
229
198
290
224
310
527
293
280
557
221
294
403
580
373
348
509
438
272
318
721
328
704
581
705
517
626
713
365
387
555
486
422
414
461
345
417
628
592

PENTLAND FIRTH
North Hd.
Swona
Barth Hd.
Dundas Ho.
Burwick
Nklater
Halcro Hd.
Cleat
TOMB OF THE EAGLES AND BRONZE AGE HOUSE
Old Hd.
Liddel
Brough Ness
B904
A96
112
Langaton Point
Muckle Skerry
Pentland Skerries
Nethertown
Red Head
Island of Stroma
Mell Head
Uppertown
0:45
DUNNET HEAD
Briga Hd.
STROMNESS 1:45
Holborn Hd.
The Thirl
Scarfskerry Pt.
Scarfskerry
Men of Mey
St. John's Pt.
Boars of Duncansby
East Mey
Gills Bay
Brough
Ham
Hunspow
St. John's Loch
Rattar
MARY ANN'S COTTAGE
Corsback
Barrock
Mey
Gills
Kirkstyle
Huna
DUNCANSBY HEAD
A836
JOHN O' GROATS
Canisbay
John o' Groats
Stacks of Duncansby
Dunnet
Clardon Hd.
Thurso Bay
DUNNET BAY
THURSO CASTLE
THURSO MUSEUM
FLAGSTONE INTERPRETATIVE TRAIL
Castlehill
Inkstack
Brabster
Clardon
Murkle
Thurso
Thurso East
Haimer
Castletown
Greenland
Loch Heilen
Lochend
Gill Burn
Tofts
Skirza
Skirza Head
Freswick
Freswick Bay
Olrig Ho.
Tain
Slickly
Ness Head
BUCHOLLY CASTLE
Geise
Hilliclay
Durran
Weydale
Reaster
Alterwall
NORTHLANDS VIKING CENTRE
Auckengill
Bowermadden
Lyth
LYTH ARTS CENTRE
Sortat
Barrock Ho.
Nybster
Brough Head
Buckies
Achingills
Sordale
Stemster
Knockdee
Bowertower
Howe
Keiss
KEISS CASTLE
Braal Castle
Stemster Ho.
Halcro
Hastigrow
Mireland
Roadside
Clayock
Loch Scarmclate
Gillock
Kirk
Loch of Wester
Halkirk
North Watten
Myrelandhorn
SINCLAIR'S BAY
A882
Banniskirk Ho.
Mains of Watten
Killimster
B876
B870
B874
Harpsdale
Loch Watten
Scotscalder Station
Ighmore
CASTLE GIRNIGOE
Noss Head
Reiss
Spittal
Backlass
Watten
Winless
CASTLE SINCLAIR
Sealky Head
A99
Ackergill
Bilbster
WICK
Staxigoe
Mybster
Loch of Toftingall
WICK HERITAGE CENTRE
Papigoe
Westerdale
Strath
Wick
Acharole
Broadhaven
Burn of Acharole
Strath Burn
Stirkoke Ho.
Milton
Wick Bay
Old Wick
Newton
South Hd.
CASTLE OF OLD WICK
Badlipster
Achairn Burn
Whiterow
Gote O'Tram
Strathmore Lodge
Little River
Tannach
Hempriggs House
Loch Hempriggs
Helman Hd.
Camster Burn
HILL OF OLICLETT
Rangag
Thrumster
GREY CAIRNS OF CAMSTER
Gansclet
Sarclet
Loch Ruard
Achavanich
Loch of Yarrows
Sarclet Hd.
Loch Thulachan
STEMSTER HILL
Loch Rangag
Camster
Ulbster
CAIRN OF GET
Whaligoe
Roster
Crofts of Benachielt
MILL O' MANY STANES
Bruan
Rumster Forest
Upper Lybster
Mid Clyth
Braehungie
Reisgill Burn
West Clyth
CONANH CONACHREAG
Forse Ho.
Swiney
Lybster
Houstry
WAG OF FORSE
Burn of Houstry
Smerral
Forse
Latheron
CLAN GUNN HERITAGE CENTRE
Latheronwheel Ho.
Latheronwheel
LAIDHAY CROFT MUSEUM
Balnabruich
DUNBEATH HERITAGE CENTRE
Dunbeath
Knockally
Dunbeath Bay
DUNBEATH CASTLE
Ramscraigs
Borgue
Newport
Ceann Leathad nam Bò
Berriedale
A
B
C
D
E
F
G
H
6
7
8
9
10

Orkney
Papa Westray
Holm of Papa
North Ronaldsay
Hollandstoun
NORTH RONALDSAY FIRTH
NOUP HEAD
Pierowall
WESTRAY
THE NORTH SOUND
Sanday
Lettan
START PT.
WESTRAY FIRTH
Calf of Eday
EDAY
SANDAY SOUND
ROUSAY
Egilsay
Wyre
Eynhallow
Muckle Green Holm
Papa Stronsay
Linga Holm
STRONSAY
Gairsay
Shapinsay
STRONSAY FIRTH
Auskerry
BROUGH HEAD
MAINLAND
Kirkwall
Stromness
Copinsay
SCAPA FLOW
HOY
Cava
Rysa Little
Fara
Flotta
Switha
SOUTH WALLS
Burray
SOUTH RONALDSAY
Swona
PENTLAND FIRTH
OLD MAN OF HOY
RORA HEAD
Island of Stroma
DUNNET HEAD
DUNCANSBY HEAD
DUNNET BAY
Thurso
Halkirk
SINCLAIR'S BAY
Wick
Scale : 1:450 000
(approx 7 miles to 1 inch)
0 5 10 15 miles
0 5 10 15 20 25 km

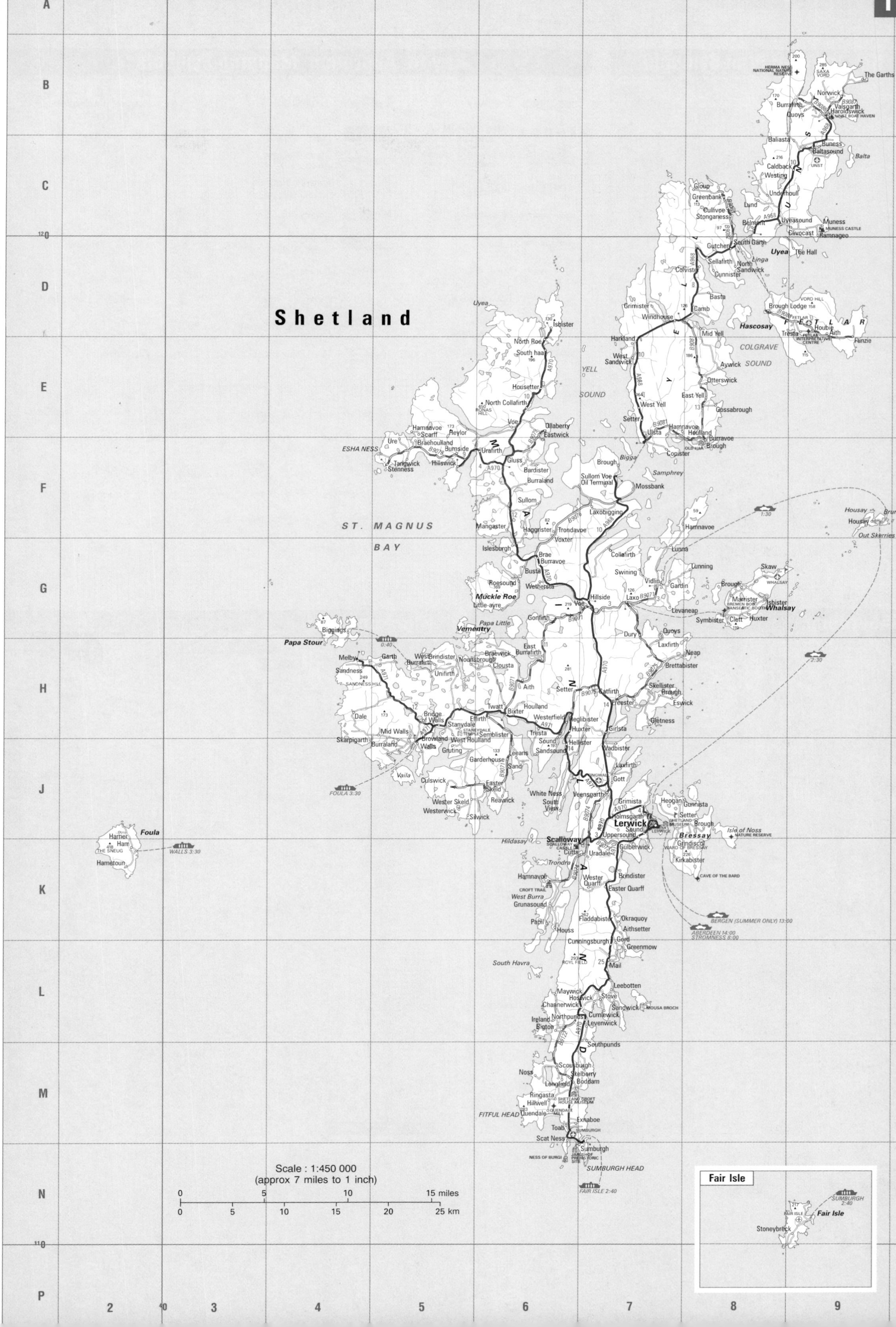
Shetland
ST. MAGNUS
BAY
YELL
SOUND
COLGRAVE
SOUND
Hascosay
Uyea
Unst
Burrafirth
Norwick
Haroldswick
Valsgarth
Baliasta
Buness
Baltasound
Balta
Caldback
Westing
Underhoull
Lund
Belmont
Uyeasound
Muness
Clivocast
Bamnageo
The Hall
The Garths
Gloup
Greenbank
Cullivoe
Stonganess
Gutcher
South Garth
Sellafirth
North Sandwick
Cunnister
Linga
Basta
Camb
Grimister
Windhouse
Mid Yell
Harkland
West Sandwick
Aywick
Otterswick
East Yell
West Yell
Gossabrough
Setter
Ulsta
Hamnavoe
Hogland
Burravoe
Brough
Copister
Brough Lodge
Vord Hill
Fetlar
Houbie
Tresta
Aith
Funzie
Isbister
North Roe
South haa
Housetter
North Collafirth
Ronas Hill
Voe
Ollaberry
Eastwick
Hamnavoe
Scarff
Heylor
Ure
Braehoulland
Burnside
Urafirth
Esha Ness
Tangwick
Stenness
Hillswick
Gluss
Bardister
Burraland
Sullom
Sullom Voe Oil Terminal
Brough
Bigga
Samphrey
Mossbank
Laxobigging
Mangaster
Haggrister
Trondavoe
Voxter
Islesburgh
Brae
Burravoe
Busta
Wethersta
Roesound
Muckle Roe
Little-ayre
Hamnavoe
Lunna
Lunning
Collafirth
Swining
Vidlin
Gardin
Laxo
Hillside
Voe
Skaw
Brough
Marrister
Isbister
Whalsay
Symbister
Clett
Huxter
Levaneap
Housay
Bruray
Out Skerries
Gonfirth
Papa Little
Vementry
Biggings
Papa Stour
Melby
Sandness
Garth
West Burrafirth
Brindister
Noonsbrough
Clousta
Unifirth
East Burrafirth
Aith
Dury
Quoys
Laxfirth
Neap
Brettabister
Skellister
Brough
Eswick
Setter
Catfirth
Freester
Girlsta
Gletness
Dale
Bridge of Walls
Mid Walls
Skarpigarth
Burraland
Browland
Walls
Stanydale
Effirth
Twatt
Bixter
Semblister
West Houlland
Gruting
Houlland
Westerfield
Tresta
Sound
Sandsound
Tagliblster
Huxter
Hellister
Vadbister
Laxfirth
Garderhouse
Sand
Gott
Vaila
Culswick
Easter Skeld
Wester Skeld
Reawick
Westerwick
Silwick
White Ness
South View
Veensgarth
Grimista
Heogan
Gunnista
Setter
Lerwick
Sound
Bressay
Brough
Grindiscol
Isle of Noss
Kirkabister
Gulberwick
Hildasay
Scalloway
Cutts
Uradale
Trondra
Hamnavoe
West Burra
Grunasound
Wester Quarff
Easter Quarff
Bondister
Papil
Houss
Fladdabister
Okraquoy
Aithsetter
Cunningsburgh
Greenmow
South Havra
Mail
Leebotten
Maywick
Hoswick
Stove
Channerwick
Sandwick
Ireland
Bigton
Northpund
Cumlewick
Levenwick
Southpunds
Noss
Scousburgh
Skelberry
Boddam
Ringasta
Hillwell
Quendale
Fitful Head
Exnaboe
Toab
Scat Ness
Sumburgh
Sumburgh Head
Foula
Harrier
Ham
Hametoun
The Sneug
Walls 3:30
Foula 3:30
Fair Isle 2:40
Aberdeen 14:00
Stromness 8:00
Bergen (summer only) 13:00
Fair Isle
Stoneybreck
Sumburgh 2:40
Scale : 1:450 000
(approx 7 miles to 1 inch)
0 5 10 15 miles
0 5 10 15 20 25 km

Key to Town Plan Symbols

- Through Route
- Shopping Streets
- Secondary Road
- Railway
- Minor Road
- Railway/ Bus Station
- Pedestrian Roads
- Shopping Precinct
- Restricted Access Roads
- Park

- Abbey/Cathedral
- Preserved Railway
- Ancient Monument
- Railway Station
- Aquarium
- Roman Antiquity
- Art Gallery
- Safari Park
- Bird Garden
- Theatre
- Building of Public Interest
- Tourist Information Centre open all year/summer only
- Castle
- Zoo
- Church of interest
- Other Place of Interest
- Garden
- Hospital
- Historic Ship
- Parking
- House
- Police
- House & Garden
- Post Office
- Museum
- Youth Hostel

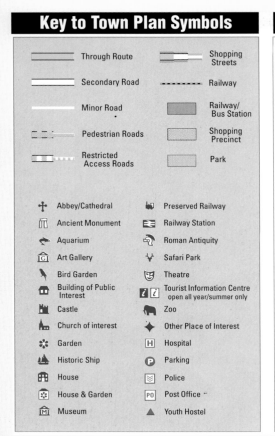

Key to Approach Mapping Symbols

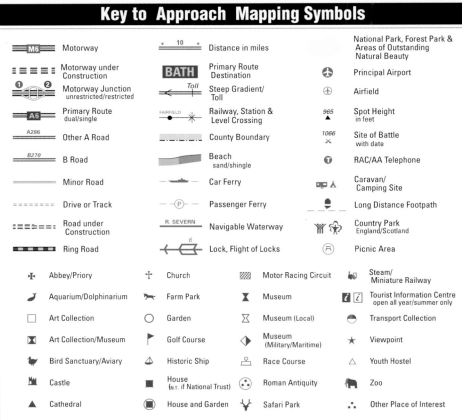

- M6 Motorway
- 10 Distance in miles
- National Park, Forest Park & Areas of Outstanding Natural Beauty
- Motorway under Construction
- BATH Primary Route Destination
- Principal Airport
- 1 2 Motorway Junction unrestricted/restricted
- Toll Steep Gradient/ Toll
- Airfield
- A6 Primary Route dual/single
- FAIRFIELD Railway, Station & Level Crossing
- 965 Spot Height in feet
- A286 Other A Road
- County Boundary
- 1066 Site of Battle with date
- B270 B Road
- Beach sand/shingle
- RAC/AA Telephone
- Minor Road
- Car Ferry
- Caravan/ Camping Site
- Drive or Track
- P Passenger Ferry
- Long Distance Footpath
- Road under Construction
- R. SEVERN Navigable Waterway
- Country Park England/Scotland
- Ring Road
- 6 Lock, Flight of Locks
- Picnic Area

- Abbey/Priory
- Church
- Motor Racing Circuit
- Steam/ Miniature Railway
- Aquarium/Dolphinarium
- Farm Park
- Museum
- Tourist Information Centre open all year/summer only
- Art Collection
- Garden
- Museum (Local)
- Transport Collection
- Art Collection/Museum
- Golf Course
- Museum (Military/Maritime)
- Viewpoint
- Bird Sanctuary/Aviary
- Historic Ship
- Race Course
- Youth Hostel
- Castle
- House (N.T. if National Trust)
- Roman Antiquity
- Zoo
- Cathedral
- House and Garden
- Safari Park
- Other Place of Interest

Aberdeen

0 Miles ¼

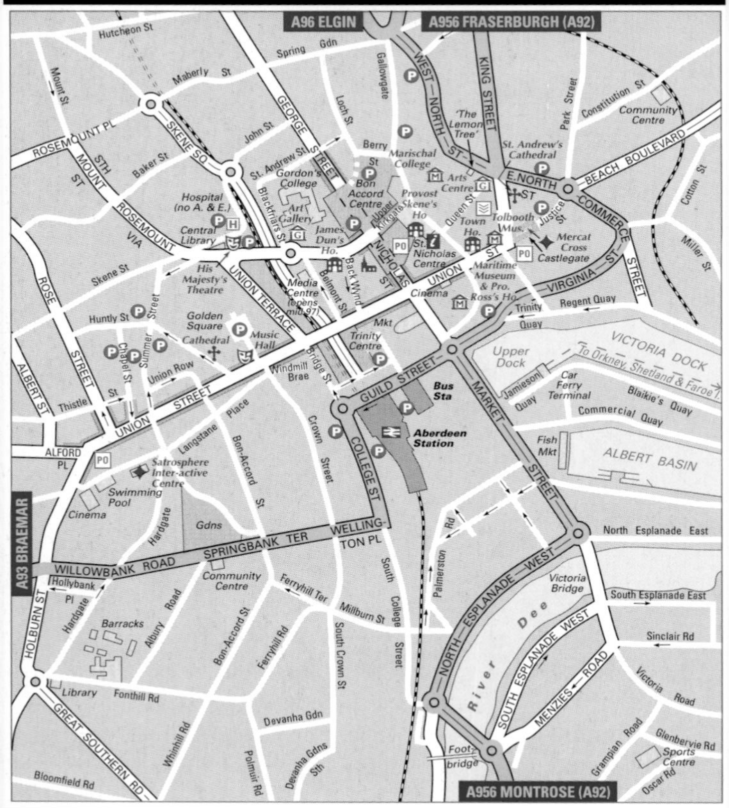

Blackpool

0 Miles ¼

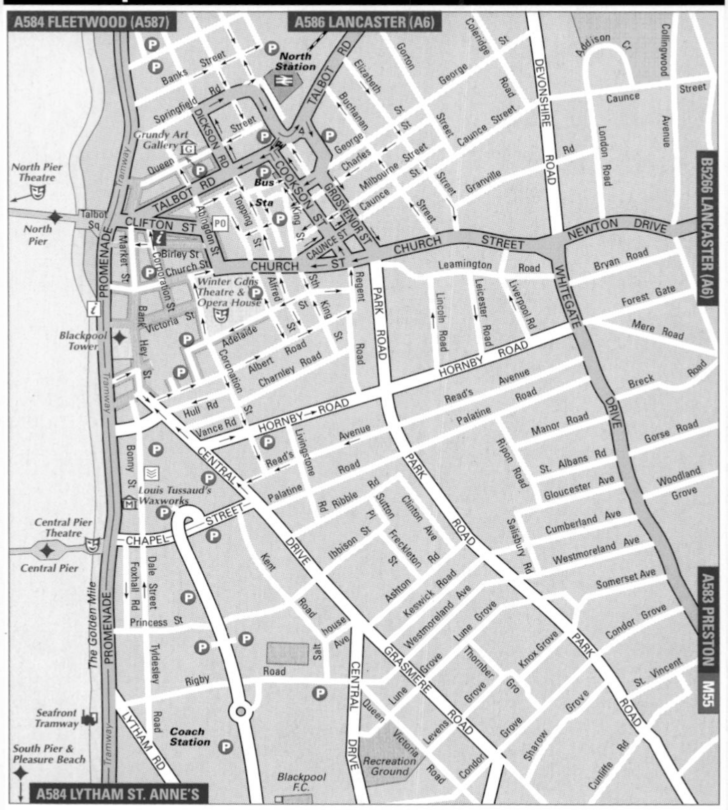

Bath see page 125
Birmingham see page 122

Bournemouth

0 Miles ¼

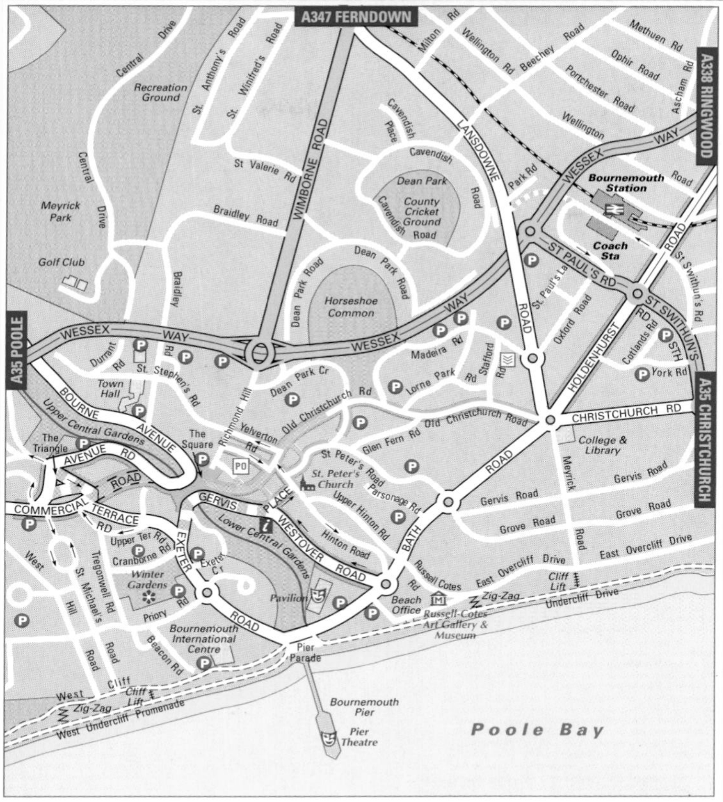

Brighton

0 Miles ¼

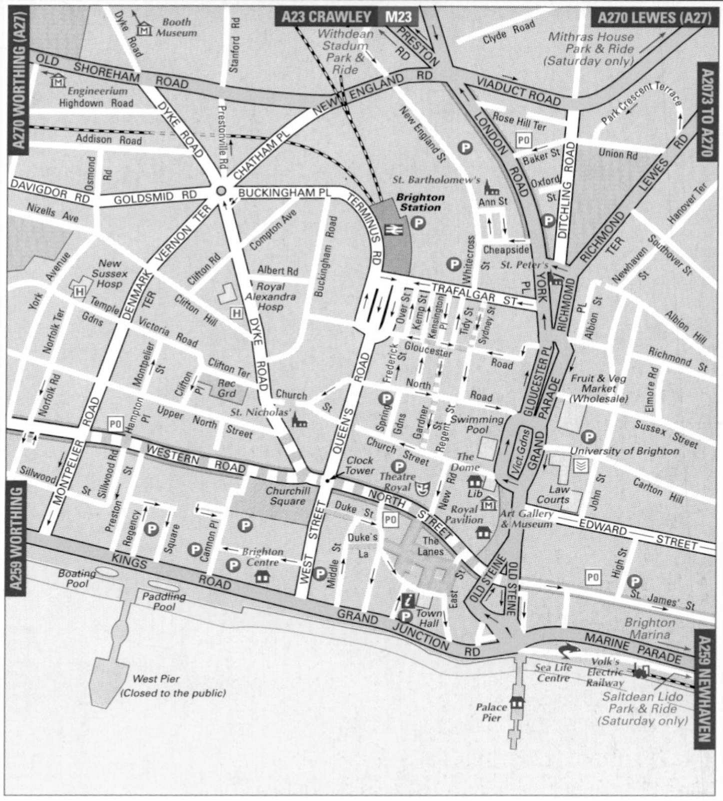

Cambridge

0 Miles ¼

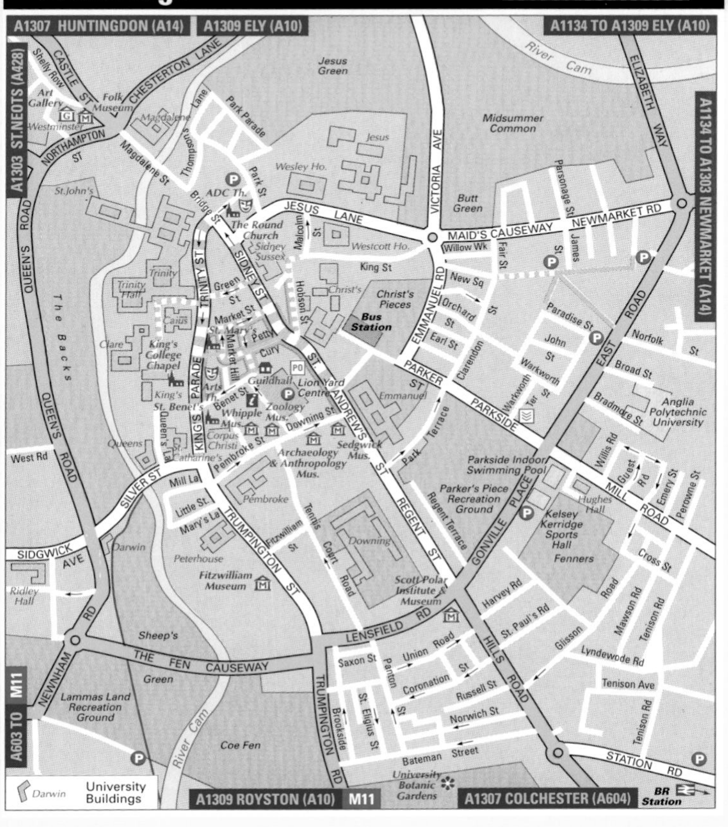

Canterbury

0 Miles ¼

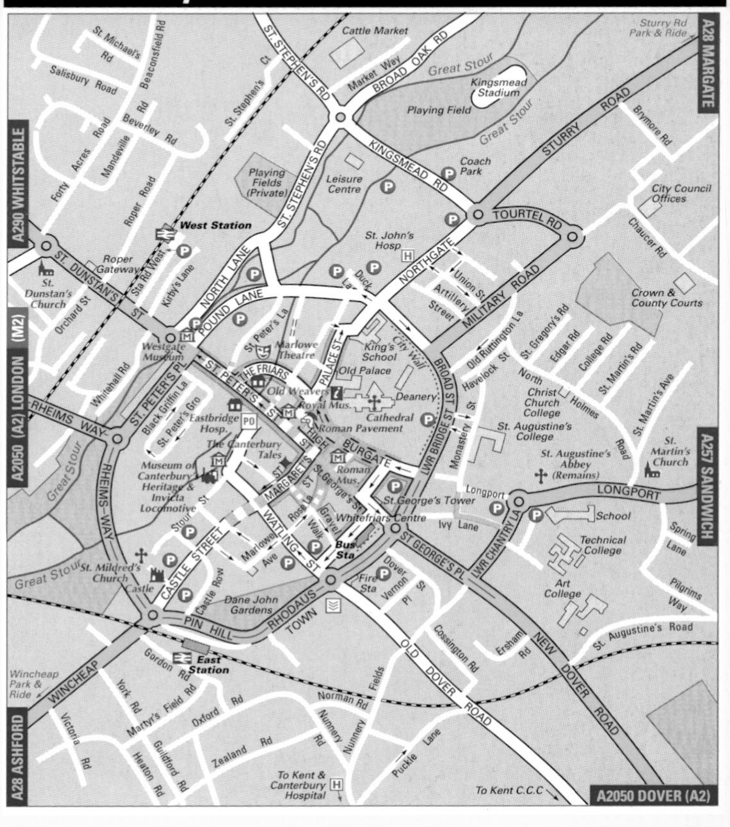

Bradford see page 136
Bristol see page 124
Cardiff see page 127

Cheltenham

0 Miles ¼

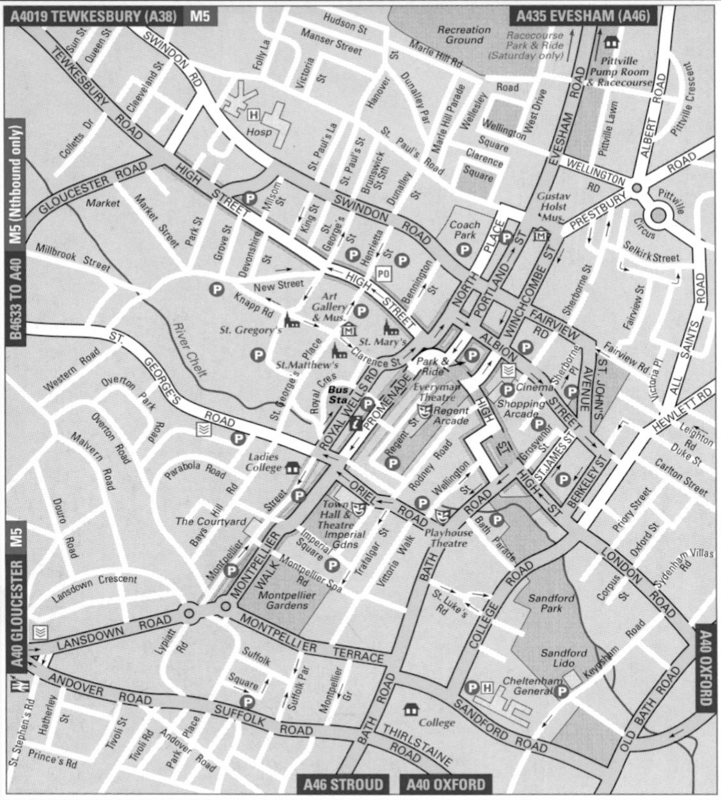

Chester

0 Miles ¼

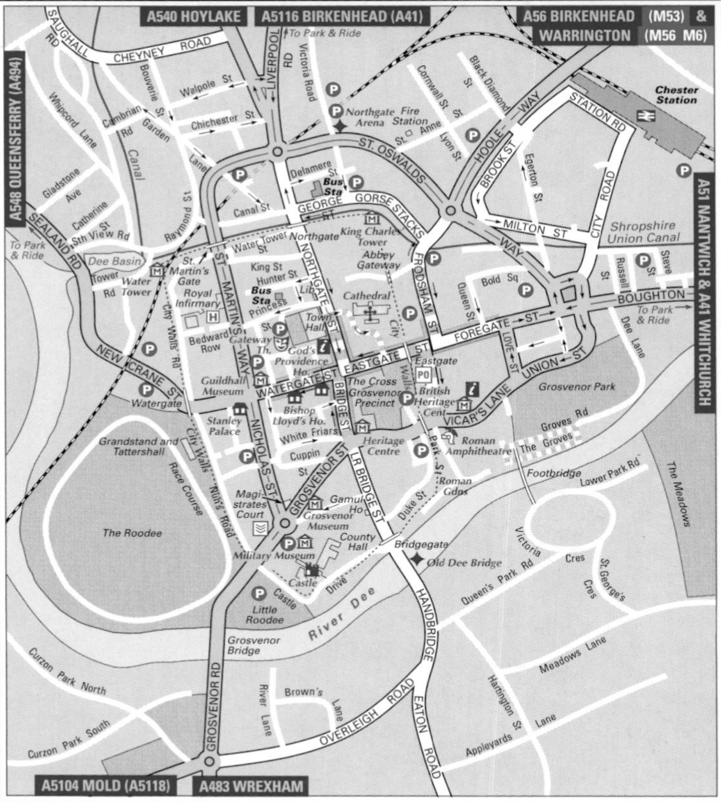

Colchester

0 Miles ¼

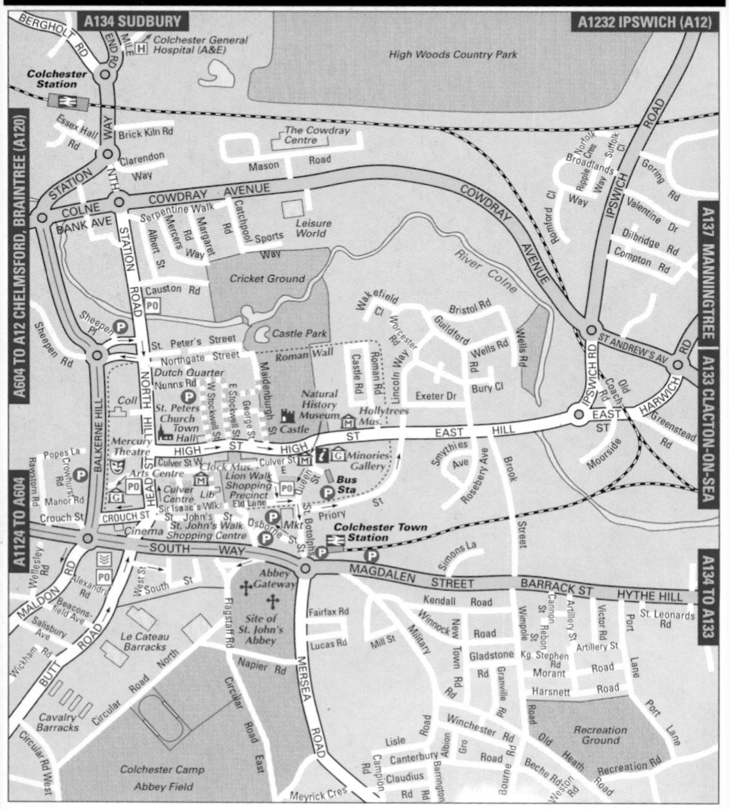

Croydon

0 Miles ¼

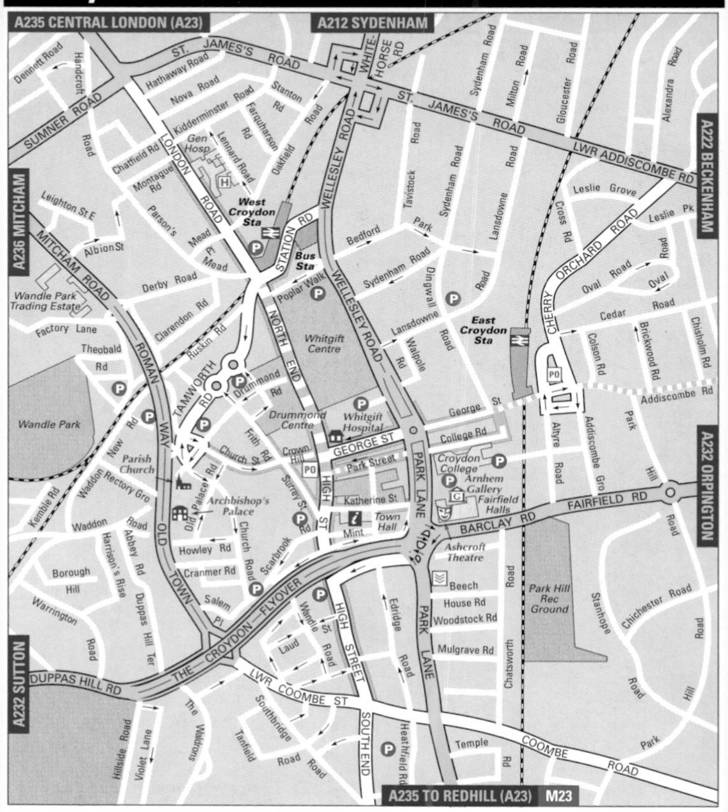

Coventry see page 128

Dundee

0 Miles ¼

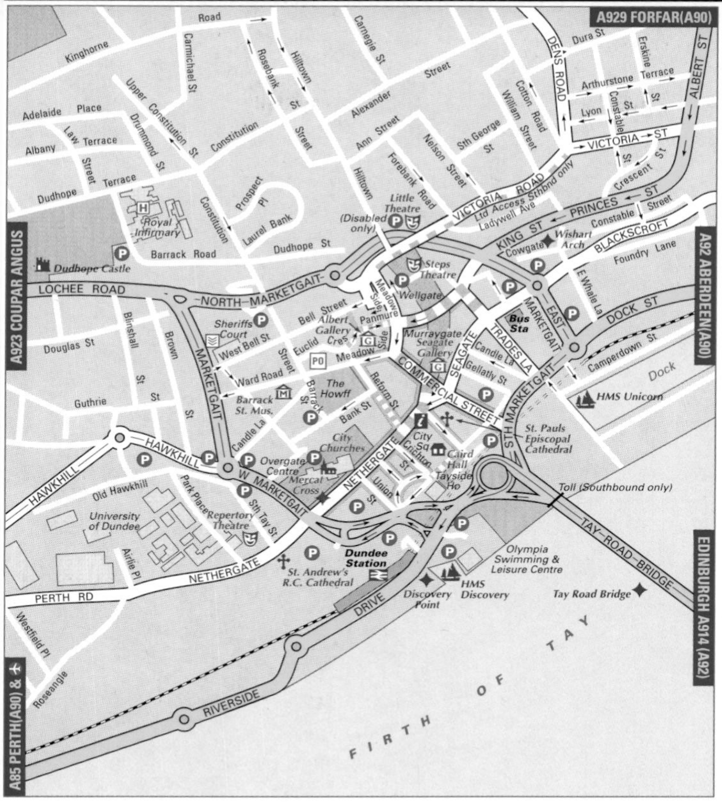

Durham

0 Miles ¼

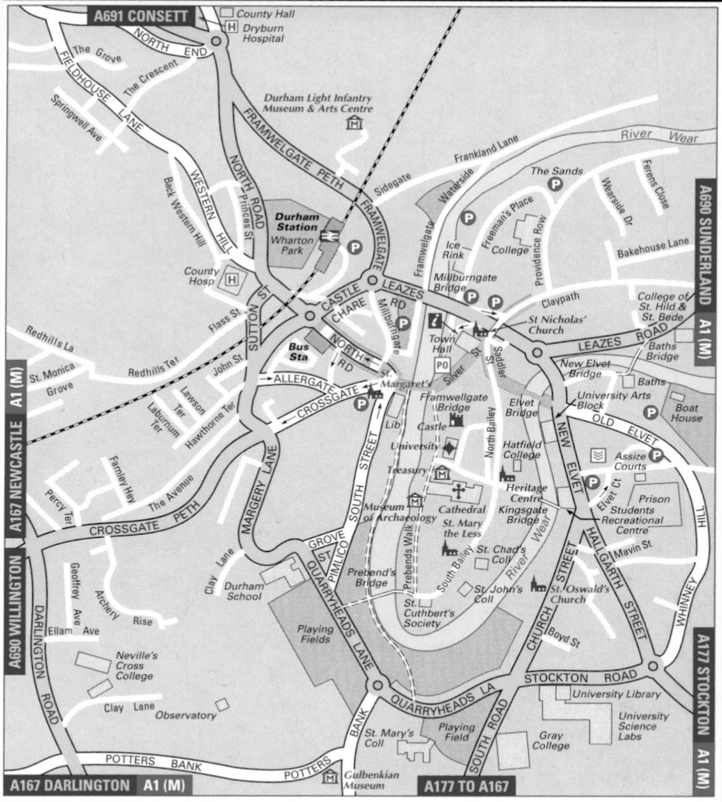

Exeter

0 Miles ¼

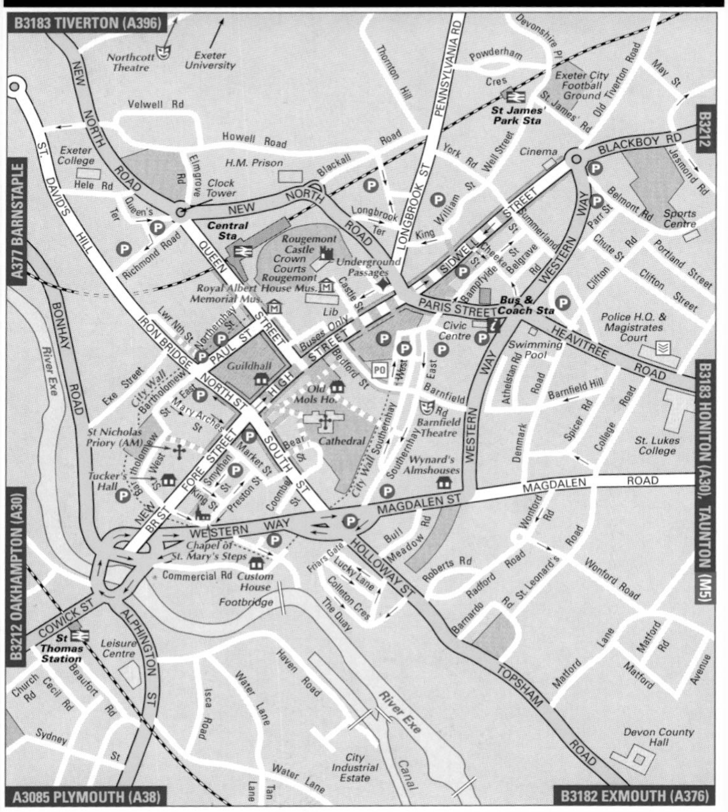

Gloucester

0 Miles ¼

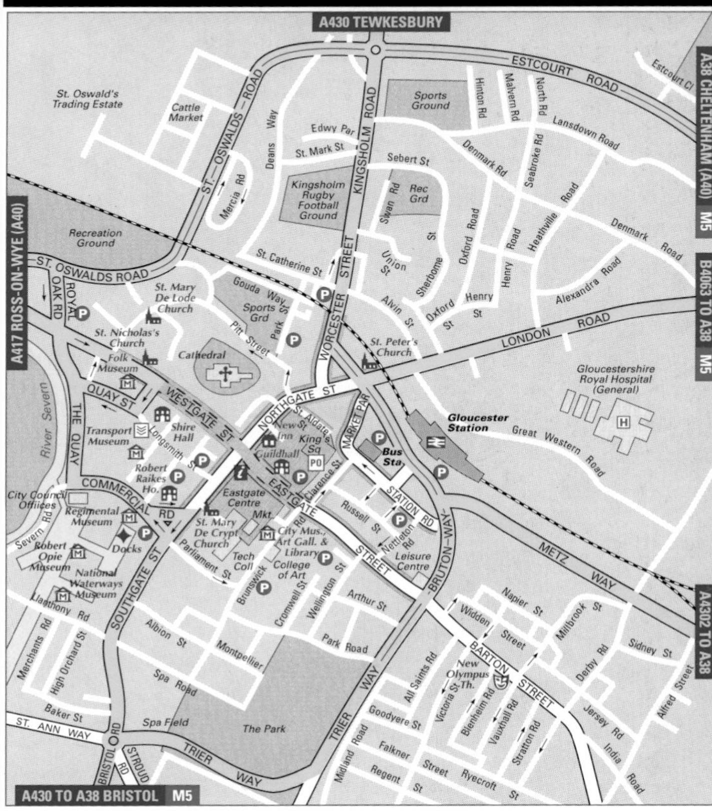

Derby see page 130
Edinburgh see page 133
Glasgow see page 134

Hull

0 Miles ¼

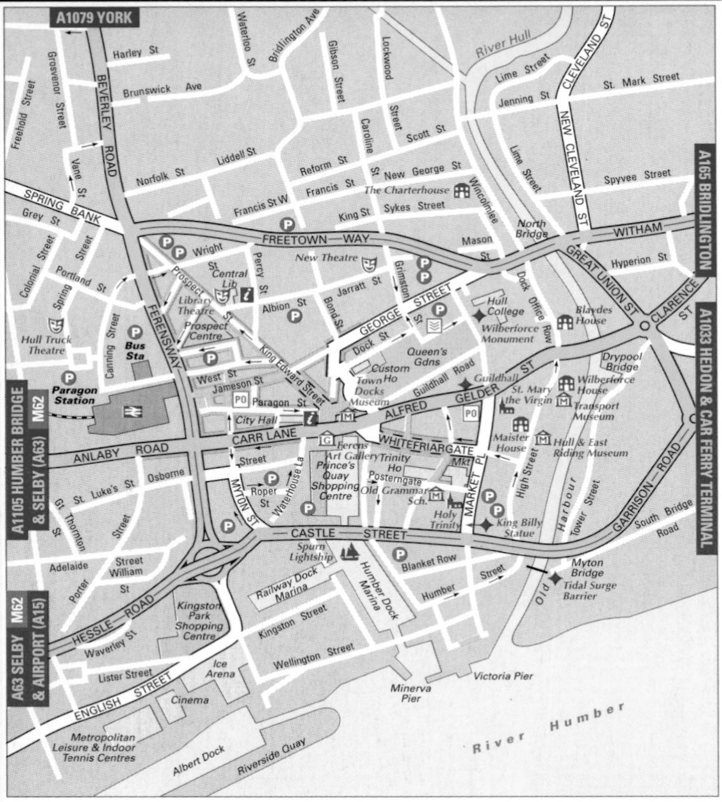

Ipswich

0 Miles ¼

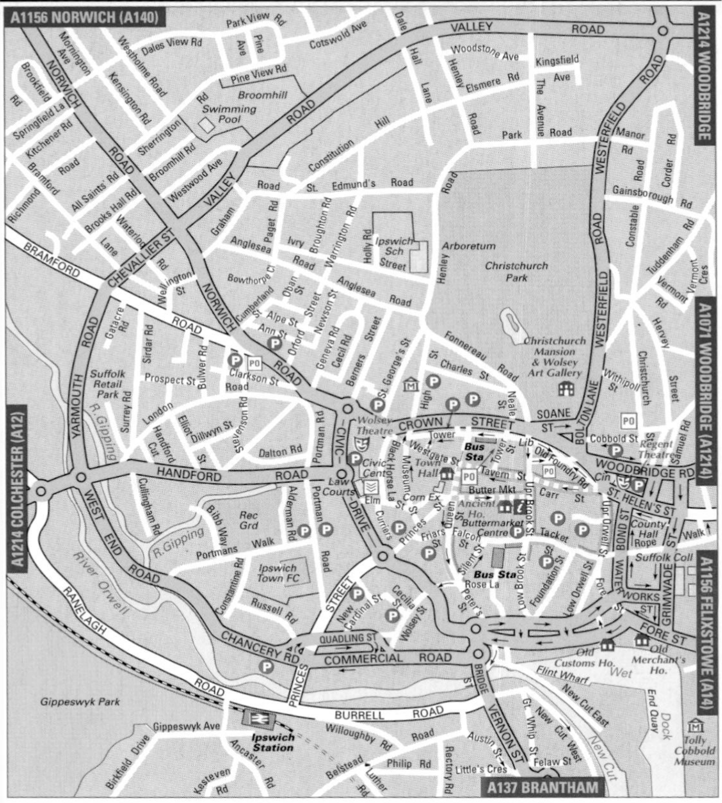

Lincoln

0 Miles ¼

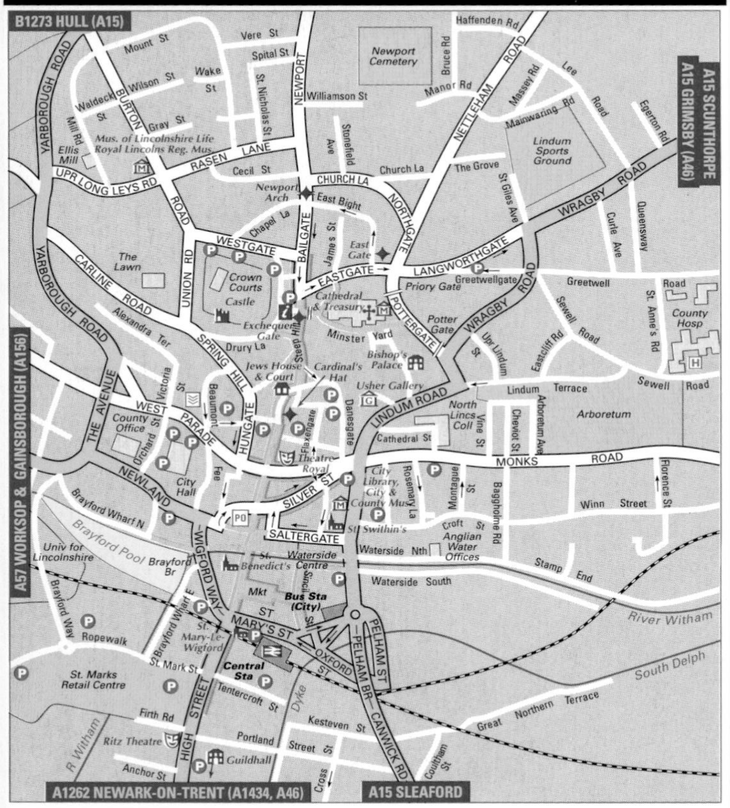

Middlesbrough

0 Miles ½

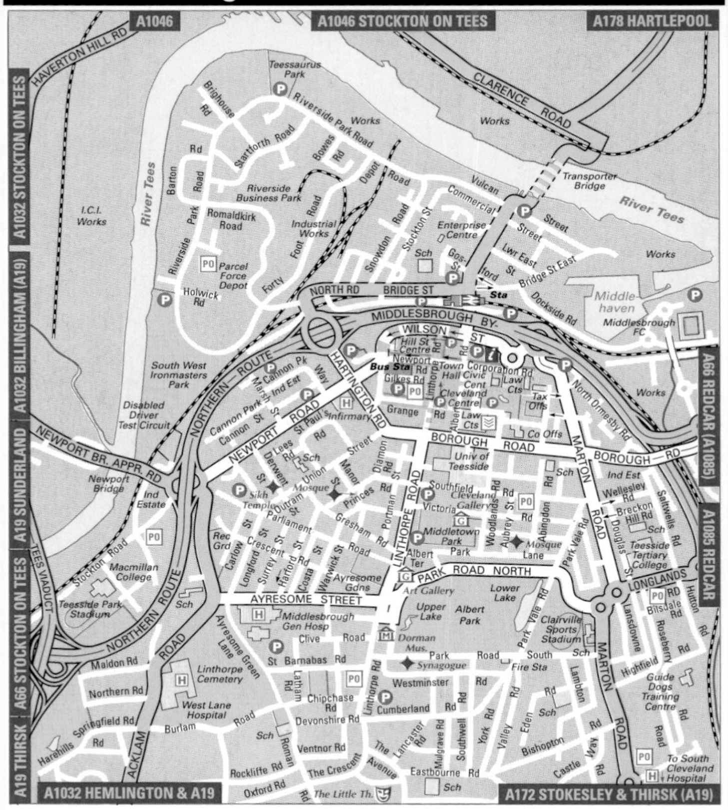

Hanley see page **156**
Leicester see page **129**
London see page **140-145**
Milton Keynes see page **150**
Leeds see page **137**
Liverpool see page **138**
Manchester see page **147**

Norwich

0 Miles ¼

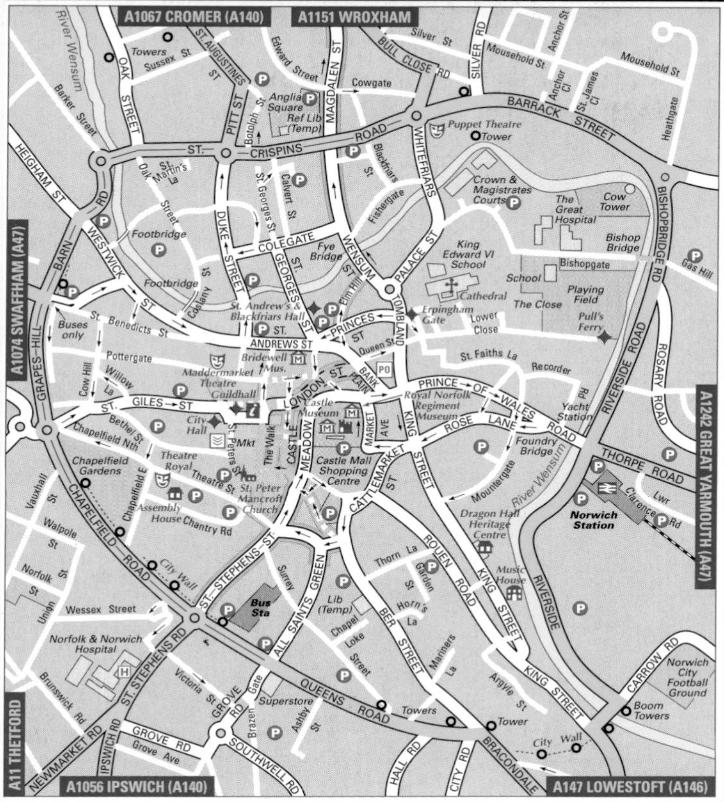

Oxford

0 Miles ¼

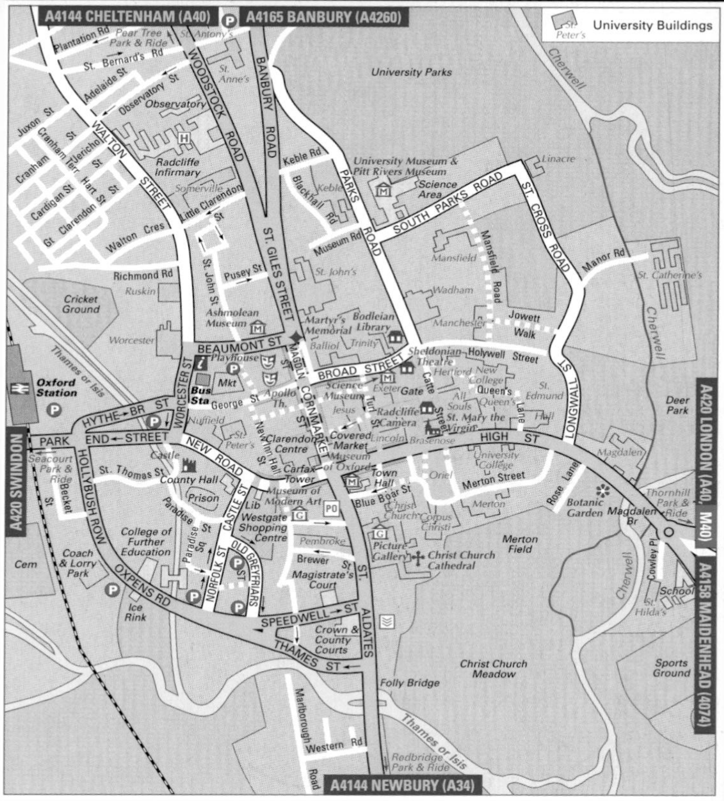

Reading

0 Miles ¼

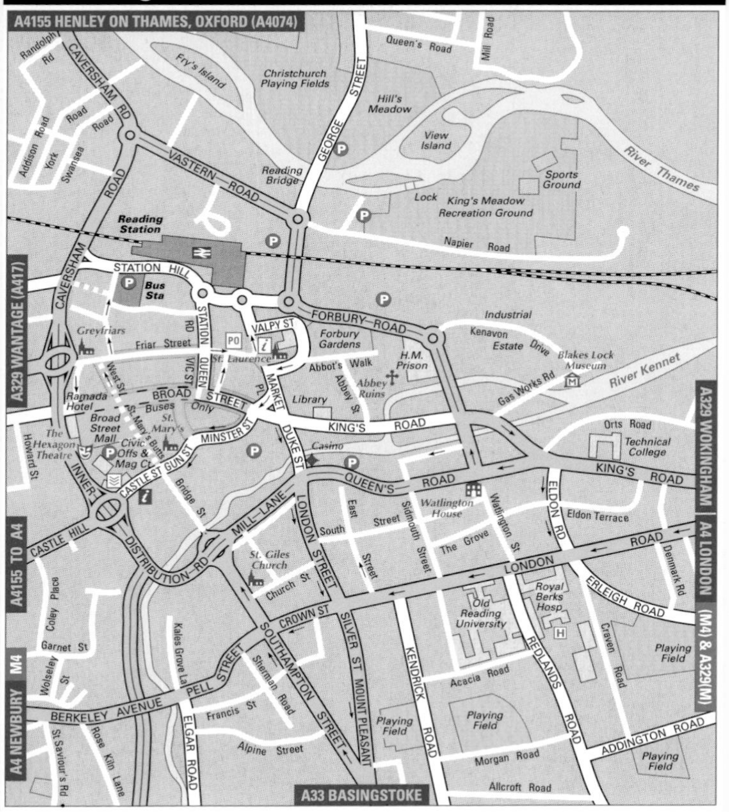

Salisbury

0 Miles ¼

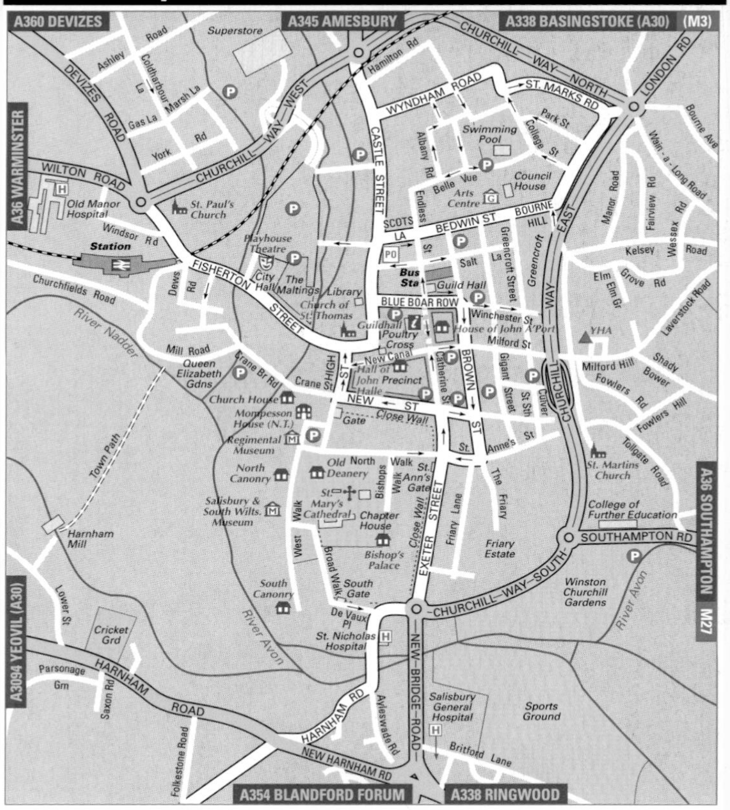

Newcastle see page **148**
Northampton see page **150**
Nottingham see page **131**
Portsmouth see page **155**
Plymouth see page **151**

Scarborough

0 Miles ¼

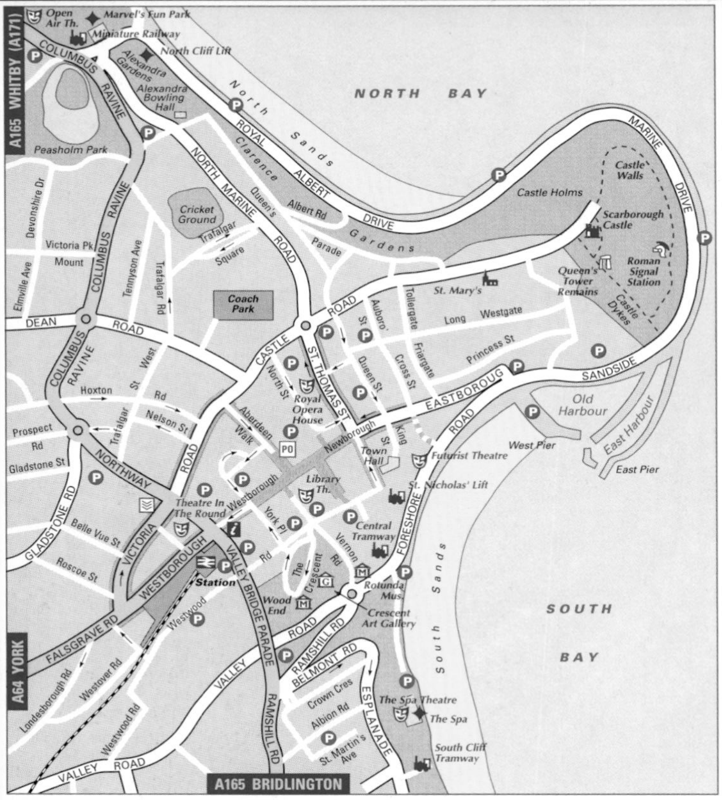

Southend

0 Miles ¼

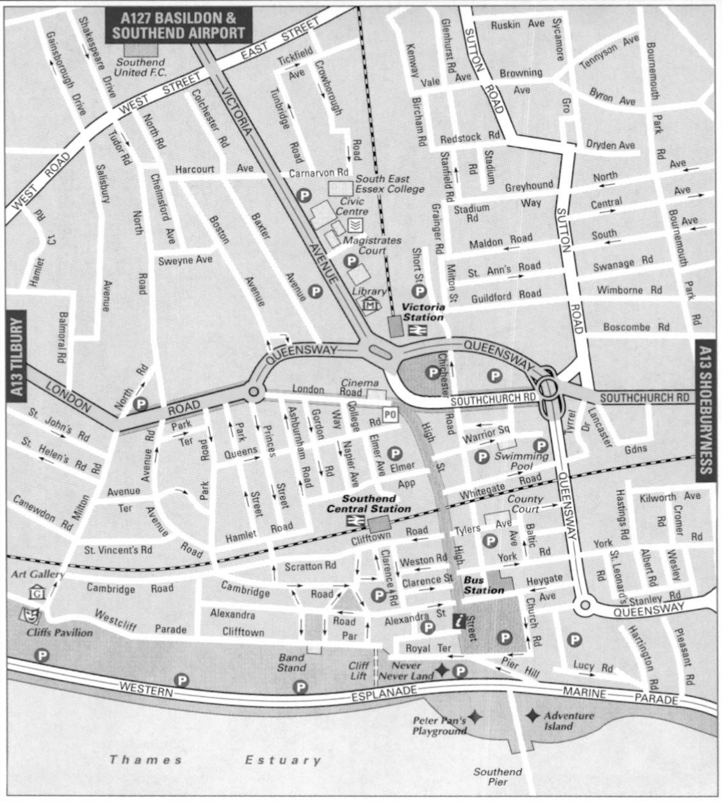

Stratford-upon-Avon

0 Miles ¼

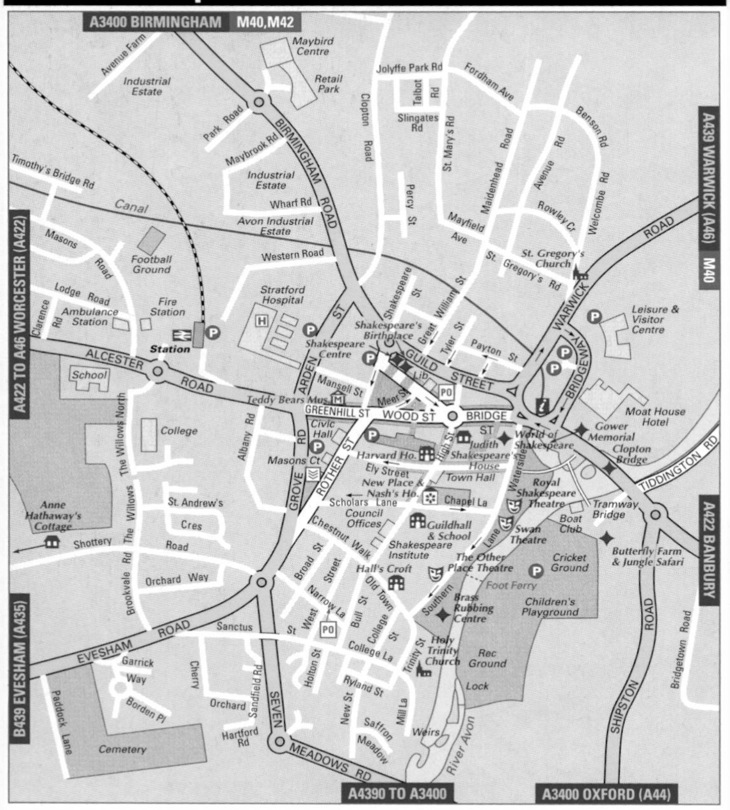

Swansea

0 Miles ¼

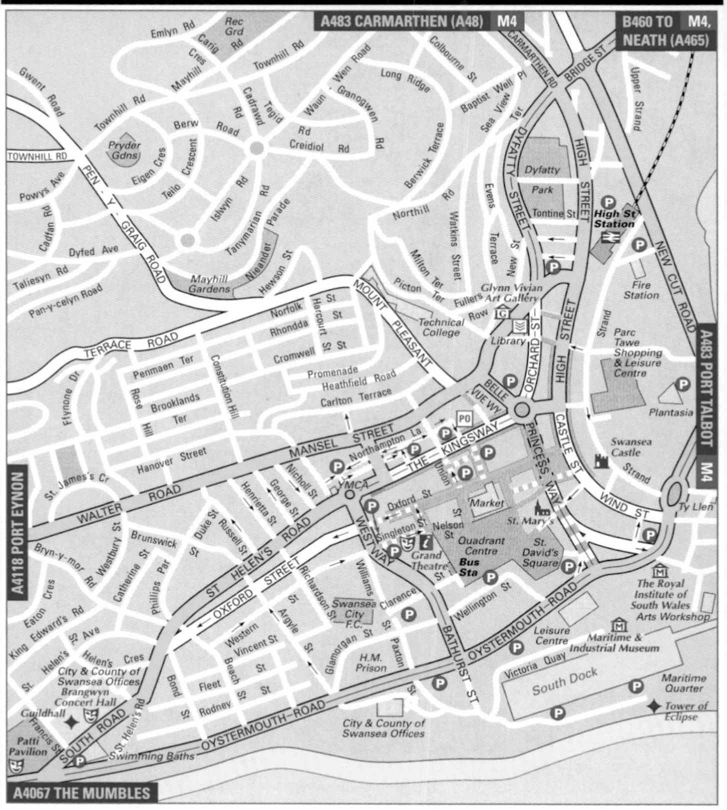

Sheffield see page **153**
Southampton see page **154**
Stoke see page **156**
Sunderland see page **148**

Torquay

0 Miles ¼

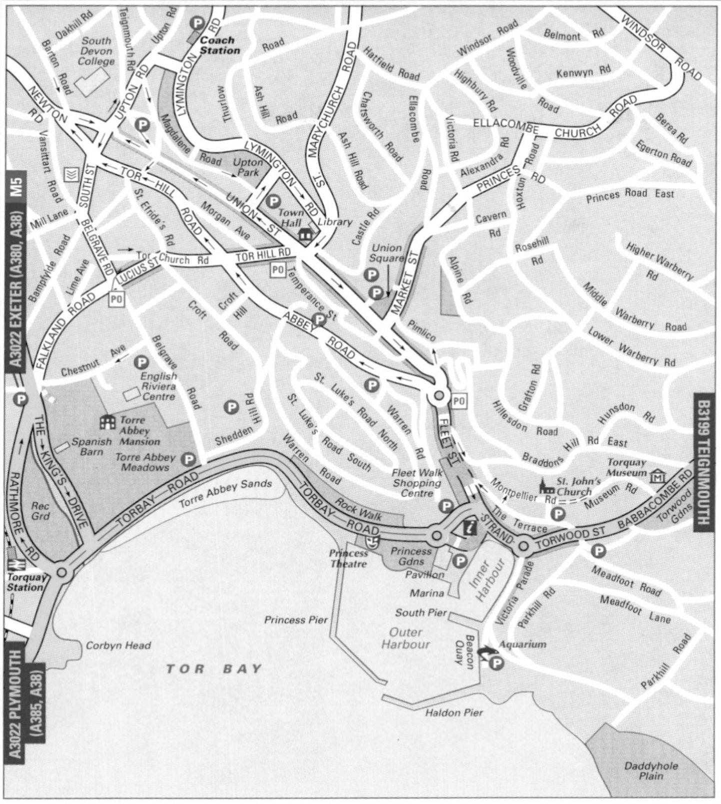

Windsor

0 Miles ¼

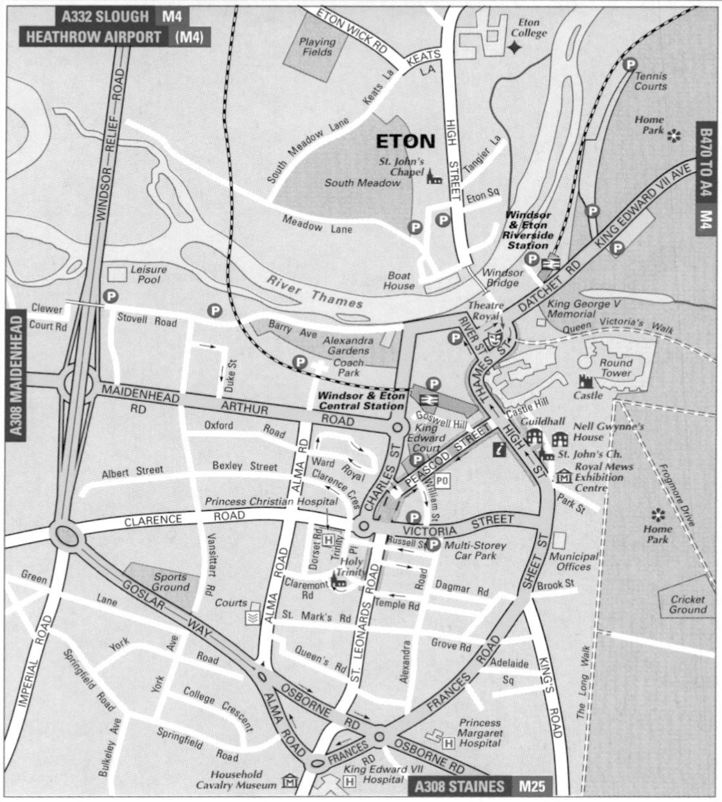

Worcester

0 Miles ¼

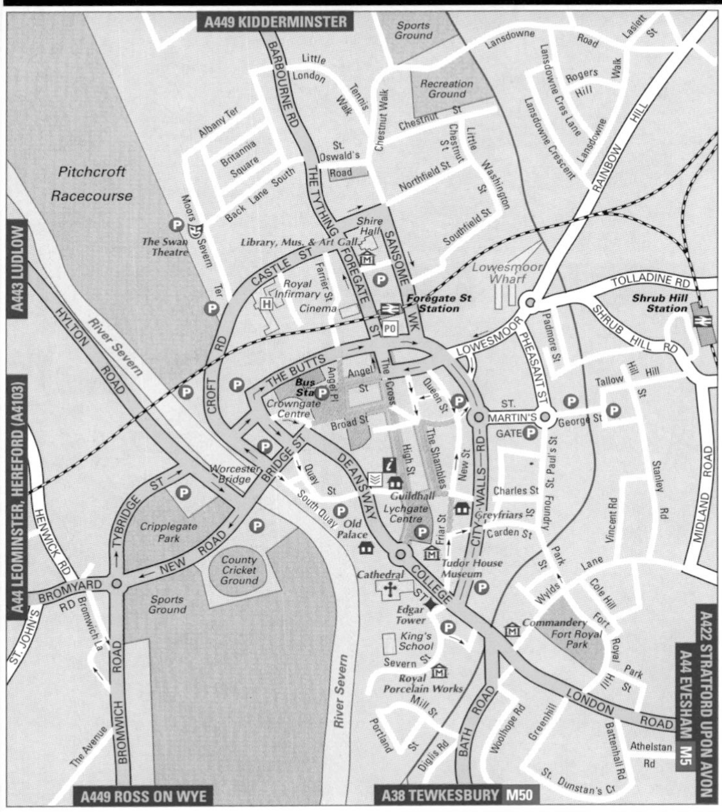

York

0 Miles ¼

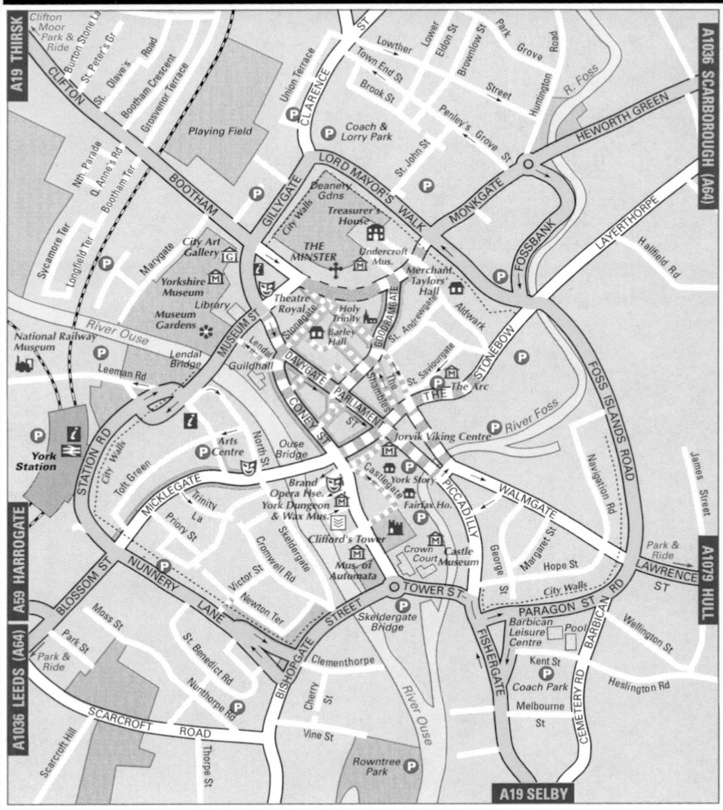

Winchester see page 154

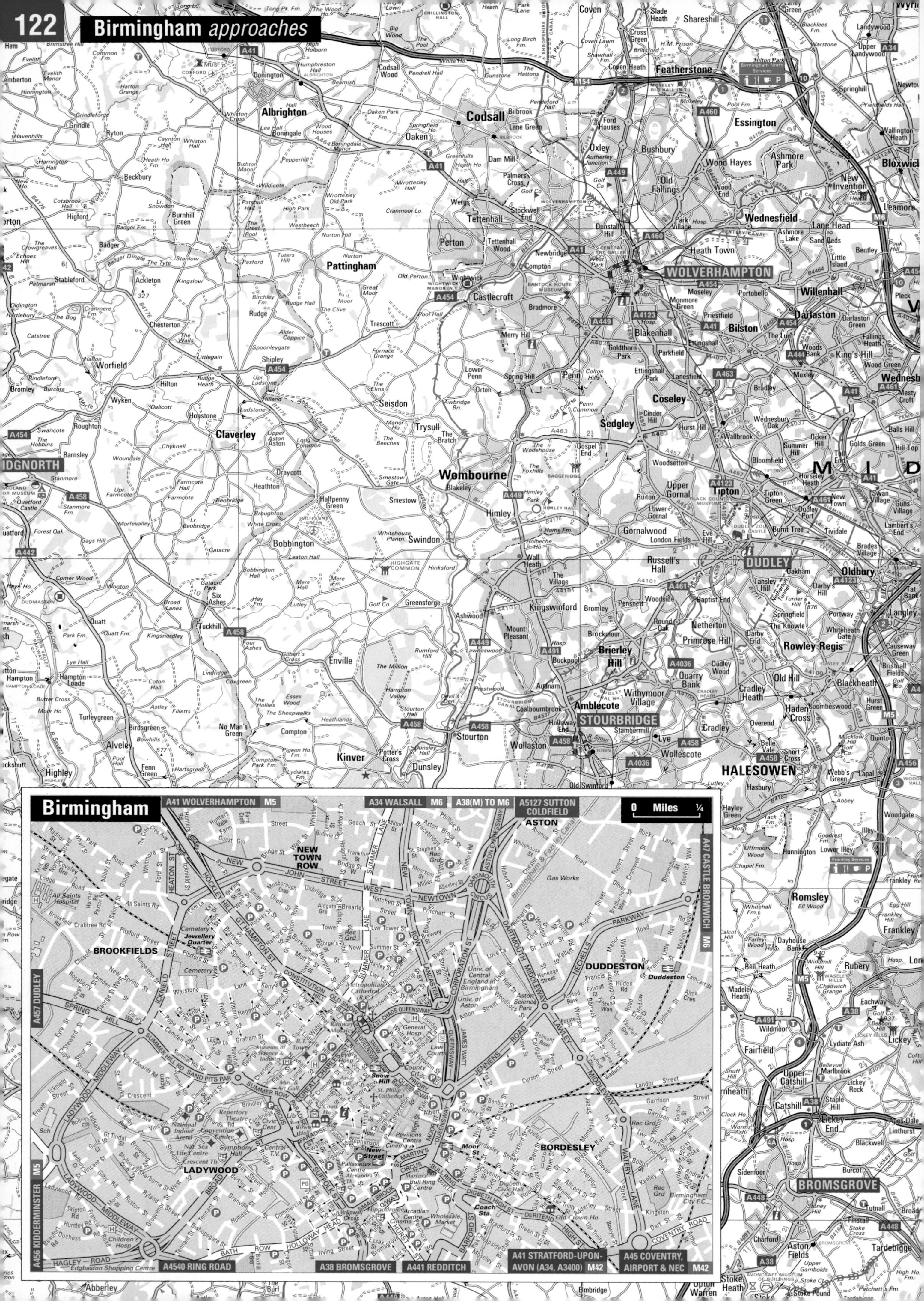

Albrighton
Codsall
Featherstone
Essington
Bloxwich
Pattingham
Tettenhall
Wednesfield
WOLVERHAMPTON
Willenhall
Darlaston
Bilston
Coseley
Sedgley
Claverley
Wombourne
Tipton
Himley
DUDLEY
Oldbury
Bobbington
Swindon
Kingswinford
Brierley Hill
Rowley Regis
Enville
Amblecote
STOURBRIDGE
Kinver
HALESOWEN
Romsley
Frankley
Rubery
BROMSGROVE
Birmingham
A41 WOLVERHAMPTON M5
A34 WALSALL M6
A38(M) TO M6
A5127 SUTTON COLDFIELD
ASTON
A47 CASTLE BROMWICH M6
A457 DUDLEY
A456 KIDDERMINSTER M5
A4540 RING ROAD
A38 BROMSGROVE
A441 REDDITCH
A41 STRATFORD-UPON-AVON (A34, A3400) M42
A45 COVENTRY, AIRPORT & NEC M42
NEW TOWN ROW
BROOKFIELDS
DUDDESTON
LADYWOOD
BORDESLEY

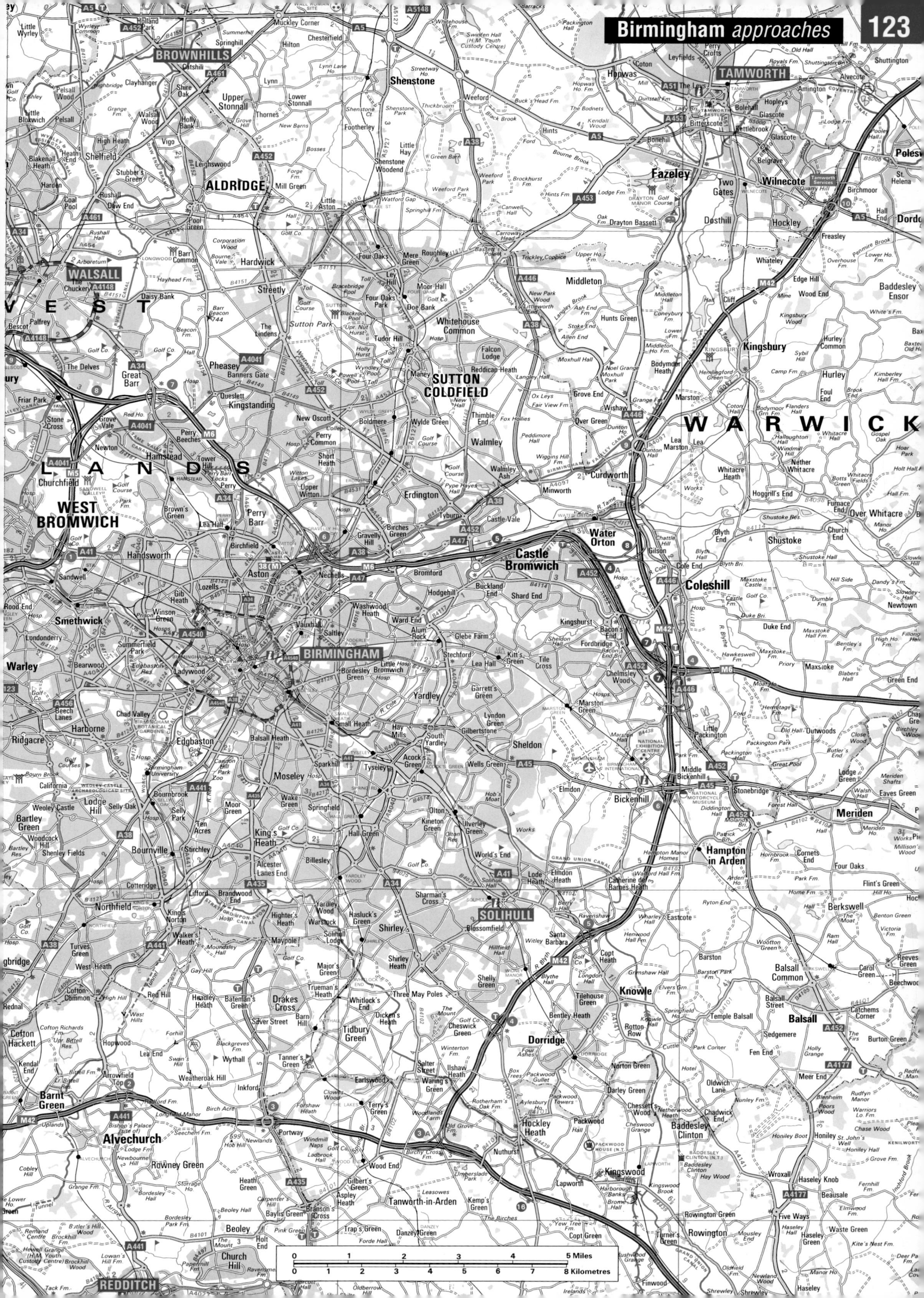
BROWNHILLS
TAMWORTH
Shenstone
Fazeley
Wilnecote
ALDRIDGE
WALSALL
WEST
MIDLANDS
WARWICK
SUTTON COLDFIELD
WEST BROMWICH
Castle Bromwich
Water Orton
Coleshill
Kingsbury
Middleton
Curdworth
Erdington
Aston
Handsworth
Smethwick
BIRMINGHAM
Yardley
Sheldon
Solihull
SOLIHULL
Shirley
Moseley
Edgbaston
Harborne
Northfield
Bournville
Kings Heath
Knowle
Dorridge
Hampton in Arden
Meriden
Balsall
Berkswell
Alvechurch
REDDITCH
Barnt Green
Tanworth-in-Arden
Hockley Heath
Kingswood
Baddesley Clinton
Rowington
Church Hill
Beoley
Warley
Sandwell
Bickenhill
Great Barr
Perry Barr
Kingstanding
Streetly
Pheasey
Walmley
Whitehouse Common
0 1 2 3 4 5 Miles
0 1 2 3 4 5 6 7 8 Kilometres

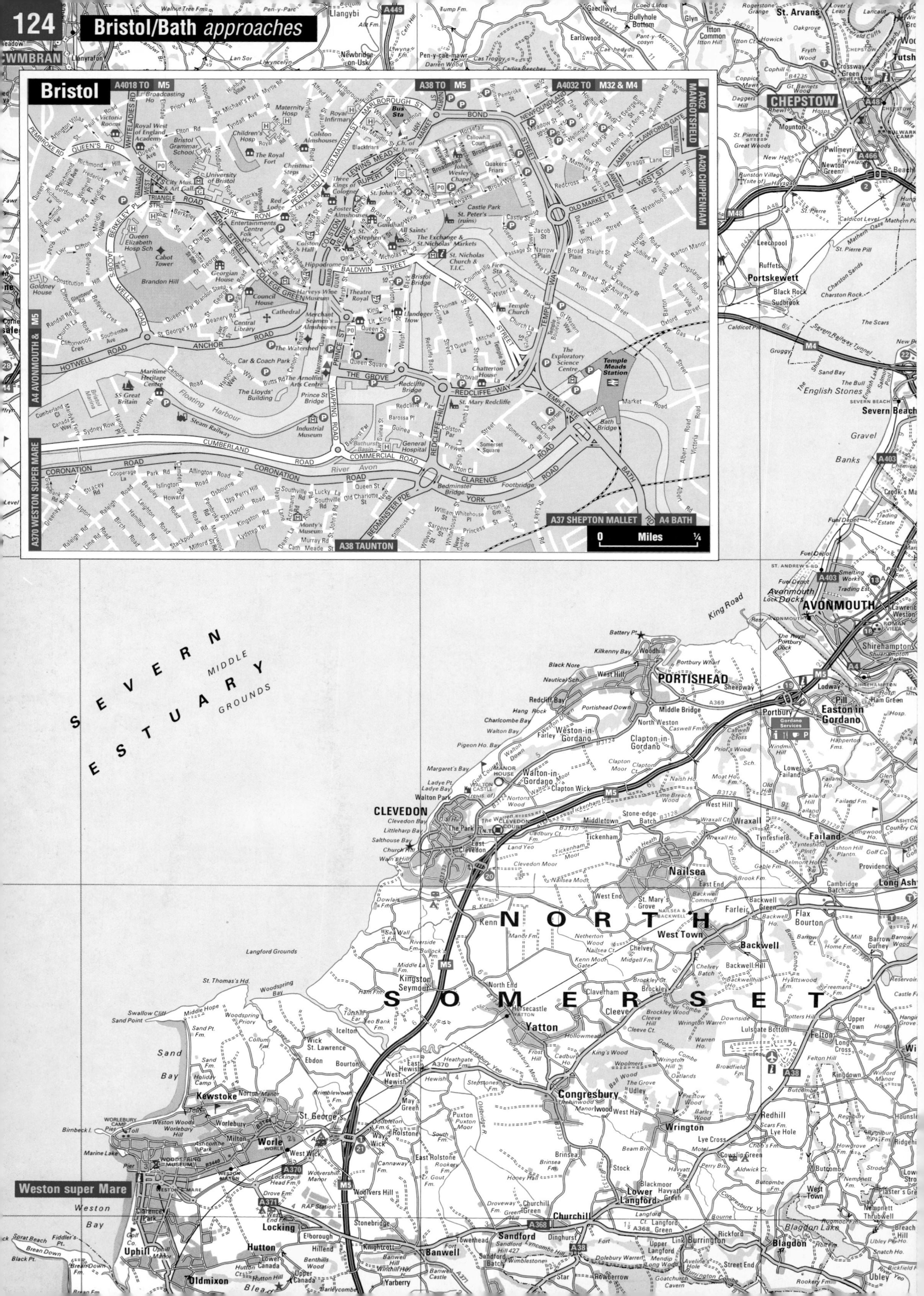

Bristol
A4018 TO M5
A38 TO M5
A4032 TO M32 & M4
A432 MANGOTSFIELD
A420 CHIPPENHAM
A4 AVONMOUTH & M5
A370 WESTON SUPER MARE
A38 TAUNTON
A37 SHEPTON MALLET
A4 BATH
0 Miles ¼
Temple Meads Station
Cabot Tower
Brandon Hill
Cathedral
Floating Harbour
River Avon
Queen Square
St. Mary Redcliffe
Industrial Museum
SS Great Britain
The Watershed
Castle Park
CWMBRAN
CHEPSTOW
St. Arvans
Portskewett
Caldicot
The English Stones
Severn Beach
AVONMOUTH
Shirehampton
PORTISHEAD
Easton in Gordano
Portbury
Pill
Weston-in-Gordano
Clapton-in-Gordano
Walton-in-Gordano
CLEVEDON
Nailsea
Wraxall
Failand
Long Ashton
Flax Bourton
Backwell
West Town
Tickenham
Kenn
Yatton
Cleeve
Congresbury
Wrington
Felton
Redhill
Blagdon
Churchill
Lower Langford
Sandford
Banwell
Locking
Hutton
Uphill
Oldmixon
Kewstoke
Worle
St. George's
Sand Bay
Weston Bay
Weston super Mare
SEVERN ESTUARY
MIDDLE GROUNDS
NORTH SOMERSET
M5
M4
M48
A38
A370
A368
A371
A369
A403

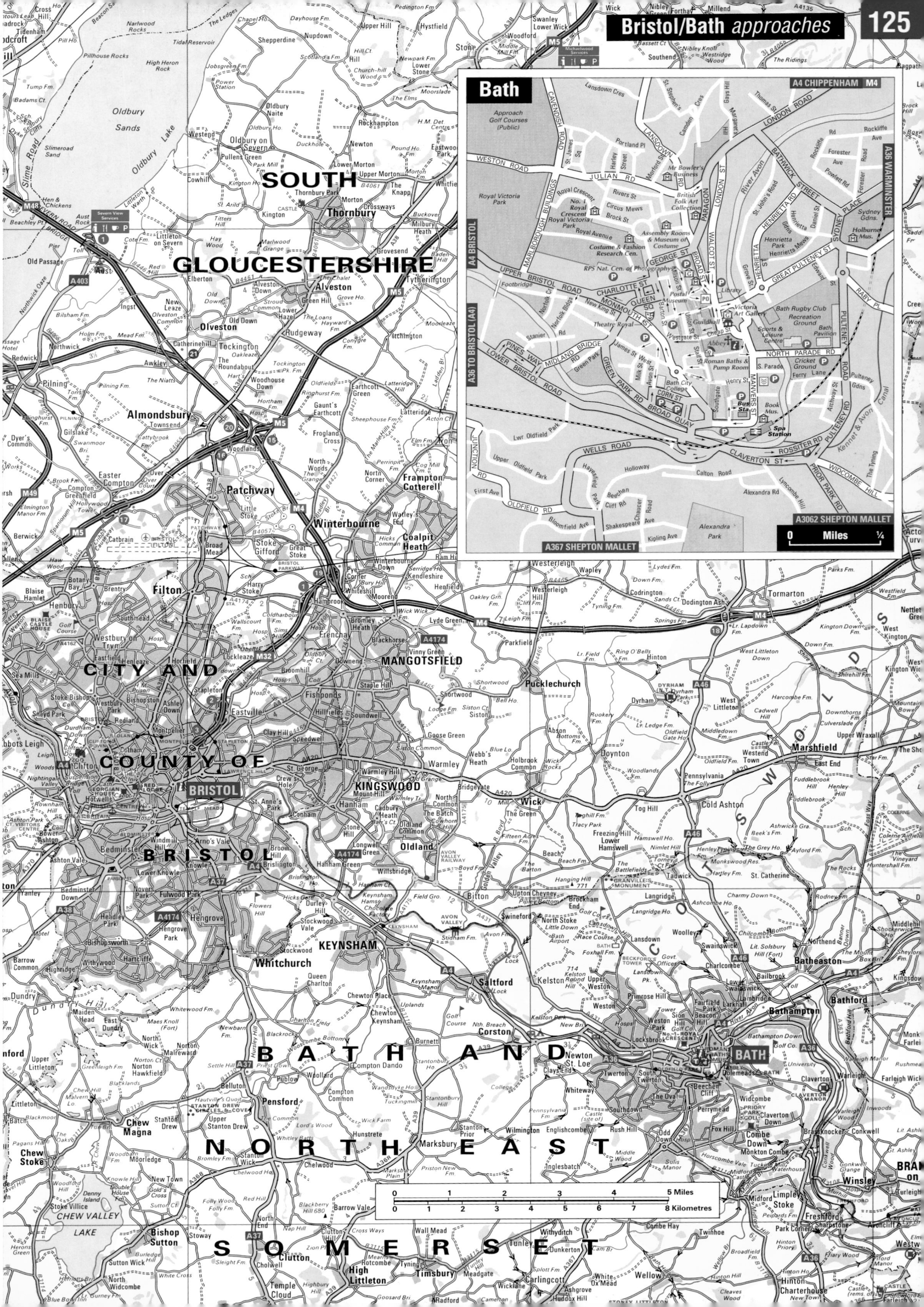
SOUTH
GLOUCESTERSHIRE
CITY AND
COUNTY OF
BRISTOL
BATH AND
NORTH EAST
SOMERSET
COTSWOLDS
Bath
A4 CHIPPENHAM M4
A36 WARMINSTER
A4 BRISTOL
A36 TO BRISTOL (A4)
A3062 SHEPTON MALLET
A367 SHEPTON MALLET
Miles
Approach Golf Courses (Public)
Royal Victoria Park
Royal Crescent
Circus Mews
Assembly Rooms & Museum of Costume
Costume & Fashion Research Cen.
Victoria Art Gallery
Guildhall
Abbey
Roman Baths & Pump Room
Theatre Royal
Bath Rugby Club Recreation Ground
Sports & Leisure Centre
Cricket Ground
Bus Sta.
Spa Station
Holburne Mus.
Alexandra Park
Oldbury Sands
Severn View Services
Michaelwood Services
Thornbury
Alveston
Olveston
Tockington
Almondsbury
Patchway
Filton
Winterbourne
Frampton Cotterell
Coalpit Heath
Mangotsfield
Pucklechurch
Kingswood
Warmley
Keynsham
Whitchurch
Saltford
Bitton
Wick
Dyrham
Marshfield
Cold Ashton
Tormarton
Bristol Parkway
Bristol Filton
Henbury
Westbury on Trym
Clifton
Bedminster
Hengrove
Bishopsworth
Hartcliffe
Withywood
Stockwood
Chew Magna
Chew Stoke
Chew Valley Lake
Pensford
Bishop Sutton
Clutton
High Littleton
Timsbury
Marksbury
Compton Dando
Corston
Newton St. Loe
Kelston
Weston
Twerton
Combe Down
Bathampton
Batheaston
Bathford
Limpley Stoke
Freshford
Winsley
Wellow
Dunkerton
Carlingcott
Batheaston
Claverton
BATH
BRISTOL
M4
M5
M32
M48
M49
A4
A36
A37
A38
A39
A46
A420
A4174
0 1 2 3 4 5 Miles
0 1 2 3 4 5 6 7 8 Kilometres

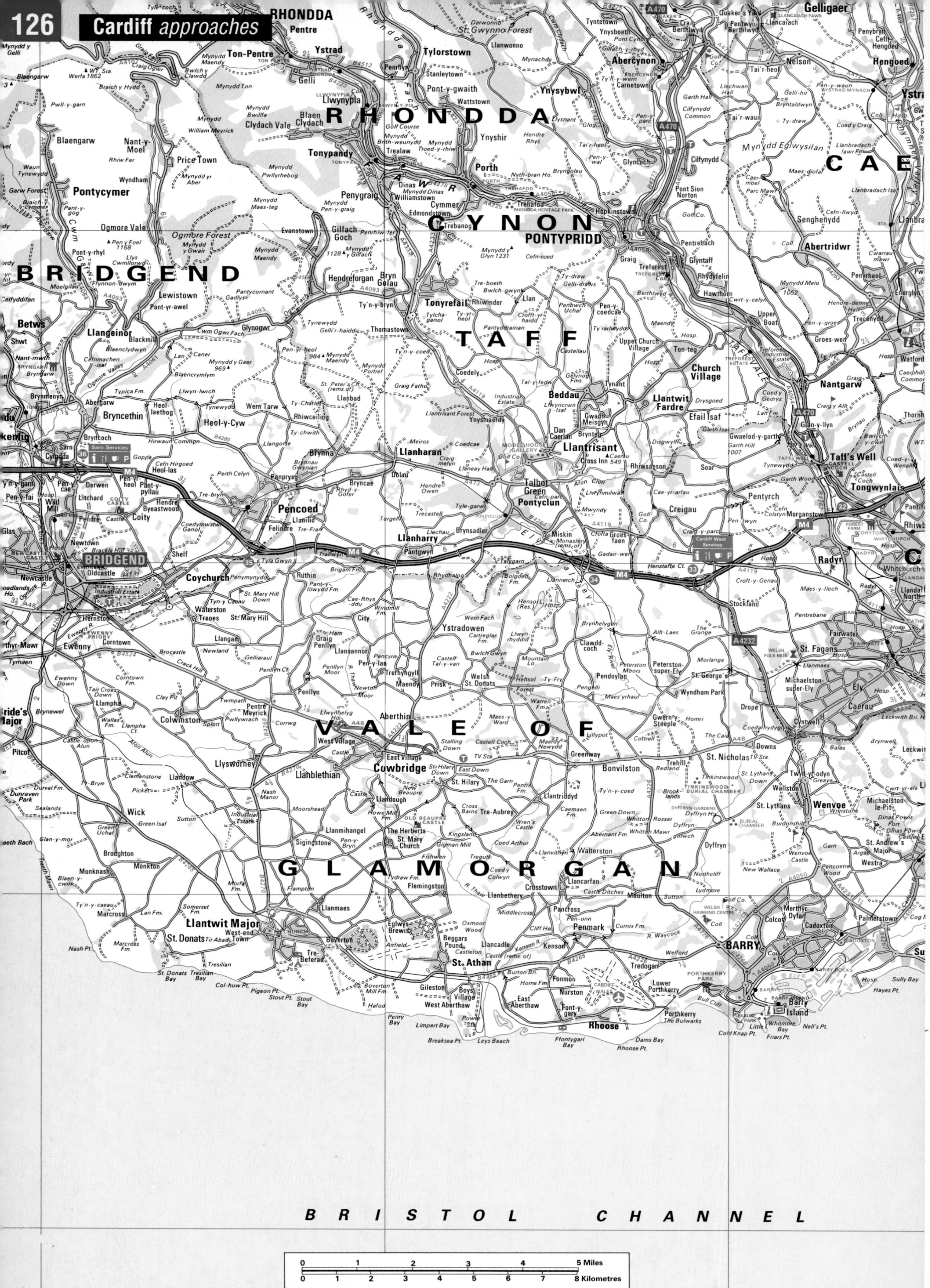
RHONDDA
CYNON
TAFF
BRIDGEND
VALE OF GLAMORGAN
BRISTOL CHANNEL
Pontypridd
Bridgend
Cowbridge
Llantwit Major
Barry
Barry Island
Llantrisant
Pontyclun
Pencoed
Tonypandy
Porth
Ystrad
Ton-Pentre
Tylorstown
Abercynon
Nelson
Gelligaer
Hengoed
Ynysybwl
Llanharan
Llanharry
Tonyrefail
Beddau
Church Village
Llantwit Fardre
Taff's Well
Tongwynlais
Radyr
Pentyrch
Creigau
Morganstown
St. Fagans
Ely
Caerau
Culverhouse Cross
Wenvoe
Cadoxton
St. Athan
Rhoose
St. Nicholas
Bonvilston
Llandough
St. Hilary
Llanblethian
Colwinston
Llysworney
Wick
St. Donats
Boverton
Llancarfan
Penmark
Fonmon
Coychurch
Coity
Bryncethin
Sarn
Pontycymer
Blaengarw
Ogmore Vale
Llangeinor
Betws
Ewenny
Corntown
Pentyrch
Ystradowen
Aberthin
M4
A470
A48
A4232
A4119
A4050
Sarn Services
Cardiff West Services
0 1 2 3 4 5 Miles
0 1 2 3 4 5 6 7 8 Kilometres

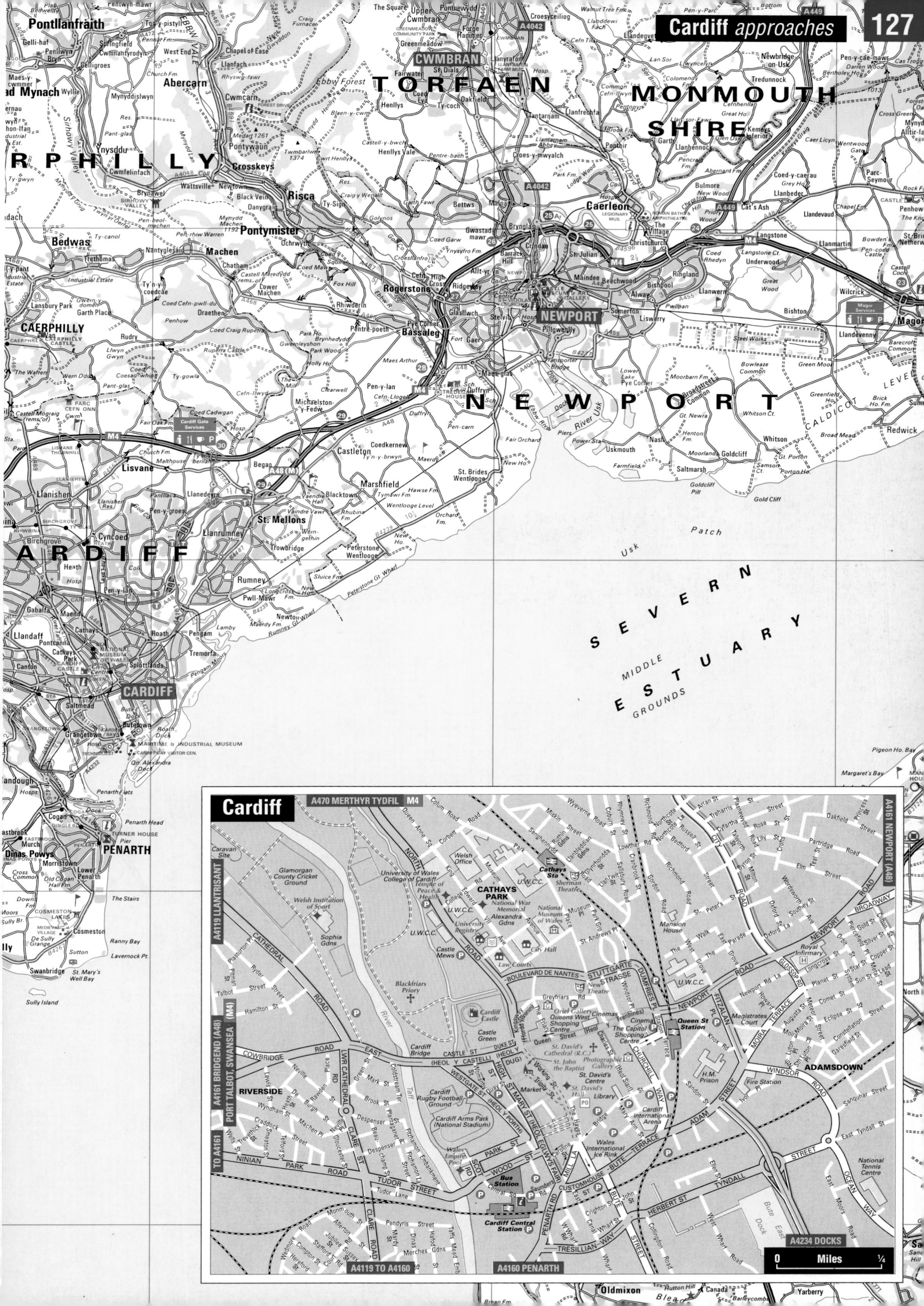
TORFAEN
MONMOUTH SHIRE
RPHILLY
NEWPORT
ARDIFF
SEVERN ESTUARY
MIDDLE GROUNDS
Usk Patch
CWMBRAN
NEWPORT
CARDIFF
Pontllanfraith
Abercarn
Crosskeys
Risca
Pontymister
Machen
Bedwas
CAERPHILLY
Caerleon
Rogerstone
Bassaleg
Castleton
Marshfield
St. Mellons
Lisvane
Llanishen
Cyncoed
Llanrumney
Rumney
Penarth
PENARTH
Dinas Powys
Sully Island
Goldcliff
Whitson
Redwick
Magor
Langstone
Llanmartin
Christchurch
Maindee
Malpas
Bettws
Cardiff Gate Services
Magor Services
Cardiff
A470 MERTHYR TYDFIL M4
A4161 NEWPORT (A48)
A4119 LLANTRISANT
A4161 BRIDGEND (A48) PORT TALBOT, SWANSEA (M4)
TO A4161
A4119 TO A4160
A4160 PENARTH
A4234 DOCKS
CATHAYS PARK
Cathays Sta
City Hall
Cardiff Castle
Queen St Station
Cardiff Central Station
Bus Station
Cardiff Arms Park (National Stadium)
Cardiff Rugby Football Ground
RIVERSIDE
ADAMSDOWN
H.M. Prison
Royal Infirmary
Glamorgan County Cricket Ground
Welsh Institution of Sport
Sophia Gdns
Blackfriars Priory
Castle Mews
Law Courts
Welsh Office
University of Wales College of Cardiff
National Museum of Wales
St. David's Centre
Cardiff International Arena
Wales International Ice Rink
Wales Empire Pool
National Tennis Centre
Bute East Dock
0 Miles 1/4

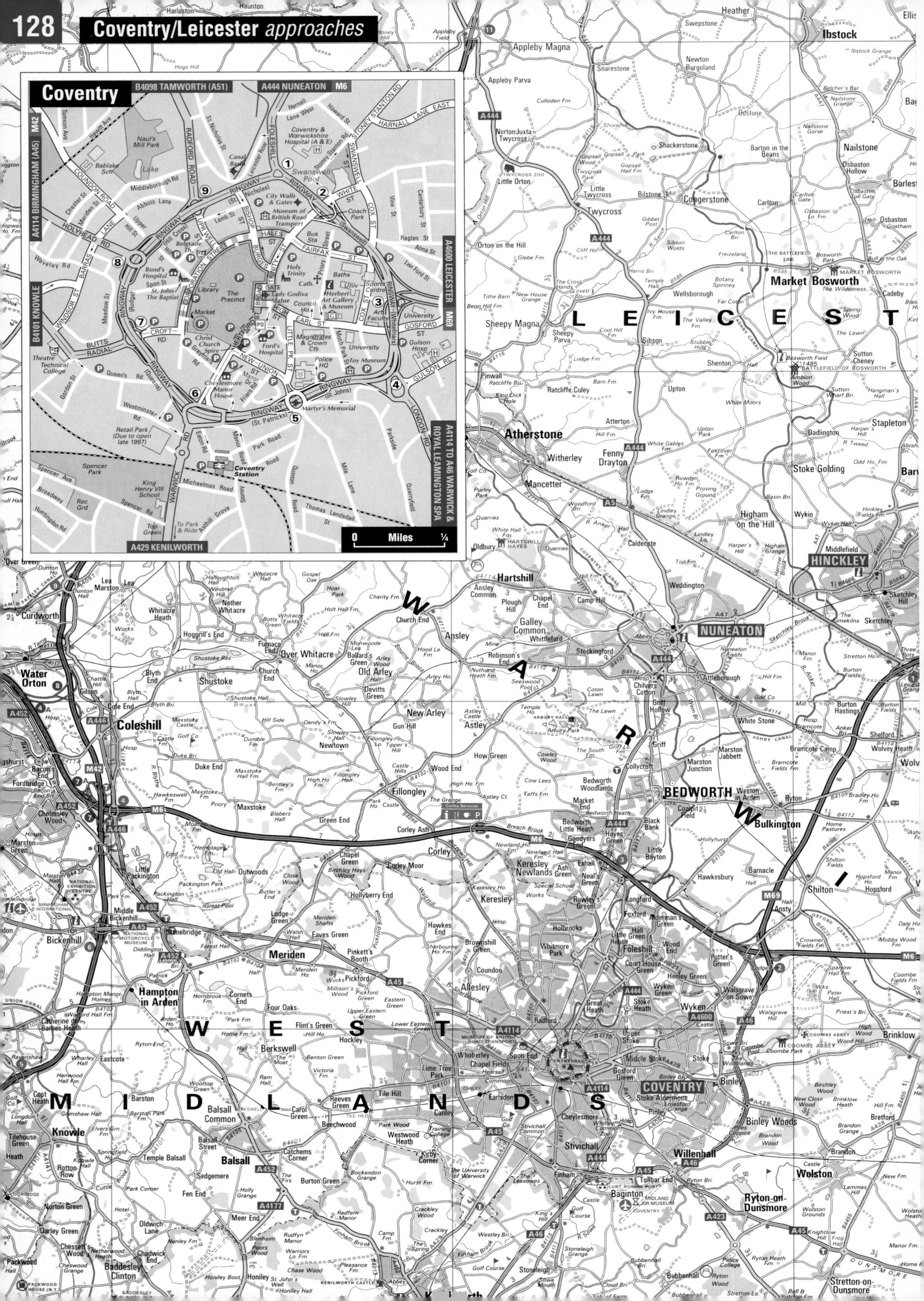
Coventry
B4098 TAMWORTH (A51)
A444 NUNEATON
M6
A4114 BIRMINGHAM (A45)
M42
A4600 LEICESTER
M69
B4101 KNOWLE
A4114 TO A46 WARWICK & ROYAL LEAMINGTON SPA
A429 KENILWORTH
RINGWAY
Coventry Station
Martyr's Memorial
Miles
LEICEST
WARWI
WEST MIDLANDS
Ibstock
Appleby Magna
Market Bosworth
Atherstone
HINCKLEY
NUNEATON
Hartshill
BEDWORTH
Bulkington
Coleshill
Water Orton
Curdworth
Meriden
Hampton in Arden
Knowle
Balsall
COVENTRY
Binley Woods
Willenhall
Wolston
Ryton-on-Dunsmore
Stretton-on-Dunsmore
Brinklow
Baginton
Kenilworth
Stoke Golding
Shilton

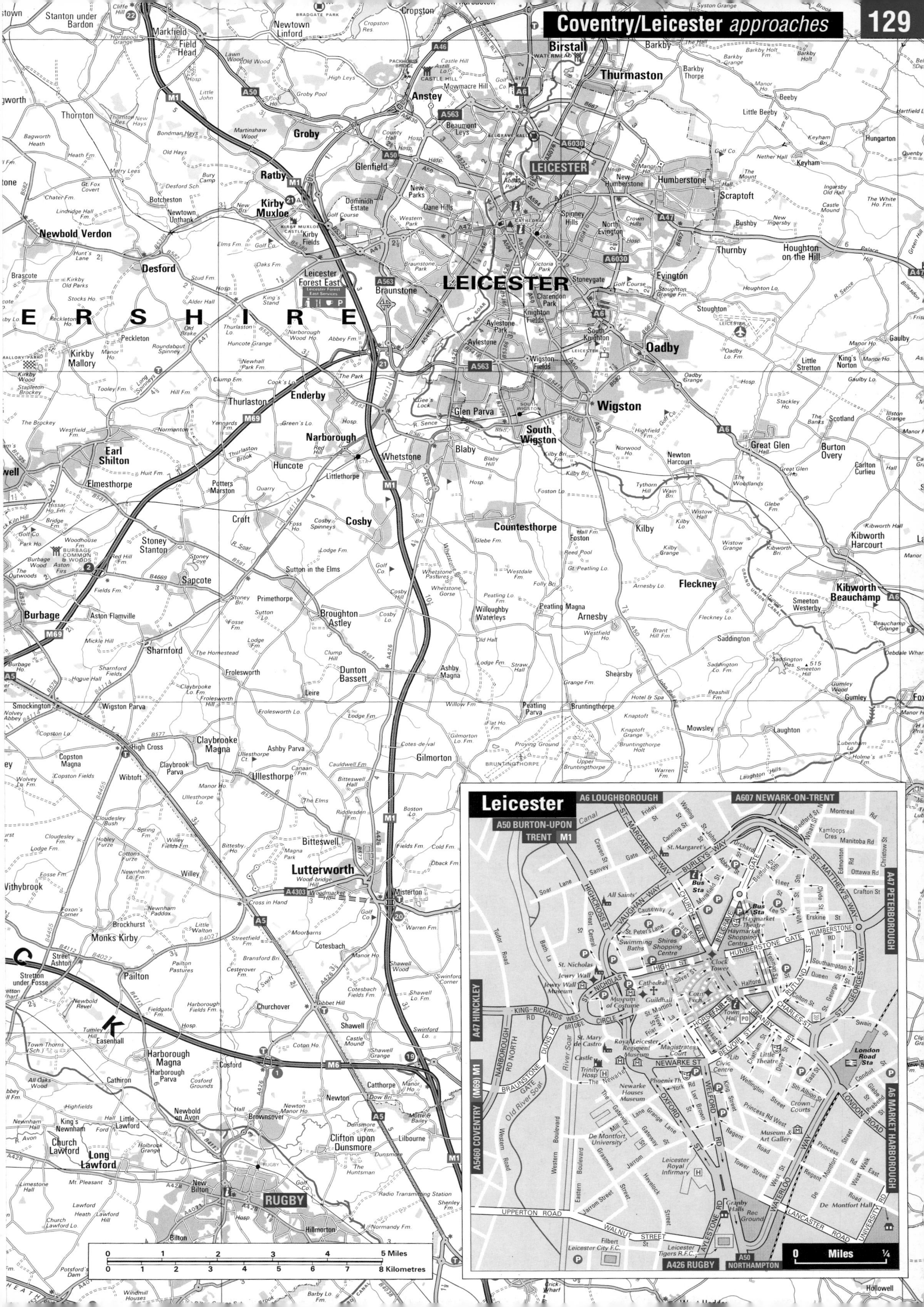
LEICESTER
Birstall
Thurmaston
Anstey
Groby
Glenfield
Ratby
Kirby Muxloe
Newbold Verdon
Desford
Leicester Forest East
Braunstone
Humberstone
Scraptoft
Thurnby
Houghton on the Hill
Evington
Oadby
Wigston
South Wigston
Glen Parva
Blaby
Enderby
Narborough
Whetstone
Earl Shilton
Elmesthorpe
Countesthorpe
Kilby
Fleckney
Kibworth Harcourt
Kibworth Beauchamp
Great Glen
Cosby
Croft
Stoney Stanton
Sapcote
Burbage
Sharnford
Broughton Astley
Dunton Bassett
Arnesby
Peatling Magna
Claybrooke Magna
Ullesthorpe
Gilmorton
Lutterworth
Bitteswell
Monks Kirby
Pailton
Harborough Magna
Newbold on Avon
Clifton upon Dunsmore
Long Lawford
RUGBY
Leicester
A6 LOUGHBOROUGH
A607 NEWARK-ON-TRENT
A50 BURTON-UPON TRENT M1
A47 PETERBOROUGH
A47 HINCKLEY
A5460 COVENTRY (M69) M1
A6 MARKET HARBOROUGH
A426 RUGBY
A50 NORTHAMPTON
0 Miles ¼
0 1 2 3 4 5 Miles
0 1 2 3 4 5 6 7 8 Kilometres

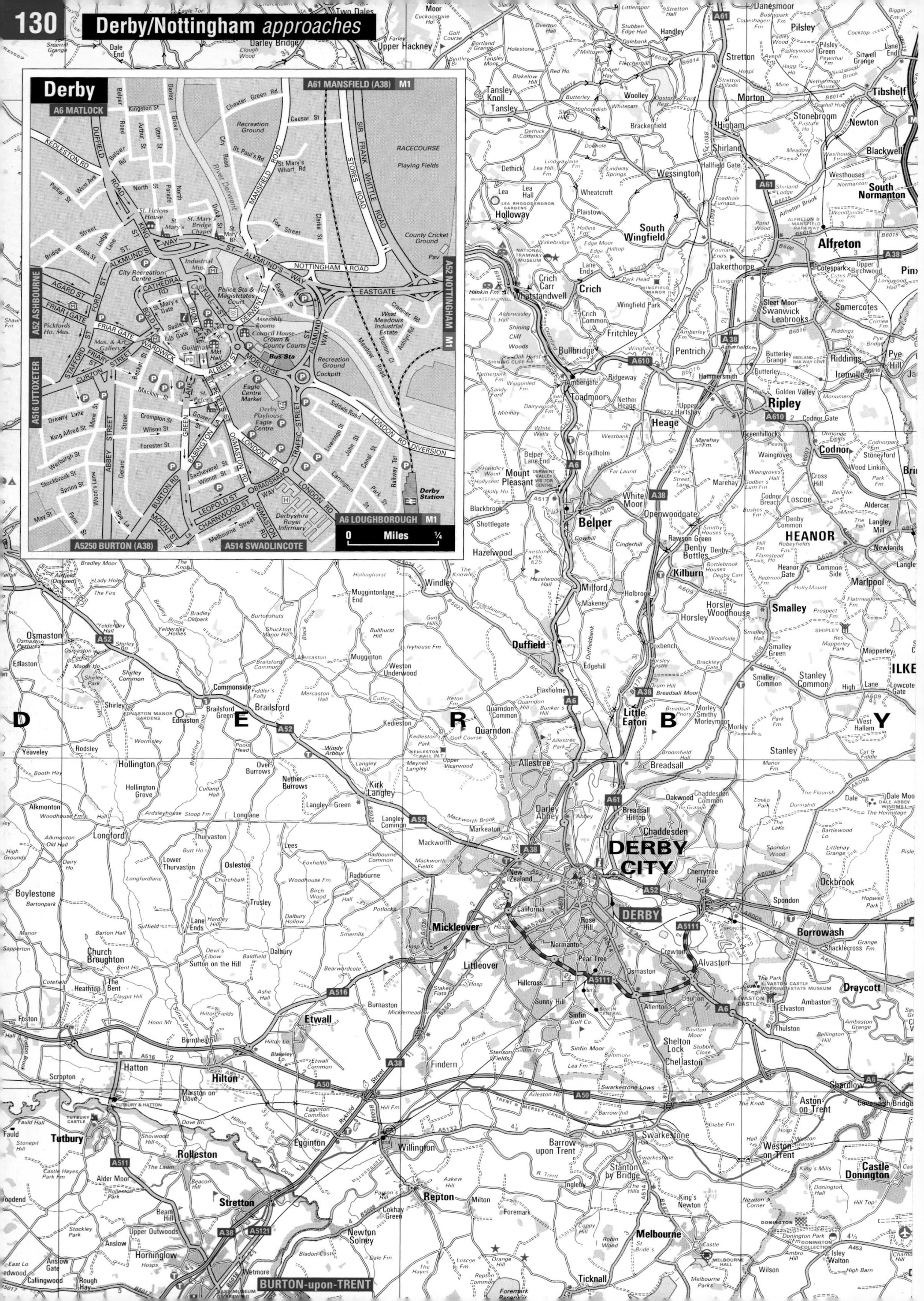
Derby
A6 MATLOCK
A61 MANSFIELD (A38) M1
A52 NOTTINGHAM
M1
A6 LOUGHBOROUGH M1
A514 SWADLINCOTE
A5250 BURTON (A38)
A516 UTTOXETER
A52 ASHBOURNE
0 Miles 1/4
Derby Station
Derbyshire Royal Infirmary
Council House
Bus Sta
Cathedral
River Derwent
Racecourse Playing Fields
County Cricket Ground
Eagle Centre Market
Derby Playhouse
Nottingham Road
Eastgate
London Rd
Osmaston Rd
Friar Gate
Kedleston Rd
Duffield Road
Mansfield Road
Sir Frank Whittle Road
Stores Road
Alfreton
Ripley
Heanor
Belper
Crich
Duffield
Allestree
Mickleover
Littleover
DERBY CITY
DERBY
Chaddesden
Spondon
Borrowash
Alvaston
Chellaston
Melbourne
Castle Donington
Repton
Willington
Etwall
Hilton
Tutbury
Rolleston
Stretton
Brailsford
Kirk Langley
Quarndon
Little Eaton
Kilburn
Smalley
Ilkeston
Tibshelf
South Normanton
Somercotes
Shardlow
Aston-on-Trent
Weston-on-Trent
Swarkestone
Draycott
BURTON-upon-TRENT
D E R B Y

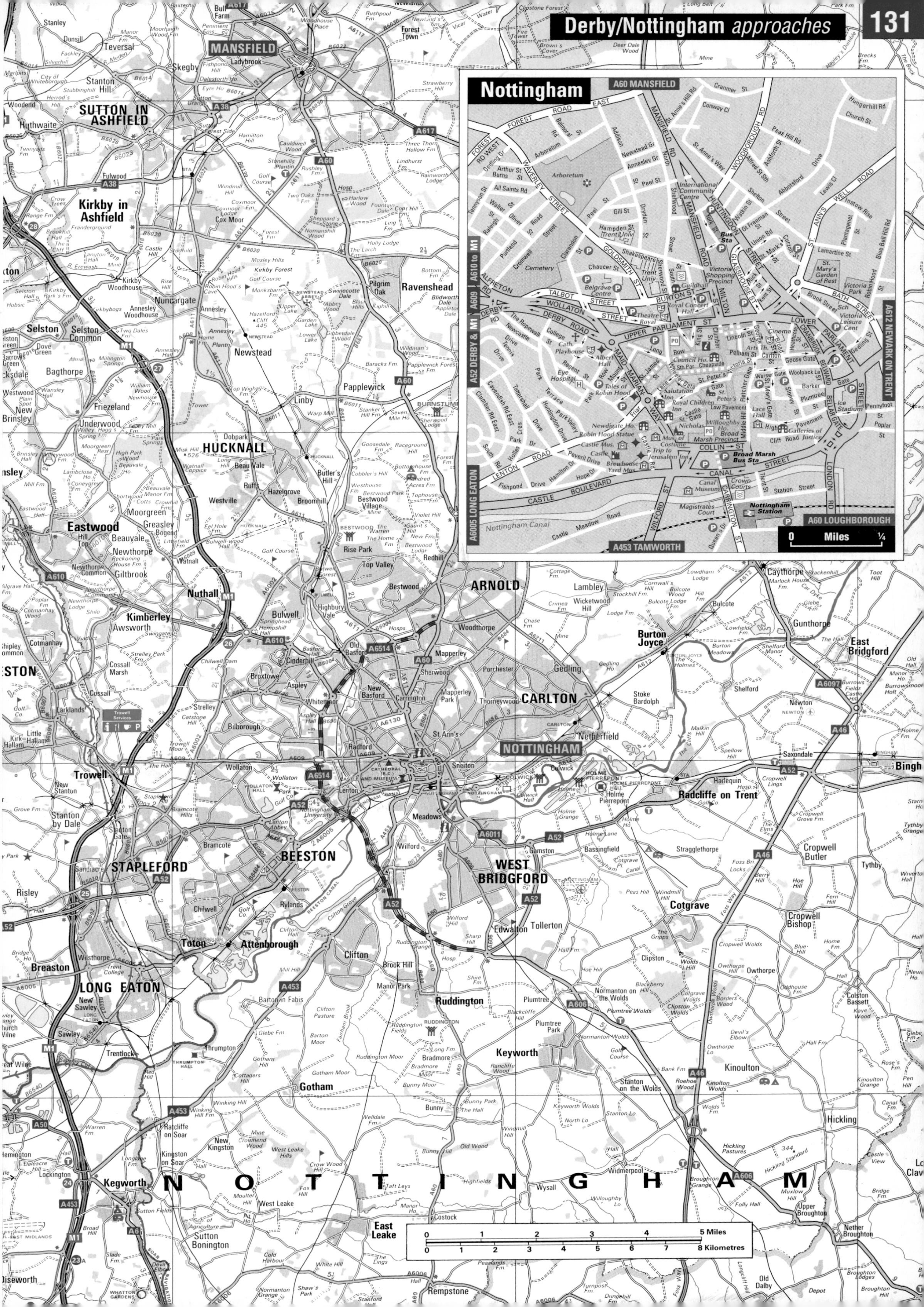
Nottingham
A60 MANSFIELD
A610 to M1
A609
A52 DERBY & M1
A612 NEWARK ON TRENT
A6005 LONG EATON
A453 TAMWORTH
A60 LOUGHBOROUGH
0 Miles ¼
Arboretum
Nottingham Station
Broad Marsh Bus Sta
Victoria Shopping Precinct
Castle Mus.
Nottingham Canal
MANSFIELD
SUTTON IN ASHFIELD
Kirkby in Ashfield
Ravenshead
Newstead
Papplewick
Linby
HUCKNALL
Eastwood
Kimberley
Nuthall
Bulwell
ARNOLD
Gedling
CARLTON
NOTTINGHAM
West Bridgford
WEST BRIDGFORD
BEESTON
STAPLEFORD
LONG EATON
Trowell
Ilkeston
Burton Joyce
East Bridgford
Radcliffe on Trent
Cotgrave
Ruddington
Keyworth
Clifton
Gotham
Kegworth
East Leake
Sutton Bonington
Kinoulton
Hickling
Cropwell Bishop
Cropwell Butler
Tollerton
Edwalton
Attenborough
Toton
Breaston
N O T T I N G H A M
0 1 2 3 4 5 Miles
0 1 2 3 4 5 6 7 8 Kilometres

FIFE REGIONAL PARK
F I F E
Lochore
Crosshill
Auchterderran
Cardenden
Kelty
Lochgelly
Cowdenbeath
Lumphinnans
KIRKCALDY
Kingseat
Townhill
DUNFERMLINE
Crossford
Cairneyhill
Charlestown
Limekilns
Rosyth
Inverkeithing
Dalgety Bay
Aberdour
Burntisland
Kinghorn
Crossgates
North Queensferry
Forth Road Bridge
F I R T H O F F O
Queensferry
Dalmeny
Kirkliston
Winchburgh
Broxburn
Uphall
LIVINGSTON
Pumpherston
East Calder
Mid Calder
Ratho
Currie
Balerno
Kirknewton
Cramond
Muirhouse
Granton
Newhaven
Leith
EDINBURGH
CITY OF EDINBURGH
Corstorphine
Colinton
Liberton
Loanhead
Bonnyrigg
Bilston
Roslin
Penicuik
WEST LOTHIAN
PENTLAND HILLS REGIONAL PARK
MID
M90
M9
M8
A90
A92
A720
A702
A701
A71
0 1 2 3 4 5 Miles
0 1 2 3 4 5 6 7 8 Kilometres

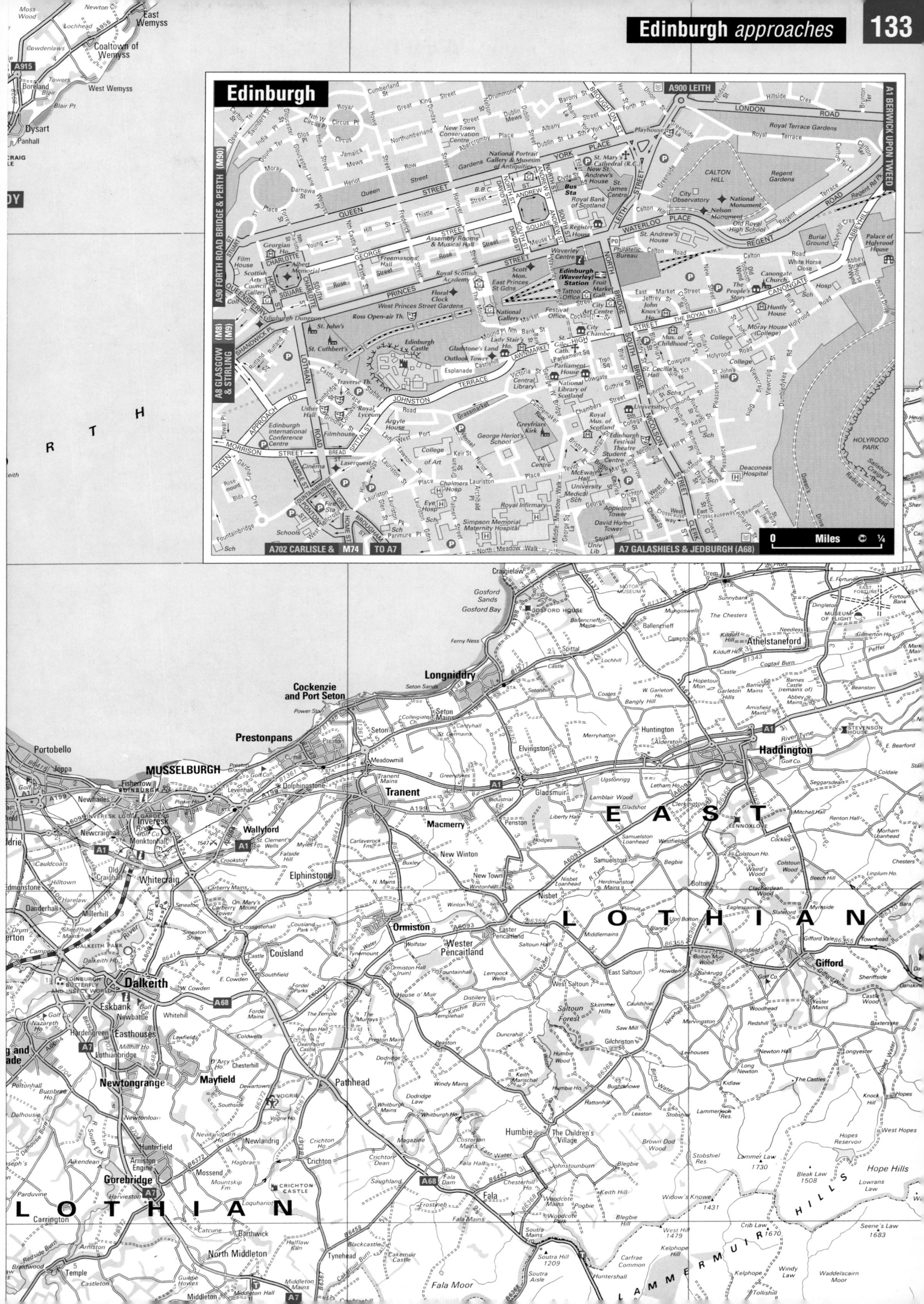
Edinburgh
A900 LEITH
A1 BERWICK UPON TWEED
A90 FORTH ROAD BRIDGE & PERTH (M90)
A8 GLASGOW & STIRLING (M8) (M9)
A702 CARLISLE & M74
TO A7
A7 GALASHIELS & JEDBURGH (A68)
0 Miles 1/4
PRINCES STREET
GEORGE STREET
QUEEN STREET
YORK PLACE
WATERLOO PLACE
REGENT ROAD
LONDON ROAD
CANONGATE
THE ROYAL MILE
HIGH STREET
LAWNMARKET
NORTH BRIDGE
SOUTH BRIDGE
NICOLSON STREET
LOTHIAN ROAD
JOHNSTON TERRACE
MORRISON STREET
Royal Terrace Gardens
CALTON HILL
Regent Gardens
City Observatory
National Monument
Nelson Monument
Old Royal High School
St. Andrew's House
Burial Ground
Palace of Holyrood House
HOLYROOD PARK
Salisbury Crags
National Portrait Gallery & Museum of Antiquities
St. Mary's Cathedral (R.C.)
Bus Sta
Royal Bank of Scotland
Register House
Waverley Centre
Edinburgh (Waverley) Station
Fruit Market Gall.
Philatelic Bureau
Scott Mon.
East Princes St Gdns
West Princes Street Gardens
Floral Clock
Royal Scottish Academy
National Gallery
Ross Open-air Th.
Edinburgh Castle
Esplanade
Outlook Tower
Gladstone's Land
Lady Stair's Ho.
St. Giles Cath.
Parliament House
City Chambers
National Library of Scotland
Royal Mus. of Scotland
Greyfriars Kirk
George Heriot's School
College of Art
Royal Infirmary
Simpson Memorial Maternity Hospital
Edinburgh Festival Theatre
McEwan Hall
University
Deaconess Hospital
Moray House (College)
Huntly House
Canongate Church
The People's Story
John Knox's Ho.
Mus. of Childhood
Usher Hall
Royal Lyceum
Traverse Th.
Filmhouse
Edinburgh International Conference Centre
Edinburgh Dungeon
St. John's
St. Cuthbert's
Albert Memorial
Scottish Arts Council Gallery
Film House
Georgian Ho.
Assembly Rooms & Musical Hall
Freemasons' Hall
Tattoo Office
Festival Office
Cockburn St
Laserquest
Cinema
East Wemyss
Coaltown of Wemyss
West Wemyss
Dysart
Gosford Sands
Gosford Bay
Gosford House
Drem
Museum of Flight
Athelstaneford
Longniddry
Cockenzie and Port Seton
Prestonpans
Portobello
Joppa
MUSSELBURGH
Inveresk
Wallyford
Tranent
Macmerry
Seton
Meadowmill
Elphinstone
New Winton
Gladsmuir
Haddington
Huntington
Stevenson House
Lennoxlove
EAST LOTHIAN
Ormiston
Wester Pencaitland
Samuelston
Nisbet
East Saltoun
West Saltoun
Saltoun Forest
Gifford
Bolton
Cousland
Whitecraig
Dalkeith
Eskbank
Newbattle
Easthouses
Newtongrange
Mayfield
Pathhead
Gorebridge
Newlandrig
Crichton
Crichton Castle
Humbie
The Children's Village
Fala
Fala Moor
Soutra Hill 1209
Carrington
Temple
North Middleton
Middleton
LOTHIAN
LAMMERMUIR HILLS
Hope Hills
Lammer Law 1730
Bleak Law 1508
Crib Law 1670
Seene's Law 1683
Hopes Reservoir
Lammerloch Res.
A1
A7
A68
A199
A6093
A6124
A6094

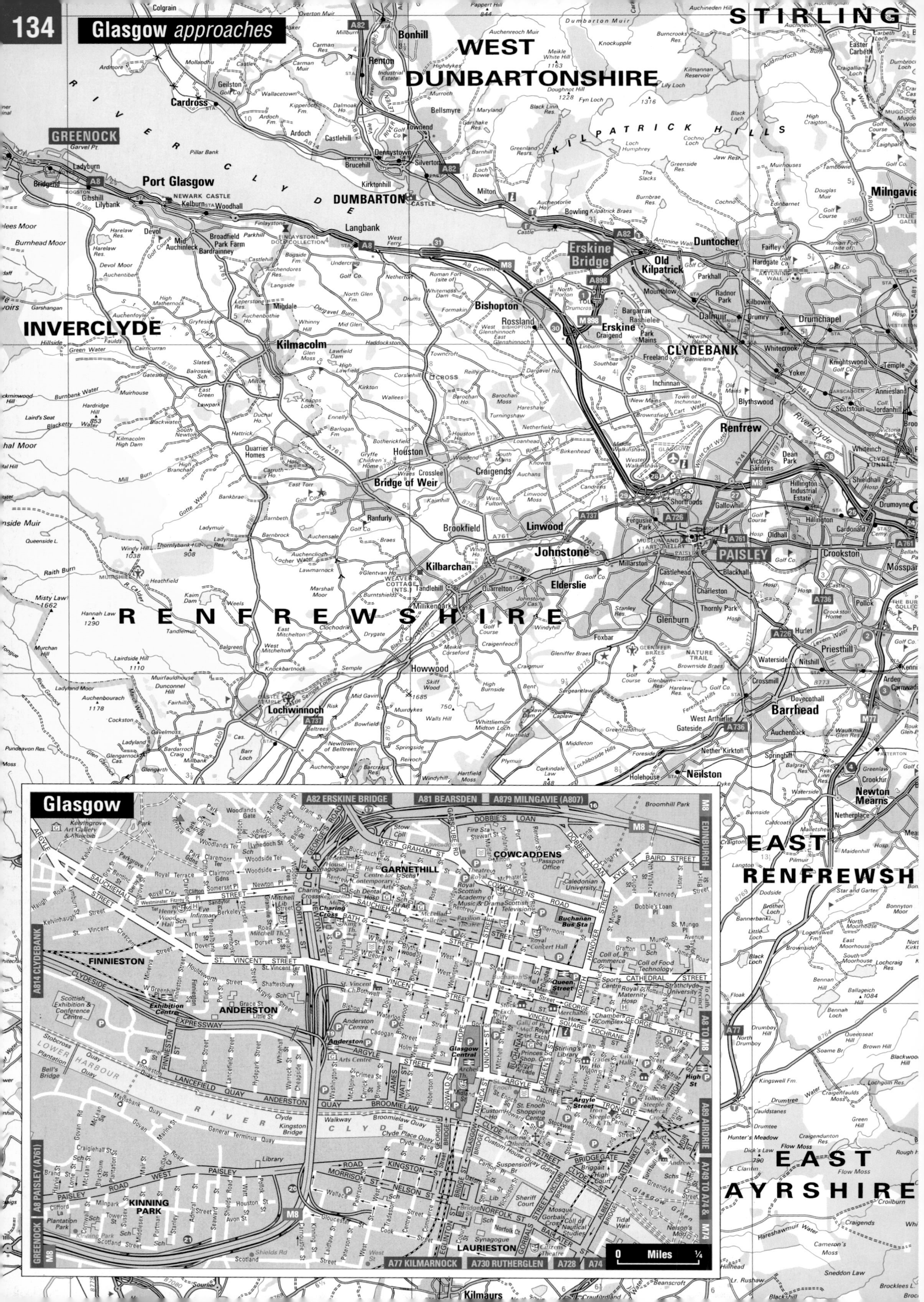
STIRLING
WEST DUNBARTONSHIRE
KILPATRICK HILLS
RIVER CLYDE
GREENOCK
Port Glasgow
DUMBARTON
Cardross
Bonhill
Renton
Milngavie
Erskine Bridge
Old Kilpatrick
Duntocher
CLYDEBANK
INVERCLYDE
Kilmacolm
Bishopton
Erskine
Renfrew
Houston
Bridge of Weir
Linwood
Johnstone
PAISLEY
Elderslie
Kilbarchan
RENFREWSHIRE
Lochwinnoch
Howwood
Barrhead
Neilston
Newton Mearns
EAST RENFREWSH
EAST AYRSHIRE
Glasgow
A82 ERSKINE BRIDGE
A81 BEARSDEN
A879 MILNGAVIE (A807)
M8 EDINBURGH
COWCADDENS
GARNETHILL
FINNIESTON
ANDERSTON
KINNING PARK
LAURIESTON
A814 CLYDEBANK
A8 PAISLEY (A761)
GREENOCK M8
A8 TO M8
A89 AIRDRIE
A749 TO A74 & M74
A77 KILMARNOCK
A730 RUTHERGLEN
A728
A74
0 Miles 1/4

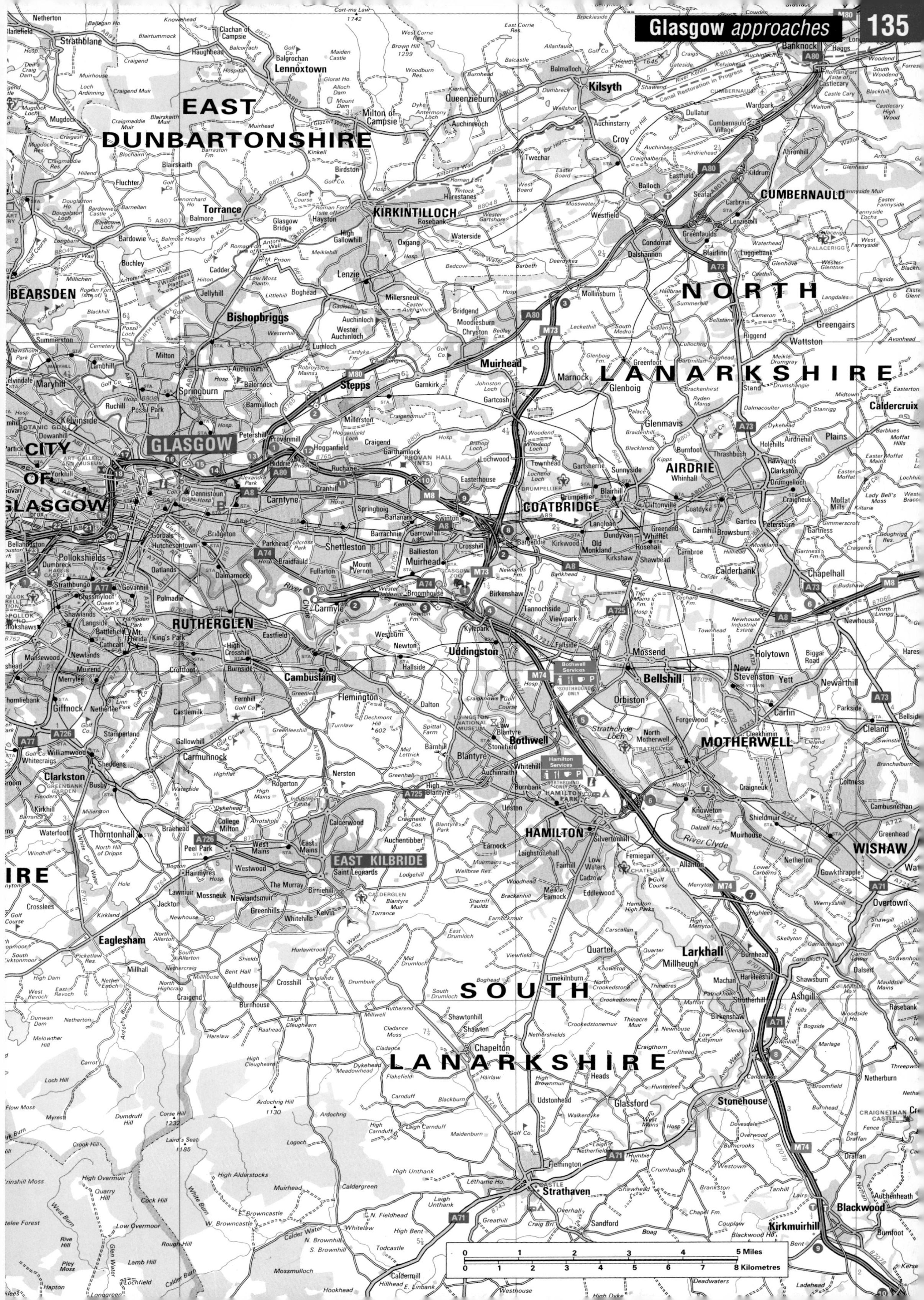
EAST
DUNBARTONSHIRE
CITY
OF
GLASGOW
GLASGOW
NORTH
LANARKSHIRE
SOUTH
LANARKSHIRE
Strathblane
Lennoxtown
Milton of Campsie
Kilsyth
Queenzieburn
Banknock
Torrance
KIRKINTILLOCH
Lenzie
BEARSDEN
Bishopbriggs
Milngavie
Croy
CUMBERNAULD
Stepps
Muirhead
Glenboig
Glenmavis
Caldercruix
Plains
AIRDRIE
COATBRIDGE
Springburn
Maryhill
Rutherglen
RUTHERGLEN
Cambuslang
Uddingston
Bellshill
Bothwell
Blantyre
MOTHERWELL
WISHAW
HAMILTON
Larkhall
EAST KILBRIDE
Clarkston
Giffnock
Eaglesham
Carmunnock
Stonehouse
Strathaven
Glassford
Blackwood
Kirkmuirhill
Chapelton
Holytown
New Stevenson
Newarthill
Carfin
Cleland
Overtown
Ashgill
Bothwell Services
Hamilton Services
0 1 2 3 4 5 Miles
0 1 2 3 4 5 6 7 8 Kilometres

Bradford
A650 SKIPTON (A629)
A6037 OTLEY (A6038)
A658 HARROGATE (A61)
TO A647
A647 LEEDS
A650 WAKEFIELD
M62 M1
A641 HUDDERSFIELD
A647 HALIFAX
0 Miles ¼
Forster Sq Sta
Interchange Sta
Bus Station
Colour Museum
Kirkgate Centre
Alhambra Theatre
University of Bradford
Bradford College
Nat. Mus. of Photography Film & Television
Jacob's Well Municipal Offices
St. Luke's Hosp
Bolling Hall
St. Mary's R.C. Church
Menston
Guiseley
Yeadon
Rawdon
Baildon
Horsforth
Calverley
SHIPLEY
BRADFORD
PUDSEY
Gildersome
W
E
Y O R K
Hebden Bridge
Northowram
Luddenden
Halifax
Sowerby Bridge
Hipperholme
Cleckheaton
Gomersal
Birkenshaw
BATLEY
Heckmondwike
Liversedge
BRIGHOUSE
Elland
Greetland
Ripponden
Mirfield
Dewsbury
HUDDERSFIELD
Kirkheaton
Slaithwaite
Marsden
Honley
Meltham
Holmfirth
Kirkburton
Emley
Skelmanthorpe
Denby Dale
Flockton
Shepley
Golcar
0 1 2 3 4 5 Miles
0 1 2 3 4 5 6 7 8 Kilometres

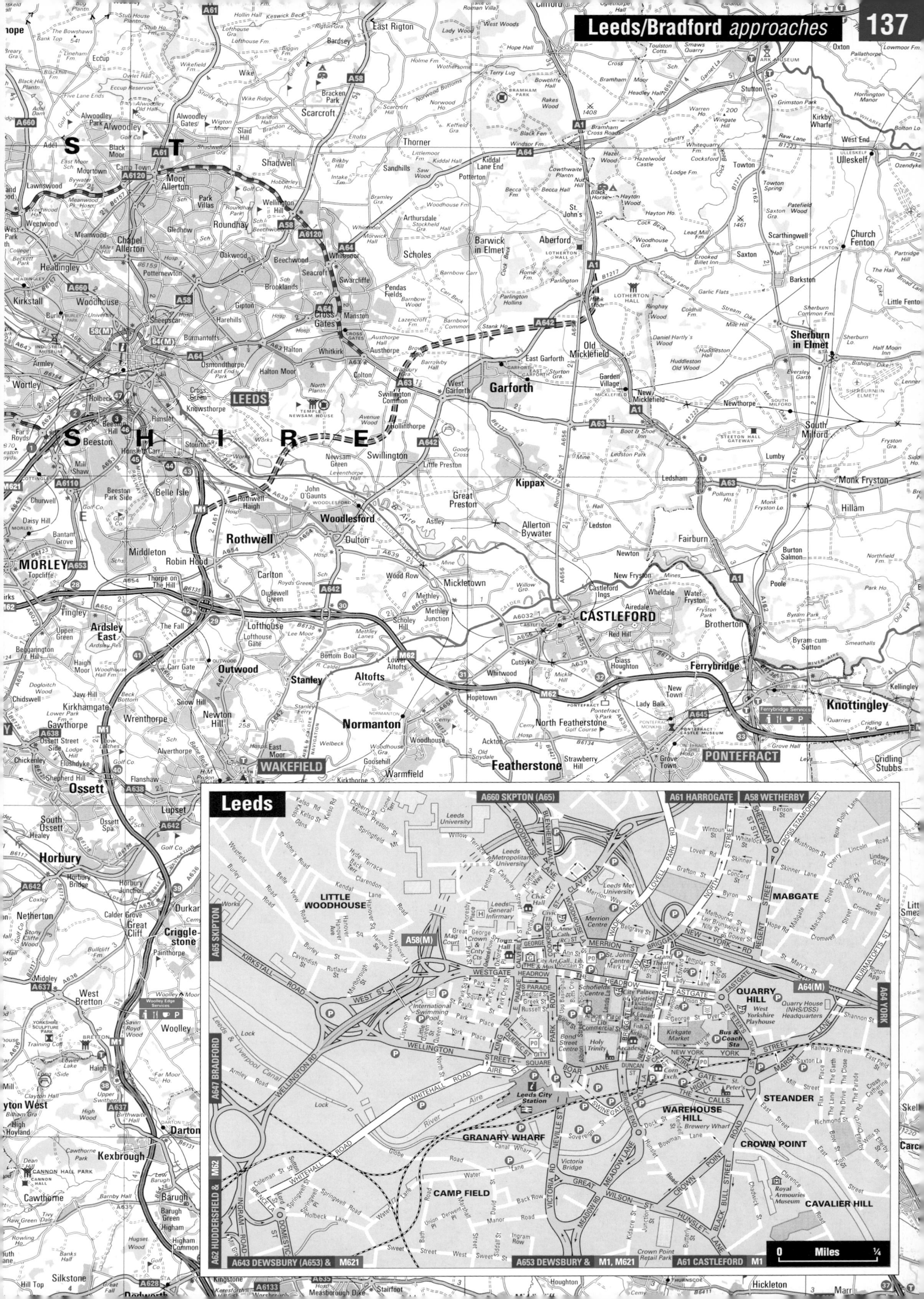
Leeds
LEEDS
WAKEFIELD
PONTEFRACT
CASTLEFORD
MORLEY
Ossett
Horbury
Rothwell
Garforth
Normanton
Featherstone
Knottingley
Ferrybridge
Sherburn in Elmet
Aberford
Kippax
Woodlesford
Ulleskelf
Scarcroft
Shadwell
Thorner
Moor Allerton
Roundhay
Headingley
Kirkstall
Beeston
Middleton
Crigglestone
Kexbrough
Cawthorne
Silkstone
Barugh
West Bretton
Woolley
Netherton
Ardsley East
Outwood
Stanley
Altofts
Swillington
Barwick in Elmet
Scholes
Church Fenton
South Milford
Monk Fryston
Hillam
Saxton
Towton
Oxton
LITTLE WOODHOUSE
MABGATE
QUARRY HILL
STEANDER
WAREHOUSE HILL
GRANARY WHARF
CROWN POINT
CAMP FIELD
CAVALIER HILL
Leeds City Station
A660 SKPTON (A65)
A61 HARROGATE
A58 WETHERBY
A64 YORK
A65 SKIPTON
A647 BRADFORD
A62 HUDDERSFIELD & M62
A643 DEWSBURY (A653) & M621
A653 DEWSBURY & M1, M621
A61 CASTLEFORD M1
0 Miles ¼

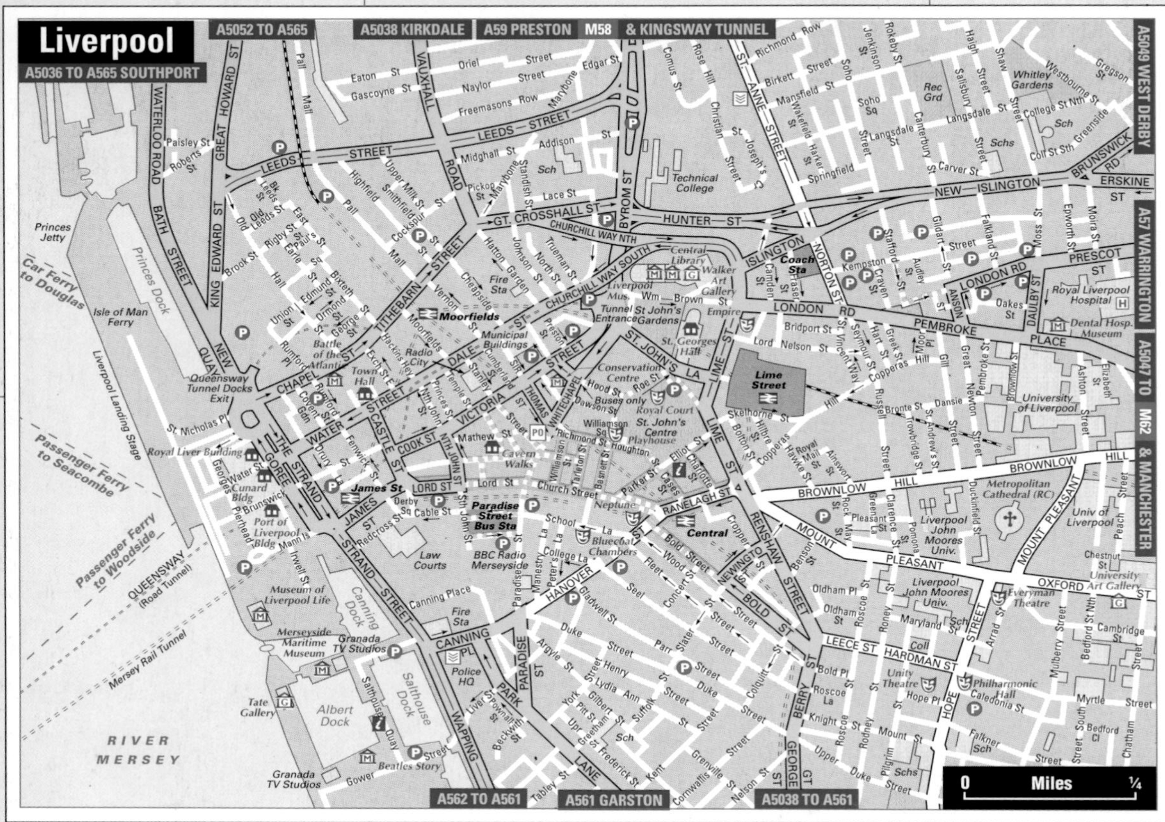
Liverpool
A5036 TO A565 SOUTHPORT
A5052 TO A565
A5038 KIRKDALE
A59 PRESTON
M58 & KINGSWAY TUNNEL
A5049 WEST DERBY
A57 WARRINGTON
A5047 TO M62 & MANCHESTER
A562 TO A561
A561 GARSTON
A5038 TO A561
0 Miles ¼
Moorfields
Lime Street
James St.
Central
Paradise Street Bus Sta
Coach Sta
Technical College
Central Library
Walker Art Gallery
St. George's Hall
St. John's Gardens
Royal Liverpool Hospital
University of Liverpool
Metropolitan Cathedral (RC)
Liverpool John Moores Univ.
Philharmonic Hall
Everyman Theatre
Unity Theatre
Law Courts
BBC Radio Merseyside
Bluecoat Chambers
Cavern Walks
Royal Court
Conservation Centre
Municipal Buildings
Town Hall
Battle of the Atlantic
Queensway Tunnel Docks Exit
Royal Liver Building
Cunard Bldg
Port of Liverpool Bldg
Museum of Liverpool Life
Merseyside Maritime Museum
Granada TV Studios
Tate Gallery
Albert Dock
Salthouse Dock
Canning Dock
Beatles Story
Princes Dock
Princes Jetty
Isle of Man Ferry
Car Ferry to Douglas
Liverpool Landing Stage
Passenger Ferry to Seacombe
Passenger Ferry to Woodside
QUEENSWAY (Road Tunnel)
Mersey Rail Tunnel
RIVER MERSEY
LEEDS STREET
HUNTER ST
LONDON RD
PEMBROKE PLACE
BROWNLOW HILL
MOUNT PLEASANT
OXFORD ST
HARDMAN ST
LEECE ST
HANOVER
CANNING
STRAND STREET
WATERLOO ROAD
BATH STREET
KING EDWARD ST
GREAT HOWARD ST
TITHEBARN STREET
VICTORIA
DALE
WATER ST
CHAPEL ST
RANELAGH ST
BOLD ST
RENSHAW STREET
ISLINGTON
NEW ISLINGTON
ERSKINE ST
PRESCOT ST
BRUNSWICK
BYROM ST
VAUXHALL ROAD
WAPPING
PARK LANE
BERRY ST
GREAT GEORGE ST
HOPE ST

Formby
Freshfield
Formby Pt.
Taylor's Bank
Formby Bank
CROSBY CHANNEL
Blundellsands
Brighton le
Great Burbo Bank
WALLASEY
Leasowe
Moreton
Bidston
East Hoyle Bank
Dove Point
Meols
HOYLAKE
Red Rocks
Hilbre Island
Little Hilbre Island
West Kirby
Little Eye
Grange
Newton
Saughall Massie
Upton
Greasby
Frankby
Arrowe Hill
Woodchurch
BIRKEN
Irby
Caldy
Thurstaston
Pensby
Thingwall
Landican
M53
Barnston
HESWALL
Gayton
Parkgate
Neston
Little Neston
Dawpool Bank
Salisbury Bank
Salisbury Middle
Mostyn Bank
Holywell Bank
Gayton Sands
Bagillt Bank
POINT OF AYR
Wild Road
Talacre
The Warren
Gronant
PRESTATYN
Meliden
Gwaenysgor
Dyserth
Rhuddlan
DENBIGHSHIRE
Llanasa
Ffynnongroyw
Pen-y-ffordd
Mostyn-Quay
Mostyn
Trelogan
Rhewl-Mostyn
Tre-Mostyn
Glan-y-don
Llannerch-y-môr
Berthengam
Whitford
Lloc
Carmel
Greenfield
Holywell
Bagillt
Brynford
FLINTSHIRE
Caerwys
Flint
Halkyn
Ysceifiog
Afon-wen
Tremeirchion
Rhuallt
Trefnant
Bodfari
A55
A548
A540
Oakenholt
Kelsterton

LANCASHIRE
MERSEYSIDE
CHESHIRE
ORMSKIRK
SKELMERSDALE
WIGAN
Orrell
Maghull
Rainford
Billinge
KIRKBY
Knowsley
ST. HELENS
BOOTLE
Litherland
Aintree
Crosby
LIVERPOOL
HUYTON-WITH-ROBY
Huyton
Prescot
Widnes
RUNCORN
Garston
Speke
BEBINGTON
Port Sunlight
ELLESMERE PORT
Frodsham
Helsby
Willaston
Kingsley
RIVER MERSEY
MANCHESTER SHIP CANAL
0 1 2 3 4 5 Miles
0 1 2 3 4 5 6 7 8 Kilometres

Paddington
Marylebone
EALING
Hanwell
Acton
Yiewsley
Hayes
Southall
HAMMERSMITH
West Drayton
Richings Park
Langley
Harlington
Heston
Chiswick
Kew Bridge
Westminster
Harmondsworth
Sipson
Cranford
Brentford
Fulham
Battersea
Colnbrook
Longford
Heathrow Airport
Hounslow
Isleworth
Putney
Clapham
Stanwell
Wraysbury
East Bedfont
RICHMOND
Roehampton
Wandsworth
Feltham
Twickenham
RICHMOND PARK
Petersham
Balham
STAINES
Egham
Ashford
Hanworth
Teddington
Sunbury
Hampton
WIMBLEDON
Merton
Thorpe
Laleham
Littleton
Shepperton
Hampton Wick
KINGSTON
Mitcham
Raynes Park
West Molesey
East Molesey
New Malden
Morden
Thames Ditton
Surbiton
Chertsey
Walton on Thames
Long Ditton
Tolworth
St. Helier
Addlestone
Weybridge
Hersham
Esher
Hook
Worcester Park
Carshalton
Sutton
Claygate
Chessington
Ewell
Cheam
Wallington
Ottershaw
Woodham
Byfleet
West Byfleet
Cobham
Oxshott
EPSOM
Banstead
WOKING
Stoke D'Abernon
Ripley
Ockham
LEATHERHEAD
Ashtead
Chipstead
Burgh Heath
Tadworth
Send
Fetcham
Little Bookham
Kingswood
Walton on the Hill
West Horsley
East Horsley
Effingham
Great Bookham
Mickleham
Headley
Merstham
S U R R E Y
Westhumble
Redhill
REIGATE
DORKING
Brockham
Betchworth
Westcott
GUILDFORD
Albury
Gomshall
Shere
Wotton
North Holmwood
Salfords
Wonersh
Shamley Green
ABINGER FOREST
South Holmwood
Peaslake
Holmbury St. Mary
HORLEY
Newdigate
Charlwood
Gatwick Airport
Ewhurst
Capel
Ockley
Cranleigh

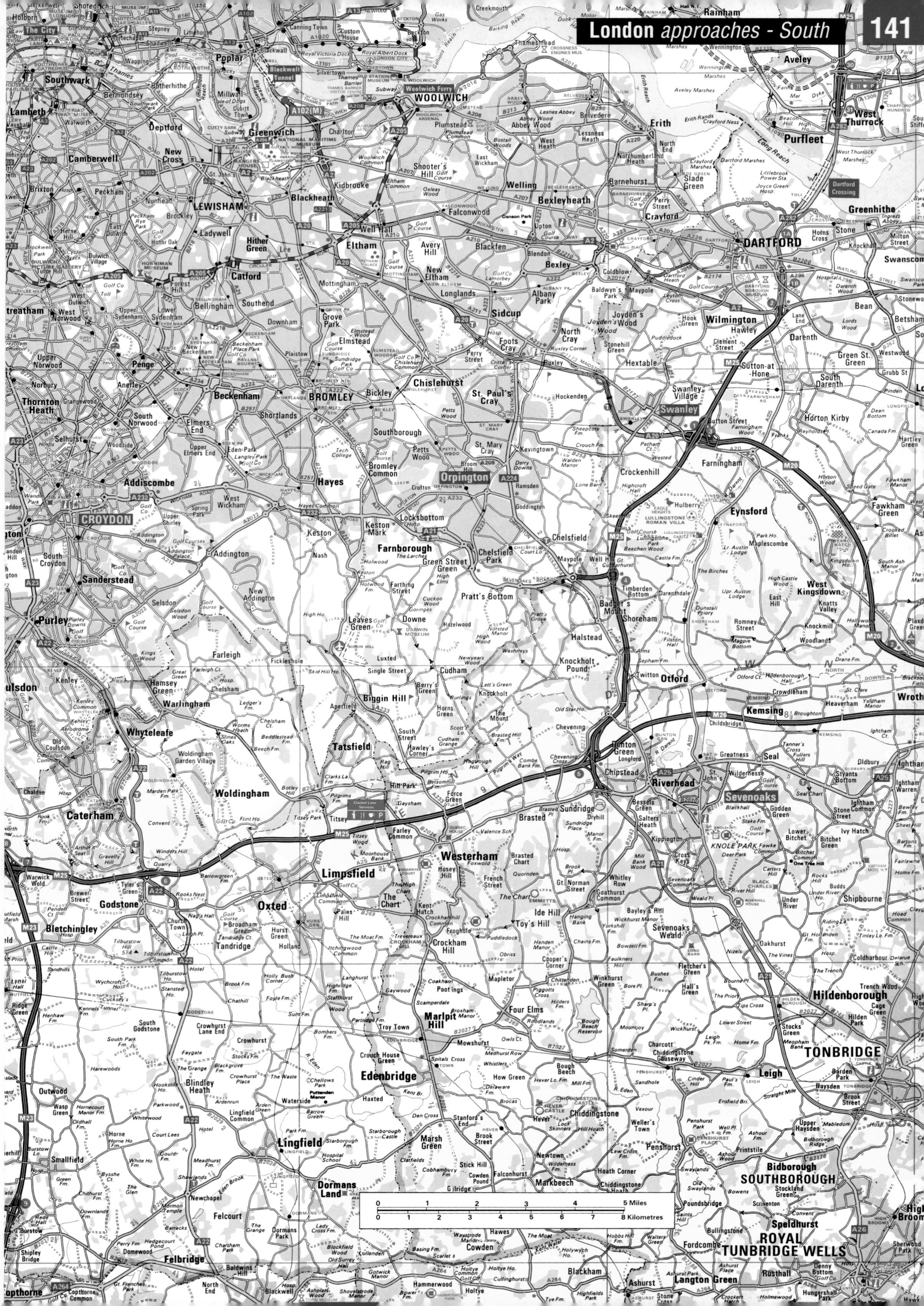
Southwark
Lambeth
Camberwell
Brixton
Peckham
Deptford
Greenwich
WOOLWICH
Poplar
LEWISHAM
Blackheath
Eltham
Catford
Welling
Bexleyheath
Erith
Purfleet
West Thurrock
Crayford
DARTFORD
Greenhithe
Sidcup
Bexley
Wilmington
BROMLEY
Beckenham
Chislehurst
Orpington
Swanley
CROYDON
Addiscombe
Purley
Sanderstead
Farnborough
Eynsford
Otford
Kemsing
Warlingham
Whyteleafe
Caterham
Biggin Hill
Tatsfield
Westerham
Limpsfield
Oxted
Godstone
Bletchingley
Riverhead
Sevenoaks
Edenbridge
Lingfield
Dormans Land
Felbridge
Hildenborough
TONBRIDGE
Leigh
Penshurst
SOUTHBOROUGH
ROYAL TUNBRIDGE WELLS
Langton Green
Ashurst
0 1 2 3 4 5 Miles
0 1 2 3 4 5 6 7 8 Kilometres

HARPENDEN
Wheathampstead
WELWYN GARDEN CITY
Hertingfordbury
Gt. Gaddesden
Sandridge
H
E
R
T
F
O
Potten End
RKHAMSTED
Hatfield
Essendon
Little Berkhamsted
HEMEL HEMPSTEAD
ST. ALBANS
Chiswell Green
London Colney
Colney Heath
Brookmans Park
Bovingdon
Kings Langley
Abbots Langley
Bricket Wood
Shenley
POTTERS BAR
Chipperfield
Sarratt
Radlett
WATFORD
Bushey
Borehamwood
Elstree
BARNET
New Barnet
Cockfosters
East Barnet
Chorleywood
RICKMANSWORTH
Oxhey
Totteridge
South Oxhey
Northwood
Edgware
Mill Hill
Friern Barnet
Finchley
Pinner
HARROW
Hendon
G
R
E
A
Ruislip
Denham
Wembley
Willesden
Hampstead
Highgate
L
O
N
UXBRIDGE
Hillingdon
Greenford
EALING
Acton
Paddington
Marylebone
Iver
Yiewsley
Hayes
Southall
Hanwell
HAMMERSMITH
Kensington
West Drayton
Harlington
Heston
Chiswick
Brentford
Fulham
Battersea
Chelsea
Heathrow Airport
Hounslow
Isleworth
Putney
Wandsworth
Stanwell
Feltham
Twickenham
RICHMOND
RICHMOND PARK
STAINES
Ashford
Hanworth
Teddington
Egham
Wraysbury
Heathrow Services
Heston Services
South Mimms Services
Scratchwood Services
Kew Bridge

0 1 2 3 4 5 Miles
0 1 2 3 4 5 6 7 8 Kilometres
HERTFORD
HARLOW
Great Amwell
Stanstead Abbotts
Hoddesdon
Lower Nazeing
Cheshunt
Waltham Cross
Waltham Abbey
Epping
North Weald Bassett
High Ongar
Chipping Ongar
ENFIELD
Edmonton
Chingford
Theydon Bois
High Beach
Loughton
Debden
Abridge
Chigwell
Kelvedon Hatch
Doddinghurst
Stapleford Abbotts
Harold Hill
ROMFORD
Tottenham
Walthamstow
Woodford
Wanstead
ILFORD
Leyton
Stoke Newington
Islington
Hackney
West Ham
East Ham
BARKING
Dagenham
Hornchurch
Upminster
Rainham
Poplar
Southwark
Lambeth
WOOLWICH
Erith
Purfleet
West Thurrock
Greenwich
Deptford
Camberwell
LEWISHAM
Blackheath
Welling
Bexleyheath
Crayford
DARTFORD
Greenhithe
Eltham
Catford
Bexley
Sidcup
Wilmington
Dartford Crossing
Blackwell Tunnel
Woolwich Ferry
The City
M11
M25
A10
A12
A13
A406
A414

REGENT'S PARK
REGENTS PARK
SOMERS TOWN
EUSTON
KINGS CROSS
ST. PANCRAS
BRITISH LIB.
MARYLEBONE
FITZROVIA
BLOOMSBURY
BRITISH MUSEUM
UNIVERSITY OF LONDON
SOHO
MAYFAIR
ST. JAMES'S
HYDE PARK
THE SERPENTINE
Rotten Row
GREEN PARK
ST. JAMES'S PARK
BUCKINGHAM PALACE GARDENS
BUCKINGHAM PALACE
KNIGHTSBRIDGE
BROMPTON
BELGRAVIA
VICTORIA
WESTMINSTER
WESTMINSTER ABBEY
TATE GALLERY
NATIONAL GALLERY
ROYAL ACADEMY
WALLACE COLLECTION
MADAME TUSSAUD'S
PLANETARIUM
SHERLOCK HOLMES MUSEUM
WELLINGTON MUSEUM
QUEEN MARY'S GARDENS
MARYLEBONE ROAD
EUSTON ROAD
PARK ROAD
EDGWARE ROAD
BAYSWATER ROAD
PARK LANE
Oxford Street
Regent Street
Piccadilly
The Mall
Whitehall
Victoria Street
Belgrave Road
Vauxhall Bridge Road
Millbank
Grosvenor Place
Brompton Road
Knightsbridge
Kensington Road
Tottenham Court Road
Charing Cross Road
Shaftesbury Avenue
Baker Street
Albany Street
Hampstead Road
Eversholt Street
Strand
Constitution Hill

KING'S CROSS
FINSBURY
CLERKENWELL
HOLBORN
HOXTON
SHOREDITCH
CITY OF LONDON
SOUTHWARK
SOUTH BANK
LAMBETH
RIVER THAMES
KING'S REACH
PENTONVILLE ROAD
CITY ROAD
EAST ROAD
OLD STREET
GREAT EASTERN STREET
COMMERCIAL STREET
KINGSLAND ROAD
BOROUGH ROAD
LONG LANE
LONDON ROAD
NEWINGTON CAUSEWAY
NEWINGTON BUTTS
KENNINGTON LANE
KENNINGTON ROAD
TOWER BRIDGE ROAD
MINORIES
BLACKFRIARS
WATERLOO
LONDON BRIDGE
LIVERPOOL STREET
FENCHURCH STREET
ST. PAUL'S CATHEDRAL
THE TOWER OF LONDON
THE BARBICAN CENTRE FOR ARTS
MUSEUM OF LONDON
BANK OF ENGLAND
IMPERIAL WAR MUSEUM
ROYAL NATIONAL THEATRE
MUSEUM OF THE MOVING IMAGE
SOUTHWARK CATHEDRAL
HMS BELFAST
Primary Route
Inner Ring Road
Bus Route within Inner Ring Rd.
Closed at all times except for access
One Way Street
Street Market
Buses & Taxis Only 7am - 7pm, Mon-Sat.
British Rail Station
EUSTON
Public Buildings
Buildings of Interest open to the public
Underground Station
Main Post Office
Church
Hospital
Youth Hostel
Scale 3¼ inches to 1 mile
0
¼
½
miles
0
½
1 kms

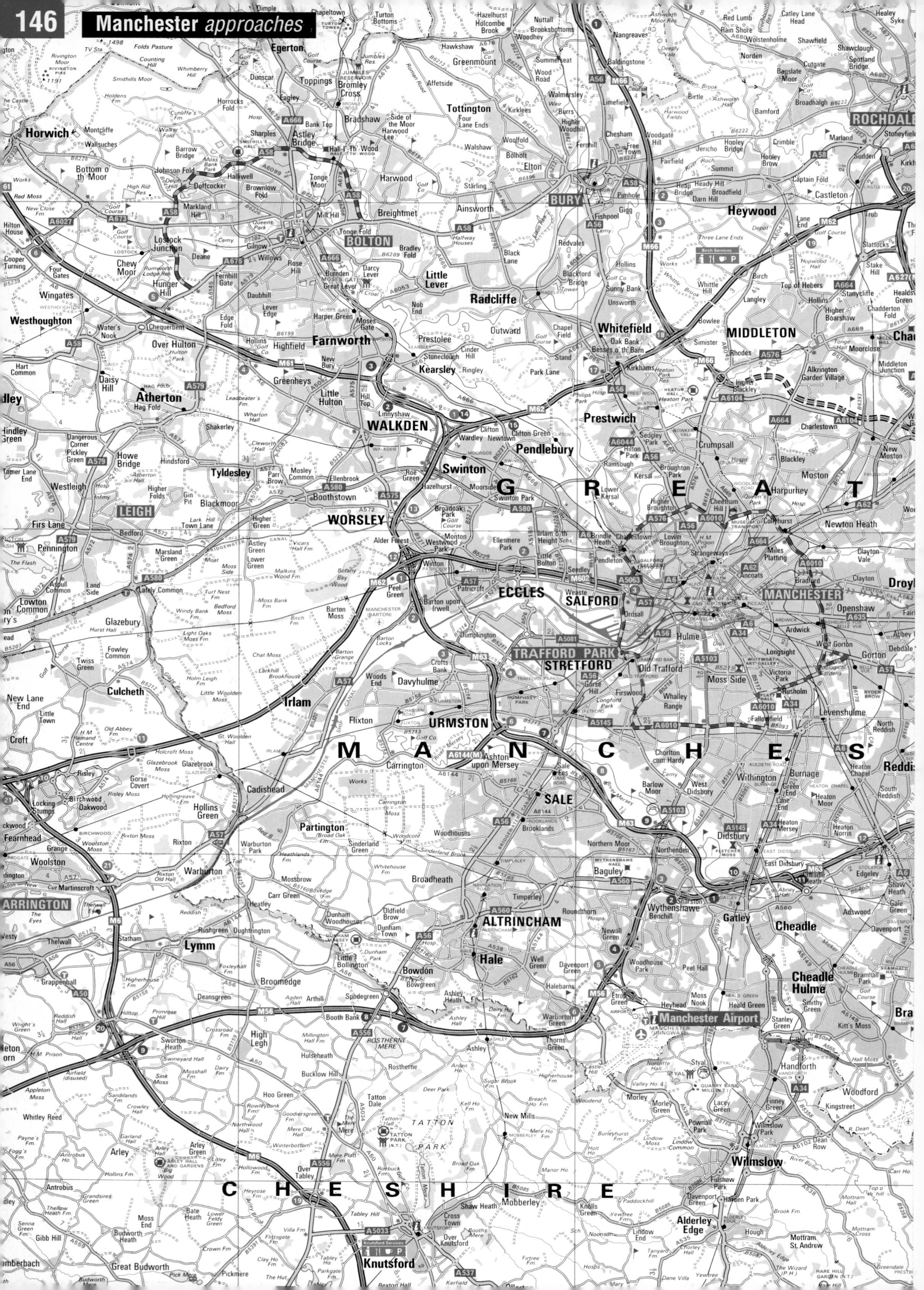

Horwich
Egerton
Bolton
Bury
Rochdale
Heywood
Middleton
Whitefield
Radcliffe
Farnworth
Kearsley
Walkden
Atherton
Westhoughton
Tyldesley
Leigh
Worsley
Swinton
Pendlebury
Prestwich
Eccles
Salford
Manchester
Trafford Park
Stretford
Urmston
Irlam
Cadishead
Partington
Sale
Altrincham
Hale
Lymm
Warrington
Wythenshawe
Gatley
Cheadle
Cheadle Hulme
Manchester Airport
Wilmslow
Alderley Edge
Knutsford
Mobberley
Greater Manchester
Cheshire

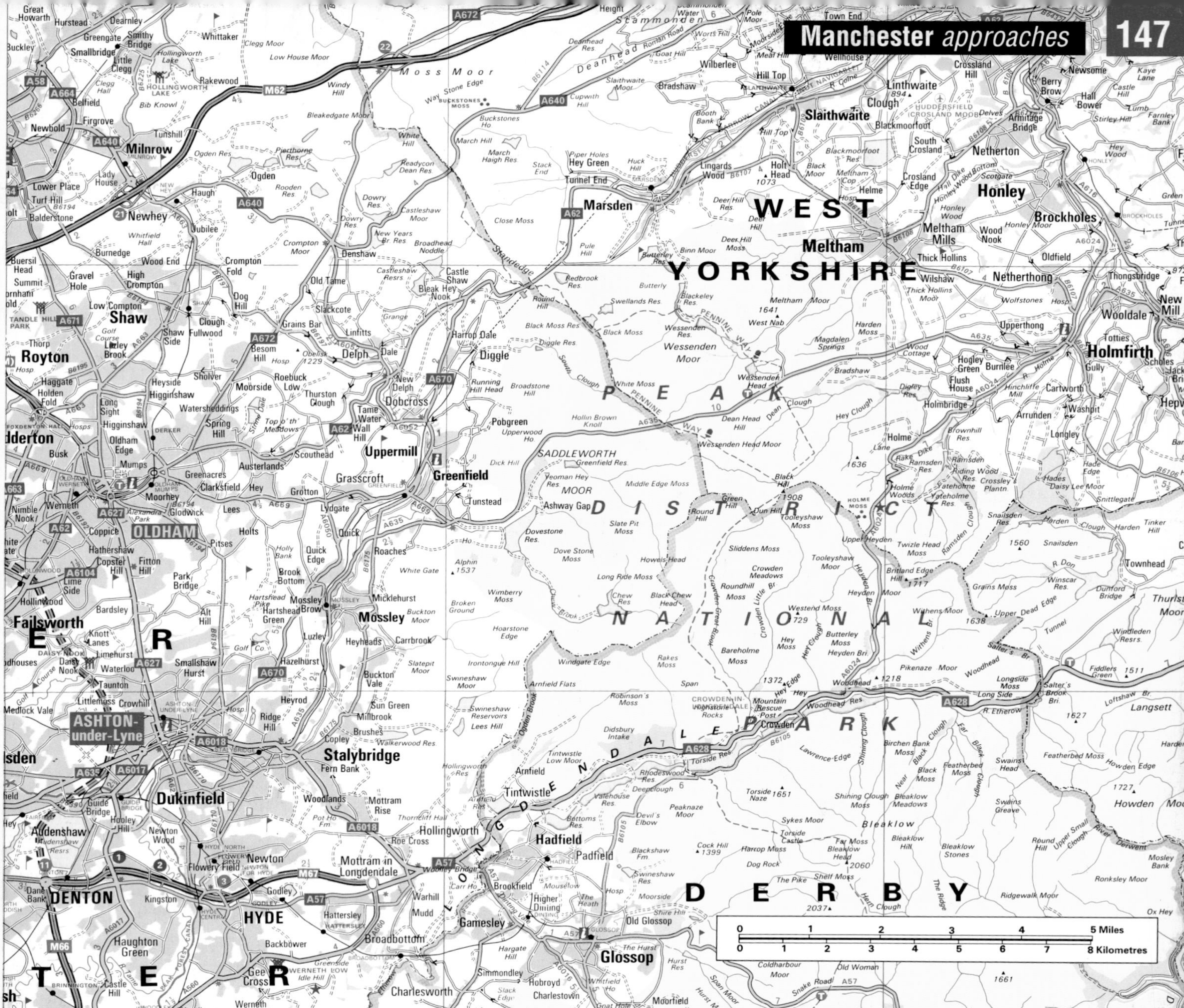
WEST YORKSHIRE
PEAK DISTRICT NATIONAL PARK
DERBY
LONGDENDALE
OLDHAM
ASHTON-under-Lyne
STOCKPORT
Rochdale
Milnrow
Shaw
Royton
Failsworth
Denton
Hyde
Dukinfield
Stalybridge
Mossley
Uppermill
Greenfield
Delph
Diggle
Dobcross
Marsden
Slaithwaite
Meltham
Honley
Holmfirth
Netherton
Brockholes
Hollingworth
Hadfield
Glossop
Tintwistle
Mottram in Longdendale
Bredbury
Romiley
Marple
Hazel Grove
Poynton
Adlington
Bollington
Woodley
Broadbottom
Charlesworth
Padfield
Crowden
Holme
Langsett
M62
M67
M66
A62
A635
A628
A57
A6
0 1 2 3 4 5 Miles
0 1 2 3 4 5 6 7 8 Kilometres

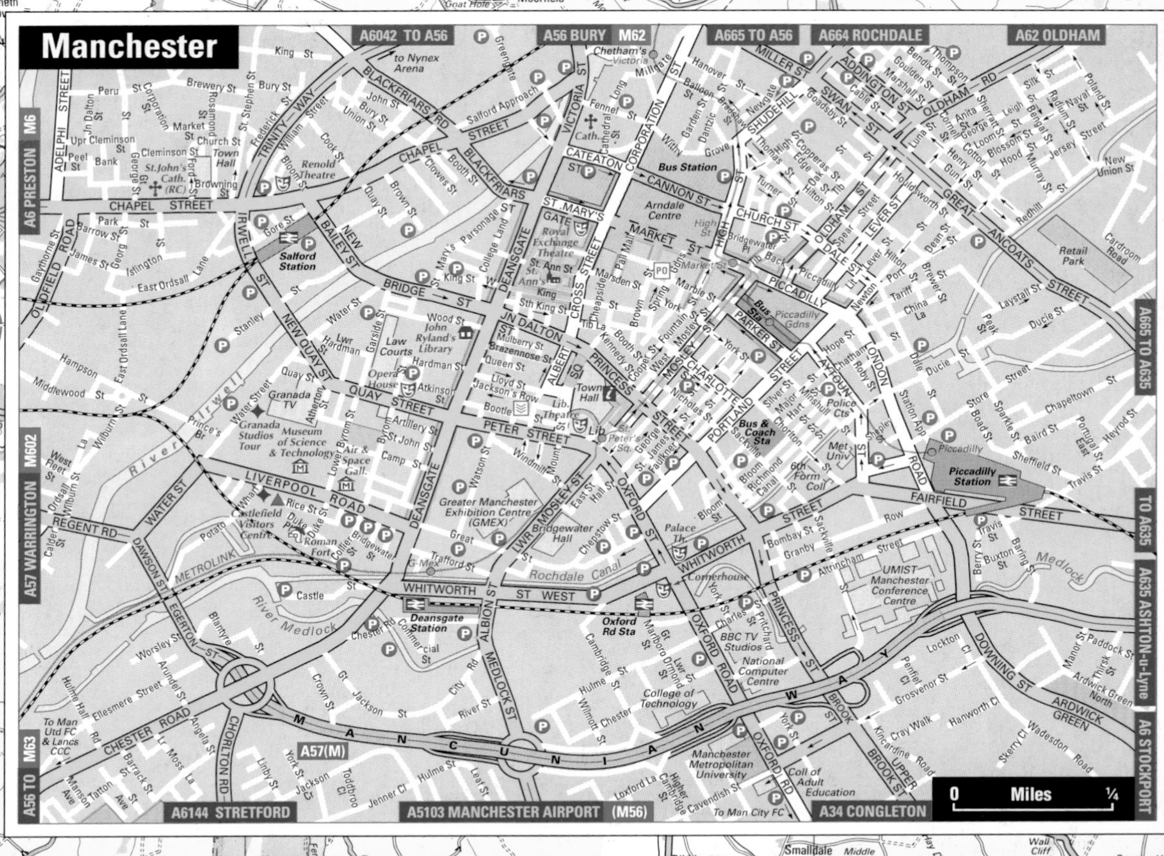
Manchester
A6042 TO A56
A56 BURY
M62
A665 TO A56
A664 ROCHDALE
A62 OLDHAM
A6 PRESTON
M6
M602
A57 WARRINGTON
A56 TO M63
A6144 STRETFORD
A5103 MANCHESTER AIRPORT (M56)
A34 CONGLETON
A6 STOCKPORT
A635 ASHTON-u-Lyne
TO A635
A665 TO A635
MANCUNIAN WAY
A57(M)
Salford Station
Deansgate Station
Oxford Rd Sta
Piccadilly Station
Victoria
Bus Station
Arndale Centre
Piccadilly Gdns
Town Hall
Greater Manchester Exhibition Centre (GMEX)
Bridgewater Hall
Museum of Science & Technology
Granada Studios Tour
UMIST Manchester Conference Centre
Manchester Metropolitan University
River Irwell
River Medlock
Rochdale Canal
0 Miles ¼

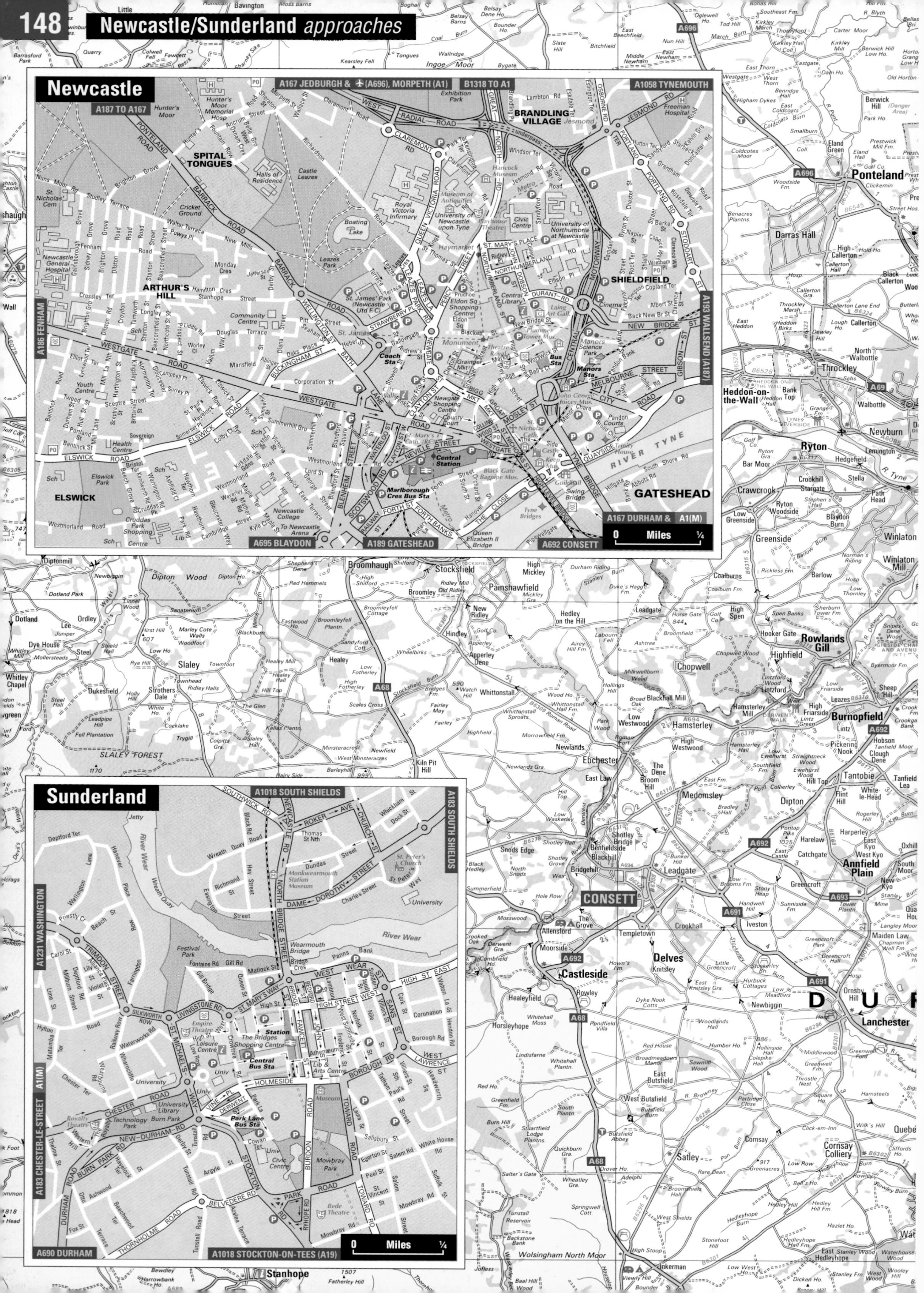
Newcastle
A167 JEDBURGH & (A696), MORPETH (A1)
B1318 TO A1
A1058 TYNEMOUTH
A187 TO A167
A186 FENHAM
A193 WALLSEND (A187)
A695 BLAYDON
A189 GATESHEAD
A692 CONSETT
A167 DURHAM & A1(M)
0 Miles ¼
SPITAL TONGUES
BRANDLING VILLAGE
ARTHUR'S HILL
SHIELDFIELD
ELSWICK
GATESHEAD
RIVER TYNE
Central Station
Coach Sta
Bus Sta
Manors Sta
Sunderland
A1018 SOUTH SHIELDS
A183 SOUTH SHIELDS
A1231 WASHINGTON
A1(M)
A183 CHESTER-LE-STREET
A690 DURHAM
A1018 STOCKTON-ON-TEES (A19)
0 Miles ¼
River Wear
Central Bus Sta
Park Lane Bus Sta
Ponteland
Darras Hall
Throckley
Heddon-on-the-Wall
Newburn
Ryton
Crawcrook
Greenside
Winlaton
Stocksfield
Broomhaugh
Slaley
SLALEY FOREST
Ebchester
Chopwell
Rowlands Gill
Burnopfield
Hamsterley
Medomsley
Dipton
Annfield Plain
CONSETT
Leadgate
Castleside
Delves
Lanchester
Satley
Cornsay Colliery
Stanhope
A696
A69
A68
A692
A694
A691
A693
D U R

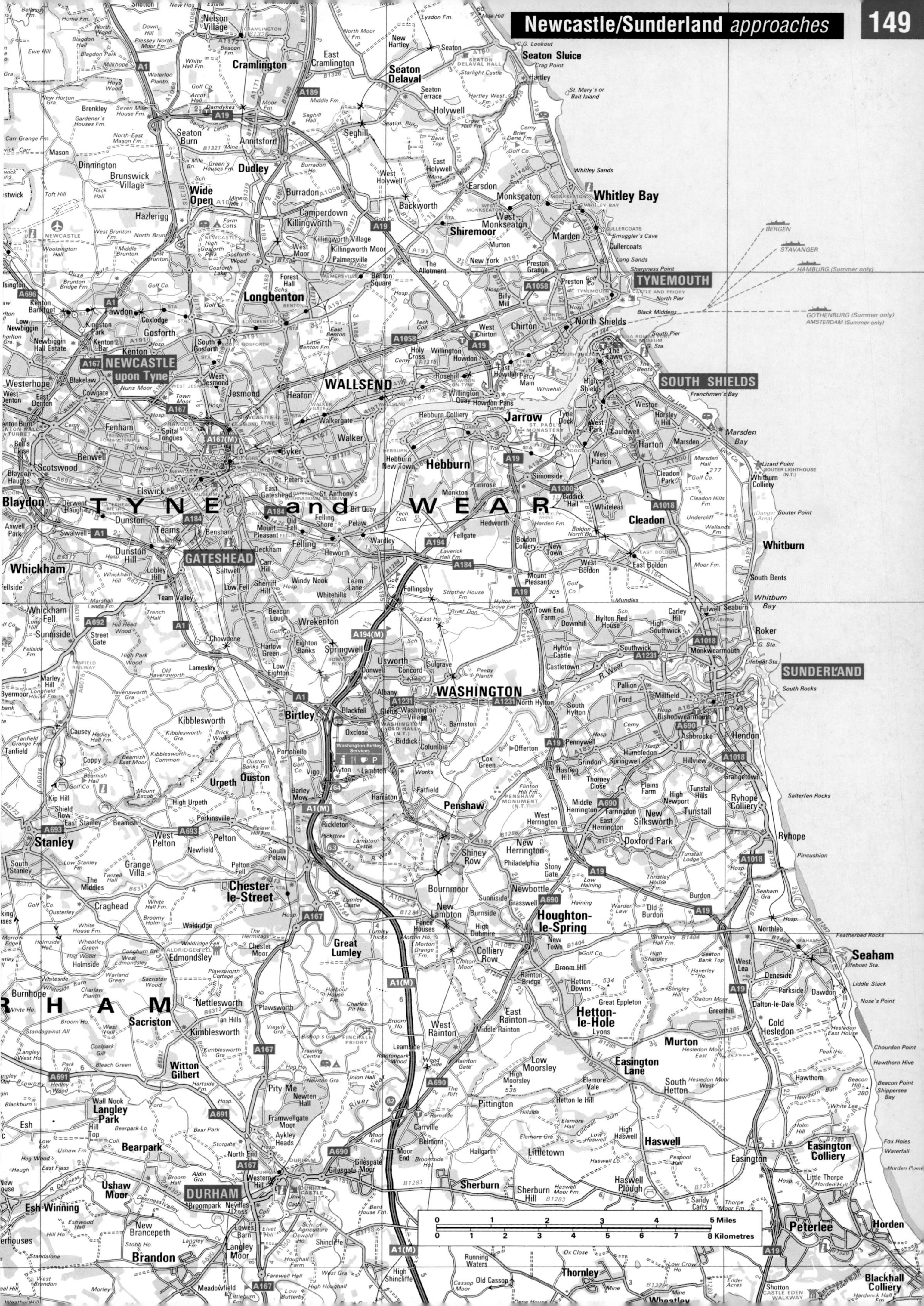
TYNE and WEAR
DURHAM
NEWCASTLE upon Tyne
GATESHEAD
SUNDERLAND
SOUTH SHIELDS
TYNEMOUTH
WALLSEND
WASHINGTON
DURHAM
Cramlington
Seaton Delaval
Seaton Sluice
Whitley Bay
Dudley
Wide Open
Longbenton
Shiremoor
North Shields
Jarrow
Hebburn
Cleadon
Whitburn
Blaydon
Whickham
Stanley
Birtley
Chester-le-Street
Penshaw
Houghton-le-Spring
Hetton-le-Hole
Seaham
Murton
Easington Lane
Easington Colliery
Haswell
Sherburn
Peterlee
Horden
Blackhall Colliery
Thornley
Wheatley Hill
Brandon
Ushaw Moor
Esh Winning
Bearpark
Langley Park
Sacriston
Witton Gilbert
Pity Me
Great Lumley
Urpeth
Ouston
Sunniside
Wrekenton
Springwell
Kibblesworth
Craghead
Ryhope
Doxford Park
New Silksworth
Tunstall
Roker
Gosforth
Jesmond
Heaton
Byker
Walker
Felling
Fenham
Benwell
Scotswood
Elswick
Dunston
Teams
Low Fell
Whickham
Newcastle/Sunderland approaches
0 1 2 3 4 5 Miles
0 1 2 3 4 5 6 7 8 Kilometres
BERGEN
STAVANGER
HAMBURG (Summer only)
GOTHENBURG (Summer only)
AMSTERDAM (Summer only)
A1
A1(M)
A19
A167
A184
A194
A690
A693
A1018
A1058
A1231

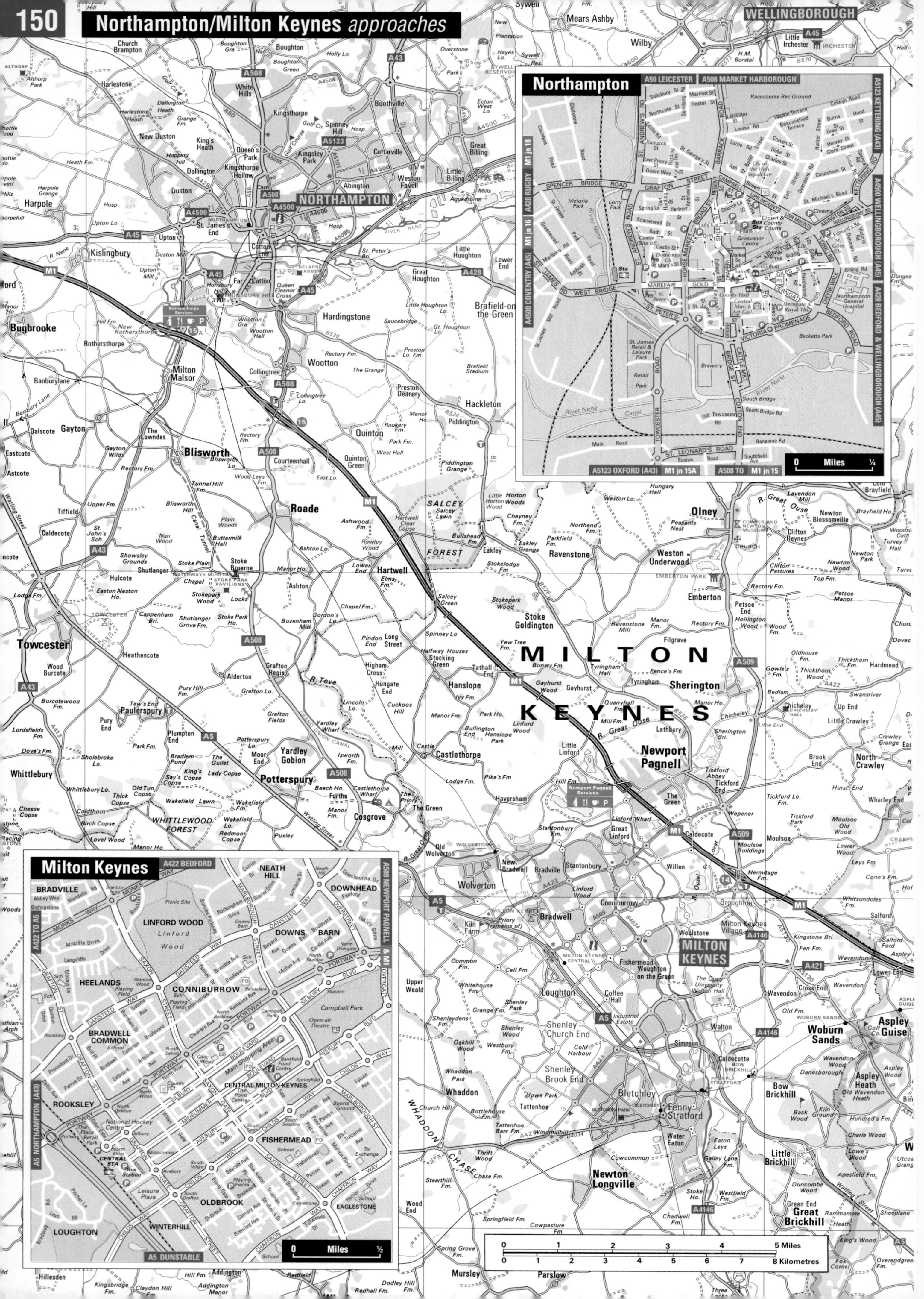
Northampton
A50 LEICESTER
A508 MARKET HARBOROUGH
A5123 KETTERING (A43)
A4500 WELLINGBOROUGH (A45)
A428 BEDFORD & WELLINGBOROUGH (A45)
A5123 OXFORD (A43) M1 jn 15A
A508 TO M1 jn 15
A4500 COVENTRY (A45) M1 jn 16
A428 RUGBY M1 jn 18
SPENCER BRIDGE ROAD
GRAFTON STREET
ST. ANDREW'S ROAD
MAREFAIR
GOLD ST
WEST BRIDGE
ST. PETER'S WAY
VICTORIA PROMENADE
ST. LEONARD'S ROAD
TOWCESTER ROAD
COTTON END
River Nene
Canal
Racecourse Rec Ground
Victoria Park
Becketts Park
Brewery
Northampton General Hospital
0 Miles ¼
Milton Keynes
A422 BEDFORD
A509 NEWPORT PAGNELL & M1
A422 TO A5
A5 NORTHAMPTON (A43)
A5 DUNSTABLE
BRADVILLE
NEATH HILL
DOWNHEAD
LINFORD WOOD
DOWNS BARN
HEELANDS
CONNIBURROW
BRADWELL COMMON
CENTRAL MILTON KEYNES
ROOKSLEY
FISHERMEAD
OLDBROOK
EAGLESTONE
WINTERHILL
LOUGHTON
Campbell Park
Main Shopping Area
National Hockey Centre
Leisure Plaza
CENTRAL STA
0 Miles ½
NORTHAMPTON
WELLINGBOROUGH
MILTON KEYNES
Mears Ashby
Wilby
Little Irchester
Church Brampton
Boughton
Harlestone
New Duston
Duston
Harpole
Kislingbury
Upton
St. James's End
Kingsthorpe
Spinney Hill
Kingsley Park
Cottarville
Weston Favell
Abington
Great Billing
Little Billing
Little Houghton
Great Houghton
Hardingstone
Brafield-on-the-Green
Wootton
Collingtree
Bugbrooke
Rothersthorpe
Milton Malsor
Gayton
Blisworth
Courteenhall
Quinton
Hackleton
Piddington
Roade
Tiffield
Stoke Bruerne
Shutlanger
Hartwell
Towcester
Paulerspury
Alderton
Grafton Regis
Hanslope
Castlethorpe
Yardley Gobion
Potterspury
Cosgrove
Whittlebury
WHITTLEWOOD FOREST
SALCEY FOREST
Olney
Weston Underwood
Ravenstone
Emberton
Stoke Goldington
Sherington
Newport Pagnell
Chicheley
North Crawley
Little Linford
Haversham
Great Linford
Wolverton
Bradwell
Stantonbury
Willen
Woolstone
Broughton
Milton Keynes Village
Loughton
Shenley Church End
Shenley Brook End
Bletchley
Fenny Stratford
Whaddon
WHADDON CHASE
Newton Longville
Walton
Simpson
Woburn Sands
Aspley Guise
Aspley Heath
Bow Brickhill
Little Brickhill
Great Brickhill
Mursley
Parslow
M1
A5
A43
A45
A428
A508
A509
A422
A421
A4146
0 1 2 3 4 5 Miles
0 1 2 3 4 5 6 7 8 Kilometres

Plymouth
A386 LISKEARD (A38)
B3250 TAVISTOCK A386
A374 DEVONPORT
A374 EXETER (A38) & KINGSBRIDGE (A379)
Plymouth Station
NORTH ROAD WEST
NORTH ROAD EAST
MAYFLOWER STREET
ROYAL PARADE
UNION STREET
NOTTE STREET
EXETER ST
Sutton Harbour
The Hoe
Royal Citadel
Continental Ferry Port
Deadman's Bay
0 Miles ¼
TAVISTOCK
PLYMOUTH
SALTASH
Torpoint
Devonport
St. Germans
Princetown
Horrabridge
Yelverton
Yealmpton
Newton Ferrers
Noss Mayo
Wembury
Plympton
Millbrook
Kingsand
Cawsand
Landrake
Mary Tavy
Peter Tavy
DARTMOOR
NATIONAL
PARK
DEVON
TAMAR VALLEY
RIVER TAMAR
RIVER TAVY
The Sound
Rame Head
ROSCOFF SANTANDER (Mar-Nov) ST MALO (Nov-Mar)
A38
A386
A388
A374
A379
0 1 2 3 4 5 Miles
0 1 2 3 4 5 6 7 8 Kilometres

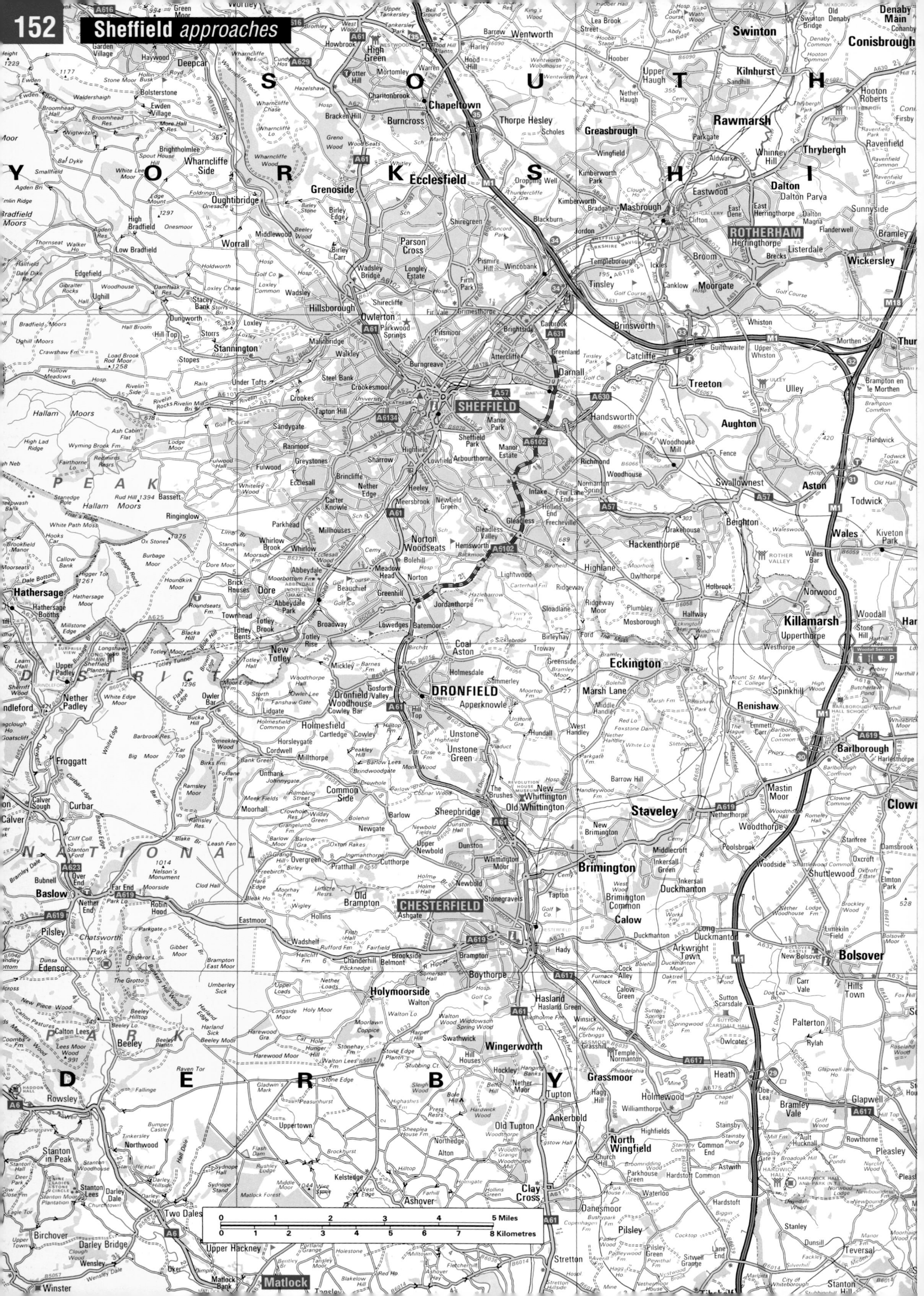
SOUTH YORKSHIRE
PEAK DISTRICT NATIONAL PARK
DERBYSHIRE
SHEFFIELD
ROTHERHAM
CHESTERFIELD
DRONFIELD
Matlock
Swinton
Conisbrough
Wentworth
Deepcar
Chapeltown
Burncross
High Green
Rawmarsh
Greasbrough
Thrybergh
Ecclesfield
Grenoside
Oughtibridge
Wharncliffe Side
Dalton
Masbrough
Wickersley
Bramley
Worrall
Hillsborough
Stannington
Moorgate
Tinsley
Brinsworth
Catcliffe
Treeton
Darnall
Handsworth
Ulley
Aughton
Swallownest
Aston
Todwick
Wales
Beighton
Hackenthorpe
Killamarsh
Eckington
Renishaw
Barlborough
Spinkhill
Norton Woodseats
Dore
Totley
Hathersage
Nether Padley
Froggatt
Curbar
Baslow
Pilsley
Edensor
Beeley
Rowsley
Staveley
Brimington
Calow
Duckmanton
Bolsover
Old Brampton
Holymoorside
Wingerworth
Grassmoor
Heath
Tupton
North Wingfield
Ashover
Clay Cross
Pilsley
Stretton
Two Dales
Darley Bridge
Upper Hackney
Wensley
Winster
Stanton in Peak
Glapwell
Pleasley
Teversal
0 1 2 3 4 5 Miles
0 1 2 3 4 5 6 7 8 Kilometres

New Edlington
Loversall
Old Edlington
Wadworth
Clifton
Braithwell
Stainton
Tickhill
Maltby
Hellaby
Hooton Levitt
Rossington
New Rossington
Wellingley
Harworth
Bircotes
Bawtry
Austerfield
Misson
Misterton
Scaftworth
Everton
Walkeringham
Gringley on the Hill
Styrrup
Scrooby
Mattersey
Wiseton
Oldcotes
Firbeck
Laughton en le Morthen
Laughton Common
Throapham
Langold
Blyth
Ranskill
Torworth
Clayworth
Dinnington
Gildingwells
North Anston
South Anston
North Carlton
Carlton in Lindrick
Woodsetts
Lound
Sutton
Barnby Moor
Hayton
North Wheatley
Clarborough
Welham
Thorpe Salvin
Shireoaks
Rhodesia
Netherthorpe
WORKSOP
Manton
Ranby
RETFORD
Ordsall
Grove
Eaton
Whitwell
Hodthorpe
Creswell
Elmton
Whaley Thorns
Nether Langwith
Langwith
Langwith Junction
Shirebrook
Mansfield Woodhouse
MANSFIELD
Gamston
Bilsthorpe
Maplebeck
Caunton
N O T T S .
R E
Sheffield
A61 BARNSLEY M1
A6135 BARNSLEY
A6109 ROTHERHAM M1
A630 ROTHERHAM M1
A57 WORKSOP M1
A616 ECKINGTON M1
B6070 TO A6135
A621 TO A61
A61 CHESTERFIELD
A625 HATHERSAGE
A57 MANCHESTER
Recreation Ground
Bramwell Gardens
Crookes Valley Park
Weston Park
Sheffield University
Industrial Museum
Castle
Cath.
Cathedral
City Hall
Transport Exchange
Ponds Forge Sports Centre
Sheffield Station
Playing Field
Royal Hallamshire Hosp
The Leadmill
Sheffield Ice Sports Centre
College
0 Miles ¼

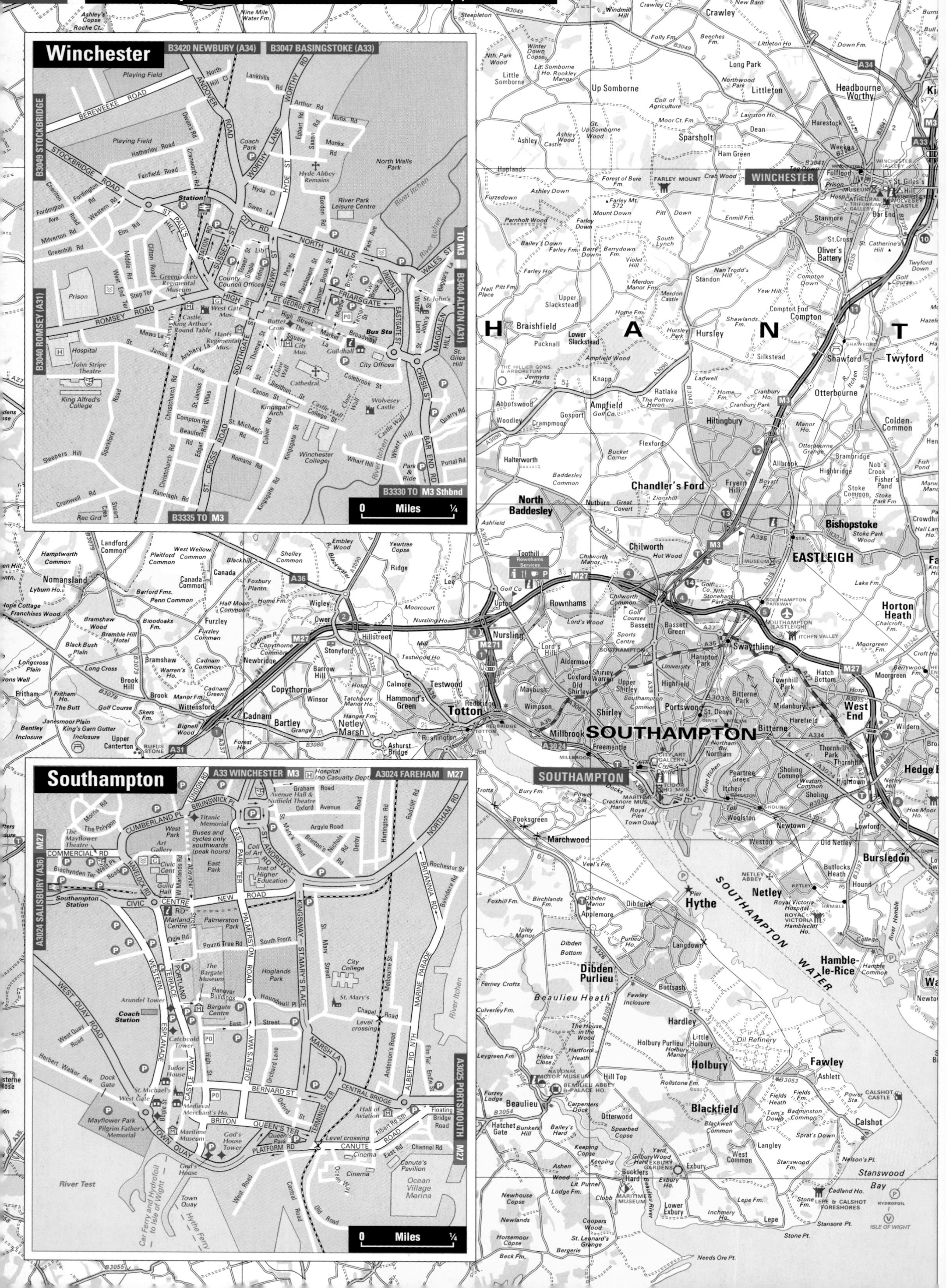
Winchester
B3420 NEWBURY (A34)
B3047 BASINGSTOKE (A33)
B3049 STOCKBRIDGE
B3040 ROMSEY (A31)
B3404 ALTON (A31)
TO M3
B3330 TO M3 Sthbnd
B3335 TO M3
Miles
Southampton
A33 WINCHESTER M3
A3024 FAREHAM M27
A3024 SALISBURY (A36) M27
A3025 PORTSMOUTH M27
SOUTHAMPTON
WINCHESTER
EASTLEIGH
Chandler's Ford
North Baddesley
Totton
Hythe
Netley
Bursledon
Hamble-le-Rice
Fawley
Calshot
Holbury
Blackfield
Beaulieu
Dibden Purlieu
Twyford
Bishopstoke
West End
Hedge End
Horton Heath
Chilworth
Nursling
Rownhams
Ampfield
Hursley
Compton
Otterbourne
Sparsholt
Crawley
Littleton
Headbourne Worthy
Cadnam
Bartley
Copythorne
Netley Marsh
Ashurst
Marchwood
Braishfield
Canada
Nomansland
SOUTHAMPTON WATER
Beaulieu Heath
Stanswood Bay
H A N T

Portsmouth
A3 PETERSFIELD & SOUTHAMPTON (M27)
Continental Ferries Port
H.M. Naval Base
Mary Rose Ship Hall
H.M.S. Victory
Royal Naval Museum
Mary Rose Exhibition
H.M.S. Nelson (Royal Naval Barracks)
Cathedral (RC)
Victory Gate
H.M.S. Warrior
Bus Station
Portsmouth Harbour Station
Passenger Ferry to Gosport
Passenger Ferry to Isle of Wight
Isle of White Ferry Terminal
Car Ferry to Isle of Wight
University of Portsmouth
Victoria Park Swimming Pool
Portsmouth & Southsea Station
Guildhall
Civic Offices
Law Courts
Library
United Services Recreation Ground (Officers)
United Services Recreation Ground (Men)
College of Art
City Museum & Art Gallery
Buckingham House
Cathedral
Camber Dock
Round Tower
Point Battery
Jetty
Square Tower
Garrison Church
Pembroke Gardens
Town Fortifications
Car & Coach Park
Naval Recreation Ground
Clarence Pier
Southsea Common
Hovercraft to Isle of Wight
Hovercraft Terminal
A288 SOUTHSEA
0 Miles 1/4
0 1 2 3 4 5 Miles
0 1 2 3 4 5 6 7 8 Kilometres
Four Marks
New Alresford
Old Alresford
Itchen Abbas
Kings Worthy
Bishops Sutton
Cheriton
New Cheriton
Hinton Ampner
Owslebury
Marwell Zoological Gdns.
Bishop's Waltham
Droxford
Meonstoke
Exton
Corhampton
Warnford
Swanmore
Waltham Chase
Shirrell Heath
Soberton
Soberton Heath
Hambledon
Clanfield
Catherington
Horndean
Denmead
Forest of Bere
Wickham
Botley
Shedfield
Curdridge
Durley
Meon Valley
Waterlooville
Purbrook
Cowplain
Rowland's Castle
Havant
Emsworth
Westbourne
Southwick
Locks Heath
Park Gate
Sarisbury
Fareham
Titchfield
Titchfield Common
Portchester
Portsmouth
Portsmouth Harbour
Portsea Island
Langstone Harbour
Hilsea
Cosham
Drayton
Farlington
Wymering
Paulsgrove
North End
Copnor
Baffins
Fratton
Milton
Eastney
Southsea
Gosport
Alverstoke
Stubbington
Hill Head
Lee-on-the-Solent
Bridgemary
Hayling Island
South Hayling
North Hayling
Chichester Harbour
Thorney Island
Stokes Bay
Hayling Bay
Langstone
Bedhampton
Ports Down

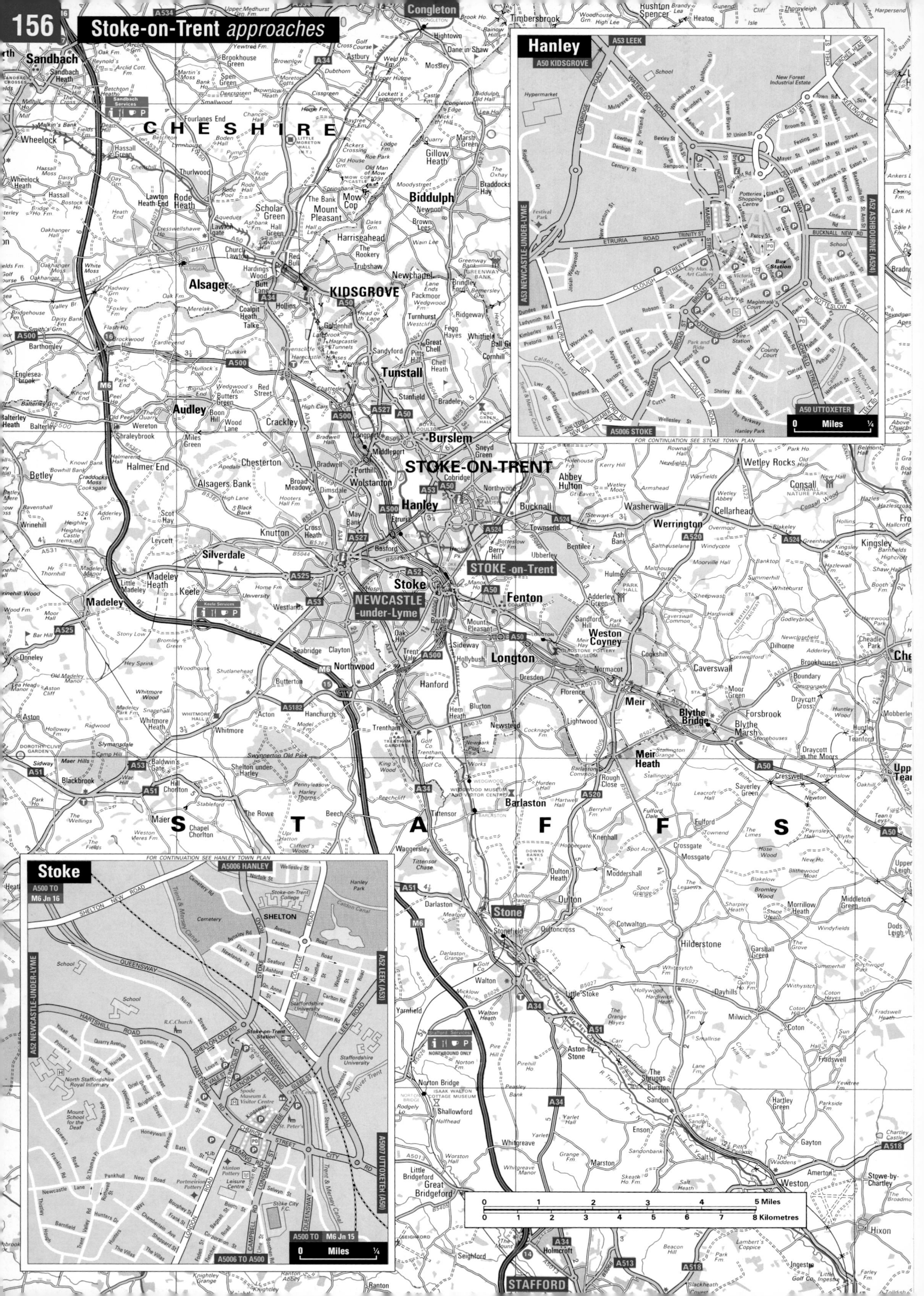
Hanley
A53 LEEK
A50 KIDSGROVE
A52 ASHBOURNE (A524)
A53 NEWCASTLE-UNDER-LYME
A5006 STOKE
A50 UTTOXETER
FOR CONTINUATION SEE STOKE TOWN PLAN
Stoke
A5006 HANLEY
A500 TO M6 Jn 16
A52 LEEK (A53)
A52 NEWCASTLE-UNDER-LYME
A5007 UTTOXETER (A50)
A500 TO M6 Jn 15
A5006 TO A500
FOR CONTINUATION SEE HANLEY TOWN PLAN
CHESHIRE
STAFFS
Congleton
Sandbach
Alsager
KIDSGROVE
Biddulph
Tunstall
Burslem
STOKE-ON-TRENT
Hanley
STOKE-on-Trent
Stoke
NEWCASTLE -under-Lyme
Fenton
Longton
Madeley
Audley
Silverdale
Meir
Blythe Bridge
Barlaston
Stone
STAFFORD
0 1 2 3 4 5 Miles
0 1 2 3 4 5 6 7 8 Kilometres

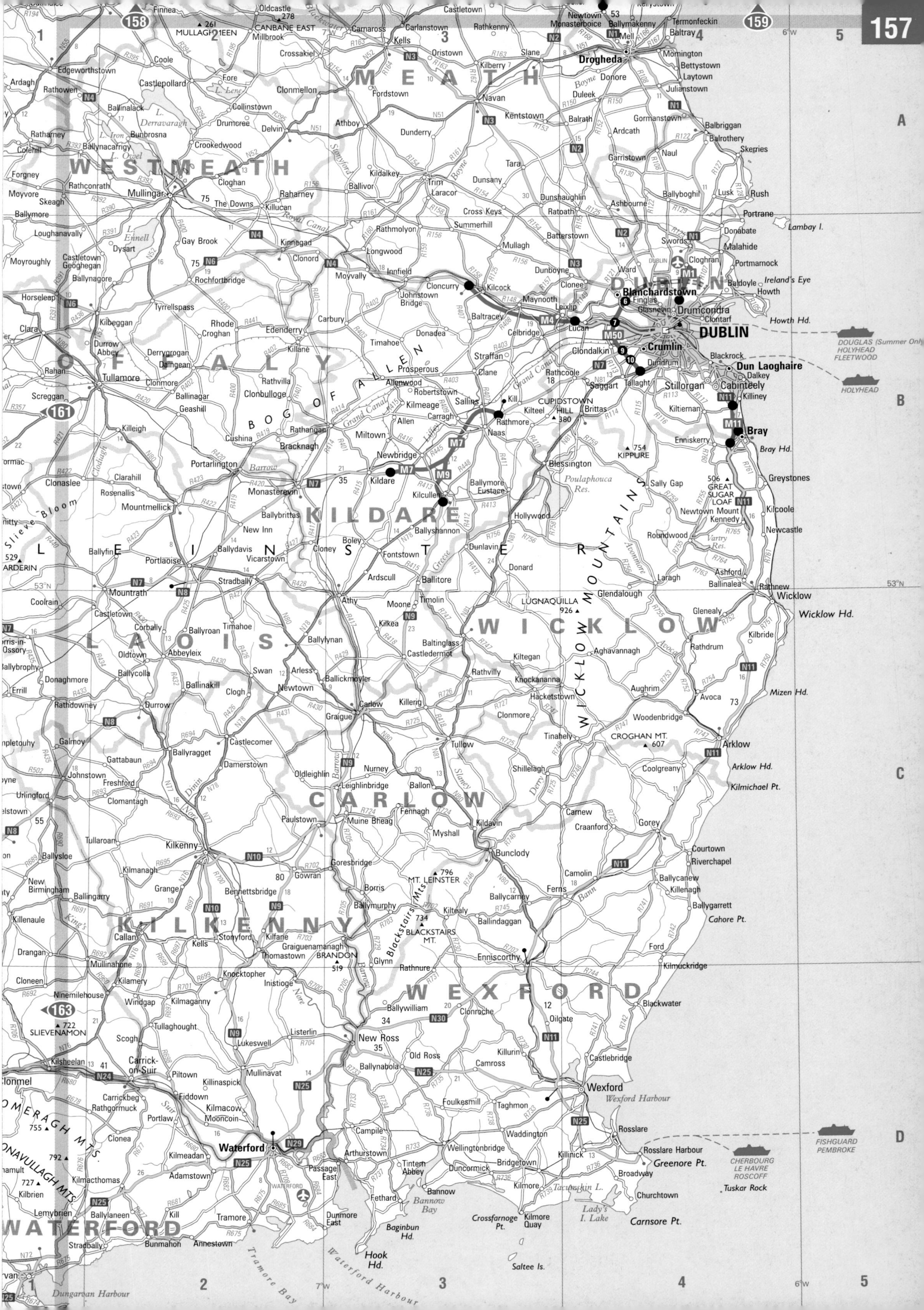
158
159
161
163
MEATH
WESTMEATH
OFFALY
KILDARE
LAOIS
CARLOW
WICKLOW
KILKENNY
WEXFORD
WATERFORD
LEINSTER
BOG OF ALLEN
WICKLOW MOUNTAINS
Blackstairs Mts.
COMERAGH MTS.
MONAVULLAGH MTS.
Slieve Bloom
DUBLIN
Dun Laoghaire
Drogheda
Blanchardstown
Drumcondra
Crumlin
Dundrum
Stillorgan
Cabinteely
Dalkey
Killiney
Bray
Greystones
Wicklow
Arklow
Gorey
Enniscorthy
Wexford
Rosslare
Rosslare Harbour
New Ross
Waterford
Tramore
Kilkenny
Carlow
Athy
Kildare
Newbridge
Naas
Portlaoise
Tullamore
Mullingar
Navan
Trim
Kells
Maynooth
Leixlip
Lucan
Clondalkin
Tallaght
Swords
Malahide
Skerries
Balbriggan
Howth
Carrick-on-Suir
Clonmel
Callan
Thomastown
Mountmellick
Portarlington
Edenderry
Tullow
Bunclody
Ferns
Baltinglass
Blessington
Rathdrum
Avoca
Lambay I.
Ireland's Eye
Howth Hd.
Bray Hd.
Wicklow Hd.
Mizen Hd.
Arklow Hd.
Kilmichael Pt.
Cahore Pt.
Greenore Pt.
Carnsore Pt.
Tuskar Rock
Saltee Is.
Hook Hd.
Baginbun Hd.
Crossfarnoge Pt.
Wexford Harbour
Waterford Harbour
Tramore Bay
Dungarvan Harbour
Bannow Bay
Lady's I. Lake
Tacumshin L.
Poulaphouca Res.
Vartry Res.
Grand Canal
Royal Canal
LUGNAQUILLA 926
KIPPURE 754
MT. LEINSTER 796
BLACKSTAIRS MT. 734
BRANDON 519
CROGHAN MT. 607
GREAT SUGAR LOAF 506
CUPIDSTOWN HILL 380
SLIEVENAMON 722
ARDERIN 529
DOUGLAS (Summer Only)
HOLYHEAD
FLEETWOOD
HOLYHEAD
FISHGUARD
PEMBROKE
CHERBOURG
LE HAVRE
ROSCOFF
53°N
7°W
6°W
1
2
3
4
5
A
B
C
D

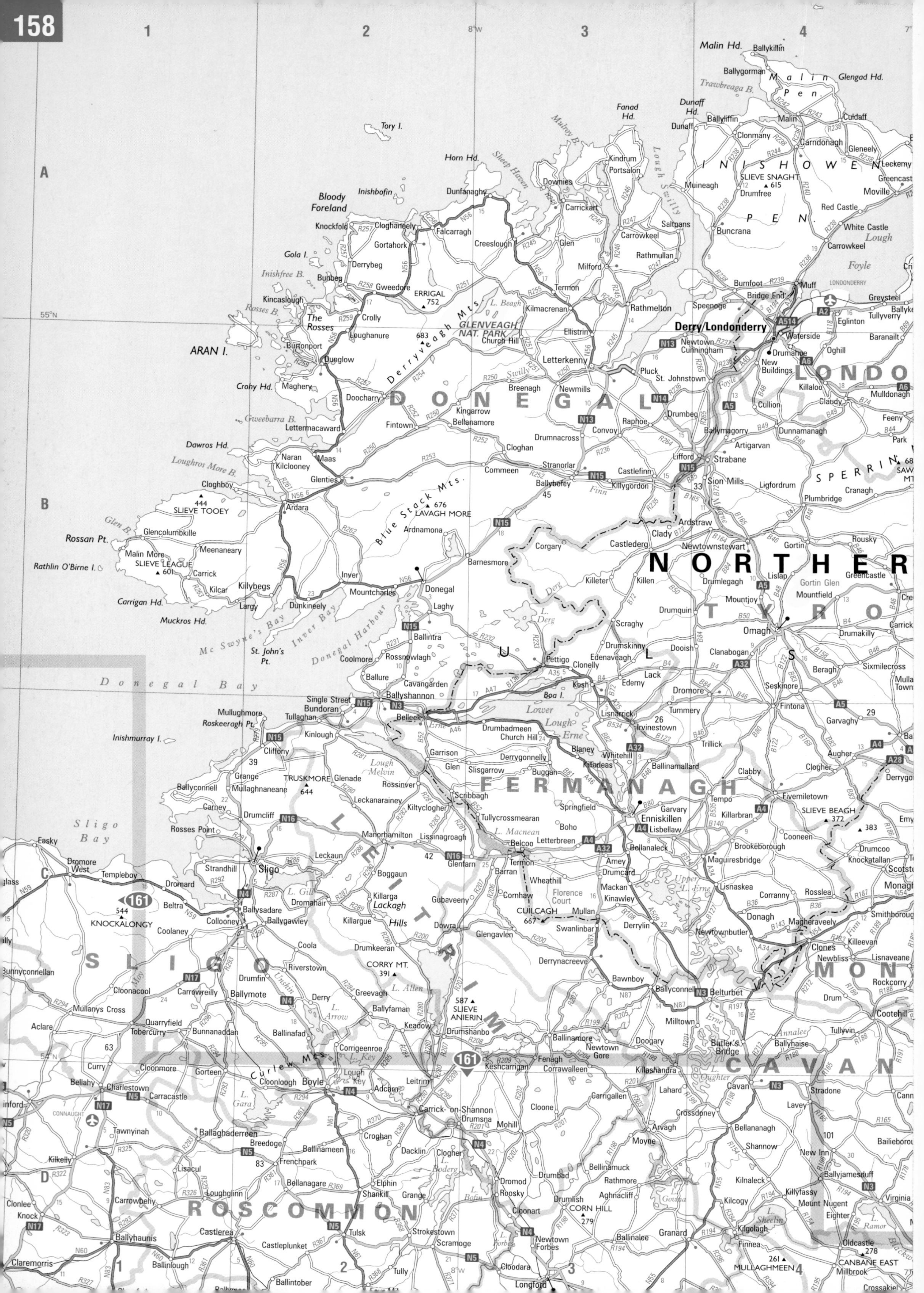
1
2
3
4
A
B
C
D
55°N
54°N
8°W
7°
Malin Hd.
Ballykillin
Ballygorman
Malin Pen.
Glengad Hd.
Trawbreaga B.
Dunaff Hd.
Fanad Hd.
Tory I.
Horn Hd.
Sheep Haven
Mulroy B.
Lough Swilly
INISHOWEN PEN.
SLIEVE SNAGHT 615
Bloody Foreland
Inishbofin
Dunfanaghy
Falcarragh
Creeslough
Gortahork
Knockfola
Gola I.
Inishfree B.
Bunbeg
Derrybeg
Gweedore
ERRIGAL 752
Kincaslough
Crolly
The Rosses
Derryveagh Mts
GLENVEAGH NAT. PARK
Church Hill
ARAN I.
Burtonport
Dunglow
Loughanure
Crohy Hd.
Maghery
Doocharry
DONEGAL
Letterkenny
Kilmacrenan
Rathmelton
Ramelton
Milford
Carrickart
Downies
Kindrum
Portsalon
Glen
Carrowkeel
Rathmullan
Saltpans
Buncrana
Muineagh
Drumfree
Clonmany
Ballyliffin
Dunaff
Malin
Carndonagh
Culdaff
Gleneely
Leckemy
Greencastle
Moville
Red Castle
White Castle
Carrowkeel
Lough Foyle
Muff
Burnfoot
Bridge End
Derry/Londonderry
Waterside
Eglinton
Greysteel
Tullyverry
Ballykelly
Baranailt
Oghill
Drumahoe
New Buildings
Killaloo
Claudy
Mulldonagh
Newtown Cunningham
St. Johnstown
Pluck
Newmills
Breenagh
Kingarrow
Bellanamore
Fintown
Lettermacaward
Gweebarra B.
Dawros Hd.
Loughros More B.
Naran
Kilclooney
Maas
Glenties
Cloghan
Drumnacross
Convoy
Raphoe
Drumbeg
Lifford
Strabane
Sion Mills
Ballymagorry
Artigarvan
Dunnamanagh
Feeny
Park
Cullion
Ballybofey
Stranorlar
Castlefinn
Killygordon
Commeen
Finn
Cloghboy
SLIEVE TOOEY 444
Ardara
Blue Stack Mts.
LAVAGH MORE 676
Ardnamona
Glen B.
Glencolumbkille
Rossan Pt.
Malin More
SLIEVE LEAGUE 601
Meenaneary
Rathlin O'Birne I.
Carrick
Kilcar
Killybegs
Carrigan Hd.
Largy
Dunkineely
Inver
Mountcharles
Donegal
Barnesmore
Muckros Hd.
Mc Swyne's Bay
Inver Bay
St. John's Pt.
Donegal Harbour
Laghy
Ballintra
Rossnowlagh
Coolmore
Ballure
Cavangarden
Ballyshannon
Donegal Bay
Single Street
Bundoran
Tullaghan
Mullaghmore
Roskeeragh Pt.
Inishmurray I.
Kinlough
Belleek
Pettigo
Lough Derg
Corgary
Castlederg
Killeter
Clady
Ardstraw
Newtownstewart
Killen
Drumlegagh
Mountjoy
Lislap
Gortin
Gortin Glen
Mountfield
Greencastle
Rousky
Omagh
Drumquin
NORTHERN
TYRONE
SPERRIN
Ligfordrum
Cranagh
Plumbridge
Scraghy
Drumskinny
Edenaveagh
Dooish
Clanabogan
Drumakilly
Sixmilecross
Beragh
Seskinore
Fintona
Clonelly
Lack
Kesh
Ederny
Boa I.
Dromore
Tummery
Garvaghy
Lower Lough Erne
Lisnarrick
Irvinestown
Trillick
Augher
Clogher
Drumbadmeen
Church Hill
Derrygonnelly
Garrison
Lough Melvin
Glen
Slisgarrow
Buggan
Blaney
Killadeas
Whitehill
Ballinamallard
Clabby
Fivemiletown
FERMANAGH
Tempo
Enniskillen
Lisbellaw
Garvary
Killarbran
SLIEVE BEAGH 372
383
Cliffony
Grange
TRUSKMORE 644
Glenade
Mullaghnaneane
Ballyconnell
Rossinver
Leckanarainey
Kiltyclogher
Scribbagh
Tullycrossmearan
Springfield
Boho
Carney
Drumcliff
Rosses Point
Sligo Bay
Manorhamilton
Lissinagroagh
L. Macnean
Belcoo
Letterbreen
Ballanaleck
Brookeborough
Cooneen
Drumcoo
Knockatallan
Scotstown
Easky
Dromore West
Templeboy
Dromard
Strandhill
Sligo
Leckaun
Glenfarn
Termon
Barran
Arney
Drumcard
Maguiresbridge
Lisnaskea
Corranny
Rosslea
Monaghan
L. Gill
Boggaun
Killarga
Dromahair
Lackagh Hills
Gubaveeny
Cornhaw
Wheathill
Florence Court
Mackan
Kinawley
Upper L. Erne
Beltra
Ballysadare
Ballygawley
KNOCKALONGY 544
Collooney
Coolaney
Killargue
CUILCAGH 667
Mullan
Swanlinbar
Derrylin
Newtownbutler
Donagh
Magheraveely
Smithborough
Killeevan
Clones
Newbliss
Lisnaveane
Rockcorry
SLIGO
LEITRIM
Dowra
Glengavlen
Coola
Drumkeeran
Derrynacreeve
Riverstown
CORRY MT. 391
L. Allen
Bawnboy
Ballyconnell
Belturbet
Drum
Cootehill
MONAGHAN
Bunnyconnellan
Cloonacool
Carrowreilly
Drumfin
Ballymote
Derry
Greevagh
L. Arrow
Ballyfarnan
SLIEVE ANIERIN 587
Mullanys Cross
Quarryfield
Tobercurry
Bunnanaddan
Aclare
Ballinafad
Keadow
Drumshanbo
Milltown
Ballinamore
Newtown Gore
Doogary
Butler's Bridge
Annalee
Ballyhaise
Tullyvin
CAVAN
Curry
Cloonmore
Gorteen
Curlew Mts.
Corrigeenroe
L. Key
Cloonlough
Boyle
Lough Key
Adcarn
Leitrim
Keshcarrigan
Fenagh
Corrawalleen
Killashandra
Lough Oughter
Cavan
Stradone
Bellahy
Charlestown
Carracastle
L. Gara
CONNAUGHT
Carrick-on-Shannon
Drumsna
Mohill
Cloone
Carrigallen
Lahard
Crossdoney
Lavey
Arvagh
Bellananagh
Tawnyinah
Ballaghaderreen
Breedoge
Ballinameen
Croghan
Dacklin
Clogher
Moyne
Shannow
Kilkelly
Frenchpark
Lisacul
Bellanagare
Elphin
Shankill
Grange
L. Boderg
Dromod
Roosky
Drumbad
Bellinamuck
Rathmore
Aghnacliff
L. Gowna
Kilnaleck
New Inn
Ballyjamesduff
Baillieborough
Loughglinn
Carrowbehy
Clonlee
Knock
ROSCOMMON
Cloonart
Drumlish
CORN HILL 279
Killyfassy
Mount Nugent
Kilcogy
Virginia
Ballyhaunis
Castlerea
Tulsk
Strokestown
Scramoge
Newtown Forbes
Ballinalee
Granard
L. Sheelin
Kilgolagh
Eighter
Finnea
Oldcastle
CANBANE EAST 278
MULLAGHMEEN 261
Millbrook
Claremorris
Ballinlough
Castleplunket
Tully
Cloodara
Longford
Ballintober
Crossakiel

Campbeltown
Machrihanish
Earadale Pt.
446 CNOC MOY
Johnston's Pt.
Southend
Rathlin Island
Mull of Kintyre
BALLYCASTLE (Summer only)
Sanda I.
Ailsa Craig 334
Giants Causeway
Benbane Hd.
CAMPBELTOWN (Summer only)
Ballintroohan
Inishowen Hd.
Stroove
The Skerries
Portballintrae
Ballintoy
Fair Hd.
Ballycastle
Ballyvoy
Magilligan Pt.
Portstewart
Portrush
Bushmills
Ballinlea
Carrowreagh
517 KNOCKLAYD
Loughran
Runabay Hd.
Bennane Hd.
Lendalfoot
Downhill
Castlerock
Moss-side
Derrykeighan
Armoy
Cushendun
Ballantrae
Articlave
Coleraine
Ballybogy
Dervock
Mullarts
Cushendall
Red B.
Garron Pt.
Eargantea
Dirtagh
Macosquin
Drumdallagh
Bolea
Ballymoney
Glenariff
Limavady
Drumramer
Milltown
Loughguile
554 TROSTAN
Milleur Pt.
Ringsend
Ardreagh
Corsewall Pt.
Drumsurn
Killykergan
Finvoy
Dunloy
Newtown Crommelin
Glenariff
Carnlough
Kirkcolm
Cairnryan
Drumaduff
Garvagh
Rasharkin
Cullinane
Glenarm
Gortnacross
Drumsaragh
Clogh
436 Islandtown
Leswalt
L. Ryan
STRANRAER
Innermessan
LONDONDERRY
ANTRIM
MOUNTAINS OF ANTRIM
Kilrea
Parkview
Milltown
Dungiven
The Sheddings
Swatragh
Teeshan
Carncastle
Lochans
Fincarn
Inishrush
Portglenone
Broughshane
Larne
Larne Lough
554
Maghera
Ballymena
AGNEWS HILL 476
Portpatrick
Stoneykirk
Lisnamusk
Gulladuff
Ahoghill
Moorfields
Glynn
Moneyneany
Tobermore
L. Beg
Connor
I. Magee
Sandhead
Sperrin
Bellaghy
Kells
Glenoe
Black Hd.
Draperstown
Castledawson
Ballycarry
Ardwell
Labby
Desertmartin
Moneyglass
Randalstown
Ballyclare
Ballynure
Toome
Doagh
Whitehead
Magherafelt
Eden
Port Logan
Broughderg
Davagh
The Loup
Ballyronan
Antrim
Carrickfergus
Moneymore
Creeve
Templepatrick
Mossley
Greenisland
NORTHERN IRELAND
North Channel
Belfast Lough
Groomsport
Copeland I.
Glengormley
Bangor
Cookstown
Coagh
BELFAST INTERNATIONAL
Nutts Corner
Newtownabbey
Donaghadee
LIVERPOOL DOUGLAS (Summer Only)
Drum Manor
Arboe
Crumlin
Dundrod
Leggniel
Holywood
Conlig
Millisle
Lough Neagh
Glenavy
BELFAST
Dundonald
Newtownards
Tullaghoge
Pomeroy
Stewartstown
Newtownbreda
Coalisland
Killeen
Ballinderry Upr.
Dunmurry
Comber
Greyabbey
Ballywalter
Donaghmore
Aghalee
Drumbeg
Carryduff
Lisbane
Parkanaur
Granville
Dungannon
Maghery
Derrytrasna
Magheragall
Lisburn
Ballygowan
Ballyhalbert
Kircubbin
Glastry
Cabragh
Moira
The Temple
Ardkeen
Portavogie
Ballygawley
Eglish
Moy
Charlemont
Craigavon
Lurgan
Hillsborough
Saintfield
Strangford Lough
Ards Peninsula
Benburb
Portadown
Waringstown
Annahilt
Derryboy
Shrigley
Cloghy
Aughnacloy
Loughall
Dromore
Crossgar
Ballynahinch
Killyleagh
Portaferry
Dyan
Drumsallan
Rich Hill
Gilford
Lawrencetown
Mount Ida
DOWN
Strangford
Caledon
Killylea
Armagh
Tandragee
Banbridge
Garvaghy
Dromara
Annacloy
Tynan
Millford
Hamiltownbawn
Finnis
Frankville
Scarva
Downpatrick
Ballyquintin Pt.
Glaslough
ARMAGH
Loughbrickland
Katesbridge
Tobermoney
Killard Pt.
Markethill
Acton
Castlewellan
Ballyward
Clough
Ballydugan
Ballyhornan
Middletown
Poyntz Pass
Clady Milltown
Mountnorris
Diamond
Ballyroney
Ardglass
Silverstream
Keady
Dundrum
Killough
Beech Hill
Square
St. John's Pt.
Drumbear
Whitecross
Rathfriland
Kilcoo
Dundrum Bay
Ardaghy
Darkley
Newtown Hamilton
Tollymore
Newcastle
Bessbrook
Hilltown
MOURNE MTS.
852 SLIEVE DONARD
Milltown
Belleek
Scotch Corner
Creaghanroe
Camlough
Newry
Mayo Bridge
Corvoy
Glasdrumman
MONAGHAN
744
Lislea
Burren
Ballybay
Cullyhanna
Tullymacreeve
Meigh
577 SLIEVE GULLION
Rostrevor
Castleblaney
Annalong
Attical
Moyad
Warrenpoint
Omeath
Crossmaglen
Forkill
Killowen
Broomfield
Ballymartin
Cullaville
Drumbilla
Ravensdale
Carlingford
Lisnacree
Kilkeel
Shantonagh
590 SLIEVE FOYE
Greencastle
Kilcurry
Greenore
Lisgall
Cranfield Pt.
Inishkeen
Carlingford Lough
Corvally
Dundalk
Rampark
Rathcor
Ballagan Pt.
Shercock
Essexford
Channonrock
Carrickmacross
Louth
Black Rock
Kingstown
LOUTH
Lurgangreen
Dundalk Bay
Bracklin
Drumbo
Tallanstown
Dromiskin
Kingscourt
Manfieldstown
Castlebellingham
Edmondstown
Gudderstown
Annagassan
Dunheeda
Killsaran
Salterstown
Ardee
Dunany Pt.
Drumcondra
Dromin
Dunleer
Togher
Nobber
Grangebellew
Woodtown
Ashville
Clogher Head
Mullagh
Moynalty
Lobinstown
Collon
Clogher Hd.
Castletown
Kellystown
Carlanstown
Rathkenny
Newtown Monasterboice
Ballymakenny
Termonfeckin
Carnaross
Baltray
Kells
Mell
Oristown
Slane
Drogheda
Mornington
157
54°N
55°N
6°W
5
6
7
8
A
B
C
D

Broad Haven
Benwee Hd.
Portacloy
Erris Hd.
Belderg
Downpatrick Hd.
Rathlacken
Lenadoon Pt.
Killala Bay
MAUMAKEOGH 380
Ballycastle
Corlogh
Graghil
Annagh Hd.
Mullet Pen.
Belmullet
Knockalina
Glenamoy
Creeragh
Killala
Inishcrone
An Geata Mór
Bunahowen
Carrowmore L.
Inishkea North
Inishkea South
Blacksod Bay
Srahmore
Bangor
Largan
Beville
Owenmore
Bellacorick
Crossmolina
Ballina
Crockets Town
Ardnaree
Fallmore
Gweesalia
Blacksod Pt.
NEPHIN BEG RANGE
722
627
Deel
L. Conn
Ridge Pt.
Saddle Hd.
SLIEVEMORE 672
Ballycroy
Lahardaun
806 NEPHIN
54°N
Doogort
Castlehill
Achill Hd.
Dooagh
Keel
Chasel
714
Pontoon
L. Cullin
Foxford
Callow
ACHILL I.
Achill
L. Feeagh
Beltra
Strade Friary
Dooega Hd.
Mallaranny
Corraun Pen.
Rosturk
Beltra L.
Bellavary
Bohola
Achill Sd.
Achillbeg I.
Newport B.
Newport
Castlebar
Derrycoosh
Kiltamagh
Manulla
CLARE I.
Clew Bay
Westport B.
Westport
Balla
Louisburgh
Killadangan
765 CROAGH PATRICK
Aghagower
Ballyhean
Killavally
Ballintober
Mayo
Ballyglass
Lugatemple
Caher I.
Inishturk
Killadoon
Cregganbaun
Sheeffry Hills
Carrowkennedy
392
M A
C Y
Cornanagh
Partry
L. Carra
763
819 MWEELREA
PARTRY MTS.
683
Toomakeady
Hollymount
Killary Harbour
Inishbofin
Inishshark
Lough Mask
Srahnalong
Ballinrobe
Kilmaine
Tully Cross
Gowlaun
Leenaun
Joyce Country
Neale
Cleggan
Moyard
Streamstown
Letterfrack
BENBAUN 730
CONNEMARA NAT. PARK
MAUMTURK MTS.
Clonbur
Cornamona
Cong
Maum
Shrule
Clifden
Clifden B.
Recess
660
Maam Cross
Lough Corrib
Headford
Ballyconneely
CONNEMARA
Toombeola
Oughterard
Ballyhale
Slyne Hd.
Roundstone
Kilgarrif
Callow
Derryrush
Screeb
Rosscahill
Ballyconneely Bay
Glinsk
Kylesa
Kilbrickan
G A L
Bertraghboy Bay
Kilkieran
Moycullen
Carna
Kilkieran Bay
Lettermore I.
Lettermore
Costelloe
Ballagh
Menlough
Ardmore
Galway
Carraroe
Rossaveel
Lettermullan
Gorumna I.
Inveran
Caher
Spiddle
Barna
Salthill
Cashla Bay
Galway Bay
North Sound
Black Hd.
Burren
Kilmurvy
Kilronan
INISHMORE
Murrooogh
Ballyvaghan
Inishmaan
ARAN IS.
South Sd.
345 SL. ELVA
Carran
Inisheer
53°N
Lisdoonvarna
Doolin
Kilfenora
Kilshanny
Killinaboy
Cliffs of Moher
Hags Hd.
Ennistimon
Corrofin
Liscannor
Lehinch
Liscannor Bay
C L A
Spanish Pt.
Milltown Malbay
Inagh
Fountain Cross
Mal Bay
SLIEVECALLEN 391
Kilmaley
Ennis
Mutton I.
Quilty
Shanovogh
Kilmurry
Darragh
162
10°W
9°
A
B
C
D
1
2
3
4

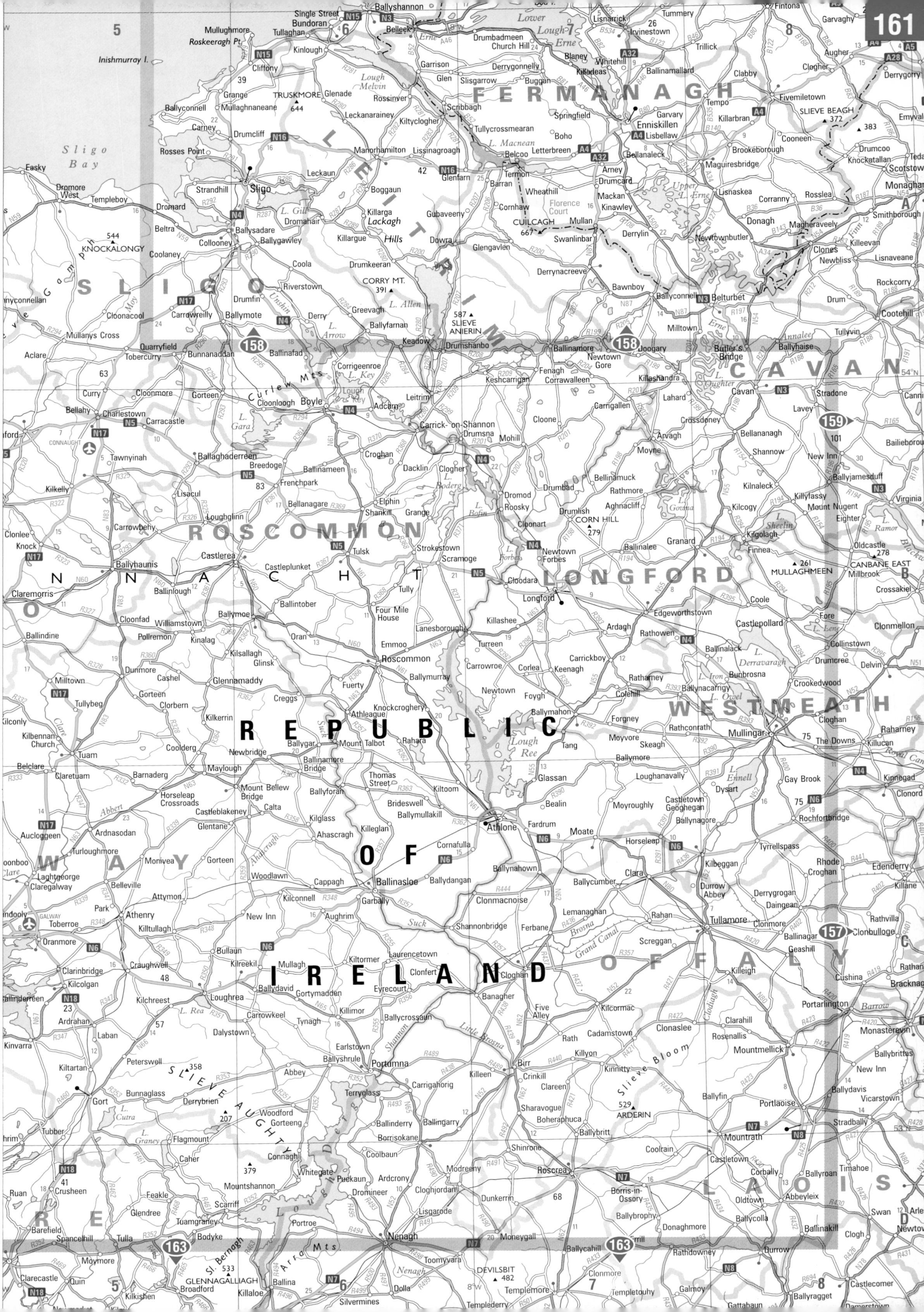
FERMANAGH
LEITRIM
SLIGO
CAVAN
ROSCOMMON
LONGFORD
WESTMEATH
OFFALY
LAOIS
REPUBLIC OF IRELAND
Sligo Bay
Inishmurray I.
Mullaghmore
Roskeeragh Pt.
Bundoran
Single Street
Ballyshannon
Belleek
Tullaghan
Kinlough
Cliffony
Grange
Lough Melvin
Rossinver
Garrison
Glen
Lower Lough Erne
Drumbadmeen
Church Hill
Derrygonnelly
Slisgarrow
Buggan
Lisnarrick
Irvinestown
Tummery
Blaney
Whitehill
Killadeas
Ballinamallard
Trillick
Clabby
Tempo
Fivemiletown
Clogher
Augher
Fintona
Garvaghy
Derrygorry
Enniskillen
Lisbellaw
Garvary
Springfield
Killarbran
SLIEVE BEAGH
Emyvale
Cooneen
Brookeborough
Maguiresbridge
Lisnaskea
Upper L. Erne
Corranny
Rosslea
Monaghan
Smithborough
Magheraveely
Donagh
Newtownbutler
Clones
Newbliss
Killeevan
Lisnaveane
Rockcorry
Drum
Cootehill
TRUSKMORE
Glenade
Leckanarainey
Kiltyclogher
Scribbagh
Tullycrossmearan
Boho
L. Macnean
Belcoo
Letterbreen
Bellanaleck
Arney
Drumcard
Mackan
Kinawley
Florence Court
Derrylin
Swanlinbar
CUILCAGH
Mullan
Ballymote
Drumfin
Riverstown
Coola
Collooney
Ballysadare
Beltra
Dromard
Templeboy
Dromore West
Easky
Strandhill
Rosses Point
Drumcliff
Carney
Ballyconnell
Mullaghnaneane
Manorhamilton
Lissinagroagh
Glenfarn
Leckaun
Boggaun
Dromahair
Killarga
Lackagh Hills
Gubaveeny
Dowra
Killargue
Drumkeeran
Glengavlen
CORRY MT.
L. Allen
Greevagh
Ballyfarnan
Keadow
Drumshanbo
SLIEVE ANIERIN
Derrynacreeve
Bawnboy
Ballyconnell
Belturbet
Milltown
Ballinamore
Doogary
Butler's Bridge
Ballyhaise
Tullyvin
KNOCKALONGY
Coolaney
Cloonacool
Carrowreilly
Mullanys Cross
Aclare
Tobercurry
Quarryfield
Bunnanaddan
Ballinafad
Corrigeenroe
L. Key
Curlew Mts
Cloonloogh
Boyle
Adcarn
Leitrim
Fenagh
Keshcarrigan
Corrawalleen
Newtown Gore
Killashandra
Cavan
Stradone
Lavey
Curry
Cloonmore
Gorteen
Charlestown
Bellahy
Carracastle
L. Gara
Carrick-on-Shannon
Drumsna
Mohill
Cloone
Carrigallen
Lahard
Crossdoney
Arvagh
Bellananagh
Shannow
Bailieborough
Ballaghaderreen
Tawnyinah
Breedoge
Frenchpark
Ballinameen
Croghan
Dacklin
Clogher
L. Boderg
Moyne
New Inn
Ballyjamesduff
Kilkelly
Lisacul
Bellanagare
Elphin
Shankill
Grange
Dromod
Roosky
Drumlish
Bellinamuck
Rathmore
Aghnacliff
CORN HILL
Kilnaleck
Kilcogy
Killyfassy
Mount Nugent
Eighter
Virginia
Loughglinn
Carrowbehy
Knock
Clonlee
Ballyhaunis
Castlerea
Castleplunket
Tulsk
Strokestown
Scramoge
Cloonart
Newtown Forbes
Ballinalee
Granard
L. Sheelin
Kilgolagh
Finnea
Oldcastle
CANBANE EAST
MULLAGHMEEN
Millbrook
Claremorris
Ballinlough
Tully
Cloodara
Longford
Coole
Crossakiel
Ballintober
Four Mile House
Edgeworthstown
Castlepollard
Fore
Clonmellon
Cloonfad
Williamstown
Ballymoe
Oran
Lanesborough
Killashee
Ardagh
Rathowen
L. Derravaragh
Collinstown
Ballindine
Pollremon
Kinalag
Kilsallagh
Glinsk
Emmoo
Roscommon
Turreen
Carrickboy
Ballinalack
Drumcree
Delvin
Milltown
Dunmore
Cashel
Glennamaddy
Fuerty
Ballymurray
Carrowroe
Corlea
Keenagh
Rathamey
Ballynacarrigy
Bunbrosna
Crookedwood
Tullybeg
Gorteen
Clorbern
Creggs
Knockcroghery
Newtown
Foygh
Colehill
Kilconly
Kilkerrin
Athleague
Ballymahon
Forgney
Rathconrath
Mullingar
Cloghan
Raharney
Kilbennan Church
Tuam
Coolderg
Ballygar
Mount Talbot
Rahara
Lough Ree
Tang
Moyvore
Skeagh
The Downs
Killucan
Belclare
Claretuam
Barnaderg
Maylough
Newbridge
Ballinamore Bridge
Thomas Street
Kiltoom
Glassan
Ballymore
Loughanavally
L. Ennell
Dysart
Gay Brook
Kinnegad
Clonard
Mount Bellew Bridge
Horseleap Crossroads
Ballyforan
Brideswell
Ballymullakill
Bealin
Moyroughly
Castletown Geoghegan
Ballynagore
Rochfortbridge
Castleblakeney
Calta
Glentane
Kilglass
Ahascragh
Killeglan
Athlone
Fardrum
Moate
Horseleap
Tyrrellspass
Auclogeen
Ardnasodan
Turloughmore
Monivea
Gorteen
Cornafulla
Ballynahown
Kilbeggan
Rhode
Croghan
Edenderry
Lackagh
Claregalway
Belleville
Woodlawn
Cappagh
Ballinasloe
Ballydangan
Ballycumber
Clara
Durrow Abbey
Derrygrogan
Daingean
Kilcornell
Garbally
Clonmacnoise
Lemanaghan
Rahan
Tullamore
Clonmore
Rathvilla
Clonbullogue
Attymon
Park
Athenry
New Inn
Aughrim
Shannonbridge
Ferbane
Screggan
Ballinagar
Geashill
Toberroe
Killtullagh
Brosna
Grand Canal
Oranmore
Craughwell
Bullaun
Kilreekil
Mullagh
Kiltormer
Laurencetown
Clonfert
Cloghan
Killeigh
Cushina
Clarinbridge
Kilcolgan
Kilchreest
Loughrea
Ballydavid
Gortymadden
Eyrecourt
Banagher
Five Alley
Kilcormac
Portarlington
Ardrahan
L. Rea
Carrowkeel
Tynagh
Killimor
Ballycrossaun
Little Brosna
Clonaslee
Clarahill
Rosenallis
Monasterevin
Kinvarra
Laban
Dalystown
Earlstown
Rath
Cadamstown
Mountmellick
Ballybrittas
Kiltartan
Peterswell
SLIEVE AUGHTY
Ballyshrule
Portumna
Birr
Killyon
Kinnitty
Slieve Bloom
New Inn
Gort
Bunnaglass
Derrybrien
Abbey
Terryglass
Carrigahorig
Killeen
Crinkill
Clareen
Ballyfin
Portlaoise
Ballydavis
Vicarstown
L. Cutra
Woodford
Gorteeng
Ballinderry
Ballingarry
Sharavogue
Boheraphuca
ARDERIN
Stradbally
Tubber
L. Graney
Flagmount
Borrisokane
Ballybritt
Mountrath
Caher
Connagh
Coolbaun
Shinrone
Coolrain
Castletown
Timahoe
Whitegate
Puckaun
Ardcrony
Modreeny
Roscrea
Corbally
Ballyroan
Crusheen
Mountshannon
Dromineer
Cloghjordan
Dunkerrin
Borris-in-Ossory
Oldtown
Abbeyleix
Ruan
Feakle
Scarriff
Lough Derg
Lisgarode
Ballybrophy
Ballycolla
Swan
Barefield
Glendree
Tuamgraney
Portroe
Donaghmore
Ballinakill
Newtown
Spancelhill
Tulla
Bodyke
Nenagh
Moneygall
Ballycahill
Errill
Rathdowney
Durrow
Clogh
Moymore
Sl. Bernagh
Arra Mts
Toomyvara
DEVILSBIT
Clonmore
Clarecastle
Quin
GLENNAGALLIAGH
Broadford
Ballina
Killaloe
Silvermines
Dolla
Templemore
Templetouhy
Galmoy
Castlecomer
Ballyragget
Kilkishen
Templederry
Gattabaun
CONNAUGHT
GALWAY
158
159
157
163

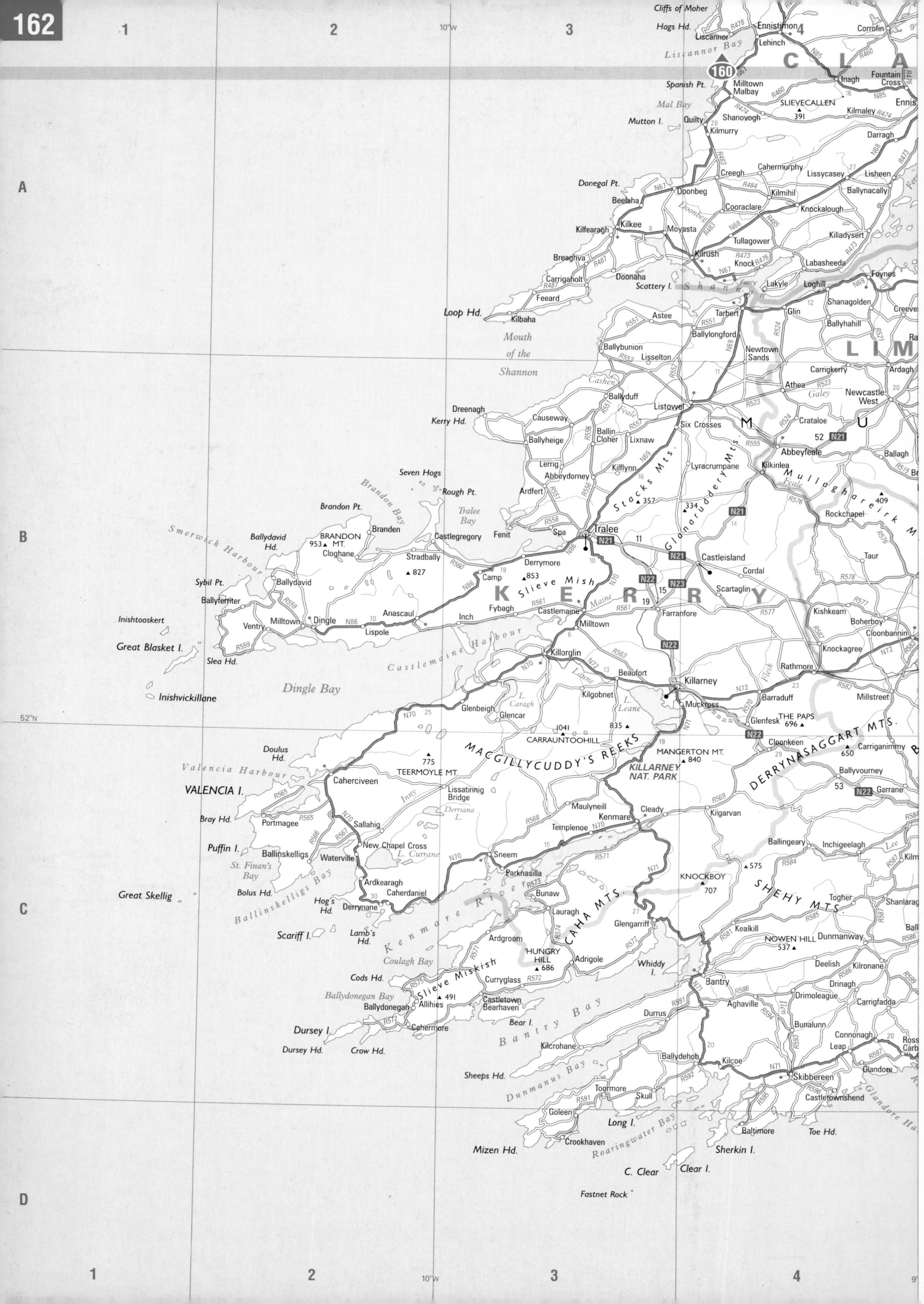

1
2
3
4
A
B
C
D
10°W
52°N
9°
Cliffs of Moher
Hags Hd.
Liscannor
Liscannor Bay
Ennistimon
Lehinch
Corrofin
160
CLA
Spanish Pt.
Milltown Malbay
Inagh
Fountain Cross
Mal Bay
SLIEVECALLEN
391
Kilmaley
Ennis
Mutton I.
Quilty
Shanovogh
Kilmurry
Darragh
Creegh
Cahermurphy
Lissycasey
Lisheen
Donegal Pt.
Doonbeg
Kilmihil
Ballynacally
Beelaha
Cooraclare
Knockalough
Kilkee
Moyasta
Kilfearagh
Tullagower
Killadysert
Kilrush
Knock
Labasheeda
Breaghva
Carrigaholt
Doonaha
Scattery I.
Lakyle
Loghill
Foynes
Feeard
Shannon
Loop Hd.
Kilbaha
Tarbert
Glin
Shanagolden
Astee
Ballyhahill
Mouth of the Shannon
Ballylongford
Ballybunion
Newtown Sands
LIM
Lisselton
Carrigkerry
Ardagh
Cashen
Athea
Galey
Newcastle West
Ballyduff
Dreenagh
Kerry Hd.
Listowel
Causeway
Six Crosses
Crataloe
Ballin Cloher
Lixnaw
Abbeyfeale
Ballagh
Ballyheige
Lerrig
Abbeydorney
Kilflynn
Lyracrumpane
Kilkinlea
Mullaghareirk Mts.
Seven Hogs
Brandon Bay
Rough Pt.
Ardfert
Stacks Mts.
Glanaruddery Mts.
Feale
409
Tralee Bay
357
334
Rockchapel
Brandon Pt.
Smerwick Harbour
Ballydavid Hd.
BRANDON MT.
953
Branden
Castlegregory
Fenit
Spa
Tralee
Cloghane
Stradbally
Derrymore
Castleisland
Cordal
Taur
827
Camp
853
Sybil Pt.
Ballydavid
KERRY
Slieve Mish
Scartaglin
Ballyferriter
Inishtooskert
Ventry
Milltown
Dingle
Anascaul
Inch
Fybagh
Castlemaine
Farranfore
Kishkeam
Boherboy
Lispole
Maine
Cloonbannin
Great Blasket I.
Slea Hd.
Castlemaine Harbour
Killorglin
Knockagree
Beaufort
Rathmore
Dingle Bay
Laune
Killarney
Flesk
Barraduff
Millstreet
Inishvickillane
Kilgobnet
Glenbeigh
L. Caragh
Glencar
L. Leane
Muckross
Glenfesk
THE PAPS
696
1041
835
CARRAUNTOOHILL
Cloonkeen
Carriganimmy
Doulus Hd.
MACGILLYCUDDY'S REEKS
MANGERTON MT.
840
DERRYNASAGGART MTS.
650
775
Valencia Harbour
TEERMOYLE MT.
KILLARNEY NAT. PARK
Ballyvourney
Caherciveen
Lissatinnig Bridge
Garrane
VALENCIA I.
Inny
Derriana L.
Maulyneill
Cleady
Kilgarvan
Bray Hd.
Portmagee
Sallahig
Kenmare
Templenoe
New Chapel Cross
Ballingeary
Inchigeelagh
Lee
Puffin I.
Ballinskelligs
Waterville
L. Currane
Sneem
St. Finan's Bay
Parknasilla
575
Ballinskelligs Bay
Ardkearagh
Caherdaniel
KNOCKBOY
707
SHEHY MTS.
Great Skellig
Bolus Hd.
Bunaw
Togher
Shanlaragh
Hog's Hd.
Derrynane
Kenmare River
CAHA MTS.
Lauragh
Glengarriff
Kealkill
Scariff I.
Lamb's Hd.
Ardgroom
NOWEN HILL
537
Dunmanway
HUNGRY HILL
686
Adrigole
Coulagh Bay
Whiddy I.
Deelish
Kilronane
Cods Hd.
Slieve Miskish
Curryglass
Bantry
Drinagh
Ballydonegan Bay
491
Castletown Bearhaven
Drimoleague
Carrigfadda
Ballydonegan
Allihies
Aghaville
Ilen
Bear I.
Bantry Bay
Durrus
Bunalunn
Dursey I.
Cahermore
Connonagh
Leap
Dursey Hd.
Crow Hd.
Kilcrohane
Ballydehob
Kilcoe
Glandore
Sheeps Hd.
Dunmanus Bay
Skibbereen
Toormore
Skull
Castletownshend
Glandore Harbour
Goleen
Long I.
Roaringwater Bay
Baltimore
Toe Hd.
Crookhaven
Mizen Hd.
Sherkin I.
C. Clear
Clear I.
Fastnet Rock
N21
N22
N23
N67
N68
N69
N70
N71
N72
N85
N86

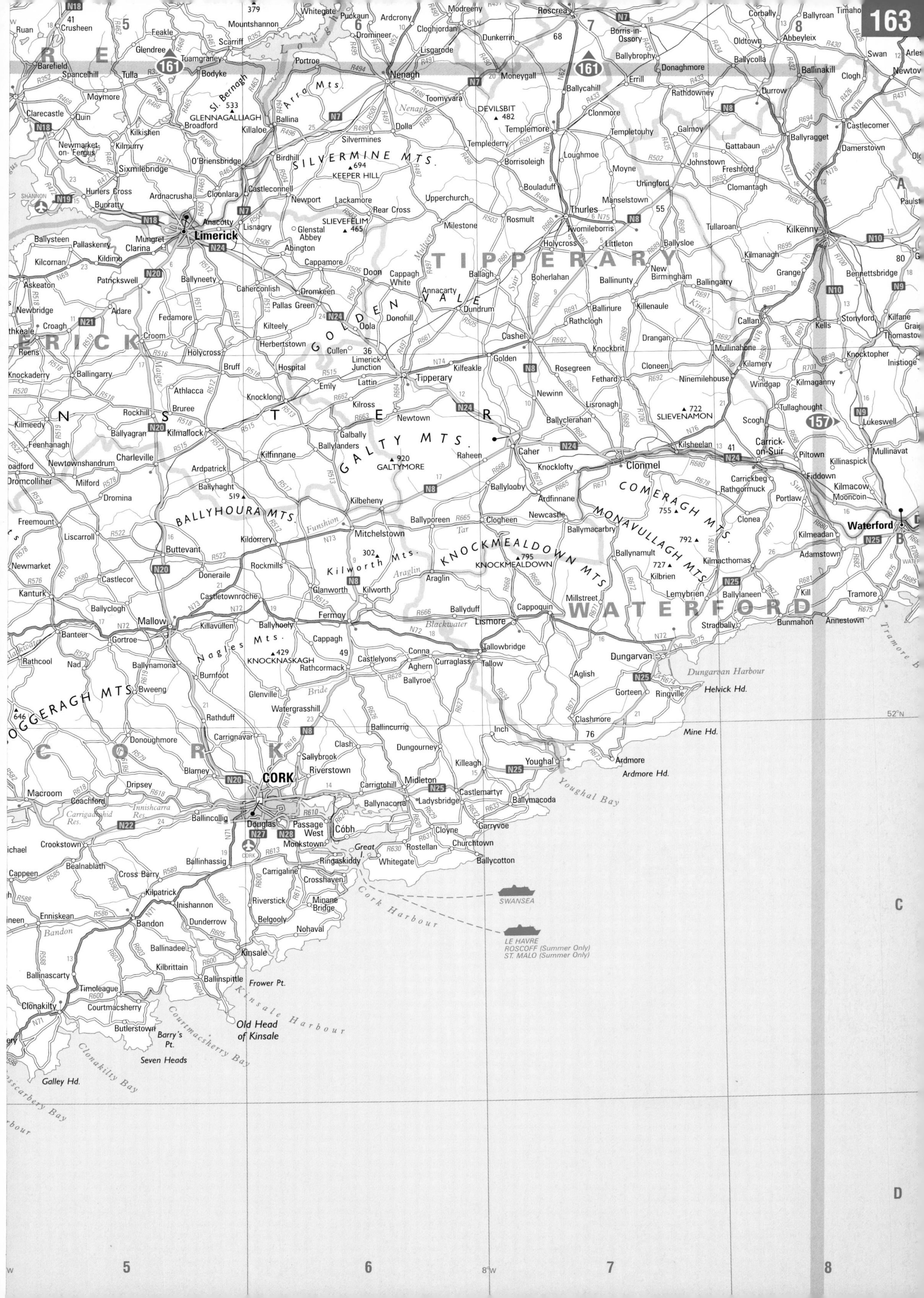
TIPPERARY
WATERFORD
CORK
GOLDEN VALE
SILVERMINE MTS.
GALTY MTS.
BALLYHOURA MTS.
KNOCKMEALDOWN MTS.
COMERAGH MTS.
MONAVULLAGH MTS.
BOGGERAGH MTS
Nagles Mts.
Kilworth Mts.
Arra Mts.
Sl. Bernagh
KEEPER HILL
GALTYMORE
SLIEVENAMON
KNOCKNASKAGH
KNOCKMEALDOWN
DEVILSBIT
SLIEVEFELIM
GLENNAGALLIAGH
Limerick
Cork
Waterford
Kilkenny
Clonmel
Tipperary
Thurles
Nenagh
Cashel
Mallow
Youghal
Dungarvan
Kinsale
Mitchelstown
Fermoy
Lismore
Carrick-on-Suir
Cóbh
Midleton
Bandon
Clonakilty
Dungarvan Harbour
Youghal Bay
Cork Harbour
Kinsale Harbour
Courtmacsherry Bay
Clonakilty Bay
Old Head of Kinsale
Seven Heads
Galley Hd.
Ardmore Hd.
Helvick Hd.
Mine Hd.
SWANSEA
LE HAVRE
ROSCOFF (Summer Only)
ST. MALO (Summer Only)
52°N
8°W
5
6
7
8
A
B
C
D

Belfast

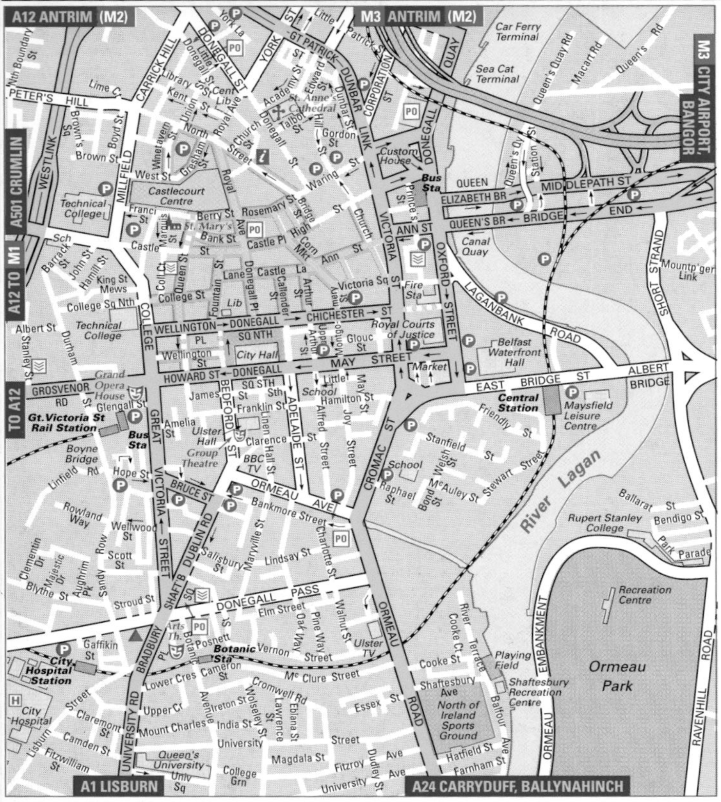

Cork

Derry / Londonderry

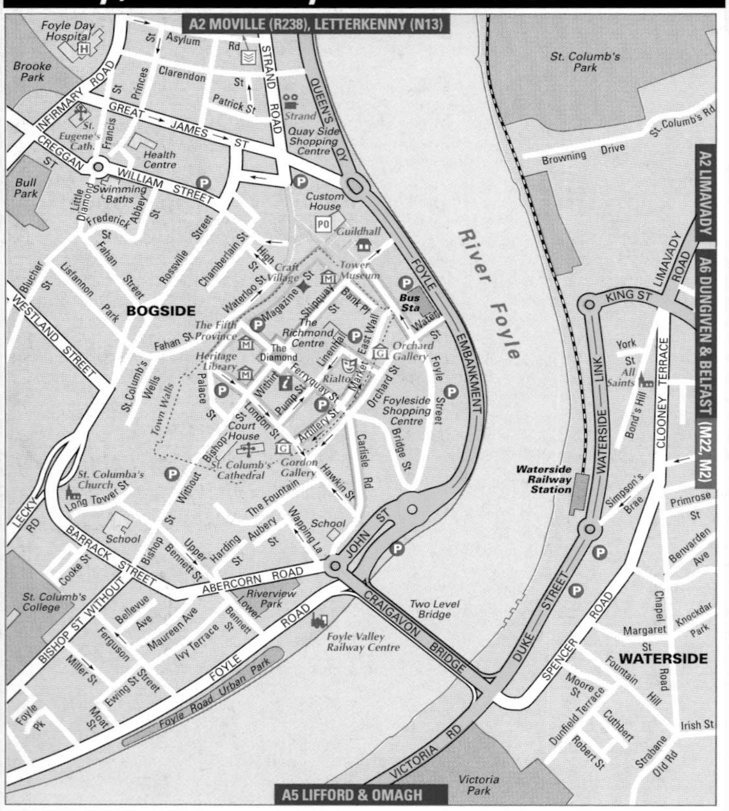

Dublin

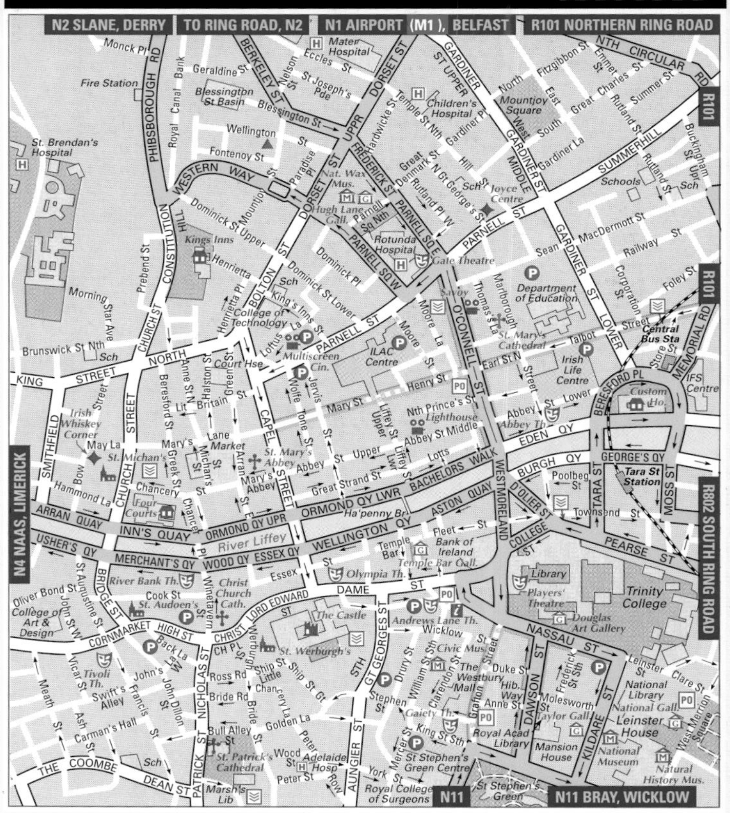

A

Abbey Galway 161 C6
Abbeydorney Kerry 162 B3
Abbeyfeale Limerick 162 B4
Abbeyleix Laois 157 C2
Abington Limerick 163 A6
Achill Mayo 160 B3
Aclare Sligo 161 A5
Acton Armagh 159 C6
Adamstown Waterford 157 D2
Adare Limerick 163 A5
Adcarn Roscommon 161 B6
Adrigole Cork 162 C3
Aghagower Mayo 160 B4
Aghalee Antrim 159 B6
Aghavannagh Wicklow 157 C4
Aghaville Cork 162 C4
Aghern Cork 163 B6
Aghnacliff Longford 161 B7
Aglish Waterford 163 B7
Ahascragh Galway 161 C6
Ahoghill Antrim 159 B6
Allen Kildare 157 B3
Allenwood Kildare 157 B3
Allihies Cork 162 C2
An Geata Mór Mayo 160 A2
Anacotty Limerick 163 A5
Anascaul Kerry 162 B2
Annacarty Tipperary 163 A6
Annacloy Down 159 C7
Annagassan Louth 159 D6
Annahilt Down 159 C7
Annalong Down 159 C7
Annestown Waterford 157 D2
Antrim Antrim 159 B6
Araglin Tipperary 163 B6
Arboe Tyrone 159 B5
Ardagh Limerick 162 B4
Ardagh Longford 161 B7
Ardahy Monaghan 159 C5
Ardara Donegal 158 B2
Ardcath Meath 157 A4
Ardcrony Tipperary 161 D6
Ardee Louth 159 D5
Ardfert Kerry 162 B3
Ardfinnane Tipperary 163 B7
Ardglass Down 159 C7
Ardgroom Cork 162 C3
Ardkearagh Kerry 162 C2
Ardkeen Down 159 C7
Ardmore Galway 160 C3
Ardmore Waterford 163 C7
Ardnacrusha Clare 163 A5
Ardnamona Donegal 158 B2
Ardnaree Mayo 160 A4
Ardnasodan Galway 161 C5
Ardpatrick Limerick 163 B5
Ardrahan Galway 161 C5
Ardreagh Londonderry 159 A5
Ardscull Kildare 157 B3
Ardstraw Tyrone 158 B4
Arklow Wicklow 157 C4
Arless Laois 157 C2
Armagh Armagh 159 C5
Armoy Antrim 159 A6
Arney Fermanagh 158 C3
Arthurstown Wexford 157 D3
Articlave Londonderry 159 A5
Artigarvan Tyrone 158 B4
Arvagh Cavan 161 B7
Ashbourne Meath 157 A4
Ashford Wicklow 157 B4
Ashville Louth 159 D5
Askeaton Limerick 163 A5
Astee Kerry 162 A3
Athboy Meath 157 A3
Athea Limerick 162 B4
Athenry Galway 161 C5
Athlacca Limerick 163 B5
Athleague Roscommon 161 B6
Athlone Westmeath 161 C7
Athy Kildare 157 C3
Attical Down 159 C6
Attymon Galway 161 C5
Aucloggeen Galway 161 C5
Augher Tyrone 158 C4
Aughnacloy Tyrone 159 C5
Aughrim Clare 161 C5
Aughrim Galway 161 C6
Aughrim Wicklow 157 C4
Avoca Wicklow 157 C4

B

Bailieborough Cavan 159 D5
Balbriggan Dublin 157 A4
Baldoyle Dublin 157 B4
Balla Mayo 160 B4
Ballagh Galway 160 C4
Ballagh Limerick 162 B4
Ballagh Tipperary 163 A7
Ballaghaderreen Roscommon 161 B5
Ballickmoyler Laois 157 C2
Ballin Cloher Kerry 162 B3
Ballina Mayo 160 A4
Ballina Tipperary 163 A6
Ballinadee Cork 163 C5
Ballinafad Sligo 158 C2
Ballinagar Offaly 157 B2
Ballinakill Laois 157 C2
Ballinalack Westmeath 157 A2
Ballinalea Wicklow 157 B4
Ballinalee Longford 161 B7
Ballinamallard Fermanagh 158 C3
Ballinameen Roscommon 161 B6
Ballinamore Leitrim 158 C3
Ballinamore Bridge Galway 161 C6
Ballinascarty Cork 163 C5
Ballinasloe Galway 161 C6
Ballincollig Cork 163 C5
Ballincurrig Cork 163 C6
Ballindaggan Wexford 157 C3
Ballinderreen Galway 161 C5
Ballinderry Tipperary 161 C6
Ballinderry Upr. Antrim 159 B6
Ballindine Mayo 161 B5
Ballindooly Galway 160 C4
Ballineen Cork 163 C5
Ballingarry Limerick 163 B5
Ballingarry Tipperary 163 A7
Ballingarry Tipperary 161 C6
Ballingeary Cork 162 C4
Ballinhassig Cork 163 C5
Ballinlea Antrim 159 A6
Ballinlough Roscommon 161 B5
Ballinrobe Mayo 160 B4
Ballinskelligs Kerry 162 C2
Ballinspittle Cork 163 C5
Ballintober Mayo 160 B4
Ballintober Roscommon 161 B6
Ballintoy Antrim 159 A6
Ballintra Donegal 158 B2
Ballintroohan Donegal 158 A4
Ballinunty Tipperary 163 A7
Ballinure Tipperary 163 A7
Ballitore Kildare 157 B3
Ballivor Meath 157 A3
Ballon Carlow 157 C3
Ballure Donegal 158 B2
Ballyagran Limerick 163 B5
Ballybay Monaghan 159 C5
Ballybofey Donegal 158 B3
Ballyboghil Dublin 157 A4
Ballybogy Antrim 159 A5
Ballybritt Offaly 161 C7
Ballybrittas Laois 157 B2
Ballybrophy Laois 161 D7
Ballybunion Kerry 162 A3
Ballycahill Tipperary 163 A7
Ballycanew Wexford 157 C4
Ballycarney Wexford 157 C3
Ballycarry Antrim 159 B7
Ballycastle Mayo 160 A4
Ballycastle Antrim 159 A6
Ballyclare Antrim 159 B7
Ballyclerahan Tipperary 163 B7
Ballyclogh Cork 163 B5
Ballycolla Laois 157 C2
Ballyconneely Galway 160 C2
Ballyconnell Cavan 158 C3
Ballyconnell Sligo 158 C1
Ballycotton Cork 163 C6
Ballycrossaun Galway 161 C6
Ballycroy Mayo 160 A3
Ballycumber Offaly 161 C7
Ballydangan Roscommon 161 C6
Ballydavid Galway 161 C6
Ballydavid Kerry 162 B2
Ballydavis Laois 157 B2
Ballydehob Cork 162 C4
Ballydonegan Cork 162 C2
Ballyduff Kerry 162 B3
Ballyduff Waterford 163 B6
Ballydugan Down 159 C7
Ballyfarnan Roscommon 158 C2
Ballyferriter Kerry 162 B2
Ballyfin Laois 157 B2
Ballyforan Roscommon 161 C6
Ballygar Galway 161 B6
Ballygarrett Wexford 157 C4
Ballygawley Sligo 158 C2
Ballygawley Tyrone 158 C4
Ballyglass Mayo 160 B4
Ballygorman Donegal 158 A4
Ballygowan Down 159 B7
Ballyhaght Limerick 163 B5
Ballyhahill Limerick 162 A4
Ballyhaise Cavan 158 C4
Ballyhalbert Down 159 C8
Ballyhale Galway 160 C4
Ballyhaunis Mayo 161 B5
Ballyhean Mayo 160 B4
Ballyheige Kerry 162 B3
Ballyhooly Cork 163 B6
Ballyhornan Down 159 C7
Ballyjamesduff Cavan 158 D4
Ballykelly Londonderry 158 A4
Ballykillin Donegal 158 A4
Ballylanders Limerick 163 B6
Ballylaneen Waterford 157 D2
Ballyliffin Donegal 158 A4
Ballylongford Kerry 162 A4
Ballylooby Tipperary 163 B7
Ballylynan Laois 157 C2
Ballymacarbry Waterford 163 B7
Ballymacoda Cork 163 C7
Ballymagorry Tyrone 158 B4
Ballymahon Longford 161 B7
Ballymakenny Louth 159 D6
Ballymartin Down 159 C7
Ballymena Antrim 159 B6
Ballymoe Galway 161 B6
Ballymoney Antrim 159 A5
Ballymore Westmeath 161 C7
Ballymore Eustace Kildare 157 B3
Ballymote Sligo 158 C1
Ballymullakill Roscommon 161 C6
Ballymurphy Carlow 157 C3
Ballymurray Roscommon 161 B6
Ballynabola Wexford 157 D3
Ballynacally Clare 162 A4
Ballynacarrigy Westmeath 161 B7
Ballynacorra Cork 163 C6
Ballynagore Westmeath 157 B2
Ballynahinch Down 159 C7
Ballynahown Westmeath 161 C7
Ballynamona Cork 163 B5
Ballynamult Waterford 163 B7
Ballyneety Limerick 163 A5
Ballynure Antrim 159 B7
Ballyporeen Tipperary 163 B6
Ballyragget Kilkenny 157 C2
Ballyroan Laois 157 C2
Ballyroe Cork 163 B6
Ballyronan Londonderry 159 B5
Ballyroney Down 159 C6
Ballysadare Sligo 158 C1
Ballyshannon Donegal 158 C2
Ballyshannon Kildare 157 B3
Ballyshrule Galway 161 C6
Ballysloe Tipperary 163 A7
Ballysteen Limerick 163 A5
Ballyvaghan Clare 160 C4
Ballyvourney Cork 162 C4
Ballyvoy Antrim 159 A6
Ballywalter Down 159 B8
Ballyward Down 159 C6
Ballywilliam Wexford 157 D3
Balrath Meath 157 A4
Balrothery Dublin 157 A4
Baltimore Cork 162 D4
Baltinglass Wicklow 157 C3
Baltracey Kildare 157 B3
Baltray Louth 157 A4
Banagher Offaly 161 C7
Banbridge Down 159 C6
Bandon Cork 163 C5
Bangor Mayo 160 A3
Bangor Down 159 B7
Bannow Wexford 157 D3
Banteer Cork 163 B5
Bantry Cork 162 C4
Baranailt Londonderry 158 B4
Barefield Clare 161 D5
Barna Galway 160 C4
Barnaderg Galway 161 C5
Barnesmore Donegal 158 B2
Barraduff Kerry 162 B4
Barran Cavan 158 C3
Batterstown Meath 157 B3
Bawnboy Cavan 158 C3
Bealin Westmeath 161 C7
Bealnablath Cork 163 C5
Beaufort Kerry 162 B3
Beech Hill Down 159 C6
Beelaha Clare 162 A3
Belclare Galway 161 C5
Belcoo Fermanagh 158 C3
Belderg Mayo 160 A3
Belfast Antrim 159 B7
Belgooly Cork 163 C6
Bellacorick Mayo 160 A3
Bellaghy Londonderry 159 B5
Bellahy Sligo 161 B5
Bellanagare Roscommon 161 B6
Bellanaleck Fermanagh 158 C3
Bellanamore Donegal 158 B2
Bellananagh Cavan 158 D4
Bellavary Mayo 160 B4
Belleek Donegal 158 C2
Belleek Armagh 159 C6
Belleville Galway 161 C5
Bellinamuck Longford 161 B7
Belmullet Mayo 160 A3
Beltra Mayo 160 B4
Beltra Sligo 158 C1
Belturbet Cavan 158 C4
Benburb Tyrone 159 C5
Bennettsbridge Kilkenny 157 C2
Beragh Tyrone 158 B4
Bessbrook Armagh 159 C6
Bettystown Meath 157 A4
Beville Mayo 160 A4
Birdhill Tipperary 163 A6
Birr Offaly 161 C7
Black Rock Louth 159 D6
Blackrock Dublin 157 B4
Blackwater Wexford 157 D4
Blanchardstown Dublin 157 B4
Blaney Fermanagh 158 C3
Blarney Cork 163 C5
Blessington Wicklow 157 B3
Bodyke Clare 161 D5
Boggaun Leitrim 158 C2
Boheraphuca Offaly 161 C7
Boherboy Cork 162 B4
Boherlahan Tipperary 163 A7
Boho Fermanagh 158 C3
Bohola Mayo 160 B4
Bolea Londonderry 159 A5
Boley Kildare 157 B3
Borris Carlow 157 C3
Borris-in-Ossory Laois 161 D7
Borrisokane Tipperary 161 D6
Borrisoleigh Tipperary 163 A7
Bouladuff Tipperary 163 A7
Boyle Roscommon 161 B6
Bracklin Cavan 159 D5
Bracknagh Offaly 157 B2
Branden Kerry 162 B2
Bray Wicklow 157 B4
Breaghva Clare 162 A3
Breedoge Roscommon 161 B6
Breenagh Donegal 158 B3
Brideswell Roscommon 161 C6
Bridge End Donegal 158 A4
Bridgetown Wexford 157 D3
Brittas Dublin 157 B4
Broadford Clare 163 A5
Broadford Limerick 163 B5
Broadway Wexford 157 D4
Brookeborough Fermanagh 158 C4
Broomfield Monaghan 159 C5
Broughderg Tyrone 159 B5
Broughshane Antrim 159 B6
Bruff Limerick 163 B5
Bruree Limerick 163 B5
Buggan Fermanagh 158 C3
Bullaun Galway 161 C5
Bunahowen Mayo 160 A3
Bunalunn Cork 162 C4
Bunaw Kerry 162 C3
Bunbeg Donegal 158 A2
Bunbrosna Westmeath 157 A2
Bunclody Wexford 157 C3
Buncrana Donegal 158 A4
Bundoran Donegal 158 C2
Bunmahon Waterford 157 D2
Bunnaglass Galway 161 C5
Bunnanaddan Sligo 161 B5
Bunnyconnellan Mayo 160 A4
Bunratty Clare 163 A5
Burnfoot Cork 163 B5
Burnfoot Donegal 158 A4
Burren Clare 160 C4
Burren Down 159 C6
Burtonport Donegal 158 B2
Bushmills Antrim 159 A5
Butler's Bridge Cavan 158 C4
Butlerstown Cork 163 C5
Buttevant Cork 163 B5
Bweeng Cork 163 B5

C

Cabinteely Dublin 157 B4
Cabragh Tyrone 159 C5
Cadamstown Offaly 161 C7
Caher Clare 161 D5
Caher Galway 160 C4
Caher Tipperary 163 B7
Caherciveen Kerry 162 C2
Caherconlish Limerick 163 A6
Caherdaniel Kerry 162 C2
Cahermore Cork 162 C3
Cahermurphy Clare 162 A4
Caledon Tyrone 159 C5
Callan Kilkenny 157 C2
Callow Galway 160 C2
Callow Mayo 160 B4
Calta Galway 161 C6
Camlough Armagh 159 C6
Camolin Wexford 157 C4
Camp Kerry 162 B3
Campile Wexford 157 D3
Camross Wexford 157 D3
Canningstown Cavan 158 D4
Cappagh Cork 163 B6
Cappagh Galway 161 C6
Cappagh White Tipperary 163 A6
Cappamore Limerick 163 A6
Cappeen Cork 163 C5
Cappoquin Waterford 163 B7
Carbury Kildare 157 B3
Carlanstown Meath 159 D5
Carlingford Louth 159 C6
Carlow Carlow 157 C3
Carna Galway 160 C3
Carnaross Meath 157 A3
Carncastle Antrim 159 B7
Carndonagh Donegal 158 A4
Carnew Wicklow 157 C4
Carney Sligo 158 C1
Carnlough Antrim 159 B7
Carracastle Mayo 161 B5
Carragh Kildare 157 B3
Carran Clare 160 C4
Carraroe Galway 160 C3
Carrick Donegal 158 B1
Carrick-on-Shannon Roscommon 161 B6
Carrick-on-Suir Tipperary 157 D2
Carrickart Donegal 158 A3
Carrickbeg Waterford 157 D2
Carrickboy Longford 161 B7
Carrickfergus Antrim 159 B7
Carrickmacross Monaghan 159 D5
Carrickmore Tyrone 158 B4
Carrigaholt Clare 162 A3
Carrigahorig Tipperary 161 C6
Carrigaline Cork 163 C6
Carrigallen Leitrim 161 B7
Carriganimmy Cork 162 C4
Carrigfadda Cork 162 C4
Carrigkerry Limerick 162 B4
Carrignavar Cork 163 C6
Carrigtohill Cork 163 C6
Carrowbehy Roscommon 161 B5
Carrowkeel Donegal 158 A4
Carrowkeel Donegal 158 A4
Carrowkeel Galway 161 C6
Carrowkennedy Mayo 160 B3
Carrowreagh Antrim 159 A6
Carrowreilly Sligo 158 C1
Carrowroe Longford 161 B7
Carryduff Down 159 B7
Cashel Galway 161 B5
Cashel Tipperary 163 A7
Castlebar Mayo 160 B4
Castlebellingham Louth 159 D6
Castleblakeney Galway 161 C6
Castleblayney Monaghan 159 C5
Castlebridge Wexford 157 D4
Castlecomer Kilkenny 157 C2
Castleconnell Limerick 163 A6
Castlecor Cork 163 B5
Castledawson Londonderry 159 B5
Castlederg Tyrone 158 B3
Castledermot Kildare 157 C3
Castlefinn Donegal 158 B3
Castlegregory Kerry 162 B2
Castlehill Mayo 160 A3
Castleisland Kerry 162 B4
Castlelyons Cork 163 B6
Castlemaine Kerry 162 B3
Castlemartyr Cork 163 C6
Castleplunket Roscommon 161 B6
Castlepollard Westmeath 157 A2
Castlerea Roscommon 161 B6
Castlerock Londonderry 159 A5
Castletown Laois 157 C2
Castletown Meath 159 D5
Castletown Bearhaven Cork 162 C3
Castletown Geoghegan Westmeath 157 B2
Castletownroche Cork 163 B6
Castletownshend Cork 162 C4
Castlewellan Down 159 C7
Causeway Kerry 162 B3
Cavan Cavan 158 D4
Cavangarden Donegal 158 B2
Celbridge Kildare 157 B3
Chanonrock Louth 159 D5
Charlemont Armagh 159 C5
Charlestown Mayo 161 B5
Charleville Cork 163 B5
Chasel Mayo 160 B3
Church Hill Donegal 158 B3
Church Hill Fermanagh 158 C3
Churchtown Cork 163 C6
Churchtown Wexford 157 D4
Clabby Fermanagh 158 C4
Clady Tyrone 158 B3
Clady Milltown Armagh 159 C5
Clanabogan Tyrone 158 B4
Clane Kildare 157 B3
Clara Offaly 161 C7
Clarahill Laois 157 B2
Clarecastle Clare 163 A5
Clareen Offaly 161 C7
Claregalway Galway 161 C5
Claremorris Mayo 161 B4
Claretuam Galway 161 C5
Clarina Limerick 163 A5
Clarinbridge Galway 161 C5
Clash Cork 163 C6
Clashmore Waterford 163 B7
Claudy Londonderry 158 B4
Cleady Kerry 162 C3
Cleggan Galway 160 B2
Clifden Galway 160 C2
Cliffony Sligo 158 C2
Clogh Kilkenny 157 C2
Clogh Antrim 159 B6
Cloghan Donegal 158 B3
Cloghan Offaly 161 C7
Cloghan Westmeath 157 A2
Cloghane Kerry 162 B2
Cloghaneely Donegal 158 A2
Cloghboy Donegal 158 B1
Clogheen Tipperary 163 B7
Clogher Roscommon 161 B6
Clogher Tyrone 158 C4
Clogher Head Louth 159 D6
Cloghjordan Tipperary 161 D6
Cloghran Dublin 157 B4
Cloghy Down 159 C8
Clomantagh Kilkenny 157 C2
Clonakilty Cork 163 C5
Clonaslee Laois 161 C7
Clonbulloge Offaly 157 B2
Clonbur Galway 160 B4
Cloncurry Kildare 157 B3
Clondalkin Dublin 157 B4
Clonea Waterford 157 D2
Clonee Meath 157 B4
Cloneen Tipperary 163 B7
Clonelly Fermanagh 158 B3
Clones Monaghan 158 C4
Cloney Kildare 157 B2
Clonfert Galway 161 C6
Clonlee Mayo 161 B5
Clonmacnoise Offaly 161 C7
Clonmany Donegal 158 A4
Clonmel Tipperary 163 B7
Clonmellon Westmeath 157 A2
Clonmore Carlow 157 C3
Clonmore Offaly 157 B2
Clonmore Tipperary 163 A7
Clonord Meath 157 B2
Clonroche Wexford 157 D3
Clontarf Dublin 157 B4
Cloodara Longford 161 B7
Cloonacool Sligo 161 A5
Cloonart Longford 161 B7
Cloonbannin Cork 162 B4
Cloonboo Galway 160 C4
Cloone Leitrim 161 B7
Cloonfad Roscommon 161 B5
Cloonkeen Kerry 162 C4
Cloonlara Clare 163 A5
Cloonloogh Sligo 161 B6
Cloonmore Mayo 161 B5
Clorbern Galway 161 B5
Clough Down 159 C7
Cloyne Cork 163 C6
Coachford Cork 163 C5
Coagh Tyrone 159 B5
Coalisland Tyrone 159 B5
Cóbh Cork 163 C6
Colehill Longford 161 B7
Coleraine Londonderry 159 A5
Collinstown Westmeath 157 A2
Collon Louth 159 D6
Collooney Sligo 158 C2
Comber Down 159 B7
Commeen Donegal 158 B3
Cong Mayo 160 B4
Conlig Down 159 B7
Conna Cork 163 B6
Connagh Galway 161 D6
Connonagh Cork 162 C4
Connor Antrim 159 B6
Convoy Donegal 158 B3
Cookstown Tyrone 159 B5
Coola Sligo 158 C2
Coolaney Sligo 158 C1
Coolbaun Tipperary 161 D6
Coolderg Galway 161 B5
Coole Westmeath 157 A2
Coolgreany Wexford 157 C4
Coolmore Donegal 158 B2
Coolrain Laois 161 D7
Cooneen Fermanagh 158 C4
Cooraclare Clare 162 A4
Cootehill Cavan 158 C4
Corbally Laois 157 C2
Corbally Sligo 160 A4
Cordal Kerry 162 B4
Corgary Tyrone 158 B3
Cork Cork 163 C6
Corlea Longford 161 B7
Corlogh Mayo 160 A2
Cornafulla Roscommon 161 C7
Cornamona Galway 160 B4
Cornanagh Mayo 160 B4
Cornhaw Cavan 158 C3
Corranny Fermanagh 158 C4
Corrawalleen Leitrim 158 C3
Corrigeenroe Roscommon 158 C2
Corrofin Clare 160 D4
Corvally Monaghan 159 D5
Corvoy Monaghan 159 C5
Costelloe Galway 160 C3
Courtmacsherry Cork 163 C5
Courtown Wexford 157 C4
Craanford Wexford 157 C4
Craigavon Armagh 159 C6
Cranagh Tyrone 158 B4
Crataloe Limerick 162 B4
Craughwell Galway 161 C5
Creaghanroe Monaghan 159 C5
Creegh Clare 162 A4
Creeragh Mayo 160 A4
Creeslough Donegal 158 A3
Creeve Tyrone 159 B5
Creeves Limerick 162 A4
Creggan Tyrone 158 B4
Cregganbaun Mayo 160 B3
Creggs Galway 161 B6
Crindle Londonderry 159 A5
Crinkill Offaly 161 C7
Croagh Limerick 163 A5
Crockets Town Mayo 160 A4
Croghan Offaly 157 B2
Croghan Roscommon 161 B6
Crolly Donegal 158 A2
Crookedwood Westmeath 157 A2
Crookhaven Cork 162 D3
Crookstown Cork 163 C5
Croom Limerick 163 A5
Cross Barry Cork 163 C5
Cross Keys Meath 157 A3
Crossakiel Meath 157 A2
Crossdoney Cavan 158 D4
Crossgar Down 159 C7
Crosshaven Cork 163 C6
Crossmaglen Armagh 159 C5
Crossmolina Mayo 160 A4
Crumlin Dublin 157 B4
Crumlin Antrim 159 B6
Crusheen Clare 161 D5
Culdaff Donegal 158 A4
Cullaville Armagh 159 C5
Cullen Tipperary 163 A6
Cullinane Antrim 159 B6
Cullion Tyrone 158 B4
Cullyhanna Armagh 159 C5
Curraglass Cork 163 B6
Curry Sligo 161 B5
Curryglass Cork 162 C3
Cushendall Antrim 159 A6
Cushendun Antrim 159 A6
Cushina Offaly 157 B2

D

Dacklin Roscommon 161 B6
Daingean Offaly 157 B2
Dalkey Dublin 157 B4
Dalystown Galway 161 C6
Damerstown Kilkenny 157 C2
Darkley Armagh 159 C5
Darragh Clare 162 A4
Deelish Cork 162 C4
Delvin Westmeath 157 A2
Derry Sligo 158 C2
Derry/Londonderry Londonderry 158 B4
Derrybeg Donegal 158 A2
Derryboy Down 159 C7
Derrybrien Galway 161 C5
Derrycoosh Mayo 160 B4
Derrygonnelly Fermanagh 158 C3
Derrygorry Monaghan 158 C4
Derrygrogan Offaly 157 B2
Derrykeighan Antrim 159 A5
Derrylin Fermanagh 158 C3
Derrymore Kerry 162 B3
Derrynacreeve Cavan 158 C3
Derrynane Kerry 162 C2
Derryrush Galway 160 C3
Derrytrasna Armagh 159 B6
Dervock Antrim 159 A6
Desertmartin Londonderry 159 B5
Diamond Down 159 C6
Dingle Kerry 162 B2
Dirtagh Londonderry 159 A5
Doagh Antrim 159 B6
Dolla Tipperary 163 A6
Donabate Dublin 157 B4
Donadea Kildare 157 B3
Donagh Fermanagh 158 C4
Donaghadee Down 159 B7
Donaghmore Laois 161 D7
Donaghmore Tyrone 159 B5
Donard Wicklow 157 B3
Donegal Donegal 158 B2
Doneraile Cork 163 B5
Donohill Tipperary 163 A6
Donore Meath 157 A4
Donoughmore Cork 163 C5
Dooagh Mayo 160 B2
Doocharry Donegal 158 B2
Doogary Cavan 158 C3
Doogort Mayo 160 A2
Dooish Tyrone 158 B4
Doolin Clare 160 C4
Doon Limerick 163 A6
Doonaha Clare 162 A3
Doonbeg Clare 162 A3
Douglas Cork 163 C6
Downhill Londonderry 159 A5
Downies Donegal 158 A3
Downpatrick Down 159 C7
Dowra Cavan 158 C2
Drangan Tipperary 163 A7
Draperstown Londonderry 159 B5
Dreenagh Kerry 162 B3
Drimoleague Cork 162 C4
Drinagh Cork 162 C4
Dripsey Cork 163 C5
Drogheda Louth 157 A4
Dromahair Leitrim 158 C2
Dromara Down 159 C6
Dromard Sligo 158 C1
Dromcolliher Limerick 163 B5
Dromin Louth 159 D6
Dromina Cork 163 B5
Dromineer Tipperary 161 D6
Dromiskin Louth 159 D6
Dromkeen Limerick 163 A6
Dromod Leitrim 161 B7
Dromore Down 159 C6
Dromore Tyrone 158 B4
Dromore West Sligo 161 A5
Drum Monaghan 158 C4
Drumaduff Londonderry 159 B5
Drumahoe Londonderry 158 B4
Drumakilly Tyrone 158 B4
Drumbad Longford 161 B7
Drumbadmeen Fermanagh 158 C3
Drumbear Monaghan 159 C5
Drumbeg Donegal 158 B3
Drumbeg Down 159 B7
Drumbilla Louth 159 C6
Drumbo Monaghan 159 D5
Drumcard Fermanagh 158 C3
Drumcliff Sligo 158 C1
Drumcondra Dublin 157 B4
Drumcondra Meath 159 D5
Drumcoo Monaghan 158 C4
Drumcree Westmeath 157 A2
Drumdallagh Antrim 159 A6
Drumfin Sligo 158 C2
Drumfree Donegal 158 A4
Drumkeeran Leitrim 158 C2
Drumlegagh Tyrone 158 B4
Drumlish Longford 161 B7
Drumnacross Donegal 158 B3
Drumquin Tyrone 158 B4
Drumramer Londonderry 159 A5
Drumsallan Armagh 159 C5
Drumsaragh Londonderry 159 B5
Drumshanbo Leitrim 158 C2
Drumskinny Fermanagh 158 B3
Drumsna Leitrim 161 B6
Drumsurn Londonderry 159 A5
Dublin Dublin 157 B4
Duleek Meath 157 A4
Dun Laoghaire Dublin 157 B4
Dunaff Donegal 158 A4
Dunboyne Meath 157 B4
Duncormick Wexford 157 D3
Dundalk Louth 159 C6
Dunderrow Cork 163 C5
Dunderry Meath 157 A3
Dundonald Down 159 B7
Dundrod Antrim 159 B6
Dundrum Dublin 157 B4
Dundrum Tipperary 163 A6
Dundrum Down 159 C7
Dunfanaghy Donegal 158 A3
Dungannon Tyrone 159 B5
Dungarvan Waterford 163 B7
Dungiven Londonderry 159 B5
Dunglow Donegal 158 B2
Dungourney Cork 163 C6
Dunheeda Meath 159 D5
Dunkerrin Offaly 161 D7
Dunkineely Donegal 158 B2
Dunlavin Wicklow 157 B3
Dunleer Louth 159 D6
Dunloy Antrim 159 A6
Dunmanway Cork 162 C4
Dunmore Galway 161 B5
Dunmore East Waterford 157 D3
Dunmurry Antrim 159 B6
Dunnamanagh Tyrone 158 B4
Dunsany Meath 157 A3
Dunshaughlin Meath 157 A3
Durrow Laois 157 C2
Durrow Abbey Offaly 161 C7
Durrus Cork 162 C3
Dyan Tyrone 159 C5
Dysart Westmeath 157 B2

E

Eargantea Londonderry 159 A5
Earlstown Galway 161 C6
Easky Sligo 161 A5
Eden Antrim 159 B7
Edenaveagh Fermanagh 158 B3
Edenderry Offaly 157 B2
Ederny Fermanagh 158 B3
Edgeworthstown Longford 161 B7
Edmondstown Louth 159 D5
Eglinton Londonderry 158 A4
Eglish Tyrone 159 C5
Eighter Cavan 158 D4
Ellistrin Donegal 158 B3
Elphin Roscommon 161 B6
Emly Tipperary 163 B6
Emmoo Roscommon 161 B6
Emyvale Monaghan 159 C5
Ennis Clare 163 A5
Enniscorthy Wexford 157 C3
Enniskean Cork 163 C5
Enniskerry Wicklow 157 B4
Enniskillen Fermanagh 158 C3
Ennistimon Clare 160 D4
Errill Laois 163 A7
Essexford Monaghan 159 D5
Eyrecourt Galway 161 C6

F

Falcarragh Donegal 158 A2
Fallmore Mayo 160 A2
Fardrum Westmeath 161 C7
Farranfore Kerry 162 B3
Feakle Clare 161 D5
Fedamore Limerick 163 A5
Feeard Clare 162 A3
Feenhanagh Limerick 163 B5
Feeny Londonderry 158 B4
Fenagh Leitrim 158 C3
Fenit Kerry 162 B3
Fennagh Carlow 157 C3
Ferbane Offaly 161 C7
Fermoy Cork 163 B6
Ferns Wexford 157 C4
Fethard Tipperary 163 B7
Fethard Wexford 157 D3
Fiddown Kilkenny 157 D2
Fincarn Londonderry 159 B5
Finglas Dublin 157 B4
Finnea Westmeath 158 D4
Finnis Down 159 C6
Fintona Tyrone 158 C4
Fintown Donegal 158 B2
Finvoy Antrim 159 A6
Five Alley Offaly 161 C7
Fivemiletown Tyrone 158 C4
Flagmount Clare 161 C5
Fontstown Kildare 157 C4
Ford Wexford 157 C4
Fordstown Meath 157 A3
Fore Westmeath 157 A2
Forgney Longford 161 B7
Forkill Armagh 159 C6
Foulkesmill Wexford 157 D3
Fountain Cross Clare 162 A4
Four Mile House Roscommon 161 B6
Foxford Mayo 160 B4
Foygh Longford 161 B7
Foynes Limerick 162 A4
Frankville Down 159 C7
Freemount Cork 163 B5
Frenchpark Roscommon 161 B6
Freshford Kilkenny 157 C2
Fuerty Roscommon 161 B6
Fybagh Kerry 162 B3

G

Galbally Limerick 163 B6
Galmoy Kilkenny 163 A7
Galway Galway 160 C4
Garbally Galway 161 C6
Garrane Cork 162 C4
Garrison Fermanagh 158 C2
Garristown Dublin 157 A4
Garryvoe Cork 163 C6
Garvagh Londonderry 159 B5
Garvaghy Down 159 C6
Garvaghy Tyrone 158 C4
Garvary Fermanagh 158 C3
Gattabaun Kilkenny 157 C2
Gay Brook Westmeath 157 B2
Geashill Offaly 157 B2
Gilford Down 159 C6
Glandore Cork 162 C4
Glanworth Cork 163 B6
Glasdrumman Down 159 C7
Glaslough Monaghan 159 C5
Glasnevin Dublin 157 B4
Glassan Westmeath 161 C7
Glastry Down 159 C8
Glen Donegal 158 A3
Glen Fermanagh 158 C2
Glenade Leitrim 158 C2
Glenamoy Mayo 160 A3
Glenariff Antrim 159 A6
Glenarm Antrim 159 B7
Glenavy Antrim 159 B6
Glenbeigh Kerry 162 B3
Glencar Kerry 162 B3
Glencolumbkille Donegal 158 B1
Glendalough Wicklow 157 B4
Glendree Clare 161 D5
Glenealy Wicklow 157 C4
Gleneely Donegal 158 A4
Glenfarn Leitrim 158 C3
Glenfesk Kerry 162 B4
Glengarriff Cork 162 C3
Glengavlen Cavan 158 C3
Glengormly Antrim 159 B7
Glennamaddy Galway 161 B5
Glenoe Antrim 159 B7
Glenstal Abbey Limerick 163 A6
Glentane Galway 161 C5
Glenties Donegal 158 B2
Glenville Cork 163 B6
Glin Limerick 162 A4
Glinsk Galway 161 B6
Glinsk Galway 160 C3

Glynn *Carlow* 157 C3
Glynn *Antrim* 159 B7
Golden *Tipperary* 163 B7
Goleen *Cork* 162 D3
Goresbridge *Kilkenny* 157 C3
Gorey *Wexford* 157 C4
Gormanstown *Meath* 157 A4
Gort *Galway* 161 C5
Gortahork *Donegal* 158 A2
Gorteen *Galway* 161 B5
Gorteen *Galway* 161 C5
Gorteen *Sligo* 161 B5
Gorteen *Waterford* 163 B7
Gorteeng *Galway* 161 C6
Gortin *Tyrone* 158 B4
Gortnacross *Londonderry* 159 B5
Gortroe *Cork* 163 B5
Gortymadden *Galway* 161 C6
Gowlaun *Galway* 160 B3
Gowran *Kilkenny* 157 C2
Graghil *Mayo* 160 A3
Graigue *Laois* 157 C3
Graiguenamanagh *Kilkenny* 157 C3
Granard *Longford* 158 D4
Grange *Kilkenny* 157 C2
Grange *Roscommon* 161 B6
Grange *Sligo* 158 C1
Grangebellew *Louth* 159 D6
Granville *Tyrone* 159 C5
Greencastle *Donegal* 159 A5
Greencastle *Down* 159 C6
Greencastle *Tyrone* 158 B4
Greenisland *Antrim* 159 B7
Greenore *Louth* 159 C6
Greevagh *Sligo* 158 C2
Greyabbey *Down* 159 B7
Greysteel *Londonderry* 158 A4
Greystones *Wicklow* 157 B4
Groomsport *Down* 159 B7
Gubaveeny *Cavan* 158 C3
Gudderstown *Louth* 159 D5
Gulladuff *Londonderry* 159 B5
Gweedore *Donegal* 158 A2
Gwessalia *Mayo* 160 A3

H

Hacketstown *Carlow* 157 C3
Hamiltonsbawn *Armagh* 159 C5
Headford *Galway* 160 C4
Herbertstown *Limerick* 163 A6
Hillsborough *Down* 159 C6
Hilltown *Down* 159 C6
Hollymount *Mayo* 160 B4
Hollywood *Wicklow* 157 B3
Holycross *Limerick* 163 A5
Holycross *Tipperary* 163 A7
Holywood *Down* 159 B7
Horseleap *Offaly* 161 C7
Horseleap Crossroads *Galway* 161 C5
Hospital *Limerick* 163 B6
Howth *Dublin* 157 B4
Hurlers Cross *Clare* 163 A5

I

Inagh *Clare* 162 A4
Inch *Cork* 163 C7
Inch *Kerry* 162 B3
Inchigeelagh *Cork* 162 C4
Inishannon *Cork* 163 C5
Inishcrone *Sligo* 160 A4
Inishkeen *Monaghan* 159 C5
Inishrush *Londonderry* 159 B5
Inistioge *Kilkenny* 157 D2
Innfield *Meath* 157 B3
Inver *Donegal* 158 B2
Inveran *Galway* 160 C4
Irvinestown *Fermanagh* 158 C3
Islandtown *Antrim* 159 B6

J

Johnstown *Kilkenny* 163 A7
Johnstown Bridge *Kildare* 157 B3
Julianstown *Meath* 157 A4

K

Kanturk *Cork* 163 B5
Katesbridge *Down* 159 C6
Keadow *Roscommon* 158 C2
Keady *Armagh* 159 C5
Kealkill *Cork* 162 C4
Keel *Mayo* 160 B2
Keenagh *Longford* 161 B7
Kells *Kilkenny* 157 C2
Kells *Meath* 157 A3
Kells *Antrim* 159 B6
Kellystown *Louth* 159 D6
Kenmare *Kerry* 162 C3
Kentstown *Meath* 157 A3
Kesh *Fermanagh* 158 B3
Keshcarrigan *Leitrim* 158 C3
Kilamery *Kilkenny* 157 D2
Kilbaha *Clare* 162 A3
Kilbeggan *Westmeath* 157 B2
Kilbeheny *Limerick* 163 B6
Kilbennan Church *Galway* 161 B5
Kilberry *Meath* 157 A3
Kilbrickan *Galway* 160 C3
Kilbride *Wicklow* 157 C4
Kilbrien *Waterford* 163 B7
Kilbrittain *Cork* 163 C5
Kilcar *Donegal* 158 B1
Kilchreest *Galway* 161 C5
Kilclooney *Donegal* 158 B2
Kilcock *Kildare* 157 B3
Kilcoe *Cork* 162 C4
Kilcogy *Cavan* 158 D4
Kilcolgan *Galway* 161 C5
Kilconly *Galway* 160 B4
Kilconnell *Galway* 161 C6
Kilcoo *Down* 159 C6
Kilcoole *Wicklow* 157 B4
Kilcormac *Offaly* 161 C7
Kilcornan *Limerick* 163 A5
Kilcrohane *Cork* 162 C3
Kilcullen *Kildare* 157 B3
Kilcurry *Louth* 159 C6
Kildalkey *Meath* 157 A3
Kildare *Kildare* 157 B3
Kildavin *Carlow* 157 C3
Kildimo *Limerick* 163 A5
Kildorrery *Cork* 163 B6
Kilfane *Kilkenny* 157 C2
Kilfeakle *Tipperary* 163 B6
Kilfearagh *Clare* 162 A3
Kilfenora *Clare* 160 D4
Kilfinnane *Limerick* 163 B6
Kilflynn *Kerry* 162 B3
Kilgarrif *Galway* 160 C4
Kilgarvan *Kerry* 162 C4
Kilglass *Galway* 161 C6
Kilglass *Sligo* 160 A4
Kilgobnet *Kerry* 162 B3
Kilgolagh *Cavan* 158 D4
Kilkea *Kildare* 157 C3
Kilkee *Clare* 162 A3
Kilkeel *Down* 159 C6
Kilkelly *Mayo* 161 B5
Kilkenny *Kilkenny* 157 C2
Kilkerrin *Galway* 161 B5
Kilkieran *Galway* 160 C3
Kilkinlea *Kerry* 162 B4
Kilkishen *Clare* 163 A5
Kill *Kildare* 157 B3
Kill *Waterford* 157 D2
Killadangan *Mayo* 160 B3
Killadeas *Fermanagh* 158 C3
Killadoon *Mayo* 160 B3
Killadysert *Clare* 162 A4
Killala *Mayo* 160 A4
Killaloe *Clare* 163 A6
Killaloo *Londonderry* 158 B4
Killane *Offaly* 157 B2
Killarbran *Fermanagh* 158 C4
Killarga *Leitrim* 158 C2
Killargue *Leitrim* 158 C2
Killarney *Kerry* 162 B3
Killashandra *Cavan* 158 C3
Killashee *Longford* 161 B7
Killavally *Mayo* 160 B4
Killavullen *Cork* 163 B5
Killeagh *Cork* 163 C7
Killeen *Tipperary* 161 C7
Killeen *Tyrone* 159 B5
Killeevan *Monaghan* 158 C4
Killeglan *Roscommon* 161 C6
Killeigh *Offaly* 157 B2
Killen *Tyrone* 158 B3
Killenagh *Wexford* 157 C4
Killenaule *Tipperary* 163 A7
Killerig *Carlow* 157 C3
Killeter *Tyrone* 158 B3
Killimor *Galway* 161 C6
Killinaboy *Clare* 160 D4
Killinaspick *Kilkenny* 157 D2
Killiney *Dublin* 157 B4
Killinick *Wexford* 157 D4
Killorglin *Kerry* 162 B3
Killough *Down* 159 C7
Killowen *Down* 159 C6
Killsaran *Louth* 159 D6
Killtullagh *Galway* 161 C5
Killucan *Westmeath* 157 A2
Killurin *Wexford* 157 D3
Killybegs *Donegal* 158 B2
Killyfassy *Cavan* 158 D4
Killygordon *Donegal* 158 B3
Killykergan *Londonderry* 159 A5
Killylea *Armagh* 159 C5
Killyleagh *Down* 159 C7
Killyon *Offaly* 161 C7
Kilmacow *Kilkenny* 157 D2
Kilmacrenan *Donegal* 158 A3
Kilmacthomas *Waterford* 157 D2
Kilmaganny *Kilkenny* 157 D2
Kilmaine *Mayo* 160 B4
Kilmaley *Clare* 162 A4
Kilmallock *Limerick* 163 B5
Kilmanagh *Kilkenny* 157 C2
Kilmeadan *Waterford* 157 D2
Kilmeage *Kildare* 157 B3
Kilmeedy *Limerick* 163 B5
Kilmichael *Cork* 162 C4
Kilmihil *Clare* 162 A4
Kilmore *Wexford* 157 D3
Kilmore Quay *Wexford* 157 D3
Kilmuckridge *Wexford* 157 C4
Kilmurry *Clare* 162 A4
Kilmurry *Clare* 163 A5
Kilmurvy *Galway* 160 C3
Kilnaleck *Cavan* 158 D4
Kilpatrick *Cork* 163 C5
Kilrea *Londonderry* 159 B5
Kilreekil *Galway* 161 C6
Kilronan *Galway* 160 C3
Kilronane *Cork* 162 C4
Kilross *Tipperary* 163 B6
Kilrush *Clare* 162 A4
Kilsallagh *Galway* 161 B5
Kilshanny *Clare* 160 D4
Kilsheelan *Tipperary* 163 B7
Kiltamagh *Mayo* 160 B4
Kiltartan *Galway* 161 C5
Kiltealy *Wexford* 157 C3
Kilteel *Kildare* 157 B3
Kilteely *Limerick* 163 A6
Kiltegan *Wicklow* 157 C3
Kiltiernan *Dublin* 157 B4
Kiltoom *Roscommon* 161 C6
Kiltormer *Galway* 161 C6
Kiltyclogher *Leitrim* 158 C2
Kilworth *Cork* 163 B6
Kinalag *Galway* 161 B5
Kinawley *Fermanagh* 158 C3
Kincaslough *Donegal* 158 A2
Kindrum *Donegal* 158 A3
Kingarrow *Donegal* 158 B2
Kingscourt *Cavan* 159 D5
Kinlough *Leitrim* 158 C2
Kinnegad *Westmeath* 157 B2
Kinnitty *Offaly* 161 C7
Kinsale *Cork* 163 C5
Kinvarra *Galway* 161 C5
Kircubbin *Down* 159 C7
Kishkeam *Cork* 162 B4
Knock *Clare* 162 A4
Knock *Mayo* 161 B5
Knockaderry *Limerick* 163 B5
Knockagree *Cork* 162 B4
Knockalina *Mayo* 160 A3
Knockalough *Clare* 162 A4
Knockananna *Wicklow* 157 C4
Knockatallan *Monaghan* 158 C4
Knockbrit *Tipperary* 163 B7
Knockcroghery *Roscommon* 161 B6
Knockfold *Donegal* 158 A2
Knocklofty *Tipperary* 163 B7
Knocklong *Limerick* 163 B6
Knocktopher *Kilkenny* 157 D2
Kylesa *Galway* 160 C3

L

Laban *Galway* 161 C5
Labasheeda *Clare* 162 A4
Labby *Londonderry* 159 B5
Lack *Fermanagh* 158 B3
Lackamore *Tipperary* 163 A6
Ladysbridge *Cork* 163 C6
Laghtgeorge *Galway* 161 C5
Laghy *Donegal* 158 B2
Lahard *Cavan* 161 B7
Lahardaun *Mayo* 160 A4
Lakyle *Clare* 162 A4
Lanesborough *Longford* 161 B7
Laracor *Meath* 157 A3
Laragh *Wicklow* 157 B4
Largan *Mayo* 160 A3
Largy *Donegal* 158 B1
Larne *Antrim* 159 B7
Lattin *Tipperary* 163 B6
Lauragh *Kerry* 162 C3
Laurencetown *Galway* 161 C6
Lavey *Cavan* 158 D4
Lawrencetown *Down* 159 C6
Laytown *Meath* 157 A4
Leap *Cork* 162 C4
Leckanarainey *Leitrim* 158 C2
Leckaun *Leitrim* 158 C2
Leckemy *Donegal* 158 A4
Leenaun *Galway* 160 B3
Legoniel *Antrim* 159 B7
Lehinch *Clare* 160 D4
Leighlinbridge *Carlow* 157 C3
Leitrim *Leitrim* 161 B6
Leixlip *Kildare* 157 B4
Lemanaghan *Offaly* 161 C7
Lemybrien *Waterford* 163 B7
Lerrig *Kerry* 162 B3
Letterbreen *Fermanagh* 158 C3
Letterfrack *Galway* 160 B3
Letterkenny *Donegal* 158 B3
Lettermacaward *Donegal* 158 B2
Lettermore *Galway* 160 C3
Lettermullan *Galway* 160 C3
Lifford *Donegal* 158 B4
Ligfordrum *Tyrone* 158 B4
Limavady *Londonderry* 159 A5
Limerick *Limerick* 163 A5
Limerick Junction *Tipperary* 163 B6
Lisacul *Roscommon* 161 B5
Lisbane *Down* 159 B7
Lisbellaw *Fermanagh* 158 C3
Lisburn *Antrim* 159 B6
Liscannor *Clare* 160 D4
Liscarroll *Cork* 163 B5
Lisdoonvarna *Clare* 160 C4
Lisgall *Monaghan* 159 C5
Lisgarode *Tipperary* 161 D6
Lisheen *Clare* 162 A4
Lislap *Tyrone* 158 B4
Lislea *Armagh* 159 C6
Lismore *Waterford* 163 B7
Lisnacree *Down* 159 C6
Lisnagry *Limerick* 163 A5
Lisnamusk *Londonderry* 159 B5
Lisnarick *Fermanagh* 158 C3
Lisnaskea *Fermanagh* 158 C4
Lisnaveane *Monaghan* 158 C4
Lispole *Kerry* 162 B2
Lisronagh *Tipperary* 163 B7
Lissatinnig Bridge *Kerry* 162 C3
Lisselton *Kerry* 162 B3
Lissinagroagh *Leitrim* 158 C2
Lissycasey *Clare* 162 A4
Listerlin *Kilkenny* 157 D2
Listowel *Kerry* 162 B4
Littleton *Tipperary* 163 A7
Lixnaw *Kerry* 162 B3
Lobinstown *Meath* 159 D5
Loghill *Limerick* 162 A4
Longford *Longford* 161 B7
Longwood *Meath* 157 B3
Loughall *Armagh* 159 C5
Loughanavally *Westmeath* 161 C7
Loughanure *Donegal* 158 B2
Loughbrickland *Down* 159 C6
Loughglinn *Roscommon* 161 B5
Loughguile *Antrim* 159 A6
Loughmoe *Tipperary* 163 A7
Loughran *Antrim* 159 A6
Loughrea *Galway* 161 C5
Louisburgh *Mayo* 160 B3
Louth *Louth* 159 D5
Lucan *Dublin* 157 B4
Lugatemple *Mayo* 160 B4
Lukeswell *Kilkenny* 157 D2
Lurgan *Armagh* 159 C6
Lurgangreen *Louth* 159 D6
Lusk *Dublin* 157 A4
Lyracrumpane *Kerry* 162 B4

M

Maam Cross *Galway* 160 C3
Maas *Donegal* 158 B2
Mackan *Fermanagh* 158 C3
Macosquin *Londonderry* 159 A5
Macroom *Cork* 163 C5
Maghera *Londonderry* 159 B5
Magherafelt *Londonderry* 159 B5
Magheragall *Antrim* 159 B6
Magheraveely *Fermanagh* 158 C4
Maghery *Donegal* 158 B2
Maghery *Armagh* 159 B5
Maguiresbridge *Fermanagh* 158 C4
Malahide *Dublin* 157 B4
Malin *Donegal* 158 A4
Malin More *Donegal* 158 A1
Mallaranny *Mayo* 160 B3
Mallow *Cork* 163 B5
Manfieldstown *Louth* 159 D6
Manorhamilton *Leitrim* 158 C2
Manselstown *Tipperary* 163 A7
Manulla *Mayo* 160 B4
Markethill *Armagh* 159 C5
Maulyneill *Kerry* 162 C3
Maum *Galway* 160 B3
Maylough *Galway* 161 C5
Maynooth *Kildare* 157 B3
Mayo *Mayo* 160 B4
Mayo Bridge *Down* 159 C6
Meenaneary *Donegal* 158 B1
Meigh *Armagh* 159 C6
Mell *Louth* 157 A4
Menlough *Galway* 160 C4
Middletown *Armagh* 159 C5
Midleton *Cork* 163 C6
Milestone *Tipperary* 163 A6
Milford *Cork* 163 B5
Milford *Donegal* 158 A3
Millbrook *Meath* 157 A2
Milford *Armagh* 159 C5
Millisle *Down* 159 B7
Millstreet *Cork* 162 B4
Millstreet *Waterford* 163 B7
Milltown *Cavan* 158 C4
Milltown *Galway* 161 B5
Milltown *Kerry* 162 B2
Milltown *Kerry* 162 B3
Milltown *Monaghan* 159 C5
Milltown *Antrim* 159 B7
Milltown *Londonderry* 159 A5
Milltown Malbay *Clare* 162 A4
Miltown *Kildare* 157 B3
Minane Bridge *Cork* 163 C6
Mitchelstown *Cork* 163 B6
Moate *Westmeath* 161 C7
Modreeny *Tipperary* 161 D6
Mohill *Leitrim* 161 B7
Moira *Down* 159 C6
Monaghan *Monaghan* 159 C5
Monasterevin *Kildare* 157 B2
Moneygall *Offaly* 161 D7
Moneyglass *Antrim* 159 B6
Moneymore *Londonderry* 159 B5
Moneyneany *Londonderry* 159 B5
Monivea *Galway* 161 C5
Monkstown *Cork* 163 C6
Mooncoin *Kilkenny* 157 D2
Moone *Kildare* 157 C3
Moorfields *Antrim* 159 B6
Mornington *Meath* 157 A4
Moss-side *Antrim* 159 A6
Mossley *Antrim* 159 B7
Mount Bellew Bridge *Galway* 161 C6
Mount Ida *Down* 159 C6
Mount Nugent *Cavan* 158 D4
Mount Talbot *Roscommon* 161 B6
Mountcharles *Donegal* 158 B2
Mountfield *Tyrone* 158 B4
Mountjoy *Tyrone* 158 B4
Mountmellick *Laois* 157 B2
Mountnorris *Armagh* 159 C6
Mountrath *Laois* 157 B2
Mountshannon *Clare* 161 D6
Moville *Donegal* 158 A4
Moy *Tyrone* 159 C5
Moyad *Down* 159 C6
Moyard *Galway* 160 B2
Moyasta *Clare* 162 A3
Moycullen *Galway* 160 C4
Moymore *Clare* 163 A5
Moynalty *Meath* 159 D5
Moyne *Longford* 161 B7
Moyne *Tipperary* 163 A7
Moyroughly *Westmeath* 161 C7
Moyvally *Kildare* 157 B3
Moyvore *Westmeath* 161 B7
Muckross *Kerry* 162 B4
Muff *Donegal* 158 A4
Muine Bheag *Carlow* 157 C3
Muineagh *Donegal* 158 A3
Mullagh *Cavan* 159 D5
Mullagh *Galway* 161 C6
Mullagh *Meath* 157 B3
Mullaghnaneane *Sligo* 158 C1
Mullan *Fermanagh* 158 C3
Mullans Town *Tyrone* 158 B4
Mullanys Cross *Sligo* 161 A5
Mullarts *Antrim* 159 A6
Mulldonagh *Londonderry* 158 B4
Mullinahone *Tipperary* 157 C1
Mullinavat *Kilkenny* 157 D2
Mullingar *Westmeath* 157 A2
Mullughmore *Sligo* 158 C2
Mungret *Limerick* 163 A5
Murroogh *Clare* 160 C4
Myshall *Carlow* 157 C3

N

Naas *Kildare* 157 B3
Nad *Cork* 163 B5
Naran *Donegal* 158 B2
Naul *Dublin* 157 A4
Navan *Meath* 157 A3
Neale *Mayo* 160 B4
Nenagh *Tipperary* 163 A6
New Birmingham *Tipperary* 163 A7
New Buildings *Londonderry* 158 B4
New Chapel Cross *Kerry* 162 C2
New Inn *Cavan* 158 D4
New Inn *Galway* 161 C6
New Inn *Laois* 157 B2
New Ross *Wexford* 157 D3
Newbliss *Monaghan* 158 C4
Newbridge *Galway* 161 B6
Newbridge *Kildare* 157 B3
Newbridge *Limerick* 163 A5
Newcastle *Tipperary* 163 B7
Newcastle *Wicklow* 157 B4
Newcastle *Down* 159 C7
Newcastle West *Limerick* 162 B4
Newinn *Tipperary* 163 B7
Newmarket *Cork* 163 B5
Newmarket-on-Fergus *Clare* 163 A5
Newmills *Donegal* 158 B3
Newport *Mayo* 160 B3
Newport *Tipperary* 163 A6
Newry *Down* 159 C6
Newtown *Laois* 157 C2
Newtown *Longford* 161 B7
Newtown *Tipperary* 163 B6
Newtown Crommelin *Antrim* 159 B6
Newtown Cunningham *Donegal* 158 B3
Newtown Forbes *Longford* 161 B7
Newtown Gore *Leitrim* 158 C3
Newtown Hamilton *Armagh* 159 C5
Newtown Monasterboice *Louth* 159 D6
Newtown Mount Kennedy *Wicklow* 157 B4
Newtown Sands *Kerry* 162 A4
Newtownabbey *Antrim* 159 B7
Newtownards *Down* 159 B7
Newtownbreda *Down* 159 B7
Newtownbutler *Fermanagh* 158 C4
Newtownshandrum *Cork* 163 B5
Newtownstewart *Tyrone* 158 B4
Ninemilehouse *Tipperary* 157 D2
Nobber *Meath* 159 D5
Nohaval *Cork* 163 C6
Nurney *Carlow* 157 C3
Nutts Corner *Antrim* 159 B6

O

O'Briensbridge *Clare* 163 A6
Ogill *Londonderry* 158 B4
Oilgate *Wexford* 157 D3
Old Ross *Wexford* 157 D3
Oldcastle *Meath* 158 D4
Oldleighlin *Carlow* 157 C2
Oldtown *Laois* 157 C2
Omagh *Tyrone* 158 B4
Omeath *Louth* 159 C6
Oola *Limerick* 163 A6
Oran *Roscommon* 161 B6
Oranmore *Galway* 161 C5
Oristown *Meath* 157 A3
Oughterard *Galway* 160 C4

P

Pallas Green *Limerick* 163 A6
Pallaskenry *Limerick* 163 A5
Park *Galway* 161 C5
Park *Londonderry* 158 B4
Parknasilla *Kerry* 162 C3
Parkview *Antrim* 159 B7
Partry *Mayo* 160 B4
Passage East *Waterford* 157 D3
Passage West *Cork* 163 C6
Patrickswell *Limerick* 163 A5
Paulstown *Kilkenny* 157 C2
Peterswell *Galway* 161 C5
Pettigo *Donegal* 158 B3
Piltown *Kilkenny* 157 D2
Pluck *Donegal* 158 B3
Plumbridge *Tyrone* 158 B4
Pollremon *Galway* 161 B5
Pomeroy *Tyrone* 159 B5
Pontoon *Mayo* 160 B4
Portacloy *Mayo* 160 A3
Portadown *Armagh* 159 C6
Portaferry *Down* 159 C7
Portarlington *Offaly* 157 B2
Portavogie *Down* 159 C8
Portballintrae *Antrim* 159 A5
Portglenone *Antrim* 159 B6
Portlaoise *Laois* 157 B2
Portlaw *Waterford* 157 D2
Portmagee *Kerry* 162 C2
Portmarnock *Dublin* 157 B4
Portrane *Dublin* 157 B4
Portroe *Tipperary* 161 D6
Portrush *Antrim* 159 A5
Portsalon *Donegal* 158 A3
Portstewart *Londonderry* 159 A5
Portumna *Galway* 161 C6
Poyntz Pass *Armagh* 159 C6
Prosperous *Kildare* 157 B3
Puckaun *Tipperary* 161 D6

Q

Quarryfield *Sligo* 158 C1
Quilty *Clare* 162 A4
Quin *Clare* 163 A5

R

Rahan *Offaly* 161 C7
Rahara *Roscommon* 161 B6
Raharney *Westmeath* 157 A2
Raheen *Tipperary* 163 B7
Rampark *Louth* 159 C6
Randalstown *Antrim* 159 B6
Raphoe *Donegal* 158 B3
Rasharkin *Antrim* 159 B6
Rath *Offaly* 161 C7
Rathangan *Kildare* 157 B3
Ratharney *Longford* 161 B7
Rathclogh *Tipperary* 163 A7
Rathconrath *Westmeath* 161 B7
Rathcool *Cork* 163 B5
Rathcoole *Dublin* 157 B4
Rathcor *Louth* 159 D6
Rathcormack *Cork* 163 B6
Rathdowney *Laois* 163 A7
Rathdrum *Wicklow* 157 C4
Rathduff *Cork* 163 B5
Rathfriland *Down* 159 C6
Rathgormuck *Waterford* 157 D2
Rathkeale *Limerick* 163 A5
Rathkenny *Meath* 157 A3
Rathlacken *Mayo* 160 A4
Rathmelton *Donegal* 158 A3
Rathmolyon *Meath* 157 B3
Rathmore *Kerry* 162 B4
Rathmore *Kildare* 157 B3
Rathmore *Longford* 161 B7
Rathmullan *Donegal* 158 A3
Rathnew *Wicklow* 157 C4
Rathnure *Wexford* 157 D3
Rathowen *Westmeath* 161 B7
Rathvilla *Offaly* 157 B2
Rathvilly *Carlow* 157 C3
Ratoath *Meath* 157 A4
Ravensdale *Louth* 159 C6
Rear Cross *Tipperary* 163 A6
Recess *Galway* 160 C3
Red Castle *Donegal* 158 A4
Reens *Limerick* 163 A5
Rhode *Offaly* 157 B2
Rich Hill *Armagh* 159 C5
Ringaskiddy *Cork* 163 C6
Ringsend *Londonderry* 159 A5
Ringville *Waterford* 163 B7
Riverchapel *Wexford* 157 C4
Riverstick *Cork* 163 C6
Riverstown *Cork* 163 C6
Riverstown *Sligo* 158 C2
Robertstown *Kildare* 157 B3
Rochfortbridge *Westmeath* 157 B2
Rockchapel *Cork* 162 B4
Rockcorry *Monaghan* 158 C4
Rockhill *Limerick* 163 B5
Rockmills *Cork* 163 B6
Roosky *Leitrim* 161 B7
Roscommon *Roscommon* 161 B6
Roscrea *Tipperary* 161 D7
Rosegreen *Tipperary* 163 B7
Rosenallis *Laois* 157 B2
Rosmult *Tipperary* 163 A7
Ross Carbery *Cork* 162 C4
Rossaveel *Galway* 160 C3
Rosscahill *Galway* 160 C4
Rosses Point *Sligo* 158 C1
Rossinver *Leitrim* 158 C2
Rosslare *Wexford* 157 D4
Rosslare Harbour *Wexford* 157 D4
Rosslea *Fermanagh* 158 C4
Rossnowlagh *Donegal* 158 B2
Rostellan *Cork* 163 C6
Rostrevor *Down* 159 C6
Rosturk *Mayo* 160 B3
Roundstone *Galway* 160 C3
Roundwood *Wicklow* 157 B4
Rousky *Tyrone* 158 B4
Ruan *Clare* 161 D5
Rush *Dublin* 157 A4

S

Saggart *Dublin* 157 B4
St. Johnstown *Donegal* 158 B4
Saintfield *Down* 159 C7
Sallahig *Kerry* 162 C2
Sallins *Kildare* 157 B3
Sally Gap *Wicklow* 157 B4
Sallybrook *Cork* 163 C6
Salterstown *Louth* 159 D6
Salthill *Galway* 160 C4
Saltpans *Donegal* 158 A3
Scarriff *Clare* 161 D5
Scartaglin *Kerry* 162 B4
Scarva *Down* 159 C6
Scogh *Kilkenny* 157 D2
Scotch Corner *Monaghan* 159 C5
Scotstown *Monaghan* 158 C4
Scraghy *Tyrone* 158 B3
Scramoge *Roscommon* 161 B6
Screeb *Galway* 160 C3
Screggan *Offaly* 161 C7
Scribbagh *Fermanagh* 158 C2
Seskinore *Tyrone* 158 B4
Shanagolden *Limerick* 162 A4
Shankill *Roscommon* 161 B6
Shanlaragh *Cork* 162 C4
Shannonbridge *Offaly* 161 C6
Shannow *Cavan* 158 D4
Shanovogh *Clare* 162 A4
Shantonagh *Monaghan* 159 C5
Sharavogue *Offaly* 161 C7
Shercock *Cavan* 159 D5
Shillelagh *Wicklow* 157 C3
Shinrone *Offaly* 161 D7
Shrigley *Down* 159 C7
Shrule *Mayo* 160 B4
Silvermines *Tipperary* 163 A6
Silverstream *Monaghan* 159 C5
Single Street *Donegal* 158 C2
Sion Mills *Tyrone* 158 B4
Six Crosses *Kerry* 162 B3
Sixmilebridge *Clare* 163 A5
Sixmilecross *Tyrone* 158 B4
Skeagh *Westmeath* 161 B7
Skerries *Dublin* 157 A4
Skibbereen *Cork* 162 C4
Skull *Cork* 162 C3
Slane *Meath* 157 A3
Sligo *Sligo* 158 C2
Slisgarrow *Fermanagh* 158 C3
Smithborough *Monaghan* 158 C4
Sneem *Kerry* 162 C3
Spa *Kerry* 162 B3
Spancelhill *Clare* 163 A5
Speenoge *Donegal* 158 A4
Sperrin *Tyrone* 158 B4
Spiddle *Galway* 160 C4
Springfield *Fermanagh* 158 C3
Square *Down* 159 C6
Srahmore *Mayo* 160 A3
Srahnalong *Mayo* 160 B4
Stewartstown *Tyrone* 159 B5
Stillorgan *Dublin* 157 B4
Stonyford *Kilkenny* 157 C2
Strabane *Tyrone* 158 B4
Stradbally *Kerry* 162 B2
Stradbally *Laois* 157 B2
Stradbally *Waterford* 157 D2
Strade Friary *Mayo* 160 B4
Stradone *Cavan* 158 D4
Straffan *Kildare* 157 B3
Strandhill *Sligo* 158 C1
Strangford *Down* 159 C7
Stranorlar *Donegal* 158 B3
Streamstown *Galway* 160 B2
Strokestown *Roscommon* 161 B6
Stroove *Donegal* 159 A5
Summerhill *Meath* 157 B3
Swan *Laois* 157 C2
Swanlinbar *Cavan* 158 C3
Swatragh *Londonderry* 159 B5
Swinford *Mayo* 161 B5
Swords *Dublin* 157 B4

T

Taghmon *Wexford* 157 D3
Tallaght *Dublin* 157 B4
Tallanstown *Louth* 159 D5
Tallow *Waterford* 163 B6
Tallowbridge *Waterford* 163 B6
Tandragee *Armagh* 159 C6
Tang *Westmeath* 161 B7
Tara *Meath* 157 A3
Tarbert *Kerry* 162 A4
Taur *Cork* 162 B4
Tawnyinah *Mayo* 161 B5
Tedavnet *Monaghan* 158 C4
Teeshan *Antrim* 159 B6
Templeboy *Sligo* 161 A5
Templederry *Tipperary* 163 A6
Templemore *Tipperary* 163 A7
Templenoe *Kerry* 162 C3
Templepatrick *Antrim* 159 B6
Templetouhy *Tipperary* 163 A7
Tempo *Fermanagh* 158 C4
Termon *Cavan* 158 C3
Termon *Donegal* 158 A3
Termonfeckin *Louth* 159 D6
Terryglass *Tipperary* 161 C6
The Downs *Westmeath* 157 A2
The Loup *Londonderry* 159 B5
The Sheddings *Antrim* 159 B6
The Temple *Down* 159 C7
Thomas Street *Roscommon* 161 C6
Thomastown *Kilkenny* 157 C2
Thurles *Tipperary* 163 A7
Timahoe *Kildare* 157 B3
Timahoe *Laois* 157 C2
Timoleague *Cork* 163 C5
Timolin *Kildare* 157 C3
Tinahely *Wicklow* 157 C4
Tintern Abbey *Wexford* 157 D3
Tipperary *Tipperary* 163 B6
Tobercurry *Sligo* 161 A5
Tobermoney *Down* 159 C7
Tobermore *Londonderry* 159 B5
Toberroe *Galway* 161 C5
Togher *Cork* 162 C4
Togher *Louth* 159 D6
Toomakeady *Mayo* 160 B4
Toombeola *Galway* 160 C3
Toome *Antrim* 159 B6
Toomyvara *Tipperary* 163 A6
Toormore *Cork* 162 C3
Tralee *Kerry* 162 B3
Tramore *Waterford* 157 D2
Trillick *Tyrone* 158 C4
Trim *Meath* 157 A3
Tuam *Galway* 161 B5
Tuamgraney *Clare* 161 D5
Tubber *Galway* 161 C5
Tulla *Clare* 163 A5
Tullaghan *Leitrim* 158 C2
Tullaghoge *Tyrone* 159 B5
Tullaghought *Kilkenny* 157 D2
Tullagower *Clare* 162 A4
Tullamore *Offaly* 157 B2
Tullaroan *Kilkenny* 157 C2
Tullow *Carlow* 157 C3
Tully *Roscommon* 161 B6
Tully Cross *Galway* 160 B3
Tullybeg *Galway* 161 B5
Tullycrossmearan *Fermanagh* 158 C3
Tullymacreeve *Armagh* 159 C6
Tullyverry *Londonderry* 158 A4
Tullyvin *Cavan* 158 C4
Tulsk *Roscommon* 161 B6
Tummery *Tyrone* 158 C3
Turloughmore *Galway* 161 C5
Turreen *Longford* 161 B7
Twomileborris *Tipperary* 163 A7
Tynagh *Galway* 161 C6
Tynan *Armagh* 159 C5
Tyrrellspass *Westmeath* 157 B2

U

Upperchurch *Tipperary* 163 A6
Urlingford *Kilkenny* 163 A7

V

Ventry *Kerry* 162 B2
Vicarstown *Laois* 157 B2
Virginia *Cavan* 158 D4

W

Waddington *Wexford* 157 D3
Ward *Dublin* 157 B4
Waringstown *Down* 159 C6
Warrenpoint *Down* 159 C6
Waterford *Waterford* 157 D2
Watergrasshill *Cork* 163 B6
Waterside *Londonderry* 158 B4
Waterville *Kerry* 162 C2
Wellingtonbridge *Wexford* 157 D3
Westport *Mayo* 160 B3
Wexford *Wexford* 157 D4
Wheathill *Fermanagh* 158 C3
White Castle *Donegal* 158 A4
Whitecross *Armagh* 159 C6
Whitegate *Clare* 161 D6
Whitegate *Cork* 163 C6
Whitehead *Antrim* 159 B7
Whitehill *Fermanagh* 158 C3
Wicklow *Wicklow* 157 C4
Williamstown *Galway* 161 B5
Windgap *Kilkenny* 157 D2
Woodenbridge *Wicklow* 157 C4
Woodford *Galway* 161 C6
Woodlawn *Galway* 161 C6
Woodtown *Meath* 159 D5

Y

Youghal *Cork* 163 C7

How to use the index

Example: Westcott Devon 8 D2

- grid square
- page number
- county or unitary authority

Places of special interest are highlighted in red

Abbreviations

Aberd C	Aberdeen City
Aberds	Aberdeenshire
Angl	Isle of Anglesey
Arg/Bute	Argyll & Bute
Bath/NE Som'set	Bath & North East Somerset
Beds	Bedfordshire
Berks	Berkshire
Bl Gwent	Blaenau Gwent
Bournem'th	Bournemouth
Bridg	Bridgend
Brighton/Hove	Brighton and Hove
Bristol	City & County of Bristol
Bucks	Buckinghamshire
C of Edinb	City of Edinburgh
C of Glasg	City of Glasgow
C of York	City of York
Caerph	Caerphilly
Cambs	Cambridgeshire
Card	Cardiff
Carms	Carmarthenshire
Ceredig'n	Ceredigion
Ches	Cheshire
Clack	Clackmannanshire
Cornw'l	Cornwall
Cumb	Cumbria
Denbs	Denbighshire
Derby	Derbyshire
Derby C	Derby City
D'lington	Darlington
Dumf/Gal	Dumfries & Galloway
Dundee C	Dundee City
E Ayrs	East Ayrshire
E Dunb	East Dunbartonshire
E Loth	East Lothian
E Renf	East Renfrewshire
E Riding Yorks	East Riding of Yorkshire
E Sussex	East Sussex
Falk	Falkirk
Flints	Flintshire
Glos	Gloucestershire
Gtr Lon	Greater London
Gtr Man	Greater Manchester
Gwyn	Gwynedd
Hants	Hampshire
Hartlep'l	Hartlepool
Heref/Worcs	Hereford and Worcester
Herts	Hertfordshire
H'land	Highland
I of Man	Isle of Man
I of Scilly	Isles of Scilly
I of Wight	Isle of Wight
Invercl	Inverclyde
Kingston/Hull	Kingston upon Hull
Lancs	Lancashire
Leics	Leicestershire
Leics C	Leicester City
Lincs	Lincolnshire
Luton	Luton
Mersey	Merseyside
Merth Tyd	Merthyr Tydfil
Middlesbro'	Middlesbrough
Midloth	Midlothian
M/Keynes	Milton Keynes
Monmouths	Monmouthshire
Moray	Moray
N Ayrs	North Ayrshire
N Lanarks	North Lanarkshire
N Lincs	North Lincolnshire
N Som'set	North Somerset
N Yorks	North Yorkshire
NE Lincs	North East Lincolnshire
Neath P Talb	Neath Port Talbot
Newp	Newport
Northants	Northamptonshire
Northum	Northumberland
Notts	Nottinghamshire
Oxon	Oxfordshire
Pembs	Pembrokeshire
Perth/Kinr	Perth & Kinross
Poole	Poole
Portsm'th	Portsmouth
Redcar/Clevel'd	Redcar & Cleveland
Renf	Renfrewshire
Rh Cyn Taff	Rhondda Cynon Taff
Rutl'd	Rutland
S Ayrs	South Ayrshire
S Gloucs	South Gloucestershire
S Lanarks	South Lanarkshire
S Yorks	South Yorkshire
Scot Borders	Scottish Borders
Shetl'd	Shetland
Shrops	Shropshire
Som'set	Somerset
Staffs	Staffordshire
S'thampton	Southampton
Stirl	Stirling
Stockton	Stockton on Tees
Stoke	Stoke-on-Trent
Swan	Swansea
Thamesd'n	Thamesdown
Torf	Torfaen
Tyne/Wear	Tyne & Wear
V of Glam	Vale of Glamorgan
W Dunb	West Dunbartonshire
W Isles	Western Isles
W Loth	West Lothian
W Midlands	West Midlands
W Sussex	West Sussex
W Yorks	West Yorkshire
Warwick	Warwickshire
Wilts	Wiltshire
Wrex	Wrexham

A

Astwood Bank Heref/Worcs 30 B2
Aswarby Lincs 42 B3
Aswardby Lincs 53 E6
Atch Lench Heref/Worcs 30 C2
Atcham Shrops 39 E6
Athelhampton Dorset 9 E9
Athelington Suffolk 35 A6
Athelney Som'set 8 B5
Athelstaneford E Loth 85 G7
Atherington Devon 7 D6
Atherstone Warwick 40 F5
Atherstone on Stour Warwick 30 C4
Atherton Gtr Man 49 B7
Atley Hill N Yorks 63 D7
Atlow Derbys 50 H4
Attadale H'land 95 C6
Attadale Ho. H'land 95 C6
Attenborough Notts 41 B7
Atterby Lincs 52 C2
Attercliffe S Yorks 50 D5
Attleborough Norfolk 44 F4
Attleborough Warwick 40 F5
Attlebridge Norfolk 44 D5
Atwick E Riding Yorks 59 C7
Atworth Wilts 18 E5
Aubourn Lincs 52 F2
Auchagallon N Ayrs 73 D8
Auchallater Aberds 90 C2
Aucharnie Aberds 98 D6
Auchattie Aberds 91 B7
Auchavan Angus 90 E2
Auchbraad Arg/Bute 81 F8
Auchbreck Moray 98 F2
Auchenback E Renf 75 B7
Auchenbainzie Dumf/Gal 75 H10
Auchenblae Aberds 91 D8
Auchenbrack Dumf/Gal 75 H9
Auchenbreck Arg/Bute 81 F10
Auchencairn Dumf/Gal 67 E9
Auchencairn Dumf/Gal 68 B2
Auchencairn N Ayrs 74 E2
Auchencrosh S Ayrs 66 C3
Auchencrow Scot Borders 78 A3
Auchendinny Midloth 76 A5
Auchengray S Lanarks 76 B2
Auchenhalrig Moray 98 B3
Auchenheath S Lanarks 75 C10
Auchenlochan Arg/Bute 81 G9
Auchensoul S Ayrs 66 A4
Auchentiber N Ayrs 74 C5
Auchertyre H'land 94 D5
Auchgourish H'land 97 E7
Auchincarroch W Dunb 82 F5
Auchindrain Arg/Bute 81 D10
Auchindrean H'land 103 D9
Auchininna Aberds 98 D6
Auchinleck E Ayrs 75 E7
Auchinloch N Lanarks 83 G7
Auchinroath Moray 98 C2
Auchintoul Aberds 98 G5
Auchiries Aberds 99 E10
Auchlee Aberds 91 B9
Auchleven Aberds 98 F6
Auchlochan S Lanarks 75 D10
Auchlossan Aberds 91 A6
Auchlunies Aberds 91 B9
Auchlyne Stirl 83 B6
Auchmacoy Aberds 99 E9
Auchmair Moray 98 F3
Auchmantle Dumf/Gal 66 D3
Auchmillan E Ayrs 75 E7
Auchmithie Angus 91 G7
Auchmuirbridge Fife 84 D4
Auchmull Angus 91 D6
Auchnacree Angus 90 E5
Auchnagallin H'land 97 C8
Auchnagatt Aberds 99 D9
Auchnaha Arg/Bute 81 F9
Auchnashelloch Perth/Kinr 83 C8
Aucholzie Aberds 90 B4
Auchroisk H'land 97 D8
Auchronie Angus 90 C5
Auchterarder Perth/Kinr 83 C10
Auchteraw H'land 96 F1
Auchterderran Fife 84 E4
Auchterhouse Angus 90 H4
Auchtermuchty Fife 84 C4
Auchterneed H'land 104 G3
Auchtertool Fife 84 E4
Auchtertyre Moray 105 G10
Auchtubh Stirl 83 B6
Auckengill H'land 111 C8
Auckley S Yorks 51 B8
Audenshaw Gtr Man 49 C10
Audlem Ches 39 A7
Audley Staffs 49 G8
Audley End Essex 34 E2
Audley End House Essex 33 E8
Auds Aberds 99 B6
Aughton E Riding Yorks 58 E3
Aughton Lancs 48 B4
Aughton Lancs 55 B5
Aughton S Yorks 51 D6
Aughton Wilts 19 F9
Aughton Park Lancs 48 B5
Auldearn H'land 105 G8
Aulden Heref/Worcs 28 C5
Auldgirth Dumf/Gal 68 B2
Auldhame E Loth 85 F7
Auldhouse S Lanarks 75 B8
Ault a'chruinn H'land 95 D6
Aultanrynie H'land 109 F6
Aultbea H'land 103 D6
Aultdearg H'land 104 F1
Aultgrishan H'land 102 D5
Aultguish Inn H'land 104 E2
Aultibea H'land 110 G5
Aultiphurst H'land 110 C3
Aultmore Moray 98 C4
Aultnagoire H'land 96 D3
Aultnamain Inn H'land 104 D5
Aultnaslat H'land 95 F8
Aulton Aberds 98 F6
Aundorach H'land 97 E7
Aunsby Lincs 42 B3
Auquhorthies Aberds 99 F8
Aust S Gloucs 18 C2
Austendike Lincs 42 C5
Austerfield S Yorks 51 C8
Austrey Warwick 40 E4
Austwick N Yorks 56 B2
Authorpe Lincs 53 D7
Authorpe Row Lincs 53 E8
Avebury Wilts 19 E8
Aveley Essex 22 C5
Avening Glos 18 B5
Averham Notts 51 G9
Aveton Gifford Devon 5 F7
Avielochan H'land 97 E7
Aviemore H'land 97 E6
Avington Berks 20 E1
Avington Hants 11 A8
Avoch H'land 104 G6
Avon Hants 10 E4
Avon Dassett Warwick 31 D6
Avonbridge Falk 83 G10
Avonmouth Bristol 18 D2
Avonwick Devon 5 E8
Awbridge Hants 11 B6
Awhirk Dumf/Gal 66 E2
Awkley S Gloucs 18 C2
Awliscombe Devon 8 D3
Awre Glos 29 H8
Awsworth Notts 41 A6
Axbridge Som'set 17 F9
Axford Hants 20 G4
Axford Wilts 19 D9
Axminster Devon 8 E4
Axmouth Devon 8 E4
Axton Flints 48 D2
Aycliff Kent 15 D8
Aycliffe Durham 63 B7
Aydon Northum 70 D5
Aylburton Glos 18 A3
Ayle Northum 70 F2
Aylesbeare Devon 8 E2
Aylesbury Bucks 31 G10
Aylesby NE Lincs 52 B5
Aylesford Kent 14 C2
Aylesham Kent 15 C7
Aylestone Leics C 41 E7
Aylmerton Norfolk 44 B5
Aylsham Norfolk 44 C5
Aylton Heref/Worcs 29 E7
Aymestrey Heref/Worcs 28 B5
Aynho Northants 31 E7
Ayot St. Lawrence Herts 32 G4
Ayot St. Peter Herts 32 G5
Ayr S Ayrs 74 E5
Aysgarth N Yorks 62 F5
Ayside Cumb 61 F6
Ayston Rutl'd 42 E1
Aythorpe Roding Essex 33 G8
Ayton Scot Borders 78 A4
Aywick Shetl'd 113 E8
Azerley N Yorks 63 G7

B

Babbacombe Devon 5 D10
Babbinswood Shrops 38 B4
Babcary Som'set 9 B7
Babel Carms 27 E8
Babell Flints 48 E2
Babraham Cambs 33 C8
Babworth Notts 51 D8
Bac W Isles 107 E8
Bachau Angl 46 D4
Back of Keppoch H'land 87 C6
Back Rogerton E Ayrs 75 E7
Backaland Orkney 112 E6
Backaskaill Orkney 112 C5
Backbarrow Cumb 61 F6
Backe Carms 25 E7
Backfolds Aberds 99 C10
Backford Ches 48 E5
Backford Cross Ches 48 E4
Backhill Aberds 99 E7
Backhill Aberds 99 E10
Backhill of Clackriach Aberds 99 D9
Backhill of Fortree Aberds 99 D9
Backhill of Trustach Aberds 91 B7
Backies H'land 105 B7
Backlass H'land 111 D7
Backwell N Som'set 17 E9
Backworth Tyne/Wear 71 C8
Bacon End Essex 33 G9
Baconsthorpe Norfolk 44 B5
Bacton Heref/Worcs 28 E4
Bacton Norfolk 45 B7
Bacton Suffolk 34 B4
Bacton Green Suffolk 34 B4
Bacup Lancs 56 F3
Badachro H'land 102 E5
Badanloch Lodge H'land 110 F2
Badavanich H'land 103 G9
Badbury Thamesd'n 19 C8
Badby Northants 31 C7
Badcall H'land 108 D5
Badcaul H'land 103 C8
Baddeley Green Stoke 49 G10
Baddesley Clinton Warwick 30 A4
Baddesley Clinton Hall Warwick 30 A4
Baddesley Ensor Warwick 40 F4
Baddidarach H'land 108 G3
Baddoch Aberds 90 C2
Baddock H'land 105 G6
Badenscoth Aberds 99 E7
Badenyon Aberds 98 G3
Badger Shrops 39 F8
Badger's Mount Kent 22 E4
Badgeworth Glos 29 G10
Badgworth Som'set 17 F8
Badicaul H'land 94 D4
Badingham Suffolk 35 B7
Badlesmere Kent 14 C5
Badlipster H'land 111 E7
Badluarach H'land 103 C7
Badninish H'land 105 C6
Badrallach H'land 103 C8
Badsey Heref/Worcs 30 D2
Badshot Lea Surrey 21 G6
Badsworth W Yorks 57 G9
Badwell Ash Suffolk 34 B3
Bag Enderby Lincs 53 E6
Bagby N Yorks 63 F9
Bagendon Glos 30 H2
Bagh a Chaisteil W Isles 92 F2
Bagh Mor W Isles 100 G4
Bagh Shiarabhagh W Isles 92 E3
Baghasdal W Isles 92 D3
Bagillt Flints 48 E3
Baginton Warwick 30 A5
Baglan Neath P Talb 16 B2
Bagley Shrops 38 C5
Bagnall Staffs 49 G10
Bagnor Berks 20 E2
Bagshot Surrey 21 E7
Bagshot Wilts 19 E10
Bagthorpe Norfolk 44 B1
Bagthorpe Notts 51 G6
Bagworth Leics 41 E6
Bagwy Llydiart Heref/Worcs 28 F5
Bail Uachdraich W Isles 100 F4
Baildon W Yorks 57 E6
Baile W Isles 92 D3
Baile W Isles 100 D5
Baile a Mhanaich W Isles 100 G3
Baile Ailein W Isles 107 G6
Baile an Truiseil W Isles 107 D7
Baile Ard W Isles 107 D8
Baile Boidheach Arg/Bute 81 G7
Baile Glas W Isles 100 G4
Baile Mhartainn W Isles 100 E3
Baile MhicPhail W Isles 100 E4
Baile Mor Arg/Bute 80 B2
Baile Mor W Isles 100 F3
Baile na Creige W Isles 92 E2
Baile nan Cailleach W Isles 100 G3
Baile Raghaill W Isles 100 E3
Baile Ur W Isles 107 E9
Bailebeag H'land 96 E3
Baileyhead Cumb 69 C8
Bailiesward Aberds 98 E4
Baillieston C of Glasg 75 A8
Bainbridge N Yorks 62 E4
Bainsford Falk 83 F9
Bainshole Aberds 98 E6
Bainton Cambs 42 E3
Bainton E Riding Yorks 58 C5
Bairnkine Scot Borders 77 F9
Baker Street Essex 23 C6
Baker's End Herts 33 G6
Bakewell Derbys 50 F4
Bala Gwyn 37 B9
Balachuirn H'land 94 B2
Balavil H'land 96 F5
Balbeg H'land 96 D2
Balbeg H'land 96 C2
Balbeggie Perth/Kinr 84 B3
Balbithan Aberds 99 G7
Balbithan Ho. Aberds 99 G8
Balblair H'land 104 F6
Balby S Yorks 51 B7
Balchers Aberds 99 C7
Balchladich H'land 108 F3
Balchraggan H'land 96 C3
Balchraggan H'land 96 B3
Balchrick H'land 108 D4
Balchrystie Fife 85 D6
Balcombe W Sussex 13 B7
Balcombe Lane W Sussex 13 B7
Balcomie Fife 85 C8
Balcurvie Fife 84 D5
Baldersby N Yorks 63 G8
Baldersby St. James N Yorks 63 G8
Balderstone Lancs 56 E1
Balderton Ches 48 F4
Balderton Notts 51 G10
Baldhu Cornw'l 3 E6
Baldinnie Fife 84 C6
Baldock Herts 32 E5
Baldovie Dundee C 85 A6
Baldrine I of Man 54 E4
Baldslow E Sussex 14 G2
Baldwin I of Man 54 E3
Baldwinholme Cumb 69 E6
Baldwin's Gate Staffs 39 A8
Bale Norfolk 44 B4
Balearn Aberds 99 C10
Balemartine Arg/Bute 86 D1
Balephuil Arg/Bute 86 D1
Balerno C of Edinb 84 H3
Balevullin Arg/Bute 86 D1
Balfield Angus 91 E6
Balfour Orkney 112 G5
Balfron Stirl 83 F6
Balfron Station Stirl 83 F6
Balgaveny Aberds 99 D6
Balgavies Angus 91 F6
Balgonar Fife 84 E2
Balgove Aberds 99 E8
Balgowan H'land 89 B7
Balgown H'land 101 F9
Balgrochan E Dunb 83 G7
Balgy H'land 103 G6
Balhaldie Stirl 83 D9
Balhalgardy Aberds 99 F7
Balham Gtr Lon 22 D2
Balhary Perth/Kinr 90 G3
Baliasta Shetl'd 113 C9
Baligill H'land 110 C3
Balintore Angus 90 F3
Balintore H'land 105 E7
Balintraid H'land 104 E6
Balk N Yorks 63 F9
Balkeerie Angus 90 G4
Balkemback Angus 90 H4
Balkholme E Riding Yorks 58 F3
Balkissock S Ayrs 66 B3
Ball Shrops 38 C4
Ball Haye Green Staffs 50 G1
Ball Hill Hants 20 E2
Ballabeg I of Man 54 F2
Ballacannel I of Man 54 E4
Ballachulish H'land 88 F1
Ballajora I of Man 54 D4
Ballaleigh I of Man 54 E3
Ballamodha I of Man 54 F2
Ballantrae S Ayrs 66 B2
Ballaquine I of Man 54 E4
Ballards Gore Essex 23 B9
Ballasalla I of Man 54 D3
Ballasalla I of Man 54 F2
Ballater Aberds 90 B4
Ballaugh I of Man 54 D3
Ballaveare I of Man 54 F3
Ballcorach Moray 97 D9
Ballechin Perth/Kinr 89 F10
Balleigh H'land 104 D6
Ballencrieff E Loth 85 G6
Ballentoul Perth/Kinr 89 E9
Ballidon Derbys 50 G4
Balliemore Arg/Bute 82 F1
Balliemore Arg/Bute 81 B8
Ballikinrain Stirl 83 F6
Ballimeanoch Arg/Bute 81 C10
Ballimore Arg/Bute 81 F9
Ballimore Stirl 83 C6
Ballinaby Arg/Bute 80 H2
Ballindean Perth/Kinr 84 B4
Ballingdon Suffolk 34 D2
Ballinger Common Bucks 21 A7
Ballingham Heref/Worcs 29 E6
Ballingry Fife 84 E3
Ballinlick Perth/Kinr 89 G10
Ballinluig Perth/Kinr 89 F10
Ballintuim Perth/Kinr 90 F2
Balloch Angus 90 F4
Balloch W Dunb 82 F4
Balloch H'land 96 B5
Balloch N Lanarks 83 G8
Balloch Perth/Kinr 83 C9
Ballochan Aberds 91 B6
Ballochford Moray 98 E3
Ballochmorrie S Ayrs 66 B4
Ballochroy Arg/Bute 73 B7
Balls Cross W Sussex 12 C3
Balls Green Essex 34 F4
Ballygown Arg/Bute 86 G4
Ballygrant Arg/Bute 80 H3
Ballyhaugh Arg/Bute 86 F1
Ballymichael N Ayrs 73 D9
Balmacara H'land 94 D5
Balmacara Square H'land 94 D5
Balmaclellan Dumf/Gal 67 C8
Balmacneil Perth/Kinr 89 F10
Balmacqueen H'land 101 E10
Balmae Dumf/Gal 67 F8
Balmaha Stirl 82 E5
Balmalcolm Fife 84 D5
Balmeanach H'land 94 B2
Balmedie Aberds 99 G9
Balmer Heath Shrops 38 B5
Balmerino Fife 84 B5
Balmerlawn Hants 11 D6
Balmirmer Angus 91 H6
Balmoral Castle and Gardens Aberds 90 B3
Balmore H'land 93 A8
Balmore H'land 96 C1
Balmore H'land 97 B6
Balmore Perth/Kinr 89 F10
Balmule Fife 84 F4
Balmullo Fife 84 B6
Balmungie H'land 104 G6
Balnaboth Angus 90 E4
Balnabruaich H'land 105 F6
Balnabruich H'land 111 G6
Balnacoil H'land 105 A7
Balnacra H'land 95 B6
Balnafoich H'land 96 C4
Balnagall H'land 105 D7
Balnaguard Perth/Kinr 89 F10
Balnaguisich H'land 104 E5
Balnahard Arg/Bute 80 E4
Balnahard Arg/Bute 80 A4
Balnain H'land 96 C2
Balnakeil H'land 109 C6
Balnaknock H'land 101 F10
Balnapaling H'land 105 F6
Balne N Yorks 58 G1
Balone Fife 85 C6
Balornock C of Glasg 83 H7
Balquharn Perth/Kinr 89 H11
Balquhidder Stirl 83 B6
Balsall W Midlands 40 H4
Balsall Common W Midlands 40 H4
Balsall Hth. W Midlands 40 G2
Balscott Oxon 30 D5
Balsham Cambs 33 C8
Baltasound Shetl'd 113 C9
Balterley Staffs 49 G8
Baltersan Dumf/Gal 67 D6
Balthangie Aberds 99 C8
Baltonsborough Som'set 9 A7
Balvaird H'land 104 G4
Balvicar Arg/Bute 81 C7
Balvraid H'land 94 E5
Balvraid H'land 97 C6
Bamber Bridge Lancs 55 F5
Bambers Green Essex 33 F8
Bamburgh Northum 79 D6
Bamburgh Castle Northum 79 D6
Bamff Perth/Kinr 90 F3
Bamford Derbys 50 D4
Bamford Gtr Man 56 G3
Bampton Cumb 61 C8
Bampton Devon 8 B1
Bampton Oxon 19 A10
Bampton Grange Cumb 61 C8
Banavie H'land 88 D2
Banbury Oxon 31 D6
Bancffosfelen Carms 25 E9
Banchory Aberds 91 B7
Banchory-Devenick Aberds 91 A10
Bancycapel Carms 25 E9
Bancyfelin Carms 25 E8
Bancyffordd Carms 25 C9
Banff Aberds 99 B6
Bangor Gwyn 46 E5
Bangor-is-y-coed Wrex 48 H4
Banham Norfolk 44 G4
Banham Zoo, Diss Norfolk 44 G4
Bank Hants 10 D5
Bank Newton N Yorks 56 C4
Bank Street Heref/Worcs 29 B7
Bankend Dumf/Gal 68 D3
Bankfoot Perth/Kinr 90 H1
Bankglen E Ayrs 75 F8
Bankhead Aberd C 99 G8
Bankhead Aberds 99 H6
Banknock Falk 83 G8
Banks Cumb 69 D8
Banks Lancs 55 F3
Bankshill Dumf/Gal 68 B4
Banningham Norfolk 45 C6
Banniskirk Ho. H'land 111 D6
Bannister Green Essex 33 F9
Bannockburn Stirl 83 E9
Banstead Surrey 22 F2
Bantham Devon 5 F7
Banton N Lanarks 83 G8
Banwell N Som'set 17 F8
Banyard's Green Suffolk 35 A6
Bapchild Kent 14 B4
Bar Hill Cambs 33 B6
Barabhas W Isles 107 E7
Barabhas Iarach W Isles 107 E7
Barabhas Uarach W Isles 107 D7
Barachandroman Arg/Bute 81 B6
Barassie S Ayrs 74 D5
Baravullin Arg/Bute 87 H8
Barbaraville H'land 104 E6
Barber Booth Derbys 50 D3
Barbieston S Ayrs 75 F6
Barbon Cumb 61 F9
Barbridge Ches 49 G7
Barbrook Devon 7 B8
Barby Northants 31 A7
Barcaldine Arg/Bute 87 G9
Barcaldine Sea Life Centre Arg/Bute 87 G9
Barcheston Warwick 30 E4
Barcombe E Sussex 13 D8
Barcombe Cross E Sussex 13 D8
Barden N Yorks 63 E6
Barden Scale N Yorks 56 C5
Bardennoch Dumf/Gal 67 A7
Bardfield Saling Essex 33 F9
Bardister Shetl'd 113 F6
Bardney Lincs 52 F4
Bardon Leics 41 D6
Bardon Mill Northum 70 D2
Bardowie E Dunb 83 G6
Bardrainney Invercl 82 G4
Bardsea Cumb 61 G6
Bardsey W Yorks 57 D8
Bardwell Suffolk 34 A3
Bare Lancs 55 B4
Barfad Arg/Bute 81 H8
Barford Norfolk 44 E5
Barford Warwick 30 B4
Barford St. John Oxon 31 E6
Barford St. Martin Wilts 10 A3
Barford St. Michael Oxon 31 E6
Barfreston Kent 15 C7
Bargoed Caerph 17 B6
Bargrennan Dumf/Gal 66 C5
Barham Cambs 42 H4
Barham Kent 15 C7
Barham Suffolk 34 C5
Barharrow Dumf/Gal 67 E8
Barhill Dumf/Gal 67 D10
Barholm Lincs 42 D3
Barkby Leics 41 E8
Barkestone-le-Vale Leics 41 B9
Barkham Berks 20 E5
Barking Gtr Lon 22 C4
Barking Suffolk 34 C4
Barking Tye Suffolk 34 C4
Barkingside Gtr Lon 22 C4
Barkisland W Yorks 56 G5
Barkston Lincs 42 A2
Barkston N Yorks 57 E9
Barkway Herts 33 E6
Barlaston Staffs 39 B9
Barlavington W Sussex 12 D3
Barlborough Derbys 51 E6
Barlby N Yorks 58 E2
Barlestone Leics 41 E6
Barley Herts 33 E6
Barley Lancs 56 D3
Barley Mow Tyne/Wear 71 E7
Barleythorpe Rutl'd 41 E10
Barling Essex 23 C9
Barlow Derbys 50 E5
Barlow N Yorks 58 F2
Barlow Tyne/Wear 71 D6
Barmby Moor E Riding Yorks 58 D3
Barmby on the Marsh E Riding Yorks 58 F2
Barmer Norfolk 44 B2
Barmoor Castle Northum 78 D4
Barmoor Lane End Northum 78 D5
Barmouth Gwyn 37 D6
Barmpton Durham 63 C8
Barmston E Riding Yorks 59 C7
Barnack Cambs 42 E3
Barnacle Warwick 40 G5
Barnard Castle Durham 62 C5
Barnard Gate Oxon 31 G6
Barnardiston Suffolk 33 D10
Barnbarroch Dumf/Gal 67 E10
Barnburgh S Yorks 51 B6
Barnby Suffolk 45 G8
Barnby Dun S Yorks 51 B8
Barnby in the Willows Notts 52 G1
Barnby Moor Notts 51 D8
Barnes Street Kent 23 G6
Barnet Gtr Lon 22 B2
Barnetby le Wold N Lincs 52 B3
Barney Norfolk 44 B3
Barnham Suffolk 44 H2
Barnham W Sussex 12 E3
Barnham Broom Norfolk 44 E4
Barnhead Angus 91 F7
Barnhill Ches 48 G5
Barnhill Dundee C 85 A6
Barnhill Moray 105 G10
Barnhills Dumf/Gal 66 C1
Barningham Durham 62 C5
Barningham Suffolk 44 H3
Barnoldby le Beck NE Lincs 52 B5
Barnoldswick Lancs 56 D3
Barns Green W Sussex 12 C5
Barnsley Glos 30 H2
Barnsley S Yorks 50 B5
Barnstaple Devon 7 C6
Barnston Essex 33 G9
Barnston Mersey 48 D3
Barnstone Notts 41 B9
Barnt Green Heref/Worcs 30 A2
Barnton Ches 49 E7
Barnton C of Edinb 84 G3
Barnwell All Saints Northants 42 G3
Barnwell St. Andrew Northants 42 G3
Barnwood Glos 29 G9
Barochreal Arg/Bute 81 B8
Barons Cross Heref/Worcs 28 C5
Barr S Ayrs 66 A4
Barra Castle Aberds 99 F7
Barrachan Dumf/Gal 66 F5
Barrack Aberds 99 D8
Barraglom W Isles 106 F5
Barrahormid Arg/Bute 81 F7
Barran Arg/Bute 81 B8
Barrapol Arg/Bute 86 D1
Barras Aberds 91 C9
Barras Cumb 62 C3
Barrasford Northum 70 C4
Barravullin Arg/Bute 81 D8
Barregarrow I of Man 54 E3
Barrhead E Renf 75 B6
Barrhill S Ayrs 66 B4
Barrington Cambs 33 D6
Barrington Som'set 8 C5
Barripper Cornw'l 2 F5
Barrmill N Ayrs 74 B5
Barrock H'land 111 B7
Barrock Ho. H'land 111 C7
Barrow Lancs 56 E2
Barrow Rutl'd 42 D1
Barrow Suffolk 34 B1
Barrow Green Kent 14 B4
Barrow Gurney N Som'set 18 E2
Barrow Haven N Lincs 59 F6
Barrow-in-Furness Cumb 55 B2
Barrow Island Cumb 55 B1
Barrow Nook Lancs 48 B5
Barrow Street Wilts 9 A10
Barrow upon Humber N Lincs 59 F6
Barrow upon Soar Leics 41 D7
Barrow upon Trent Derbys 40 C5
Barroway Drove Norfolk 43 E8
Barrowburn Northum 78 F3
Barrowby Lincs 42 B1
Barrowcliff N Yorks 65 F8
Barrowden Rutl'd 42 E2
Barrowford Lancs 56 E3
Barrows Green Ches 49 G7
Barrow's Green Ches 49 D6
Barrows Green Cumb 61 F8
Barry Angus 85 A7
Barry V of Glam 17 E6
Barry Island V of Glam 17 E6
Barsby Leics 41 D8
Barsham Suffolk 45 G7
Barston W Midlands 40 H4
Bartestree Heref/Worcs 29 D6
Barthol Chapel Aberds 99 E8
Barthomley Ches 49 G8
Bartley Hants 11 C6
Bartley Green W Midlands 40 G2
Bartlow Cambs 33 D8
Barton Cambs 33 C7
Barton Ches 48 G5
Barton Devon 5 D10
Barton Glos 30 F3
Barton Lancs 48 B4
Barton Lancs 55 E5
Barton N Yorks 63 D7
Barton Oxon 31 H7
Barton Warwick 30 C3
Barton Bendish Norfolk 43 E10
Barton Hartshorn Bucks 31 E8
Barton in Fabis Notts 41 B7
Barton in the Beans Leics 40 E5
Barton-le-Clay Beds 32 E3
Barton-le-Street N Yorks 64 G5
Barton-le-Willows N Yorks 58 B3
Barton Mills Suffolk 33 A10
Barton on Sea Hants 10 E5
Barton on the Heath Warwick 30 E4
Barton Seagrave Northants 42 H1
Barton St. David Som'set 9 A7
Barton Stacey Hants 20 G2
Barton Turf Norfolk 45 C7
Barton-under-Needwood Staffs 40 D3
Barton-upon-Humber N Lincs 59 F6
Barton Waterside N Lincs 59 F6
Barugh S Yorks 50 B5
Barway Cambs 43 H8
Barwell Leics 41 F6
Barwick Herts 33 G6
Barwick Som'set 9 C7
Barwick in Elmet W Yorks 57 E8
Baschurch Shrops 38 C5
Bascote Warwick 31 B6
Basford Green Staffs 50 G1
Bashall Eaves Lancs 56 D1
Bashley Hants 10 E5
Basildon Essex 23 C7
Basingstoke Hants 20 F4
Baslow Derbys 50 E4
Bason Bridge Som'set 17 G8
Bassaleg Newp 17 C7
Bassenthwaite Cumb 68 G5
Bassett S'thampton 11 C7
Bassingbourn Cambs 33 D6
Bassingfield Notts 41 B8
Bassingham Lincs 52 F2
Bassingthorpe Lincs 42 C2
Basta Shetl'd 113 D8
Baston Lincs 42 D4
Bastwick Norfolk 45 D8
Baswick Steer E Riding Yorks 59 D6
Batchworth Heath Herts 21 B8
Batcombe Dorset 9 D8
Batcombe Som'set 18 H3
Bate Heath Ches 49 E7
Bateman's, Burwash E Sussex 14 F1
Batford Herts 32 G4
Bath Bath/NE Som'set 18 E4
Bath Abbey Bath/NE Som'set 18 E4
Bathampton Bath/NE Som'set 18 E4
Bathealton Som'set 8 B2
Batheaston Bath/NE Som'set 18 E4
Bathford Bath/NE Som'set 18 E4
Bathgate W Loth 83 H10
Bathley Notts 51 G9
Bathpool Cornw'l 4 C3
Bathpool Som'set 8 B4
Bathville W Loth 83 H10
Batley W Yorks 57 F7
Batsford Glos 30 E3
Battersby N Yorks 64 D3
Battersea Gtr Lon 22 D2
Battisborough Cross Devon 5 F6
Battisford Suffolk 34 C4
Battisford Tye Suffolk 34 C4
Battle E Sussex 14 G2
Battle Powys 27 E10
Battle Abbey E Sussex 14 G2
Battledown Glos 30 F1
Battlefield Shrops 39 D6
Battlesbridge Essex 23 B7
Battlesden Beds 32 F2
Battlesea Green Suffolk 45 H6
Battleton Som'set 7 D10
Battramsley Hants 11 E6
Baughton Heref/Worcs 29 D9
Baughurst Hants 20 F3
Baulking Oxon 19 B10
Baumber Lincs 52 E5
Baunton Glos 19 A7
Baverstock Wilts 10 A3
Bawburgh Norfolk 44 E5
Bawdeswell Norfolk 44 C4
Bawdrip Som'set 17 H8
Bawdsey Suffolk 35 D7
Bawtry S Yorks 51 C8
Baxenden Lancs 56 F2
Baxterley Warwick 40 F4
Baybridge Hants 11 B8
Baycliff Cumb 60 G5
Baydon Wilts 19 D9
Bayford Herts 33 H6
Bayford Som'set 9 B9
Bayles Cumb 70 F2
Baylham Suffolk 34 C5
Baynard's Green Oxon 31 F7
Bayston Hill Shrops 38 E5
Baythorn End Essex 33 D10
Bayton Heref/Worcs 29 A7
Beach H'land 87 F7
Beachampton Bucks 31 E9
Beachamwell Norfolk 44 E1
Beachans Moray 97 B8
Beachborough Kent 15 E6
Beachley Glos 18 B2
Beachmenach Arg/Bute 73 C6
Beacon Devon 8 D3
Beacon End Essex 34 F3
Beacon Hill Surrey 12 B2
Beacon's Bottom Bucks 20 B5
Beaconsfield Bucks 21 C7
Beadlam N Yorks 64 F4
Beadlow Beds 32 E4
Beadnell Northum 79 E7
Beaford Devon 7 E6
Beal Northum 78 C5
Beal N Yorks 57 F10
Beale Park, Goring Berks 20 D4
Beamhurst Staffs 40 B2
Beaminster Dorset 9 D6
Beamish Durham 71 E7
Beamish Open Air Museum, Stanley Durham 71 E7
Beamsley N Yorks 56 C5
Bean Kent 22 D5
Beanacre Wilts 19 E6
Beanley Northum 78 F5
Beaquoy Orkney 112 F4
Bear Cross Bournem'th 10 E3
Beardwood Lancs 56 F1
Beare Green Surrey 21 G9
Bearley Warwick 30 B3
Bearnus Arg/Bute 86 G3
Bearpark Durham 71 F7
Bearsbridge Northum 70 E2
Bearsden E Dunb 83 G6
Bearsted Kent 14 C2
Bearstone Shrops 39 B8
Bearwood Heref/Worcs 28 C4
Bearwood Poole 10 E3
Bearwood W Midlands 40 G2
Beattock Dumf/Gal 76 G3
Beauchamp Roding Essex 33 G8
Beauchief S Yorks 50 D5
Beaufort Bl Gwent 28 G2
Beaufort Castle H'land 96 B3
Beaulieu Hants 11 D6
Beauly H'land 96 B3
Beaumaris Angl 47 E6
Beaumaris Castle Angl 47 E6
Beaumont Cumb 69 E6
Beaumont Essex 34 F5
Beaumont Hill Durham 63 C7
Beausale Warwick 30 A4
Beauworth Hants 11 B8
Beaworthy Devon 6 G5
Beazley End Essex 33 F10
Bebington Mersey 48 D4
Bebside Northum 71 B7
Beccles Suffolk 45 F8
Becconsall Lancs 55 F4
Beck Foot Cumb 61 E9
Beck Hole N Yorks 65 D6
Beck Row Suffolk 43 H9
Beck Side Cumb 60 F5
Beckbury Shrops 39 E8
Beckenham Gtr Lon 22 E3
Beckermet Cumb 60 D3
Beckfoot Cumb 60 D4
Beckfoot Cumb 68 F3
Beckford Heref/Worcs 30 E1
Beckhampton Wilts 19 E7
Beckingham Lincs 52 G1
Beckingham Notts 51 D9
Beckington Som'set 18 F5
Beckley E Sussex 14 F3
Beckley Hants 10 E5
Beckley Oxon 31 G7
Beckton Gtr Lon 22 C4
Beckwithshaw N Yorks 57 C7
Becontree Gtr Lon 22 C4
Bed-y-coedwr Gwyn 37 C7
Bedale N Yorks 63 F7
Bedburn Durham 71 G6
Bedchester Dorset 10 C1
Beddau Caerph 17 C6
Beddau Rh Cyn Taff 16 C5
Beddgelert Gwyn 46 H5
Beddingham E Sussex 13 E8
Beddington Gtr Lon 22 E3
Bedfield Suffolk 35 B6
Bedford Beds 32 C3
Bedham W Sussex 12 C4
Bedhampton Hants 11 D10
Bedingfield Suffolk 34 B5
Bedlam N Yorks 57 B7
Bedlington Northum 71 B7
Bedlington Station Northum 71 B7
Bedlinog Merth Tyd 16 A5
Bedminster Bristol 18 D2
Bedmond Herts 21 A8
Bednall Staffs 40 D1
Bedrule Scot Borders 77 F9
Bedstone Shrops 38 H4
Bedwas Caerph 17 C6
Bedworth Warwick 40 G5
Bedworth Little Heath Warwick 40 G5
Beeby Leics 41 E8
Beech Hants 20 H4
Beech Staffs 39 B9
Beech Hill Berks 20 E4
Beech Hill Gtr Man 49 B6
Beechingstoke Wilts 19 F7
Beedon Berks 20 D2
Beeford E Riding Yorks 59 C7
Beeley Derbys 50 F4
Beelsby NE Lincs 52 B5
Beenham Berks 20 E3
Beeny Cornw'l 6 G2
Beer Devon 8 F4
Beer Hackett Dorset 9 C7
Beercrocombe Som'set 8 B5
Beesands Devon 5 F9
Beesby Lincs 53 D7
Beeson Devon 5 F9
Beeston Beds 32 D4
Beeston Ches 49 G6
Beeston Norfolk 44 D3
Beeston Notts 41 B7
Beeston W Yorks 57 E7
Beeston Castle Ches 49 G6
Beeston Regis Norfolk 44 A5
Beeswing Dumf/Gal 68 D1
Beetham Cumb 61 G7
Beetley Norfolk 44 D3
Begbroke Oxon 31 G6
Begelly Pembs 24 F6
Beggar's Bush Powys 28 B3
Beguildy Powys 38 H2
Beicribhig W Isles 101 C7
Beighton Norfolk 45 E7
Beighton S Yorks 51 D6
Beighton Hill Derbys 50 G4
Beith N Ayrs 74 B5
Bekesbourne Kent 15 C6
Bekonscot Model Village, Beaconsfield Bucks 21 B7
Belaugh Norfolk 45 D6
Belbroughton Heref/Worcs 39 H10
Belchamp Otten Essex 34 D2
Belchamp St. Paul Essex 34 D1
Belchamp Walter Essex 34 D2
Belchford Lincs 52 E5
Belford Northum 79 D6
Belhelvie Aberds 99 G9
Belhinnie Aberds 98 F4
Bell Bar Herts 32 H5
Bell Busk N Yorks 56 C4
Bell End Heref/Worcs 39 H10
Bell o'th'Hill Ches 49 H6
Bellabeg Aberds 98 G3
Bellanoch Arg/Bute 81 E7
Bellaty Angus 90 F3
Belleau Lincs 53 E7
Bellehiglash Moray 97 C9
Bellerby N Yorks 63 E6
Bellever Devon 5 C7
Bellhaven E Loth 85 G8
Belliehill Angus 91 E6
Bellingdon Bucks 32 H2
Bellingham Northum 70 B3
Belloch Arg/Bute 73 D6
Bellochantuy Arg/Bute 73 D6
Bells Yew Green E Sussex 13 B10
Bellsbank E Ayrs 75 G6
Bellshill N Lanarks 75 A9
Bellshill Northum 79 D6
Bellspool Scot Borders 76 D4
Bellsquarry W Loth 84 H2
Bellymore S Ayrs 66 B4
Belmaduthy H'land 104 G5
Belmesthorpe Rutl'd 42 D3
Belmont Gtr Lon 22 E2
Belmont Lancs 56 G1
Belmont S Ayrs 74 E5
Belmont Shetl'd 113 C8
Belnacraig Aberds 98 G3
Belowda Cornw'l 3 C8
Belper Derbys 50 H5
Belper Lane End Derbys 50 H5
Belsay Northum 71 C6
Belsay Hall Northum 70 C5
Belses Scot Borders 77 E8
Belsford Devon 5 E8
Belstead Suffolk 34 D5
Belston S Ayrs 74 E5
Belstone Devon 7 G7
Belthorn Lancs 56 F2
Beltinge Kent 15 B6
Beltoft N Lincs 51 B10
Belton Leics 41 C6
Belton Lincs 42 B2
Belton N Lincs 51 B9
Belton Norfolk 45 E8
Belton House, Grantham Lincs 42 B2
Belton in Rutland Rutl'd 41 E10
Beltring Kent 14 D1
Belvedere Gtr Lon 22 D4
Belvoir Leics 41 B10
Belvoir Leics 41 B10
Bembridge I of Wight 11 F9
Bemersyde Scot Borders 77 D8
Bemerton Wilts 10 A4
Bempton E Riding Yorks 65 G9
Ben Alder Lodge H'land 89 D6
Ben Armine Lodge H'land 110 H2
Ben Casgro W Isles 107 G8
Benacre Suffolk 45 G9
Benbuie Dumf/Gal 75 H9
Bendronaig Lodge H'land 95 C7
Benenden Kent 14 E3
Benfield Dumf/Gal 66 D5
Bengate Norfolk 45 C7
Bengeworth Heref/Worcs 30 D2
Benhall Green Suffolk 35 B7
Benhall Street Suffolk 35 B7
Benholm Aberds 91 E9
Beningbrough N Yorks 57 C10
Beningbrough Hall N Yorks 57 C10
Benington Herts 32 F5
Benington Lincs 53 H6
Benllech Angl 46 D5
Benmore Arg/Bute 82 F2
Benmore Stirl 82 B5
Benmore Lodge H'land 104 A2
Bennacott Cornw'l 6 G3
Bennan N Ayrs 73 E9
Benniworth Lincs 52 D5
Benover Kent 14 D2
Bensham Tyne/Wear 71 D7
Benson Oxon 20 B4
Bent Aberds 91 D7
Bent Gate Lancs 56 F2
Benthall Northum 79 E7
Benthall Shrops 39 E7
Bentham Glos 29 G10
Benthoul Aberd C 91 A9
Bentlawnt Shrops 38 E4
Bentley E Riding Yorks 59 E6
Bentley Hants 20 G5
Bentley Heref/Worcs 30 B1
Bentley Suffolk 34 E5
Bentley S Yorks 51 B7
Bentley Warwick 40 F4
Bentley Heath W Midlands 40 H3
Benton Devon 7 C7
Bentpath Dumf/Gal 69 A6
Bents W Loth 76 A2
Bentworth Hants 20 G4
Benvie Dundee C 84 A5
Benwick Cambs 43 F6
Beoley Heref/Worcs 30 B2
Beoraidbeg H'land 87 B6
Bepton W Sussex 12 D2
Berden Essex 33 F7
Bere Alston Devon 4 D5
Bere Ferrers Devon 4 D5
Bere Regis Dorset 9 E10
Berepper Cornw'l 2 G5
Bergh Apton Norfolk 45 E7
Berinsfield Oxon 20 B3
Berkeley Glos 18 B3
Berkhamsted Herts 32 H2
Berkley Som'set 18 G5
Berkswell W Midlands 40 H4
Bermondsey Gtr Lon 22 D3
Bernera H'land 94 D5
Bernice Arg/Bute 82 E2
Bernisdale H'land 101 G10
Berrick Salome Oxon 20 B4
Berriedale H'land 111 G6
Berrier Cumb 61 B6
Berriew Powys 38 E2
Berrington Northum 78 C5
Berrington Shrops 39 E6
Berrow Som'set 17 F8
Berrow Green Heref/Worcs 29 C8
Berry Down Cross Devon 7 B6
Berry Hill Glos 29 G6
Berry Hill Pembs 24 B5
Berry Pomeroy Devon 5 D9
Berryhillock Moray 98 B5
Berrynarbor Devon 7 B6
Bersham Wrex 48 H4
Berstane Orkney 112 G5
Berwick E Sussex 13 E9
Berwick Bassett Wilts 19 D7
Berwick Hill Northum 71 C6
Berwick St. James Wilts 19 H7
Berwick St. John Wilts 10 B2
Berwick St. Leonard Wilts 10 A2
Berwick-upon-Tweed Northum 78 B4
Bescar Lancs 55 G3
Besford Heref/Worcs 29 D10
Bessacarr S Yorks 51 B8
Bessels Leigh Oxon 20 A2
Bessingby E Riding Yorks 59 B7
Bessingham Norfolk 44 B5
Bestbeech Hill E Sussex 13 B10
Besthorpe Norfolk 44 F4
Besthorpe Notts 51 F10
Bestwood Notts 41 A7
Bestwood Village Notts 51 H7
Beswick E Riding Yorks 59 D6
Betchworth Surrey 22 G2
Bethania Ceredig'n 26 B5
Bethania Gwyn 47 G6
Bethania Gwyn 47 H7
Bethel Angl 46 E3
Bethel Gwyn 46 F5
Bethel Gwyn 37 B9
Bethersden Kent 14 D4
Bethesda Gwyn 47 F6
Bethesda Pembs 24 E5
Bethlehem Carms 27 F6
Bethnal Green Gtr Lon 22 C3
Betley Staffs 49 H8
Betsham Kent 23 D6
Betteshanger Kent 15 C8
Bettiscombe Dorset 8 E5
Bettisfield Wrex 38 B5
Betton Shrops 38 E4
Betton Shrops 39 B7
Bettws Newp 17 B7
Bettws Cedewain Powys 38 F2
Bettws Gwerfil Goch Denbs 47 H10
Bettws Ifan Ceredig'n 25 B8
Bettws Newydd Monmouths 28 H4
Bettws-y-crwyn Shrops 38 G3
Bettyhill H'land 110 C2
Betws Bridg 16 C4
Betws Carms 27 G6
Betws Bledrws Ceredig'n 26 C5
Betws-Garmon Gwyn 46 G5
Betws-y-coed Conwy 47 G7
Betws-yn-Rhos Conwy 47 E9
Beulah Ceredig'n 25 B7
Beulah Powys 27 C9
Bevendean Brighton/Hove 13 E7
Bevercotes Notts 51 E8
Beverley E Riding Yorks 59 E6
Beverley Minster E Riding Yorks 59 E6
Beverston Glos 18 B5
Bevington Glos 18 B3
Bewaldeth Cumb 68 G5
Bewcastle Cumb 69 C8
Bewdley Heref/Worcs 39 H8
Bewerley N Yorks 57 B6
Bewholme E Riding Yorks 59 C7
Bexhill E Sussex 14 H2
Bexley Gtr Lon 22 D4
Bexleyheath Gtr Lon 22 D4
Bexwell Norfolk 43 E9
Beyton Suffolk 34 B3
Bhaltos W Isles 106 F4
Bhatarsaigh W Isles 92 F2
Bibury Glos 30 H3
Bicester Oxon 31 F7
Bickenhall Som'set 8 C4
Bickenhill W Midlands 40 G3
Bicker Lincs 42 B5
Bickershaw Gtr Man 49 B7
Bickerstaffe Lancs 48 B5
Bickerton Ches 49 G6
Bickerton N Yorks 57 C9
Bickington Devon 5 C8
Bickington Devon 7 C6
Bickleigh Devon 7 F10
Bickleigh Devon 5 D6
Bickleton Devon 7 C6
Bickley Gtr Lon 22 E4
Bickley Moss Ches 49 H6
Bicknacre Essex 23 A7
Bicknoller Som'set 17 H6
Bicknor Kent 14 C3
Bickton Hants 10 C4
Bicton Shrops 38 D5
Bicton Shrops 38 G3
Bicton Park Gradens Devon 8 F2
Bidborough Kent 22 G5
Biddenden Kent 14 E3
Biddenham Beds 32 D3
Biddestone Wilts 18 D5
Biddisham Som'set 17 F8
Biddlesden Bucks 31 D8
Biddlestone Northum 78 G4
Biddulph Staffs 49 G9
Biddulph Moor Staffs 49 G10
Bideford Devon 6 D5
Bidford on Avon Warwick 30 C3
Bidston Mersey 48 C3
Bielby E Riding Yorks 58 D3
Bieldside Aberd C 91 A9
Bierley I of Wight 11 G8
Bierly W Yorks 57 E6
Bierton Bucks 31 G10
Big Sand H'land 102 E5
Bigbury Devon 5 F7
Bigbury on Sea Devon 5 F7
Bigby Lincs 52 B3
Biggar Cumb 55 B1
Biggar S Lanarks 76 D3
Biggin Derbys 50 G3
Biggin Derbys 50 H4
Biggin N Yorks 57 E10
Biggin Hill Gtr Lon 22 F4
Biggings Shetl'd 113 G4
Biggleswade Beds 32 D4
Bighouse H'land 110 C3
Bighton Hants 11 A9
Bignor W Sussex 12 D3
Bigton Shetl'd 113 L6
Bilberry Cornw'l 3 C9
Bilborough Notts 41 A7
Bilbrook Som'set 16 G5
Bilbrough N Yorks 57 D10
Bilbster H'land 111 D7
Bildershaw Durham 63 B7
Bildeston Suffolk 34 D3
Billericay Essex 23 B6
Billesdon Leics 41 E9
Billesley Warwick 30 C3
Billingborough Lincs 42 B4
Billinge Mersey 49 B6
Billingford Norfolk 44 C4
Billingham Stockton 63 B9
Billinghay Lincs 52 G4
Billingley S Yorks 51 B6
Billingshurst W Sussex 12 C4
Billingsley Shrops 39 G8
Billington Beds 32 F2
Billington Lancs 56 E2
Billockby Norfolk 45 D8
Billy Row Durham 71 G6
Bilsborrow Lancs 55 E5
Bilsby Lincs 53 E7
Bilsham W Sussex 12 E3
Bilsington Kent 14 E5
Bilson Green Glos 29 G7
Bilsthorpe Notts 51 F8
Bilsthorpe Moor Notts 51 G8
Bilston Midloth 76 A5
Bilston W Midlands 40 F1
Bilstone Leics 40 E5
Bilting Kent 14 D5
Bilton E Riding Yorks 59 E7
Bilton Northum 79 F7
Bilton N Yorks 57 D9
Bilton Warwick 31 A6
Bimbister Orkney 112 G4
Binbrook Lincs 52 C5
Binchester Blocks Durham 71 G7
Bincombe Dorset 9 F8
Bindal H'land 105 D8
Binegar Som'set 18 G3
Binfield Berks 21 D6
Binfield Hth. Oxon 20 D5
Bingfield Northum 70 C4
Bingham Notts 41 B9
Bingley W Yorks 57 E6
Bings Heath Shrops 39 D6
Binham Norfolk 44 B3
Binley Hants 20 F2
Binley W Midlands 40 H5
Binley Woods Warwick 40 H5
Binniehill Falk 83 G9
Binsoe N Yorks 63 G7
Binstead I of Wight 11 E8
Binsted Hants 20 G5
Binton Warwick 30 C3
Bintree Norfolk 44 C4
Binweston Shrops 38 E4
Birch Essex 34 G3
Birch Gtr Man 49 B9
Birch Green Essex 34 G3
Birch Heath Ches 49 F6
Birch Hill Ches 49 E6
Birch Vale Derbys 50 D2
Bircham Newton Norfolk 44 B1
Bircham Tofts Norfolk 44 B1
Birchanger Essex 33 F8
Birchencliffe W Yorks 57 G6
Bircher Heref/Worcs 28 B5
Birchfield H'land 97 D7
Birchgrove Card 17 D6
Birchgrove Swan 16 B2
Birchington Kent 15 B7
Birchmoor Warwick 40 E4
Birchover Derbys 50 F4
Birchwood Ches 49 C7
Birchwood Lincs 52 F2
Bircotes Notts 51 C8
Birdbrook Essex 33 D10
Birdforth N Yorks 63 G9
Birdham W Sussex 12 F2
Birdholme Derbys 50 F5
Birdingbury Warwick 31 B6
Birdland Park, Bourton-on-the-Water Glos 30 F3
Birdlip Glos 29 G10
Birds Edge W Yorks 50 B4
Birdsall N Yorks 58 B4
Birdsgreen Shrops 39 G8
Birdsmoor Gate Dorset 8 D5
Birdston E Dunb 83 G7
Birdwell S Yorks 50 B5
Birdwood Glos 29 G8
Birdworld and Underwaterworld, Farnham Hants 21 G6
Birgham Scot Borders 78 D2
Birkby N Yorks 63 D8
Birkdale Mersey 55 G3
Birkenhead Mersey 48 D4
Birkenhills Aberds 99 D7
Birkenshaw N Lanarks 75 A8
Birkenshaw W Yorks 57 F7
Birkhall Aberds 90 B4
Birkhill Angus 84 A5
Birkhill Dumf/Gal 76 F5
Birkholme Lincs 42 C2
Birkin N Yorks 57 F10
Birley Heref/Worcs 28 C5
Birling Kent 14 B1
Birling Northum 79 G7
Birling Gap E Sussex 13 F9
Birlingham Heref/Worcs 29 D10
Birmingham W Midlands 40 G2
Birmingham Botanical Gardens W Midlands 40 G2
Birmingham Museum and Art Gallery W Midlands 40 G2
Birmingham Museum of Science and Technology W Midlands 40 G2
Birnam Perth/Kinr 90 G1
Birse Aberds 91 B6
Birsemore Aberds 91 B6
Birstall Leics 41 E7
Birstall W Yorks 57 F7
Birstwith N Yorks 57 C7
Birthorpe Lincs 42 B4
Birtley Heref/Worcs 28 B4
Birtley Northum 70 C3
Birtley Tyne/Wear 71 E7
Birts Street Heref/Worcs 29 E8
Bisbrooke Rutl'd 42 F1
Biscathorpe Lincs 52 D5
Biscot Luton 32 F3
Bish Mill Devon 7 D8
Bisham Berks 21 C6
Bishampton Heref/Worcs 30 C1
Bishop Auckland Durham 63 B7
Bishop Burton E Riding Yorks 58 E5
Bishop Middleham Durham 71 G8
Bishop Monkton N Yorks 57 B8
Bishop Norton Lincs 52 C2
Bishop Sutton Bath/NE Som'set 18 F2
Bishop Thornton N Yorks 57 B7
Bishop Wilton E Riding Yorks 58 C3
Bishopbridge Lincs 52 C3
Bishopbriggs E Dunb 83 H7
Bishopmill Moray 98 B2
Bishops Cannings Wilts 19 E7
Bishop's Castle Shrops 38 G4
Bishop's Caundle Dorset 9 C8
Bishop's Cleeve Glos 30 F1
Bishop's Frome Heref/Worcs 29 D7
Bishop's Green Essex 33 G9
Bishop's Hull Som'set 8 B4
Bishop's Itchington Warwick 30 C5
Bishop's Lydeard Som'set 8 B3
Bishops Nympton Devon 7 D8
Bishop's Offley Staffs 39 C8
Bishop's Stortford Herts 33 F7
Bishops Sutton Hants 11 A9
Bishop's Tachbrook Warwick 30 B5
Bishops Tawton Devon 7 C6
Bishops Waltham Hants 11 C8
Bishop's Wood Staffs 39 E9
Bishopsbourne Kent 15 C6
Bishopsteignton Devon 5 C10
Bishopstoke Hants 11 C7
Bishopston Swan 25 H10
Bishopstone Bucks 31 G10
Bishopstone E Sussex 13 E8
Bishopstone Heref/Worcs 28 D5
Bishopstone Thamesd'n 19 C9
Bishopstone Wilts 10 B3
Bishopstrow Wilts 18 G5
Bishopswood Som'set 8 C4
Bishopsworth Bristol 18 E2
Bishopthorpe C of York 58 D1
Bishopton Dumf/Gal 67 F6
Bishopton Durham 63 B8
Bishopton N Yorks 63 G8
Bishopton Renf 82 G5
Bishopton Warwick 30 C3
Bishton Newp 17 C8
Bisley Glos 29 H10
Bisley Surrey 21 F7
Bispham Lancs 55 D3
Bispham Green Lancs 55 G4
Bissoe Cornw'l 3 E6
Bisterne Close Hants 10 D5
Bitchfield Lincs 42 C2
Bittadon Devon 7 B6
Bittaford Devon 5 E7
Bittering Norfolk 44 D3
Bitterley Shrops 39 H6
Bitterne S'thampton 11 C7
Bitteswell Leics 41 G7
Bitton S Gloucs 18 E3
Bix Oxon 20 C5
Bixter Shetl'd 113 H6
Blaby Leics 41 F7
Black Bourton Oxon 19 A9
Black Callerton Tyne/Wear 71 D6
Black Clauchrie S Ayrs 66 B4
Black Corries Lodge H'land 88 F3
Black Country Castle & Zoo, Dudley W Midlands 39 F10
Black Crofts Arg/Bute 81 A9
Black Dog Devon 7 F9
Black Heddon Northum 70 C5
Black Lane Gtr Man 49 B8
Black Marsh Shrops 38 F4
Black Mount Arg/Bute 88 G3
Black Notley Essex 34 F1
Black Pill Swan 25 G11
Black Tar Pembs 24 F4
Black Torrington Devon 6 F5
Blackacre Dumf/Gal 68 A3
Blackadder West Scot Borders 78 B3
Blackawton Devon 5 E9
Blackborough Devon 8 D2
Blackborough End Norfolk 43 D9
Blackboys E Sussex 13 C9
Blackbrook Derbys 50 H5
Blackbrook Mersey 49 C6
Blackbrook Staffs 39 B8
Blackburn Aberds 98 E5
Blackburn Aberds 99 G8
Blackburn Lancs 56 F1
Blackburn W Loth 84 H1
Blackcraig Dumf/Gal 67 B9
Blackden Heath Ches 49 E8
Blackdog Aberds 99 G9
Blackfell Tyne/Wear 71 E7
Blackfield Hants 11 D7
Blackford Cumb 69 D6
Blackford Perth/Kinr 83 D9

Buckland Devon 5 F7
Buckland Glos 30 E2
Buckland Hants 11 E6
Buckland Herts 33 E6
Buckland Kent 15 D8
Buckland Oxon 19 B10
Buckland Surrey 22 F2
Buckland Abbey Devon 4 D5
Buckland Brewer Devon 6 D5
Buckland Common Bucks 32 H2
Buckland Dinham Som'set 18 F4
Buckland Filleigh Devon 6 F5
Buckland in the Moor Devon 5 C8
Buckland Monachorum Devon 4 D5
Buckland Newton Dorset 9 D8
Buckland St. Mary Som'set 8 C4
Bucklebury Berks 20 D3
Bucklegate Lincs 43 B6
Bucklerheads Angus 90 H5
Bucklers Hard Hants 11 E7
Bucklers Hard Hants 11 E7
Bucklesham Suffolk 35 D6
Buckley Flints 48 F3
Bucklow Hill Ches 49 D8
Buckminster Leics 42 C1
Bucknall Lincs 52 F4
Bucknall Stoke 49 H10
Bucknell Oxon 31 F7
Bucknell Shrops 28 A4
Buckpool Moray 98 B4
Buck's Cross Devon 6 D4
Bucks Green W Sussex 12 B4
Bucks Horn Oak Hants 21 G6
Buck's Mills Devon 6 D4
Bucksburn Aberd C 99 H8
Buckskin Hants 20 F4
Buckton E Riding Yorks 65 G9
Buckton Heref/Worcs 28 A4
Buckton Northum 78 D5
Buckworth Cambs 42 H4
Budbrooke Warwick 30 B4
Budby Notts 51 F8
Budd's Titson Cornw'l 6 F3
Bude Cornw'l 6 F3
Budlake Devon 8 E1
Budle Northum 79 D6
Budleigh Salterton Devon 8 F2
Budock Water Cornw'l 3 F6
Buerton Ches 39 A7
Buffler's Holt Bucks 31 E8
Bugbrooke Northants 31 C8
Buglawton Ches 49 F9
Bugle Cornw'l 3 D9
Bugley Wilts 18 G5
Bugthorpe E Riding Yorks 58 C3
Buildwas Shrops 39 E7
Builth Road Powys 27 C10
Builth Wells Powys 27 C10
Buirgh W Isles 101 C6
Bulby Lincs 42 C3
Bulcote Notts 41 A8
Buldoo H'land 110 C4
Bulford Wilts 19 G8
Bulford Camp Wilts 19 G8
Bulkeley Ches 49 G6
Bulkington Warwick 40 G5
Bulkington Wilts 19 F6
Bulkworthy Devon 6 E4
Bull Hill Hants 11 E6
Bullamoor N Yorks 63 E8
Bullbridge Derbys 50 G5
Bullbrook Berks 21 E6
Bulley Glos 29 G8
Bullgill Cumb 68 G3
Bullington Hants 20 G2
Bullington Lincs 52 E3
Bull's Green Herts 32 G5
Bullwood Arg/Bute 82 G2
Bulmer Essex 34 D2
Bulmer N Yorks 58 B2
Bulmer Tye Essex 34 E2
Bulphan Essex 23 C6
Bulverhythe E Sussex 14 H2
Bulwark Aberds 99 D9
Bulwell Notts 51 H7
Bulwick Northants 42 F2
Bumbles Green Essex 33 H7
Bun Abhainn Eadarra W Isles 101 B7
Bun Loyne H'land 95 F9
Bunacaimb H'land 87 C6
Bunarkaig H'land 88 C2
Bunbury Ches 49 G6
Bunbury Heath Ches 49 G6
Bunchrew H'land 96 B4
Bundalloch H'land 94 D5
Buness Shetl'd 113 C9
Bunessan Arg/Bute 80 B3
Bungay Suffolk 45 G7
Bunker's Hill Lincs 52 E2
Bunker's Hill Lincs 52 G5
Bunkers Hill Oxon 31 G6
Bunloit H'land 96 D3
Bunnahabhain Arg/Bute 80 G4
Bunny Notts 41 C7
Buntait H'land 96 C1
Buntingford Herts 33 F6
Bunwell Norfolk 44 F5
Burbage Derbys 50 E2
Burbage Leics 41 F6
Burbage Wilts 19 E9
Burchett's Green Berks 21 C6
Burcombe Wilts 10 A3
Burcot Oxon 20 B3
Burcott Bucks 32 F1
Burdon Tyne/Wear 71 E8
Bures Suffolk 34 E3
Bures Green Suffolk 34 E3
Burford Ches 49 G7
Burford Oxon 30 G4
Burford Shrops 29 B6
Burg Arg/Bute 86 G3
Burgar Orkney 112 F4
Burgate Hants 10 C4
Burgate Suffolk 44 H4
Burgess Hill W Sussex 13 D7
Burgh Suffolk 35 C6
Burgh-by-Sands Cumb 69 E6
Burgh Castle Norfolk 45 E8
Burgh Heath Surrey 22 F2
Burgh le Marsh Lincs 53 F8
Burgh Muir Aberds 99 F7
Burgh next Aylsham Norfolk 45 C6
Burgh on Bain Lincs 52 D5
Burgh St. Margaret Norfolk 45 D8
Burgh St. Peter Norfolk 45 F8
Burghclere Hants 20 E2
Burghead Moray 105 F10
Burghfield Berks 20 E4
Burghfield Common Berks 20 E4
Burghfield Hill Berks 20 E4
Burghill Heref/Worcs 28 D5
Burghwallis S Yorks 57 G10
Burham Kent 14 B2
Buriton Hants 11 B10
Burland Ches 49 G7
Burlawn Cornw'l 3 B8
Burleigh Berks 21 E6
Burlescombe Devon 8 C2
Burleston Dorset 9 E9
Burley Hants 10 D5
Burley Rutl'd 42 D1
Burley W Yorks 57 E7
Burley Gate Heref/Worcs 29 D6
Burley in Wharfedale W Yorks 57 D6
Burley Lodge Hants 10 D5
Burley Street Hants 10 D5
Burleydam Ches 39 A7
Burlingjobb Powys 28 C3
Burlow E Sussex 13 D9
Burlton Shrops 38 C5
Burmarsh Kent 14 E5
Burmington Warwick 30 E4
Burn N Yorks 58 F1
Burn of Cambus Stirl 83 D8
Burnaston Derbys 40 B4
Burnbank S Lanarks 75 B9
Burnby E Riding Yorks 58 D4
Burncross S Yorks 50 C5
Burneside Cumb 61 E8
Burness Orkney 112 D7
Burneston N Yorks 63 F8
Burnett Bath/NE Som'set 18 E3
Burnfoot Scot Borders 77 F7
Burnfoot Scot Borders 77 F8
Burnfoot E Ayrs 75 G6
Burnfoot Perth/Kinr 84 D1
Burnham Bucks 21 C7
Burnham N Lincs 59 G6
Burnham Deepdale Norfolk 44 A2
Burnham Green Herts 32 G5
Burnham Market Norfolk 44 A2
Burnham Norton Norfolk 44 A2
Burnham on Crouch Essex 23 B9
Burnham on Sea Som'set 17 G8
Burnham Overy Staithe Norfolk 44 A2
Burnham Overy Town Norfolk 44 A2
Burnham Thorpe Norfolk 44 A2
Burnhaven Aberds 99 D11
Burnhead Dumf/Gal 76 H1
Burnhead S Ayrs 74 G4
Burnhervie Aberds 99 G7
Burnhill Green Staffs 39 E8
Burnhope Durham 71 F6
Burnhouse N Ayrs 74 B5
Burniston N Yorks 65 E8
Burnlee W Yorks 50 B3
Burnley Lancs 56 E3
Burnley Lane Lancs 56 E3
Burnmouth Scot Borders 78 A4
Burnopfield Durham 71 E6
Burnsall N Yorks 56 B5
Burnside Angus 91 F6
Burnside E Ayrs 75 F7
Burnside Fife 84 D3
Burnside Shetl'd 113 F5
Burnside S Lanarks 75 A8
Burnside W Loth 84 G2
Burnside of Duntrune Angus 84 A6
Burnswark Dumf/Gal 68 C4
Burnt Heath Derbys 50 E4
Burnt Houses Durham 63 B6
Burnt Yates N Yorks 57 B7
Burntcommon Surrey 21 F8
Burnthouse Cornw'l 3 F6
Burntisland Fife 84 F4
Burnton E Ayrs 75 G6
Burntwood Staffs 40 E2
Burnwynd C of Edinb 84 H3
Burpham Surrey 21 F8
Burpham W Sussex 12 E4
Burradon Northum 78 G4
Burradon Tyne/Wear 71 C7
Burrafirth Shetl'd 113 B9
Burraland Shetl'd 113 F6
Burraland Shetl'd 113 J5
Burras Cornw'l 2 F5
Burravoe Shetl'd 113 G6
Burravoe Shetl'd 113 F8
Burrells Cumb 61 C9
Burrelton Perth/Kinr 90 H3
Burridge Devon 7 C6
Burridge Hants 11 C8
Burrill N Yorks 63 F7
Burringham N Lincs 51 B10
Burrington Devon 7 E7
Burrington Heref/Worcs 28 A5
Burrington N Som'set 17 F9
Burrough Green Cambs 33 C9
Burrough on the Hill Leics 41 D9
Burrow Bridge Som'set 8 B5
Burrowhill Surrey 21 E7
Burry Swan 25 G9
Burry Green Swan 25 G9
Burry Port Carms 25 F9
Burscough Lancs 55 G4
Burscough Bridge Lancs 55 G4
Bursea E Riding Yorks 58 E4
Burshill E Riding Yorks 59 D6
Bursledon Hants 11 D7
Burslem Stoke 49 H9
Burstall Suffolk 34 D4
Burstock Dorset 9 D6
Burston Norfolk 44 G5
Burston Staffs 39 B10
Burstow Surrey 22 G3
Burstwick E Riding Yorks 59 F8
Burtersett N Yorks 62 F3
Burtle Som'set 17 G8
Burton Ches 48 E4
Burton Ches 49 F6
Burton Dorset 10 E4
Burton Lincs 52 E2
Burton Northum 79 D6
Burton Pembs 24 F4
Burton Som'set 17 G6
Burton Wilts 18 D5
Burton Agnes E Riding Yorks 59 B7
Burton Bradstock Dorset 9 F6
Burton Dassett Warwick 30 C5
Burton Fleming E Riding Yorks 65 G8
Burton Green W Midlands 40 H4
Burton Green Wrex 48 G4
Burton Hastings Warwick 41 F6
Burton-in-Kendal Cumb 61 G8
Burton in Lonsdale N Yorks 61 G9
Burton Joyce Notts 41 A8
Burton Latimer Northants 32 A2
Burton Lazars Leics 41 D9
Burton-le-Coggles Lincs 42 C2
Burton Leonard N Yorks 57 B8
Burton on the Wolds Leics 41 C7
Burton Overy Leics 41 F8
Burton Pedwardine Lincs 42 A4
Burton Pidsea E Riding Yorks 59 E8
Burton Salmon N Yorks 57 F9
Burton Stather N Lincs 58 G4
Burton upon Stather N Lincs 58 G4
Burton-upon-Trent Staffs 40 C4
Burtonwood Ches 49 C6
Burwardsley Ches 49 G6
Burwarton Shrops 39 G7
Burwash E Sussex 14 F1
Burwash Common E Sussex 13 C10
Burwash Weald E Sussex 13 C10
Burwell Cambs 33 B8
Burwell Lincs 53 E6
Burwen Angl 46 C4
Burwick Orkney 112 K5
Bury Cambs 42 G5
Bury Gtr Man 56 G3
Bury Som'set 7 D10
Bury W Sussex 12 D4
Bury Green Herts 33 F7
Bury St. Edmunds Suffolk 34 B2
Burythorpe N Yorks 58 B3
Busby S Lanarks 75 B7
Buscot Oxon 19 B9
Bush Bank Heref/Worcs 28 C5
Bush Crathie Aberds 90 B3
Bush Green Norfolk 45 G6
Bushbury W Midlands 39 E10
Bushby Leics 41 E8
Bushey Herts 21 B9
Bushey Heath Herts 21 B9
Bushley Heref/Worcs 29 E9
Bushton Wilts 19 D7
Buslingthorpe Lincs 52 D3
Busta Shetl'd 113 G6
Butcher's Cross E Sussex 13 C9
Butcher's Pasture Essex 33 F9
Butcombe N Som'set 18 E2
Butetown Card 17 D6
Butleigh Som'set 9 A7
Butleigh Wootton Som'set 18 H2
Butler's Cross Bucks 31 H10
Butler's End Warwick 40 G4
Butler's Marston Warwick 30 D5
Butley Suffolk 35 C7
Butley High Corner Suffolk 35 D7
Butt Green Ches 49 G7
Butterburn Cumb 69 C9
Buttercrambe N Yorks 58 C3
Butterknowle Durham 63 B6
Butterleigh Devon 8 D1
Buttermere Cumb 60 C4
Buttermere Wilts 19 E10
Buttershaw W Yorks 57 F6
Butterstone Perth/Kinr 90 G1
Butterton Staffs 50 G2
Butterwick Durham 63 B8
Butterwick Lincs 53 H6
Butterwick N Yorks 64 G5
Butterwick N Yorks 65 G7
Buttington Powys 38 E3
Buttock's Booth Northants 31 B9
Buttonoak Shrops 39 H8
Butt's Green Hants 11 B6
Buttsash Hants 11 D7
Buxhall Suffolk 34 C4
Buxhall Fen Street Suffolk 34 C4
Buxley Scot Borders 78 B3
Buxted E Sussex 13 C8
Buxton Derbys 50 E2
Buxton Norfolk 45 C6
Buxworth Derbys 50 D2
Bwlch Powys 28 F2
Bwlch-Llan Ceredig'n 26 C5
Bwlch-y-cibau Powys 38 D2
Bwlch-y-fadfa Ceredig'n 25 B9
Bwlch-y-ffridd Powys 38 F1
Bwlch-y-sarnau Powys 27 A10
Bwlchgwyn Wrex 48 G3
Bwlchnewydd Carms 25 D8
Bwlchtocyn Gwyn 36 C3
Bwlchyddar Powys 38 C2
Bwlchygroes Pembs 25 C7
Byermoor Tyne/Wear 71 E6
Byers Green Durham 71 G7
Byfield Northants 31 C7
Byfleet Surrey 21 E8
Byford Heref/Worcs 28 D4
Bygrave Herts 32 E5
Byker Tyne/Wear 71 D7
Bylchau Conwy 47 F9
Byley Ches 49 F8
Bynea Carms 25 G10
Byrness Northum 78 G2
Bythorn Cambs 42 H3
Byton Heref/Worcs 28 B4
Byworth W Sussex 12 C3

C

Cabharstadh W Isles 107 G7
Cablea Perth/Kinr 89 H10
Cabourne Lincs 52 B4
Cabrach Arg/Bute 72 A4
Cabrach Moray 98 F3
Cabus Lancs 55 D4
Cackle Street E Sussex 13 C8
Cadbury Devon 7 F10
Cadbury Barton Devon 7 E7
Cadbury World, Bourneville W Midlands 40 G2
Cadder E Dunb 83 G7
Caddington Beds 32 G3
Caddonfoot Scot Borders 77 D7
Cade Street E Sussex 13 C10
Cadeby Leics 41 E6
Cadeby S Yorks 51 B7
Cadeleigh Devon 7 F10
Cadgwith Cornw'l 3 H6
Cadham Fife 84 D4
Cadishead Gtr Man 49 C8
Cadle Swan 16 B1
Cadley Lancs 55 E5
Cadley Wilts 19 F9
Cadley Wilts 19 E9
Cadmore End Bucks 20 B5
Cadnam Hants 10 C5
Cadney N Lincs 52 B3
Cadole Flints 48 F3
Cadoxton V of Glam 17 E6
Cadoxton-Juxta-Neath Neath P Talb 16 B2
Cadshaw Lancs 56 G2
Cadzow S Lanarks 75 B9
Caeathraw Gwyn 46 F4
Caehopkin Powys 27 G8
Caenby Lincs 52 D3
Caenby Corner Lincs 52 D2
Caer-bryn Carms 26 G5
Caer Llan Monmouths 28 H5
Caerau Bridg 16 B3
Caerau Card 17 D6
Caerdeon Gwyn 37 D6
Caerfarchell Pembs 24 D2
Caergeiliog Angl 46 E3
Caergwrle Flints 48 G4
Caerleon Newp 17 B8
Caernarfon Castle Gwyn 46 F4
Caernarfon Gwyn 46 F4
Caernarfon Castle Gwyn 46 F4
Caerphilly Caerph 17 C6
Caersws Powys 37 F10
Caerwedros Ceredig'n 26 C3
Caerwent Monmouths 17 B9
Caerwych Gwyn 37 B6
Caerwys Flints 48 E2
Caethle Gwyn 37 F6
Cairn Angl 47 D6
Caio Carms 27 E6
Cairinis W Isles 100 F4
Cairisiadar W Isles 106 F4
Cairminis W Isles 101 D6
Cairnbaan Arg/Bute 81 E8
Cairnbanno Ho. Aberds 99 D8
Cairnborrow Aberds 98 D4
Cairnbrogie Aberds 99 F8
Cairnbulg Castle Aberds 99 B10
Cairncross Angus 90 D5
Cairncross Scot Borders 78 A3
Cairndow Arg/Bute 82 C2
Cairness Aberds 99 B10
Cairneyhill Fife 84 F2
Cairnfield Ho. Moray 98 B4
Cairngaan Dumf/Gal 66 G3
Cairngarroch Dumf/Gal 66 F2
Cairnhill Aberds 99 E6
Cairnie Aberds 98 D4
Cairnie Aberds 99 H8
Cairnorrie Aberds 99 D8
Cairnpark Aberds 99 G8
Cairnryan Dumf/Gal 66 D2
Cairnton Orkney 112 H4
Caister-on-Sea Norfolk 45 D9
Caistor Lincs 52 B4
Caistor St. Edmund Norfolk 45 E6
Caistron Northum 78 G4
Caitha Bowland Scot Borders 77 C7
Caithness Glass, Perth Perth/Kinr 84 B2
Calais Street Suffolk 34 E3
Calanais W Isles 107 F6
Calbost W Isles 107 H8
Calbourne I of Wight 11 F7
Calceby Lincs 53 E6
Calcot Row Berks 20 D4
Calcott Kent 15 B6
Caldback Shetl'd 113 C9
Caldbeck Cumb 69 G6
Caldbergh N Yorks 62 F5
Caldecot Rutl'd 42 F1
Caldecote Cambs 33 C6
Caldecote Cambs 42 G4
Caldecote Herts 32 E5
Caldecote Northants 31 C8
Caldecott Northants 32 B2
Caldecott Oxon 20 B2
Calder Bridge Cumb 60 D3
Calder Hall Cumb 60 D3
Calder Mains H'land 110 D5
Calder Vale Lancs 55 D5
Calderbank N Lanarks 75 A9
Calderbrook Gtr Man 56 G4
Caldercruix N Lanarks 83 H9
Caldermill S Lanarks 75 C8
Calderwood S Lanarks 75 B8
Caldhame Angus 90 G5
Caldicot Monmouths 17 C9
Caldwell Derbys 40 D4
Caldwell N Yorks 63 C6
Caldy Mersey 48 D3
Caledrhydiau Ceredig'n 26 C4
Calfsound Orkney 112 E6
Calgary Arg/Bute 86 F3
Califer Moray 105 G9
California Falk 83 G10
California Norfolk 45 D9
Calke Derbys 40 C5
Callaly Northum 78 G5
Callander Stirl 83 D7
Callaughton Shrops 39 F7
Callestick Cornw'l 3 D6
Callestock Cider Farm, Truro Cornw'l 3 D6
Calligarry H'land 94 F3
Callington Cornw'l 4 D4
Callow Heref/Worcs 28 E5
Callow End Heref/Worcs 29 D9
Callow Hill Heref/Worcs 29 A8
Callow Hill Wilts 19 C7
Callows Grave Heref/Worcs 29 B6
Calmore Hants 11 C6
Calmsden Glos 30 H2
Calne Wilts 19 D7
Calow Derbys 51 E6
Calshot Hants 11 D7
Calstock Cornw'l 4 D5
Calstone Wellington Wilts 19 E7
Calthorpe Norfolk 44 B5
Calthwaite Cumb 69 F7
Calton N Yorks 56 C4
Calton Staffs 50 G3
Calveley Ches 49 G6
Calver Derbys 50 E4
Calver Hill Heref/Worcs 28 D4
Calverhall Shrops 39 B7
Calverleigh Devon 7 E10
Calverley W Yorks 57 E7
Calvert Bucks 31 F8
Calverton M/Keynes 31 E9
Calverton Notts 51 H8
Calvine Perth/Kinr 89 E9
Calvo Cumb 68 E4
Calzeat Scot Borders 76 D4
Cam Glos 18 B4
Camas-luinie H'land 95 D6
Camasnacroise H'land 87 F8
Camastianavaig H'land 94 C2
Camasunary H'land 94 E2
Camault Muir H'land 96 B3
Camb Shetl'd 113 D8
Camber E Sussex 14 G4
Camberley Surrey 21 E6
Camberwell Gtr Lon 22 D3
Camblesforth N Yorks 58 F2
Cambo Northum 70 B5
Cambois Northum 71 B8
Camborne Cornw'l 2 E5
Cambridge Cambs 33 C7
Cambridge Glos 18 A4
Cambridge Town Essex 23 C9
Cambus Stirl 83 E9
Cambusavie Farm H'land 105 C6
Cambusbarron Stirl 83 E8
Cambuskenneth Stirl 83 E9
Cambuslang S Lanarks 75 A8
Cambusmore Lodge H'land 105 C6
Camden Gtr Lon 22 C2
Camelford Cornw'l 4 B2
Camelot Theme Park, Chorley Lancs 55 G5
Camelsdale W Sussex 12 B2
Camerory H'land 97 C8
Camer's Green Heref/Worcs 29 E8
Camerton Bath/NE Som'set 18 F3
Camerton Cumb 68 G3
Camerton E Riding Yorks 59 F8
Camghouran Perth/Kinr 88 F6
Cammachmore Aberds 91 B10
Cammeringham Lincs 52 D2
Camp Hill Warwick 40 F5
Campbeltown Arg/Bute 73 E7
Camperdown Tyne/Wear 71 C7
Campmuir Perth/Kinr 90 H3
Campsall S Yorks 57 G10
Campsey Ash Suffolk 35 C7
Campton Beds 32 E4
Camptown Scot Borders 77 F9
Camrose Pembs 24 D4
Camserney Perth/Kinr 89 G9
Camster H'land 111 E7
Camuschoirk H'land 87 E7
Camuscross H'land 94 E3
Camusnagaul H'land 88 D1
Camusnagaul H'land 103 D8
Camusrory H'land 94 G5
Camusteel H'land 94 B4
Camusterrach H'land 94 B4
Camusvrachan Perth/Kinr 89 G7
Canada Hants 10 C5
Canadia E Sussex 14 G2
Canal Side S Yorks 58 G2
Candacraig Aberds 90 B4
Candacraig Ho. Aberds 98 G3
Candlesby Lincs 53 F7
Candy Mill Scot Borders 76 C3
Cane End Oxon 20 D4
Canewdon Essex 23 B8
Canford Bottom Dorset 10 D3
Canford Cliffs Poole 10 F3
Canford Magna Poole 10 E3
Canham's Green Suffolk 34 B4
Canholes Derbys 50 E2
Canisbay H'land 111 B8
Cann Dorset 10 B1
Cann Common Dorset 10 B1
Cannard's Grave Som'set 18 G3
Cannich H'land 95 C10
Cannington Som'set 17 H7
Cannock Staffs 40 E1
Cannock Wood Staffs 40 D2
Canon Bridge Heref/Worcs 28 D5
Canon Frome Heref/Worcs 29 D7
Canon Pyon Heref/Worcs 28 D5
Canonbie Dumf/Gal 69 C6
Canons Ashby Northants 31 C7
Canonstown Cornw'l 2 F4
Canterbury Kent 15 C6
Canterbury Cathedral Kent 15 C6
Canterbury Tales Kent 15 C6
Canterbury Tales Kent 15 C6
Cantley Norfolk 45 E7
Cantley S Yorks 51 B8
Cantlop Shrops 39 E6
Canton Card 17 D6
Cantraybruich H'land 96 B5
Cantraydoune H'land 96 B5
Cantraywood H'land 96 B5
Cantsfield Lancs 61 G9
Canvey Island Essex 23 C7
Canwick Lincs 52 F2
Canworthy Water Cornw'l 6 G3
Caol H'land 88 D2
Caolas Arg/Bute 86 D2
Caolas Scalpaigh W Isles 101 C8
Caolas Stocinis W Isles 101 C7
Capel Surrey 21 G9
Capel Bangor Ceredig'n 37 G6
Capel Betws Lleucu Ceredig'n 27 C6
Capel Carmel Gwyn 36 C1
Capel Coch Angl 46 D4
Capel Curig Conwy 47 G7
Capel Cynon Ceredig'n 25 B8
Capel Dewi Ceredig'n 25 B9
Capel Dewi Ceredig'n 37 G6
Capel Dewi Carms 25 D9
Capel Garmon Conwy 47 G8
Capel-gwyn Angl 46 E3
Capel Gwyn Carms 25 D9
Capel Gwynfe Carms 27 F7
Capel Hendre Carms 26 G5
Capel Hermon Gwyn 37 C7
Capel Isaac Carms 26 F5
Capel Iwan Carms 25 C7
Capel le Ferne Kent 15 E7
Capel Llanilltern Card 16 C5
Capel Mawr Angl 46 E4
Capel Seion Ceredig'n 37 H6
Capel St. Andrew Suffolk 35 D7
Capel St. Mary Suffolk 34 E4
Capel Tygwydd Ceredig'n 25 B7
Capel Uchaf Gwyn 46 H4
Capel-y-graig Gwyn 46 F5
Capelulo Conwy 47 E7
Capenhurst Ches 48 E4
Capernwray Lancs 61 G8
Capheaton Northum 70 B5
Cappercleuch Scot Borders 76 E5
Capplegill Dumf/Gal 76 G4
Capton Devon 5 E9
Caputh Perth/Kinr 90 H1
Car Colston Notts 41 A9
Carbis Bay Cornw'l 2 F4
Carbost H'land 93 B9
Carbost H'land 101 H10
Carbrook S Yorks 50 D5
Carbrooke Norfolk 44 E3
Carburton Notts 51 E8
Carcant Scot Borders 77 B6
Carcary Angus 91 F7
Carclaze Cornw'l 3 D9
Carcroft S Yorks 57 G10
Cardenden Fife 84 E4
Cardeston Shrops 38 D4
Cardiff Card 17 D6
Cardiff Castle Card 17 D6
Cardigan Ceredig'n 25 B6
Cardington Beds 32 D3
Cardington Shrops 39 F6
Cardinham Cornw'l 4 D2
Cardonald C of Glasg 75 A7
Cardow Moray 97 B9
Cardrona Scot Borders 77 D6
Cardross Arg/Bute 82 G4
Cardurnock Cumb 68 E4
Careby Lincs 42 D3
Careston Angus 91 F6
Carew Pembs 24 F5
Carew Cheriton Pembs 24 F5
Carew Newton Pembs 24 F5
Carey Heref/Worcs 29 E6
Carfrae E Loth 85 H7
Cargenbridge Dumf/Gal 68 C2
Cargill Perth/Kinr 90 H2
Cargo Cumb 69 E6
Cargreen Cornw'l 4 D5
Carham Northum 78 D3
Carhampton Som'set 16 G5
Carharrack Cornw'l 3 E6
Carie Perth/Kinr 89 H7
Carie Perth/Kinr 89 F7
Carines Cornw'l 3 D6
Carisbrooke I of Wight 11 F7
Carisbrooke Castle I of Wight 11 F7
Cark Cumb 61 G6
Carlabhagh W Isles 107 E6
Carland Cross Cornw'l 3 D7
Carlby Lincs 42 D3
Carlecotes S Yorks 50 B3
Carlesmoor N Yorks 63 G6
Carleton Cumb 61 B8
Carleton Cumb 69 E7
Carleton Lancs 55 E3
Carleton N Yorks 56 D4
Carleton Forehoe Norfolk 44 E4
Carleton Rode Norfolk 44 F5
Carlin How Redcar/Clevel'd 64 C5
Carlingcott Bath/NE Som'set 18 F3
Carlisle Cumb 69 E7
Carlisle Cathedral Cumb 69 E6
Carlops Scot Borders 76 B4
Carlton Beds 32 C2
Carlton Cambs 33 C9
Carlton Leics 40 E5
Carlton Notts 41 A8
Carlton N Yorks 64 F4
Carlton N Yorks 58 F2
Carlton N Yorks 62 F5
Carlton N Yorks 63 C6
Carlton Stockton 63 B8
Carlton Suffolk 35 B7
Carlton S Yorks 57 G8
Carlton W Yorks 57 F8
Carlton Colville Suffolk 45 G9
Carlton Curlieu Leics 41 F8
Carlton Husthwaite N Yorks 63 G9
Carlton in Cleveland N Yorks 64 D3
Carlton in Lindrick Notts 51 D7
Carlton le Moorland Lincs 52 G2
Carlton Miniott N Yorks 63 F8
Carlton on Trent Notts 51 F9
Carlton Scroop Lincs 42 A2
Carluke S Lanarks 75 B10
Carmarthen Carms 25 D9
Carmel Angl 46 D3
Carmel Carms 26 G5
Carmel Flints 48 E2
Carmel Guernsey 4
Carmel Gwyn 46 G4
Carmont Aberds 91 C9
Carmunnock C of Glasg 75 B8
Carmyle C of Glasg 75 A8
Carmyllie Angus 91 G6
Carn-gorm H'land 95 D6
Carnaby E Riding Yorks 59 B7
Carnach H'land 103 C8
Carnach H'land 95 D7
Carnach W Isles 101 C8
Carnachy H'land 110 D2
Carnbee Fife 85 D7
Carnbo Perth/Kinr 84 D2
Carnbrea Cornw'l 2 E5
Carnduff S Lanarks 75 C8
Carnduncan Arg/Bute 80 H2
Carne Cornw'l 3 F8
Carnforth Lancs 61 G7
Carnhedryn Pembs 24 D3
Carnhell Green Cornw'l 2 F5
Carnkie Cornw'l 3 F6
Carnkie Cornw'l 2 F5
Carno Powys 37 F9
Carnoch H'land 96 C1
Carnoch H'land 103 G10
Carnock Fife 84 F2
Carnon Downs Cornw'l 3 E6
Carnousie Aberds 99 C6
Carnoustie Angus 85 A7
Carnwath S Lanarks 76 C2
Carnyorth Cornw'l 2 F2
Carperby N Yorks 62 F5
Carpley Green N Yorks 62 F4
Carr S Yorks 51 C7
Carr Hill Tyne/Wear 71 D7
Carradale Arg/Bute 73 D8
Carragraich W Isles 101 C7
Carrbridge H'land 97 D7
Carrefour Selous Jersey 4
Carreg-wen Pembs 25 B7
Carreglefn Angl 46 D3
Carrick Arg/Bute 81 F9
Carrick Fife 84 B6
Carrick Castle Arg/Bute 82 E2
Carrick Ho. Orkney 112 E6
Carriden Falk 84 F2
Carrington Gtr Man 49 C8
Carrington Lincs 53 G6
Carrington Midloth 77 A6
Carrog Conwy 47 H7
Carrog Denbs 38 A2
Carron Falk 83 F9
Carron Moray 98 D2
Carron Bridge N Lanarks 83 F8
Carronbridge Dumf/Gal 76 H1
Carrshield Northum 70 F3
Carrutherstown Dumf/Gal 68 C4
Carrville Durham 71 F8
Carsaig Arg/Bute 80 B5
Carscreugh Dumf/Gal 66 E4
Carse Gray Angus 90 F5
Carse Ho. Arg/Bute 73 A7
Carsegown Dumf/Gal 67 E6
Carseriggan Dumf/Gal 66 D5
Carsethorn Dumf/Gal 68 E2
Carshalton Gtr Lon 22 E2
Carsington Derbys 50 G4
Carskiey Arg/Bute 73 G6
Carsluith Dumf/Gal 67 E6
Carsphairn Dumf/Gal 67 A7
Carstairs S Lanarks 76 C2
Carstairs Junction S Lanarks 76 C2
Carswell Marsh Oxon 19 B10
Carter's Clay Hants 11 B6
Carterton Oxon 30 H4
Carterway Heads Northum 70 E5
Carthew Cornw'l 3 D9
Carthorpe N Yorks 63 F8
Cartington Northum 78 G5
Cartland S Lanarks 76 C1
Cartmel Cumb 61 G6
Cartmel Fell Cumb 61 F7
Carway Carms 25 F9
Cary Fitzpaine Som'set 9 B7
Cascob Powys 28 B3
Cashlie Perth/Kinr 88 G5
Cashmere Visitor Centre, Elgin Moray 98 B2
Cashmoor Dorset 10 C2
Cassey Compton Glos 30 G2
Cassington Oxon 31 G6
Cassop Durham 71 G8
Castell Denbs 48 F2
Castell Coch Card 17 C6
Castell-Howell Ceredig'n 25 B9
Castell-y-bwch Torf 17 B7
Castellau Rh Cyn Taff 16 C5
Casterton Cumb 61 G9
Castle Acre Norfolk 44 D2
Castle Ashby Northants 32 C1
Castle Bolton N Yorks 62 E5
Castle Bromwich W Midlands 40 G3
Castle Bytham Lincs 42 D2
Castle Caereinion Powys 38 E2
Castle Camps Cambs 33 D9
Castle Carrock Cumb 69 E8
Castle Cary Som'set 9 A8
Castle Combe Wilts 18 D5
Castle Craig Scot Borders 76 C4
Castle Donington Leics 41 C6
Castle Douglas Dumf/Gal 67 D9
Castle Drogo, Exeter Devon 7 G8
Castle Eaton Thamesd'n 19 B8
Castle Eden Durham 71 G9
Castle Forbes Aberds 98 G6
Castle Frome Heref/Worcs 29 D7
Castle Green Surrey 21 E7
Castle Gresley Derbys 40 D4
Castle Heaton Northum 78 C4
Castle Hedingham Essex 34 E1
Castle Hill Kent 14 D1
Castle Howard, Malton N Yorks 64 G5
Castle Huntly Perth/Kinr 84 B5
Castle Kennedy Dumf/Gal 66 E3
Castle Museum, York C of York 58 C2
Castle O'er Dumf/Gal 68 A5
Castle Pulverbatch Shrops 38 E5
Castle Rising Norfolk 43 C9
Castle Stuart H'land 96 B5
Castlebythe Pembs 24 D5
Castlecary N Lanarks 83 G8
Castlecraig H'land 105 F7
Castlefairn Dumf/Gal 67 B9
Castleford W Yorks 57 F9
Castlehill Scot Borders 76 D5
Castlehill W Dunb 82 G4
Castlehill H'land 111 C6
Castlemaddy Dumf/Gal 67 B7
Castlemartin Pembs 24 G4
Castlemilk Dumf/Gal 68 C4
Castlemilk C of Glasg 75 B8
Castlemorris Pembs 24 C4
Castlemorton Heref/Worcs 29 E8
Castleside Durham 70 F5
Castlethorpe M/Keynes 31 D10
Castleton Angus 90 G4
Castleton Arg/Bute 81 F8
Castleton Derbys 50 D3
Castleton Gtr Man 56 G3
Castleton Newp 17 C7
Castleton N Yorks 64 D4
Castletown Ches 48 G5
Castletown H'land 111 C6
Castletown H'land 96 B5
Castletown I of Man 54 G2
Castletown Tyne/Wear 71 E8
Castleweary Scot Borders 77 G7
Castley N Yorks 57 D7
Caston Norfolk 44 F3
Castor Cambs 42 F4
Catacol N Ayrs 73 C9
Catbrain S Gloucs 18 C2
Catbrook Monmouths 18 A2
Catchall Cornw'l 2 G3
Catchems Corner W Midlands 40 H4
Catchgate Durham 71 E6
Catcleugh Northum 78 G2
Catcliffe S Yorks 51 D6
Catcott Som'set 17 H8
Caterham Surrey 22 F3
Catfield Norfolk 45 C7
Catfirth Shetl'd 113 H7
Catford Gtr Lon 22 D3
Catforth Lancs 55 E4
Cathays Card 17 D6
Cathcart C of Glasg 75 A7
Cathedine Powys 28 F2
Catherington Hants 11 C9
Catherton Shrops 39 H7
Catlodge H'land 89 B7
Catlowdy Cumb 69 C7
Catmore Berks 20 C2
Caton Lancs 55 B5
Caton Green Lancs 55 B5
Catrine E Ayrs 75 E7
Cat's Ash Newp 17 B8
Catsfield E Sussex 14 G2
Catshill Heref/Worcs 30 A1
Cattal N Yorks 57 C9
Cattawade Suffolk 34 E5
Catterall Lancs 55 D4
Catterick N Yorks 63 E7
Catterick Bridge N Yorks 63 E7
Catterick Garrison N Yorks 63 E6
Catterlen Cumb 69 G7
Catterline Aberds 91 D9
Catterton N Yorks 57 D10
Catthorpe Leics 41 H7
Cattistock Dorset 9 E7
Catton Northum 70 E3
Catton N Yorks 63 G8
Catwick E Riding Yorks 59 D7
Catworth Cambs 32 A3
Caudlesprings Norfolk 44 E3
Caudwell's Mill, Matlock Derbys 50 F4
Caulcott Oxon 31 F7
Cauldcots Angus 91 G7
Cauldhame Stirl 83 E7
Cauldmill Scot Borders 77 F8
Cauldon Staffs 50 H2
Caulkerbush Dumf/Gal 68 E2
Caulside Dumf/Gal 69 B7
Caunsall Heref/Worcs 39 G9
Caunton Notts 51 G9
Causeway End Dumf/Gal 67 D6
Causeway Foot W Yorks 56 E5
Causeway-head Stirl 83 E8
Causewayend S Lanarks 76 D3
Causewayhead Cumb 68 E4
Causey Park Bridge Northum 71 A6
Causeyend Aberds 99 G9
Cautley Cumb 61 E9
Cavendish Suffolk 34 D2
Cavendish Bridge Leics 41 C6
Cavenham Suffolk 34 B1
Caversfield Oxon 31 F7
Caversham Berks 20 D5
Caverswall Staffs 40 A1
Cavil E Riding Yorks 58 E3
Cawdor H'land 105 G7
Cawdor Castle and Gardens H'land 97 B6
Cawkwell Lincs 52 E5
Cawood N Yorks 58 E1
Cawsand Cornw'l 4 E5
Cawston Norfolk 44 C5
Cawthorne S Yorks 50 B4
Cawthorpe Lincs 42 C3
Cawton N Yorks 64 G4
Caxton Cambs 33 C6
Caynham Shrops 29 A6
Caythorpe Lincs 52 H2
Caythorpe Notts 51 H8
Cayton N Yorks 65 F8
Ceann a Bhaigh W Isles 100 F3
Ceann Loch Shiphoirt W Isles 107 H6
Ceannacroc Lodge H'land 95 E9
Cearsiadar W Isles 107 G7
Cefn Berain Conwy 47 F9
Cefn-brith Conwy 47 G9
Cefn Canol Powys 38 B3
Cefn-coch Conwy 47 F8
Cefn Coch Powys 38 C2
Cefn-coed-y-cymmer Merth Tyd 27 H10
Cefn Cribbwr Bridg 16 C3
Cefn Cross Bridg 16 C3
Cefn-ddwysarn Gwyn 37 B9
Cefn Einion Shrops 38 G3
Cefn-gorwydd Powys 27 D9
Cefn-mawr Wrex 38 A3
Cefn-y-bedd Flints 48 G4
Cefn-y-pant Carms 25 D6
Cefneithin Carms 26 G5
Cei-bach Ceredig'n 26 C4
Ceint Angl 46 E4
Cellan Ceredig'n 27 D6
Cellarhead Staffs 50 H1
Cemaes Angl 46 C3
Cemmaes Powys 37 E8
Cemmaes Road Powys 37 E8
Cenarth Carms 25 B7
Cenin Gwyn 46 H4
Central Invercl 82 G3
Ceos W Isles 107 G7
Ceres Fife 84 C6
Cerne Abbas Dorset 9 D8
Cerney Wick Glos 19 B7
Cerrigceinwen Angl 46 E4
Cerrigydrudion Conwy 47 H9
Cessford Scot Borders 78 E2
Ceunant Gwyn 46 F5
Chaceley Glos 29 E9
Chacewater Cornw'l 3 E6
Chackmore Bucks 31 E8
Chacombe Northants 31 D6
Chad Valley W Midlands 40 G2
Chadderton Gtr Man 49 B10
Chadderton Fold Gtr Man 49 B9
Chaddesden Derby C 40 B5
Chaddesley Corbett Heref/Worcs 29 A9
Chaddleworth Berks 20 D2
Chadlington Oxon 30 F5
Chadshunt Warwick 30 C5
Chadwell Leics 41 C9
Chadwell St. Mary Essex 23 D6
Chadwick End W Midlands 30 A4
Chadwick Green Mersey 49 C6
Chaffcombe Som'set 8 C5
Chagford Devon 5 B8
Chailey E Sussex 13 D7
Chain Bridge Lincs 43 A6
Chainbridge Cambs 43 E7
Chainhurst Kent 14 D2
Chalbury Dorset 10 D3
Chalbury Common Dorset 10 D3
Chaldon Surrey 22 F3
Chaldon Herring or Dorset 9 F9
Chale I of Wight 11 G7
Chale Green I of Wight 11 G7
Chalfont Common Bucks 21 B8
Chalfont St. Giles Bucks 21 B7
Chalfont St. Peter Bucks 21 B8
Chalford Glos 18 A5
Chalgrove Oxon 20 B4
Chalk Kent 23 D6
Challacombe Devon 7 B7
Challoch Dumf/Gal 66 D5
Challock Lees Kent 14 C5
Chalton Beds 32 F3
Chalton Hants 11 C10
Chalvington E Sussex 13 E9
Champany Falk 84 G2
Chancery Ceredig'n 36 H5
Chandler's Ford Hants 11 B7
Channerwick Shetl'd 113 L7
Chantry Som'set 18 G4
Chantry Suffolk 34 D5
Chapel Fife 84 E4
Chapel Allerton Som'set 17 F9
Chapel Allerton W Yorks 57 E8
Chapel Amble Cornw'l 3 B8
Chapel Brampton Northants 31 B9
Chapel Chorlton Staffs 39 B9
Chapel-en-le-Frith Derbys 50 D2
Chapel End Warwick 40 F5
Chapel Green Warwick 40 G4
Chapel Green Warwick 31 B6
Chapel Haddlesey N Yorks 58 F1
Chapel Head Cambs 43 G6
Chapel Hill Aberds 99 E10
Chapel Hill Lincs 52 G5
Chapel Hill Monmouths 18 B2
Chapel Hill N Yorks 57 D8
Chapel Lawn Shrops 38 H4
Chapel-le-Dale N Yorks 62 G2
Chapel Milton Derbys 50 D2
Chapel of Garioch Aberds 99 F7
Chapel Row Berks 20 E3
Chapel St. Leonards Lincs 53 E8
Chapel Stile Cumb 61 D6
Chapelgate Lincs 43 C7
Chapelhall N Lanarks 75 A9
Chapelhill Dumf/Gal 68 A3
Chapelhill H'land 105 E7
Chapelhill N Ayrs 74 C4
Chapelhill Perth/Kinr 84 B4
Chapelhill Perth/Kinr 84 A2
Chapelknowe Dumf/Gal 69 C6
Chapelton Angus 91 G7
Chapelton Devon 7 D6
Chapelton H'land 97 E7
Chapelton S Lanarks 75 C8
Chapeltown Lancs 56 G2
Chapeltown Moray 98 F2
Chapeltown S Yorks 50 C5
Chapmans Well Devon 6 G4
Chapmanslade Wilts 18 G5
Chapmore End Herts 33 G6
Chappel Essex 34 F2
Chard Som'set 8 D5
Chardstock Devon 8 D5
Charfield S Gloucs 18 B4
Charing Kent 14 D4
Charing Cross Dorset 10 C4
Charing Heath Kent 14 D4
Charingworth Glos 30 E4
Charlbury Oxon 30 G5
Charlcombe Bath/NE Som'set 18 E4
Charlecote Warwick 30 C4
Charlecote Park, Wellesbourne Warwick 30 C4
Charles Devon 7 C7
Charles Manning's Amusement Park, Felixstowe Suffolk 35 E6
Charles Tye Suffolk 34 C4
Charlesfield Dumf/Gal 68 D4
Charleston Angus 90 G4
Charleston Renf 75 A6
Charlestown Aberd C 91 A10
Charlestown Cornw'l 3 D9
Charlestown Derbys 50 C2
Charlestown Dorset 9 G8
Charlestown Fife 84 F2
Charlestown Gtr Man 49 B9
Charlestown H'land 96 B4
Charlestown H'land 103 E6
Charlestown W Yorks 56 F4
Charlestown of Aberlour Moray 98 D2
Charlesworth Derbys 50 C2
Charleton Devon 5 F8
Charlton Gtr Lon 22 D4
Charlton Hants 20 G1
Charlton Herts 32 F4
Charlton Heref/Worcs 30 D2
Charlton Northants 31 E7
Charlton Northum 70 B3
Charlton Shrops 39 D6
Charlton Som'set 18 F3
Charlton Wilts 10 B2
Charlton Wilts 19 F8
Charlton Wilts 19 C6
Charlton W Sussex 12 D2
Charlton Abbots Glos 30 F2
Charlton Adam Som'set 9 B7
Charlton All Saints Wilts 10 B4
Charlton Horethorne Som'set 9 B8
Charlton Kings Glos 30 F1
Charlton Mackerell Som'set 9 B7
Charlton Marshall Dorset 10 D1
Charlton Musgrove Som'set 9 B9
Charlton on Otmoor Oxon 31 G7
Charltons Redcar/Clevel'd 64 C4
Charlwood Surrey 22 G2
Charlynch Som'set 17 H7
Charminster Dorset 9 E8
Charmouth Dorset 8 E5
Charndon Bucks 31 F8
Charney Bassett Oxon 20 B1
Charnock Richard Lancs 55 G5
Charsfield Suffolk 35 C6
Chart Corner Kent 14 C2
Chart Sutton Kent 14 D3
Charter Alley Hants 20 F3
Charterhouse Som'set 17 F9
Charterville Allotments Oxon 30 G5
Chartham Kent 15 C6
Chartham Hatch Kent 15 C6
Chartridge Bucks 21 A7
Chartwell, Westerham Kent 22 F4
Charvil Berks 20 D5
Charwelton Northants 31 C7
Chasetown Staffs 40 E2
Chastleton Oxon 30 F4
Chasty Devon 6 F4
Chatburn Lancs 56 D2
Chatcull Staffs 39 B8
Chatham Kent 14 B2
Chathill Northum 79 E6
Chatsworth, Bakewell Derbys 50 E4
Chattenden Kent 23 D7
Chatteris Cambs 43 G6
Chattisham Suffolk 34 D4
Chatto Scot Borders 78 F2
Chatton Northum 78 E5
Chawleigh Devon 7 E8
Chawley Oxon 20 A2
Chawston Beds 32 C4
Chawton Hants 20 H5
Cheadle Gtr Man 49 D9
Cheadle Staffs 40 A2
Cheadle Heath Gtr Man 49 D9
Cheadle Hulme Gtr Man 49 D9
Cheam Gtr Lon 22 E2
Cheapside Surrey 21 F8
Chearsley Bucks 31 G9
Chebsey Staffs 39 C9
Checkendon Oxon 20 C4
Checkley Ches 49 H8
Checkley Heref/Worcs 29 E6
Checkley Staffs 40 B2
Chedburgh Suffolk 34 C1
Cheddar Som'set 17 F9
Cheddar Showcaves and Gorge Som'set 17 F9
Cheddington Bucks 32 G2
Cheddleton Staffs 50 G1
Cheddon Fitzpaine Som'set 8 B4
Chedglow Wilts 19 B6
Chedgrave Norfolk 45 F7
Chedington Dorset 9 D6
Chediston Suffolk 45 H7
Chedworth Glos 30 G2
Chedworth Roman Villa Glos 30 G2
Chedzoy Som'set 17 H8
Cheeklaw Scot Borders 78 B2
Cheeseman's Green Kent 14 E5
Cheglinch Devon 7 B6
Cheldon Devon 7 E8
Chelford Ches 49 E9
Chell Heath Stoke 49 G9
Chellaston Derby C 40 B5
Chellington Beds 32 C2
Chelmarsh Shrops 39 G8
Chelmer Village Essex 33 H10
Chelmondiston Suffolk 35 E6
Chelmorton Derbys 50 F3
Chelmsford Essex 33 H10
Chelsea Gtr Lon 22 D2
Chelsfield Gtr Lon 22 E4
Chelsworth Suffolk 34 D3
Cheltenham Glos 29 F10
Chelveston Northants 32 B2
Chelvey N Som'set 17 E9
Chelwood Bath/NE Som'set 18 E3
Chelwood Common E Sussex 13 C8
Chelwood Gate E Sussex 13 C8
Chelworth Wilts 19 B6
Chelworth Green Wilts 19 B7
Chemistry Shrops 39 A6
Chenies Bucks 21 B8
Cheny Longville Shrops 38 G5
Chepstow Monmouths 18 B2
Chequerfield W Yorks 57 F9
Cherhill Wilts 19 D7
Cherington Glos 19 B6
Cherington Warwick 30 E4
Cheriton Devon 7 B8
Cheriton Hants 11 B8
Cheriton Kent 15 E6
Cheriton Swan 25 G9
Cheriton Bishop Devon 7 G8
Cheriton Fitzpaine Devon 7 F9
Cheriton or Stackpole Elidor Pembs 24 G4
Cherrington Shrops. 39 C7
Cherry Burton E Riding Yorks 58 D5
Cherry Hinton Cambs 33 C7
Cherry Orchard Heref/Worcs 29 C9
Cherry Willingham Lincs 52 E3
Cherrybank Perth/Kinr 84 B3
Chertsey Surrey 21 E8
Cheselbourne Dorset 9 E9
Chesham Bucks 21 A7
Chesham Bois Bucks 21 B7
Cheshire Candle Workshops, Burwardsley Ches 49 G6
Cheshunt Herts 22 A3
Cheslyn Hay Staffs 40 E1
Chessington Gtr Lon 21 E9
Chessington World of Adventures Gtr Lon 21 E9
Chester Ches 48 F5
Chester Cathedral Ches 48 F4
Chester Le Street Durham 71 E7
Chester Moor Durham 71 F7
Chester Zoo Ches 48 E5
Chesterblade Som'set 18 G3
Chesterfield Derbys 50 E5
Chesters Scot Borders 77 F9
Chesters Scot Borders 77 E9
Chesters Roman Fort Northum 70 C4
Chesterton Cambs 42 F4
Chesterton Cambs 33 B7
Chesterton Glos 19 A7
Chesterton Oxon 31 F7
Chesterton Shrops 39 F8
Chesterton Staffs 49 H9
Chesterton Warwick 30 C5
Chesterwood Northum 70 D3
Chestfield Kent 15 B6
Cheston Devon 5 E7
Cheswardine Shrops 39 C8
Cheswick Northum 78 C5
Chetnole Dorset 9 D8
Chettiscombe Devon 8 C1
Chettisham Cambs 43 G8
Chettle Dorset 10 C2
Chetton Shrops 39 F7
Chetwode Bucks 31 F8
Chetwynd Aston Shrops 39 D8
Cheveley Cambs 33 B9
Chevening Kent 22 F4
Chevington Suffolk 34 C1
Chevithorne Devon 8 C1
Chew Magna Bath/NE Som'set 18 E2
Chew Stoke Bath/NE Som'set 18 E2
Chewton Keynsham Bath/NE Som'set 18 E3
Chewton Mendip Som'set 18 F2
Chicheley M/Keynes 32 D2
Chichester W Sussex 12 E2
Chichester Cathedral W Sussex 12 E2
Chickerell Dorset 9 F8
Chicklade Wilts 10 A2
Chicksgrove Wilts 10 A2
Chidden Hants 11 C9
Chiddingfold Surrey 12 B3
Chiddingly E Sussex 13 D9
Chiddingstone Kent 22 G4
Chiddingstone Causeway Kent 22 G5
Chiddingstone Hoath Kent 22 G4
Chideock Dorset 9 E6
Chidham W Sussex 12 E1
Chidswell W Yorks 57 F7
Chieveley Berks 20 D2
Chignall Smealy Essex 33 G9
Chignall St. James Essex 33 H9
Chigwell Essex 22 B4
Chigwell Row Essex 22 B4
Chilbolton Hants 20 H1
Chilcomb Hants 11 B8
Chilcombe Dorset 9 E7
Chilcompton Som'set 18 F3
Chilcote Leics 40 D4
Child Okeford Dorset 9 C10
Childer Thornton Ches 48 E4
Childrey Oxon 20 C1
Child's Ercall Shrops 39 C7
Childswickham Heref/Worcs 30 E2
Childwall Mersey 48 D5
Childwick Green Herts 32 G4
Chilfrome Dorset 9 E7
Chilgrove W Sussex 12 D2
Chilham Kent 14 C5
Chilhampton Wilts 10 A3
Chilla Devon 6 F5
Chillaton Devon 4 B5
Chillenden Kent 15 C7
Chillerton I of Wight 11 F7
Chillesford Suffolk 35 C7
Chillingham Northum 78 E5
Chillington Devon 5 F8
Chillington Som'set 8 C5
Chilmark Wilts 10 A2
Chilson Oxon 30 G5
Chilsworthy Cornw'l 4 C5
Chilsworthy Devon 6 F4
Chilthorne Domer Som'set 9 C7
Chiltington E Sussex 13 D7
Chilton Bucks 31 G8
Chilton Durham 63 B7
Chilton Oxon 20 C2
Chilton Cantelo Som'set 9 B7
Chilton Foliat Wilts 19 D10
Chilton Lane Durham 71 G8
Chilton Polden Som'set 17 H8
Chilton Street Suffolk 34 D1
Chilton Trinity Som'set 17 H7
Chilvers Coton Warwick 40 F5
Chilwell Notts 41 B7
Chilworth Hants 11 C7
Chilworth Surrey 21 G8
Chimney Oxon 20 A1
Chineham Hants 20 F4
Chingford Gtr Lon 22 B3
Chinley Derbys 50 D2
Chinley Head Derbys 50 D2
Chinnor Oxon 20 A5
Chipnall Shrops 39 B8
Chippenhall Green Suffolk 45 H6
Chippenham Cambs 33 B9
Chippenham Wilts 19 D6
Chipperfield Herts 21 A8

D

E

F

Friskney Lincs 53 G7
Friskney Eaudike Lincs 53 G7
Friskney Tofts Lincs 53 G7
Friston E Sussex 13 F9
Friston Suffolk 35 B8
Fritchley Derbys 50 G5
Frith Bank Lincs 53 H6
Frith Common Heref/Worcs 29 B7
Fritham Hants 10 C5
Frithelstock Devon 6 E5
Frithelstock Stone Devon 6 E5
Frithville Lincs 53 G6
Frittenden Kent 14 D3
Frittiscombe Devon 5 F9
Fritton Norfolk 45 F6
Fritton Norfolk 45 E8
Fritwell Oxon 31 F7
Frizinghall W Yorks 57 E6
Frizington Cumb 60 C3
Frocester Glos 18 A4
Frodesley Shrops 39 E6
Frodingham N Lincs 58 G4
Frodsham Ches 49 E6
Frogden Scot Borders 78 E2
Froggatt Derbys 50 E4
Froghall Staffs 50 H2
Frogmore Devon 5 F8
Frogmore Hants 21 F6
Frognall Lincs 42 D4
Frogshail Norfolk 45 B6
Frolesworth Leics 41 F7
Frome Som'set 18 G4
Frome St. Quintin Dorset 9 D7
Fromes Hill Heref/Worcs 29 D7
Fron Denbs 48 F1
Fron Gwyn 46 G5
Fron Gwyn 36 B3
Fron Powys 28 B1
Fron Powys 38 E3
Fron Powys 38 F2
Froncysyllte Wrex 38 A3
Frongoch Gwyn 37 B9
Frontierland Western Theme Park, Morecambe Lancs 55 B4
Frostenden Suffolk 45 G8
Frosterley Durham 70 G5
Frotoft Orkney 112 F5
Froxfield Wilts 19 E9
Froxfield Green Hants 11 B10
Froyle Hants 20 G5
Fryerning Essex 23 A6
Fryton N Yorks 64 G4
Fulbeck Lincs 52 G2
Fulbourn Cambs 33 C8
Fulbrook Oxon 30 G4
Fulford Som'set 8 B4
Fulford Staffs 40 B1
Fulford C of York 58 D2
Fulham Gtr Lon 22 D2
Fulking W Sussex 13 D6
Full Sutton E Riding Yorks 58 C3
Fullarton C of Glasg 75 A8
Fullarton N Ayrs 74 D5
Fuller Street Essex 33 G10
Fuller's Moor Ches 48 G5
Fullerton Hants 20 H1
Fulletby Lincs 52 E5
Fullwood E Ayrs 75 B6
Fulmer Bucks 21 C7
Fulmodestone Norfolk 44 B3
Fulnetby Lincs 52 E3
Fulstow Lincs 53 C6
Fulwell Tyne/Wear 71 E8
Fulwood Lancs 55 E5
Fulwood S Yorks 50 D5
Fundenhall Norfolk 44 F5
Fundenhall Street Norfolk 44 F5
Funtington W Sussex 12 E1
Funtley Hants 11 D8
Funtullich Perth/Kinr 83 B8
Funzie Shetl'd 113 D9
Furley Devon 8 D4
Furnace Arg/Bute 81 D10
Furnace Carms 25 F10
Furnace End Warwick 40 F4
Furneaux Pelham Herts 33 F7
Furness Vale Derbys 50 D2
Furze Platt Berks 21 C6
Furzehill Devon 7 B8
Fyfett Som'set 8 C4
Fyfield Essex 33 H8
Fyfield Glos 19 A9
Fyfield Hants 19 G9
Fyfield Oxon 20 B2
Fyfield Wilts 19 E8
Fylingthorpe N Yorks 65 D7
Fyvie Aberds 99 E7

G

Gabhsann bho Dheas W Isles 107 D8
Gabhsann bho Thuath W Isles 107 D8
Gablon H'land 104 C6
Gabroc Hill E Ayrs 75 B6
Gaddesby Leics 41 D8
Gadebridge Herts 32 H3
Gaer Powys 28 F2
Gaerllwyd Monmouths 17 B9
Gaerwen Angl 46 E4
Gagingwell Oxon 31 F6
Gaick Lodge H'land 89 C8
Gailey Staffs 39 D10
Gainford Durham 63 C6
Gainsborough Lincs 51 C10
Gainsborough Suffolk 34 D5
Gainsford End Essex 33 E10
Gairloch H'land 103 E6
Gairlochy H'land 88 C2
Gairney Bank Perth/Kinr 84 E3
Gairnshiel Lodge Aberds 90 A3
Gaisgill Cumb 61 D9
Gaitsgill Cumb 69 F6
Galashiels Scot Borders 77 D7
Galgate Lancs 55 C4
Galhampton Som'set 9 B8
Gallaberry Dumf/Gal 68 B2
Gallachoille Arg/Bute 81 F7
Gallanach Arg/Bute 81 B8
Gallanach Arg/Bute 86 E2
Gallantry Bank Ches 49 G6
Gallatown Fife 84 E4
Galley Common Warwick 40 F5
Galley Hill Cambs 33 B6
Galleyend Essex 23 A7
Galleywood Essex 23 A7
Gallowfauld Angus 90 G5
Gallows Green Staffs 40 A2
Galltair H'land 94 D5
Galmisdale H'land 86 C4
Galmpton Devon 5 F7
Galmpton Devon 5 E9
Galphay N Yorks 63 G7
Galston E Ayrs 75 D7
Galtrigill H'land 101 G7
Gamblesby Cumb 69 G9
Gamesley Derbys 50 C2
Gamlingay Cambs 32 C5
Gammersgill N Yorks 62 F5
Gamrie Aberds 99 B7
Gamston Notts 51 E9
Ganarew Heref/Worcs 29 G6
Ganavan Arg/Bute 81 A8
Gang Cornw'l 4 D4
Ganllwyd Gwyn 37 C7
Gannochy Angus 91 D6
Gannochy Perth/Kinr 84 B3
Gansclet H'land 111 E8
Ganstead E Riding Yorks 59 E7
Ganthorpe N Yorks 64 G4
Ganton N Yorks 65 G7
Garbat H'land 104 F3
Garbhallt Arg/Bute 81 E10
Garboldisham Norfolk 44 G4
Garden City Flints 48 F4
Garden Village Wrex 48 G4
Garden Village W Yorks 57 E9
Gardenstown Aberds 99 B7
Garderhouse Shetl'd 113 J6
Gardham E Riding Yorks 58 D5
Gardin Shetl'd 113 G7
Gare Hill Som'set 18 G4
Garelochhead Arg/Bute 82 E3
Garford Oxon 20 B2
Garforth W Yorks 57 E9
Gargrave N Yorks 56 C4
Gargunnock Stirl 83 E8
Garlic Street Norfolk 45 G6
Garlieston Dumf/Gal 67 F6
Garlinge Green Kent 15 C6
Garlogie Aberds 99 H7
Garmond Aberds 99 C8
Garmony Arg/Bute 87 G6
Garmouth Moray 98 B3
Garn-yr-erw Torf 28 G3
Garnant Carms 27 G6
Garndiffaith Torf 17 A7
Garndolbenmaen Gwyn 36 A4
Garnedd Conwy 47 G7
Garnett Bridge Cumb 61 E8
Garnfadryn Gwyn 36 B2
Garnkirk N Lanarks 83 H7
Garnlydan Bl Gwent 28 G2
Garnswllt Swan 27 H6
Garrabost W Isles 107 F9
Garragie Lodge H'land 96 E3
Garraron Arg/Bute 81 D8
Garras Cornw'l 3 G6
Garreg Gwyn 37 A6
Garrick Perth/Kinr 83 C9
Garrigill Cumb 70 F2
Garriston N Yorks 63 E6
Garroch Dumf/Gal 67 B7
Garros H'land 102 F2
Garrow Perth/Kinr 89 G9
Garryhorn Dumf/Gal 67 A7
Garsdale Cumb 62 F2
Garsdale Head Cumb 62 E2
Garsdon Wilts 19 C6
Garshall Green Staffs 40 B1
Garsington Oxon 20 A3
Garstang Lancs 55 D4
Garston Mersey 48 D5
Garswood Mersey 49 C6
Gartcosh N Lanarks 83 H7
Garth Bridg 16 B3
Garth Gwyn 46 E5
Garth Powys 27 D9
Garth Shetl'd 113 H5
Garth Wrex 38 A3
Garth Row Cumb 61 E8
Garthamlock C of Glasg 83 H7
Garthbrengy Powys 27 E10
Garthdee Aberd C 91 A10
Gartheli Ceredig'n 26 C5
Garthmyl Powys 38 F2
Garthorpe Leics 41 C10
Garthorpe N Lincs 58 G4
Gartly Aberds 98 E5
Gartmore Stirl 83 E6
Gartnagrenach Arg/Bute 73 B7
Gartness N Lanarks 75 A9
Gartness Stirl 83 F6
Gartocharn W Dunb 82 F5
Garton E Riding Yorks 59 E8
Garton-on-the-Wolds E Riding Yorks 58 C5
Gartsherrie N Lanarks 83 H8
Gartymore H'land 105 A9
Garvald E Loth 85 G7
Garvamore H'land 88 B6
Garvard Arg/Bute 80 E3
Garvault Hotel H'land 110 F2
Garve H'land 104 F2
Garvestone Norfolk 44 E4
Garvock Aberds 91 D8
Garvock Invercl 82 G3
Garway Heref/Worcs 28 F5
Garway Hill Heref/Worcs 28 F5
Gaskan H'land 87 D7
Gastard Wilts 18 E5
Gasthorpe Norfolk 44 G3
Gatcombe I of Wight 11 F7
Gate Burton Lincs 51 D10
Gate Helmsley N Yorks 58 C2
Gateacre Mersey 48 D5
Gatebeck Cumb 61 F8
Gateford Notts 51 D7
Gateforth N Yorks 58 F1
Gatehead E Ayrs 74 D5
Gatehouse Northum 70 B2
Gatehouse of Fleet Dumf/Gal 67 E8
Gatelawbridge Dumf/Gal 76 H2
Gateley Norfolk 44 C3
Gatenby N Yorks 63 F8
Gateshead Tyne/Wear 71 D7
Gatesheath Ches 48 F5
Gateside Aberds 98 G6
Gateside Angus 90 G5
Gateside E Renf 75 B6
Gateside Fife 84 D3
Gateside N Ayrs 74 B5
Gathurst Gtr Man 49 B6
Gatley Gtr Man 49 D9
Gattonside Scot Borders 77 D8
Gaufron Powys 27 B9
Gaulby Leics 41 E8
Gauldry Fife 84 B5
Gaunt's Common Dorset 10 D3
Gautby Lincs 52 E4
Gavinton Scot Borders 78 B2
Gawber S Yorks 50 B5
Gawcott Bucks 31 E8
Gawsworth Ches 49 F9
Gawthorpe W Yorks 57 F7
Gawthrop Cumb 61 F9
Gawthwaite Cumb 60 F5
Gay Street W Sussex 12 C4
Gaydon Warwick 30 C5
Gayfield Orkney 112 C5
Gayhurst M/Keynes 31 D10
Gayle N Yorks 62 F3
Gayles N Yorks 63 D6
Gayton Mersey 48 D3
Gayton Norfolk 43 D10
Gayton Northants 31 C9
Gayton Staffs 40 C1
Gayton le Marsh Lincs 53 D7
Gayton le Wold Lincs 52 D5
Gayton Thorpe Norfolk 43 D10
Gaywood Norfolk 43 C9
Gazeley Suffolk 33 B10
Geanies House H'land 105 E7
Gearraidh Bhailteas W Isles 92 C3
Gearraidh Bhaird W Isles 107 G7
Gearraidh na h-Aibhne W Isles 107 F6
Gearraidh na Monadh W Isles 92 D3
Gearrannan W Isles 106 E5
Geary H'land 101 F8
Geddes House H'land 105 G7
Gedding Suffolk 34 C3
Geddington Northants 42 G1
Gedintailor H'land 94 C2
Gedling Notts 41 A8
Gedney Lincs 43 C7
Gedney Broadgate Lincs 43 C7
Gedney Drove End Lincs 43 C7
Gedney Dyke Lincs 43 C7
Gedney Hill Lincs 43 D6
Gee Cross Gtr Man 50 C1
Geilston Arg/Bute 82 G4
Geirinis W Isles 92 A3
Geise H'land 111 C6
Geisiadar W Isles 106 F5
Geldeston Norfolk 45 F7
Gell Conwy 47 F8
Gelli Pembs 24 E5
Gelli Rh Cyn Taff 16 B4
Gellideg Merth Tyd 27 H10
Gellifor Denbs 48 F2
Gelligaer Caerph 17 B6
Gellilydan Gwyn 37 B6
Gellinudd Neath P Talb 16 A2
Gellyburn Perth/Kinr 90 H1
Gellywen Carms 25 D7
Gelston Dumf/Gal 67 E9
Gelston Lincs 42 A2
Gembling E Riding Yorks 59 C7
Gentleshaw Staffs 40 D2
Geocrab W Isles 101 C7
George Green Bucks 21 C8
George Nympton Devon 7 D8
George Town Bl Gwent 28 H2
Georgefield Dumf/Gal 68 A5
Georgeham Devon 6 C5
Georth Orkney 112 F4
Gerlan Gwyn 47 F6
Germansweek Devon 6 G5
Germoe Cornw'l 2 G4
Gerrans Cornw'l 3 F7
Gerrards Cross Bucks 21 C8
Gestingthorpe Essex 34 E2
Geuffordd Powys 38 D3
Gib Hill Ches 49 E7
Gibbet Hill Warwick 41 G7
Gibbshill Dumf/Gal 67 C9
Gidea Park Gtr Lon 22 C5
Gidleigh Devon 5 B7
Giffnock E Renf 75 B7
Gifford E Loth 85 H7
Giffordland N Ayrs 74 C4
Giffordtown Fife 84 C4
Giggleswick N Yorks 56 B3
Gilberdyke E Riding Yorks 58 F4
Gilchriston E Loth 85 H6
Gilcrux Cumb 68 G4
Gildersome W Yorks 57 F7
Gildingwells S Yorks 51 D7
Gileston V of Glam 16 E5
Gilfach Caerph 17 B6
Gilfach Goch Rh Cyn Taff 16 C4
Gilfachrheda Ceredig'n 26 C4
Gillamoor N Yorks 64 F4
Gillar's Green Mersey 48 C5
Gillen H'land 101 G8
Gilling East N Yorks 64 G4
Gilling West N Yorks 63 D6
Gillingham Dorset 9 B10
Gillingham Kent 14 B2
Gillingham Norfolk 45 F8
Gillock H'land 111 D7
Gillow Heath Staffs 49 G9
Gills H'land 111 B8
Gill's Green Kent 14 E2
Gilmanscleuch Scot Borders 77 E6
Gilmerton C of Edinb 84 H4
Gilmerton Perth/Kinr 83 B9
Gilmonby Durham 62 C4
Gilmorton Leics 41 G7
Gilmourton S Lanarks 75 C8
Gilsland Cumb 69 D9
Gilsland Spa Cumb 69 D9
Gilston Scot Borders 77 B7
Gilwern Monmouths 28 G3
Gimingham Norfolk 45 B6
Giosla W Isles 106 G5
Gipping Suffolk 34 B4
Gipsey Bridge Lincs 52 H5
Girdle Toll N Ayrs 74 C5
Girlsta Shetl'd 113 H7
Girsby N Yorks 63 D8
Girtford Beds 32 C4
Girthon Dumf/Gal 67 E8
Girton Cambs 33 B7
Girton Notts 51 F10
Girvan S Ayrs 74 H3
Gisburn Lancs 56 D3
Gisleham Suffolk 45 G9
Gislingham Suffolk 34 A4
Gissing Norfolk 44 G5
Gittisham Devon 8 E3
Gladestry Powys 28 C3
Gladsmuir E Loth 85 G6
Glais Swan 16 A2
Glaisdale N Yorks 64 D5
Glame H'land 94 B2
Glamis Angus 90 G4
Glamis Castle Angus 90 G4
Glan Adda Gwyn 46 E5
Glan-Conwy Conwy 47 G8
Glan Conwy Conwy 47 E8
Glan-Duar Carms 26 D5
Glan-Dwyfach Gwyn 36 A4
Glan Gors Angl 46 E4
Glan-rhyd Gwyn 46 G4
Glan-traeth Angl 46 E2
Glan-y-don Flints 48 E2
Glan-y-nant Powys 37 G9
Glan-y-wern Gwyn 37 B6
Glan-yr-afon Angl 47 D6
Glan-yr-afon Gwyn 37 A9
Glan-yr-afon Gwyn 37 A10
Glanaman Carms 27 G6
Glandford Norfolk 44 A4
Glandwr Bl Gwent 17 A7
Glandwr Pembs 25 D6
Glandy Cross Carms 24 D6
Glandyfi Ceredig'n 37 F6
Glangrwyney Powys 28 G3
Glanmule Powys 38 F2
Glanrafon Ceredig'n 37 G6
Glanrhyd Gwyn 36 B2
Glanrhyd Pembs 24 B6
Glanton Northum 78 F5
Glanton Pike Northum 78 F5
Glanvilles Wootton Dorset 9 D8
Glapthorn Northants 42 F3
Glapwell Derbys 51 F6
Glas-allt Shiel Aberds 90 C3
Glasbury Powys 28 E2
Glaschoil H'land 97 C8
Glascoed Denbs 47 E9
Glascoed Monmouths 17 A8
Glascoed Powys 38 D2
Glascorrie Aberds 90 B4
Glascote Staffs 40 E4
Glascwm Powys 28 C2
Glasdrum Arg/Bute 87 G10
Glasfryn Conwy 47 G9
Glasgow C of Glasg 83 H6
Glasgow Art Gallery & Museum C of Glasg 83 H6
Glasgow Botanic Gardens C of Glasg 83 H6
Glasgow Cathedral C of Glasg 83 H7
Glashvin H'land 102 F2
Glasinfryn Gwyn 46 F5
Glasnacardoch H'land 94 G3
Glasnakille H'land 94 E2
Glasphein H'land 101 H7
Glaspwll Powys 37 F7
Glassburn H'land 96 C1
Glasserton Dumf/Gal 67 G6
Glassford S Lanarks 75 C9
Glasshouse Hill Glos 29 F8
Glasshouses N Yorks 57 B6
Glasslie Fife 84 D4
Glasson Cumb 68 D5
Glasson Lancs 55 C4
Glassonby Cumb 69 G8
Glasterlaw Angus 91 F6
Glaston Rutl'd 42 E1
Glastonbury Som'set 18 H2
Glastonbury Abbey Som'set 17 H9
Glatton Cambs 42 G4
Glazebrook Ches 49 C7
Glazebury Ches 49 C7
Glazeley Shrops 39 G8
Gleadless S Yorks 50 D5
Gleadsmoss Ches 49 F9
Gleann Ghrabhair W Isles 107 H7
Gleann Tholastaidh W Isles 107 E9
Gleaston Cumb 60 G5
Gleiniant Powys 37 F9
Glemsford Suffolk 34 D2
Glen Dumf/Gal 67 E7
Glen Dumf/Gal 67 C10
Glen Auldyn I of Man 54 D4
Glen Bernisdale H'land 101 H10
Glen House Scot Borders 76 D5
Glen Mona I of Man 54 E4
Glen Nevis House H'land 88 D2
Glen of Luce Dumf/Gal 66 E4
Glen Parva Leics 41 F7
Glen Tanar House Aberds 90 B5
Glen Trool Lodge Dumf/Gal 67 B6
Glen Village Falk 83 G9
Glen Vine I of Man 54 F3
Glenamachrie Arg/Bute 81 B9
Glenbarr Arg/Bute 73 D6
Glenbeg H'land 86 E5
Glenbeg H'land 97 D8
Glenbervie Aberds 91 C8
Glenboig N Lanarks 83 H8
Glenborrodale H'land 87 E6
Glenbranter Arg/Bute 82 E2
Glenbreck Scot Borders 76 E3
Glenbrein Lodge H'land 96 E2
Glenbrittle House H'land 93 C10
Glenbuchat Lodge Aberds 98 G3
Glenbuck E Ayrs 75 E9
Glenburn Renf 75 A6
Glencalvie Lodge H'land 104 D3
Glencanisp Lodge H'land 108 G4
Glencaple Dumf/Gal 68 D2
Glencarron Lodge H'land 103 G8
Glencarse Perth/Kinr 84 B3
Glencassley Castle H'land 104 B3
Glenceitlein H'land 88 G2
Glencoe H'land 88 F1
Glencraig Fife 84 E3
Glencripesdale H'land 87 F6
Glencrosh Dumf/Gal 67 B9
Glendavan Ho. Aberds 90 A5
Glendevon Perth/Kinr 84 D1
Glendoe Lodge H'land 96 F2
Glendoebeg H'land 96 F2
Glendoick Perth/Kinr 84 B4
Glendoll Lodge Angus 90 D3
Glenduckie Fife 84 C4
Glendye Lodge Aberds 91 C7
Gleneagles Hotel Perth/Kinr 83 C10
Gleneagles House Perth/Kinr 83 D10
Glenegedale Arg/Bute 72 B3
Glenelg H'land 94 E5
Glenernie Moray 97 B8
Glenfarg Perth/Kinr 84 C3
Glenfarquhar Lodge Aberds 91 C8
Glenferness House H'land 97 B7
Glenfeshie Lodge H'land 89 B9
Glenfiddich Distillery, Dufftown Moray 98 D3
Glenfield Leics 41 E7
Glenfinnan H'land 87 C8
Glenfoot Perth/Kinr 84 C3
Glenfyne Lodge Arg/Bute 82 C3
Glengarnock N Ayrs 74 B5
Glengorm Castle Arg/Bute 86 F4
Glengrasco H'land 93 A10
Glenhead Farm Angus 90 E3
Glenhoul Dumf/Gal 67 B8
Glenhurich H'land 87 E8
Glenkerry Scot Borders 76 F5
Glenkiln Dumf/Gal 67 C10
Glenkindie Aberds 98 G4
Glenlatterach Moray 105 G10
Glenlee Dumf/Gal 67 B8
Glenlichorn Perth/Kinr 83 C8
Glenlivet Moray 97 D9
Glenlochsie Perth/Kinr 90 D1
Glenloig N Ayrs 73 D9
Glenluce Dumf/Gal 66 E4
Glenmallan Arg/Bute 82 E3
Glenmarskie H'land 104 G2
Glenmassan Arg/Bute 82 F2
Glenmavis N Lanarks 83 H8
Glenmaye I of Man 54 F2
Glenmidge Dumf/Gal 68 B1
Glenmore Arg/Bute 81 C8
Glenmore H'land 93 A10
Glenmore Lodge H'land 97 F7
Glenmoy Angus 90 E5
Glenogil Angus 90 E5
Glenprosen Lodge Angus 90 E3
Glenprosen Village Angus 90 E4
Glenquiech Angus 90 E5
Glenreasdell Mains Arg/Bute 73 B8
Glenree N Ayrs 73 E9
Glenridding Cumb 61 C6
Glenrossal H'land 104 B3
Glenrothes Fife 84 D4
Glensanda H'land 87 G8
Glensaugh Aberds 91 D7
Glenshero Lodge H'land 88 B6
Glensluain Arg/Bute 82 E1
Glenstockadale Dumf/Gal 66 D2
Glenstriven Arg/Bute 82 G1
Glentaggart S Lanarks 75 E10
Glentham Lincs 52 C3
Glentirranmuir Stirl 83 E7
Glenton Aberds 98 F6
Glentress Scot Borders 76 D5
Glentromie Lodge H'land 96 G5
Glentrool Village Dumf/Gal 66 C5
Glentruan I of Man 54 C4
Glentruim House H'land 89 B7
Glenturret Distillery, Crieff Perth/Kinr 83 B9
Glentworth Lincs 52 D2
Glenuig H'land 87 D6
Glenurquhart H'land 104 F6
Glespin S Lanarks 75 E10
Gletness Shetl'd 113 H7
Glewstone Heref/Worcs 29 F6
Glinton Cambs 42 E4
Glooston Leics 41 F9
Glororum Northum 79 D6
Glossop Derbys 50 C2
Gloster Hill Northum 79 G7
Gloucester Glos 29 G9
Gloucester Cathedral Glos 29 G9
Gloup Shetl'd 113 C8
Glusburn N Yorks 56 D5
Gluss Shetl'd 113 F6
Glutt Lodge H'land 110 F4
Glutton Bridge Derbys 50 F2
Glympton Oxon 31 F6
Glyn-Ceiriog Wrex 38 B3
Glyn-cywarch Gwyn 37 B6
Glyn-Neath Neath P Talb 27 H8
Glynarthen Ceredig'n 25 B8
Glynbrochan Powys 37 G9
Glyncoch Rh Cyn Taff 16 B5
Glyncorrwg Neath P Talb 16 B3
Glynde E Sussex 13 E8
Glyndebourne E Sussex 13 D8
Glyndyfrdwy Denbs 38 A2
Glynogwr Bridg 16 C4
Glyntaff Rh Cyn Taff 16 C5
Glyntawe Powys 27 G8
Gnosall Staffs 39 C9
Gnosall Heath Staffs 39 C9
Goadby Leics 41 F9
Goadby Marwood Leics 41 C9
Goat Lees Kent 14 D5
Goatacre Wilts 19 D7
Goathill Dorset 9 C8
Goathland N Yorks 65 D6
Goathurst Som'set 8 A4
Gobernuisgach Lodge H'land 109 E7
Gobhaig W Isles 101 B6
Gobowen Shrops 38 B4
Godalming Surrey 21 G7
Godley Gtr Man 50 C1
Godmanchester Cambs 32 A5
Godmanston Dorset 9 E8
Godmersham Kent 14 C5
Godney Som'set 17 G9
Godolphin Cross Cornw'l 2 F5
Godre'r-graig Neath P Talb 27 H7
Godshill Hants 10 C4
Godshill I of Wight 11 F8
Godstone Surrey 22 F3
Godstone Farm Surrey 22 F3
Godwinscroft Hants 10 E4
Goetre Monmouths 28 H4
Goferydd Angl 46 D2
Goff's Oak Herts 22 A3
Gogar C of Edinb 84 G3
Goginan Ceredig'n 37 G6
Golan Gwyn 36 A5
Golant Cornw'l 4 E2
Golberdon Cornw'l 4 C4
Golborne Gtr Man 49 C7
Golcar W Yorks 57 G6
Gold Hill Norfolk 43 F8
Goldcliff Newp 17 C8
Golden Cross E Sussex 13 D9
Golden Green Kent 23 G6
Golden Grove Carms 26 G5
Golden Hill Hants 10 E5
Golden Pot Hants 20 G5
Golden Valley Glos 29 F10
Goldenhill Stoke 49 G9
Golders Green Gtr Lon 22 C2
Goldhanger Essex 34 H3
Golding Shrops 39 E6
Goldington Beds 32 C3
Goldsborough N Yorks 57 C8
Goldsborough N Yorks 65 C6
Goldsithney Cornw'l 2 F4
Goldsworthy Devon 6 D4
Goldthorpe S Yorks 51 B6
Gollanfield H'land 105 G7
Golspie H'land 105 B7
Golval H'land 110 C3
Gomeldon Wilts 19 H8
Gomersal W Yorks 57 F7
Gomshall Surrey 21 G8
Gonalston Notts 51 H8
Gonfirth Shetl'd 113 G6
Good Easter Essex 33 G9
Gooderstone Norfolk 44 E1
Goodleigh Devon 7 C7
Goodmanham E Riding Yorks 58 D4
Goodnestone Kent 14 B5
Goodnestone Kent 15 C7
Goodrich Heref/Worcs 29 G6
Goodrington Devon 5 E9
Goodshaw Lancs 56 F3
Goodwick Pembs 24 C4
Goodworth Clatford Hants 20 G1
Goole E Riding Yorks 58 F3
Goonbell Cornw'l 3 E6
Goonhavern Cornw'l 3 D6
Goose Eye W Yorks 56 D5
Goose Green Gtr Man 49 B6
Goose Green Norfolk 44 G5
Goose Green W Sussex 12 D5
Gooseham Cornw'l 6 E3
Goosey Oxon 20 B1
Goosnargh Lancs 55 E5
Goostrey Ches 49 E8
Gorcott Hill Warwick 30 B2
Gord Shetl'd 113 L7
Gordon Scot Borders 77 C9
Gordonbush H'land 105 B7
Gordonsburgh Moray 98 B4
Gordonstoun Moray 105 F10
Gordonstown Aberds 98 C5
Gordonstown Aberds 99 E7
Gore Kent 15 C8
Gore Cross Wilts 19 F7
Gore Pit Essex 34 G2
Gorebridge Midloth 77 A6
Gorefield Cambs 43 D7
Gorey Jersey 4
Gorgie C of Edinb 84 G4
Goring Oxon 20 C4
Goring by Sea W Sussex 12 E5
Goring Heath Oxon 20 D4
Gorleston on Sea Norfolk 45 E9
Gornalwood W Midlands 39 F10
Gorrachie Aberds 99 C7
Gorran Churchtown Cornw'l 3 E8
Gorran Haven Cornw'l 3 E9
Gorrenberry Scot Borders 77 H7
Gors Ceredig'n 37 H6
Gorse Hill Thamesd'n 19 C8
Gorsedd Flints 48 E2
Gorseinon Swan 25 G10
Gorseness Orkney 112 G5
Gorsgoch Ceredig'n 26 C4
Gorslas Carms 26 G5
Gorsley Glos 29 F7
Gorstan H'land 104 F2
Gorstanvorran H'land 87 D8
Gorsteyhill Staffs 49 G8
Gorsty Hill Staffs 40 C3
Gortantaoid Arg/Bute 80 G3
Gorton Gtr Man 49 C9
Gosbeck Suffolk 34 C5
Gosberton Lincs 42 B5
Gosberton Clough Lincs 42 C4
Gosfield Essex 34 F1
Gosford Heref/Worcs 29 B6
Gosforth Cumb 60 D3
Gosforth Tyne/Wear 71 D7
Gosmore Herts 32 F4
Gosport Hants 11 E9
Gossabrough Shetl'd 113 E8
Gossington Glos 18 A4
Goswick Northum 78 C5
Gotham Notts 41 B7
Gotherington Glos 30 F1
Gott Shetl'd 113 J7
Goudhurst Kent 14 E2
Goulceby Lincs 52 E5
Gourdas Aberds 99 D7
Gourdon Aberds 91 D9
Gourock Invercl 82 G3
Govan C of Glasg 83 H6
Govanhill C of Glasg 75 A7
Goveton Devon 5 F8
Govilon Monmouths 28 G3
Gowanhill Aberds 99 B10
Gowdall E Riding Yorks 58 F2
Gowerton Swan 25 G10
Gowkhall Fife 84 F2
Gowthorpe E Riding Yorks 58 C3
Goxhill E Riding Yorks 59 D7
Goxhill N Lincs 59 F7
Goxhill Haven N Lincs 59 F7
Goybre Neath P Talb 16 C2
Grabhair W Isles 107 H7
Graby Lincs 42 C3
Grade Cornw'l 3 H6
Graffham W Sussex 12 D3
Grafham Cambs 32 B4
Grafham Surrey 21 G8
Grafton Heref/Worcs 28 E5
Grafton Heref/Worcs 29 B6
Grafton N Yorks 57 B9
Grafton Oxon 19 A9
Grafton Shrops 38 D5
Grafton Flyford Heref/Worcs 30 C1
Grafton Regis Northants 31 D9
Grafton Underwood Northants 42 G2
Grafty Green Kent 14 D3
Graianrhyd Denbs 48 G3
Graig Conwy 47 E8
Graig Denbs 48 E1
Graig-fechan Denbs 48 G2
Grain Kent 23 D8
Grainsby Lincs 52 C5
Grainthorpe Lincs 53 C6
Grampound Cornw'l 3 E8
Grampound Road Cornw'l 3 D8
Gramsdal W Isles 100 G4
Granborough Bucks 31 F9
Granby Notts 41 B9
Grandborough Warwick 31 B6
Grandtully Perth/Kinr 89 F10
Grange Cumb 60 C5
Grange E Ayrs 75 D6
Grange Kent 14 B2
Grange Mersey 48 D3
Grange Perth/Kinr 84 B4
Grange Crossroads Moray 98 C4
Grange Hall Moray 105 F9
Grange Hill Essex 22 B4
Grange Moor W Yorks 57 G7
Grange of Lindores Fife 84 C4
Grange over Sands Cumb 61 G7
Grange Villa Durham 71 E7
Grangemill Derbys 50 G4
Grangemouth Falk 83 F10
Grangepans Falk 84 F2
Grangetown Card 17 D6
Grangetown Redcar/Clevel'd 64 B3
Granish H'land 97 E7
Gransmoor E Riding Yorks 59 C7
Granston Pembs 24 C3
Grantchester Cambs 33 C7
Grantham Lincs 42 B2
Grantley N Yorks 57 B7
Grantlodge Aberds 99 G7
Granton Dumf/Gal 76 G3
Granton C of Edinb 84 G4
Grantown-on-Spey H'land 97 D8
Grantshouse Scot Borders 85 H10
Grappenhall Ches 49 D7
Grasby Lincs 52 B3
Grasmere Cumb 61 D6
Grasscroft Gtr Man 50 B1
Grassendale Mersey 48 D4
Grassholme Durham 62 B4
Grassington N Yorks 56 B5
Grassmoor Derbys 51 F6
Grassthorpe Notts 51 F9
Grateley Hants 19 G9
Gratwich Staffs 40 B2
Graveley Cambs 32 B5
Graveley Herts 32 F5
Gravelly Hill W Midlands 40 F3
Gravels Shrops 38 E4
Graveney Kent 14 B5
Gravesend Kent 23 D6
Grayingham Lincs 52 C2
Grayrigg Cumb 61 E8
Grays Essex 23 D6
Grayshott Hants 12 B2
Grayswood Surrey 12 B3
Graythorp Hartlep'l 64 B3
Grazeley Berks 20 E4
Greasbrough S Yorks 51 C6
Greasby Mersey 48 D3
Great Abington Cambs 33 D8
Great Addington Northants 32 A2
Great Alne Warwick 30 C3
Great Altcar Lancs 48 B4
Great Amwell Herts 33 G6
Great Asby Cumb 61 C9
Great Ashfield Suffolk 34 B3
Great Ayton N Yorks 64 C3
Great Baddow Essex 23 A7
Great Badminton S Gloucs 18 C5
Great Bardfield Essex 33 E9
Great Barford Beds 32 C4
Great Barr W Midlands 40 F2
Great Barrington Glos 30 G4
Great Barrow Ches 48 F5
Great Barton Suffolk 34 B2
Great Barugh N Yorks 64 G5
Great Bavington Northum 70 B4
Great Bealings Suffolk 35 D6
Great Bedwyn Wilts 19 E9
Great Bentley Essex 34 F5
Great Billing Northants 31 B10
Great Bircham Norfolk 44 B1
Great Blakenham Suffolk 34 C5
Great Blencow Cumb 69 G7
Great Bolas Shrops 39 C7
Great Bookham Surrey 21 F9
Great Bourton Oxon 31 D6
Great Bowden Leics 41 G9
Great Bradley Suffolk 33 C9
Great Braxted Essex 34 G2
Great Bricett Suffolk 34 C4
Great Brickhill Bucks 32 E2
Great Bridgeford Staffs 39 C9
Great Brington Northants 31 B8
Great Bromley Essex 34 F4
Great Broughton Cumb 68 G3
Great Broughton N Yorks 64 D3
Great Budworth Ches 49 E7
Great Burdon D'lington 63 C8
Great Burgh Surrey 22 F2
Great Burstead Essex 23 B6
Great Busby N Yorks 64 D3
Great Canfield Essex 33 G8
Great Carlton Lincs 53 D7
Great Casterton Rutl'd 42 E3
Great Chart Kent 14 D4
Great Chatwell Staffs 39 D8
Great Chesterford Essex 33 D8
Great Cheverell Wilts 19 F6
Great Chishill Cambs 33 E7
Great Clacton Essex 34 G5
Great Cliff W Yorks 57 G8
Great Clifton Cumb 60 B3
Great Coates NE Lincs 52 B5
Great Comberton Heref/Worcs 30 D1
Great Corby Cumb 69 E7
Great Cornard Suffolk 34 D2
Great Cowden E Riding Yorks 59 D8
Great Coxwell Oxon 19 B9
Great Crakehall N Yorks 63 E7
Great Cransley Northants 41 H10
Great Cressingham Norfolk 44 E2
Great Crosby Mersey 48 C4
Great Cubley Derbys 40 B3
Great Dalby Leics 41 D9
Great Doddington Northants 32 B1
Great Dunham Norfolk 44 D2
Great Dunmow Essex 33 F9
Great Durnford Wilts 19 H8
Great Easton Essex 33 F9
Great Easton Leics 41 F10
Great Eccleston Lancs 55 D4
Great Edstone N Yorks 64 F5
Great Ellingham Norfolk 44 F4
Great Elm Som'set 18 G4
Great Everdon Northants 31 C7
Great Eversden Cambs 33 C6
Great Fencote N Yorks 63 E7
Great Finborough Suffolk 34 C4
Great Fransham Norfolk 44 D2
Great Gaddesden Herts 32 G3
Great Gidding Cambs 42 G4
Great Givendale E Riding Yorks 58 C4
Great Glemham Suffolk 35 B7
Great Glen Leics 41 F8
Great Gonerby Lincs 42 B1
Great Gransden Cambs 32 C5
Great Green Norfolk 45 G6
Great Green Suffolk 34 C3
Great Habton N Yorks 64 G5
Great Hale Lincs 42 A4
Great Hampden Bucks 21 A6
Great Harrowden Northants 32 A1
Great Harwood Lancs 56 E2
Great Haseley Oxon 20 A4
Great Hatfield E Riding Yorks 59 D7
Great Haywood Staffs 40 C2
Great Heath W Midlands 40 G5
Great Heck N Yorks 58 F1
Great Henny Essex 34 E2
Great Hinton Wilts 19 F6
Great Hockham Norfolk 44 F3
Great Holland Essex 35 G6
Great Horkesley Essex 34 E3
Great Hormead Herts 33 F6
Great Horton W Yorks 57 E6
Great Horwood Bucks 31 E9
Great Houghton Northants 31 C9
Great Houghton S Yorks 51 B6
Great Hucklow Derbys 50 E3
Great Kelk E Riding Yorks 59 C7
Great Kimble Bucks 31 H10
Great Kingshill Bucks 21 B6
Great Langton N Yorks 63 E7
Great Leighs Essex 33 G10
Great Lever Gtr Man 49 B8
Great Limber Lincs 52 B4
Great Linford M/Keynes 32 D1
Great Livermere Suffolk 34 A2
Great Longstone Derbys 50 E4
Great Lumley Durham 71 F7
Great Lyth Shrops 38 E5
Great Malvern Heref/Worcs 29 D8
Great Maplestead Essex 34 E2
Great Marton Lancs 55 E3
Great Massingham Norfolk 44 C1
Great Melton Norfolk 44 E5
Great Milton Oxon 20 A4
Great Missenden Bucks 21 A6
Great Mitton Lancs 56 E2
Great Mongeham Kent 15 C8
Great Moulton Norfolk 44 F5
Great Munden Herts 33 F6
Great Musgrave Cumb 62 C2
Great Ness Shrops 38 D4
Great Oakley Essex 34 F5
Great Oakley Northants 42 G1
Great Offley Herts 32 F4
Great Orme Tramway, Llandudno Conwy 47 D7
Great Ormside Cumb 62 C2
Great Orton Cumb 69 E6
Great Ouseburn N Yorks 57 B9
Great Oxendon Northants 41 G9
Great Oxney Green Essex 33 H9
Great Palgrave Norfolk 44 D2
Great Paxton Cambs 32 B5
Great Plumpton Lancs 55 E3
Great Plumstead Norfolk 45 D7
Great Ponton Lincs 42 B2
Great Preston W Yorks 57 F9
Great Raveley Cambs 42 G5
Great Rissington Glos 30 G3
Great Rollright Oxon 30 E5
Great Ryburgh Norfolk 44 C3
Great Ryle Northum 78 F5
Great Ryton Shrops 38 E5
Great Saling Essex 33 F10
Great Salkeld Cumb 69 G8
Great Sampford Essex 33 E9
Great Sankey Ches 49 D6
Great Saxham Suffolk 34 B1
Great Shefford Berks 20 D1
Great Shelford Cambs 33 C7
Great Smeaton N Yorks 63 D8
Great Snoring Norfolk 44 B3
Great Somerford Wilts 19 C6
Great Stainton Durham 63 B8
Great Stambridge Essex 23 B8
Great Staughton Cambs 32 B4
Great Steeping Lincs 53 F7
Great Stonar Kent 15 C8
Great Strickland Cumb 61 B8
Great Stukeley Cambs 32 A5
Great Sturton Lincs 52 E5
Great Sutton Ches 48 E4
Great Sutton Shrops 39 G6
Great Swinburne Northum 70 C4
Great Tew Oxon 30 F5
Great Tey Essex 34 F2
Great Thurkleby N Yorks 63 G9
Great Thurlow Suffolk 33 C9
Great Torrington Devon 6 E5
Great Tosson Northum 78 G5
Great Totham Essex 34 G2
Great Totham Essex 34 G2
Great Tows Lincs 52 C5
Great Urswick Cumb 60 G5
Great Wakering Essex 23 C9
Great Waldingfield Suffolk 34 D3
Great Walsingham Norfolk 44 B3
Great Waltham Essex 33 G9
Great Warley Essex 22 B5
Great Washbourne Glos 30 E1
Great Weldon Northants 42 G2
Great Welnetham Suffolk 34 C2
Great Wenham Suffolk 34 E4
Great Whittington Northum 70 C5
Great Wigborough Essex 34 G3
Great Wilbraham Cambs 33 C8
Great Wishford Wilts 19 H7
Great Witcombe Glos 29 G10
Great Witley Heref/Worcs 29 B8
Great Wolford Warwick 30 E4
Great Wratting Suffolk 33 D9
Great Wymondley Herts 32 F5
Great Wyrley Staffs 40 E1
Great Wytheford Shrops 39 D6
Great Yarmouth Norfolk 45 E9
Great Yarmouth Sea Life Centre Norfolk 45 E9
Great Yeldham Essex 34 E1
Greater Doward Heref/Worcs 29 G6
Greatford Lincs 42 D3
Greatgate Staffs 40 A2
Greatham Hants 12 B1
Greatham Hartlep'l 63 B9
Greatham W Sussex 12 D4
Greatstone on Sea Kent 14 F5
Greatworth Northants 31 D7
Greave Lancs 56 F3
Greeba I of Man 54 E3
Green Denbs 48 F1
Green End Beds 32 C4
Green Hammerton N Yorks 57 C9
Green Lane Powys 38 F2
Green Ore Som'set 18 F2
Green St. Green Gtr Lon 22 E4
Green Street Herts 21 B9
Greenbank Shetl'd 113 C8
Greenburn W Loth 76 A2
Greendikes Northum 78 E5
Greenfield Beds 32 E3
Greenfield Flints 48 E2
Greenfield Gtr Man 50 B1
Greenfield H'land 95 F9
Greenfield Oxon 20 B5
Greenford Gtr Lon 21 C9
Greengairs N Lanarks 83 G8
Greenham Berks 20 E2
Greenhaugh Northum 70 B2
Greenhead Northum 69 D9
Greenhill Falk 83 G9
Greenhill Gtr Lon 21 C9
Greenhill Kent 15 B6
Greenhill Leics 41 D6
Greenhills N Ayrs 74 B5
Greenhithe Kent 22 D5
Greenholm E Ayrs 75 D7
Greenholme Cumb 61 D8
Greenhouse Scot Borders 77 E8
Greenhow Hill N Yorks 57 B6
Greenigo Orkney 112 H5
Greenland H'land 111 C7
Greenlands Bucks 20 C5
Greenlaw Aberds 99 C6
Greenlaw Scot Borders 78 C2
Greenlea Dumf/Gal 68 C3
Greenloaning Perth/Kinr 83 D9
Greenmeadow Community Farm, Pontnewydd Torf 17 B7
Greenmount Gtr Man 56 G2
Greenmow Shetl'd 113 L7
Greenock Invercl 82 G3
Greenock West Invercl 82 G3
Greenodd Cumb 61 F6
Greenrow Cumb 68 E4
Greens Norton Northants 31 D8
Greenside Tyne/Wear 71 D6
Greensidehill Northum 78 F4
Greenstead Green Essex 34 F2
Greensted Essex 22 A5
Greenway Pembs 24 C5
Greenwich Gtr Lon 22 D3
Greet Glos 30 E2
Greete Shrops 29 A6
Greetham Lincs 53 E6
Greetham Rutl'd 42 D2
Greetland W Yorks 56 F5
Gregg Hall Cumb 61 E7
Gregson Lane Lancs 55 F5
Greinetobht W Isles 100 E4
Greinton Som'set 17 H9
Grenaby I of Man 54 F2
Grendon Northants 32 B1
Grendon Warwick 40 E4
Grendon Common Warwick 40 F4
Grendon Green Heref/Worcs 29 C6
Grendon Underwood Bucks 31 F8
Grenofen Devon 4 C5
Grenoside S Yorks 50 C5
Greosabhagh W Isles 101 C7
Gresford Wrex 48 G4
Gresham Norfolk 44 B5
Greshornish H'land 101 G9
Gressenhall Norfolk 44 D3
Gressingham Lancs 55 B5
Gresty Green Ches 49 G8
Greta Bridge Durham 62 C5
Gretna Dumf/Gal 69 D6
Gretna Green Dumf/Gal 69 D6
Gretton Glos 30 E2
Gretton Northants 42 F1
Gretton Shrops 39 F6
Grewelthorpe N Yorks 63 G7
Grey Green N Lincs 51 B9
Greygarth N Yorks 63 G6
Greynor Carms 25 F10
Greysouthen Cumb 60 B3
Greystoke Cumb 69 G7
Greystone Angus 91 G6
Greystone Dumf/Gal 68 C2
Greywell Hants 20 F5
Griais W Isles 107 E8
Grianan W Isles 107 F8
Gribthorpe E Riding Yorks 58 E3
Gridley Corner Devon 6 G4
Griff Warwick 40 G5
Griffithstown Torf 17 B7
Grimbister Orkney 112 G4
Grimblethorpe Lincs 52 D5
Grimeford Village Lancs 55 G6
Grimethorpe S Yorks 51 B6
Griminis W Isles 100 G3
Grimista Shetl'd 113 J7
Grimister Shetl'd 113 D7
Grimley Heref/Worcs 29 B9
Grimness Orkney 112 J5
Grimoldby Lincs 53 D6
Grimpo Shrops 38 C4
Grimsargh Lancs 55 E5
Grimsbury Oxon 31 D6
Grimsby NE Lincs 59 G8
Grimscote Northants 31 C8
Grimscott Cornw'l 6 F3
Grimsthorpe Lincs 42 C3
Grimston E Riding Yorks 59 E8
Grimston Leics 41 C8
Grimston Norfolk 43 C10
Grimston C of York 58 C2
Grimstone Dorset 9 E8
Grinacombe Moor Devon 6 G5
Grindale E Riding Yorks 65 G9
Grindigair Orkney 112 H6
Grindiscol Shetl'd 113 K7
Grindle Shrops 39 E8
Grindleford Derbys 50 E4
Grindleton Lancs 56 D2
Grindley Staffs 40 C2
Grindley Brook Shrops 39 A6
Grindlow Derbys 50 E3
Grindon Northum 78 C4
Grindon Staffs 50 G2
Grindonmoor Gate Staffs 50 G2
Gringley on the Hill Notts 51 C9
Grinsdale Cumb 69 E6
Grinshill Shrops 39 C6
Grinton N Yorks 62 E5
Griomsiadar W Isles 107 G7
Grishipoll Arg/Bute 86 F1
Grisling Common E Sussex 13 C8
Gristhorpe N Yorks 65 F8
Griston Norfolk 44 F3
Gritley Orkney 112 H6
Grittenham Wilts 19 C7
Grittleton Wilts 18 C5
Grizebeck Cumb 60 F5
Grizedale Cumb 61 E6
Grobister Orkney 112 F7
Groby Leics 41 E7
Groes Conwy 47 F10
Groes Neath P Talb 16 C2
Groes faen Rh Cyn Taff 16 C5
Groes-lwyd Powys 38 D3
Groesffordd Marli Denbs 47 E10
Groeslon Gwyn 46 F5
Groeslon Gwyn 46 G4
Grogport Arg/Bute 73 C8
Gromford Suffolk 35 C7
Gronant Flints 48 D1
Groombridge E Sussex 13 B9
Grosmont Monmouths 28 F5
Grosmont N Yorks 65 D6
Grosvenor Museum, Chester Ches 48 F5
Groton Suffolk 34 D3
Grouville Jersey 4
Grove Dorset 9 G9
Grove Kent 15 B7
Grove Notts 51 E9
Grove Oxon 20 B2
Grove Park Gtr Lon 22 D4
Grove Vale W Midlands 40 F2
Grovesend Swan 25 F10
Grudie H'land 104 F2
Gruids H'land 104 B4
Gruinard House H'land 103 C7
Grula H'land 93 C9
Gruline Arg/Bute 86 G5
Grunasound Shetl'd 113 K6
Grundisburgh Suffolk 35 C6
Grunsagill Lancs 56 C2
Gruting Shetl'd 113 J5
Gt. Bridge W Midlands 40 F1
Gt. Hallingbury Essex 33 G8
Gt. Parndon Essex 33 H7
Gualachulain H'land 88 G2
Gualin Ho. H'land 109 D6
Guardbridge Fife 85 C6
Guarlford Heref/Worcs 29 D9
Guay Perth/Kinr 89 G11
Guestling Green E Sussex 14 G3
Guestling Thorn E Sussex 14 G3
Guestwick Norfolk 44 C4
Guestwick Green Norfolk 44 C4
Guide Lancs 56 F2
Guide Post Northum 71 B7
Guilden Morden Cambs 32 D5
Guilden Sutton Ches 48 F5
Guildford Surrey 21 G7
Guildtown Perth/Kinr 84 A3
Guilsborough Northants 31 A8
Guilsfield Powys 38 D3
Guilton Kent 15 C7
Guineaford Devon 7 C6
Guisborough Redcar/Clevel'd 64 C4
Guiseley W Yorks 57 D6
Guist Norfolk 44 C3
Guith Orkney 112 E6
Guiting Power Glos 30 F2
Gulberwick Shetl'd 113 K7
Gullane E Loth 85 F6
Gulval Cornw'l 2 F3
Gulworthy Devon 4 C5
Gumfreston Pembs 24 F6
Gumley Leics 41 F8
Gummow's Shop Cornw'l 3 D7
Gun Hill E Sussex 13 D9
Gunby E Riding Yorks 58 E3
Gunby Lincs 42 C2
Gundleton Hants 11 A9
Gunn Devon 7 C7
Gunnerside N Yorks 62 E4
Gunnerton Northum 70 C4
Gunness N Lincs 58 G4
Gunnislake Cornw'l 4 C5
Gunnista Shetl'd 113 J8
Gunthorpe Cambs 42 E4
Gunthorpe Norfolk 44 B4
Gunthorpe Notts 41 A8
Gunville I of Wight 11 F7
Gunwalloe Cornw'l 2 G5
Gurnard I of Wight 11 E7
Gurnett Ches 49 E10
Gurney Slade Som'set 18 G3
Gurnos Powys 27 H7
Gussage All Saints Dorset 10 C3
Gussage St. Michael Dorset 10 C2
Guston Kent 15 D8
Gutcher Shetl'd 113 D8
Guthrie Angus 91 F6
Guyhirn Cambs 43 E6
Guyhirn Gull Cambs 43 E6
Guy's Head Lincs 43 C7
Guy's Marsh Dorset 9 B10
Guyzance Northum 79 G7
Gwaenysgor Flints 48 D1
Gwalchmai Angl 46 E3
Gwaun-Cae-Gurwen Neath P Talb 27 G7
Gwaun-Leision Neath P Talb 27 G7
Gwbert Ceredig'n 25 B6
Gweek Cornw'l 3 G6
Gwehelog Monmouths 17 A8
Gwenddwr Powys 28 D1
Gwennap Cornw'l 3 F6
Gwenter Cornw'l 3 H6
Gwernaffield Flints 48 F3
Gwernesney Monmouths 17 A9
Gwernogle Carms 26 E5
Gwernymynydd Flints 48 F3
Gwersyllt Wrex 48 G4
Gwespyr Flints 48 D2
Gwithian Cornw'l 2 E4
Gwredog Angl 46 D4
Gwyddelwern Denbs 48 H1
Gwyddgrug Carms 25 C9
Gwydyr Uchaf Conwy 47 F7
Gwynfryn Wrex 48 G3
Gwystre Powys 28 B1
Gwytherin Conwy 47 F8
Gyfelia Wrex 48 H4
Gyffin Conwy 47 E7
Gyrn-goch Gwyn 46 H4

H

Habberley Shrops 38 E4
Habergham Lancs 56 E3
Habrough NE Lincs 59 G7
Haceby Lincs 42 B3
Hacheston Suffolk 35 C7
Hackbridge Gtr Lon 22 E2
Hackenthorpe S Yorks 51 D6
Hackford Norfolk 44 E4
Hackforth N Yorks 63 E7
Hackland Orkney 112 F4
Hackleton Northants 31 C10
Hackness N Yorks 65 E7
Hackness Orkney 112 J4
Hackney Gtr Lon 22 C3
Hackthorn Lincs 52 D2
Hackthorpe Cumb 61 B8
Haconby Lincs 42 C4
Hacton Gtr Lon 22 C5
Hadden Scot Borders 78 D2
Haddenham Bucks 31 H9
Haddenham Cambs 43 H7
Haddington E Loth 85 G7
Haddington Lincs 52 F2
Haddiscoe Norfolk 45 F8
Haddon Cambs 42 F4
Haddon Ches 50 F1
Haddon Hall Derbys 50 F4
Hade Edge W Yorks 50 B3
Hademore Staffs 40 E3
Hadfield Derbys 50 C2
Hadham Cross Herts 33 G7
Hadham Ford Herts 33 F7
Hadleigh Essex 23 C8
Hadleigh Suffolk 34 D4
Hadley Shrops 39 D7
Hadley End Staffs 40 C3
Hadlow Kent 23 G6
Hadlow Down E Sussex 13 C9
Hadnall Shrops 39 D6
Hadstock Essex 33 D8
Hady Derbys 50 E5
Hadzor Heref/Worcs 29 B10
Haffenden Quarter Kent 14 D3
Hafod-Dinbych Conwy 47 G8
Hafod-lom Conwy 47 E8
Haggate Lancs 56 E3
Haggbeck Cumb 69 C7
Haggerston Northum 78 C5
Haggrister Shetl'd 113 F6
Hagley Heref/Worcs 29 D6
Hagley Heref/Worcs 39 G10
Hagworthingham Lincs 53 F6
Haigh Gtr Man 49 B7
Haigh S Yorks 57 G7
Haigh Moor W Yorks 57 F7
Haighton Green Lancs 55 E5
Hail Weston Cambs 32 B4
Haile Cumb 60 D3
Hailes Glos 30 E2
Hailey Herts 33 G6
Hailey Oxon 30 G5
Hailsham E Sussex 13 E9
Haimer H'land 111 C6
Hainault Gtr Lon 22 B4
Hainford Norfolk 45 D6
Hainton Lincs 52 D4
Hairmyers S Lanarks 75 B8
Haisthorpe E Riding Yorks 59 B7
Hakin Pembs 24 F3
Halam Notts 51 G8
Halbeath Fife 84 F3
Halberton Devon 8 C2
Halcro H'land 111 C7

Hopley's Green Heref/Worcs 28 C4
Hopperton N Yorks 57 C9
Hopstone Shrops 39 F8
Hopton Shrops 38 C4
Hopton Shrops 39 C6
Hopton Staffs 39 C10
Hopton Suffolk 44 H3
Hopton Cangeford Shrops 39 G6
Hopton Castle Shrops 38 H4
Hopton on Sea Norfolk 45 E9
Hopton Wafers Shrops 39 H7
Hoptonheath Shrops 38 H4
Hopwas Staffs 40 E3
Hopwood Gtr Man 49 B9
Hopwood Heref/Worcs 40 H2
Horam E Sussex 13 D9
Horbling Lincs 42 B4
Horbury W Yorks 57 G7
Horcott Glos 19 A8
Horden Durham 71 F9
Horderley Shrops 38 G5
Hordle Hants 10 E5
Hordley Shrops 38 B4
Horeb Ceredig'n 25 B8
Horeb Carms 25 F9
Horeb Carms 26 F5
Horfield Bristol 18 D3
Horham Suffolk 35 A6
Horkesley Heath Essex 34 F3
Horkstow N Lincs 58 G5
Horley Oxon 31 D6
Horley Surrey 22 G2
Hornblotton Green Som'set 9 A7
Hornby Lancs 55 B5
Hornby N Yorks 63 E7
Hornby N Yorks 63 D8
Horncastle Lincs 52 F5
Hornchurch Gtr Lon 22 C5
Horncliffe Northum 78 C4
Horndean Scot Borders 78 C3
Horndean Hants 11 C10
Horndon Devon 5 C6
Horndon on the Hill Essex 23 C6
Horne Surrey 22 G3
Horniehaugh Angus 90 E5
Horning Norfolk 45 D7
Horninghold Leics 41 F10
Horninglow Staffs 40 C4
Horningsea Cambs 33 B7
Horningsham Wilts 18 G5
Horningtoft Norfolk 44 C3
Horns Corner Kent 14 F2
Horns Cross Devon 6 D4
Horns Cross E Sussex 14 F3
Hornsby Cumb 69 E8
Hornsea E Riding Yorks 59 D8
Hornsea Bridge E Riding Yorks 59 D8
Hornsea Freeport E Riding Yorks 59 D8
Hornsey Gtr Lon 22 C3
Hornton Oxon 30 D5
Horrabridge Devon 5 D6
Horringer Suffolk 34 B2
Horringford I of Wight 11 F8
Horse Bridge Staffs 50 G1
Horsebridge Devon 4 C5
Horsebridge Hants 11 A6
Horsebrook Staffs 39 D9
Horsehay Shrops 39 E7
Horseheath Cambs 33 D9
Horsehouse N Yorks 62 F5
Horsell Surrey 21 F7
Horseman's Green Wrex 38 A5
Horseway Cambs 43 G7
Horsey Norfolk 45 C8
Horsford Norfolk 44 D5
Horsforth W Yorks 57 E7
Horsham Heref/Worcs 29 C8
Horsham W Sussex 12 B5
Horsham St. Faith Norfolk 45 D6
Horsington Lincs 52 F4
Horsington Som'set 9 B9
Horsley Derbys 40 A5
Horsley Glos 18 B5
Horsley Northum 70 D5
Horsley Northum 78 H3
Horsley Cross Essex 34 F5
Horsley Woodhouse Derbys 40 A5
Horsleycross Street Essex 34 F5
Horsleyhill Scot Borders 77 F8
Horsleyhope Durham 70 F5
Horsmonden Kent 14 D1
Horspath Oxon 20 A3
Horstead Norfolk 45 D6
Horsted Keynes W Sussex 13 C7
Horton Berks 21 D8
Horton Bucks 32 G2
Horton Dorset 10 D3
Horton Lancs 56 C3
Horton Northants 31 C10
Horton Shrops 38 C5
Horton S Gloucs 18 C4
Horton Som'set 8 C5
Horton Staffs 49 G10
Horton Swan 25 H9
Horton Wilts 19 E7
Horton-cum-Studley Oxon 31 G7
Horton Green Ches 48 H5
Horton Heath Hants 11 C7
Horton-in-Ribblesdale N Yorks 62 G3
Horton Kirby Kent 22 E5
Hortonlane Shrops 38 D5
Horwich Gtr Man 56 G1
Horwich End Derbys 50 D2
Horwood Devon 7 D6
Hose Leics 41 C9
Hoselaw Scot Borders 78 D3
Hoses Cumb 60 E5
Hosh Perth/Kinr 83 B9
Hosta W Isles 100 E3
Hoswick Shetl'd 113 L7
Hotham E Riding Yorks 58 E4
Hothfield Kent 14 D4
Hoton Leics 41 C7
Houbie Shetl'd 113 D9
Houdston S Ayrs 74 H3
Hough Ches 49 G8
Hough Ches 49 E9
Hough Green Ches 48 D5
Hough-on-the-Hill Lincs 52 H2
Hougham Lincs 42 A1
Houghton Cambs 32 A5
Houghton Cumb 69 E7
Houghton Hants 11 A6
Houghton Pembs 24 F4
Houghton W Sussex 12 D4
Houghton Conquest Beds 32 D3
Houghton Green Ches 49 C7
Houghton Green E Sussex 14 F4
Houghton-le-Side Durham 63 B7
Houghton-Le-Spring Tyne/Wear 71 F8
Houghton on the Hill Leics 41 E8
Houghton Regis Beds 32 F3
Houghton St. Giles Norfolk 44 B3
Houlland Shetl'd 113 H6
Houlland Shetl'd 113 F8
Houlsyke N Yorks 64 D5
Hound Hants 11 D7
Hound Green Hants 20 F5
Houndslow Scot Borders 77 C9
Houndwood Scot Borders 78 A3
Hounslow Gtr Lon 21 D9
Hounslow Grn. Essex 33 G9
Housay Shetl'd 113 F9
House of Daviot H'land 96 B5
House of Glenmuick Aberds 90 B4
Housesteads Roman Fort Northum 70 D2
Housetter Shetl'd 113 E6
Houss Shetl'd 113 K6
Houston Renf 82 H5
Houstry H'land 111 F6
Houth Orkney 112 H4
Hove Brighton/Hove 13 E6
Hoveringham Notts 51 H8
Hoveton Norfolk 45 D7
Hovingham N Yorks 64 G4
How Cumb 69 E8
How Caple Heref/Worcs 29 E7
How End Beds 32 D3
How Green Kent 22 G4
Howbrook S Yorks 50 C5
Howden Scot Borders 77 E9
Howden E Riding Yorks 58 F3
Howden-le-Wear Durham 71 G6
Howe H'land 111 C8
Howe Norfolk 45 E6
Howe N Yorks 63 F8
Howe Bridge Gtr Man 49 B7
Howe Green Essex 23 A7
Howe of Teuchar Aberds 99 D7
Howe Street Essex 33 G9
Howe Street Essex 33 E9
Howell Lincs 52 H4
Howey Powys 28 C1
Howgate Midloth 76 B5
Howick Northum 79 F7
Howle Durham 62 B5
Howle Shrops 39 C7
Howlett End Essex 33 E8
Howley Som'set 8 D4
Hownam Scot Borders 78 F2
Hownam Mains Scot Borders 78 E2
Howpasley Scot Borders 77 G6
Howsham N Lincs 52 B3
Howsham N Yorks 58 B3
Howtel Northum 78 D3
Howton Heref/Worcs 28 F5
Howtown Cumb 61 C7
Howwood Renf 74 A5
Hoxa Orkney 112 J5
Hoxne Suffolk 44 H5
Hoylake Mersey 48 D3
Hoyland S Yorks 50 B5
Hoylandswaine S Yorks 50 B4
Hubberholme N Yorks 62 G4
Hubbert's Bridge Lincs 42 A5
Huby N Yorks 57 D7
Huby N Yorks 58 B1
Hucclecote Glos 29 G9
Hucking Kent 14 C3
Hucknall Notts 51 H7
Huddersfield W Yorks 57 G6
Huddington Heref/Worcs 29 C10
Hudswell N Yorks 63 D6
Huggate E Riding Yorks 58 C4
Hugglescote Leics 41 D6
Hugh Town I of Scilly 2 C3
Hughenden Valley Bucks 21 B6
Hughley Shrops 39 F6
Huish Devon 7 E6
Huish Wilts 19 E8
Huish Champflower Som'set 8 B2
Huish Episcopi Som'set 9 B6
Huisinis W Isles 100 A5
Hulcott Bucks 32 G1
Hulland Derbys 50 H4
Hulland Ward Derbys 50 H4
Hullavington Wilts 18 C5
Hullbridge Essex 23 B8
Hulme Gtr Man 49 C9
Hulme End Staffs 50 G3
Hulme Walfield Ches 49 F9
Hulver Street Suffolk 45 G8
Hulverstone I of Wight 11 F6
Humber Court Heref/Worcs 29 C6
Humberston NE Lincs 53 B6
Humbie E Loth 77 A7
Humbleton E Riding Yorks 59 E8
Humbleton Northum 78 E4
Humby Lincs 42 B3
Hume Scot Borders 78 C2
Humshaugh Northum 70 C4
Huna H'land 111 B8
Huncoat Lancs 56 E2
Huncote Leics 41 F7
Hundalee Scot Borders 77 F9
Hunderthwaite Durham 62 B4
Hundle Houses Lincs 52 G5
Hundleby Lincs 53 F6
Hundleton Pembs 24 F4
Hundon Suffolk 33 D10
Hundred Acres Hants 11 C8
Hundred End Lancs 55 F4
Hundred House Powys 28 C2
Hungarton Leics 41 E8
Hungerford Berks 19 E10
Hungerford Hants 10 C4
Hungerford Newtown Berks 20 D1
Hungerton Lincs 42 C1
Hungladder H'land 101 E9
Hunmanby N Yorks 65 G8
Hunmanby Moor N Yorks 65 G9
Hunningham Warwick 30 B5
Hunny Hill I of Wight 11 F7
Hunsdon Herts 33 G7
Hunsingore N Yorks 57 C9
Hunslet W Yorks 57 E8
Hunsonby Cumb 69 G8
Hunspow H'land 111 B7
Hunstanton Norfolk 43 A9
Hunstanworth Durham 70 F4
Hunsterson Ches 49 H7
Hunston Suffolk 34 B3
Hunston W Sussex 12 E2
Hunstrete Bath/NE Som'set 18 E3
Hunt End Heref/Worcs 30 B2
Hunter's Quay Arg/Bute 82 G2
Hunthill Lodge Angus 90 D5
Hunting-tower Perth/Kinr 84 B2
Huntingdon Cambs 32 A5
Huntingfield Suffolk 35 A7
Huntingford Dorset 9 A10
Huntington E Loth 85 G6
Huntington Heref/Worcs 28 C3
Huntington Staffs 40 D1
Huntington C of York 58 C2
Huntley Glos 29 G8
Huntly Aberds 98 E5
Huntlywood Scot Borders 77 C9
Hunton Kent 14 D2
Hunton N Yorks 63 E6
Hunt's Corner Norfolk 44 G4
Hunt's Cross Mersey 48 D5
Huntsham Devon 8 B2
Huntspill Som'set 17 G8
Huntworth Som'set 8 A5
Hunwick Durham 71 G6
Hunworth Norfolk 44 B4
Hurdsfield Ches 49 E10
Hurley Berks 21 C6
Hurley Warwick 40 F4
Hurlford E Ayrs 75 D6
Hurliness Orkney 112 K3
Hurn Dorset 10 E4
Hurn's End Lincs 53 H7
Hursley Hants 11 B7
Hurst Berks 20 D5
Hurst N Yorks 62 D5
Hurst Som'set 9 C6
Hurst Green E Sussex 14 F2
Hurst Green Lancs 56 E1
Hurst Wickham W Sussex 13 D6
Hurstbourne Priors Hants 20 G2
Hurstbourne Tarrant Hants 20 F1
Hurstpierpoint W Sussex 13 D6
Hurstway Common Heref/Worcs 28 D3
Hurstwood Lancs 56 E3
Hurtmore Surrey 21 G7
Hurworth Place Durham 63 D7
Hury Durham 62 C4
Husabost Pier H'land 101 G8
Husbands Bosworth Leics 41 G8
Husborne Crawley Beds 32 E2
Husthwaite N Yorks 64 G3
Hutchwns Bridg 16 D3
Huthwaite Notts 51 G6
Huttoft Lincs 53 E8
Hutton Scot Borders 78 B4
Hutton Cumb 61 B7
Hutton E Riding Yorks 59 C6
Hutton Essex 23 B6
Hutton Lancs 55 F4
Hutton N Som'set 17 F8
Hutton Buscel N Yorks 65 F7
Hutton Conyers N Yorks 63 G8
Hutton Cranswick E Riding Yorks 59 C6
Hutton End Cumb 69 G7
Hutton Gate Redcar/Clevel'd 64 C3
Hutton Henry Durham 71 G9
Hutton-le-Hole N Yorks 64 E5
Hutton Magna Durham 63 C6
Hutton Roof Cumb 69 G6
Hutton Roof Cumb 61 G8
Hutton Rudby N Yorks 63 D9
Hutton Sessay N Yorks 63 G9
Hutton Village Redcar/Clevel'd 64 C3
Hutton Wandesley N Yorks 57 C10
Huxley Ches 49 F6
Huxter Shetl'd 113 H6
Huxter Shetl'd 113 G8
Huxton Scot Borders 85 H10
Huyton Mersey 48 C5
Hycemoor Cumb 60 F3
Hyde Glos 18 A5
Hyde Gtr Man 49 C10
Hyde Hants 10 C4
Hyde Heath Bucks 21 A7
Hyde Park S Yorks 51 B7
Hydestile Surrey 21 G7
Hylton Castle Tyne/Wear 71 E8
Hyndford Bridge S Lanarks 76 C2
Hynish Arg/Bute 86 E1
Hyssington Powys 38 F4
Hythe Hants 11 D7
Hythe Kent 15 E6
Hythe End Berks 21 D8
Hythie Aberds 99 C10

I

Ibberton Dorset 9 D9
Ible Derbys 50 G4
Ibsley Hants 10 D4
Ibstock Leics 41 D6
Ibstone Bucks 20 B5
Ibthorpe Hants 20 F1
Ibworth Hants 20 F3
Ichrachan Arg/Bute 81 A10
Ickburgh Norfolk 44 F2
Ickenham Gtr Lon 21 C8
Ickford Bucks 31 H8
Ickham Kent 15 C7
Ickleford Herts 32 E4
Icklesham E Sussex 14 G3
Ickleton Cambs 33 D7
Icklingham Suffolk 34 A1
Ickwell Green Beds 32 D4
Ickworth House Suffolk 34 B2
Icomb Glos 30 F4
Idbury Oxon 30 G4
Iddesleigh Devon 7 F6
Ide Devon 7 G9
Ide Hill Kent 22 F4
Ideford Devon 5 C9
Iden E Sussex 14 F4
Iden Green Kent 14 E3
Iden Green Kent 14 E2
Idle W Yorks 57 E6
Idlicote Warwick 30 D4
Idmiston Wilts 19 H8
Idole Carms 25 E9
Idridgehay Derbys 50 H4
Idrigill H'land 101 F9
Idstone Oxon 19 C9
Idvies Angus 91 G6
Iffley Oxon 20 A3
Ifield W Sussex 13 B6
Ifold W Sussex 12 B4
Iford E Sussex 13 E8
Ifton Heath Shrops 38 B4
Ightfield Shrops 39 B6
Ightham Kent 22 F5
Ightham Mote, Sevenoaks Kent 22 F5
Iken Suffolk 35 C8
Ilam Staffs 50 G3
Ilchester Som'set 9 B7
Ilderton Northum 78 E5
Ilford Gtr Lon 22 C4
Ilfracombe Devon 7 B6
Ilkeston Derbys 41 A6
Ilketshall St. Andrew Suffolk 45 G7
Ilketshall St. Lawrence Suffolk 45 G7
Ilketshall St. Margaret Suffolk 45 G7
Ilkley W Yorks 57 D6
Illey W Midlands 40 G1
Illingworth W Yorks 56 F5
Illogan Cornw'l 2 E5
Illston on the Hill Leics 41 F9
Ilmer Bucks 31 H9
Ilmington Warwick 30 D4
Ilminster Som'set 8 C5
Ilsington Devon 5 C8
Ilston Swan 25 G10
Ilton N Yorks 63 G6
Ilton Som'set 8 C5
Imachar N Ayrs 73 C8
Imeraval Arg/Bute 72 C3
Immingham NE Lincs 59 G7
Imperial War Museum Gtr Lon 22 D3
Impington Cambs 33 B7
Ince Ches 48 E5
Ince Blundell Mersey 48 B4
Ince in Makerfield Gtr Man 49 B6
Inch of Arnhall Aberds 91 D7
Inchbare Angus 91 E7
Inchberry Moray 98 C3
Inchbraoch Angus 91 F8
Incheril H'land 103 F8
Inchgrundle Angus 90 D5
Inchina H'land 103 C7
Inchinnan Renf 82 H5
Inchkinloch H'land 109 E8
Inchlaggan H'land 95 F8
Inchlumpie H'land 104 E4
Inchmore H'land 96 B1
Inchnacardoch Hotel H'land 96 E1
Inchnadamph H'land 108 G5
Inchture Perth/Kinr 84 B4
Inchyra Perth/Kinr 84 B3
Indian Queens Cornw'l 3 D8
Inerval Arg/Bute 72 C3
Ingatestone Essex 23 B6
Ingbirchworth S Yorks 50 B4
Ingestre Staffs 40 C1
Ingham Lincs 52 D2
Ingham Norfolk 45 C7
Ingham Suffolk 34 A2
Ingham Corner Norfolk 45 C7
Ingleborough Norfolk 43 D7
Ingleby Derbys 40 C5
Ingleby Lincs 52 E1
Ingleby Arncliffe N Yorks 63 D9
Ingleby Barwick Stockton 63 C9
Ingleby Greenhow N Yorks 64 D3
Inglemire Kingston/Hull 59 E6
Inglesbatch Bath/NE Som'set 18 E4
Inglesham Thamesd'n 19 B9
Ingleton Durham 63 B6
Ingleton N Yorks 61 G9
Inglewhite Lancs 55 D5
Ingliston C of Edinb 84 G3
Ingoe Northum 70 C5
Ingol Lancs 55 E5
Ingoldisthorpe Norfolk 43 B9
Ingoldmells Lincs 53 F8
Ingoldsby Lincs 42 B3
Ingon Warwick 30 C4
Ingram Northum 78 F5
Ingrave Essex 23 B6
Ingrow W Yorks 56 E5
Ings Cumb 61 E7
Ingst S Gloucs 18 C2
Ingworth Norfolk 44 C5
Inham's End Cambs 42 F5
Inkberrow Heref/Worcs 30 C2
Inkpen Berks 20 E1
Inkstack H'land 111 B7
Inn Cumb 61 D7
Innellan Arg/Bute 82 H2
Innerleithen Scot Borders 77 D6
Innerleven Fife 84 D5
Innermessan Dumf/Gal 66 D2
Innerwick E Loth 85 G9
Innerwick Perth/Kinr 89 G6
Innis Chonain Arg/Bute 82 B2
Insch Aberds 98 F6
Insh H'land 97 F6
Inshore H'land 109 C6
Inskip Lancs 55 E4
Instoneville S Yorks 58 G1
Instow Devon 6 C5
Intake S Yorks 51 B7
Inver Aberds 90 B3
Inver H'land 105 D7
Inver Perth/Kinr 89 G11
Inver Mallie H'land 88 C2
Inverailort H'land 87 C7
Inveralligin H'land 103 G6
Inverallochy Aberds 99 B10
Inveran H'land 104 C4
Inveraray Arg/Bute 82 D1
Inveraray Jail Arg/Bute 82 D1
Inverarish H'land 94 C2
Inverarity Angus 90 G5
Inverarnan Stirl 82 C4
Inverasdale H'land 103 D6
Inverbeg Arg/Bute 82 E4
Inverbervie Aberds 91 D9
Inverboyndie Aberds 99 B6
Inverbroom H'land 103 D9
Invercassley H'land 104 B3
Invercauld House Aberds 90 B2
Inverchaolain Arg/Bute 82 G1
Invercharnan H'land 88 G2
Inverchoran H'land 103 G10
Invercreran Arg/Bute 87 G10
Inverdruie H'land 97 E7
Inverebrie Aberds 99 E9
Invereck Arg/Bute 82 F2
Inverernan Ho. Aberds 98 G3
Invereshie House H'land 97 F6
Inveresk E Loth 84 G5
Inverewe Gardens, Gairloch H'land 103 D6
Inverey Aberds 90 C1
Inverfarigaig H'land 96 D3
Invergarry H'land 95 F10
Invergeldie Perth/Kinr 83 B8
Invergordon H'land 104 F6
Invergowrie Perth/Kinr 84 A5
Inverguseran H'land 94 F4
Inverhadden Perth/Kinr 89 F7
Inverharroch Moray 98 E3
Inverherive Stirl 82 B4
Inverie H'land 94 G4
Inverinan Arg/Bute 81 C9
Inverinate H'land 95 D6
Inverkeilor Angus 91 G7
Inverkeithing Fife 84 F3
Inverkeithny Aberds 98 D6
Inverkip Invercl 82 G3
Inverkirkaig H'land 108 H3
Inverlael H'land 103 D9
Inverlochlarig Stirl 82 C5
Inverlochy Arg/Bute 82 B2
Inverlochy H'land 88 D2
Inverlussa Arg/Bute 81 F6
Invermark Lodge Angus 90 C5
Invermoidart H'land 87 D6
Invermoriston H'land 96 E2
Invernaver H'land 110 C2
Inverneill Arg/Bute 81 F8
Inverness H'land 96 B4
Invernoaden Arg/Bute 82 E2
Inveroran Hotel Arg/Bute 88 G3
Inverpolly Lodge H'land 103 A8
Inverquharity Angus 90 F5
Inverquhomery Aberds 99 D10
Inverroy H'land 88 C3
Inversanda H'land 87 F9
Invershiel H'land 95 E6
Invershin H'land 104 C4
Inversnaid Hotel Stirl 82 D4
Inverugie Aberds 99 D11
Inveruglas Arg/Bute 82 D4
Inveruglass H'land 97 F6
Inverurie Aberds 99 F7
Invervar Perth/Kinr 89 G7
Inverythan Aberds 99 D7
Inwardleigh Devon 7 G6
Inworth Essex 34 G2
Iochdar W Isles 100 H3
Iona Abbey and Cathedral Arg/Bute 80 B2
Iping W Sussex 12 C2
Ipplepen Devon 5 D9
Ipsden Oxon 20 C4
Ipsley Heref/Worcs 30 B2
Ipstones Staffs 50 G2
Ipswich Suffolk 34 D5
Irby Mersey 48 D3
Irby in the Marsh Lincs 53 F7
Irby upon Humber NE Lincs 52 B4
Irchester Northants 32 B2
Ireby Cumb 68 G5
Ireby Lancs 61 G9
Ireland Orkney 112 H4
Ireland Shetl'd 113 L6
Ireland's Cross Shrops 39 A8
Ireleth Cumb 60 G5
Ireshopeburn Durham 70 G3
Irlam Gtr Man 49 C8
Irnham Lincs 42 C3
Iron Acton S Gloucs 18 C3
Iron Cross Warwick 30 C2
Ironbridge Shrops 39 E7
Ironbridge Gorge Museum, Telford Shrops 39 E7
Ironmacannie Dumf/Gal 67 C8
Ironside Aberds 99 C8
Ironville Derbys 51 G6
Irstead Norfolk 45 C7
Irthington Cumb 69 D7
Irthlingborough Northants 32 A2
Irton N Yorks 65 F8
Irvine N Ayrs 74 D5
Isauld H'land 110 C4
Isbister Orkney 112 F3
Isbister Orkney 112 G4
Isbister Shetl'd 113 D6
Isbister Shetl'd 113 G8
Isfield E Sussex 13 D8
Isham Northants 32 A1
Isle Abbotts Som'set 8 B5
Isle Brewers Som'set 8 B5
Isle of Whithorn Dumf/Gal 67 G6
Isleham Cambs 33 A9
Isleornsay H'land 94 E3
Islesburgh Shetl'd 113 G6
Islesteps Dumf/Gal 68 C2
Isleworth Gtr Lon 21 D9
Isley Walton Leics 41 C6
Islibhig W Isles 106 G3
Islington Gtr Lon 22 C3
Islip Northants 42 H2
Islip Oxon 31 G7
Istead Rise Kent 23 E6
Isycoed Wrex 48 G5
Itchen S'thampton 11 C7
Itchen Abbas Hants 11 A8
Itchen Stoke Hants 11 A8
Itchingfield W Sussex 12 C5
Itchington S Gloucs 18 C3
Itteringham Norfolk 44 B5
Itton Devon 7 G7
Itton Common Monmouths 17 B9
Ivegill Cumb 69 F7
Iver Bucks 21 C8
Iver Heath Bucks 21 C8
Iveston Durham 71 E6
Ivinghoe Bucks 32 G2
Ivinghoe Aston Bucks 32 G2
Ivington Heref/Worcs 28 C5
Ivington Green Heref/Worcs 28 C5
Ivy Chimneys Essex 22 A4
Ivy Cross Dorset 10 B1
Ivy Hatch Kent 22 F5
Ivybridge Devon 5 E7
Ivychurch Kent 14 F5
Iwade Kent 14 B4
Iwerne Courtney or Shroton Dorset 10 C1
Iwerne Minster Dorset 10 C1
Ixworth Suffolk 34 A3
Ixworth Thorpe Suffolk 34 A3

J

Jack Hill N Yorks 57 C7
Jack in the Green Devon 8 E2
Jacksdale Notts 51 G6
Jackstown Aberds 99 E7
Jacobstow Cornw'l 6 G2
Jacobstowe Devon 7 F6
Jameston Pembs 24 G5
Jamestown W Dunb 82 F4
Jamestown Dumf/Gal 77 H6
Jamestown H'land 104 G3
Jarrow Tyne/Wear 71 D8
Jarvis Brook E Sussex 13 C9
Jasper's Green Essex 33 F10
Jawcraig Falk 83 G9
Jaywick Essex 34 G5
Jealott's Hill Berks 21 D6
Jedburgh Scot Borders 77 E9
Jeffreyston Pembs 24 F5
Jellyhill E Dunb 83 G7
Jemimaville H'land 104 F6
Jersey Farm Herts 32 H4
Jersey Zoo & Wildlife Park Jersey 4
Jesmond Tyne/Wear 71 D7
Jevington E Sussex 13 E9
Jockey End Herts 32 G3
Jodrell Bank Science Centre, Holmes Chapel Ches 49 E8
John o'Groats H'land 111 B8
Johnby Cumb 69 G7
John's Cross E Sussex 14 F2
Johnshaven Aberds 91 E8
Johnston Pembs 24 E4
Johnstone Renf 75 A6
Johnstonebridge Dumf/Gal 68 A3
Johnstown Carms 25 E8
Johnstown Wrex 48 H4
Joppa C of Edinb 84 G5
Joppa S Ayrs 75 F6
Jordans Bucks 21 B7
Jordanthorpe S Yorks 50 D5
Jorvik Centre, York C of York 58 C2
Jump S Yorks 50 B5
Jumpers Green Dorset 10 E4
Juniper Green C of Edinb 84 H3
Jurby East I of Man 54 D3
Jurby West I of Man 54 D3

K

Kaber Cumb 62 C2
Kaimend S Lanarks 76 C2
Kaimes C of Edinb 84 H4
Kalemouth Scot Borders 78 E2
Kalnakill H'land 102 G4
Kames Arg/Bute 81 G9
Kames Arg/Bute 81 C8
Kames E Ayrs 75 E8
Kea Cornw'l 3 E7
Keadby N Lincs 58 G4
Keal Cotes Lincs 53 F6
Kearsley Gtr Man 49 B8
Kearstwick Cumb 61 F9
Kearton N Yorks 62 E4
Kearvaig H'land 108 B5
Keasden N Yorks 56 B2
Keckwick Ches 49 D6
Keddington Lincs 53 D6
Kedington Suffolk 33 D10
Kedleston Derbys 40 A5
Kedleston Hall Derbys 40 A5
Keelby Lincs 59 G7
Keele Staffs 49 H9
Keeley Green Beds 32 D3
Keeston Pembs 24 E4
Keevil Wilts 19 F6
Kegworth Leics 41 C6
Kehelland Cornw'l 2 E5
Keig Aberds 98 G6
Keighley W Yorks 56 D5
Keighley and Worth Valley Railway W Yorks 56 E5
Keil H'land 87 F9
Keilarsbrae Clack 83 E9
Keilhill Aberds 99 C7
Keillmore Arg/Bute 81 F6
Keillor Perth/Kinr 90 G3
Keillour Perth/Kinr 84 B1
Keills Arg/Bute 80 H4
Keils Arg/Bute 80 H5
Keinton Mandeville Som'set 9 A7
Keir Mill Dumf/Gal 68 A1
Keisby Lincs 42 C3
Keiss H'land 111 C8
Keith Moray 98 C4
Keith Inch Aberds 99 D11
Keithock Angus 91 E7
Kelbrook Lancs 56 D4
Kelby Lincs 42 A3
Keld Cumb 61 C8
Keld N Yorks 62 D3
Keldholme N Yorks 64 F5
Kelfield N Lincs 51 B10
Kelfield N Yorks 58 E1
Kelham Notts 51 G9
Kellan Arg/Bute 86 G5
Kellas Angus 90 H5
Kellas Moray 105 G10
Kellaton Devon 5 G9
Kelleth Cumb 61 D9
Kelleythorpe E Riding Yorks 58 C5
Kelling Norfolk 44 A4
Kellingley N Yorks 57 F10
Kellington N Yorks 58 F1
Kelloe Durham 71 G8
Kelloholm Dumf/Gal 75 F9
Kelly Devon 4 B4
Kelly Bray Cornw'l 4 C4
Kelmarsh Northants 41 H9
Kelmscot Oxon 19 B9
Kelsale Suffolk 35 B7
Kelsall Ches 49 F6
Kelsall Hill Ches 49 F6
Kelshall Herts 33 E6
Kelsick Cumb 68 E4
Kelso Scot Borders 78 D2
Kelstedge Derbys 50 F5
Kelstern Lincs 52 C5
Kelston Bath/NE Som'set 18 E4
Keltneyburn Perth/Kinr 89 G8
Kelton Dumf/Gal 68 C2
Kelty Fife 84 E3
Kelvedon Essex 34 G2
Kelvedon Hatch Essex 22 B5
Kelvin S Lanarks 75 B8
Kelvinside C of Glasg 83 H6
Kelynack Cornw'l 2 F2
Kemback Fife 84 C6
Kemberton Shrops 39 E8
Kemble Glos 19 B6
Kemerton Heref/Worcs 29 E10
Kemeys Commander Monmouths 17 A8
Kemnay Aberds 99 G7
Kemp Town Brighton/Hove 13 E7
Kempley Glos 29 F7
Kemps Green Warwick 30 A3
Kempsey Heref/Worcs 29 D9
Kempsford Glos 19 B8
Kempshott Hants 20 F4
Kempston Beds 32 D3
Kempston Hardwick Beds 32 D3
Kempton Shrops 38 G4
Kemsing Kent 22 F5
Kemsley Kent 14 B4
Kenardington Kent 14 E4
Kenchester Heref/Worcs 28 D5
Kencot Oxon 19 A9
Kendal Cumb 61 E8
Kendray S Yorks 50 B5
Kenfig Bridg 16 C3
Kenfig Hill Bridg 16 C3
Kenilworth Warwick 30 A4
Kenilworth Castle Warwick 30 A4
Kenknock Stirl 88 H5
Kenley Gtr Lon 22 F3
Kenley Shrops 39 E6
Kenmore H'land 102 G5
Kenmore Perth/Kinr 89 G8
Kenn Devon 5 B10
Kenn N Som'set 17 E9
Kennacley W Isles 101 C7
Kennacraig Arg/Bute 73 A8
Kennerleigh Devon 7 F9
Kennet Clack 83 E10
Kennethmont Aberds 98 F5
Kennett Cambs 33 B9
Kennford Devon 5 B10
Kenninghall Norfolk 44 G4
Kenninghall Heath Norfolk 44 G4
Kennington Kent 14 D5
Kennington Oxon 20 A3
Kennoway Fife 84 D5
Kenny Hill Suffolk 43 H9
Kennythorpe N Yorks 58 B3
Kenovay Arg/Bute 86 D1
Kensaleyre H'land 101 G10
Kensington Gtr Lon 22 D2
Kensworth Beds 32 G3
Kensworth Common Beds 32 G3
Kent Street E Sussex 14 G2
Kent Street Kent 14 C1
Kent Street W Sussex 13 C6
Kentallen H'land 87 F10
Kentchurch Heref/Worcs 28 F5
Kentford Suffolk 33 B10
Kentisbeare Devon 8 D2
Kentisbury Devon 7 B7
Kentisbury Ford Devon 7 B7
Kentmere Cumb 61 D7
Kenton Devon 8 F1
Kenton Suffolk 34 B5
Kenton Tyne/Wear 71 D7
Kenton Bankfoot Tyne/Wear 71 D7
Kentra H'land 87 E6
Kents Bank Cumb 61 G6
Kent's Green Glos 29 F8
Kent's Oak Hants 11 B6
Kenwick Shrops 38 B5
Kenwyn Cornw'l 3 E7
Keoldale H'land 109 C6
Keppanach H'land 87 E10
Keppoch H'land 95 D6
Keprigan Arg/Bute 73 F6
Kepwick N Yorks 63 E9
Kerchesters Scot Borders 78 D2
Keresley W Midlands 40 G5
Kernborough Devon 5 F8
Kerne Bridge Heref/Worcs 29 G6
Kerris Cornw'l 2 G3
Kerry Powys 38 G2
Kerrycroy Arg/Bute 74 A3
Kerry's Gate Heref/Worcs 28 E4
Kerrysdale H'land 103 E6
Kersall Notts 51 F9
Kersey Suffolk 34 D4
Kershope Foot Cumb 69 B7
Kersoe Heref/Worcs 30 E1
Kerswell Devon 8 D2
Kerswell Grn. Heref/Worcs 29 D9
Kesgrave Suffolk 35 D6
Kessingland Suffolk 45 G9
Kessingland Beach Suffolk 45 G9
Kessington E Dunb 83 G6
Kestle Cornw'l 3 E8
Kestle Mill Cornw'l 3 D7
Keston Gtr Lon 22 E4
Keswick Cumb 60 B5
Keswick Norfolk 45 E6
Keswick Norfolk 45 B7
Ketley Shrops 39 D7
Ketley Bank Shrops 39 D7
Ketsby Lincs 53 E6
Kettering Northants 42 H1
Ketteringham Norfolk 44 E5
Kettins Perth/Kinr 90 H3
Kettlebaston Suffolk 34 C3
Kettlebridge Fife 84 D5
Kettleburgh Suffolk 35 B6
Kettlehill Fife 84 D5
Kettleholm Dumf/Gal 68 C4
Kettleness N Yorks 65 C6
Kettleshume Ches 50 E1
Kettlesing Bottom N Yorks 57 C7
Kettlesing Head N Yorks 57 C7
Kettlestone Norfolk 44 B3
Kettlethorpe Lincs 51 E10
Kettletoft Orkney 112 E7
Kettlewell N Yorks 62 G4
Ketton Rutl'd 42 E2
Kew Gtr Lon 21 D9
Kew Gardens Gtr Lon 21 D9
Kewstoke N Som'set 17 E8
Kexbrough S Yorks 50 B5
Kexby Lincs 52 D1
Kexby C of York 58 C3
Key Green Ches 49 F9
Keyham Leics 41 E8
Keyhaven Hants 11 E6
Keyingham E Riding Yorks 59 F8
Keymer W Sussex 13 D7
Keynsham Bath/NE Som'set 18 E3
Keysoe Beds 32 B3
Keysoe Row Beds 32 B3
Keyston Cambs 42 H3
Keyworth Notts 41 B8
Kibblesworth Tyne/Wear 71 E7
Kibworth Beauchamp Leics 41 F8
Kibworth Harcourt Leics 41 F8
Kidbrooke Gtr Lon 22 D4
Kiddemore Green Staffs 39 E9
Kidderminster Heref/Worcs 39 H9
Kiddington Oxon 31 F6
Kidlington Oxon 31 G6
Kidmore End Oxon 20 D4
Kidsgrove Staffs 49 G9
Kidstones N Yorks 62 F4
Kidwelly Carms 25 F9
Kiel Crofts Arg/Bute 87 H9
Kielder Northum 69 A9
Kielder Castle Visitor Centre Northum 69 A9
Kierfiold House Orkney 112 G3
Kilbagie Clack 83 F10
Kilbarchan Renf 75 A6
Kilbeg H'land 94 F3
Kilberry Arg/Bute 73 A7
Kilbirnie N Ayrs 74 B5
Kilbride Arg/Bute 81 B8
Kilbride Arg/Bute 81 B9
Kilbride H'land 94 D2
Kilburn Angus 90 E4
Kilburn Derbys 50 H5
Kilburn Gtr Lon 22 C2
Kilburn N Yorks 64 G3
Kilby Leics 41 F8
Kilchamaig Arg/Bute 73 A8
Kilchattan Arg/Bute 80 E3
Kilchattan Bay Arg/Bute 74 B3
Kilchenzie Arg/Bute 73 E6
Kilcheran Arg/Bute 87 H8
Kilchiaran Arg/Bute 72 A2
Kilchoan Arg/Bute 81 C7
Kilchoan H'land 86 E4
Kilchoman Arg/Bute 72 A2
Kilchrenan Arg/Bute 81 B10
Kilconquhar Fife 85 D6
Kilcot Glos 29 F7
Kilcoy H'land 104 G4
Kilcreggan Arg/Bute 82 F3
Kildale N Yorks 64 D4
Kildalloig Arg/Bute 73 F7
Kildary H'land 105 E6
Kildermorie Lodge H'land 104 E4
Kildonan N Ayrs 74 E2
Kildonan Lodge H'land 110 G4
Kildonnan H'land 86 C4
Kildrummy Aberds 98 G4
Kildwick N Yorks 56 D5
Kilfinan Arg/Bute 81 G9
Kilfinnan H'land 95 G9
Kilgetty Pembs 24 F6
Kilgwrrwg Common Monmouths 17 B9
Kilham E Riding Yorks 59 B6
Kilham Northum 78 D3
Kilkenneth Arg/Bute 86 D1
Kilkerran Arg/Bute 73 F7
Kilkhampton Cornw'l 6 E3
Killamarsh Derbys 51 D6
Killay Swan 25 G11
Killbeg Arg/Bute 87 G6
Killean Arg/Bute 73 C6
Killearn Stirl 83 F6
Killen H'land 104 G5
Killerby Durham 63 C6
Killerton House, Exeter Devon 8 D1
Killichonan Perth/Kinr 88 F6
Killiechonate H'land 88 C3
Killiechronan Arg/Bute 86 G5
Killiecrankie Perth/Kinr 89 E10
Killiemor Arg/Bute 86 H4
Killiemore House Arg/Bute 80 B4
Killilan H'land 95 C6
Killimster H'land 111 D8
Killin Stirl 83 A6
Killin Lodge H'land 96 F3
Killinallan Arg/Bute 80 G3
Killinghall N Yorks 57 C7
Killington Cumb 61 F9
Killingworth Tyne/Wear 71 C7
Killmahumaig Arg/Bute 81 E7
Killochyett Scot Borders 77 C7
Killocraw Arg/Bute 73 D6
Killundine H'land 86 G5
Kilmacolm Invercl 82 H4
Kilmaha Arg/Bute 81 D9
Kilmahog Stirl 83 D7
Kilmalieu H'land 87 F8
Kilmaluag H'land 101 E10
Kilmany Fife 84 B5
Kilmarie H'land 94 E2
Kilmarnock E Ayrs 75 D6
Kilmaron Castle Fife 84 C5
Kilmartin Arg/Bute 81 E8
Kilmaurs E Ayrs 75 C6
Kilmelford Arg/Bute 81 C8
Kilmeny Arg/Bute 80 H3
Kilmersdon Som'set 18 F3
Kilmeston Hants 11 B8
Kilmichael Arg/Bute 73 E6
Kilmichael Glassary Arg/Bute 81 E8
Kilmichael of Inverlussa Arg/Bute 81 F7
Kilmington Devon 8 E4
Kilmington Wilts 18 H4
Kilmonivaig H'land 88 C2
Kilmorack H'land 96 B2
Kilmore Arg/Bute 81 B8
Kilmore H'land 94 F3
Kilmory Arg/Bute 81 G7
Kilmory H'land 86 D5
Kilmory H'land 93 E9
Kilmory N Ayrs 73 E9
Kilmuir H'land 101 H8
Kilmuir H'land 96 B4
Kilmuir H'land 105 E6
Kilmuir H'land 101 E9
Kilmun Arg/Bute 82 F2
Kilmun Arg/Bute 81 C9
Kiln Pit Hill Northum 70 E5
Kilncadzow S Lanarks 76 C1
Kilndown Kent 14 E2
Kilnhurst S Yorks 51 C6
Kilninian Arg/Bute 86 G3
Kilninver Arg/Bute 81 B8
Kilnsea E Riding Yorks 59 G10
Kilnsey N Yorks 56 B4
Kilnwick E Riding Yorks 58 D5
Kilnwick Percy E Riding Yorks 58 C4
Kiloran Arg/Bute 80 E3
Kilpatrick N Ayrs 73 E9
Kilpeck Heref/Worcs 28 E5
Kilphedir H'land 110 H4
Kilpin E Riding Yorks 58 F3
Kilpin Pike E Riding Yorks 58 F3
Kilrenny Fife 85 D7
Kilsby Northants 31 A7
Kilspindie Perth/Kinr 84 B4
Kilsyth N Lanarks 83 G8
Kiltarlity H'land 96 B3
Kilton Notts 51 E7
Kilton Som'set 17 G6
Kilton Thorpe Redcar/Clevel'd 64 C4
Kilvaxter H'land 101 F9
Kilve Som'set 17 G6
Kilvington Notts 41 A9
Kilwinning N Ayrs 74 C5
Kimber worth S Yorks 51 C6
Kimberley Norfolk 44 E4
Kimberley Notts 41 A7
Kimble Wick Bucks 31 H10
Kimblesworth Durham 71 F7
Kimbolton Cambs 32 B3
Kimbolton Heref/Worcs 29 B6
Kimcote Leics 41 G7
Kimmeridge Dorset 10 G2
Kimmerston Northum 78 D4
Kimpton Hants 19 G9
Kimpton Herts 32 G4
Kinbrace H'land 110 F3
Kinbuck Stirl 83 D8
Kincaple Fife 85 C6
Kincardine Fife 83 F10
Kincardine H'land 104 D5
Kincardine O'Neil Aberds 91 B6
Kinclaven Perth/Kinr 90 H2
Kincorth Aberd C 91 A10
Kincorth Ho. Moray 105 F9
Kincraig H'land 97 F6
Kincraigie Perth/Kinr 89 G10
Kindallachan Perth/Kinr 89 G10
Kinderland, Scarborough N Yorks 65 E8
Kineton Glos 30 F2
Kineton Warwick 30 C5
Kinfauns Perth/Kinr 84 B3
King Sterndale Derbys 50 E2
Kingairloch H'land 87 F8
Kingarth Arg/Bute 74 B2
Kingcoed Monmouths 28 H5
Kingerby Lincs 52 C3
Kingham Oxon 30 F4
Kingholm Quay Dumf/Gal 68 C2
Kinghorn Fife 84 F4
Kinglassie Fife 84 E4
Kingoodie Perth/Kinr 84 B5
King's Acre Heref/Worcs 28 D5
King's Bromley Staffs 40 D3
King's Caple Heref/Worcs 29 F6
King's Cliffe Northants 42 F3
Kings College Chapel, Cambridge Cambs 33 C7
King's Coughton Warwick 30 C2
King's Heath W Midlands 40 G2
Kings Hedges Cambs 33 B7
Kings Langley Herts 21 A8
King's Meaburn Cumb 61 B9
Kings Muir Scot Borders 76 D5
King's Newnham Warwick 41 H6
King's Newton Derbys 40 C5
King's Norton Leics 41 E8
King's Norton W Midlands 40 H2
King's Nympton Devon 7 E7
King's Pyon Heref/Worcs 28 C5
King's Ripton Cambs 42 H5
King's Somborne Hants 11 A6
King's Stag Dorset 9 C9
King's Stanley Glos 18 A5
King's Sutton Northants 31 E6
Kings Thorn Heref/Worcs 29 E6
King's Walden Herts 32 F4
Kings Worthy Hants 11 A7
Kingsand Cornw'l 4 E5
Kingsbarns Fife 85 C7
Kingsbridge Devon 5 F8
Kingsbridge Som'set 16 H4
Kingsburgh H'land 101 G9
Kingsbury Gtr Lon 22 C2
Kingsbury Warwick 40 F4
Kingsbury Episcopi Som'set 9 B6
Kingsclere Hants 20 F3
Kingscote Glos 18 B5
Kingscott Devon 7 E6
Kingscross N Ayrs 74 E2
Kingsdon Som'set 9 B7
Kingsdown Kent 15 D8
Kingseat Fife 84 E3
Kingsey Bucks 31 H9
Kingsfold W Sussex 12 B5
Kingsford E Ayrs 75 C6
Kingsford Heref/Worcs 39 G9
Kingsforth N Lincs 59 G6
Kingsgate Kent 15 A8
Kingsheanton Devon 7 C6
Kingshouse Hotel H'land 88 F3
Kingside Hill Cumb 68 E4
Kingskerswell Devon 5 D9
Kingskettle Fife 84 D5
Kingsland Angl 46 D2
Kingsland Heref/Worcs 28 B5
Kingsley Ches 49 E6
Kingsley Hants 12 B1
Kingsley Staffs 50 H2
Kingsley Green W Sussex 12 B2
Kingsley Holt Staffs 50 H2
Kingsley Park Northants 31 B9
Kingsmuir Angus 90 G5
Kingsmuir Fife 85 D7
Kingsnorth Kent 14 E5
Kings's Lynn Norfolk 43 C9
Kings's Mills Wrex 48 H4
Kingstanding W Midlands 40 F2
Kingsteignton Devon 5 C9
Kingsthorpe Northants 31 B9
Kingston Cambs 33 C6
Kingston Devon 5 F7
Kingston Dorset 9 D9
Kingston Dorset 10 G2
Kingston E Loth 85 F7
Kingston Hants 10 D4
Kingston I of Wight 11 F7
Kingston Kent 15 C6
Kingston Moray 98 B3
Kingston Bagpuize Oxon 20 B2
Kingston Blount Oxon 20 B5
Kingston by Sea W Sussex 13 E6
Kingston Deverill Wilts 18 H5
Kingston Gorse W Sussex 12 E4
Kingston Lacey, Wimborne Minster Dorset 10 D2
Kingston Lisle Oxon 19 C10
Kingston Maurward Dorset 9 E9
Kingston near Lewes E Sussex 13 E7
Kingston on Soar Notts 41 C7
Kingston Russell Dorset 9 E7
Kingston Seymour N Som'set 17 E9
Kingston St. Mary Som'set 8 B4
Kingston Upon Hull Kingston/Hull 59 F6
Kingston upon Thames Gtr Lon 21 E9
Kingston Vale Gtr Lon 22 D2
Kingstone Heref/Worcs 28 E5
Kingstone Som'set 8 C5
Kingstone Staffs 40 C2
Kingstown Cumb 69 E6
Kingswear Devon 5 E9
Kingswells Aberd C 99 H8
Kingswinford W Midlands 39 G9
Kingswood Bucks 31 G8
Kingswood Glos 18 B4
Kingswood Heref/Worcs 28 C3
Kingswood Kent 14 C3
Kingswood Powys 38 E3
Kingswood S Gloucs 18 D3
Kingswood Surrey 22 F2
Kingswood Warwick 30 A3
Kingthorpe Lincs 52 E4
Kington Heref/Worcs 28 C3
Kington Heref/Worcs 30 C1
Kington Langley Wilts 19 D6
Kington Magna Dorset 9 B9
Kington St. Michael Wilts 19 D6
Kingussie H'land 96 F5
Kingweston Som'set 9 A7
Kininvie Ho. Moray 98 D3
Kinkell Bridge Perth/Kinr 83 C10
Kinknockie Aberds 99 D10
Kinlet Shrops 39 G8
Kinloch Fife 84 C4
Kinloch H'land 93 F9
Kinloch H'land 109 F6
Kinloch H'land 94 E3
Kinloch Perth/Kinr 90 G2
Kinloch Perth/Kinr 90 G3
Kinloch Hourn H'land 95 F6
Kinloch Laggan H'land 88 C6
Kinloch Lodge H'land 109 D8
Kinloch Rannoch Perth/Kinr 89 F7
Kinlochan H'land 87 E8
Kinlochard Stirl 82 D5
Kinlochbeoraid H'land 87 C8
Kinlochbervie H'land 108 D5
Kinlocheil H'land 87 D9
Kinlochewe H'land 103 F8
Kinlochleven H'land 88 E2
Kinlochmoidart H'land 87 D7
Kinlochmorar H'land 87 B8
Kinlochmore H'land 88 E2
Kinlochspelve Arg/Bute 81 B6
Kinloss Moray 105 F9
Kinmel Bay Conwy 47 D9
Kinmuck Aberds 99 G8
Kinmundy Aberds 99 G8
Kinnadie Aberds 99 D9
Kinnaird Perth/Kinr 84 B4
Kinnaird Castle Angus 91 F7
Kinneff Aberds 91 D9
Kinnelhead Dumf/Gal 76 G3
Kinnell Angus 91 F7
Kinnerley Shrops 38 C4
Kinnersley Heref/Worcs 28 D4
Kinnersley Heref/Worcs 29 D9
Kinnerton Powys 28 B3
Kinnesswood Perth/Kinr 84 D3
Kinninvie Durham 62 B5
Kinnordy Angus 90 F4
Kinoulton Notts 41 B8
Kinross Perth/Kinr 84 D3
Kinrossie Perth/Kinr 84 A3
Kinsbourne Green Herts 32 G4
Kinsey Heath Ches 39 A7
Kinsham Heref/Worcs 28 B4
Kinsham Heref/Worcs 29 E10
Kinsley W Yorks 57 G9
Kinson Bournem'th 10 E3
Kintarvie W Isles 107 H6
Kintbury Berks 20 E1
Kintessack Moray 105 F8
Kintillo Perth/Kinr 84 C3
Kintocher Aberds 98 H5
Kinton Heref/Worcs 28 A5
Kinton Shrops 38 D4
Kintore Aberds 99 G7
Kintour Arg/Bute 72 B4
Kintra Arg/Bute 80 B3
Kintra Arg/Bute 72 C3
Kintraw Arg/Bute 81 D8
Kinuachdrachd Arg/Bute 81 E7
Kinveachy H'land 97 E7
Kinver Staffs 39 G9
Kippax W Yorks 57 E9
Kippen Stirl 83 E7
Kippford or Scaur Dumf/Gal 67 E10
Kirbister Orkney 112 H4
Kirbister Orkney 112 F7
Kirbuster Orkney 112 F3
Kirby Bedon Norfolk 45 E6
Kirby Bellars Leics 41 D9
Kirby Cane Norfolk 45 F7
Kirby Cross Essex 35 F6
Kirby Grindalythe N Yorks 58 B5
Kirby Hill N Yorks 57 B8
Kirby Hill N Yorks 63 D6
Kirby Knowle N Yorks 63 F9
Kirby le Soken Essex 35 F6
Kirby Misperton N Yorks 64 G5
Kirby Muxloe Leics 41 E7
Kirby Overblow N Yorks 57 D8
Kirby Row Norfolk 45 F7
Kirby Sigston N Yorks 63 E9
Kirby Underdale E Riding Yorks 58 C4
Kirby Wiske N Yorks 63 F8
Kirdford W Sussex 12 C4
Kirk H'land 111 D7
Kirk Bramwith S Yorks 58 G2
Kirk Deighton N Yorks 57 C8
Kirk Ella E Riding Yorks 59 F6
Kirk Hallam Derbys 41 A6
Kirk Hammerton N Yorks 57 C9
Kirk Ireton Derbys 50 G4
Kirk Langley Derbys 40 B4
Kirk Merrington Durham 71 G7
Kirk Michael I of Man 54 D3
Kirk of Shotts N Lanarks 75 A10
Kirk Sandall S Yorks 51 B8
Kirk Smeaton N Yorks 57 G10
Kirk Yetholm Scot Borders 78 E3
Kirkabister Shetl'd 113 K7
Kirkandrews Dumf/Gal 67 F8
Kirkandrews upon Eden Cumb 69 E6
Kirkbampton Cumb 69 E6
Kirkbean Dumf/Gal 68 E2
Kirkbride Cumb 68 E5
Kirkbuddo Angus 91 G6
Kirkburn Scot Borders 76 D5
Kirkburn E Riding Yorks 58 C5
Kirkburton W Yorks 57 G6
Kirkby Lincs 52 C3
Kirkby Mersey 48 C5
Kirkby N Yorks 64 D3
Kirkby Fleetham N Yorks 63 E7
Kirkby Green Lincs 52 G3
Kirkby In Ashfield Notts 51 G7
Kirkby-in-Furness Cumb 60 F5
Kirkby la Thorpe Lincs 52 H4
Kirkby Lonsdale Cumb 61 G9
Kirkby Malham N Yorks 56 B3
Kirkby Mallory Leics 41 E6
Kirkby Malzeard N Yorks 63 G7
Kirkby Mills N Yorks 64 F5
Kirkby on Bain Lincs 52 F5
Kirkby Stephen Cumb 62 D2
Kirkby Thore Cumb 61 B9
Kirkby Underwood Lincs 42 C3
Kirkby Wharfe N Yorks 57 D10
Kirkbymoorside N Yorks 64 F4
Kirkcaldy Fife 84 E4
Kirkcambeck Cumb 69 D8
Kirkcarswell Dumf/Gal 67 F9
Kirkcolm Dumf/Gal 66 D2
Kirkconnel Dumf/Gal 75 F9
Kirkconnell Dumf/Gal 68 D2
Kirkcowan Dumf/Gal 66 D5
Kirkcudbright Dumf/Gal 67 E8
Kirkdale Mersey 48 C4
Kirkfieldbank S Lanarks 76 C1
Kirkgunzeon Dumf/Gal 68 D1
Kirkham Lancs 55 E4
Kirkham N Yorks 58 B3
Kirkhamgate W Yorks 57 F7
Kirkharle Northum 70 B5
Kirkheaton Northum 70 C5
Kirkheaton W Yorks 57 G6
Kirkhill Angus 91 E7
Kirkhill H'land 96 B3
Kirkhill Midloth 76 A5
Kirkhill Moray 98 E2
Kirkhope Scot Borders 77 E6
Kirkhouse Scot Borders 77 D6
Kirkiboll H'land 109 D8
Kirkibost H'land 94 E2
Kirkinch Angus 90 G4
Kirkinner Dumf/Gal 67 E6
Kirkintilloch E Dunb 83 G7
Kirkland Cumb 60 C3
Kirkland Cumb 69 G9
Kirkland Dumf/Gal 67 A10
Kirkland Dumf/Gal 75 F9
Kirkleatham Redcar/Clevel'd 64 B3
Kirklevington Stockton 63 D9
Kirkley Suffolk 45 F9
Kirklington Notts 51 G8
Kirklington N Yorks 63 F8
Kirklinton Cumb 69 D7
Kirkliston C of Edinb 84 G3
Kirkmaiden Dumf/Gal 66 G3
Kirkmichael Perth/Kinr 90 F1
Kirkmichael S Ayrs 74 G5
Kirkmuirhill S Lanarks 75 C9
Kirknewton Northum 78 D4
Kirknewton W Loth 84 H3
Kirkney Aberds 98 E5
Kirkoswald Cumb 69 F8
Kirkoswald S Ayrs 74 G4
Kirkpatrick Durham Dumf/Gal 67 C9
Kirkpatrick-Fleming Dumf/Gal 68 C5
Kirksanton Cumb 60 F4
Kirkstall W Yorks 57 E7
Kirkstead Lincs 52 F4
Kirkstile Aberds 98 E5
Kirkstile Dumf/Gal 69 A6
Kirkstyle H'land 111 B8
Kirkton Aberds 98 F6
Kirkton Aberds 99 D6

N

Newton W Loth 84 G2
Newton Abbot Devon 5 C9
Newton Arlosh Cumb 68 E4
Newton Aycliffe Durham 63 B7
Newton Bewley Hartlep'l 63 B9
Newton Blossomville M/Keynes 32 C2
Newton Bromshold Northants 32 B2
Newton Burgoland Leics 40 E5
Newton by Toft Lincs 52 D3
Newton Ferrers Devon 5 F6
Newton Flotman Norfolk 45 F6
Newton Hall Northum 70 D5
Newton Harcourt Leics 41 F8
Newton Heath Gtr Man 49 B9
Newton Ho. Aberds 99 F6
Newton Kyme N Yorks 57 D9
Newton-le-Willows Mersey 49 C6
Newton-le-Willows N Yorks 63 F7
Newton Longville Bucks 31 E10
Newton Mearns E Renf 75 B7
Newton Morrell N Yorks 63 D7
Newton Mulgrave N Yorks 64 C5
Newton of Ardtoe H'land 87 D6
Newton of Balcanquhal Perth/Kinr 84 C3
Newton of Falkland Fife 84 D4
Newton on Ayr S Ayrs 74 E5
Newton on Ouse N Yorks 57 C10
Newton-on-Rawcliffe N Yorks 65 E6
Newton-on-the-Moor Northum 79 G6
Newton on Trent Lincs 51 E10
Newton Poppleford Devon 8 F2
Newton Purcell Oxon 31 E8
Newton Regis Warwick 40 E4
Newton Reigny Cumb 69 G7
Newton Solney Derbys 40 C4
Newton St. Cyres Devon 7 G9
Newton St. Faith Norfolk 45 D6
Newton St. Loe Bath/NE Som'set 18 E4
Newton St. Petrock Devon 6 E5
Newton Stacey Hants 20 G2
Newton Stewart Dumf/Gal 67 D6
Newton Toney Wilts 19 G9
Newton Tracey Devon 7 D6
Newton under Roseberry Redcar/Clevel'd 64 C3
Newton upon Derwent E Riding Yorks 58 D3
Newton Valence Hants 11 A10
Newtonairds Dumf/Gal 68 B1
Newtongrange Midloth 77 A6
Newtonhill Aberds 91 B10
Newtonhill H'land 96 B3
Newtonmill Angus 91 E7
Newtonmore H'land 96 G5
Newtown Ches 49 E6
Newtown Cornw'l 3 G6
Newtown Cumb 68 F3
Newtown Cumb 69 D8
Newtown Derbys 50 D1
Newtown Devon 7 D8
Newtown Glos 18 A3
Newtown Glos 29 E10
Newtown Hants 10 C5
Newtown Hants 11 B6
Newtown Hants 11 C9
Newtown Hants 20 E2
Newtown Hants 11 C8
Newtown Hants 11 D7
Newtown Heref/Worcs 29 D7
Newtown H'land 96 F1
Newtown I of Man 54 F3
Newtown I of Wight 11 E7
Newtown Lancs 55 G5
Newtown Northum 78 G5
Newtown Northum 78 E5
Newtown Northum 78 D4
Newtown Poole 10 E3
Newtown Powys 38 F2
Newtown Shrops 38 B5
Newtown Staffs 49 F10
Newtown Staffs 50 F2
Newtown Wilts 10 B2
Newtown Linford Leics 41 E7
Newtown St. Boswells Scot Borders 77 D8
Newtown Unthank Leics 41 E6
Newtyle Angus 90 G3
Neyland Pembs 24 F4
Niarbyl I of Man 54 F2
Nibley S Gloucs 18 C3
Nibley Green Glos 18 B4
Nicholashayne Devon 8 C3
Nicholaston Swan 25 H10
Nidd N Yorks 57 B8
Nigg Aberd C 91 A10
Nigg H'land 105 E7
Nightcott Som'set 7 D9
Nilig Denbs 47 G10
Nine Ashes Essex 22 A5
Nine Mile Burn Midloth 76 B4
Nine Wells Pembs 24 D2
Ninebanks Northum 70 E2
Ninfield E Sussex 14 G2
Ningwood I of Wight 11 F6
Nisbet Scot Borders 77 E9
Nisthouse Orkney 112 G4
Niton I of Wight 11 G8
Nitshill C of Glasg 75 A7
No Man's Heath Ches 49 H6
No Man's Heath Warwick 40 E4
No Man's Land Devon 7 E9
Noak Hill Gtr Lon 22 B5
Noblethorpe S Yorks 50 B4
Nobottle Northants 31 B8
Nocton Lincs 52 F3
Noke Oxon 31 G7
Nolton Pembs 24 E3
Nolton Haven Pembs 24 E3
Nomansland Wilts 10 C5
Noneley Shrops 38 C5
Nonington Kent 15 C7
Norbreck Lancs 55 D3
Norbridge Heref/Worcs 29 D8
Norbury Ches 49 H6
Norbury Derbys 40 A3
Norbury Shrops 38 F4
Norbury Staffs 39 C8
Nordelph Norfolk 43 E8
Norden Gtr Man 56 G3
Norden Heath Dorset 10 F2
Nordley Shrops 39 F7
Norham Northum 78 C4
Norley Ches 49 E6
Norleywood Hants 11 E6
Norman Cross Cambs 42 F4
Normanby N Lincs 58 G4
Normanby N Yorks 64 F5
Normanby Redcar/Clevel'd 64 C3
Normanby-by-Spital Lincs 52 D3
Normanby by Stow Lincs 52 D1
Normanby le Wold Lincs 52 C4
Normandy Surrey 21 F7
Norman's Bay E Sussex 14 H1
Norman's Green Devon 8 D2
Normanstone Suffolk 45 F9
Normanton Derby C 40 B5
Normanton Leics 41 A10
Normanton Lincs 52 H2
Normanton Notts 51 G9
Normanton Rutl'd 42 E2
Normanton W Yorks 57 F8
Normanton le Heath Leics 40 D5
Normanton on Soar Notts 41 C7
Normanton-on-the-Wolds Notts 41 B8
Normanton on Trent Notts 51 F9
Normoss Lancs 55 E3
Norney Surrey 21 G7
Norrington Common Wilts 18 E5
Norris Green Mersey 48 C4
Norris Hill Leics 40 D5
North Anston S Yorks 51 D7
North Aston Oxon 31 F6
North Baddesley Hants 11 C6
North Ballachulish H'land 87 E10
North Barrow Som'set 9 B8
North Barsham Norfolk 44 B3
North Benfleet Essex 23 C7
North Bersted W Sussex 12 E3
North Berwick E Loth 85 F7
North Boarhunt Hants 11 C9
North Bovey Devon 5 B8
North Bradley Wilts 18 F5
North Brentor Devon 4 B5
North Brewham Som'set 18 H4
North Buckland Devon 6 B5
North Burlingham Norfolk 45 D7
North Cadbury Som'set 9 B8
North Cairn Dumf/Gal 66 C1
North Carlton Lincs 52 E2
North Carrine Arg/Bute 73 G6
North Cave E Riding Yorks 58 E4
North Cerney Glos 30 H2
North Charford Wilts 10 C4
North Charlton Northum 79 E6
North Cheriton Som'set 9 B8
North Cliff E Riding Yorks 59 D8
North Cliffe E Riding Yorks 58 E4
North Clifton Notts 51 E10
North Coates Lincs 53 B6
North Cockerington Lincs 53 C6
North Coker Som'set 9 C7
North Collafirth Shetl'd 113 E6
North Common E Sussex 13 C7
North Cornelly Bridg 16 C3
North Cove Suffolk 45 G8
North Cowton N Yorks 63 D7
North Crawley M/Keynes 32 D2
North Cray Gtr Lon 22 D4
North Creake Norfolk 44 B2
North Curry Som'set 8 B5
North Dalton E Riding Yorks 58 C5
North Dawn Orkney 112 H5
North Deighton N Yorks 57 C8
North Duffield N Yorks 58 E2
North Elkington Lincs 52 C5
North Elmham Norfolk 44 C3
North Elmshall W Yorks 57 G9
North End Bath/NE Som'set 18 E4
North End Bucks 31 F10
North End E Riding Yorks 59 E8
North End Essex 33 G9
North End Hants 20 E2
North End Lincs 42 A5
North End N Som'set 17 E9
North End Portsm'th 11 D9
North End Som'set 8 B4
North End W Sussex 12 E5
North Erradale H'land 102 D5
North Fambridge Essex 23 B8
North Fearns H'land 94 C2
North Featherstone W Yorks 57 F9
North Ferriby E Riding Yorks 58 F5
North Frodingham E Riding Yorks 59 C7
North Gorley Hants 10 C4
North Green Norfolk 45 G6
North Green Suffolk 35 B7
North Greetwell Lincs 52 E3
North Grimston N Yorks 58 B4
North Halley Orkney 112 H6
North Halling Kent 14 B2
North Hayling Hants 11 D10
North Hazelrigg Northum 78 D5
North Heasley Devon 7 C8
North Heath W Sussex 12 C4
North Hill Cambs 43 H7
North Hill Cornw'l 4 C3
North Hinksey Oxon 31 H6
North Holmwood Surrey 21 G9
North Howden E Riding Yorks 58 E3
North Huish Devon 5 E8
North Hykeham Lincs 52 F2
North Johnston Pembs 24 E4
North Kelsey Lincs 52 B3
North Kelsey Moor Lincs 52 B3
North Kessock H'land 96 B4
North Killingholme N Lincs 59 G7
North Kilvington N Yorks 63 F9
North Kilworth Leics 41 G8
North Kirkton Aberds 99 C11
North Kiscadale N Ayrs 74 E2
North Kyme Lincs 52 G4
North Lancing W Sussex 12 E5
North Lee Bucks 31 H10
North Leigh Oxon 30 G5
North Leverton with Habblesthorpe Notts 51 D9
North Littleton Heref/Worcs 30 D2
North Lopham Norfolk 44 G4
North Luffenham Rutl'd 42 E2
North Marden W Sussex 12 D2
North Marston Bucks 31 F9
North Middleton Midloth 77 B6
North Middleton Northum 78 E5
North Molton Devon 7 D8
North Moreton Oxon 20 C3
North Mundham W Sussex 12 E2
North Muskham Notts 51 G9
North Newbald E Riding Yorks 58 E5
North Newington Oxon 31 E6
North Newnton Wilts 19 F8
North Newton Som'set 8 A4
North Nibley Glos 18 B4
North Norfolk Railway, Sheringham Norfolk 44 A5
North Oakley Hants 20 F3
North Ockendon Gtr Lon 22 C5
North Ormesby Middlesbro' 64 B3
North Ormsby Lincs 52 C5
North Otterington N Yorks 63 F8
North Owersby Lincs 52 C3
North Perrott Som'set 9 D6
North Petherton Som'set 8 A4
North Petherwin Cornw'l 4 B3
North Pickenham Norfolk 44 E2
North Piddle Heref/Worcs 30 C1
North Poorton Dorset 9 E7
North Port Arg/Bute 81 B10
North Queensferry Fife 84 F3
North Radworthy Devon 7 C8
North Rauceby Lincs 52 H3
North Reston Lincs 53 D6
North Rigton N Yorks 57 D7
North Rode Ches 49 F9
North Roe Shetl'd 113 E6
North Runcton Norfolk 43 D9
North Sandwick Shetl'd 113 D8
North Scale Cumb 55 B1
North Scarle Lincs 52 F1
North Seaton Northum 71 B7
North Shian Arg/Bute 87 G9
North Shields Tyne/Wear 71 D8
North Shoebury Essex 23 C9
North Shore Lancs 55 E3
North Side Cambs 42 F5
North Side Cumb 60 B3
North Skelton Redcar/Clevel'd 64 C4
North Somercotes Lincs 53 C7
North Stainley N Yorks 63 G7
North Stainmore Cumb 62 C3
North Stifford Essex 23 C6
North Stoke Bath/NE Som'set 18 E4
North Stoke Oxon 20 C4
North Stoke W Sussex 12 D4
North Street Berks 20 D4
North Street Hants 11 A9
North Street Kent 23 D8
North Street Kent 14 C5
North Sunderland Northum 79 D7
North Tamerton Cornw'l 6 G4
North Tawton Devon 7 F7
North Thoresby Lincs 52 C5
North Tidworth Wilts 19 G9
North Togston Northum 79 G7
North Tuddenham Norfolk 44 D4
North Walbottle Tyne/Wear 71 D6
North Walsham Norfolk 45 B6
North Waltham Hants 20 G3
North Warnborough Hants 20 F5
North Water Bridge Angus 91 E7
North Watten H'land 111 D7
North Weald Bassett Essex 22 A4
North Wheatley Notts 51 D9
North Whilborough Devon 5 D9
North Wick Bath/NE Som'set 18 E2
North Willingham Lincs 52 D4
North Wingfield Derbys 51 F6
North Witham Lincs 42 C2
North Woolwich Gtr Lon 22 D4
North Wootton Dorset 9 C8
North Wootton Norfolk 43 C9
North Wootton Som'set 18 G2
North Wraxall Wilts 18 D5
North Wroughton Thamesd'n 19 C8
North Yorkshire Moors Railway, Pickering N Yorks 65 F6
Northacre Norfolk 44 F3
Northallerton N Yorks 63 E8
Northam Devon 6 D5
Northam S'thampton 11 C7
Northampton Northants 31 B9
Northaw Herts 22 A2
Northbeck Lincs 42 A3
Northborough Cambs 42 E4
Northbourne Kent 15 C8
Northbridge Street E Sussex 14 F2
Northchapel W Sussex 12 C3
Northchurch Herts 32 H2
Northcott Devon 6 G4
Northdown Kent 15 A8
Northdyke Orkney 112 F3
Northend Bucks 20 B5
Northend Warwick 30 C5
Northenden Gtr Man 49 C9
Northfield Aberd C 99 H9
Northfield Scot Borders 85 H11
Northfield E Riding Yorks 59 F6
Northfield W Midlands 40 H2
Northfields Lincs 42 E3
Northfleet Kent 23 D6
Northgate Lincs 42 C4
Northhouse Scot Borders 77 G7
Northiam E Sussex 14 F3
Northill Beds 32 D4
Northington Hants 20 H3
Northlands Lincs 53 G6
Northlea Durham 71 E9
Northleach Glos 30 G3
Northleigh Devon 8 E3
Northlew Devon 7 G6
Northmoor Oxon 20 A2
Northmoor Green or Moorland Som'set 8 A5
Northmuir Angus 90 F4
Northney Hants 11 D10
Northolt Gtr Lon 21 C9
Northop Flints 48 F3
Northop Hall Flints 48 F3
Northorpe Lincs 42 D3
Northorpe Lincs 42 B5
Northorpe Lincs 52 C1
Northover Som'set 17 H9
Northover Som'set 9 B7
Northowram W Yorks 57 F6
Northport Dorset 10 F2
Northpunds Shetl'd 113 L7
Northrepps Norfolk 45 B6
Northtown Orkney 112 J5
Northumbria Craft Centre, Morpeth Northum 71 B6
Northway Glos 29 E10
Northwich Ches 49 E7
Northwick S Gloucs 18 C2
Northwold Norfolk 44 F1
Northwood Derbys 50 F4
Northwood Gtr Lon 21 B8
Northwood I of Wight 11 E7
Northwood Kent 15 B8
Northwood Shrops 38 B5
Northwood Green Glos 29 G8
Norton Ches 49 D6
Norton E Sussex 13 E8
Norton Glos 29 F9
Norton Herts 32 E5
Norton Heref/Worcs 29 C9
Norton Heref/Worcs 30 D2
Norton I of Wight 11 F6
Norton Monmouths 28 G5
Norton Notts 51 E7
Norton Northants 31 B8
Norton N Yorks 64 G5
Norton Powys 28 B4
Norton Shrops 38 G5
Norton Shrops 39 E6
Norton Shrops 39 E8
Norton Stockton 63 B9
Norton Suffolk 34 B3
Norton S Yorks 57 G10
Norton Wilts 18 C5
Norton W Sussex 12 F2
Norton W Sussex 12 E3
Norton Bavant Wilts 19 G6
Norton Bridge Staffs 39 B9
Norton Canes Staffs 40 E2
Norton Canon Heref/Worcs 28 D4
Norton Corner Norfolk 44 C4
Norton Disney Lincs 52 G1
Norton East Staffs 40 E2
Norton Ferris Wilts 18 H4
Norton Fitzwarren Som'set 8 B3
Norton Green I of Wight 11 F6
Norton Hawkfield Bath/NE Som'set 18 E2
Norton Heath Essex 23 A6
Norton in Hales Shrops 39 B8
Norton-in-the-Moors Stoke 49 G9
Norton-Juxta-Twycross Leics 40 E5
Norton-le-Clay N Yorks 63 G9
Norton Lindsey Warwick 30 B4
Norton Malreward Bath/NE Som'set 18 E3
Norton Mandeville Essex 22 A5
Norton St. Philip Som'set 18 F4
Norton sub Hamdon Som'set 9 C6
Norton Woodseats S Yorks 50 D5
Norwell Notts 51 F9
Norwell Woodhouse Notts 51 F9
Norwich Norfolk 45 E6
Norwich Castle Museum Norfolk 45 E6
Norwich Cathedral Norfolk 45 E6
Norwick Shetl'd 113 B9
Norwood Derbys 51 D6
Norwood Hill Surrey 22 G2
Norwoodside Cambs 43 F7
Noseley Leics 41 F9
Noss Shetl'd 113 M6
Noss Mayo Devon 5 F6
Nosterfield N Yorks 63 F7
Nostie H'land 94 D5
Notgrove Glos 30 F3
Nothe Fort, Weymouth Dorset 9 G8
Nottage Bridg 16 D3
Nottingham Notts 41 B7
Nottingham Castle Museum Notts 41 A7
Nottington Dorset 9 F8
Notton Wilts 19 E6
Notton W Yorks 57 G8
Nounsbrough Shetl'd 113 H5
Nounsley Essex 34 G1
Noutard's Green Heref/Worcs 29 B8
Novar House H'land 104 F5
Nox Shrops 38 D5
Nuffield Oxon 20 C4
Nun Hills Lancs 56 F3
Nun Monkton N Yorks 57 C10
Nunburnholme E Riding Yorks 58 D4
Nuncargate Notts 51 G7
Nuneaton Warwick 40 F5
Nuneham Courtenay Oxon 20 B3
Nunney Som'set 18 G4
Nunnington N Yorks 64 G4
Nunnykirk Northum 70 A5
Nunsthorpe NE Lincs 52 B5
Nunthorpe Middlesbro' 64 C3
Nunthorpe C of York 58 C2
Nunton Wilts 10 B4
Nunwick N Yorks 63 G8
Nupend Glos 29 H8
Nursling Hants 11 C6
Nursted Hants 12 C1
Nutbourne W Sussex 12 D4
Nutbourne W Sussex 12 E1
Nutfield Surrey 22 F3
Nuthall Notts 41 A7
Nuthampstead Herts 33 E7
Nuthurst W Sussex 12 C5
Nutley E Sussex 13 C8
Nutley Hants 20 G4
Nutwell S Yorks 51 B8
Nybster H'land 111 C8
Nyetimber W Sussex 12 F2
Nyewood W Sussex 12 C2
Nymans Garden, Crawley W Sussex 13 C6
Nymet Rowland Devon 7 F8
Nymet Tracey Devon 7 F8
Nympsfield Glos 18 A5
Nynehead Som'set 8 B3
Nyton W Sussex 12 E3

O

Oad Street Kent 14 B3
Oadby Leics 41 E8
Oak Cross Devon 7 G6
Oakamoor Staffs 40 A2
Oakbank W Loth 84 H2
Oakdale Caerph 17 B6
Oake Som'set 8 B3
Oaken Staffs 39 E9
Oakenclough Lancs 55 D5
Oakengates Shrops 39 D8
Oakenholt Flints 48 E3
Oakenshaw Durham 71 G7
Oakenshaw W Yorks 57 F6
Oakerthorpe Derbys 50 G5
Oakes W Yorks 57 G6
Oakfield Torf 17 B8
Oakford Ceredig'n 26 C4
Oakford Devon 7 D10
Oakfordbridge Devon 7 D10
Oakgrove Ches 49 F10
Oakham Rutl'd 42 E1
Oakhanger Hants 12 B1
Oakhill Som'set 18 G3
Oakhurst Kent 22 F5
Oakington Cambs 33 B7
Oaklands Herts 32 G5
Oaklands Powys 27 C10
Oakle Street Glos 29 G8
Oakley Beds 32 C3
Oakley Bucks 31 G8
Oakley Fife 84 F2
Oakley Hants 20 F3
Oakley Oxon 20 A5
Oakley Poole 10 E3
Oakley Suffolk 44 H5
Oakley Green Berks 21 D7
Oakley Park Powys 37 G9
Oakmere Ches 49 F6
Oakridge Glos 19 A6
Oakridge Hants 20 F4
Oaks Shrops 38 E5
Oaks Green Derbys 40 B3
Oaksey Wilts 19 B6
Oakthorpe Leics 40 D5
Oakwood Adventure Park, Narberth Pembs 24 E5
Oakwoodhill Surrey 12 B5
Oakworth W Yorks 56 E5
Oape H'land 104 B3
Oare Berks 20 D3
Oare Kent 14 B5
Oare Som'set 7 B9
Oare Wilts 19 E8
Oasby Lincs 42 B3
Oathlaw Angus 90 F5
Oatlands N Yorks 57 C8
Oban Arg/Bute 81 B8
Oban H'land 87 C8
Oborne Dorset 9 C8
Obthorpe Lincs 42 D3
Occlestone Green Ches 49 F7
Occold Suffolk 34 A5
Ocean Beach Amusement Park, Rhyl Denbs 47 D9
Ochil Hills Hospital Perth/Kinr 84 D2
Ochiltree E Ayrs 75 E7
Ochtermuthill Perth/Kinr 83 C9
Ochtertyre Perth/Kinr 83 B9
Ockbrook Derbys 41 B6
Ockham Surrey 21 F8
Ockle H'land 86 D5
Ockley Surrey 12 B5
Ocle Pychard Heref/Worcs 29 D6
Octon E Riding Yorks 59 B6
Octon Cross Roads E Riding Yorks 59 B6
Odcombe Som'set 9 C7
Odd Down Bath/NE Som'set 18 E4
Oddendale Cumb 61 C8
Odder Lincs 52 E2
Oddingley Heref/Worcs 29 C10
Oddington Glos 30 F4
Oddington Oxon 31 G7
Odell Beds 32 C2
Odie Orkney 112 F7
Odiham Hants 20 F5
Odstock Wilts 10 B4
Odstone Leics 40 E5
Offchurch Warwick 30 B5
Offenham Heref/Worcs 30 D2
Offham E Sussex 13 D7
Offham Kent 14 C1
Offham W Sussex 12 E4
Offord Cluny Cambs 32 B5
Offord Darcy Cambs 32 B5
Offton Suffolk 34 D4
Offwell Devon 8 E3
Ogbourne Maizey Wilts 19 D8
Ogbourne St. Andrew Wilts 19 D8
Ogbourne St. George Wilts 19 D9
Ogil Angus 90 E5
Ogle Northum 71 C6
Ogmore V of Glam 16 D3
Ogmore by Sea V of Glam 16 D3
Ogmore Vale Bridg 16 B4
Okeford Fitzpaine Dorset 9 C10
Okehampton Devon 7 G6
Okehampton Camp Devon 7 G6
Okraquoy Shetl'd 113 K7
Old Northants 31 A9
Old Aberdeen Aberd C 99 H9
Old Alresford Hants 11 A8
Old Arley Warwick 40 F4
Old Basford Notts 41 A7
Old Basing Hants 20 F4
Old Bewick Northum 78 E5
Old Bolingbroke Lincs 53 F6
Old Bramhope W Yorks 57 D7
Old Brampton Derbys 50 E5
Old Bridge of Urr Dumf/Gal 67 D9
Old Buckenham Norfolk 44 F4
Old Burghclere Hants 20 F2
Old Byland N Yorks 64 F3
Old Cassop Durham 71 G8
Old Castleton Scot Borders 69 A8
Old Catton Norfolk 45 D6
Old Clee NE Lincs 52 B5
Old Cleeve Som'set 16 G5
Old Clipstone Notts 51 F8
Old Colwyn Conwy 47 E8
Old Coulsdon Gtr Lon 22 F3
Old Crombie Aberds 98 C5
Old Dailly S Ayrs 74 H4
Old Dalby Leics 41 C8
Old Deer Aberds 99 D9
Old Denaby S Yorks 51 C6
Old Edlington S Yorks 51 C7
Old Eldon Durham 63 B7
Old Ellerby E Riding Yorks 59 E7
Old Felixstowe Suffolk 35 E7
Old Fletton Cambs 42 F4
Old Glossop Derbys 50 C2
Old Goole E Riding Yorks 58 F3
Old Hall Powys 37 G9
Old Heath Essex 34 F4
Old Heathfield E Sussex 13 C9
Old Hill W Midlands 40 G1
Old Hunstanton Norfolk 43 A9
Old Hutton Cumb 61 F8
Old Kea Cornw'l 3 E7
Old Kilpatrick W Dunb 82 G5
Old Kinnernie Aberds 99 H7
Old Knebworth Herts 32 F5
Old Langho Lancs 56 E2
Old Laxey I of Man 54 E4
Old Leake Lincs 53 G7
Old Malton N Yorks 64 G5
Old Micklefield W Yorks 57 E9
Old Milton Hants 10 E5
Old Milverton Warwick 30 B4
Old Monkland N Lanarks 75 A9
Old Netley Hants 11 D7
Old Philpstoun W Loth 84 G2
Old Quarrington Durham 71 G8
Old Radnor Powys 28 C3
Old Rattray Aberds 99 C10
Old Rayne Aberds 99 F6
Old Romney Kent 14 F5
Old Sarum, Salisbury Wilts 10 A4
Old Scone Perth/Kinr 84 B3
Old Smithy, Gretna Green Dumf/Gal 69 D6
Old Sodbury S Gloucs 18 C4
Old Somerby Lincs 42 B2
Old Stratford Northants 31 D9
Old Thirsk N Yorks 63 F9
Old Town Cumb 69 F7
Old Town Cumb 61 F8
Old Town Northum 70 A3
Old Town I of Scilly 2 C3
Old Trafford Gtr Man 49 C9
Old Tupton Derbys 50 F5
Old Warden Beds 32 D4
Old Weston Cambs 42 H3
Old Whittington Derbys 50 E5
Old Wick H'land 111 D8
Old Windsor Berks 21 D7
Old Wives Lees Kent 14 C5
Old Woking Surrey 21 F8
Old Woodhall Lincs 52 F5
Oldany H'land 108 F4
Oldberrow Warwick 30 B3
Oldborough Devon 7 F8
Oldbury Shrops 39 F8
Oldbury Warwick 40 F5
Oldbury W Midlands 40 G1
Oldbury-on-Severn S Gloucs 18 B3
Oldbury on the Hill Glos 18 C5
Oldcastle Bridg 16 D4
Oldcastle Monmouths 28 F4
Oldcotes Notts 51 D7
Oldfallow Staffs 40 D1
Oldfield Heref/Worcs 29 B9
Oldford Som'set 18 F4
Oldham Gtr Man 49 B10
Oldhamstocks E Loth 85 G9
Oldhurst Cambs 42 H5
Oldland S Gloucs 18 D3
Oldmeldrum Aberds 99 F8
Oldshore Beg H'land 108 D4
Oldshoremore H'land 108 D5
Oldstead N Yorks 64 F3
Oldtown Aberds 98 F5
Oldtown of Ord Aberds 98 C6
Oldway Swan 25 H10
Oldways End Devon 7 D9
Oldwhat Aberds 99 C8
Olgrinmore H'land 110 D5
Oliver's Battery Hants 11 B7
Ollaberry Shetl'd 113 E6
Ollerton Ches 49 E8
Ollerton Notts 51 F8
Ollerton Shrops 39 C7
Olmarch Ceredig'n 27 C6
Olney M/Keynes 32 C1
Olrig Ho. H'land 111 C6
Olton W Midlands 40 G3
Olveston S Gloucs 18 C3
Olwen Ceredig'n 26 D5
Ombersley Heref/Worcs 29 B9
Ompton Notts 51 F8
Onchan I of Man 54 F3
Onecote Staffs 50 G2
Onen Monmouths 28 G5
Ongar Hill Norfolk 43 C8
Ongar Street Heref/Worcs 28 B4
Onibury Shrops 38 H5
Onich H'land 87 E10
Onllwyn Neath P Talb 27 G8
Onneley Staffs 39 A8
Onslow Village Surrey 21 G7
Onthank E Ayrs 75 C6
Openwoodgate Derbys 50 H5
Opinan H'land 103 C6
Opinan H'land 102 E5
Orange Lane Scot Borders 78 C2
Orange Row Norfolk 43 C8
Orasaigh W Isles 101 A9
Orbliston Moray 98 C3
Orbost H'land 93 A8
Orby Lincs 53 F7
Orchard Hill Devon 6 D5
Orchard Portman Som'set 8 B4
Orcheston Wilts 19 G7
Orcop Heref/Worcs 28 F5
Orcop Hill Heref/Worcs 28 F5
Ord H'land 94 E3
Ordhead Aberds 99 G6
Ordie Aberds 90 A5
Ordiequish Moray 98 C3
Ordsall Notts 51 D8
Ore E Sussex 14 G3
Oreton Shrops 39 G7
Orford Ches 49 C7
Orford Suffolk 35 D8
Orgreave Staffs 40 D3
Orlestone Kent 14 E4
Orleton Heref/Worcs 29 B7
Orleton Heref/Worcs 28 B5
Orlingbury Northants 32 A1
Ormesby Redcar/Clevel'd 64 C3
Ormesby St. Margaret Norfolk 45 D8
Ormesby St. Michael Norfolk 45 D8
Ormiclate Castle W Isles 92 B3
Ormiscaig H'land 103 C6
Ormiston E Loth 84 H6
Ormsaigbeg H'land 86 E4
Ormsaigmore H'land 86 E4
Ormsary Arg/Bute 81 G7
Ormsgill Cumb 60 G4
Ormskirk Lancs 48 B5
Orphir Orkney 112 H4
Orpington Gtr Lon 22 E4
Orrell Gtr Man 49 B6
Orrell Mersey 48 C4
Orrisdale I of Man 54 D3
Orroland Dumf/Gal 67 F9
Orsett Essex 23 C6
Orslow Staffs 39 D9
Orston Notts 41 A9
Orthwaite Cumb 68 G5
Ortner Lancs 55 C5
Orton Cumb 61 D9
Orton Northants 41 H10
Orton Longueville Cambs 42 F4
Orton-on-the-Hill Leics 40 E5
Orton Waterville Cambs 42 F4
Orwell Cambs 33 C6
Osbaldeston Lancs 56 E1
Osbaldwick C of York 58 C2
Osbaston Shrops 38 C4
Osborne House I of Wight 11 E8
Osbournby Lincs 42 B3
Oscroft Ches 49 F6
Ose H'land 93 A9
Osgathorpe Leics 41 D6
Osgodby Lincs 52 C3
Osgodby N Yorks 58 E2
Osgodby N Yorks 65 F8
Oskaig H'land 94 C2
Oskamull Arg/Bute 86 G4
Osmaston Derbys 40 A4
Osmaston Derby C 40 B5
Osmington Dorset 9 F9
Osmington Mills Dorset 9 F9
Osmotherley N Yorks 63 E9
Ospisdale H'land 104 D6
Ospringe Kent 14 B5
Ossett W Yorks 57 F7
Ossington Notts 51 F9
Ostend Essex 23 B9
Oswaldkirk N Yorks 64 G4
Oswaldtwistle Lancs 56 F2
Oswestry Shrops 38 C3
Otford Kent 22 F5
Otham Kent 14 C2
Othery Som'set 8 A5
Otley Suffolk 35 C6
Otley W Yorks 57 D7
Otter Ferry Arg/Bute 81 F9
Otterbourne Hants 11 B7
Otterburn Northum 70 A3
Otterburn N Yorks 56 C3
Otterburn Camp Northum 78 H3
Otterham Cornw'l 6 G2
Otterhampton Som'set 17 G7
Ottershaw Surrey 21 E8
Otterswick Shetl'd 113 E8
Otterton Devon 8 F2
Ottery St. Mary Devon 8 E3
Ottinge Kent 15 D6
Ottringham E Riding Yorks 59 F8
Oughterby Cumb 68 E5
Oughtershaw N Yorks 62 F3
Oughterside Cumb 68 F4
Oughtibridge S Yorks 50 C5
Oughtrington Ches 49 D7
Oulston N Yorks 64 G3
Oulton Cumb 68 E5
Oulton Norfolk 44 C5
Oulton Staffs 39 B10
Oulton Suffolk 45 F9
Oulton W Yorks 57 F8
Oulton Broad Suffolk 45 F9
Oulton Street Norfolk 44 C5
Oundle Northants 42 G3
Ousby Cumb 69 G9
Ousdale H'land 110 G5
Ousden Suffolk 33 C10
Ousefleet E Riding Yorks 58 F4
Ouston Durham 71 E7
Ouston Northum 70 C5
Out Newton E Riding Yorks 59 F9
Out Rawcliffe Lancs 55 D4
Outertown Orkney 112 G3
Outgate Cumb 61 E6
Outhgill Cumb 62 D2
Outlane W Yorks 56 G5
Outwell Norfolk 43 E8
Outwick Hants 10 C4
Outwood Surrey 22 G3
Outwood W Yorks 57 F8
Outwoods Staffs 39 D8
Ovenden W Yorks 56 F5
Ovenscloss Scot Borders 77 D7
Over Cambs 33 A6
Over Ches 49 F7
Over S Gloucs 18 C2
Over Compton Dorset 9 C7
Over Green W Midlands 40 F3
Over Haddon Derbys 50 F4
Over Hulton Gtr Man 49 B7
Over Kellet Lancs 61 G8
Over Kiddington Oxon 31 F6
Over Knutsford Ches 49 E8
Over Monnow Monmouths 29 G6
Over Norton Oxon 30 F5
Over Peover Ches 49 E8
Over Silton N Yorks 63 E9
Over Stowey Som'set 17 H6
Over Stratton Som'set 9 C6
Over Tabley Ches 49 D8
Over Wallop Hants 19 H9
Over Whitacre Warwick 40 F4
Over Worton Oxon 31 F6
Overbister Orkney 112 D7
Overbury Heref/Worcs 30 E1
Overcombe Dorset 9 F8
Overgreen Derbys 50 E5
Overleigh Som'set 17 H9
Overley Green Warwick 30 C2
Overpool Ches 48 E4
Overscaig Hotel H'land 109 G7
Overseal Derbys 40 D4
Oversland Kent 14 C5
Overstone Northants 31 B10
Overstrand Norfolk 45 A6
Overthorpe Northants 31 D6
Overton Aberd C 99 G8
Overton Ches 49 E6
Overton Dumf/Gal 68 D2
Overton Hants 20 G3
Overton Lancs 55 C4
Overton N Yorks 58 C1
Overton Shrops 29 A6
Overton Swan 25 H9
Overton Wrex 38 A4
Overton W Yorks 57 G7
Overton Bridge Wrex 38 A4
Overton Green Ches 49 F8
Overtown N Lanarks 75 B10
Oving Bucks 31 F9
Oving W Sussex 12 E3
Ovingdean Brighton/Hove 13 E7
Ovingham Northum 70 D5
Ovington Durham 63 C6
Ovington Essex 34 D1
Ovington Hants 11 A8
Ovington Norfolk 44 E3
Ovington Northum 70 D5
Ower Hants 11 C6
Owermoigne Dorset 9 F9
Owlbury Shrops 38 F4
Owler Bar Derbys 50 E4
Owlerton S Yorks 50 D5
Owl's Green Suffolk 35 B6
Owlswick Bucks 31 H9
Owmby Lincs 52 B3
Owmby-by-Spital Lincs 52 D3
Owslebury Hants 11 B8
Owston Leics 41 E9
Owston S Yorks 58 G1
Owston Ferry N Lincs 51 B10
Owstwick E Riding Yorks 59 E8
Owthorne E Riding Yorks 59 F9
Owthorpe Notts 41 B8
Oxborough Norfolk 43 E10
Oxburgh Hall Norfolk 43 E10
Oxcombe Lincs 53 E6
Oxen Park Cumb 61 F6
Oxenholme Cumb 61 F8
Oxenhope W Yorks 56 E5
Oxenton Glos 30 E1
Oxenwood Wilts 19 F10
Oxford Oxon 31 H7
Oxford University Botanic Garden Oxon 31 H7
Oxhey Herts 21 B9
Oxhill Warwick 30 D5
Oxley W Midlands 39 E10
Oxley Green Essex 34 G3
Oxley's Green E Sussex 14 F1
Oxnam Scot Borders 78 F2
Oxshott Surrey 21 E9
Oxspring S Yorks 50 B4
Oxted Surrey 22 F3
Oxton Scot Borders 77 B7
Oxton Notts 51 G8
Oxwich Swan 25 H9
Oxwick Norfolk 44 C3
Oykel Bridge H'land 104 B2
Oyne Aberds 99 F6

P

Pabail Iarach W Isles 107 F9
Pabail Uarach W Isles 107 F9
Pace Gate N Yorks 57 C6
Packington Leics 40 D5
Padanaram Angus 90 F5
Padbury Bucks 31 E9
Paddington Gtr Lon 22 C2
Paddlesworth Kent 15 E6
Paddock Wood Kent 14 D1
Paddockhaugh Moray 98 C2
Paddockhole Dumf/Gal 68 B5
Padfield Derbys 50 C2
Padiham Lancs 56 E2
Padog Conwy 47 G8
Padside N Yorks 57 C6
Padstow Cornw'l 3 B8
Padworth Berks 20 E4
Page Bank Durham 71 G7
Pagelsham Eastend Essex 23 B9
Pagham W Sussex 12 F2
Paglesham Churchend Essex 23 B9
Paibeil W Isles 100 F3
Paible W Isles 101 C6
Paignton Devon 5 D9
Paignton & Dartmouth Steam Railway Devon 5 D9
Paignton Zoo Devon 5 E9
Pailton Warwick 41 G6
Painscastle Powys 28 D2
Painshawfield Northum 70 D5
Painsthorpe E Riding Yorks 58 C4
Painswick Glos 29 H9
Pairc Shiaboist W Isles 107 E6
Paisley Renf 75 A6
Pakefield Suffolk 45 F9
Pakenham Suffolk 34 B3
Palace House, Beaulieu Hants 11 D6
Palace of Holyroodhouse, Edinburgh C of Edinb 84 G4
Pale Gwyn 37 B9
Palestine Hants 19 G9
Paley Street Berks 21 D6
Palfrey W Midlands 40 F2
Palgowan Dumf/Gal 66 B5
Palgrave Suffolk 44 H5
Pallion Tyne/Wear 71 E8
Palmarsh Kent 15 E6
Palnackie Dumf/Gal 67 E10
Palnure Dumf/Gal 67 D6
Palterton Derbys 51 F6
Pamber End Hants 20 F4
Pamber Green Hants 20 F4
Pamber Heath Hants 20 E4
Pamphill Dorset 10 D2
Pampisford Cambs 33 D7
Pan Orkney 112 J4
Panbride Angus 91 H6
Pancrasweek Devon 6 F3
Pandy Gwyn 37 E6
Pandy Monmouths 28 F4
Pandy Powys 37 E9
Pandy Wrex 38 B2
Pandy Tudur Conwy 47 F8
Panfield Essex 33 F10
Pangbourne Berks 20 D4
Pannal N Yorks 57 C8
Panshanger Herts 32 G5
Pant Shrops 38 C3
Pant-glas Carms 26 F5
Pant-glas Gwyn 46 H4
Pant-glâs Powys 37 F7
Pant-glas Shrops 38 B3
Pant gwyn Carms 26 F5
Pant Mawr Powys 37 G8
Pant-teg Carms 25 D9
Pant-y-Caws Carms 25 D6
Pant-y-dwr Powys 37 H9
Pant-y-ffridd Powys 38 E2
Pant-y-Wacco Flints 48 E2
Pant-yr-awel Bridg 16 C4
Pantgwyn Ceredig'n 25 B7
Pantlasau Swan 16 B1
Panton Lincs 52 E4
Pantperthog Gwyn 37 E7
Pantyffynnon Carms 27 G6
Pantymwyn Flints 48 F2
Panxworth Norfolk 45 D7
Papcastle Cumb 68 G4
Papigoe H'land 111 D8
Papil Shetl'd 113 K6
Papley Orkney 112 J5
Papple E Loth 85 G7
Papplewick Notts 51 G7
Papworth Everard Cambs 32 B5
Papworth St. Agnes Cambs 32 B5
Par Cornw'l 3 D9
Paradise Wildlife Park, Broxbourne Herts 33 H6
Parbold Lancs 55 G4
Parbrook Som'set 18 H2
Parbrook W Sussex 12 C4
Parc Gwyn 37 B8
Parc-y-rhôs Carms 26 D5
Parcllyn Ceredig'n 26 C2
Pardshaw Cumb 60 B3
Parham Suffolk 35 B7
Park Dumf/Gal 68 A2
Park Corner Berks 21 C6
Park Corner Oxon 20 C4
Park End Middlesbro' 64 C3
Park End Northum 70 C3
Park Gate Hants 11 D8
Park Hill Notts 51 G8
Park Hill N Yorks 57 B8
Park Rose Pottery and Leisure Park, Bridlington E Riding Yorks 59 B7
Park Street W Sussex 12 B5
Parkdargue Aberds 98 D6
Parkend Glos 29 H7
Parkeston Essex 35 E6
Parkgate Ches 48 E3
Parkgate Dumf/Gal 68 B3
Parkgate Kent 14 E3
Parkgate Surrey 22 G2
Parkham Devon 6 D4
Parkham Ash Devon 6 D4
Parkhill Ho. Aberds 99 G8
Parkhouse Monmouths 17 A9
Parkhouse Green Derbys 51 F6
Parkhurst I of Wight 11 E7
Parkmill Swan 25 H10
Parkneuk Aberds 91 D8
Parkstone Poole 10 E3
Parley Cross Dorset 10 E3
Parracombe Devon 7 B7
Parrog Pembs 24 C5
Parsley Hay Derbys 50 F3
Parson Cross S Yorks 50 C5
Parson Drove Cambs 43 E6
Parsonage Green Essex 33 H10
Parsonby Cumb 68 G4
Parson's Heath Essex 34 F4
Partick C of Glasg 83 H6
Partington Gtr Man 49 C8
Partney Lincs 53 F7
Parton Cumb 60 B2
Parton Dumf/Gal 67 C8
Parton Glos 29 F9
Partridge Green W Sussex 12 D5
Parwich Derbys 50 G3
Passenham Northants 31 E9
Paston Norfolk 45 B7
Patchacott Devon 6 G5
Patcham Brighton/Hove 13 E7
Patching W Sussex 12 E4
Patchole Devon 7 B7
Patchway S Gloucs 18 C3
Pateley Bridge N Yorks 57 B6
Paternoster Heath Essex 34 G3
Path of Condie Perth/Kinr 84 C2
Pathe Som'set 8 A5
Pathhead Aberds 91 E8
Pathhead E Ayrs 75 F8
Pathhead Fife 84 E4
Pathhead Midloth 77 A6
Pathstruie Perth/Kinr 84 C2
Patmore Heath Herts 33 F7
Patna E Ayrs 75 F6
Patney Wilts 19 F7
Patrick I of Man 54 E2
Patrick Brompton N Yorks 63 E7
Patrington E Riding Yorks 59 F9
Patrixbourne Kent 15 C6
Patterdale Cumb 61 C6
Pattingham Staffs 39 F9
Pattishall Northants 31 C8
Pattiswick Green Essex 34 F2
Patton Bridge Cumb 61 E8
Paul Cornw'l 2 G3
Paulerspury Northants 31 D9
Paull E Riding Yorks 59 F7
Paulton Bath/NE Som'set 18 F3
Paultons Park, Totton Hants 11 C6
Pavenham Beds 32 C2
Pawlett Som'set 17 G8
Pawston Northum 78 D3
Paxford Glos 30 E3
Paxton Scot Borders 78 B4
Payhembury Devon 8 D2
Paythorne Lancs 56 C3
Peacehaven E Sussex 13 E8
Peak Dale Derbys 50 E2
Peak Forest Derbys 50 E3
Peakirk Cambs 42 E4
Pearsie Angus 90 F4
Pease Pottage W Sussex 13 B6
Peasedown St. John Bath/NE Som'set 18 F4
Peasemore Berks 20 D2
Peasenhall Suffolk 35 B7
Peaslake Surrey 21 G8
Peasley Cross Mersey 49 C6
Peasmarsh E Sussex 14 F3
Peaston E Loth 84 H6
Peaston Bank E Loth 84 H6
Peat Inn Fife 85 D6
Peathill Aberds 99 B9
Peatling Magna Leics 41 F7
Peatling Parva Leics 41 G7
Peaton Shrops 39 G6
Peats Corner Suffolk 34 B5
Pebmarsh Essex 34 E2
Pebworth Heref/Worcs 30 D3
Pecket Well W Yorks 56 F4
Peckforton Ches 49 G6
Peckham Gtr Lon 22 D3
Peckleton Leics 41 E6
Pedlinge Kent 15 E6
Pedmore W Midlands 39 G10
Pedwell Som'set 17 H9
Peebles Scot Borders 76 C5
Peel I of Man 54 E2
Peel Common Hants 11 D8
Peel Park S Lanarks 75 B8
Peening Quarter Kent 14 F3
Pegsdon Beds 32 E4
Pegswood Northum 71 B7
Pegwell Kent 15 B8
Peinchorran H'land 94 C2
Peinlich H'land 101 G10
Pelaw Tyne/Wear 71 D7
Pelcomb Bridge Pembs 24 E4
Pelcomb Cross Pembs 24 E4
Peldon Essex 34 G3
Pellon W Yorks 56 F5
Pelsall W Midlands 40 E2
Pelton Durham 71 E7
Pelutho Cumb 68 F4
Pelynt Cornw'l 4 E3
Pemberton Gtr Man 49 B6
Pembrey Carms 25 F9
Pembridge Heref/Worcs 28 C4
Pembroke Pembs 24 F4
Pembroke Castle Pembs 24 F4
Pembroke Dock Pembs 24 F4
Pembury Kent 23 G6
Pen-bont Rhydybeddau Ceredig'n 37 G6
Pen-clawdd Swan 25 G10
Pen-ffordd Pembs 24 D5
Pen-groes-oped Monmouths 28 H4
Pen-llyn Angl 46 D3
Pen-lon Angl 46 F4
Pen-sarn Gwyn 36 A4
Pen-sarn Gwyn 36 C5
Pen-twyn Monmouths 29 H6
Pen-y-banc Carms 27 F6
Pen-y-bont Gwyn 37 E7
Pen-y-bont Carms 25 D8
Pen-y-bont Gwyn 37 C6
Pen-y-bont Powys 38 C3
Pen-y-bryn Gwyn 37 D6
Pen-y-bryn Pembs 25 B6
Pen-y-cae Powys 27 G8
Pen-y-cae-mawr Monmouths 17 B9
Pen-y-cefn Flints 48 E2
Pen-y-clawdd Monmouths 28 H5
Pen-y-coedcae Rh Cyn Taff 16 C5
Pen-y-fai Bridg 16 C3
Pen-y-garn Ceredig'n 37 G6
Pen-y-garn Carms 26 E5
Pen-y-garnedd Angl 46 E5
Pen-y-gop Conwy 37 A9
Pen-y-graig Gwyn 36 B1
Pen-y-groes Carms 26 G5
Pen-y-groeslon Gwyn 36 B2
Pen-y-Gwryd Hotel Gwyn 47 G6
Pen-y-stryt Denbs 48 G2
Pen-yr-heol Monmouths 28 G5
Pen-yr-Heolgerrig Merth Tyd 27 H10
Penallt Monmouths 29 G6
Penally Pembs 24 G6
Penalt Heref/Worcs 29 F6
Penare Cornw'l 3 E8
Penarth V of Glam 17 D6
Penbryn Ceredig'n 26 C2
Pencader Carms 25 C9
Pencaenewydd Gwyn 36 A4
Pencarnisiog Angl 46 E3
Pencarreg Carms 26 D5
Pencelli Powys 28 F1
Pencoed Bridg 16 C4
Pencombe Heref/Worcs 29 C6
Pencoyd Heref/Worcs 29 F6
Pencraig Heref/Worcs 29 F6
Pencraig Powys 37 C10
Pendeen Cornw'l 2 F2
Pendennis Castle Cornw'l 3 F7
Penderyn Rh Cyn Taff 27 H9
Pendine Carms 25 F7
Pendlebury Gtr Man 49 B8
Pendleton Lancs 56 E2
Pendock Heref/Worcs 29 E8
Pendoggett Cornw'l 3 B9
Pendomer Som'set 9 C7
Pendoylan V of Glam 16 D5
Pendre Bridg 16 C4
Penegoes Powys 37 E7
Pengam Caerph 17 B6
Penge Gtr Lon 22 D3
Pengenffordd Powys 28 E2
Pengorffwysfa Angl 46 C4
Pengover Green Cornw'l 4 D3
Penhale Cornw'l 2 H5
Penhale Cornw'l 3 D8
Penhalvaen Cornw'l 3 F6
Penhill Thamesd'n 19 C8
Penhow Newp 17 B9
Penhurst E Sussex 14 G1
Peniarth Gwyn 37 E6
Penicuik Midloth 76 A5
Peniel Carms 25 D9
Peniel Denbs 47 F10
Penifiler H'land 94 B1
Peninver Arg/Bute 73 E7
Penisarwaun Gwyn 46 F5
Penistone S Yorks 50 B4
Penjerrick Cornw'l 3 F6
Penketh Ches 49 D6
Penkill S Ayrs 74 H4
Penkridge Staffs 39 D10
Penley Wrex 38 B5
Penllergaer Swan 25 G11
Penllyn V of Glam 16 D4
Penmachno Conwy 47 G7
Penmaen Swan 25 H10
Penmaenan Conwy 47 E7
Penmaenmawr Conwy 47 E7
Penmaenpool Gwyn 37 D6
Penmark V of Glam 16 E5
Penmarth Cornw'l 3 F6
Penmon Angl 47 D6
Penmore Mill Arg/Bute 86 F4
Penmorfa Ceredig'n 26 C3
Penmorfa Gwyn 36 A5
Penmynydd Angl 46 E5
Penn Bucks 21 B7
Penn Street Bucks 21 B7
Pennal Gwyn 37 E7
Pennan Aberds 99 B8
Pennant Ceredig'n 26 B5
Pennant Denbs 37 B10
Pennant Denbs 47 G10
Pennant Powys 37 F8
Pennant Melangell Powys 37 C10
Pennar Pembs 24 F4
Pennard Swan 25 H10
Pennerley Shrops 38 F4
Pennington Cumb 60 G5
Pennington Gtr Man 49 C7
Pennington Hants 11 E6
Penny Bridge Cumb 61 F6
Pennycross Arg/Bute 80 B5
Pennygate Norfolk 45 C7
Pennygown Arg/Bute 86 G5
Pennymoor Devon 7 E9
Pennywell Tyne/Wear 71 E8
Penparc Ceredig'n 25 B7
Penparc Pembs 24 C3
Penparcau Ceredig'n 36 G5
Penperlleni Monmouths 17 A8
Penpillick Cornw'l 3 D9
Penpol Cornw'l 3 F7
Penpoll Cornw'l 4 E2
Penpont Dumf/Gal 67 A10
Penpont Powys 27 F9
Penrherber Carms 25 C7
Penrhiw goch Carms 26 G5
Penrhiw-llan Ceredig'n 25 B8
Penrhiw-pâl Ceredig'n 25 B8
Penrhiwceiber Rh Cyn Taff 16 B5
Penrhos Gwyn 36 B3
Penrhôs Monmouths 28 G5
Penrhos Powys 27 G7
Penrhosfeilwo Angl 46 D2
Penrhyn Bay Conwy 47 D8
Penrhyn Castle Gwyn 47 E6
Penrhyn-coch Ceredig'n 37 G6
Penrhyndeudraeth Gwyn 37 B6
Penrhynside Conwy 47 D8
Penrice Swan 25 H9
Penrith Cumb 69 G8
Penrose Cornw'l 3 B7
Penruddock Cumb 61 B7
Penryn Cornw'l 3 F6
Pensarn Conwy 47 E9
Pensarn Carms 25 E9
Pensax Heref/Worcs 29 B8
Pensby Mersey 48 D3
Penscynor Park, Neath Neath P Talb 16 B2
Penselwood Som'set 9 A9
Pensford Bath/NE Som'set 18 E3
Penshaw Tyne/Wear 71 E8
Penshurst Kent 22 G5
Pensilva Cornw'l 4 D3
Penston E Loth 84 G6
Pentewan Cornw'l 3 E9
Pentir Gwyn 46 F5
Pentire Cornw'l 3 C6
Pentlow Essex 34 D2
Pentney Norfolk 43 D10
Penton Mewsey Hants 19 G10
Pentraeth Angl 46 E5
Pentre Carms 26 G5
Pentre Powys 38 G1
Pentre Powys 38 F3
Pentre Rh Cyn Taff 16 B4
Pentre Shrops 38 D4
Pentre Wrex 38 A3
Pentre Wrex 38 B2
Pentre-bâch Ceredig'n 26 D5
Pentre-bach Powys 27 E9
Pentre Berw Angl 46 E4
Pentre-bont Conwy 47 G7
Pentre-celyn Denbs 48 G2
Pentre-Celyn Powys 37 E8
Pentre-chwyth Swan 16 B1
Pentre-cwrt Carms 25 C8
Pentre Dolau-Honddu Powys 27 D9
Pentre-dwr Swan 16 B1
Pentre-galar Pembs 25 C6

Pentre-Gwenlais Carms 27 G6
Pentre Gwynfryn Gwyn 36 C5
Pentre Halkyn Flints 48 E3
Pentre-Isaf Conwy 47 F8
Pentre Llanrhaeadr Denbs 48 F1
Pentre-llwyn-llŵyd Powys 27 C9
Pentre-llyn Ceredig'n 27 A6
Pentre-llyn cymmer Conwy 47 G9
Pentre Meyrick V of Glam 16 D4
Pentre-poeth Newp 17 C7
Pentre-rhew Ceredig'n 27 C6
Pentre-tafarn-y-fedw Conwy 47 F8
Pentre-ty-gwyn Carms 27 E8
Pentrebach Merth Tyd 16 A5
Pentrebach Swan 25 F11
Pentrebeirdd Powys 38 D2
Pentrecagal Carms 25 B8
Pentredwr Denbs 48 H2
Pentrefelin Conwy 47 E8
Pentrefelin Ceredig'n 27 D6
Pentrefelin Carms 26 F5
Pentrefelin Gwyn 36 B5
Pentrefoelas Conwy 47 G8
Pentregat Ceredig'n 26 C3
Pentreheyling Shrops 38 F3
Pentre'r Felin Conwy 47 F8
Pentre'r-felin Powys 27 E9
Pentrich Derbys 50 G5
Pentridge Dorset 10 C3
Pentyrch Card 17 C6
Penuchadre V of Glam 16 D3
Penuwch Ceredig'n 26 B5
Penwithick Cornw'l 3 D9
Penwyllt Powys 27 G8
Penybanc Carms 27 G6
Penybont Powys 28 B2
Penybontfawr Powys 38 C1
Penycae Wrex 48 H3
Penycwm Pembs 24 D3
Penyffordd Flints 48 F4
Penyffridd Gwyn 46 G5
Penygarnedd Powys 38 C2
Penygraig Rh Cyn Taff 16 B4
Penygroes Gwyn 46 G4
Penygroes Pembs 25 C6
Penyrheol Caerph 17 C6
Penysarn Angl 46 C4
Penywaun Rh Cyn Taff 16 A4
Penzance Cornw'l 2 F3
People's Palace, Glasgow C of Glasg 75 A8
Peopleton Heref/Worcs 29 C10
Peover Heath Ches 49 E8
Peper Harow Surrey 21 G7
Perceton N Ayrs 74 C5
Percie Aberds 91 B6
Percyhorner Aberds 99 B9
Periton Som'set 16 G4
Perivale Gtr Lon 21 C9
Perkinsville Durham 71 E7
Perlethorpe Notts 51 E8
Perranarworthal Cornw'l 3 F6
Perranporth Cornw'l 3 D6
Perranuthnoe Cornw'l 2 G4
Perranzabuloe Cornw'l 3 D6
Perry Barr W Midlands 40 F2
Perry Green Herts 33 G7
Perry Green Wilts 19 C6
Perry Street Kent 23 D6
Perryfoot Derbys 50 D3
Pershall Staffs 39 B9
Pershore Heref/Worcs 29 D10
Pert Angus 91 E7
Pertenhall Beds 32 B3
Perth Perth/Kinr 84 B3
Perthy Shrops 38 B4
Perton Staffs 39 F9
Pertwood Wilts 18 H5
Peter Tavy Devon 5 C6
Peterborough Cambs 42 F4
Peterborough Cathedral Cambs 42 F4
Peterburn H'land 102 D5
Peterchurch Heref/Worcs 28 E4
Peterculter Aberd C 91 A9
Peterhead Aberds 99 D11
Peterlee Durham 71 F9
Peter's Green Herts 32 G4
Peters Marland Devon 6 E5
Petersfield Hants 11 B10
Peterston super-Ely V of Glam 16 D5
Peterstone Wentlooge Newp 17 C7
Peterstow Heref/Worcs 29 F6
Petertown Orkney 112 H4
Petham Kent 15 C6
Petrockstow Devon 7 F6
Pett E Sussex 14 G3
Pettaugh Suffolk 34 C5
Petteridge Kent 14 D1
Pettinain S Lanarks 76 C2
Pettistree Suffolk 35 C6
Petton Devon 8 B2
Petton Shrops 38 C5
Petts Wood Gtr Lon 22 E4
Petty Aberds 99 E7
Pettycur Fife 84 F4
Pettymuick Aberds 99 F9
Petworth W Sussex 12 C3
Petworth House W Sussex 12 C3
Pevensey E Sussex 13 E10
Pevensey Bay E Sussex 14 H1
Pewsey Wilts 19 E8
Philham Devon 6 D3
Philiphaugh Scot Borders 77 E7
Phillack Cornw'l 2 F4
Philleigh Cornw'l 3 F7
Philpstoun W Loth 84 G2
Phocle Green Heref/Worcs 29 F7
Phoenix Green Hants 20 F5
Pica Cumb 60 B3
Piccotts End Herts 32 H3
Picheon Green S Yorks 58 G2
Pickering N Yorks 64 F5
Picket Piece Hants 20 G1
Picket Post Hants 10 D4
Pickhill N Yorks 63 F8
Picklescott Shrops 38 F5
Pickletillem Fife 84 B6
Pickmere Ches 49 E7
Pickney Som'set 8 B3
Pickstock Shrops 39 C8
Pickwell Devon 6 B5
Pickwell Leics 41 D9
Pickworth Lincs 42 B3
Pickworth Rutl'd 42 D2
Picton Ches 48 E5
Picton Flints 48 D2
Picton N Yorks 63 D9
Piddinghoe E Sussex 13 E8
Piddington Northants 31 C10
Piddington Oxon 31 G8
Piddlehinton Dorset 9 E9
Piddletrenthide Dorset 9 E9
Pidley Cambs 43 H6
Piece Hall, Halifax W Yorks 57 F6
Piercebridge Durham 63 C7
Pierowall Orkney 112 D5
Pigdon Northum 71 B6
Pikehall Derbys 50 G3
Pilgrims Hatch Essex 22 B5
Pilham Lincs 52 C1
Pill N Som'set 18 D2
Pillaton Cornw'l 4 D4
Pillerton Hersey Warwick 30 D5
Pillerton Priors Warwick 30 D4
Pilleth Powys 28 B3
Pilley Hants 11 E6
Pilley S Yorks 50 B5
Pilling Lancs 55 D4
Pilling Lane Lancs 55 D3
Pillowell Glos 29 H7
Pillwell Dorset 9 C9
Pilning S Gloucs 18 C2
Pilsbury Derbys 50 F3
Pilsdon Dorset 9 E6
Pilsgate Cambs 42 E3
Pilsley Derbys 50 E4
Pilsley Derbys 51 F6
Pilton Devon 7 C6
Pilton Northants 42 G3
Pilton Rutl'd 42 E2
Pilton Som'set 18 G2
Pilton Green Swan 25 H9
Pimperne Dorset 10 D2
Pinchbeck Lincs 42 C5
Pinchbeck Bars Lincs 42 C4
Pinchbeck West Lincs 42 C5
Pinehurst Thamesd'n 19 C8
Pinfold Lancs 55 G3
Pinged Carms 25 F9
Pinhoe Devon 8 E1
Pinkneys Green Berks 21 C6
Pinley W Midlands 40 H5
Pinmill Suffolk 35 E6
Pinminnoch S Ayrs 66 A3
Pinmore S Ayrs 66 A4
Pinmore Mains S Ayrs 66 A4
Pinner Gtr Lon 21 C9
Pinvin Heref/Worcs 30 D1
Pinwherry S Ayrs 66 B3
Pinxton Derbys 51 G6
Pipe and Lyde Heref/Worcs 29 D6
Pipe Gate Shrops 39 A8
Piperhill H'land 105 G7
Piper's Pool Cornw'l 4 B3
Pipewell Northants 41 G10
Pippacott Devon 7 C6
Pipton Powys 28 E2
Pirbright Surrey 21 F7
Pirnmill N Ayrs 73 C8
Pirton Herts 32 E4
Pirton Heref/Worcs 29 D9
Pisgah Ceredig'n 37 H6
Pisgah Stirl 83 D8
Pishill Oxon 20 C5
Pistyll Gwyn 36 A3
Pitagowan Perth/Kinr 89 B9
Pitblae Aberds 99 B9
Pitcairngreen Perth/Kinr 84 B2
Pitcalnie H'land 105 E7
Pitcaple Aberds 99 F7
Pitch Green Bucks 20 A5
Pitch Place Surrey 21 F7
Pitchcombe Glos 29 H9
Pitchcott Bucks 31 F9
Pitchford Shrops 39 E6
Pitcombe Som'set 9 A8
Pitcorthie Fife 85 D7
Pitcox E Loth 85 G8
Pitcur Perth/Kinr 90 H3
Pitfichie Aberds 99 G6
Pitforthie Aberds 91 D9
Pitgrudy H'land 105 C6
Pitkennedy Angus 91 F6
Pitkevy Fife 84 D4
Pitkierie Fife 85 D7
Pitlessie Fife 84 D5
Pitlochry Perth/Kinr 89 F10
Pitmachie Aberds 99 F6
Pitmain H'land 96 F5
Pitmedden Aberds 99 F8
Pitminster Som'set 8 C4
Pitmuies Angus 91 G6
Pitmunie Aberds 99 G6
Pitney Som'set 9 B6
Pitroddie Perth/Kinr 84 B4
Pitscottie Fife 84 C6
Pitsea Essex 23 C7
Pitsford Northants 31 B9
Pitsmoor S Yorks 50 D5
Pitstone Bucks 32 G2
Pitstone Green Bucks 32 G2
Pitt Rivers Museum (See University Museum) Oxon 31 H7
Pittendreich Moray 105 F10
Pittentrail H'land 104 B6
Pittenweem Fife 85 D7
Pitteuchar Fife 84 E4
Pittington Durham 71 F8
Pittodrie Aberds 99 F6
Pitton Wilts 10 A5
Pittswood Kent 23 G6
Pittulie Aberds 99 B9
Pity Me Durham 71 E8
Pityme Cornw'l 3 B8
Pityoulish H'land 97 E7
Pixey Green Suffolk 45 H6
Pixham Surrey 21 F9
Pixley Heref/Worcs 29 E7
Place Newton N Yorks 65 G6
Plaidy Aberds 99 C7
Plains N Lanarks 83 H8
Plaish Shrops 39 F6
Plaistow W Sussex 12 B4
Plaitford Hants 10 C5
Plank Lane Gtr Man 49 C7
Plâs Carms 25 D9
Plas-canol Gwyn 36 D5
Plas Gogerddan Ceredig'n 37 G6
Plas Llwyngwern Powys 37 E7
Plas Nantyr Wrex 38 B2
Plas-yn-Cefn Denbs 47 E10
Plastow Green Hants 20 E3
Platt Kent 23 F6
Platt Bridge Gtr Man 49 B7
Platts Common S Yorks 50 B5
Plawsworth Durham 71 F7
Plaxtol Kent 23 F6
Play Hatch Oxon 20 D5
Playden E Sussex 14 F4
Playford Suffolk 35 D6
Playing Place Cornw'l 3 E7
Playley Green Glos 29 E8
Plealey Shrops 38 E5
Plean Stirl 83 F9
Pleasington Lancs 56 F1
Pleasley Derbys 51 F7
Pleasure Island, Liverpool Mersey 48 D4
Pleasure Island Theme Park NE Lincs 53 B6
Pleasureland Mersey 55 G3
Pleasurewood Hills American Theme Park, Lowestoft Suffolk 45 F9
Pleckgate Lancs 56 E1
Plenmeller Northum 70 D2
Pleshey Essex 33 G9
Plockton H'land 94 C5
Plocropol W Isles 101 C7
Ploughfield Heref/Worcs 28 D4
Plowden Shrops 38 G4
Ploxgreen Shrops 38 E4
Pluckley Kent 14 D4
Pluckley Thorne Kent 14 D4
Plumbland Cumb 68 G4
Plumley Ches 49 E8
Plumpton Cumb 69 G7
Plumpton E Sussex 13 D7
Plumpton Green E Sussex 13 D7
Plumpton Head Cumb 69 G8
Plumstead Gtr Lon 22 D4
Plumstead Norfolk 44 B5
Plumtree Notts 41 B8
Plungar Leics 41 B9
Plush Dorset 9 D9
Plwmp Ceredig'n 26 C3
Plymouth Devon 4 E5
Plympton Devon 5 E6
Plymstock Devon 5 E6
Plymtree Devon 8 D2
Pockley N Yorks 64 F4
Pocklington E Riding Yorks 58 D4
Pode Hole Lincs 42 C5
Podimore Som'set 9 B7
Podington Beds 32 B2
Podmore Staffs 39 B8
Point Clear Essex 34 G4
Pointon Lincs 42 B4
Pokesdown Bournem'th 10 E4
Pol a Charra W Isles 92 D3
Polbae Dumf/Gal 66 C4
Polbain H'land 103 A7
Polbathic Cornw'l 4 E4
Polbeth W Loth 76 A3
Polchar H'land 97 F6
Pole Elm Heref/Worcs 29 D9
Polebrook Northants 42 G3
Polegate E Sussex 13 E9
Poles H'land 105 C6
Polesden Lacey, Dorking Surrey 21 F9
Polesworth Warwick 40 E4
Polgigga Cornw'l 2 G2
Polglass H'land 103 B8
Polgooth Cornw'l 3 D8
Poling W Sussex 12 E4
Polkerris Cornw'l 3 D9
Polla H'land 109 D6
Pollington E Riding Yorks 58 G2
Polloch H'land 87 E7
Pollok C of Glasg 75 A7
Pollok House, Glasgow C of Glasg 75 A7
Pollokshields C of Glasg 75 A7
Polmassick Cornw'l 3 E8
Polmont Falk 83 G10
Polnessan E Ayrs 75 F6
Polnish H'land 87 C7
Polperro Cornw'l 4 E3
Polruan Cornw'l 4 E2
Polsham Som'set 18 G2
Polstead Suffolk 34 E3
Poltalloch Arg/Bute 81 E8
Poltimore Devon 8 E1
Polton Midloth 76 A5
Polwarth Scot Borders 78 B2
Polyphant Cornw'l 4 B3
Polzeath Cornw'l 3 B8
Ponders End Gtr Lon 22 B3
Pondersbridge Cambs 42 F5
Pondtail Hants 21 F6
Ponsanooth Cornw'l 3 F6
Ponsworthy Devon 5 C8
Pont Aber Carms 27 F7
Pont Aber-Geirw Gwyn 37 C7
Pont-ar-gothi Carms 26 F5
Pont ar Hydfer Powys 27 F8
Pont-ar-llechau Carms 27 F7
Pont Cwm Pydew Denbs 37 B10
Pont Cyfyng Conwy 47 G7
Pont Cysyllte Wrex 38 A3
Pont Dolydd Prysor Gwyn 37 B7
Pont-faen Powys 27 E9
Pont Fronwydd Gwyn 37 C8
Pont-gareg Pembs 24 B6
Pont-Henri Carms 25 F9
Pont-Llogel Powys 37 D10
Pont Pen-y-benglog Gwyn 47 F6
Pont Rhyd-goch Conwy 47 F6
Pont-Rhyd-sarn Gwyn 37 C8
Pont Rhyd-y-cyff Bridg 16 C3
Pont-rhyd-y-groes Ceredig'n 27 A7
Pont-rug Gwyn 46 F5
Pont-siân Ceredig'n 25 B9
Pont-y-gwaith Rh Cyn Taff 16 B5
Pont-y-pant Conwy 47 G7
Pont y Pennant Gwyn 37 C9
Pont yclun Rh Cyn Taff 16 C5
Pont yr Afon-Gam Gwyn 37 A7
Pont-yr-hafod Pembs 24 D4
Pontamman Carms 27 G6
Pontantwn Carms 25 E9
Pontardawe Neath P Talb 16 A2
Pontardulais Swan 25 F10
Pontarsais Carms 25 D9
Pontblyddyn Flints 48 F3
Pontbren Araeth Carms 27 F6
Pontbren Llwyd Rh Cyn Taff 27 H9
Pontefract W Yorks 57 F9
Ponteland Northum 71 C6
Ponterwyd Ceredig'n 37 G7
Pontesbury Shrops 38 E4
Pontfadog Wrex 38 B3
Pontfaen Pembs 24 C5
Pontfraith Caerph 17 B6
Pontgarreg Ceredig'n 26 C3
Ponthir Torf 17 B8
Ponthirwaun Ceredig'n 25 B7
Pontlliw Swan 25 F11
Pontllyfni Gwyn 46 G4
Pontlottyn Caerph 28 H2
Pontneddfechan Rh Cyn Taff 27 H9
Pontnewydd Torf 17 B7
Pontrhydfendigaid Ceredig'n 27 B7
Pontrhydyfen Neath P Talb 16 B2
Pontrilas Heref/Worcs 28 F4
Pontrobert Powys 38 D2
Ponts Green E Sussex 14 G1
Pontshill Heref/Worcs 29 F7
Pontsticill Merth Tyd 28 G1
Pontwgan Conwy 47 E7
Pontyates Carms 25 F9
Pontyberem Carms 26 G5
Pontycymmer Bridg 16 B4
Pontyglasier Pembs 24 C6
Pontypool Torf 17 A7
Pontypridd Rh Cyn Taff 16 C5
Pontywaun Caerph 17 B7
Pooksgreen Hants 11 C6
Pool Cornw'l 2 E5
Pool W Yorks 57 D7
Pool o'Muckhart Clack 84 D2
Pool Quay Powys 38 D3
Poole Poole 10 E3
Poole Keynes Glos 19 B6
Poolend Staffs 50 G1
Poolewe H'land 103 D6
Pooley Bridge Cumb 61 B7
Poolfold Staffs 49 G9
Poolhill Glos 29 F8
Poolsbrook Derbys 51 E6
Pootings Kent 22 G4
Pope Hill Pembs 24 E4
Popeswood Berks 21 E6
Popham Hants 20 G3
Poplar Gtr Lon 22 C3
Popley Hants 20 F4
Porchester Notts 41 A7
Porchfield I of Wight 11 E7
Porin H'land 104 G2
Poringland Norfolk 45 E6
Porkellis Cornw'l 2 F5
Porlock Som'set 7 B9
Porlock Weir Som'set 7 B9
Port Ann Arg/Bute 81 F9
Port Appin Arg/Bute 87 G9
Port Askaig Arg/Bute 80 H4
Port Bannatyne Arg/Bute 82 H1
Port Carlisle Cumb 68 D5
Port Charlotte Arg/Bute 72 B2
Port Clarence Stockton 63 B9
Port Dinorwic Gwyn 46 F5
Port Driseach Arg/Bute 81 G9
Port e Vullen I of Man 54 D4
Port Ellen Arg/Bute 72 C3
Port Elphinstone Aberds 99 G7
Port Erin I of Man 54 G1
Port Eynon Swan 25 H9
Port Gaverne Cornw'l 4 B1
Port Glasgow Invercl 82 G4
Port Henderson H'land 102 E5
Port Isaac Cornw'l 3 A8
Port Lamont Arg/Bute 82 G1
Port Lion Pembs 24 F4
Port Logan Dumf/Gal 66 F2
Port Mholair W Isles 107 F9
Port Mor H'land 86 D4
Port Mulgrave N Yorks 64 C5
Port Nan Giuran W Isles 107 F9
Port nan Long W Isles 100 E4
Port Nis W Isles 107 C9
Port of Menteith Stirl 83 D6
Port Quin Cornw'l 3 A8
Port Ramsay Arg/Bute 87 G8
Port St. Mary I of Man 54 G2
Port Sunlight Mersey 48 D4
Port Talbot Neath P Talb 16 B2
Port Tennant Swan 16 B1
Port Wemyss Arg/Bute 72 B1
Port William Dumf/Gal 66 F5
Portachoillan Arg/Bute 73 B7
Portavadie Arg/Bute 81 H9
Portbury N Som'set 18 D2
Portchester Hants 11 D9
Portclair H'land 96 E2
Portencross N Ayrs 74 C3
Portesham Dorset 9 F8
Portessie Moray 98 B4
Portfield Gate Pembs 24 E4
Portgate Devon 4 B5
Portgordon Moray 98 B3
Portgower H'land 105 A9
Porth Cornw'l 3 C7
Porth Rh Cyn Taff 16 B5
Porth Navas Cornw'l 3 G6
Porth-y-waen Shrops 38 C3
Porthallow Cornw'l 3 G6
Porthallow Cornw'l 4 E3
Porthcawl Bridg 16 D3
Porthcothan Cornw'l 3 B7
Porthcurno Cornw'l 2 G2
Porthgain Pembs 24 C3
Porthill Shrops 38 D5
Porthkerry V of Glam 16 E5
Porthleven Cornw'l 2 G5
Porthllechog Angl 46 C4
Porthmadog Gwyn 36 B5
Porthmeor Cornw'l 2 F3
Portholland Cornw'l 3 E8
Porthoustock Cornw'l 3 G7
Porthpean Cornw'l 3 D9
Porthtowan Cornw'l 2 E5
Porthyrhyd Carms 26 G5
Porthyrhyd Carms 27 E7
Portincaple Arg/Bute 82 E3
Portington E Riding Yorks 58 E3
Portinnisherrich Arg/Bute 81 C9
Portinscale Cumb 60 B5
Portishead N Som'set 17 D9
Portkil Arg/Bute 82 F3
Portknockie Moray 98 B4
Portlethen Aberds 91 B10
Portling Dumf/Gal 68 E1
Portloe Cornw'l 3 F8
Portmahomack H'land 105 D8
Portmeirion Gwyn 36 B5
Portmeirion Village Gwyn 36 B5
Portmellon Cornw'l 3 E9
Portmore Hants 11 E6
Portnacroish Arg/Bute 87 G9
Portnahaven Arg/Bute 72 B1
Portnalong H'land 93 B9
Portnaluchaig H'land 87 C6
Portnancon H'land 109 C7
Portobello C of Edinb 84 G5
Porton Wilts 19 H8
Portpatrick Dumf/Gal 66 E2
Portreath Cornw'l 2 E5
Portree H'land 94 B1
Portscatho Cornw'l 3 F7
Portsea Portsm'th 11 D9
Portskerra H'land 110 C3
Portskewett Monmouths 18 C2
Portslade Brighton/Hove 13 E6
Portslade by Sea Brighton/Hove 13 E6
Portsmouth Portsm'th 11 D9
Portsmouth W Yorks 56 F4
Portsmouth Sea Life Centre Portsm'th 11 E9
Portsonachan Arg/Bute 82 B1
Portsoy Aberds 98 B5
Portswood S'thampton 11 C7
Portuairk H'land 86 E4
Portway Heref/Worcs 28 E5
Portway Heref/Worcs 30 A2
Portwrinkle Cornw'l 4 E4
Poslingford Suffolk 34 D1
Postbridge Devon 5 C7
Postcombe Oxon 20 B5
Postling Kent 15 E6
Postwick Norfolk 45 E6
Potholm Dumf/Gal 69 B6
Potsgrove Beds 32 F2
Pott Row Norfolk 43 C10
Pott Shrigley Ches 49 E10
Potten End Herts 32 H3
Potter Brompton N Yorks 65 G7
Potter Heigham Norfolk 45 D8
Potter Street Essex 33 H7
Potterhanworth Lincs 52 F3
Potterhanworth Booths Lincs 52 F3
Potterne Wilts 19 F6
Potterne Wick Wilts 19 F7
Potternewton W Yorks 57 E8
Potters Bar Herts 22 A2
Potter's Cross Staffs 39 G9
Potterspury Northants 31 D9
Potterton Aberds 99 G9
Potterton W Yorks 57 E9
Potto N Yorks 63 D9
Potton Beds 32 D5
Poughill Cornw'l 6 F3
Poughill Devon 7 F9
Poulshot Wilts 19 F6
Poulton Glos 19 A8
Poulton Mersey 48 C4
Poulton-le-Fylde Lancs 55 E3
Pound Bank Heref/Worcs 29 A8
Pound Green E Sussex 13 C9
Pound Green Heref/Worcs 39 H8
Pound Green I of Wight 11 F6
Pound Hill W Sussex 13 B6
Poundfield E Sussex 13 B9
Poundland S Ayrs 66 B3
Poundon Bucks 31 F8
Poundsgate Devon 5 C8
Poundstock Cornw'l 6 G3
Powburn Northum 78 F5
Powderham Devon 8 F1
Powderham Castle Devon 8 F1
Powerstock Dorset 9 E7
Powfoot Dumf/Gal 68 D4
Powick Heref/Worcs 29 C9
Powis Castle, Welshpool Powys 38 E3
Powmill Perth/Kinr 84 E2
Poxwell Dorset 9 F9
Poyle Surrey 21 D8
Poynings W Sussex 13 D6
Poyntington Dorset 9 C8
Poynton Ches 49 D10
Poynton Green Shrops 39 D6
Poystreet Green Suffolk 34 C3
Praa Sands Cornw'l 2 G4
Pratt's Bottom Gtr Lon 22 E4
Praze Cornw'l 2 F4
Praze-an-Beeble Cornw'l 2 F5
Predannack Wollas Cornw'l 2 H5
Prees Shrops 39 B6
Prees Green Shrops 39 B6
Prees Heath Shrops 39 B6
Prees Higher Heath Shrops 39 B6
Prees Lower Heath Shrops 39 B6
Preesall Lancs 55 D3
Preesgweene Shrops 38 B3
Prenderguest Scot Borders 78 B4
Prendwick Northum 78 F5
Prengwyn Ceredig'n 25 B9
Prenteg Gwyn 36 A5
Prenton Mersey 48 D4
Prescot Mersey 48 C5
Prescott Shrops 38 C5
Pressen Northum 78 D3
Prestatyn Denbs 48 D1
Prestbury Ches 49 E10
Prestbury Glos 30 F1
Presteigne Powys 28 B4
Presthope Shrops 39 F6
Prestleigh Som'set 18 G3
Preston Scot Borders 78 B2
Preston Brighton/Hove 13 E7
Preston Devon 5 C9
Preston Dorset 9 F9
Preston E Loth 85 G7
Preston E Riding Yorks 59 E7
Preston Glos 19 A7
Preston Glos 29 E7
Preston Herts 32 F4
Preston Kent 14 B5
Preston Kent 15 B7
Preston Lancs 55 F5
Preston Northum 79 E6
Preston Rutl'd 42 E1
Preston Shrops 39 D6
Preston Suffolk 34 C3
Preston Wilts 19 D7
Preston Wilts 19 D9
Preston Bagot Warwick 30 B3
Preston Bissett Bucks 31 F8
Preston Bowyer Som'set 8 B3
Preston Brockhurst Shrops 39 C6
Preston Brook Ches 49 D6
Preston Candover Hants 20 G4
Preston Capes Northants 31 C7
Preston Crowmarsh Oxon 20 B4
Preston Gubbals Shrops 38 D5
Preston Hall Museum, Stockton-on-Tees Stockton 63 C9
Preston on Stour Warwick 30 D4
Preston on the Hill Ches 49 D6
Preston on Wye Heref/Worcs 28 D4
Preston Plucknett Som'set 9 C7
Preston-under-Scar N Yorks 62 E5
Preston upon the Weald Moors Shrops 39 D7
Preston Wynne Heref/Worcs 29 D6
Prestonmill Dumf/Gal 68 E2
Prestonpans E Loth 84 G6
Prestwich Gtr Man 49 B9
Prestwick Northum 71 C6
Prestwick S Ayrs 74 E5
Prestwood Bucks 21 A6
Price Town Bridg 16 B4
Prickwillow Cambs 43 G8
Priddy Som'set 18 F2
Priest Hutton Lancs 61 G8
Priest Weston Shrops 38 F3
Priesthaugh Scot Borders 77 G7
Primethorpe Leics 41 F7
Primrose Green Norfolk 44 D4
Primrose Valley N Yorks 65 G9
Primrosehill Herts 21 A8
Princes Gate Pembs 24 E6
Princes Risborough Bucks 21 A6
Princethorpe Warwick 31 A6
Princetown Caerph 28 G2
Princetown Devon 5 C6
Prinknash Abbey, Gloucester Glos 29 G9
Prion Denbs 48 F1
Prior Muir Fife 85 C7
Prior Park Northum 78 B4
Priors Frome Heref/Worcs 29 E6
Priors Hardwick Warwick 31 C6
Priors Marston Warwick 31 C6
Priorslee Shrops 39 D8
Priory Church, Lancaster Lancs 55 B4
Priory Wood Heref/Worcs 28 D3
Priston Bath/NE Som'set 18 E3
Pristow Green Norfolk 44 G5
Prittlewell Essex 23 C8
Privett Hants 11 B9
Prixford Devon 7 C6
Probus Cornw'l 3 E7
Proncy H'land 105 C6
Prospect Cumb 68 F4
Prudhoe Northum 70 D5
Ptarmigan Lodge Stirl 82 D4
Pubil Perth/Kinr 88 G5
Puckeridge Herts 33 F6
Puckington Som'set 8 C5
Pucklechurch S Gloucs 18 D3
Pucknall Hants 11 B6
Puckrup Glos 29 E9
Puddinglake Ches 49 F8
Puddington Ches 48 E4
Puddington Devon 7 E9
Puddledock Norfolk 44 F4
Puddletown Dorset 9 E9
Pudleston Heref/Worcs 29 C6
Pudsey W Yorks 57 E7
Pulborough W Sussex 12 D4
Puleston Shrops 39 C8
Pulford Ches 48 G4
Pulham Dorset 9 D9
Pulham Market Norfolk 44 G5
Pulham St. Mary Norfolk 45 G6
Pulloxhill Beds 32 E3
Pumpherston W Loth 84 H2
Pumsaint Carms 27 D6
Puncheston Pembs 24 D5
Puncknowle Dorset 9 F7
Punnett's Town E Sussex 13 C10
Purbrook Hants 11 D9
Purewell Dorset 10 E4
Purfleet Essex 22 D5
Puriton Som'set 17 G8
Purleigh Essex 23 A8
Purley Berks 20 D4
Purley Gtr Lon 22 E3
Purlogue Shrops 38 H3
Purls Bridge Cambs 43 G7
Purse Caundle Dorset 9 C8
Purslow Shrops 38 G4
Purston Jaglin W Yorks 57 G9
Purton Glos 18 A3
Purton Glos 18 A3
Purton Wilts 19 C7
Purton Stoke Wilts 19 B7
Pury End Northants 31 D9
Pusey Oxon 20 B1
Putley Heref/Worcs 29 E7
Putney Gtr Lon 22 D2
Putsborough Devon 6 B5
Puttenham Herts 32 G1
Puttenham Surrey 21 G7
Puxton N Som'set 17 E9
Pwll Carms 25 F9
Pwll-glas Denbs 48 G2
Pwll-Meyric Monmouths 18 B2
Pwll-trap Carms 25 E7
Pwll-y-glaw Neath P Talb 16 B2
Pwllcrochan Pembs 24 F4
Pwllgloyw Powys 27 E10
Pwllheli Gwyn 36 B3
Pycombe W Sussex 13 D6
Pye Corner Herts 33 G7
Pye Corner Newp 17 C8
Pye Green Staffs 40 D1
Pyewipe NE Lincs 59 G8
Pyle Bridg 16 C3
Pyle I of Wight 11 G7
Pylle Som'set 18 H3
Pymore Cambs 43 G7
Pyrford Surrey 21 F8
Pyrton Oxon 20 B4
Pytchley Northants 32 A1
Pyworthy Devon 6 F4

Q

Quabbs Shrops 38 G3
Quadring Lincs 42 B5
Quainton Bucks 31 G9
Quarley Hants 19 G9
Quarndon Derbys 40 A5
Quarrier's Homes Invercl 82 H4
Quarrington Lincs 42 A3
Quarrington Hill Durham 71 G8
Quarry Bank W Midlands 39 G10
Quarry Bank Mill, Wilmslow Ches 49 D9
Quarryford E Loth 85 H7
Quarryhill H'land 104 D6
Quarrywood Moray 105 F10
Quarter S Lanarks 75 B9
Quatford Shrops 39 F8
Quatt Shrops 39 G8
Quebec Durham 71 F6
Quedgeley Glos 29 G9
Queen Adelaide Cambs 43 G8
Queen Camel Som'set 9 B7
Queen Charlton Bath/NE Som'set 18 E3
Queen Dart Devon 7 E9
Queen Oak Dorset 9 A9
Queen Street Kent 14 D1
Queen Street Wilts 19 C7
Queenborough Kent 23 D9
Queenhill Heref/Worcs 29 E9
Queen's Head Shrops 38 C4
Queen's Park Beds 32 D3
Queen's Park Northants 31 B9
Queen's View Centre, Loch Tummel Perth/Kinr 89 F9
Queensbury W Yorks 57 E6
Queensferry C of Edinb 84 G3
Queensferry Flints 48 F4
Queenstown Lancs 55 E3
Queenzieburn N Lanarks 83 G7
Quemerford Wilts 19 E7
Quendale Shetl'd 113 M6
Quendon Essex 33 E8
Queniborough Leics 41 D8
Quenington Glos 19 A8
Quernmore Lancs 55 C5
Quethiock Cornw'l 4 D4
Quholm Orkney 112 G3
Quicks Green Berks 20 D3
Quidenham Norfolk 44 G4
Quidhampton Hants 20 F3
Quidhampton Wilts 10 A4
Quilquox Aberds 99 E9
Quina Brook Shrops 39 B6
Quindry Orkney 112 J5
Quinton Northants 31 C9
Quinton W Midlands 40 G1
Quixhill Staffs 40 A3
Quoditch Devon 6 G5
Quoig Perth/Kinr 83 B9
Quorndon Leics 41 D7
Quothquan S Lanarks 76 D2
Quoyloo Orkney 112 F3
Quoys Shetl'd 113 B9
Quoys Shetl'd 113 G7

R

Raasay Ho. H'land 94 C2
Rabbit's Cross Kent 14 D2
Raby Mersey 48 E4
Rachan Mill Scot Borders 76 D4
Rachub Gwyn 47 F6
Rackenford Devon 7 E9
Rackham W Sussex 12 D4
Rackheath Norfolk 45 D6
Racks Dumf/Gal 68 C3
Rackwick Orkney 112 J3
Rackwick Orkney 112 D5
Radbourne Derbys 40 B4
Radcliffe Gtr Man 49 B8
Radcliffe Northum 79 G7
Radcliffe on Trent Notts 41 B8
Radclive Bucks 31 E8
Radcot Oxon 19 B9
Raddery H'land 104 G6
Rademie Fife 85 D6
Radford Semele Warwick 30 B5
Radipole Dorset 9 F8
Radlett Herts 21 B9
Radley Oxon 20 B3
Radmanthwaite Notts 51 F7
Radmoor Shrops 39 C7
Radmore Green Ches 49 G6
Radnage Bucks 20 B5
Radstock Bath/NE Som'set 18 F3
Radstone Northants 31 D7
Radway Warwick 30 D5
Radway Green Ches 49 G8
Radwell Beds 32 C3
Radwell Herts 32 E5
Radwinter Essex 33 E9
Radyr Card 17 C6
Raf Museum, Hendon Gtr Lon 22 C2
Rafford Moray 105 G9
Ragdale Leics 41 D8
Raglan Monmouths 28 H5
Ragley Hall Warwick 30 C2
Ragnall Notts 51 E10
Rahane Arg/Bute 82 F3
Rainford Mersey 48 B5
Rainford Junction Mersey 48 B5
Rainham Gtr Lon 22 C5
Rainham Kent 14 B3
Rainhill Mersey 48 C5
Rainhill Stoops Mersey 49 C6
Rainow Ches 50 E1
Rainton N Yorks 63 G8
Rainworth Notts 51 G7
Raisbeck Cumb 61 D9
Raise Cumb 70 F2
Rait Perth/Kinr 84 B4
Raithby Lincs 53 D6
Raithby Lincs 53 F6
Rake W Sussex 12 C2
Rakewood Gtr Man 56 G4
Ram Carms 26 D5
Ram Lane Kent 14 D4
Ramasaig H'land 93 A7
Rame Cornw'l 3 F6
Rame Cornw'l 4 F5
Ramnageo Shetl'd 113 C9
Rampisham Dorset 9 D7
Rampside Cumb 55 B2
Rampton Cambs 33 B7
Rampton Notts 51 E9
Ramsbottom Gtr Man 56 G2
Ramsbury Wilts 19 D9
Ramscraigs H'land 111 G6
Ramsdean Hants 11 B10
Ramsdell Hants 20 F3
Ramsden Oxon 30 G5
Ramsden Bellhouse Essex 23 B7
Ramsden Heath Essex 23 B7
Ramsey Cambs 42 G5
Ramsey Essex 35 E6
Ramsey I of Man 54 D4
Ramsey Forty Foot Cambs 43 G6
Ramsey Heights Cambs 42 G5
Ramsey Island Essex 34 H3
Ramsey Mereside Cambs 42 G5
Ramsey St. Mary's Cambs 42 G5
Ramseycleuch Scot Borders 76 F5
Ramsgate Kent 15 B8
Ramsgill N Yorks 63 G6
Ramshorn Staffs 50 H2
Ramsnest Common Surrey 12 B3
Ranais W Isles 107 G8
Ranby Lincs 52 E5
Ranby Notts 51 D8
Rand Lincs 52 E4
Randwick Glos 29 H9
Ranfurly Renf 74 A5
Rangag H'land 111 E6
Rangemore Staffs 40 C3
Rangeworthy S Gloucs 18 C3
Rankinston E Ayrs 75 F6
Ranmoor S Yorks 50 D5
Ranmore Common Surrey 21 F9
Rannerdale Cumb 60 C4
Rannoch School Perth/Kinr 89 F6
Rannoch Station Perth/Kinr 88 F5
Ranochan H'land 87 C8
Ranskill Notts 51 D8
Ranton Staffs 39 C9
Ranworth Norfolk 45 D7
Raploch Stirl 83 E8
Rapness Orkney 112 D6
Rascal Moor E Riding Yorks 58 E4
Rascarrel Dumf/Gal 67 F9
Rashieriewe Aberds 99 F9
Raskelf N Yorks 63 G9
Rassau Bl Gwent 28 G2
Rastrick W Yorks 57 F6
Ratagan H'land 95 E6
Ratby Leics 41 E7
Ratcliffe Culey Leics 40 F5
Ratcliffe on Soar Leics 41 C6
Ratcliffe on the Wreake Leics 41 D8
Rathen Aberds 99 B10
Rathillet Fife 84 B5
Rathmell N Yorks 56 C3
Ratho C of Edinb 84 G3
Ratho Station C of Edinb 84 G3
Rathven Moray 98 B4
Ratley Warwick 30 D5
Ratlinghope Shrops 38 F5
Rattar H'land 111 B7
Ratten Row Lancs 55 D4
Rattery Devon 5 D8
Rattlesden Suffolk 34 C3
Rattray Perth/Kinr 90 G2
Raughton Head Cumb 69 F6
Raunds Northants 32 A2
Raven Seat N Yorks 62 D3
Ravenfield S Yorks 51 C6
Ravenglass Cumb 60 E3
Ravenglass and Eskdale Railway & Museum Cumb 60 E3
Raveningham Norfolk 45 F7
Ravenscar N Yorks 65 D7
Ravenscraig Invercl 82 G3
Ravensdale I of Man 54 D3
Ravensden Beds 32 C3
Ravenshead Notts 51 G7
Ravensmoor Ches 49 G7
Ravensthorpe Northants 31 A8
Ravensthorpe W Yorks 57 F7
Ravenstone Leics 41 D6
Ravenstone M/Keynes 31 C10
Ravenstonedale Cumb 62 D2
Ravenstown Cumb 61 G6
Ravenstruther S Lanarks 76 C2
Ravensworth N Yorks 63 D6
Raw N Yorks 65 D7
Rawcliffe E Riding Yorks 58 F2
Rawcliffe C of York 58 C1
Rawcliffe Bridge E Riding Yorks 58 F2
Rawdon W Yorks 57 E7
Rawmarsh S Yorks 51 C6
Rawreth Essex 23 B7
Rawridge Devon 8 D4
Rawtenstall Lancs 56 F3
Raxton Aberds 99 E8
Raydon Suffolk 34 E4
Raylees Northum 70 A4
Rayleigh Essex 23 B8
Rayne Essex 33 F10
Rayners Lane Gtr Lon 21 C9
Raynes Park Gtr Lon 22 E2
Reach Cambs 33 B8
Read Lancs 56 E2
Reading Berks 20 D5
Reading Street Kent 14 E4
Reagill Cumb 61 C9
Rearquhar H'land 104 C6
Rearsby Leics 41 D8
Reaster H'land 111 C7
Reawick Shetl'd 113 J6
Reay H'land 110 C4
Rechullin H'land 103 G6
Reculver Kent 15 B7
Red Dial Cumb 68 F5
Red Hill Heref/Worcs 29 C9
Red Houses Jersey 4
Red Lodge Suffolk 33 A9
Red Rail Heref/Worcs 29 F6
Red Rock Gtr Man 49 B6
Red Roses Carms 25 E7
Red Row Northum 79 H7
Red Street Staffs 49 G9
Red Wharf Bay Angl 46 D5
Redberth Pembs 24 F5
Redbourn Herts 32 G4
Redbourne N Lincs 52 C2
Redbrook Glos 29 H6
Redbrook Wrex 39 A6
Redburn H'land 104 F4
Redburn H'land 97 B7
Redburn Northum 70 D2
Redcar Redcar/Clevel'd 64 B4
Redcastle Angus 91 F7
Redcastle H'land 96 B3
Redcliff Bay N Som'set 17 D9
Redding Falk 83 G10
Reddingmuirhead Falk 83 G10
Reddish Gtr Man 49 C9
Redditch Heref/Worcs 30 B2
Rede Suffolk 34 C2
Redenhall Norfolk 45 G6
Redesdale Camp Northum 78 H3
Redesmouth Northum 70 B3
Redford Aberds 91 D8
Redford Angus 91 G6
Redford Durham 70 G5
Redfordgreen Scot Borders 77 F6
Redgorton Perth/Kinr 84 B2
Redgrave Suffolk 44 H4
Redhill Aberds 99 E6
Redhill Aberds 91 A8
Redhill N Som'set 18 E2
Redhill Surrey 22 F2
Redhouse Arg/Bute 73 A8
Redhouses Arg/Bute 72 A3
Redisham Suffolk 45 G8
Redland Bristol 18 D2
Redland Orkney 112 F4
Redlingfield Suffolk 34 A5
Redlynch Som'set 9 A9
Redlynch Wilts 10 B5
Redmarley D'Abitot Glos 29 E8
Redmarshall Stockton 63 B8
Redmile Leics 41 B9
Redmire N Yorks 62 E5
Redmoor Cornw'l 3 C9
Rednal Shrops 38 C4
Redpath Scot Borders 77 D8
Redpoint H'land 102 F5
Redruth Cornw'l 2 E5
Redvales Gtr Man 49 B9
Redwick Newp 17 C9
Redwick S Gloucs 18 C2
Redworth Durham 63 B7
Reed Herts 33 E6
Reedham Norfolk 45 E8
Reedness E Riding Yorks 58 F3
Reeds Beck Lincs 52 F5
Reepham Lincs 52 E3
Reepham Norfolk 44 C4
Reeth N Yorks 62 E5
Regaby I of Man 54 D4
Regoul H'land 105 G7
Reiff H'land 103 A7
Reigate Surrey 22 F2
Reighton N Yorks 65 G9
Reighton Gap N Yorks 65 G9
Reinigeadal W Isles 101 B8
Reiss H'land 111 D8
Rejerrah Cornw'l 3 D6
Releath Cornw'l 2 F5
Relubbus Cornw'l 2 F4
Relugas Moray 97 B7
Remenham Berks 20 C5
Remenham Hill Berks 20 C5
Remony Perth/Kinr 89 G8
Rempstone Notts 41 C7
Rendcomb Glos 30 H2
Rendham Suffolk 35 B7
Rendlesham Suffolk 35 C7
Renfrew Renf 83 H6
Renhold Beds 32 C3
Renishaw Derbys 51 E6
Rennington Northum 79 F7
Renton W Dunb 82 G4
Renwick Cumb 69 F8
Repps Norfolk 45 D8
Repton Derbys 40 C5
Rescobie Angus 91 F6
Resipole H'land 87 E7
Resolis H'land 104 F5
Resolven Neath P Talb 16 A3
Reston Scot Borders 78 A3
Reswallie Angus 91 F6
Retew Cornw'l 3 D8
Retford Notts 51 D9
Rettendon Essex 23 B7
Rettendon Place Essex 23 B7
Revesby Lincs 52 F5
Revesby Bridge Lincs 53 F6
Rew Street I of Wight 11 E7
Rewe Devon 7 G10
Reydon Suffolk 45 H8
Reydon Smear Suffolk 45 H8
Reymerston Norfolk 44 E4
Reynalton Pembs 24 F5
Reynoldston Swan 25 G9
Rezare Cornw'l 4 C4
Rhandirmwyn Carms 27 D7
Rhayader Powys 27 B9
Rhedyn Gwyn 36 B2
Rhemore H'land 86 F5
Rhencullen I of Man 54 D3
Rhes-y-cae Flints 48 E2
Rhewl Denbs 48 F2
Rhewl Denbs 38 A2
Rhian H'land 109 H8
Rhicarn H'land 108 G3
Rhiconich H'land 108 D5
Rhicullen H'land 104 E5
Rhidorroch Ho. H'land 103 C9
Rhifail H'land 110 E2
Rhigos Rh Cyn Taff 27 H9
Rhilochan H'land 104 B6
Rhiroy H'land 103 D9
Rhiw Gwyn 36 C2
Rhiwbina Card 17 C6
Rhiwbryfdir Gwyn 47 H6
Rhiwderin Newp 17 C7
Rhiwlas Gwyn 46 F5
Rhiwlas Gwyn 37 B9
Rhiwlas Powys 38 B2
Rhodes Gtr Man 49 B9
Rhodes Minnis Kent 15 D6
Rhodesia Notts 51 E7
Rhodiad Pembs 24 D2
Rhondda Rh Cyn Taff 16 B4
Rhonehouse or Kelton Hill Dumf/Gal 67 E9
Rhoose V of Glam 16 E5
Rhôs Carms 25 C8
Rhôs Neath P Talb 16 A2
Rhos-fawr Gwyn 36 B3
Rhos-hill Pembs 25 B6
Rhos-on-Sea Conwy 47 D8
Rhos-y-brithdir Powys 38 C2
Rhos-y-garth Ceredig'n 27 A6
Rhos-y-gwaliau Gwyn 37 B9
Rhos-y-llan Gwyn 36 B2
Rhos-y-Madoc Wrex 38 A4
Rhos-y-meirch Powys 28 B3
Rhosaman Carms 27 G7
Rhosbeirio Angl 46 C4
Rhoscefnhir Angl 46 E5
Rhoscolyn Angl 46 E2
Rhoscrowther Pembs 24 F4
Rhosesmor Flints 48 F3
Rhosgadfan Gwyn 46 G5
Rhosgoch Angl 46 D4
Rhosgoch Powys 28 D2
Rhoshirwaun Gwyn 36 C1
Rhoslan Gwyn 36 A4
Rhoslefain Gwyn 36 E5
Rhosllanerchrugog Wrex 48 H3
Rhosmaen Carms 27 F6
Rhosmeirch Angl 46 E4
Rhosneigr Angl 46 E3
Rhosnesni Wrex 48 G4
Rhosrobin Wrex 48 G4
Rhossili Swan 25 H9
Rhosson Pembs 24 D2
Rhostryfan Gwyn 46 G4
Rhostyllen Wrex 48 H4
Rhosybol Angl 46 D4
Rhu Arg/Bute 73 A8
Rhu Arg/Bute 82 F3
Rhualt Denbs 48 E1
Rhuddall Heath Ches 49 F6
Rhuddlan Ceredig'n 25 B9
Rhuddlan Denbs 47 E10
Rhue H'land 103 C8
Rhulen Powys 28 D2
Rhunahaorine Arg/Bute 73 C7
Rhyd Gwyn 37 A6
Rhyd Powys 37 E9
Rhyd-Ddu Gwyn 46 G5
Rhyd-moel-ddu Powys 38 H1
Rhyd-Rosser Ceredig'n 26 B5
Rhyd-uchaf Gwyn 37 B9
Rhyd-wen Gwyn 37 D7
Rhyd-y-clafdy Gwyn 36 B3
Rhyd-y-foel Conwy 47 E9
Rhyd-y-fro Neath P Talb 27 H7
Rhyd-y-gwin Swan 16 A1
Rhyd-y-meirch Monmouths 28 H4
Rhyd-y-meudwy Denbs 48 G2
Rhyd-y-sarn Gwyn 37 A6
Rhyd-yr-onen Gwyn 37 E6
Rhydargaeau Carms 25 D9
Rhydcymerau Carms 26 E5
Rhydd Heref/Worcs 29 D9
Rhydding Neath P Talb 16 B2
Rhydfudr Ceredig'n 26 B5
Rhydlewis Ceredig'n 25 B8
Rhydlios Gwyn 36 B1
Rhydlydan Conwy 47 G8
Rhydness Powys 28 D2
Rhydowen Ceredig'n 25 B9
Rhydspence Heref/Worcs 28 D3
Rhydtalog Flints 48 G3
Rhydwyn Angl 46 D3
Rhydycroesau Shrops 38 B3
Rhydyfelin Ceredig'n 36 H5
Rhydyfelin Rh Cyn Taff 16 C5
Rhydymain Gwyn 37 C8
Rhydymwyn Flints 48 F3
Rhyl Denbs 47 D10
Rhymney Caerph 28 H2
Rhynd Fife 85 B6
Rhynd Perth/Kinr 84 B3
Rhynie Aberds 98 F4
Rhynie H'land 105 E7
Ribbesford Heref/Worcs 29 A8
Ribble Head N Yorks 62 G2
Ribbleton Lancs 55 E5
Ribchester Lancs 56 E1
Ribigill H'land 109 D8
Riby Lincs 52 B4
Riby Cross Roads Lincs 52 B4
Riccall N Yorks 58 E2
Riccarton E Ayrs 75 D6
Richards Castle Heref/Worcs 28 B5
Richings Park Bucks 21 D8
Richmond Gtr Lon 21 D9
Richmond N Yorks 63 D6
Rickarton Aberds 91 C9
Rickinghall Suffolk 44 H4
Rickleton Tyne/Wear 71 E7
Rickling Essex 33 E7
Rickmansworth Herts 21 B8
Riddings Cumb 69 C7
Riddings Derbys 51 G6
Riddlecombe Devon 7 E7
Riddlesden W Yorks 56 D5
Riddrie C of Glasg 83 H7
Ridge Dorset 10 F2
Ridge Hants 11 C6
Ridge Wilts 10 A2
Ridge Green Surrey 22 G3
Ridge Lane Warwick 40 F4
Ridgebourne Powys 28 B1
Ridgehill N Som'set 18 E2
Ridgeway Cross Heref/Worcs 29 D8
Ridgewell Essex 33 D10
Ridgewood E Sussex 13 D8
Ridgmont Beds 32 E2
Riding Mill Northum 70 D5
Ridleywood Wrex 48 G5
Ridlington Norfolk 45 B7
Ridlington Rutl'd 41 E10
Ridsdale Northum 70 B4
Riechip Perth/Kinr 90 G1
Riemore Perth/Kinr 90 G1
Rienachait H'land 108 F3
Rievaulx N Yorks 64 F3
Rievaulx Abbey N Yorks 64 F3
Rift House Hartlep'l 71 G9
Rigg Dumf/Gal 68 D5
Riggend N Lanarks 83 G8
Rigsby Lincs 53 E7
Rigside S Lanarks 76 D1
Riley Green Lancs 55 F6
Rileyhill Staffs 40 D3
Rilla Mill Cornw'l 4 C3
Rillington N Yorks 65 G6
Rimington Lancs 56 D3
Rimpton Som'set 9 B8
Rimswell E Riding Yorks 59 F9
Rinaston Pembs 24 D4
Ringasta Shetl'd 113 M6
Ringford Dumf/Gal 67 E8
Ringinglow S Yorks 50 D4
Ringland Norfolk 44 D5
Ringles Cross E Sussex 13 C8
Ringmer E Sussex 13 D8
Ringmore Devon 5 F7
Ringorm Moray 98 D2
Ring's End Cambs 43 E6
Ringsfield Suffolk 45 G8
Ringsfield Corner Suffolk 45 G8
Ringshall Herts 32 G2
Ringshall Suffolk 34 C4
Ringshall Stocks Suffolk 34 C4
Ringstead Norfolk 43 A10
Ringstead Northants 42 H2
Ringwood Hants 10 D4
Ringwould Kent 15 D8
Rinmore Aberds 98 G4
Rinnigill Orkney 112 J4
Rinsey Cornw'l 2 G4
Riof W Isles 106 F5
Ripe E Sussex 13 D9
Ripley Derbys 50 G5
Ripley Hants 10 E4
Ripley N Yorks 57 B7
Ripley Surrey 21 F8
Riplingham E Riding Yorks 58 E5
Ripon N Yorks 63 G8
Ripon Cathedral N Yorks 63 G8
Rippingale Lincs 42 C3
Ripple Heref/Worcs 29 E9
Ripple Kent 15 D8
Ripponden W Yorks 56 G5
Rireavach H'land 103 C8
Risabus Arg/Bute 72 C3
Risbury Heref/Worcs 29 C6
Risby Suffolk 34 B1
Risca Caerph 17 B7
Rise E Riding Yorks 59 D7
Riseden E Sussex 13 B10
Risegate Lincs 42 C5
Riseholme Lincs 52 E2
Riseley Beds 32 B3
Riseley Berks 20 E5
Rishangles Suffolk 34 B5
Rishton Lancs 56 E2
Rishworth W Yorks 56 G5
Rising Bridge Lancs 56 F2
Risley Ches 49 C7
Risley Derbys 41 B6
Risplith N Yorks 57 B7
Rispond H'land 109 C7
Rivar Wilts 19 E10
Rivenhall End Essex 34 G2
River Bank Cambs 33 B8
Riverhead Kent 22 F5
Rivington Lancs 56 G1
Roa Island Cumb 55 B2
Roachill Devon 7 D9
Road Green Norfolk 45 F6
Roade Northants 31 C9
Roadhead Cumb 69 C8
Roadmeetings S Lanarks 76 C1
Roadside H'land 111 C6
Roadside of Catterline Aberds 91 D9
Roadside of Kinneff Aberds 91 D9
Roadwater Som'set 16 H5
Roag H'land 93 A8
Roath Card 17 D6
Rob Roy and Trossachs Visitor Centre, Callander Stirl 83 D7
Roberton Scot Borders 77 F7
Roberton S Lanarks 76 E2
Robertsbridge E Sussex 14 F2
Roberttown W Yorks 57 F6
Robeston Cross Pembs 24 F3
Robeston Wathen Pembs 24 E5
Robin Hood W Yorks 57 F8
Robin Hood's Bay N Yorks 65 D7
Roborough Devon 7 E6
Roborough Devon 5 D6
Roby Mersey 48 C5
Roby Mill Lancs 49 B6
Rocester Staffs 40 B3
Roch Pembs 24 D3
Roch Gate Pembs 24 D3
Rochdale Gtr Man 56 G3
Roche Cornw'l 3 C8
Rochester Kent 14 B2
Rochester Northum 78 H3
Rochester Castle Kent 14 B2
Rochester Cathedral Kent 14 B2
Rochford Essex 23 B8
Rock Cornw'l 3 B8
Rock Heref/Worcs 29 A8
Rock Northum 79 E7
Rock W Sussex 12 D5
Rock Ferry Mersey 48 D4
Rock Hill Heref/Worcs 30 B1
Rockbeare Devon 8 E2
Rockbourne Hants 10 C4
Rockcliffe Cumb 69 D6
Rockcliffe Dumf/Gal 68 E1
Rockfield H'land 105 D8
Rockfield Monmouths 28 G5
Rockford Hants 10 D4
Rockhampton S Gloucs 18 B3
Rockingham Northants 42 F1
Rockland All Saints Norfolk 44 F3
Rockland St. Mary Norfolk 45 E7
Rockland St. Peter Norfolk 44 F3
Rockley Wilts 19 D8
Rockwell End Bucks 20 C5
Rockwell Green Som'set 8 B3
Rodborough Glos 18 A5
Rodbourne Thamesd'n 19 C8
Rodbourne Wilts 19 C6
Rodbourne Cheney Thamesd'n 19 C8
Rodd Heref/Worcs 28 B4
Roddam Northum 78 E5
Rodden Dorset 9 F8
Rode Som'set 18 F5
Rode Heath Ches 49 G9
Rodeheath Ches 49 F9
Roden Shrops 39 D6
Rodhuish Som'set 16 H5
Rodington Shrops 39 D6
Rodley Glos 29 G8
Rodley W Yorks 57 E7
Rodmarton Glos 19 B6
Rodmell E Sussex 13 E8
Rodmersham Kent 14 B4

Rodney Stoke Som'set 17 F9
Rodsley Derbys 40 A4
Rodway Som'set 17 H7
Rodwell Dorset 9 G8
Roe Green Herts 33 E6
Roecliffe N Yorks 57 B8
Roehampton Gtr Lon 22 D2
Roesound Shetl'd 113 G6
Roffey W Sussex 12 B5
Rogart H'land 104 B6
Rogart Station H'land 104 B6
Rogate W Sussex 12 C2
Rogerstone Newp 17 C7
Roghadal W Isles 101 D6
Rogiet Monmouths 17 C9
Rogue's Alley Cambs 43 E6
Roisinis W Isles 92 D3
Roke Oxon 20 B4
Roker Tyne/Wear 71 E9
Rollesby Norfolk 45 D8
Rolleston Leics 41 E9
Rolleston Notts 51 G9
Rolleston-on-Dove Staffs 40 C4
Rolston E Riding Yorks 59 D8
Rolvenden Kent 14 E3
Rolvenden Layne Kent 14 E3
Romaldkirk Durham 62 B4
Roman Baths & Pump Room, Bath Bath/NE Som'set 18 E4
Romanby N Yorks 63 E8
Romannobridge Scot Borders 76 C4
Romansleigh Devon 7 D8
Romford Gtr Lon 22 C5
Romiley Gtr Man 49 C10
Romney, Hythe and Dymchurch Railway & Museum Kent 15 E6
Romsey Hants 11 B6
Romsey Town Cambs 33 C7
Romsley Heref/Worcs 40 H1
Romsley Shrops 39 G8
Ronague I of Man 54 F2
Rookhope Durham 70 F4
Rookley I of Wight 11 F8
Rooks Bridge Som'set 17 F8
Roos E Riding Yorks 59 E8
Roosebeck Cumb 55 B2
Rootham's Green Beds 32 C4
Rootpark S Lanarks 76 B2
Ropley Hants 11 A9
Ropley Dean Hants 11 A9
Ropsley Lincs 42 B2
Rora Aberds 99 C10
Rorandle Aberds 99 G6
Rorrington Shrops 38 E4
Roscroggan Cornw'l 2 E5
Rose Cornw'l 3 D6
Rose Ash Devon 7 D8
Rose Green W Sussex 12 F3
Rose Grove Lancs 56 E3
Rose Hill E Sussex 13 D8
Rose Hill Lancs 56 E3
Rose Hill Suffolk 34 D5
Roseacre Kent 14 C2
Roseacre Lancs 55 E4
Rosebank S Lanarks 75 C10
Rosebrough Northum 79 E6
Rosebush Pembs 24 D5
Rosecare Cornw'l 6 G2
Rosedale Abbey N Yorks 64 E5
Roseden Northum 78 E5
Rosefield H'land 105 G7
Rosehall H'land 104 B3
Rosehaugh Mains H'land 104 G5
Rosehearty Aberds 99 B9
Rosehill Shrops 39 B7
Roseisle Moray 105 F10
Roselands E Sussex 13 E10
Rosemarket Pembs 24 F4
Rosemarkie H'land 104 G6
Rosemary Lane Devon 8 C3
Rosemount Perth/Kinr 90 G2
Rosenannon Cornw'l 3 C8
Rosewell Midloth 76 A5
Roseworth Stockton 63 B9
Roseworthy Cornw'l 2 F5
Rosgill Cumb 61 C8
Roshven H'land 87 D7
Roskhill H'land 101 H8
Roskill House H'land 104 G5
Rosley Cumb 69 F6
Roslin Midloth 76 A5
Rosliston Derbys 40 D4
Rosneath Arg/Bute 82 F3
Ross Dumf/Gal 67 F8
Ross Northum 79 D6
Ross Perth/Kinr 83 B8
Ross-on-Wye Heref/Worcs 29 F7
Rossett Wrex 48 G4
Rossett Green N Yorks 57 C8
Rossie Ochill Perth/Kinr 84 C2
Rossie Priory Perth/Kinr 84 A4
Rossington S Yorks 51 C8
Rosskeen H'land 104 F5
Rossland Renf 82 G5
Roster H'land 111 F7
Rostherne Ches 49 D8
Rosthwaite Cumb 60 C5
Roston Derbys 40 A3
Rosyth Fife 84 F3
Rothbury Northum 78 G5
Rotherby Leics 41 D8
Rotherfield E Sussex 13 C9
Rotherfield Greys Oxon 20 C5
Rotherfield Peppard Oxon 20 C5
Rotherham S Yorks 51 C6
Rothersthorpe Northants 31 C9
Rotherwick Hants 20 F5
Rothes Moray 98 D2
Rothesay Arg/Bute 74 A2
Rothiebrisbane Aberds 99 E7
Rothiemurchus Estate Visitor Centre H'land 97 F7
Rothienorman Aberds 99 E7
Rothiesholm Orkney 112 F7
Rothley Leics 41 D7
Rothley Northum 70 B5
Rothley Shield East Northum 70 A5
Rothmaise Aberds 99 E6
Rothwell Lincs 52 C4
Rothwell Northants 41 G10
Rothwell W Yorks 57 F8
Rothwell Haigh W Yorks 57 F8
Rotsea E Riding Yorks 59 C6
Rottal Angus 90 E4
Rotten End Suffolk 35 B7
Rottingdean Brighton/Hove 13 E7
Rottington Cumb 60 C2
Rotunda, Folkestone Kent 15 E7
Roud I of Wight 11 F8
Rough Close Staffs 39 B10
Rough Common Kent 15 C6
Rougham Norfolk 44 C2
Rougham Suffolk 34 B3
Rougham Green Suffolk 34 B3
Roughburn H'land 88 C4
Roughlee Lancs 56 D3
Roughley W Midlands 40 F3
Roughsike Cumb 69 C8
Roughton Lincs 52 F5
Roughton Norfolk 45 B6
Roughton Shrops 39 F8
Roughton Moor Lincs 52 F5
Roundhay W Yorks 57 E8
Roundstonefoot Dumf/Gal 76 G4
Roundstreet Common W Sussex 12 C4
Roundway Wilts 19 E7
Rous Lench Heref/Worcs 30 C2
Rousdon Devon 8 E4
Routenburn N Ayrs 74 A3
Routh E Riding Yorks 59 D6
Row Cornw'l 3 B9
Row Cumb 61 F7
Row Green Essex 33 F10
Row Heath Essex 34 G5
Rowanburn Dumf/Gal 69 C7
Rowardennan Stirl 82 E4
Rowde Wilts 19 E6
Rowen Conwy 47 E7
Rowfoot Northum 69 D9
Rowhedge Essex 34 F4
Rowhook W Sussex 12 B5
Rowington Warwick 30 B4
Rowland Derbys 50 E4
Rowland's Castle Hants 11 C10
Rowland's Gill Tyne/Wear 71 E6
Rowledge Surrey 21 G6
Rowley E Riding Yorks 58 E5
Rowley Shrops 38 E4
Rowley Hill W Yorks 57 G6
Rowley Regis W Midlands 40 G1
Rowlstone Heref/Worcs 28 F4
Rowly Surrey 21 G8
Rowney Green Heref/Worcs 30 A2
Rownhams Hants 11 C6
Rowrah Cumb 60 C3
Rowsham Bucks 31 G10
Rowsley Derbys 50 F4
Rowstock Oxon 20 C2
Rowston Lincs 52 G3
Rowton Ches 48 F5
Rowton Shrops 39 D7
Rowton Shrops 38 D4
Roxburgh Scot Borders 78 D2
Roxby N Lincs 58 G5
Roxby N Yorks 64 C5
Roxton Beds 32 C4
Roxwell Essex 33 H9
Royal Botanic Gardens, Edinburgh C of Edinb 84 G4
Royal Leamington Spa Warwick 30 B5
Royal Museum of Scotland, Edinburgh C of Edinb 84 G4
Royal Oak Durham 63 B7
Royal Oak Lancs 48 B5
Royal Pavilion, Brighton Brighton/Hove 13 E7
Royal Tunbridge Wells Kent 13 B9
Royal Welch Fusiliers Regimental Museum (See Caernarfon Castle) Gwyn 46 F4
Royal Worcester Porcelain, Worcester Heref/Worcs 29 C9
Roybridge H'land 88 C3
Roydhouse W Yorks 57 G7
Roydon Essex 33 H7
Roydon Norfolk 43 C10
Roydon Norfolk 44 G4
Roydon Hamlet Essex 33 H7
Royston Herts 33 D6
Royston S Yorks 57 G8
Royton Gtr Man 49 B10
Rozel Jersey 4
Ruabon Wrex 38 A4
Ruadh-phort Mor Arg/Bute 80 G4
Ruaig Arg/Bute 86 D2
Ruan Lanihorne Cornw'l 3 E7
Ruan Minor Cornw'l 3 H6
Ruarach H'land 95 D6
Ruardean Glos 29 G7
Ruardean Woodside Glos 29 G7
Rubery W Midlands 40 H1
Ruckcroft Cumb 69 F8
Ruckhall Common Heref/Worcs 28 E5
Ruckinge Kent 14 E5
Ruckland Lincs 53 E6
Ruckley Shrops 39 E6
Rudbaxton Pembs 24 D4
Rudby N Yorks 63 D9
Ruddington Notts 41 B7
Rudford Glos 29 F8
Rudge Shrops 39 F9
Rudge Som'set 18 F5
Rudgeway S Gloucs 18 C3
Rudgwick W Sussex 12 B4
Rudhall Heref/Worcs 29 F7
Rudheath Ches 49 E7
Rudley Green Essex 23 A8
Rudry Caerph 17 C6
Rudston E Riding Yorks 59 B6
Rudyard Staffs 50 G1
Rufford Lancs 55 G4
Rufforth C of York 57 C10
Rugby Warwick 41 H7
Rugeley Staffs 40 D2
Ruglen S Ayrs 74 G4
Ruilick H'land 96 B3
Ruishton Som'set 8 B4
Ruisigearraidh W Isles 100 D5
Ruislip Gtr Lon 21 C8
Ruislip Common Gtr Lon 21 C8
Rumbling Bridge Perth/Kinr 84 E2
Rumburgh Suffolk 45 G7
Rumford Cornw'l 3 B7
Rumney Card 17 D7
Runcorn Ches 49 D6
Runcton W Sussex 12 E2
Runcton Holme Norfolk 43 E9
Rundlestone Devon 5 C6
Runfold Surrey 21 G6
Runhall Norfolk 44 E4
Runham Norfolk 45 E9
Runham Norfolk 45 D8
Runnington Som'set 8 B3
Runsell Green Essex 34 H1
Runswick Bay N Yorks 65 C6
Runwell Essex 23 B7
Ruscombe Berks 20 D5
Rush Green Gtr Lon 22 C5
Rushall Heref/Worcs 29 E7
Rushall Norfolk 44 G5
Rushall Wilts 19 F8
Rushall W Midlands 40 E2
Rushbrooke Suffolk 34 B2
Rushbury Shrops 39 F6
Rushden Herts 33 E6
Rushden Northants 32 B2
Rushenden Kent 23 D9
Rushford Norfolk 44 G3
Rushlake Green E Sussex 13 D10
Rushmere Suffolk 45 G8
Rushmere St. Andrew Suffolk 35 D6
Rushmoor Surrey 21 G6
Rushmoor Wilts 10 C2
Rushock Heref/Worcs 29 A9
Rusholme Gtr Man 49 C9
Rushton Ches 49 F6
Rushton Northants 41 G10
Rushton Shrops 39 E7
Rushton Spencer Staffs 49 F10
Rushwick Heref/Worcs 29 C9
Rushyford Durham 63 B7
Ruskie Stirl 83 D7
Ruskington Lincs 52 G3
Rusland Cumb 61 F6
Rusper W Sussex 13 B6
Ruspidge Glos 29 G7
Russell's Water Oxon 20 C5
Russel's Green Suffolk 35 A6
Rusthall Kent 13 B9
Rustington W Sussex 12 E4
Ruston N Yorks 65 F7
Ruston Parva E Riding Yorks 59 B6
Ruswarp N Yorks 65 D6
Rutherford Scot Borders 77 D9
Rutherglen S Lanarks 75 A8
Ruthernbridge Cornw'l 3 C9
Ruthin Denbs 48 G2
Ruthin Craft Centre Denbs 48 G2
Ruthrieston Aberd C 91 A10
Ruthven Aberds 98 D5
Ruthven Angus 90 G3
Ruthven H'land 97 C6
Ruthven H'land 96 G5
Ruthven House Angus 90 G4
Ruthvoes Cornw'l 3 C8
Ruthwell Dumf/Gal 68 D3
Ruyton-XI-Towns Shrops 38 C4
Ryal Northum 70 C5
Ryal Fold Lancs 56 F1
Ryall Dorset 9 E6
Ryarsh Kent 14 C1
Rydal Cumb 61 D6
Ryde I of Wight 11 E8
Rye E Sussex 14 F4
Rye Foreign E Sussex 14 F3
Rye Harbour E Sussex 14 G4
Rye Park Herts 33 G6
Rye Street Heref/Worcs 29 E8
Ryecroft Gate Staffs 49 F10
Ryehill E Riding Yorks 59 F8
Ryhall Rutl'd 42 D3
Ryhill W Yorks 57 G8
Ryhope Tyne/Wear 71 E9
Rylstone N Yorks 56 C4
Ryme Intrinseca Dorset 9 C7
Ryther N Yorks 58 E1
Ryton Glos 29 E8
Ryton N Yorks 64 G5
Ryton Shrops 39 E8
Ryton Tyne/Wear 71 D6
Ryton on Dunsmore Warwick 30 A5

S

Sabden Lancs 56 E2
Sacombe Herts 33 G6
Sacriston Durham 71 F7
Sadberge Durham 63 C8
Saddell Arg/Bute 73 D7
Saddington Leics 41 F8
Saddle Bow Norfolk 43 D9
Saddlescombe W Sussex 13 D6
Sadgill Cumb 61 D7
Saffron Walden Essex 33 E8
Sageston Pembs 24 F5
Saham Hills Norfolk 44 E3
Saham Toney Norfolk 44 E3
Saighdinis W Isles 100 F4
Saighton Ches 48 F5
Saint Hill W Sussex 13 B7
Saint Leonards S Lanarks 75 B8
Saintbury Glos 30 E3
Salcombe Devon 5 G8
Salcombe Regis Devon 8 F3
Salcott Essex 34 G3
Sale Gtr Man 49 C8
Sale Green Heref/Worcs 29 C10
Saleby Lincs 53 E7
Salehurst E Sussex 14 F2
Salem Ceredig'n 37 G6
Salem Carms 27 F6
Salen Arg/Bute 86 G5
Salen H'land 87 E6
Salesbury Lancs 56 E1
Salford Beds 32 E2
Salford Gtr Man 49 C9
Salford Oxon 30 F4
Salford Priors Warwick 30 C2
Salfords Surrey 22 G2
Salhouse Norfolk 45 D7
Saline Fife 84 E2
Salisbury Wilts 10 B4
Salisbury Cathedral Wilts 10 B4
Sallachan H'land 87 E9
Sallachy H'land 95 C6
Sallachy H'land 104 B4
Salle Norfolk 44 C5
Salmonby Lincs 53 E6
Salmond's Muir Angus 91 H6
Salperton Glos 30 F2
Salph End Beds 32 C3
Salsburgh N Lanarks 75 A10
Salt Staffs 40 C1
Salt End E Riding Yorks 59 F7
Saltaire W Yorks 57 E6
Saltaire 1853 Gallery W Yorks 57 E6
Saltash Cornw'l 4 E5
Saltburn H'land 104 F6
Saltburn-by-the-Sea Redcar/Clevel'd 64 B4
Saltby Leics 42 C1
Saltcoats Cumb 60 E3
Saltcoats N Ayrs 74 C4
Saltdean Brighton/Hove 13 E7
Salter Lancs 55 B6
Salterforth Lancs 56 D3
Salterswall Ches 49 F7
Saltfleet Lincs 53 C7
Saltfleetby All Saints Lincs 53 C7
Saltfleetby St. Clements Lincs 53 C7
Saltfleetby St. Peter Lincs 53 D7
Saltford Bath/NE Som'set 18 E3
Salthouse Norfolk 44 A4
Saltmarshe E Riding Yorks 58 F3
Saltney Flints 48 F4
Salton N Yorks 64 G5
Saltwick Northum 71 C6
Saltwood Kent 15 E6
Salum Arg/Bute 86 D2
Salvington W Sussex 12 E5
Salwarpe Heref/Worcs 29 B9
Salway Ash Dorset 9 E6
Sambourne Warwick 30 B2
Sambrook Shrops 39 C8
Samhla W Isles 100 F3
Samlesbury Lancs 55 E5
Samlesbury Bottoms Lancs 55 F6
Sampford Arundel Som'set 8 C3
Sampford Brett Som'set 16 G5
Sampford Courtenay Devon 7 F7
Sampford Peverell Devon 8 C2
Sampford Spiney Devon 5 C6
Sampool Bridge Cumb 61 F7
Samuelston E Loth 85 G6
Sanachan H'land 94 B5
Sanaigmore Arg/Bute 80 G2
Sancreed Cornw'l 2 G3
Sancton E Riding Yorks 58 E5
Sand H'land 103 C7
Sand Shetl'd 113 J6
Sand Hole E Riding Yorks 58 E4
Sand Hutton N Yorks 58 C2
Sandaig H'land 94 F4
Sandal Magna W Yorks 57 G8
Sandale Cumb 68 F5
Sandbach Ches 49 F8
Sandbank Arg/Bute 82 F2
Sandbanks Poole 10 F3
Sandend Aberds 98 B5
Sanderstead Gtr Lon 22 E3
Sandfields Glos 29 F10
Sandford Cumb 62 C2
Sandford Devon 7 F9
Sandford Dorset 10 F2
Sandford I of Wight 11 F8
Sandford N Som'set 17 F9
Sandford Shrops 39 B6
Sandford S Lanarks 75 C9
Sandford on Thames Oxon 20 A3
Sandford Orcas Dorset 9 B8
Sandford St. Martin Oxon 31 F6
Sandfordhill Aberds 99 D11
Sandgarth Orkney 112 G6
Sandgate Kent 15 E6
Sandgreen Dumf/Gal 67 E7
Sandhaven Aberds 99 B9
Sandhead Dumf/Gal 66 F2
Sandhills Surrey 12 B3
Sandhoe Northum 70 D4
Sandholme E Riding Yorks 58 E4
Sandholme Lincs 43 B6
Sandhurst Berks 21 E6
Sandhurst Glos 29 F9
Sandhurst Kent 14 F2
Sandhurst Cross Kent 14 F2
Sandhutton N Yorks 63 F8
Sandiacre Derbys 41 B6
Sandilands Lincs 53 D8
Sandilands S Lanarks 76 D1
Sandiway Ches 49 E7
Sandleheath Hants 10 C4
Sandleigh Oxon 20 A2
Sandling Kent 14 C2
Sandlow Green Ches 49 F8
Sandness Shetl'd 113 H4
Sandon Essex 23 A7
Sandon Herts 33 E6
Sandon Staffs 39 B10
Sandown I of Wight 11 F8
Sandplace Cornw'l 4 E3
Sandridge Herts 32 G4
Sandridge Wilts 19 E6
Sandringham Norfolk 43 C9
Sandsend N Yorks 65 C6
Sandside Ho. H'land 110 C4
Sandsound Shetl'd 113 J6
Sandtoft N Lincs 51 B9
Sandway Kent 14 C3
Sandwell W Midlands 40 G2
Sandwich Kent 15 C8
Sandwick Cumb 61 C7
Sandwick Orkney 112 K5
Sandwick Shetl'd 113 L7
Sandwith Cumb 60 C2
Sandy Beds 32 D4
Sandy Carms 25 F9
Sandy Bank Lincs 52 G5
Sandy Haven Pembs 24 F3
Sandy Lane Wilts 19 E6
Sandy Lane Wrex 38 A4
Sandycroft Flints 48 F4
Sandyford Dumf/Gal 68 A5
Sandyford Stoke 49 G9
Sandygate I of Man 54 D3
Sandyhills Dumf/Gal 68 E1
Sandylands Lancs 55 B4
Sandypark Devon 5 B8
Sandysike Cumb 69 D6
Sangobeg H'land 109 C7
Sangomore H'land 109 C7
Sanna H'land 86 E4
Sanndabhaig W Isles 107 F8
Sanndabhaig W Isles 92 A4
Sannox N Ayrs 74 C2
Sanquhar Dumf/Gal 75 G9
Santon N Lincs 58 G5
Santon Bridge Cumb 60 D4
Santon Downham Suffolk 44 G2
Sapcote Leics 41 F6
Sapey Common Heref/Worcs 29 B8
Sapiston Suffolk 44 H3
Sapley Cambs 32 A5
Sapperton Glos 19 A6
Sapperton Lincs 42 B3
Saracen's Head Lincs 43 C6
Sarclet H'land 111 E8
Sardis Carms 25 F10
Sarn Bridg 16 C4
Sarn Powys 38 F3
Sarn Bach Gwyn 36 C3
Sarn Meyllteyrn Gwyn 36 B2
Sarnau Ceredig'n 26 C3
Sarnau Carms 25 E8
Sarnau Gwyn 37 B9
Sarnau Powys 27 E10
Sarnau Powys 38 D3
Sarnesfield Heref/Worcs 28 C4
Saron Carms 25 C8
Saron Carms 27 G6
Saron Denbs 47 F10
Saron Gwyn 46 G4
Saron Gwyn 46 F5
Sarratt Herts 21 B8
Sarre Kent 15 B7
Sarsden Oxon 30 F4
Sarsgrum H'land 109 C6
Satley Durham 71 F6
Satron N Yorks 62 E4
Satterleigh Devon 7 D7
Satterthwaite Cumb 61 E6
Satwell Oxon 20 C5
Sauchen Aberds 99 G6
Saucher Perth/Kinr 84 A3
Sauchieburn Aberds 91 E7
Saughall Ches 48 E4
Saughtree Scot Borders 77 H8
Saul Glos 29 H8
Saundby Notts 51 D9
Saundersfoot Pembs 24 F6
Saunderton Bucks 20 A5
Saunton Devon 6 C5
Sausthorpe Lincs 53 F6
Saval H'land 104 B4
Savary H'land 87 G6
Savile Park W Yorks 56 F5
Sawbridge Warwick 31 B7
Sawbridgeworth Herts 33 G7
Sawdon N Yorks 65 F7
Sawley Derbys 41 B6
Sawley Lancs 56 D2
Sawley N Yorks 57 B7
Sawston Cambs 33 D7
Sawtry Cambs 42 G4
Saxby Leics 41 D10
Saxby Lincs 52 D3
Saxby All Saints N Lincs 58 G5
Saxelby Leics 41 C9
Saxham Street Suffolk 34 B4
Saxilby Lincs 52 E1
Saxlingham Norfolk 44 B4
Saxlingham Green Norfolk 45 F6
Saxlingham Nethergate Norfolk 45 F6
Saxlingham Thorpe Norfolk 45 F6
Saxmundham Suffolk 35 B7
Saxon Street Cambs 33 C9
Saxondale Notts 41 B8
Saxtead Suffolk 35 B6
Saxtead Green Suffolk 35 B6
Saxthorpe Norfolk 44 B5
Saxton N Yorks 57 E9
Sayers Common W Sussex 13 D6
Scackleton N Yorks 64 G4
Scadabhagh W Isles 101 C7
Scaftworth Notts 51 C8
Scagglethorpe N Yorks 65 G6
Scaitcliffe Lancs 56 F2
Scalasaig Arg/Bute 80 E3
Scalby E Riding Yorks 58 F4
Scalby N Yorks 65 E8
Scaldwell Northants 31 A9
Scale Houses Cumb 69 F8
Scaleby Cumb 69 D7
Scaleby Hill Cumb 69 D7
Scales Cumb 60 G5
Scales Cumb 61 B6
Scales Lancs 55 E4
Scalford Leics 41 C9
Scaling N Yorks 64 C5
Scaling Dam Redcar/Clevel'd 64 C5
Scallastle Arg/Bute 87 H6
Scalloway Shetl'd 113 K7
Scalpay Ho. H'land 94 D3
Scalpsie Arg/Bute 74 B2
Scamadale H'land 87 B7
Scamblesby Lincs 52 E5
Scamodale H'land 87 D8
Scampston N Yorks 65 G6
Scampton Lincs 52 E2
Scapa Orkney 112 H5
Scapegoat Hill W Yorks 56 G5
Scar Orkney 112 D7
Scarborough N Yorks 65 F8
Scarborough Sea Life Centre N Yorks 65 E8
Scarcliffe Derbys 51 F6
Scarcroft W Yorks 57 D8
Scarcroft Hill W Yorks 57 D8
Scardroy H'land 103 G10
Scarff Shetl'd 113 E5
Scarfskerry H'land 111 B7
Scargill Durham 62 C5
Scarinish Arg/Bute 86 D2
Scarisbrick Lancs 55 G3
Scarning Norfolk 44 D3
Scarrington Notts 41 A9
Scartho NE Lincs 52 B5
Scarwell Orkney 112 F3
Scat Ness Shetl'd 113 M6
Scatraig H'land 96 C5
Scawby N Lincs 52 B2
Scawsby S Yorks 51 B7
Scawton N Yorks 64 F3
Scayne's Hill W Sussex 13 C7
Scethrog Powys 28 F2
Scholar Green Ches 49 G9
Scholes W Yorks 50 B3
Scholes W Yorks 57 F6
Scholes W Yorks 57 E8
School Green Ches 49 F7
Science & Industry Museum, Manchester Gtr Man 49 C9
Science Museum Gtr Lon 22 D2
Scleddau Pembs 24 C4
Sco Ruston Norfolk 45 C6
Scofton Notts 51 D8
Scole Norfolk 44 H5
Scolpaig W Isles 100 E3
Scone Palace, Perth Perth/Kinr 84 B3
Sconser H'land 94 C2
Scoonie Fife 84 D5
Scoor Arg/Bute 80 C4
Scopwick Lincs 52 G3
Scoraig H'land 103 C8
Scorborough E Riding Yorks 59 D6
Scorrier Cornw'l 3 E6
Scorton Lancs 55 D5
Scorton N Yorks 63 D7
Scotbheinn W Isles 100 G4
Scotby Cumb 69 E7
Scotforth Lancs 55 C4
Scothern Lincs 52 E3
Scotland Gate Northum 71 B7
Scotlandwell Perth/Kinr 84 D3
Scotney Castle Garden Kent 14 E1
Scotsburn H'land 104 E6
Scotscalder Station H'land 110 D5
Scotscraig Fife 84 B6
Scots'Gap Northum 70 B5
Scotston Aberds 91 D8
Scotston Perth/Kinr 89 G10
Scotstoun C of Glasg 83 H6
Scotstown H'land 87 E8
Scotswood Tyne/Wear 71 D6
Scottas H'land 94 F4
Scotter Lincs 52 B1
Scotterthorpe Lincs 52 B1
Scottlethorpe Lincs 42 C3
Scotton Lincs 52 C1
Scotton N Yorks 63 E6
Scotton N Yorks 57 C8
Scottow Norfolk 45 C6
Scoughall E Loth 85 F8
Scoulag Arg/Bute 74 B3
Scoulton Norfolk 44 E3
Scourie H'land 108 E4
Scourie More H'land 108 E4
Scousburgh Shetl'd 113 M6
Scrabster H'land 110 B5
Scrafield Lincs 53 F6
Scrainwood Northum 78 G4
Scrane End Lincs 43 A6
Scraptoft Leics 41 E8
Scratby Norfolk 45 D9
Scrayingham N Yorks 58 B3
Scredington Lincs 42 A3
Scremby Lincs 53 F7
Scremerston Northum 78 C5
Screveton Notts 41 A9
Scrivelsby Lincs 52 F5
Scriven N Yorks 57 C8
Scrooby Notts 51 C8
Scropton Derbys 40 B3
Scrub Hill Lincs 52 G5
Scruton N Yorks 63 E7
Sculcoates Kingston/Hull 59 E6
Sculthorpe Norfolk 44 B2
Scunthorpe N Lincs 58 G4
Scurlage Swan 25 H9
Sea Palling Norfolk 45 C8
Sea Zoo Angl 46 F4
Seaborough Dorset 9 D6
Seacombe Mersey 48 C4
Seacroft Lincs 53 F8
Seacroft W Yorks 57 E8
Seadyke Lincs 43 B6
Seafield S Ayrs 74 E5
Seafield W Loth 84 H2
Seaford E Sussex 13 F8
Seaforth Mersey 48 C4
Seagrave Leics 41 D8
Seaham Durham 71 F9
Seahouses Northum 79 D7
Seal Kent 22 F5
Seal Sanctuary, Gweek Cornw'l 3 G6
Sealand Flints 48 F4
Seale Surrey 21 G6
Seamer N Yorks 63 C9
Seamer N Yorks 65 F8
Seamill N Ayrs 74 C3
Searby Lincs 52 B3
Seasalter Kent 14 B5
Seascale Cumb 60 D3
Seater Orkney 112 D8
Seathorne Lincs 53 F8
Seathwaite Cumb 60 E5
Seathwaite Cumb 60 C5
Seatoller Cumb 60 C5
Seaton Cornw'l 4 E4
Seaton Cumb 68 G3
Seaton Devon 8 F4
Seaton Durham 71 E8
Seaton E Riding Yorks 59 D7
Seaton Northum 71 C8
Seaton Rutl'd 42 F2
Seaton Burn Tyne/Wear 71 C7
Seaton Carew Hartlep'l 64 B3
Seaton Delaval Northum 71 C8
Seaton Ross E Riding Yorks 58 D3
Seaton Sluice Northum 71 C8
Seatown Aberds 98 B5
Seave Green N Yorks 64 D3
Seaview I of Wight 11 E9
Seaville Cumb 68 E4
Seavington St. Mary Som'set 9 C6
Seavington St. Michael Som'set 9 C6
Sebergham Cumb 69 F6
Seckington Warwick 40 E4
Second Coast H'land 103 C7
Sedbergh Cumb 61 E9
Sedbury Glos 18 B2
Sedbusk N Yorks 62 E3
Sedgeberrow Heref/Worcs 30 E2
Sedgebrook Lincs 42 B1
Sedgefield Durham 63 B8
Sedgeford Norfolk 43 B10
Sedgehill Wilts 10 B1
Sedgley W Midlands 39 F10
Sedgwick Cumb 61 F8
Sedlescombe E Sussex 14 G2
Sedlescombe Street E Sussex 14 G2
Seend Wilts 19 E6
Seend Cleeve Wilts 19 E6
Seer Green Bucks 21 B7
Seething Norfolk 45 F7
Sefton Mersey 48 B4
Seghill Northum 71 C7
Seifton Shrops 38 G5
Seighford Staffs 39 C9
Seilebost W Isles 101 C6
Seion Gwyn 46 F5
Seisdon Staffs 39 F9
Seisiadar W Isles 107 F9
Selattyn Shrops 38 B3
Selborne Hants 11 A10
Selby N Yorks 58 E2
Selham W Sussex 12 C3
Selhurst Gtr Lon 22 E3
Selkirk Scot Borders 77 E7
Sellack Heref/Worcs 29 F6
Sellafield Station Cumb 60 D3
Sellafield Visitors Centre Cumb 60 D3
Sellafirth Shetl'd 113 D8
Sellindge Kent 14 E5
Sellindge Lees Kent 15 E6
Selling Kent 14 C5
Sells Green Wilts 19 E6
Selly Oak W Midlands 40 G2
Selmeston E Sussex 13 E9
Selsdon Gtr Lon 22 E3
Selsey W Sussex 12 F2
Selsfield Common W Sussex 13 B7
Selsted Kent 15 D7
Selston Notts 51 G6
Selworthy Som'set 7 B10
Semblister Shetl'd 113 H6
Semer Suffolk 34 D3
Semington Wilts 18 E5
Semley Wilts 10 B1
Send Surrey 21 F8
Send Marsh Surrey 21 F8
Senghenydd Caerph 17 B6
Sennen Cornw'l 2 G2
Sennen Cove Cornw'l 2 G2
Sennybridge Powys 27 F9
Serlby Notts 51 D8
Sessay N Yorks 63 G9
Setchey Norfolk 43 D9
Setley Hants 11 D6
Setter Shetl'd 113 H6
Setter Shetl'd 113 E7
Setter Shetl'd 113 J8
Settiscarth Orkney 112 G4
Settle N Yorks 56 B3
Settrington N Yorks 65 G6
Seven Kings Gtr Lon 22 C4
Seven Sisters Neath P Talb 27 H8
Sevenhampton Glos 30 F2
Sevenoaks Kent 22 F5
Sevenoaks Weald Kent 22 F5
Severn Beach S Gloucs 18 C2
Severn Stoke Heref/Worcs 29 D9
Severn Valley Railway Heref/Worcs 39 H8
Severnhampton Thamesd'n 19 B9
Sevington Kent 14 D5
Sewards End Essex 33 E8
Sewardstone Essex 22 B3
Sewardstonebury Essex 22 B3
Sewerby E Riding Yorks 59 B7
Sewerby Hall and Gardens, Bridlington E Riding Yorks 59 B8
Seworgan Cornw'l 3 F6
Sewstern Leics 42 C1
Sezincote Glos 30 E3
Sgarasta Mhor W Isles 101 C6
Sgiogarstaigh W Isles 107 C9
Shabbington Bucks 31 H8
Shackerstone Leics 40 E5
Shackleford Surrey 21 G7
Shade W Yorks 56 F4
Shadforth Durham 71 F8
Shadingfield Suffolk 45 G8
Shadoxhurst Kent 14 E4
Shadsworth Lancs 56 F2
Shadwell Norfolk 44 G3
Shadwell W Yorks 57 E8
Shaftesbury Dorset 10 B1
Shafton S Yorks 57 G8
Shakespeare's Birthplace, Stratford-upon-Avon Warwick 30 C4
Shalbourne Wilts 19 E10
Shalcombe I of Wight 11 F6
Shalden Hants 20 G4
Shaldon Devon 5 C10
Shalfleet I of Wight 11 F7
Shalford Essex 33 F10
Shalford Surrey 21 G8
Shalford Green Essex 33 F10
Shallowford Devon 7 B8
Shalmsford Street Kent 14 C5
Shalstone Bucks 31 E8
Shamley Green Surrey 21 G8
Shandon Arg/Bute 82 F3
Shandwick H'land 105 E7
Shangton Leics 41 F9
Shankend Scot Borders 77 G8
Shankhouse Northum 71 C7
Shanklin I of Wight 11 F8
Shanklin Chine I of Wight 11 F8
Shanquhar Aberds 98 E5
Shanzie Perth/Kinr 90 F3
Shap Cumb 61 C8
Shapwick Dorset 10 D2
Shapwick Som'set 17 H9
Shardlow Derbys 41 B6
Shareshill Staffs 39 E10
Sharlston W Yorks 57 G8
Sharlston Common W Yorks 57 G8
Sharnbrook Beds 32 C2
Sharnford Leics 41 F6
Sharoe Green Lancs 55 E5
Sharow N Yorks 63 G8
Sharp Street Norfolk 45 C7
Sharpenhoe Beds 32 E3
Sharperton Northum 78 G4
Sharpness Glos 18 A3
Sharpthorne W Sussex 13 B7
Sharrington Norfolk 44 B4
Shatterford Heref/Worcs 39 G8
Shaugh Prior Devon 5 D6
Shavington Ches 49 G8
Shaw Berks 20 E2
Shaw Gtr Man 49 B10
Shaw Wilts 18 E5
Shaw Green Lancs 55 G5
Shaw Mills N Yorks 57 B7
Shawbury Shrops 39 C6
Shawdon Hall Northum 78 F5
Shawell Leics 41 G7
Shawford Hants 11 B7
Shawforth Lancs 56 F3
Shawhead Dumf/Gal 68 C1
Shawhill Dumf/Gal 68 D5
Shawton S Lanarks 75 C8
Shawtonhill S Lanarks 75 C8
Shawwood E Ayrs 75 E7
Shear Cross Wilts 18 G5
Shearington Dumf/Gal 68 D3
Shearsby Leics 41 F8
Shebbear Devon 6 F5
Shebdon Staffs 39 C8
Shebster H'land 110 C5
Sheddens E Renf 75 B7
Shedfield Hants 11 C8
Sheen Staffs 50 F3
Sheepscar W Yorks 57 E8
Sheepscombe Glos 29 G9
Sheepstor Devon 5 D6
Sheepwash Devon 6 F5
Sheepway N Som'set 17 D9
Sheepy Magna Leics 40 E5
Sheepy Parva Leics 40 E5
Sheering Essex 33 G8
Sheerness Kent 23 D9
Sheet Hants 12 C1
Sheffield S Yorks 50 D5
Sheffield Bottom Berks 20 E4
Sheffield Green E Sussex 13 C8
Sheffield Park, Uckfield E Sussex 13 C8
Shefford Beds 32 E4
Shefford Woodlands Berks 20 D1
Sheigra H'land 108 C4
Sheinton Shrops 39 E7
Shelderton Shrops 38 H5
Sheldon Derbys 50 F3
Sheldon Devon 8 D3
Sheldon W Midlands 40 G3
Sheldwich Kent 14 C5
Shelf W Yorks 57 F6
Shelfanger Norfolk 44 G5
Shelfield Warwick 30 B3
Shelfield W Midlands 40 E2
Shelford Notts 41 A8
Shellacres Northum 78 C3
Shelley Essex 22 A5
Shelley Suffolk 34 E4
Shelley W Yorks 57 G7
Shellingford Oxon 19 B10
Shellow Bowells Essex 33 H9
Shelsley Beauchamp Heref/Worcs 29 B8
Shelsley Walsh Heref/Worcs 29 B8
Shelthorpe Leics 41 D7
Shelton Beds 32 B3
Shelton Norfolk 45 F6
Shelton Notts 41 A9
Shelton Shrops 38 D5
Shelton Green Norfolk 45 F6
Shelve Shrops 38 F4
Shelwick Heref/Worcs 29 D6
Shenfield Essex 23 B6
Shenington Oxon 30 D5
Shenley Herts 21 A9
Shenley Brook End M/Keynes 31 E10
Shenley Church End M/Keynes 31 E10
Shenleybury Herts 21 A9
Shenmore Heref/Worcs 28 E4
Shennanton Dumf/Gal 66 D5
Shenstone Heref/Worcs 29 A9
Shenstone Staffs 40 E3
Shenton Leics 40 E5
Shenval H'land 96 D2
Shenval Moray 98 F2
Shepeau Stow Lincs 43 D6
Shephall Herts 32 F5
Shepherd's Green Oxon 20 C5
Shepherd's Port Norfolk 43 B9
Shepherdswell Kent 15 D7
Shepley W Yorks 50 B3
Shepperdine S Gloucs 18 B3
Shepperton Surrey 21 E8
Shepreth Cambs 33 D6
Shepshed Leics 41 D6
Shepton Beauchamp Som'set 9 C6
Shepton Mallet Som'set 18 G3
Shepton Montague Som'set 9 A8
Shepway Kent 14 C2
Sheraton Durham 71 G9
Sherborne Dorset 9 C8
Sherborne Glos 30 G3
Sherborne St. John Hants 20 F4
Sherbourne Warwick 30 B4
Sherburn Durham 71 F8
Sherburn N Yorks 65 G7
Sherburn Hill Durham 71 F8
Sherburn in Elmet N Yorks 57 E9
Shere Surrey 21 G8
Shereford Norfolk 44 C2
Sherfield English Hants 10 B5
Sherfield on Loddon Hants 20 F4
Sherford Devon 5 F8
Sheriff Hutton N Yorks 58 B2
Sheriffhales Shrops 39 D8
Sheringham Norfolk 44 A5
Sherington M/Keynes 32 D1
Shernal Green Heref/Worcs 29 B10
Shernborne Norfolk 43 B10
Sherrington Wilts 19 H6
Sherston Wilts 18 C5
Sherwood Green Devon 7 D6
Shettleston C of Glasg 75 A8
Shevington Gtr Man 49 B6
Shevington Moor Gtr Man 55 G5
Shevington Vale Gtr Man 49 B6
Sheviock Cornw'l 4 E4
Shide I of Wight 11 F7
Shiel Bridge H'land 95 E6
Shieldaig H'land 103 G6
Shieldaig H'land 103 E6
Shieldhill Falk 83 G9
Shieldhill S Lanarks 76 C3
Shielfoot H'land 87 E6
Shielhill Angus 90 F5
Shielhill Invercl 82 G3
Shifford Oxon 20 A1
Shifnal Shrops 39 E8
Shilbottle Northum 79 G6
Shildon Durham 63 B7
Shillingford Devon 8 B1
Shillingford Oxon 20 B3
Shillingford St. George Devon 5 B10
Shillingstone Dorset 9 C10
Shillington Beds 32 E4
Shillmoor Northum 78 G3
Shilton Oxon 30 H4
Shilton Warwick 41 G6
Shilvington Northum 71 B6
Shimpling Norfolk 44 G5
Shimpling Suffolk 34 C2
Shimpling Street Suffolk 34 C2
Shincliffe Durham 71 F7
Shiney Row Tyne/Wear 71 E8
Shinfield Berks 20 E5
Shingham Norfolk 44 E1
Shingle Street Suffolk 35 D7
Shinner's Bridge Devon 5 D8
Shinness H'land 104 A4
Shipbourne Kent 22 F5
Shipdham Norfolk 44 E3
Shipham Som'set 17 F9
Shiphay Devon 5 D9
Shiplake Oxon 20 D5
Shipley Derbys 41 A6
Shipley Northum 79 F6
Shipley Shrops 39 F9
Shipley W Sussex 12 C5
Shipley W Yorks 57 E6
Shipley Shiels Northum 70 A2
Shipmeadow Suffolk 45 G7
Shippea Hill Sta. Cambs 43 G9
Shippon Oxon 20 B2
Shipston on Stour Warwick 30 D4
Shipton Glos 30 G2
Shipton N Yorks 58 C1
Shipton Shrops 39 F6
Shipton Bellinger Hants 19 G9
Shipton Gorge Dorset 9 E6
Shipton Green W Sussex 12 E2
Shipton Moyne Glos 18 C5
Shipton on Cherwell Oxon 31 G6
Shipton Solers Glos 30 G2
Shipton-under-Wychwood Oxon 30 G4
Shiptonthorpe E Riding Yorks 58 D4
Shirburn Oxon 20 B4
Shirdley Hill Lancs 55 G3
Shire Horse Centre, Stratford-upon-Avon Warwick 30 C4
Shirebrook Derbys 51 F7
Shiregreen S Yorks 50 C5
Shirehampton Bristol 18 D2
Shiremoor Tyne/Wear 71 C8
Shirenewton Monmouths 17 B9
Shireoaks Notts 51 D7
Shirkoak Kent 14 E4
Shirl Heath Heref/Worcs 28 C5
Shirland Derbys 50 G5
Shirley Derbys 40 A4
Shirley Gtr Lon 22 E3
Shirley S'thampton 11 C7
Shirley W Midlands 40 H3
Shirrell Heath Hants 11 C8
Shirwell Devon 7 C6
Shirwell Cross Devon 7 C6
Shiskine N Ayrs 73 E9
Shobdon Heref/Worcs 28 B5
Shobnall Staffs 40 C4
Shobrooke Devon 7 F9
Shoby Leics 41 D8
Shocklach Ches 48 H5
Shoeburyness Essex 23 C9
Sholden Kent 15 C8
Sholing S'thampton 11 C7
Shoot Hill Shrops 38 D5
Shop Cornw'l 6 E3
Shop Cornw'l 3 B7
Shop Corner Suffolk 35 E6
Shore Mill H'land 105 F6
Shoreditch Gtr Lon 22 C3
Shoreham Kent 22 E5
Shoreham By Sea W Sussex 13 E6
Shoresdean Northum 78 C4
Shoreswood Northum 78 C4
Shoreton H'land 104 F5
Shorncote Glos 19 B7
Shorne Kent 23 D6
Short Heath W Midlands 40 E1
Shortacombe Devon 5 B6
Shortgate E Sussex 13 D8
Shortlanesend Cornw'l 3 E7
Shortlees E Ayrs 75 D6
Shortstown Beds 32 D3
Shorwell I of Wight 11 F7
Shoscombe Bath/NE Som'set 18 F4
Shotatton Shrops 38 C4
Shotesham Norfolk 45 F6
Shotgate Essex 23 B7
Shotley Suffolk 35 E6
Shotley Bridge Durham 70 E5
Shotley Gate Suffolk 35 E6
Shotleyfield Northum 70 E5
Shottenden Kent 14 C5
Shottermill Surrey 12 B2
Shottery Warwick 30 C3
Shotteswell Warwick 31 D6
Shottisham Suffolk 35 D7
Shottle Derbys 50 H5
Shottlegate Derbys 50 H5
Shotton Durham 71 G9
Shotton Flints 48 F4
Shotton Northum 78 D3
Shotton Colliery Durham 71 F8
Shotts N Lanarks 76 A1
Shotwick Ches 48 E4
Shouldham Norfolk 43 E9
Shouldham Thorpe Norfolk 43 E9
Shoulton Heref/Worcs 29 C9
Shover's Green E Sussex 14 E1
Shrawardine Shrops 38 D5
Shrawley Heref/Worcs 29 B9
Shrewley Common Warwick 30 B4
Shrewsbury Shrops 38 D5
Shrewton Wilts 19 G7
Shripney W Sussex 12 E3
Shrivenham Oxon 19 C9
Shropham Norfolk 44 F3
Shrub End Essex 34 F3
Shucknall Heref/Worcs 29 D6
Shudy Camps Cambs 33 D9
Shulishaderbeg H'land 94 B1
Shurdington Glos 29 G10
Shurlock Row Berks 21 D6
Shurrery H'land 110 D5
Shurrery Lodge H'land 110 D5
Shurton Som'set 17 G7
Shustoke Warwick 40 F4
Shut End W Midlands 39 F10
Shute Devon 8 E4
Shute Devon 7 F9
Shutford Oxon 30 D5
Shuthonger Glos 29 E9
Shutlanger Northants 31 C9
Shuttington Warwick 40 E4
Shuttlewood Derbys 51 E6
Siabost bho Dheas W Isles 107 E6
Siabost bho Thuath W Isles 107 E6
Siadar W Isles 107 D7
Siadar Iarach W Isles 107 D7
Siadar Uarach W Isles 107 D7
Sibbaldbie Dumf/Gal 68 B4
Sibbertoft Northants 41 G8
Sibdon Carwood Shrops 38 G5
Sibford Ferris Oxon 30 E5
Sibford Gower Oxon 30 E5
Sible Hedingham Essex 34 E1
Sibsey Lincs 53 G6
Sibson Cambs 42 F3
Sibson Leics 40 E5
Sibthorpe Notts 51 H9
Sibton Suffolk 35 B7
Sibton Green Suffolk 35 A7
Sicklesmere Suffolk 34 B2
Sicklinghall N Yorks 57 D8
Sid Devon 8 F3
Sidbury Devon 8 E3
Sidbury Shrops 39 G7
Sidcot N Som'set 17 F9
Sidcup Gtr Lon 22 D4
Siddick Cumb 68 G3
Siddington Ches 49 E9
Siddington Glos 19 B7
Sidemoor Heref/Worcs 30 A1
Sidestrand Norfolk 45 B6
Sidford Devon 8 E3
Sidlesham W Sussex 12 F2
Sidley E Sussex 14 H2
Sidlow Surrey 22 G2
Sidmouth Devon 8 F3
Sigford Devon 5 C8
Sigglesthorne E Riding Yorks 59 D7
Sighthill C of Edinb 84 G3
Sigingstone V of Glam 16 D4
Signet Oxon 30 G4
Silchester Hants 20 E4
Sildinis W Isles 107 H6
Sileby Leics 41 D7
Silecroft Cumb 60 F4
Silfield Norfolk 44 F5
Silian Ceredig'n 26 C5
Silk Willoughby Lincs 42 A3
Silkstone S Yorks 50 B4
Silkstone Common S Yorks 50 B4
Silloth Cumb 68 E4
Sills Northum 78 G3
Sillyearn Moray 98 C5
Siloh Carms 27 E7
Silpho N Yorks 65 E7
Silsden W Yorks 56 D5
Silsoe Beds 32 E3
Silver End Essex 34 G2
Silverburn Midloth 76 A5
Silverdale Lancs 61 G7
Silverdale Staffs 49 H9
Silvergate Norfolk 44 C5
Silverhill E Sussex 14 G2
Silverley's Green Suffolk 45 H6
Silverstone Northants 31 D8
Silverton Devon 8 D1
Silvington Shrops 39 H7
Silwick Shetl'd 113 J5
Simmondley Derbys 50 C2
Simonburn Northum 70 C3
Simonsbath Som'set 7 C8
Simonstone Lancs 56 E2
Simprim Scot Borders 78 C3
Simpson M/Keynes 32 E1
Simpson Cross Pembs 24 E3
Sinclair's Hill Scot Borders 78 B3
Sinclairston E Ayrs 75 F6
Sinderby N Yorks 63 F8
Sinderhope Northum 70 E3
Sindlesham Berks 20 E5
Singdean Scot Borders 77 G8
Singleborough Bucks 31 E9
Singleton Lancs 55 E3
Singleton W Sussex 12 D2
Singlewell Kent 23 D6
Sinkhurst Green Kent 14 D3
Sinnahard Aberds 98 G4
Sinnington N Yorks 64 F5
Sinton Green Heref/Worcs 29 B9
Sipson Gtr Lon 21 D8
Sirhowy Bl Gwent 28 G2
Sisland Norfolk 45 F7
Sissinghurst Kent 14 E2
Sissinghurst, Cranbrook Kent 14 E3
Sisterpath Scot Borders 78 C2
Siston S Gloucs 18 D3
Sithney Cornw'l 2 G5
Sittingbourne Kent 14 B3
Six Ashes Shrops 39 G8
Six Hills Leics 41 C8
Six Mile Bottom Cambs 33 C8
Sixhills Lincs 52 D4
Sixpenny Handley Dorset 10 C2
Sizewell Suffolk 35 B8
Skail H'land 110 E2
Skaill Orkney 112 G3
Skaill Orkney 112 E5
Skaill Orkney 112 H6
Skares E Ayrs 75 F7
Skarpigarth Shetl'd 113 J4
Skateraw E Loth 85 G9
Skaw Shetl'd 113 G8
Skeabost H'land 101 H10
Skeabrae Orkney 112 F3
Skeeby N Yorks 63 D7
Skeffington Leics 41 E9
Skeffling E Riding Yorks 59 G9
Skegby Notts 51 F6
Skegness Lincs 53 F8
Skelberry Shetl'd 113 M6
Skelbo H'land 105 C6
Skelbrooke S Yorks 57 G10
Skeldyke Lincs 43 B6
Skellingthorpe Lincs 52 E2
Skellister Shetl'd 113 H7
Skellow S Yorks 57 G10
Skelmanthorpe W Yorks 57 G7
Skelmersdale Lancs 48 B5
Skelmonae Aberds 99 E8
Skelmorlie N Ayrs 82 H2
Skelmuir Aberds 99 D9
Skelpick H'land 110 D2
Skelton Cumb 69 G7
Skelton E Riding Yorks 58 F3
Skelton N Yorks 62 D5
Skelton Redcar/Clevel'd 64 C4
Skelton C of York 58 C1
Skelton-on-Ure N Yorks 57 B8
Skelwick Orkney 112 D5
Skelwith Bridge Cumb 61 D6
Skendleby Lincs 53 F7
Skene Ho. Aberds 99 H7
Skenfrith Monmouths 28 F5
Skerne E Riding Yorks 59 C6
Skeroblingarry Arg/Bute 73 E7
Skerray H'land 109 C9
Skerton Lancs 55 B4
Sketchley Leics 41 F6
Sketty Swan 16 B1
Skewen Neath P Talb 16 B2
Skewsby N Yorks 64 G4
Skeyton Norfolk 45 C6
Skiag Bridge H'land 108 G5
Skibo Castle H'land 104 D6
Skidbrooke Lincs 53 C7
Skidbrooke North End Lincs 53 C7
Skidby E Riding Yorks 59 E6
Skilgate Som'set 8 B1
Skillington Lincs 42 C1
Skinburness Cumb 68 E4
Skinflats Falk 83 F10
Skinidin H'land 101 H8
Skinningrove Redcar/Clevel'd 64 B5
Skipness Arg/Bute 73 B8
Skippool Lancs 55 D3
Skipsea E Riding Yorks 59 C7
Skipsea Brough E Riding Yorks 59 C7
Skipton N Yorks 56 C4
Skipton-on-Swale N Yorks 63 G8
Skipwith N Yorks 58 E2
Skirbeck Lincs 43 A6
Skirbeck Quarter Lincs 43 A6
Skirlaugh E Riding Yorks 59 E7
Skirling Scot Borders 76 D3
Skirmett Bucks 20 C5
Skirpenbeck E Riding Yorks 58 C3
Skirwith Cumb 69 G9
Skirza H'land 111 C8
Skulamus H'land 94 D3
Skullomie H'land 109 C9
Skyborry Green Shrops 28 A3
Skye of Curr H'land 97 D7
Skyreholme N Yorks 56 B5
Slackhall Derbys 50 D2
Slackhead Moray 98 B4
Slad Glos 29 H9
Slade Devon 7 B6
Slade Pembs 24 E4
Slade Green Gtr Lon 22 D5
Slaggyford Northum 69 E9
Slaidburn Lancs 56 C2
Slaithwaite W Yorks 56 G5
Slaley Northum 70 E4
Slamannan Falk 83 G9
Slapton Bucks 32 F2
Slapton Devon 5 F9
Slapton Northants 31 D8
Slatepit Dale Derbys 50 F5
Slattocks Gtr Man 49 B9
Slaugham W Sussex 13 C6
Slaughterford Wilts 18 D5
Slawston Leics 41 F9
Sleaford Hants 12 B2
Sleaford Lincs 52 H3
Sleagill Cumb 61 C8
Sleapford Shrops 39 D7
Sledge Green Heref/Worcs 29 E9
Sledmere E Riding Yorks 58 B5
Sleightholme Durham 62 C4
Sleights N Yorks 65 D6
Slepe Dorset 10 E2
Slickly H'land 111 C7
Sliddery N Ayrs 73 E9
Sligachan Hotel H'land 94 D1
Slimbridge Glos 18 A4
Slimbridge Wildfowl & Wetlands Centre, Frampton on Severn Glos 29 H8
Slindon Staffs 39 B9
Slindon W Sussex 12 E3
Slinfold W Sussex 12 B5
Sling Gwyn 47 F6
Slingsby N Yorks 64 G4
Slioch Aberds 98 E5
Slip End Beds 32 G3
Slip End Herts 32 E5
Slipton Northants 42 H2
Slitting Mill Staffs 40 D2
Slochd H'land 97 D6
Slockavullin Arg/Bute 81 E8
Sloley Norfolk 45 C6
Sloothby Lincs 53 E7
Slough Berks 21 D7
Slough Green W Sussex 13 C6
Sluggan H'land 97 D6
Slumbay H'land 94 C5
Slyfield Surrey 21 F7
Slyne Lancs 55 B4
Smailholm Scot Borders 77 D9
Small Dole W Sussex 13 D6
Small Hythe Kent 14 E3
Smallbridge Gtr Man 56 G4
Smallburgh Norfolk 45 C7
Smallburn Aberds 99 D10
Smallburn E Ayrs 75 E8
Smalley Derbys 41 A6
Smallfield Surrey 22 G3
Smallridge Devon 8 D5
Smannell Hants 20 G1
Smardale Cumb 62 D2
Smarden Kent 14 D3
Smarden Bell Kent 14 D3
Smeatharpe Devon 8 C3

Smeeth *Kent* 14 E5
Smeeton Westerby *Leics* 41 F8
Smercleit *W Isles* 92 D3
Smerral *H'land* 111 F6
Smethwick *W Midlands* 40 G2
Smirisary *H'land* 87 D6
Smisby *Derbys* 40 D5
Smith Green *Lancs* 55 C4
Smithfield *Cumb* 69 D7
Smithincott *Devon* 8 C2
Smith's Green *Essex* 33 F8
Smithstown *H'land* 102 E5
Smithton *H'land* 96 B5
Smithy Green *Ches* 49 E8
Smockington *Leics* 41 G6
Smyth's Green *Essex* 34 G3
Snaigow House *Perth/Kinr* 90 G1
Snailbeach *Shrops* 38 E4
Snailwell *Cambs* 33 B9
Snainton *N Yorks* 65 F7
Snaith *E Riding Yorks* 58 F2
Snape *N Yorks* 63 F7
Snape *Suffolk* 35 C7
Snape Green *Lancs* 55 G3
Snarestone *Leics* 40 E5
Snarford *Lincs* 52 D3
Snargate *Kent* 14 F4
Snave *Kent* 14 F5
Snead *Powys* 38 F4
Sneath Common *Norfolk* 44 G5
Sneaton *N Yorks* 65 D6
Sneatonthorpe *N Yorks* 65 D7
Snelland *Lincs* 52 D3
Snelston *Derbys* 40 A3
Snettisham *Norfolk* 43 B9
Snibston Discovery Park, Coalville *Leics* 41 D6
Snig's End *Glos* 29 F8
Sniseabhal *W Isles* 92 B3
Snitter *Northum* 78 G5
Snitterby *Lincs* 52 C2
Snitterfield *Warwick* 30 C4
Snitton *Shrops* 39 H6
Snodhill *Heref/Worcs* 28 D4
Snodland *Kent* 14 B1
Snowden Hill *S Yorks* 50 B4
Snowdon Mountain Railway, Llanberis *Gwyn* 47 G6
Snowdown *Kent* 15 C7
Snowshill *Glos* 30 E2
Snowshill Manor *Glos* 30 E2
Snydale *W Yorks* 57 G9
Soar *Angl* 46 E3
Soar *Carms* 27 F6
Soar *Devon* 5 G8
Soberton *Hants* 11 C9
Soberton Heath *Hants* 11 C9
Sockbridge *Cumb* 61 B8
Sockburn *Durham* 63 D8
Soham *Cambs* 33 A8
Soham Cotes *Cambs* 43 H8
Solas *W Isles* 100 E4
Soldon Cross *Devon* 6 E4
Soldridge *Hants* 11 A9
Sole Street *Kent* 14 B1
Sole Street *Kent* 14 D5
Solihull *W Midlands* 40 H3
Sollers Dilwyn *Heref/Worcs* 28 C5
Sollers Hope *Heref/Worcs* 29 E7
Sollom *Lancs* 55 G4
Solva *Pembs* 24 D2
Somerby *Leics* 41 D9
Somerby *Lincs* 52 B3
Somercotes *Derbys* 51 G6
Somerford *Dorset* 10 E4
Somerford Keynes *Glos* 19 B7
Somerley *W Sussex* 12 F2
Somerleyton *Suffolk* 45 F8
Somersal Herbert *Derbys* 40 B3
Somersby *Lincs* 53 E6
Somersham *Cambs* 43 H6
Somersham *Suffolk* 34 D4
Somerton *Oxon* 31 F6
Somerton *Som'set* 9 B6
Sompting *W Sussex* 12 E5
Sonning *Berks* 20 D5
Sonning Common *Oxon* 20 C5
Sonning Eye *Oxon* 20 D5
Sontley *Wrex* 48 H4
Sopley *Hants* 10 E4
Sopwell *Herts* 32 H4
Sopworth *Wilts* 18 C5
Sorbie *Dumf/Gal* 67 F6
Sordale *H'land* 111 C6
Sorisdale *Arg/Bute* 86 E2
Sorn *E Ayrs* 75 E7
Sornhill *E Ayrs* 75 D7
Sortat *H'land* 111 C7
Sotby *Lincs* 52 E5
Sots Hole *Lincs* 52 F4
Sotterley *Suffolk* 45 G8
Soudley *Shrops* 39 C8
Soughton *Flints* 48 F3
Soulbury *Bucks* 32 F1
Soulby *Cumb* 62 C2
Souldern *Oxon* 31 E7
Souldrop *Beds* 32 B2
Sound *Ches* 49 H7
Sound *Shetl'd* 113 H6
Sound *Shetl'd* 113 J7
Sound Heath *Ches* 49 H7
Soundwell *S Gloucs* 18 D3
Sourhope *Scot Borders* 78 E3
Sourin *Orkney* 112 E5
Sourton *Devon* 7 G6
Soutergate *Cumb* 60 F5
South Acre *Norfolk* 44 D2
South Allington *Devon* 5 G8
South Alloa *Falk* 83 E9
South Ambersham *W Sussex* 12 C3
South Anston *S Yorks* 51 D7
South Ascot *Berks* 21 E7
South Ballachulish *H'land* 87 F10
South Balloch *S Ayrs* 74 H5
South Bank *Redcar/Clevel'd* 64 B3
South Barrow *Som'set* 9 B8
South Beach *Gwyn* 36 B3
South Benfleet *Essex* 23 C7
South Bersted *W Sussex* 12 E3
South Brent *Devon* 5 D7
South Brewham *Som'set* 18 H4
South Broomhill *Northum* 79 H7
South Burlingham *Norfolk* 45 E7
South Cadbury *Som'set* 9 B8
South Cairn *Dumf/Gal* 66 D1
South Carlton *Lincs* 52 E2
South Cave *E Riding Yorks* 58 E5
South Cerney *Glos* 19 B7
South Chard *Som'set* 8 D5
South Charlton *Northum* 79 E6
South Cheriton *Som'set* 9 B8
South Cliffe *E Riding Yorks* 58 E4
South Clifton *Notts* 51 E10
South Cockerington *Lincs* 53 D6
South Cornelly *Bridg* 16 C3
South Cove *Suffolk* 45 G8
South Creagan *Arg/Bute* 87 G9
South Creake *Norfolk* 44 B2
South Croxton *Leics* 41 D8
South Croydon *Gtr Lon* 22 E3
South Dalton *E Riding Yorks* 58 D5
South Darenth *Kent* 22 E5
South Denmore *Aberd C* 99 G9
South Duffield *N Yorks* 58 E2
South Elkington *Lincs* 52 D5
South Elmshall *W Yorks* 57 G9
South End *Bucks* 32 F1
South End *Cumb* 55 B2
South End *N Lincs* 59 F7
South Erradale *H'land* 102 E5
South Fambridge *Essex* 23 B8
South Fawley *Berks* 20 C1
South Ferriby *N Lincs* 58 F5
South Garth *Shetl'd* 113 D8
South Garvan *H'land* 87 D9
South Glendale *W Isles* 92 D3
South Godstone *Surrey* 22 G3
South Gorley *Hants* 10 C4
South Green *Essex* 23 B6
South Green *Kent* 14 B3
South haa *Shetl'd* 113 E6
South Ham *Hants* 20 F4
South Hanningfield *Essex* 23 B7
South Harting *W Sussex* 12 D1
South Hatfield *Herts* 32 H5
South Hayling *Hants* 11 E10
South Hazelrigg *Northum* 78 D5
South Heath *Bucks* 21 A7
South Heighton *E Sussex* 13 E8
South Hetton *Durham* 71 F8
South Hiendley *W Yorks* 57 G8
South Hill *Cornw'l* 4 C4
South Hinksey *Oxon* 20 A3
South Hole *Devon* 6 D3
South Holme *N Yorks* 64 G4
South Holmwood *Surrey* 21 G9
South Hornchurch *Gtr Lon* 22 C5
South Hykeham *Lincs* 52 F2
South Hylton *Tyne/Wear* 71 E8
South Kelsey *Lincs* 52 C3
South Kessock *H'land* 96 B4
South Killingholme *N Lincs* 59 G7
South Kilvington *N Yorks* 63 F9
South Kilworth *Leics* 41 G8
South Kirkby *W Yorks* 57 G9
South Kirkton *Aberds* 99 H7
South Kiscadale *N Ayrs* 74 E2
South Kyme *Lincs* 52 H4
South Lancing *W Sussex* 12 E5
South Leigh *Oxon* 30 H5
South Leverton *Notts* 51 D9
South Littleton *Heref/Worcs* 30 D2
South Lopham *Norfolk* 44 G4
South Luffenham *Rutl'd* 42 E2
South Malling *E Sussex* 13 D8
South Marston *Thamesd'n* 19 C8
South Middleton *Northum* 78 E4
South Milford *N Yorks* 57 E9
South Millbrex *Aberds* 99 D8
South Milton *Devon* 5 F8
South Mimms *Herts* 22 A2
South Molton *Devon* 7 D8
South Moreton *Oxon* 20 C3
South Mundham *W Sussex* 12 E2
South Muskham *Notts* 51 G9
South Newbald *E Riding Yorks* 58 E5
South Newington *Oxon* 31 E6
South Newton *Wilts* 10 A3
South Normanton *Derbys* 51 G6
South Norwood *Gtr Lon* 22 E3
South Nutfield *Surrey* 22 G3
South Ockenden *Essex* 22 C5
South Ormsby *Lincs* 53 E6
South Otterington *N Yorks* 63 F8
South Owersby *Lincs* 52 C3
South Oxhey *Herts* 21 B9
South Perrott *Dorset* 9 D6
South Petherton *Som'set* 9 C6
South Petherwin *Cornw'l* 4 B4
South Pickenham *Norfolk* 44 E2
South Pool *Devon* 5 F8
South Port *Arg/Bute* 82 B1
South Radworthy *Devon* 7 C8
South Rauceby *Lincs* 52 H3
South Raynham *Norfolk* 44 C2
South Reston *Lincs* 53 D7
South Runcton *Norfolk* 43 E9
South Scarle *Notts* 51 F10
South Shian *Arg/Bute* 87 G9
South Shields *Tyne/Wear* 71 D8
South Shields Museum *Tyne/Wear* 71 D8
South Shore *Lancs* 55 E3
South Somercotes *Lincs* 53 C7
South Stainley *N Yorks* 57 B8
South Stainmore *Cumb* 62 C3
South Stifford *Essex* 23 D6
South Stoke *Bath/NE Som'set* 18 E4
South Stoke *Oxon* 20 C3
South Stoke *W Sussex* 12 E4
South Street *E Sussex* 13 D7
South Street *Gtr Lon* 22 F4
South Street *Kent* 15 B6
South Street *Kent* 14 C5
South Tawton *Devon* 7 G7
South Thoresby *Lincs* 53 E7
South Tidworth *Wilts* 19 G9
South Town *Hants* 20 H4
South View *Hants* 20 F4
South View *Shetl'd* 113 J6
South Walsham *Norfolk* 45 D7
South Warnborough *Hants* 20 G5
South Weald *Essex* 22 B5
South Weston *Oxon* 20 B5
South Wheatley *Cornw'l* 6 G3
South Wheatley *Notts* 51 D9
South Widcombe *Bath/NE Som'set* 18 F2
South Wigston *Leics* 41 F7
South Willingham *Lincs* 52 D4
South Wingfield *Derbys* 50 G5
South Witham *Lincs* 42 D2
South Wonston *Hants* 20 H2
South Woodham Ferrers *Essex* 23 B8
South Wootton *Norfolk* 43 C9
South Wraxall *Wilts* 18 E5
South Zeal *Devon* 7 G7
Southall *Gtr Lon* 21 C9
Southam *Glos* 30 F1
Southam *Warwick* 31 B6
Southampton *S'thampton* 11 C7
Southborough *Kent* 22 G5
Southbourne *Bournem'th* 10 E4
Southbourne *W Sussex* 12 E1
Southburgh *Norfolk* 44 E3
Southburn *E Riding Yorks* 58 C5
Southchurch *Essex* 23 C9
Southcott *Wilts* 19 F8
Southcourt *Bucks* 31 G10
Southdean *Scot Borders* 77 G9
Southdene *Mersey* 48 C5
Southease *E Sussex* 13 E8
Southend *Arg/Bute* 73 G6
Southend *Berks* 20 D3
Southend *Wilts* 19 D8
Southend on Sea *Essex* 23 C8
Southend Sea Life Centre *Essex* 23 C9
Southernden *Kent* 14 D3
Southerndown *V of Glam* 16 D3
Southerness *Dumf/Gal* 68 E2
Southery *Norfolk* 43 F9
Southfield *Northum* 71 C7
Southfleet *Kent* 23 D6
Southgate *Ceredig'n* 36 H5
Southgate *Gtr Lon* 22 B2
Southgate *Norfolk* 44 C5
Southgate *Swan* 25 H10
Southill *Beds* 32 D4
Southleigh *Devon* 8 E4
Southminster *Essex* 23 B9
Southmoor *Oxon* 20 B1
Southoe *Cambs* 32 B4
Southolt *Suffolk* 34 B5
Southorpe *Cambs* 42 E3
Southowram *W Yorks* 57 F6
Southport *Mersey* 55 G3
Southpunds *Shetl'd* 113 L7
Southrepps *Norfolk* 45 B6
Southrey *Lincs* 52 F4
Southrop *Glos* 19 A8
Southrope *Hants* 20 G4
Southsea *Portsm'th* 11 E9
Southtown *Norfolk* 45 E9
Southtown *Orkney* 112 J5
Southwaite *Cumb* 69 F7
Southwark *Gtr Lon* 22 D3
Southwater *W Sussex* 12 C5
Southwater Street *W Sussex* 12 C5
Southway *Som'set* 18 G2
Southwell *Dorset* 9 G8
Southwell *Notts* 51 G8
Southwell Minster *Notts* 51 G9
Southwick *Hants* 11 D9
Southwick *Northants* 42 F3
Southwick *Tyne/Wear* 71 E8
Southwick *Wilts* 18 F5
Southwick *W Sussex* 13 E6
Southwold *Suffolk* 45 H9
Southwood *Norfolk* 45 E7
Southwood *Som'set* 9 A7
Soutra Mains *Midloth* 77 B7
Soval Lodge *W Isles* 107 G7
Sowber Gate *N Yorks* 63 F8
Sowerby *N Yorks* 63 F9
Sowerby *W Yorks* 56 F5
Sowerby Bridge *W Yorks* 56 F5
Sowerby Row *Cumb* 69 G6
Sowood *W Yorks* 56 G5
Sowton *Devon* 8 E1
Spa Common *Norfolk* 45 B6
Spacey Houses *N Yorks* 57 C8
Spadeadam Farm *Cumb* 69 C8
Spalding *Lincs* 42 C5
Spaldington *E Riding Yorks* 58 E3
Spaldwick *Cambs* 32 A4
Spalford *Notts* 51 F10
Spanby *Lincs* 42 B3
Spanish City, Whitley Bay *Tyne/Wear* 71 C8
Sparham *Norfolk* 44 D4
Spark Bridge *Cumb* 61 F6
Sparkford *Som'set* 9 B8
Sparkhill *W Midlands* 40 G2
Sparkwell *Devon* 5 E6
Sparrow Green *Norfolk* 44 D3
Sparrowpit *Derbys* 50 D2
Sparsholt *Hants* 11 A7
Sparsholt *Oxon* 19 C10
Spartylea *Northum* 70 F3
Spaunton *N Yorks* 64 F5
Spaxton *Som'set* 17 H7
Spean Bridge *H'land* 88 C3
Spear Hill *W Sussex* 12 D5
Speen *Berks* 20 E2
Speen *Bucks* 21 B6
Speeton *N Yorks* 65 G9
Speke *Mersey* 48 D5
Speke Hall *Mersey* 48 D5
Speldhurst *Kent* 22 G5
Spellbrook *Herts* 33 G7
Spelsbury *Oxon* 30 F5
Spelter *Bridg* 16 B3
Spencers Wood *Berks* 20 E5
Spennithorne *N Yorks* 63 F6
Spennymoor *Durham* 71 G7
Spetchley *Heref/Worcs* 29 C9
Spetisbury *Dorset* 10 D2
Spexhall *Suffolk* 45 G7
Spey Bay *Moray* 98 B3
Speybridge *H'land* 97 D8
Speyview *Moray* 98 D2
Spilsby *Lincs* 53 F7
Spindlestone *Northum* 79 D6
Spinkhill *Derbys* 51 E6
Spinningdale *H'land* 104 D5
Spirthill *Wilts* 19 D6
Spital Hill *S Yorks* 51 C8
Spital in the Street *Lincs* 52 D2
Spitfire and Hurricane Memorial, Manston *Kent* 15 B8
Spithurst *E Sussex* 13 D8
Spittal *Dumf/Gal* 66 E5
Spittal *E Loth* 85 G6
Spittal *H'land* 111 D6
Spittal *Northum* 78 B5
Spittal *Pembs* 24 D4
Spittal *Stirl* 83 F6
Spittal of Glenmuick *Aberds* 90 C4
Spittal of Glenshee *Perth/Kinr* 90 D2
Spittalfield *Perth/Kinr* 90 G2
Spixworth *Norfolk* 45 D6
Splayne's Green *E Sussex* 13 C8
Spofforth *N Yorks* 57 C8
Spon End *W Midlands* 40 H5
Spon Green *Flints* 48 F3
Spondon *Derby C* 41 B6
Spooner Row *Norfolk* 44 F4
Sporle *Norfolk* 44 D2
Spott *E Loth* 85 G8
Spratton *Northants* 31 A9
Spreakley *Surrey* 21 G6
Spreyton *Devon* 7 G7
Spridlington *Lincs* 52 D3
Spring Vale *S Yorks* 50 B4
Spring Valley *I of Man* 54 F3
Springburn *C of Glasg* 83 H7
Springfield *Dumf/Gal* 69 D6
Springfield *Essex* 33 H10
Springfield *Fife* 84 C5
Springfield *Moray* 105 G9
Springfield *W Midlands* 40 G2
Springhill *Staffs* 40 E1
Springholm *Dumf/Gal* 67 D10
Springkell *Dumf/Gal* 68 C5
Springside *N Ayrs* 74 D5
Springthorpe *Lincs* 52 D1
Springwell *Tyne/Wear* 71 E7
Sproatley *E Riding Yorks* 59 E7
Sproston Green *Ches* 49 F8
Sprotbrough *S Yorks* 51 B7
Sproughton *Suffolk* 34 D5
Sprouston *Scot Borders* 78 D2
Sprowston *Norfolk* 45 D6
Sproxton *Leics* 42 C1
Sproxton *N Yorks* 64 F4
Spurstow *Ches* 49 G6
Spynie *Moray* 98 B2
Squires Gate *Lancs* 55 E3
Srannda *W Isles* 101 D6
Sronphadruig Lodge *Perth/Kinr* 89 D8
SS Great Britain, Bristol *Bristol* 18 D2
St Stephens *Herts* 32 H4
St. Abb's *Scot Borders* 85 H11
St. Abb's Haven *Scot Borders* 85 H11
St. Agnes *Cornw'l* 3 D6
St. Agnes *I of Scilly* 2 D2
St. Albans *Herts* 32 H4
St. Alban's Cathedral *Herts* 32 H4
St. Allen *Cornw'l* 3 D7
St. Andrews *Fife* 85 C7
St. Andrew's Major *V of Glam* 17 D6
St. Anne *Alderney* 5
St. Annes *Lancs* 55 F3
St. Ann's *Dumf/Gal* 68 A3
St. Ann's Chapel *Cornw'l* 4 C5
St. Ann's Chapel *Devon* 5 F7
St. Anthony *Cornw'l* 3 G6
St. Anthony's Hill *E Sussex* 13 E10
St. Arvans *Monmouths* 18 B2
St. Asaph *Denbs* 47 E10
St. Athan *V of Glam* 16 E5
St. Aubin *Jersey* 4
St. Austell *Cornw'l* 3 D9
St. Bees *Cumb* 60 C2
St. Blazey *Cornw'l* 3 D9
St. Boswells *Scot Borders* 77 D8
St. Brelade *Jersey* 4
St. Breock *Cornw'l* 3 B8
St. Breward *Cornw'l* 3 B9
St. Briavels *Glos* 18 A2
St. Bride's *Pembs* 24 E3
St. Brides Major *V of Glam* 16 D3
St. Bride's Netherwent *Monmouths* 17 C9
St. Brides Super Ely *V of Glam* 16 D5
St. Bride's Wentlooge *Newp* 17 C7
St. Budeaux *Devon* 4 E5
St. Buryan *Cornw'l* 2 G3
St. Catherine *Bath/NE Som'set* 18 D4
St. Catherine's *Arg/Bute* 82 D2
St. Clears *Carms* 25 E7
St. Cleer *Cornw'l* 4 D3
St. Clement *Cornw'l* 3 E7
St. Clements *Jersey* 4
St. Clement's Caves, Hastings *E Sussex* 14 G3
St. Clether *Cornw'l* 4 B3
St. Colmac *Arg/Bute* 81 H10
St. Columb Major *Cornw'l* 3 C8
St. Columb Minor *Cornw'l* 3 C7
St. Columb Road *Cornw'l* 3 D8
St. Combs *Aberds* 99 B10
St. Cross South Elmham *Suffolk* 45 G6
St. Cyrus *Aberds* 91 E8
St. David's *Pembs* 24 D2
St. David's *Perth/Kinr* 83 B10
St. Day *Cornw'l* 3 E6
St. Dennis *Cornw'l* 3 D8
St. Devereux *Heref/Worcs* 28 E5
St. Dogmaels *Pembs* 25 B6
St. Dogwells *Pembs* 24 D4
St. Dominick *Cornw'l* 4 D5
St. Donat's *V of Glam* 16 E4
St. Edith's *Wilts* 19 E6
St. Endellion *Cornw'l* 3 B8
St. Enoder *Cornw'l* 3 D7
St. Erme *Cornw'l* 3 D7
St. Erney *Cornw'l* 4 E4
St. Erth *Cornw'l* 2 F4
St. Ervan *Cornw'l* 3 B7
St. Ewe *Cornw'l* 3 E8
St. Fagans *Card* 17 D6
St. Fergus *Aberds* 99 C11
St. Fillans *Perth/Kinr* 83 B7
St. Florence *Pembs* 24 F5
St. Genny's *Cornw'l* 6 G2
St. George *Conwy* 47 E9
St. George's *V of Glam* 16 D5
St. Germans *Cornw'l* 4 E4
St. Giles *Lincs* 52 E2
St. Giles Cathedral, Edinburgh *C of Edinb* 84 G4
St. Giles in the Wood *Devon* 7 E6
St. Giles on the Hth. *Devon* 6 G4
St. Harmon *Powys* 27 A9
St. Helen Auckland *Durham* 63 B6
St. Helena *Warwick* 40 E4
St. Helen's *E Sussex* 14 G3
St. Helens *I of Wight* 11 F9
St. Helens *Mersey* 49 C6
St. Helier *Gtr Lon* 22 E2
St. Helier *Jersey* 4
St. Hilary *Cornw'l* 2 F4
St. Hilary *V of Glam* 16 D5
St. Illtyd *Bl Gwent* 17 A7
St. Ippollitts *Herts* 32 F4
St. Ishmael's *Pembs* 24 F3
St. Issey *Cornw'l* 3 B8
St. Ive *Cornw'l* 4 D4
St. Ives *Cambs* 33 A6
St. Ives *Cornw'l* 2 E4
St. Ives *Dorset* 10 D4
St. James South Elmham *Suffolk* 45 G7
St. Jidgey *Cornw'l* 3 C8
St. John *Cornw'l* 4 E5
St. John's *Heref/Worcs* 29 C9
St. John's *I of Man* 54 E2
St. John's *Jersey* 4
St. John's *Surrey* 21 F7
St. John's Chapel *Durham* 70 G3
St. John's Fen End *Norfolk* 43 D8
St. John's Highway *Norfolk* 43 D8
St. John's Town of Dalry *Dumf/Gal* 67 B8
St. Judes *I of Man* 54 D3
St. Just *Cornw'l* 2 F2
St. Just in Roseland *Cornw'l* 3 F7
St. Just In Roseland *Cornw'l* 3 F7
St. Katherine's *Aberds* 99 E7
St. Keverne *Cornw'l* 3 G6
St. Kew *Cornw'l* 3 B9
St. Kew Highway *Cornw'l* 3 B9
St. Keyne *Cornw'l* 4 D3
St. Lawrence *Cornw'l* 3 C9
St. Lawrence *Essex* 23 A9
St. Lawrence *I of Wight* 11 G8
St. Leonard's *Bucks* 32 H2
St. Leonard's *Dorset* 10 D4
St. Leonards *E Sussex* 14 H2
St. Levan *Cornw'l* 2 G2
St. Lythans *V of Glam* 17 D6
St. Mabyn *Cornw'l* 3 B9
St. Madoes *Perth/Kinr* 84 B3
St. Margaret South Elmham *Suffolk* 45 G7
St. Margarets *Herts* 33 G6
St. Margaret's *Heref/Worcs* 28 E4
St. Margaret's at Cliffe *Kent* 15 D8
St. Margaret's Hope *Orkney* 112 J5
St. Mark's *I of Man* 54 F2
St. Martin *Cornw'l* 4 E3
St. Martins *Cornw'l* 3 G6
St. Martin's *Jersey* 4
St. Martins *Perth/Kinr* 84 A3
St. Martin's *Shrops* 38 B4
St. Mary Bourne *Hants* 20 F2
St. Mary Church *V of Glam* 16 D5
St. Mary Cray *Gtr Lon* 22 E4
St. Mary Hill *V of Glam* 16 D4
St. Mary in the Marsh *Kent* 14 F5
St. Mary's *Jersey* 4
St. Mary's *Orkney* 112 H5
St. Mary's Bay *Kent* 14 F5
St. Mary's Church, Warwick *Warwick* 30 B4
St. Mary's Hoo *Kent* 23 D8
St. Maughans *Monmouths* 28 G5
St. Mawes *Cornw'l* 3 F7
St. Mawgan *Cornw'l* 3 C7
St. Mellion *Cornw'l* 4 D4
St. Mellons *Card* 17 C7
St. Merryn *Cornw'l* 3 B7
St. Mewan *Cornw'l* 3 D8
St. Michael Caerhays *Cornw'l* 3 E8
St. Michael Penkevil *Cornw'l* 3 E7
St. Michael South Elmham *Suffolk* 45 G7
St. Michaels *Heref/Worcs* 29 B6
St. Michael's *Kent* 14 E3
St. Michael's Mount, Penzance *Cornw'l* 2 F4
St. Michael's on Wyre *Lancs* 55 D4
St. Minver *Cornw'l* 3 B8
St. Monans *Fife* 85 D7
St. Neot *Cornw'l* 4 D2
St. Neots *Cambs* 32 B4
St. Nicholas *Pembs* 24 C3
St. Nicholas *V of Glam* 16 D5
St. Nicholas at Wade *Kent* 15 B7
St. Ninians *Stirl* 83 E8
St. Osyth *Essex* 34 G5
St. Osyth Heath *Essex* 34 G5
St. Ouens *Jersey* 4
St. Owens Cross *Heref/Worcs* 29 F6
St. Paul's Cathedral *Gtr Lon* 22 C3
St. Paul's Cray *Gtr Lon* 22 E4
St. Paul's Walden *Herts* 32 F4
St. Peter Port *Guernsey* 4
St. Peter's *Jersey* 4
St. Peter's *Kent* 15 B8
St. Petrox *Pembs* 24 G4
St. Pinnock *Cornw'l* 4 D3
St. Quivox *S Ayrs* 74 E5
St. Ruan *Cornw'l* 3 H6
St. Sampson *Guernsey* 4
St. Stephen *Cornw'l* 3 D8
St. Stephen's *Cornw'l* 4 B4
St. Stephens *Cornw'l* 4 E5
St. Teath *Cornw'l* 4 B1
St. Thomas *Devon* 7 G10
St. Tudy *Cornw'l* 3 B9
St. Twynnells *Pembs* 24 G4
St. Veep *Cornw'l* 4 E2
St. Vigeans *Angus* 91 G7
St. Wenn *Cornw'l* 3 C8
St. Weonards *Heref/Worcs* 28 F5
Stableford *Shrops* 39 F8
Stableford *Staffs* 39 B9
Stacey Bank *S Yorks* 50 C4
Stackhouse *N Yorks* 56 B3
Stackpole *Pembs* 24 G4
Staddiscombe *Devon* 5 E6
Staddlethorpe *E Riding Yorks* 58 F4
Stadhampton *Oxon* 20 B4
Stadhlaigearraidh *W Isles* 92 B3
Staffield *Cumb* 69 F8
Staffin *H'land* 102 F2
Stafford *Staffs* 39 C10
Stagsden *Beds* 32 D2
Stainburn *Cumb* 60 B3
Stainburn *N Yorks* 57 D7
Stainby *Lincs* 42 C2
Staincross *S Yorks* 57 G8
Staindrop *Durham* 63 B6
Staines *Surrey* 21 D8
Stainfield *Lincs* 42 C3
Stainfield *Lincs* 52 E4
Stainforth *N Yorks* 56 B3
Stainforth *S Yorks* 58 G2
Staining *Lancs* 55 E3
Stainland *W Yorks* 56 G5
Stainsacre *N Yorks* 65 D7
Stainsby *Derbys* 51 F6
Stainton *Cumb* 61 F8
Stainton *Cumb* 61 B7
Stainton *Durham* 62 C5
Stainton *Middlesbro'* 63 C9
Stainton *N Yorks* 63 E6
Stainton *S Yorks* 51 C7
Stainton by Langworth *Lincs* 52 E3
Stainton le Vale *Lincs* 52 C4
Stainton with Adgarley *Cumb* 60 G5
Staintondale *N Yorks* 65 E7
Stair *Cumb* 60 B5
Stair *E Ayrs* 75 E6
Stair Haven *Dumf/Gal* 66 E4
Staithes *N Yorks* 64 C5
Stake Pool *Lancs* 55 D4
Stakeford *Northum* 71 B7
Stalbridge *Dorset* 9 C9
Stalbridge Weston *Dorset* 9 C9
Stalham *Norfolk* 45 C7
Stalham Green *Norfolk* 45 C7
Stalisfield Green *Kent* 14 C4
Stalling Busk *N Yorks* 62 F4
Stallingborough *NE Lincs* 59 G7
Stalmine *Lancs* 55 D3
Stalybridge *Gtr Man* 50 C1
Stambourne *Essex* 33 E10
Stambourne Green *Essex* 33 E10
Stamford *Lincs* 42 E3
Stamford Bridge *Ches* 48 F5
Stamford Bridge *E Riding Yorks* 58 C3
Stamfordham *Northum* 70 C5
Stanah *Cumb* 61 C6
Stanborough *Herts* 32 G5
Stanbridge *Beds* 32 F2
Stanbridge *Dorset* 10 D3
Stanbrook *Heref/Worcs* 29 D9
Stanbury *W Yorks* 56 E5
Stand *Gtr Man* 49 B8
Stand *N Lanarks* 83 H8
Standburn *Falk* 83 G10
Standeford *Staffs* 39 E10
Standen *Kent* 14 D3
Standen, East Grinstead *W Sussex* 13 B7
Standford *Hants* 12 B2
Standingstone *Cumb* 68 G3
Standish *Gtr Man* 55 G5
Standlake *Oxon* 20 A1
Standon *Hants* 11 B7
Standon *Herts* 33 F6
Standon *Staffs* 39 B9
Stane *N Lanarks* 76 B1
Stanfield *Norfolk* 44 C3
Stanford *Beds* 32 D4
Stanford *Kent* 15 E6
Stanford Bishop *Heref/Worcs* 29 C7
Stanford Bridge *Heref/Worcs* 29 B8
Stanford Dingley *Berks* 20 D3
Stanford in the Vale *Oxon* 19 B10
Stanford le Hope *Essex* 23 C6
Stanford on Avon *Northants* 41 H7
Stanford on Soar *Notts* 41 C7
Stanford on Teme *Heref/Worcs* 29 B8
Stanford Rivers *Essex* 22 A5
Stanfree *Derbys* 51 E6
Stanghow *Redcar/Clevel'd* 64 C4
Stanground *Cambs* 42 F5
Stanhoe *Norfolk* 44 B2
Stanhope *Scot Borders* 76 E4
Stanhope *Durham* 70 G4
Stanion *Northants* 42 G2
Stanley *Derbys* 41 A6
Stanley *Durham* 71 E6
Stanley *Lancs* 48 B5
Stanley *Perth/Kinr* 84 A3
Stanley *Staffs* 49 G10
Stanley *W Yorks* 57 F8
Stanley Common *Derbys* 41 A6
Stanley Gate *Lancs* 48 B5
Stanley Hill *Heref/Worcs* 29 D7
Stanlow *Ches* 48 E5
Stanmer *Brighton/Hove* 13 E7
Stanmore *Berks* 20 D2
Stanmore *Gtr Lon* 21 B9
Stanmore *Hants* 11 B7
Stannergate *Dundee C* 84 A6
Stanningley *W Yorks* 57 E7
Stannington *Northum* 71 C7
Stannington *S Yorks* 50 D5
Stansbatch *Heref/Worcs* 28 B4
Stansfield *Suffolk* 34 C1
Stanstead *Suffolk* 34 D2
Stanstead Abbots *Herts* 33 G6
Stansted *Kent* 23 E6
Stansted Mountfitchet *Essex* 33 F8
Stanton *Glos* 30 E2
Stanton *Monmouths* 28 F4
Stanton *Northum* 71 B6
Stanton *Staffs* 50 H3
Stanton *Suffolk* 34 A3
Stanton by Bridge *Derbys* 40 C5
Stanton-by-Dale *Derbys* 41 B6
Stanton Drew *Bath/NE Som'set* 18 E2
Stanton Fitzwarren *Thamesd'n* 19 B8
Stanton Harcourt *Oxon* 31 H6
Stanton Hill *Notts* 51 F6
Stanton in Peak *Derbys* 50 F4
Stanton Lacy *Shrops* 38 H5
Stanton Long *Shrops* 39 F6
Stanton-on-the-Wolds *Notts* 41 B8
Stanton Prior *Bath/NE Som'set* 18 E3
Stanton St. Bernard *Wilts* 19 E7
Stanton St. John *Oxon* 31 H7
Stanton St. Quintin *Wilts* 19 D6
Stanton Street *Suffolk* 34 B3
Stanton under Bardon *Leics* 41 D6
Stanton upon Hine Heath *Shrops* 39 C6
Stanton Wick *Bath/NE Som'set* 18 E3
Stanwardine in the Fields *Shrops* 38 C5
Stanwardine in the Wood *Shrops* 38 C5
Stanway *Essex* 34 F3
Stanway *Glos* 30 E2
Stanway Green *Suffolk* 35 A6
Stanwell *Surrey* 21 D8
Stanwell Moor *Surrey* 21 D8
Stanwick *Northants* 32 A2
Stanwick-St-John *N Yorks* 63 C6
Stanwix *Cumb* 69 E7
Stanydale *Shetl'd* 113 H5
Staoinebrig *W Isles* 92 B3
Stape *N Yorks* 64 E5
Stapehill *Dorset* 10 D3
Stapeley *Ches* 49 H7
Stapeley Water Gardens, Nantwich *Ches* 49 G7
Stapenhill *Staffs* 40 C4
Staple *Kent* 15 C7
Staple *Som'set* 17 G6
Staple Cross *E Sussex* 14 F2
Staple Fitzpaine *Som'set* 8 C4
Staplefield *W Sussex* 13 C6
Stapleford *Cambs* 33 C7
Stapleford *Herts* 33 G6
Stapleford *Leics* 41 D10
Stapleford *Lincs* 52 G1
Stapleford *Notts* 41 B6
Stapleford *Wilts* 19 H7
Stapleford Abbotts *Essex* 22 B5
Stapleford Tawney *Essex* 22 B5
Staplegrove *Som'set* 8 B4
Staplehay *Som'set* 8 B4
Staplehurst *Kent* 14 D2
Staplers *I of Wight* 11 F8
Stapleton *Bristol* 18 D3
Stapleton *Cumb* 69 C8
Stapleton *Heref/Worcs* 28 B4
Stapleton *Leics* 41 F6
Stapleton *N Yorks* 63 C7
Stapleton *Shrops* 38 E5
Stapleton *Som'set* 9 B6
Stapley *Som'set* 8 C3
Staploe *Beds* 32 B4
Staplow *Heref/Worcs* 29 D7
Star *Fife* 84 D5
Star *Pembs* 25 C7
Star *Som'set* 17 F9
Stara *Orkney* 112 F3
Starbeck *N Yorks* 57 C8
Starbotton *N Yorks* 62 G4
Starcross *Devon* 8 F1
Stareton *Warwick* 30 A5
Starkholmes *Derbys* 50 G5
Starlings Green *Essex* 33 E7
Starston *Norfolk* 45 G6
Startforth *Durham* 62 C5
Startley *Wilts* 19 C6
Stathe *Som'set* 8 B5
Stathern *Leics* 41 B9
Station Town *Durham* 71 G9
Staughton Green *Cambs* 32 B4
Staughton Highway *Cambs* 32 B4
Staunton *Glos* 29 G6
Staunton *Glos* 29 F8
Staunton in the Vale *Notts* 41 A10
Staunton on Arrow *Heref/Worcs* 28 B4
Staunton on Wye *Heref/Worcs* 28 D4
Staveley *Cumb* 61 F6
Staveley *Cumb* 61 E7
Staveley *Derbys* 51 E6
Staveley *N Yorks* 57 B8
Staverton *Devon* 5 D8
Staverton *Glos* 29 F9
Staverton *Northants* 31 B7
Staverton *Wilts* 18 E5
Staverton Bridge *Glos* 29 F9
Stawell *Som'set* 17 H8
Staxigoe *H'land* 111 D8
Staxton *N Yorks* 65 G8
Staylittle *Powys* 37 F8
Staynall *Lancs* 55 D3
Staythorpe *Notts* 51 G9
Stean *N Yorks* 62 G5
Stearsby *N Yorks* 64 G4
Steart *Som'set* 17 G7
Stebbing *Essex* 33 F9
Stebbing Green *Essex* 33 F9
Stedham *W Sussex* 12 C2
Steele Road *Scot Borders* 69 A8
Steen's Bridge *Heref/Worcs* 29 C6
Steep *Hants* 11 B10
Steep Marsh *Hants* 12 C1
Steeple *Dorset* 10 F2
Steeple *Essex* 23 A9
Steeple Ashton *Wilts* 19 F6
Steeple Aston *Oxon* 31 F6
Steeple Barton *Oxon* 31 F6
Steeple Bumpstead *Essex* 33 D9
Steeple Claydon *Bucks* 31 F8
Steeple Gidding *Cambs* 42 G4
Steeple Langford *Wilts* 19 H7
Steeple Morden *Cambs* 32 D5
Steeton *W Yorks* 56 D5
Stein *H'land* 101 G8
Steinmanhill *Aberds* 99 D7
Stelling Minnis *Kent* 15 D6
Stemster *H'land* 111 C6
Stemster Ho. *H'land* 111 C6
Stenalees *Cornw'l* 3 D9
Stenhousemuir *Falk* 83 F9
Stenigot *Lincs* 52 D5
Stenness *Shetl'd* 113 F5
Stenscholl *H'land* 102 F2
Stenson *Derbys* 40 C5
Stenton *E Loth* 85 G8
Stenwith *Lincs* 41 B10
Stepaside *Pembs* 24 F6
Stepping Hill *Gtr Man* 49 D10
Steppingley *Beds* 32 E3
Stepps *N Lanarks* 83 H7
Sterndale Moor *Derbys* 50 F3
Sternfield *Suffolk* 35 B7
Sterridge *Devon* 7 B6
Stert *Wilts* 19 F7
Stetchworth *Cambs* 33 C9
Stevenage *Herts* 32 F5
Stevenston *N Ayrs* 74 C4
Steventon *Hants* 20 G3
Steventon *Oxon* 20 B2
Stevington *Beds* 32 C2
Stewartby *Beds* 32 D3
Stewarton *Arg/Bute* 73 F6
Stewarton *E Ayrs* 75 C6
Stewkley *Bucks* 32 F1
Stewton *Lincs* 53 D6
Steyne Cross *I of Wight* 11 F9
Steyning *W Sussex* 12 D5
Steynton *Pembs* 24 F4
Stibb *Cornw'l* 6 E3
Stibb Cross *Devon* 6 E5
Stibb Green *Wilts* 19 E9
Stibbard *Norfolk* 44 C3
Stibbington *Cambs* 42 F3
Stichill *Scot Borders* 78 D2
Sticker *Cornw'l* 3 D8
Stickford *Lincs* 53 G6
Sticklepath *Devon* 7 G7
Stickney *Lincs* 53 G6
Stiffkey *Norfolk* 44 A3
Stifford's Bridge *Heref/Worcs* 29 D8
Stillingfleet *N Yorks* 58 D1
Stillington *N Yorks* 58 B1
Stillington *Stockton* 63 B8
Stilton *Cambs* 42 G4
Stinchcombe *Glos* 18 B4
Stinsford *Dorset* 9 E9
Stirchley *Shrops* 39 E8
Stirkoke Ho. *H'land* 111 D8
Stirling *Stirl* 83 E8
Stirling Castle *Stirl* 83 E8
Stisted *Essex* 34 F1
Stithians *Cornw'l* 3 F6
Stittenham *H'land* 104 E5
Stivichall *W Midlands* 40 H5
Stixwould *Lincs* 52 F4
Stoak *Ches* 48 E5
Stobieside *S Lanarks* 75 D8
Stobo *Scot Borders* 76 D4
Stoborough *Dorset* 10 F2
Stoborough Green *Dorset* 10 F2
Stobshiel *E Loth* 77 A7
Stobswood *Northum* 71 A7
Stock *Essex* 23 B6
Stock Green *Heref/Worcs* 30 C1
Stock Wood *Heref/Worcs* 30 C2
Stockbridge *Hants* 11 A6
Stockbury *Kent* 14 B3
Stockcross *Berks* 20 E2
Stockdalewath *Cumb* 69 F6
Stockerston *Leics* 41 F10
Stockheath *Hants* 11 D10
Stockiemuir *Stirl* 83 F6
Stocking Pelham *Herts* 33 F7
Stockingford *Warwick* 40 F5
Stockland *Devon* 8 D4
Stockland Bristol *Som'set* 17 G7
Stockleigh English *Devon* 7 F9
Stockleigh Pomeroy *Devon* 7 F9
Stockley *Wilts* 19 E7
Stocklinch *Som'set* 8 C5
Stockport *Gtr Man* 49 C9
Stocksbridge *S Yorks* 50 C4
Stocksfield *Northum* 70 D5
Stockton *Heref/Worcs* 29 B6
Stockton *Norfolk* 45 F7
Stockton *Shrops* 38 E3
Stockton *Shrops* 39 F8
Stockton *Warwick* 31 B6
Stockton *Wilts* 19 H6
Stockton Heath *Ches* 49 D7
Stockton-on-Tees *Stockton* 63 C9
Stockton on Teme *Heref/Worcs* 29 B8
Stockton on the Forest *C of York* 58 C2
Stockwood Craft Museum, Luton *Luton* 32 G3
Stodmarsh *Kent* 15 B7
Stody *Norfolk* 44 B4
Stoer *H'land* 108 G3
Stoford *Som'set* 9 C7
Stoford *Wilts* 19 H7
Stogumber *Som'set* 16 H5
Stogursey *Som'set* 17 G7
Stoke *Devon* 6 D3
Stoke *Hants* 20 F2
Stoke *Hants* 11 D10
Stoke *Kent* 23 D8
Stoke *Suffolk* 34 D5
Stoke Abbott *Dorset* 9 D6
Stoke Albany *Northants* 41 G10
Stoke Ash *Suffolk* 34 A5
Stoke Bardolph *Notts* 41 A8
Stoke Bliss *Heref/Worcs* 29 B7
Stoke Bruerne *Northants* 31 D9
Stoke-by-Clare *Suffolk* 33 D10
Stoke-by-Nayland *Suffolk* 34 E3
Stoke Canon *Devon* 7 G10
Stoke Charity *Hants* 20 H2
Stoke Climsland *Cornw'l* 4 C4
Stoke D'Abernon *Surrey* 21 F9
Stoke Doyle *Northants* 42 G3
Stoke Dry *Rutl'd* 42 F1
Stoke Farthing *Wilts* 10 B3
Stoke Ferry *Norfolk* 43 F10
Stoke Fleming *Devon* 5 F9
Stoke Gabriel *Devon* 5 E9
Stoke Gifford *S Gloucs* 18 D3
Stoke Golding *Leics* 40 F5
Stoke Goldington *M/Keynes* 31 D10
Stoke Green *Bucks* 21 C7
Stoke Hammond *Bucks* 32 F1
Stoke Heath *Shrops* 39 C7
Stoke Holy Cross *Norfolk* 45 E6
Stoke Lacy *Heref/Worcs* 29 D7
Stoke Lyne *Oxon* 31 F7
Stoke Mandeville *Bucks* 31 G10
Stoke Newington *Gtr Lon* 22 C3
Stoke-on-Trent *Stoke* 49 H9
Stoke Orchard *Glos* 29 F10
Stoke Poges *Bucks* 21 C7
Stoke Prior *Heref/Worcs* 29 C6
Stoke Prior *Heref/Worcs* 30 B1
Stoke Rivers *Devon* 7 C7
Stoke Rochford *Lincs* 42 C2
Stoke Row *Oxon* 20 C4
Stoke St. Gregory *Som'set* 8 B5
Stoke St. Mary *Som'set* 8 B4
Stoke St. Michael *Som'set* 18 G3
Stoke St. Milborough *Shrops* 39 G6
Stoke sub Hamdon *Som'set* 9 C6
Stoke Talmage *Oxon* 20 B4
Stoke Trister *Som'set* 9 B9
Stoke upon Tern *Shrops* 39 C7
Stoke Wake *Dorset* 9 D9
Stokeford *Dorset* 10 F1
Stokeham *Notts* 51 E9
Stokeinteignhead *Devon* 5 C10
Stokenchurch *Bucks* 20 B5
Stokenham *Devon* 5 F9
Stokesay *Shrops* 38 G5
Stokesby *Norfolk* 45 D8
Stokesley *N Yorks* 64 D3
Stolford *Som'set* 17 G7
Ston Easton *Som'set* 18 F3
Stondon Massey *Essex* 22 A5
Stone *Bucks* 31 G9
Stone *Glos* 18 B3
Stone *Heref/Worcs* 39 H9
Stone *Kent* 14 F4
Stone *Kent* 22 D5
Stone *Staffs* 39 B10
Stone *S Yorks* 51 D7
Stone Allerton *Som'set* 17 F9
Stone Bridge Corner *Cambs* 42 E5
Stone Chair *W Yorks* 57 F6
Stone Cross *E Sussex* 13 E10
Stone Cross *Kent* 15 C8
Stone-edge Batch *N Som'set* 17 D9
Stone House *Cumb* 62 F2
Stone Street *Kent* 22 F5
Stone Street *Suffolk* 34 E3
Stone Street *Suffolk* 45 G7
Stonebroom *Derbys* 51 G6
Stoneferry *Kingston/Hull* 59 E7
Stonefield *S Lanarks* 75 B8
Stonegate *E Sussex* 14 F1
Stonegate *N Yorks* 64 D5
Stonegrave *N Yorks* 64 G4
Stonehaugh *Northum* 70 C2
Stonehaven *Aberds* 91 C9
Stonehenge, Amesbury *Wilts* 19 G8
Stonehouse *Glos* 29 H9
Stonehouse *Northum* 69 E9
Stonehouse *S Lanarks* 75 C9
Stoneleigh *Warwick* 30 A5
Stonely *Cambs* 32 B4
Stoner Hill *Hants* 11 B10
Stone's Green *Essex* 34 F5
Stonesby *Leics* 41 C10
Stonesfield *Oxon* 30 G5
Stonethwaite *Cumb* 60 C5
Stoney Cross *Hants* 10 C5
Stoney Middleton *Derbys* 50 E4
Stoney Stanton *Leics* 41 F6
Stoney Stoke *Som'set* 9 A9
Stoney Stratton *Som'set* 18 H3
Stoney Stretton *Shrops* 38 E4
Stoneybreck *Shetl'd* 113 N9
Stoneyburn *W Loth* 76 A2
Stoneygate *Aberds* 99 E10
Stoneygate *Leics C* 41 E8
Stoneyhills *Essex* 23 B9
Stoneykirk *Dumf/Gal* 66 E2
Stoneywood *Aberd C* 99 G8
Stoneywood *Falk* 83 F8
Stonganess *Shetl'd* 113 C8
Stonham Aspal *Suffolk* 34 C5
Stonnall *Staffs* 40 E2
Stonor *Oxon* 20 C5
Stonton Wyville *Leics* 41 F9
Stony Cross *Heref/Worcs* 29 D8
Stony Stratford *M/Keynes* 31 D9
Stonyfield *H'land* 104 E5
Stoodleigh *Devon* 7 E10
Stopes *S Yorks* 50 D4
Stopham *W Sussex* 12 D4
Stopsley *Luton* 32 F4
Stores Corner *Suffolk* 35 D7
Storeton *Mersey* 48 D4
Stornoway *W Isles* 107 F8
Storridge *Heref/Worcs* 29 D8
Storrington *W Sussex* 12 D4
Storrs *Cumb* 61 E6
Storth *Cumb* 61 F7
Storwood *E Riding Yorks* 58 D3
Stotfield *Moray* 98 A2
Stotfold *Beds* 32 E5
Stottesdon *Shrops* 39 G7
Stoughton *Leics* 41 E8
Stoughton *Surrey* 21 F7
Stoughton *W Sussex* 12 D2
Stoul *H'land* 87 B7
Stoulton *Heref/Worcs* 29 D10
Stour Provost *Dorset* 9 B9
Stour Row *Dorset* 9 B10
Stourbridge *W Midlands* 39 G10
Stourhead Garden *Wilts* 9 A9
Stourpaine *Dorset* 10 D1
Stourport on Severn *Heref/Worcs* 29 A9
Stourton *Staffs* 39 G9
Stourton *Warwick* 30 E4
Stourton *Wilts* 9 A9
Stourton Caundle *Dorset* 9 C9
Stove *Orkney* 112 E7
Stove *Shetl'd* 113 L7
Stoven *Suffolk* 45 G8
Stow *Scot Borders* 77 C7
Stow *Lincs* 52 D1
Stow *Lincs* 42 B3
Stow Bardolph *Norfolk* 43 E9
Stow Bedon *Norfolk* 44 F3
Stow cum Quy *Cambs* 33 B8
Stow Longa *Cambs* 32 A4
Stow Maries *Essex* 23 B8
Stow on the Wold *Glos* 30 F3
Stowbridge *Norfolk* 43 E9
Stowe *Shrops* 28 A4
Stowe-by-Chartley *Staffs* 40 C2
Stowe Green *Glos* 29 H6
Stowe School and Gardens, Buckingham *Bucks* 31 E8
Stowell *Som'set* 9 B8
Stowford *Devon* 4 B5
Stowlangtoft *Suffolk* 34 B3
Stowmarket *Suffolk* 34 C4
Stowting *Kent* 15 D6
Stowupland *Suffolk* 34 C4
Straad *Arg/Bute* 74 A2
Strachan *Aberds* 91 B7
Strachur *Arg/Bute* 82 D1
Stradbroke *Suffolk* 35 A6
Stradishall *Suffolk* 33 C10
Stradsett *Norfolk* 43 E9
Stragglethorpe *Lincs* 52 G2
Straid *S Ayrs* 66 A3
Straith *Dumf/Gal* 67 B10
Straiton *C of Edinb* 84 H4
Straiton *S Ayrs* 74 G5
Straloch *Aberds* 99 F8
Straloch *Perth/Kinr* 90 E1
Stramshall *Staffs* 40 B2
Strang *I of Man* 54 F3
Stranraer *Dumf/Gal* 66 D2
Stratfield Mortimer *Berks* 20 E4
Stratfield Saye *Hants* 20 E4
Stratfield Turgis *Hants* 20 F4
Stratford *Gtr Lon* 22 C3
Stratford St. Andrew *Suffolk* 35 B7
Stratford St. Mary *Suffolk* 34 E4
Stratford Sub Castle *Wilts* 10 A4
Stratford Tony *Wilts* 10 B3
Stratford-upon-Avon *Warwick* 30 C3
Strath *H'land* 111 D7
Strath *H'land* 102 E5
Strath Kanaird *H'land* 103 B9
Strathan *H'land* 87 B9
Strathan *H'land* 109 C8
Strathan *H'land* 108 G3
Strathaven *S Lanarks* 75 C9
Strathblane *Stirl* 83 G6
Strathcarron *H'land* 95 B6
Strathcoil *Arg/Bute* 81 A6
Strathdon *Aberds* 98 G3
Strathellie *Aberds* 99 B10
Strathkinness *Fife* 85 C6
Strathmashie House *H'land* 89 B6
Strathmiglo *Fife* 84 C4
Strathmore Lodge *H'land* 111 E6
Strathpeffer *H'land* 104 G3
Strathrannoch *H'land* 104 E2
Strathtay *Perth/Kinr* 89 F10
Strathvaich Lodge *H'land* 104 E2
Strathwhillan *N Ayrs* 74 D2
Strathy *H'land* 110 C3
Strathyre *Stirl* 83 C6
Stratton *Cornw'l* 6 F3
Stratton *Dorset* 9 E8
Stratton *Glos* 19 A7
Stratton Audley *Oxon* 31 F8
Stratton on the Fosse *Som'set* 18 F3
Stratton St. Margaret *Thamesd'n* 19 C8
Stratton St. Michael *Norfolk* 45 F6
Stratton Strawless *Norfolk* 45 C6
Stravithie *Fife* 85 C7
Streat *E Sussex* 13 D7
Streatham *Gtr Lon* 22 D3
Streatley *Beds* 32 F3
Streatley *Berks* 20 C3
Street *Lancs* 55 C5
Street *N Yorks* 64 D5
Street *Som'set* 17 H9
Street Dinas *Shrops* 38 B4
Street End *Kent* 15 C6
Street End *W Sussex* 12 F2
Street Gate *Tyne/Wear* 71 E7
Street Lydan *Wrex* 38 B5
Streethay *Staffs* 40 D3
Streetlam *N Yorks* 63 E8
Streetly *W Midlands* 40 F2
Streetly End *Cambs* 33 D9
Strefford *Shrops* 38 G5
Strelley *Notts* 41 A7
Strensall *C of York* 58 B2
Stretcholt *Som'set* 17 G7
Strete *Devon* 5 F9
Stretford *Gtr Man* 49 C9
Strethall *Essex* 33 E7
Stretham *Cambs* 33 A8
Strettington *W Sussex* 12 E2
Stretton *Ches* 48 G5
Stretton *Ches* 49 D7
Stretton *Derbys* 50 F5
Stretton *Rutl'd* 42 D2
Stretton *Staffs* 39 D9
Stretton *Staffs* 40 C4
Stretton Grandison *Heref/Worcs* 29 D7
Stretton on Dunsmore *Warwick* 31 A6
Stretton on Fosse *Warwick* 30 E4
Stretton Sugwas *Heref/Worcs* 28 D5
Stretton under Fosse *Warwick* 41 G6
Stretton Westwood *Shrops* 39 F6
Strichen *Aberds* 99 C9
Strines *Gtr Man* 50 D1
Stringston *Som'set* 17 G6
Strixton *Northants* 32 B2
Stroat *Glos* 18 B2
Stromeferry *H'land* 94 C5
Stromemore *H'land* 94 C5
Stromness *Orkney* 112 H3
Stronaba *H'land* 88 C3
Stronachlachar *Stirl* 82 C5
Stronchreggan *H'land* 87 D10
Stronchrubie *H'land* 108 H5
Strone *Arg/Bute* 82 F2
Strone *H'land* 96 D3
Strone *H'land* 88 C2
Strone *Invercl* 82 G3
Stronmilchan *Arg/Bute* 82 B2
Strontian *H'land* 87 E8
Strood *Kent* 14 B2
Strood Green *Surrey* 22 G2
Strood Green *W Sussex* 12 C4
Strood Green *W Sussex* 12 B5
Stroud *Glos* 29 H9
Stroud *Hants* 11 B10
Stroud Green *Essex* 23 B8
Stroxton *Lincs* 42 B2
Struan *H'land* 93 B9
Struan *Perth/Kinr* 89 E9
Strubby *Lincs* 53 D7
Strumpshaw *Norfolk* 45 E7
Strutherhill *S Lanarks* 75 C9
Struy *H'land* 96 C1
Stryt-issa *Wrex* 48 H3
Stuartfield *Aberds* 99 D9
Stub Place *Cumb* 60 E3
Stubbington *Hants* 11 D8
Stubbins *Lancs* 56 G2
Stubbs Cross *Kent* 14 E4
Stubb's Green *Norfolk* 45 F6
Stubbs Green *Norfolk* 45 F7
Stubhampton *Dorset* 10 C2
Stubton *Lincs* 52 H1
Stuckgowan *Arg/Bute* 82 D4
Stuckton *Hants* 10 C4
Stud Green *Berks* 21 D6
Studham *Beds* 32 G3
Studland *Dorset* 10 F3
Studley *Warwick* 30 B2
Studley *Wilts* 19 D6
Studley Roger *N Yorks* 63 G7
Stump Cross *Essex* 33 D8
Stuntney *Cambs* 43 H8
Sturbridge *Staffs* 39 B9
Sturmer *Essex* 33 D9
Sturminster Marshall *Dorset* 10 D2
Sturminster Newton *Dorset* 9 C9
Sturry *Kent* 15 B6
Sturton *N Lincs* 52 B2
Sturton by Stow *Lincs* 52 D1
Sturton le Steeple *Notts* 51 D9
Stuston *Suffolk* 44 H5
Stutton *N Yorks* 57 D9
Stutton *Suffolk* 34 E5
Styal *Ches* 49 D9
Styrrup *Notts* 51 C8
Suainebost *W Isles* 107 C9
Suardail *W Isles* 107 F8
Succoth *Aberds* 98 E4
Succoth *Arg/Bute* 82 D3
Suckley *Heref/Worcs* 29 C8
Suckquoy *Orkney* 112 K5
Sudborough *Northants* 42 G2
Sudbourne *Suffolk* 35 C8
Sudbrook *Lincs* 42 A2
Sudbrook *Monmouths* 18 C2
Sudbrooke *Lincs* 52 E3
Sudbury *Derbys* 40 B3
Sudbury *Gtr Lon* 21 C9
Sudbury *Suffolk* 34 D2
Suddie *H'land* 104 G5
Sudeley Castle and Gardens *Glos* 30 F2
Sudgrove *Glos* 29 H10
Suffield *Norfolk* 45 B6
Suffield *N Yorks* 65 E7
Sugnall *Staffs* 39 B8
Suladale *H'land* 101 G9
Sulaisiadar *W Isles* 107 F9
Sulby *I of Man* 54 D3
Sulgrave *Northants* 31 D7
Sulham *Berks* 20 D4
Sulhamstead *Berks* 20 E4
Sulland *Orkney* 112 D6
Sullington *W Sussex* 12 D4
Sullom *Shetl'd* 113 F6
Sullom Voe Oil Terminal *Shetl'd* 113 F6
Sully *V of Glam* 17 E6
Sumburgh *Shetl'd* 113 N7
Summer Bridge *N Yorks* 57 B7
Summer house *Durham* 63 C7
Summercourt *Cornw'l* 3 D7
Summerfield *Norfolk* 44 B1
Summergangs *Kingston/Hull* 59 E7
Summerleaze *Monmouths* 17 C9
Summerlee Heritage Centre, Coatbridge *N Lanarks* 83 H8

West Woodlands Som'set 18 G4
West Worldham Hants 20 H5
West Worlington Devon 7 E8
West Worthing W Sussex 12 E5
West Wratting Cambs 33 C9
West Wycombe Bucks 21 B6
West Wylam Northum 71 D6
West Yell Shetl'd 113 E7
Westacott Devon 7 C6
Westbere Kent 15 B6
Westborough Lincs 42 A1
Westbourne Bournem'th 10 E3
Westbourne Suffolk 34 D5
Westbourne W Sussex 12 E1
Westbrook Berks 20 D2
Westbury Bucks 31 E8
Westbury Shrops 38 E4
Westbury Wilts 18 F5
Westbury Leigh Wilts 18 F5
Westbury-on-Severn Glos 29 G8
Westbury on Trym Bristol 18 D2
Westbury-sub-Mendip Som'set 18 G2
Westby Lancs 55 E3
Westcliffe on Sea Essex 23 C8
Westcombe Som'set 18 H3
Westcote Glos 30 F4
Westcott Bucks 31 G9
Westcott Devon 8 D2
Westcott Surrey 21 G9
Westcott Barton Oxon 31 F6
Westdean E Sussex 13 F9
Westdene Brighton/Hove 13 E6
Wester Aberchalder H'land 96 D3
Wester Balgedie Perth/Kinr 84 D3
Wester Culbeuchly Aberds 99 B6
Wester Dechmont W Loth 84 H2
Wester Denoon Angus 90 G4
Wester Fintray Aberds 99 G8
Wester Fodderletter Moray 97 D9
Wester Gruinards H'land 104 C4
Wester Lealty H'land 104 E5
Wester Milton H'land 105 G8
Wester Newburn Fife 84 D6
Wester Pencaitland E Loth 84 H6
Wester Quarff Shetl'd 113 K7
Wester Skeld Shetl'd 113 J5
Westerdale H'land 111 D6
Westerdale N Yorks 64 D4
Westerfield Shetl'd 113 H6
Westerfield Suffolk 34 D5
Westergate W Sussex 12 E3
Westerham Kent 22 F4
Westerhope Tyne/Wear 71 D6
Westerleigh S Gloucs 18 D4
Westermill Orkney 112 J5
Westerton Angus 91 F7
Westerton Durham 71 G7
Westerton W Sussex 12 E2
Westerwick Shetl'd 113 J5
Westfield Cumb 60 B2
Westfield E Sussex 14 G3
Westfield Heref/Worcs 29 D8
Westfield H'land 110 C5
Westfield N Lanarks 83 G8
Westfield Norfolk 44 E3
Westfield W Loth 83 G10
Westfields Dorset 9 D9
Westfields of Rattray Perth/Kinr 90 G2
Westgate Durham 70 G4
Westgate N Lincs 51 B9
Westgate Norfolk 44 A3
Westgate on Sea Kent 15 A8
Westhall Aberds 99 F6
Westhall Suffolk 45 G8
Westham Dorset 9 G8
Westham E Sussex 13 E10
Westham Som'set 17 G9
Westhampnett W Sussex 12 E2
Westhay Som'set 17 G9
Westhead Lancs 48 B5
Westhide Heref/Worcs 29 D6
Westhill Aberds 99 H8
Westhill H'land 96 B5
Westhope Heref/Worcs 28 C5
Westhope Shrops 38 G5
Westhorpe Lincs 42 B5
Westhorpe Suffolk 34 B4
Westhoughton Gtr Man 49 B7
Westhouse N Yorks 61 G9
Westing Shetl'd 113 C8
Westlake Devon 5 E7
Westleigh Devon 6 D5
Westleigh Devon 8 C2
Westleigh Gtr Man 49 B7
Westleton Suffolk 35 B8
Westley Shrops 38 E4
Westley Suffolk 34 B2
Westley Waterless Cambs 33 C9
Westlington Bucks 31 G9
Westlinton Cumb 69 D6
Westmarsh Kent 15 B7
Westmeston E Sussex 13 D7
Westmill Herts 33 F6
Westminster Gtr Lon 22 D3
Westminster Cathedral Gtr Lon 22 D2
Westmuir Angus 90 F4
Westness Orkney 112 F4
Westnewton Cumb 68 F4
Westnewton Northum 78 D4
Westoe Tyne/Wear 71 D8
Weston Berks 20 D1
Weston Bath/NE Som'set 18 E4
Weston Ches 49 G8
Weston Ches 49 D6
Weston Devon 8 F3
Weston Dorset 9 G8
Weston Hants 11 B10
Weston Herts 32 E5
Weston Lincs 42 C5
Weston Notts 51 F9
Weston Northants 31 D7
Weston N Yorks 57 D6
Weston Shrops 39 F6
Weston Shrops 39 C6
Weston Staffs 40 C1
Weston Beggard Heref/Worcs 29 D6
Weston by Welland Northants 41 F9
Weston Colville Cambs 33 C9
Weston Coyney Stoke 39 A10
Weston Favell Northants 31 B9
Weston Green Cambs 33 C9
Weston Green Norfolk 44 D5
Weston Heath Shrops 39 D8
Weston Hills Lincs 42 C5
Weston-in-Gordano N Som'set 17 D9
Weston Jones Staffs 39 C8
Weston Longville Norfolk 44 D5
Weston Lullingfields Shrops 38 C5
Weston-on-the-Green Oxon 31 G7
Weston-on-Trent Derbys 41 C6
Weston Park Staffs 39 D9
Weston Patrick Hants 20 G4
Weston Rhyn Shrops 38 B3
Weston Subedge Glos 30 D3
Weston super Mare N Som'set 17 E8
Weston Turville Bucks 32 G1
Weston under Lizard Staffs 39 D9
Weston under Penyard Heref/Worcs 29 F7
Weston under Wetherley Warwick 30 B5
Weston Underwood Derbys 40 A4
Weston Underwood M/Keynes 32 C1
Westonbirt Glos 18 C5
Westonbirt Arboretum, Tetbury Glos 18 C5
Westoncommon Shrops 38 C5
Westoning Beds 32 E3
Westonzoyland Som'set 8 A5
Westow N Yorks 58 B3
Westport Arg/Bute 73 E6
Westport Som'set 8 C5
Westrigg W Loth 83 H10
Westruther Scot Borders 77 C9
Westry Cambs 43 F6
Westville Notts 51 H7
Westward Cumb 68 F5
Westward Ho! Devon 6 D5
Westwell Kent 14 D4
Westwell Oxon 30 H4
Westwell Leacon Kent 14 D4
Westwick Cambs 33 B7
Westwick Durham 62 C5
Westwick Norfolk 45 C6
Westwood Devon 8 E2
Westwood Wilts 18 F5
Westwoodside N Lincs 51 C9
Wetheral Cumb 69 E7
Wetherby W Yorks 57 D9
Wetherden Suffolk 34 B4
Wetheringsett Suffolk 34 B5
Wethersfield Essex 33 E10
Wethersta Shetl'd 113 G6
Wetherup Street Suffolk 34 B5
Wetley Rocks Staffs 50 H1
Wettenhall Ches 49 F7
Wetton Staffs 50 G3
Wetwang E Riding Yorks 58 C5
Wetwood Staffs 39 B8
Wexcombe Wilts 19 F9
Wexham Street Bucks 21 C7
Weybourne Norfolk 44 A5
Weybread Suffolk 45 G6
Weybridge Surrey 21 E8
Weycroft Devon 8 E5
Weydale H'land 111 C6
Weyhill Hants 19 G10
Weymouth Dorset 9 G8
Weymouth Sea Life Park Dorset 9 F8
Whaddon Bucks 31 E10
Whaddon Cambs 33 D6
Whaddon Glos 29 G9
Whaddon Wilts 10 B4
Whale Cumb 61 B8
Whaley Derbys 51 E7
Whaley Bridge Derbys 50 D2
Whaley Thorns Derbys 51 E7
Whaligoe H'land 111 E8
Whalley Lancs 56 E2
Whalton Northum 71 B6
Wham N Yorks 56 B2
Whaness Orkney 112 H3
Whaplode Lincs 43 C6
Whaplode Drove Lincs 43 D6
Whaplode St. Catherine Lincs 43 C6
Wharfe N Yorks 56 B2
Wharles Lancs 55 E4
Wharncliffe Side S Yorks 50 C4
Wharram-le-Street N Yorks 58 B4
Wharton Ches 49 F7
Wharton Green Ches 49 F7
Whashton N Yorks 63 D6
Whatcombe Dorset 9 D10
Whatcote Warwick 30 D5
Whatfield Suffolk 34 D4
Whatley Som'set 8 D5
Whatley Som'set 18 G4
Whatlington E Sussex 14 G2
Whatstandwell Derbys 50 G5
Whatton Notts 41 B9
Whauphill Dumf/Gal 67 F6
Whaw N Yorks 62 D4
Wheatacre Norfolk 45 F8
Wheatcroft Derbys 50 G5
Wheathampstead Herts 32 G4
Wheathill Shrops 39 G7
Wheatley Devon 7 G10
Wheatley Hants 20 G5
Wheatley Oxon 31 H7
Wheatley S Yorks 51 B7
Wheatley W Yorks 56 F5
Wheatley Hill Durham 71 G8
Wheaton Aston Staffs 39 D9
Wheddon Cross Som'set 7 C10
Wheedlemont Aberds 98 F4
Wheelerstreet Surrey 21 G7
Wheelock Ches 49 G8
Wheelock Heath Ches 49 G8
Wheelton Lancs 55 F6
Wheen Angus 90 D4
Wheldrake C of York 58 D2
Whelford Glos 19 B8
Whelpley Hill Bucks 21 A7
Whempstead Herts 33 F6
Whenby N Yorks 58 B2
Whepstead Suffolk 34 C2
Wherstead Suffolk 34 D5
Wherwell Hants 20 G1
Wheston Derbys 50 E3
Whetsted Kent 14 D1
Whetstone Leics 41 F7
Whicham Cumb 60 F4
Whichford Warwick 30 E5
Whickham Tyne/Wear 71 D7
Whiddon Down Devon 7 G7
Whigstreet Angus 90 G5
Whilton Northants 31 B8
Whim Farm Scot Borders 76 B5
Whimble Devon 6 F4
Whimple Devon 8 E2
Whimpwell Green Norfolk 45 C7
Whinburgh Norfolk 44 E4
Whinnieliggate Dumf/Gal 67 E9
Whinnyfold Aberds 99 E10
Whippingham I of Wight 11 E8
Whipsnade Beds 32 G3
Whipsnade Wild Animal Park, Dunstable Beds 32 G3
Whipton Devon 8 E1
Whirlow S Yorks 50 D5
Whisby Lincs 52 F2
Whissendine Rutl'd 41 D10
Whissonsett Norfolk 44 C3
Whistlefield Arg/Bute 82 E2
Whistlefield Arg/Bute 82 E3
Whistley Green Berks 20 D5
Whiston Mersey 48 C5
Whiston Northants 31 B10
Whiston Staffs 39 D9
Whiston Staffs 50 H2
Whiston S Yorks 51 D6
Whitbeck Cumb 60 F4
Whitbourne Heref/Worcs 29 C8
Whitbread Hop Farm, Beltring Kent 14 D1
Whitburn Tyne/Wear 71 D9
Whitburn W Loth 76 A2
Whitburn Colliery Tyne/Wear 71 D9
Whitby Ches 48 E4
Whitby N Yorks 65 C6
Whitby Abbey N Yorks 65 C7
Whitby Heath Ches 48 E4
Whitchurch Bath/NE Som'set 18 E3
Whitchurch Bucks 31 F9
Whitchurch Card 17 C6
Whitchurch Devon 4 C5
Whitchurch Hants 20 G2
Whitchurch Heref/Worcs 29 G6
Whitchurch Oxon 20 D4
Whitchurch Pembs 24 D2
Whitchurch Shrops 39 A6
Whitchurch Canonicorum Dorset 8 E5
Whitchurch Hill Oxon 20 D4
Whitcombe Dorset 9 F9
Whitcott Keysett Shrops 38 G3
White Coppice Lancs 55 G6
White Lackington Dorset 9 E9
White Ladies Aston Heref/Worcs 29 C10
White Lund Lancs 55 B4
White Mill Carms 25 D9
White Ness Shetl'd 113 J6
White Notley Essex 34 G1
White Pit Lincs 53 E6
White Post Notts 51 G8
White Post Modern Farm Centre, Farnsfield Notts 51 G8
White Rocks Heref/Worcs 28 F5
White Roding Essex 33 G8
White Waltham Berks 21 D6
Whiteacen Moray 98 D2
Whiteacre Heath Warwick 40 F4
Whitebridge H'land 96 E2
Whitebrook Monmouths 29 H6
Whiteburn Scot Borders 77 C8
Whitecairn Dumf/Gal 66 E4
Whitecairns Aberds 99 G9
Whitecastle S Lanarks 76 C3
Whitechapel Lancs 55 D5
Whitecleat Orkney 112 H6
Whitecraig E Loth 84 G5
Whitecroft Glos 29 H7
Whitecross Cornw'l 3 B8
Whitecross Falk 83 G10
Whitecross Staffs 39 C9
Whiteface H'land 104 D6
Whitefarland N Ayrs 73 C8
Whitefaulds S Ayrs 74 G4
Whitefield Gtr Man 49 B9
Whitefield Perth/Kinr 84 A3
Whiteford Aberds 99 F7
Whitegate Ches 49 F7
Whitehall Lancs 56 F1
Whitehall Orkney 112 F7
Whitehall W Sussex 12 C5
Whitehaven Cumb 60 C2
Whitehill Hants 12 B1
Whitehills Aberds 99 B6
Whitehills S Lanarks 75 B8
Whitehough Derbys 50 D2
Whitehouse Aberds 98 G6
Whitehouse Arg/Bute 73 A8
Whiteinch C of Glasg 83 H6
Whitekirk E Loth 85 F7
Whitelaw S Lanarks 75 C8
Whiteleas Tyne/Wear 71 D8
Whiteley Bank I of Wight 11 F8
Whiteley Green Ches 49 E10
Whiteley Village Surrey 21 E8
Whitemans Green W Sussex 13 C7
Whitemire Moray 105 G8
Whitemoor Cornw'l 3 D8
Whitemore Staffs 49 F9
Whitenap Hants 11 B6
Whiteoak Green Oxon 30 G5
Whiteparish Wilts 10 B5
Whiterashes Aberds 99 F8
Whiterow H'land 111 E8
Whiteshill Glos 29 H9
Whiteside Northum 70 D2
Whiteside W Loth 83 H10
Whitesmith E Sussex 13 D9
Whitestaunton Som'set 8 C4
Whitestone Devon 7 G9
Whitestone Devon 6 B5
Whitestone Warwick 40 G5
Whitestones Aberds 99 C8
Whitestreet Green Suffolk 34 E3
Whitewall Corner N Yorks 64 G5
Whiteway Glos 18 B5
Whiteway Glos 29 G10
Whitewell Aberds 99 B9
Whitewell Lancs 56 D1
Whitewell Bottom Lancs 56 F3
Whiteworks Devon 5 C7
Whitewreath Moray 98 C2
Whitfield Kent 15 D8
Whitfield Northants 31 E8
Whitfield Northum 70 E2
Whitfield S Gloucs 18 B3
Whitford Devon 8 E4
Whitford Flints 48 E2
Whitgift E Riding Yorks 58 F4
Whitgreave Staffs 39 C9
Whithorn Dumf/Gal 67 F6
Whiting Bay N Ayrs 74 E2
Whitington Norfolk 43 F10
Whitkirk W Yorks 57 E8
Whitland Carms 25 E6
Whitletts S Ayrs 74 E5
Whitley Berks 20 D5
Whitley N Yorks 58 F1
Whitley Wilts 18 E5
Whitley Bay Tyne/Wear 71 C8
Whitley Chapel Northum 70 E4
Whitley Lower W Yorks 57 G7
Whitley Row Kent 22 F4
Whitlock's End W Midlands 40 H3
Whitminster Glos 29 H8
Whitmore Staffs 39 A9
Whitnage Devon 8 C2
Whitnash Warwick 30 B5
Whitney Heref/Worcs 28 D3
Whitrigg Cumb 68 G5
Whitrigg Cumb 68 E5
Whitsbury Hants 10 C4
Whitsome Scot Borders 78 B3
Whitson Newp 17 C8
Whitstable Kent 15 B6
Whitstone Cornw'l 6 G3
Whittingham Northum 78 F5
Whittingslow Shrops 38 G5
Whittington Glos 30 F2
Whittington Heref/Worcs 29 C9
Whittington Lancs 61 G9
Whittington Shrops 38 B4
Whittington Staffs 39 G9
Whittington Staffs 40 E3
Whittle-le-Woods Lancs 55 F5
Whittlebury Northants 31 D8
Whittlesey Cambs 42 F5
Whittlesford Cambs 33 D7
Whittlestone Head Lancs 56 G2
Whitton Scot Borders 78 E2
Whitton N Lincs 58 F5
Whitton Northum 78 G5
Whitton Powys 28 B3
Whitton Shrops 29 A6
Whitton Stockton 63 B8
Whitton Suffolk 34 D5
Whittonditch Wilts 19 D9
Whittonstall Northum 70 E5
Whitway Hants 20 F2
Whitwell Derbys 51 E7
Whitwell Herts 32 F4
Whitwell I of Wight 11 G8
Whitwell N Yorks 63 E7
Whitwell Rutl'd 42 E2
Whitwell-on-the-Hill N Yorks 58 B3
Whitwell Street Norfolk 44 C5
Whitwick Leics 41 D6
Whitwood W Yorks 57 F9
Whitworth Lancs 56 G3
Whixall Shrops 39 B6
Whixley N Yorks 57 C9
Whoberley W Midlands 40 H5
Whorlton Durham 63 C6
Whorlton N Yorks 63 D9
Whygate Northum 70 C2
Whyle Heref/Worcs 29 B6
Whyteleafe Surrey 22 F3
Wibdon Glos 18 B2
Wibsey W Yorks 57 E6
Wibtoft Leics 41 G6
Wichenford Heref/Worcs 29 B8
Wichling Kent 14 C4
Wick Bournem'th 10 E4
Wick Devon 8 D3
Wick Heref/Worcs 30 D1
Wick H'land 111 D8
Wick S Gloucs 18 D4
Wick V of Glam 16 D4
Wick Wilts 10 B4
Wick W Sussex 12 E4
Wick Hill Berks 20 E5
Wick St. Lawrence N Som'set 17 E8
Wicken Cambs 33 A8
Wicken Northants 31 E9
Wicken Bonhunt Essex 33 E7
Wickenby Lincs 52 D3
Wickersley S Yorks 51 C6
Wickford Essex 23 B7
Wickham Berks 20 D1
Wickham Hants 11 C8
Wickham Bishops Essex 34 G2
Wickham Market Suffolk 35 C7
Wickham Skeith Suffolk 34 B4
Wickham St. Paul Essex 34 E2
Wickham Street Suffolk 34 C1
Wickham Street Suffolk 34 B4
Wickhambreux Kent 15 C7
Wickhambrook Suffolk 33 C10
Wickhamford Heref/Worcs 30 D2
Wickhampton Norfolk 45 E8
Wicklewood Norfolk 44 E4
Wickmere Norfolk 44 B5
Wicksteed Park, Kettering Northants 42 H1
Wickwar S Gloucs 18 C4
Widdington Essex 33 E8
Widdrington Northum 79 H7
Widdrington Station Northum 71 A7
Wide Open Tyne/Wear 71 C7
Widecombe in the Moor Devon 5 C8
Widegates Cornw'l 4 E3
Widemouth Bay Cornw'l 6 F3
Widewall Orkney 112 J5
Widford Essex 33 H9
Widford Herts 33 G7
Widham Wilts 19 C7
Widmer End Bucks 21 B6
Widmerpool Notts 41 C8
Widnes Ches 49 D6
Wigan Gtr Man 49 B6
Wigan Pier Gtr Man 49 B6
Wiggaton Devon 8 E3
Wiggenhall St. Germans Norfolk 43 D8
Wiggenhall St. Mary Magdalen Norfolk 43 D8
Wiggenhall St. Mary the Virgin Norfolk 43 D8
Wigginton Herts 32 G2
Wigginton Oxon 30 E5
Wigginton Staffs 40 E4
Wigginton C of York 58 C1
Wigglesworth N Yorks 56 C3
Wiggonby Cumb 68 E5
Wiggonholt W Sussex 12 D4
Wighill N Yorks 57 D9
Wighton Norfolk 44 B3
Wigley Hants 11 C6
Wigmore Heref/Worcs 28 B5
Wigmore Kent 14 B3
Wigsley Notts 52 E1
Wigsthorpe Northants 42 G3
Wigston Magna Leics 41 F8
Wigthorpe Notts 51 D7
Wigtoft Lincs 42 B5
Wigton Cumb 68 F5
Wigtown Dumf/Gal 67 E6
Wigtwizzle S Yorks 50 C4
Wike W Yorks 57 D8
Wike Well End S Yorks 58 G2
Wilbarston Northants 41 G10
Wilberfoss E Riding Yorks 58 C3
Wilberlee W Yorks 56 G5
Wilburton Cambs 33 A7
Wilby Norfolk 44 G4
Wilby Northants 32 B1
Wilby Suffolk 35 A6
Wilcot Wilts 19 E8
Wilcott Shrops 38 D4
Wilcrick Newp 17 C9
Wilday Green Derbys 50 E5
Wildboarclough Ches 50 F1
Wilden Beds 32 C3
Wilden Heref/Worcs 29 A9
Wildfowl and Wetland Centre, Martin Mere Lancs 55 G4
Wildhern Hants 20 F1
Wildhill Herts 32 H5
Wildlife & Dinosaur Park, Combe Martin Devon 7 B6
Wildmoor Heref/Worcs 40 H1
Wildsworth Lincs 51 C10
Wilford Notts 41 B7
Wilkesley Ches 39 A7
Wilkhaven H'land 105 D8
Wilkieston W Loth 84 H3
Willand Devon 8 C2
Willaston Ches 48 E4
Willaston Ches 49 G7
Willen M/Keynes 32 D1
Willenhall W Midlands 40 H5
Willenhall W Midlands 40 F1
Willerby E Riding Yorks 59 E6
Willerby N Yorks 65 G8
Willersey Glos 30 E3
Willersley Heref/Worcs 28 D4
Willesborough Kent 14 D5
Willesborough Lees Kent 14 D5
Willesden Gtr Lon 22 C2
Willett Som'set 8 A3
Willey Shrops 39 F7
Willey Warwick 41 G6
Willey Green Surrey 21 F7
Williamscott Oxon 31 D6
Willian Herts 32 E5
Willingale Essex 33 H8
Willingdon E Sussex 13 E9
Willingham Cambs 33 A7
Willingham by Stow Lincs 52 D1
Willington Beds 32 D4
Willington Derbys 40 C4
Willington Durham 71 G6
Willington Tyne/Wear 71 D8
Willington Warwick 30 E4
Willington Corner Ches 49 F6
Willisham Tye Suffolk 34 C4
Willitoft E Riding Yorks 58 E3
Williton Som'set 16 G5
Willoughbridge Staffs 39 A8
Willoughby Lincs 53 E7
Willoughby Warwick 31 B7
Willoughby-on-the-Wolds Notts 41 C8
Willoughby Waterleys Leics 41 F7
Willoughton Lincs 52 C2
Willows Grn. Essex 33 G10
Willsbridge S Gloucs 18 D3
Willsworthy Devon 5 B6
Wilmcote Warwick 30 C3
Wilmington Devon 8 E4
Wilmington E Sussex 13 E9
Wilmington Kent 22 D5
Wilminstone Devon 4 C5
Wilmslow Ches 49 D9
Wilnecote Staffs 40 E4
Wilpshire Lancs 56 E1
Wilsden W Yorks 56 E5
Wilsford Lincs 42 A3
Wilsford Wilts 19 F8
Wilsford Wilts 19 H8
Wilsill N Yorks 57 B6
Wilsley Pound Kent 14 E2
Wilsom Hants 20 H5
Wilson Leics 41 C6
Wilsontown S Lanarks 76 B2
Wilstead Beds 32 D3
Wilsthorpe Lincs 42 D3
Wilstone Herts 32 G2
Wilton Scot Borders 77 F7
Wilton Cumb 60 C3
Wilton N Yorks 65 F6
Wilton Redcar/Clevel'd 64 C3
Wilton Wilts 10 A3
Wilton Wilts 19 E9
Wilton House, Salisbury Wilts 10 A4
Wimbish Essex 33 E8
Wimbish Green Essex 33 E9
Wimblebury Staffs 40 D2
Wimbledon Gtr Lon 22 D2
Wimblington Cambs 43 F7
Wimborne Minster Dorset 10 E3
Wimborne Minster Dorset 10 E3
Wimborne St. Giles Dorset 10 C3
Wimbotsham Norfolk 43 E9
Wimpole Hall and Home Farm, Royston Cambs 33 C6
Wimpson S'thampton 11 C6
Wimpstone Warwick 30 D4
Wincanton Som'set 9 B9
Wincham Ches 49 E7
Winchburgh W Loth 84 G2
Winchcombe Glos 30 F2
Winchelsea E Sussex 14 G4
Winchelsea Beach E Sussex 14 G4
Winchester Hants 11 B7
Winchester Cathedral Hants 11 B7
Winchet Hill Kent 14 D2
Winchfield Hants 20 F5
Winchmore Hill Bucks 21 B7
Winchmore Hill Gtr Lon 22 B3
Wincle Ches 50 F1
Wincobank S Yorks 50 C5
Windermere Cumb 61 E7
Winderton Warwick 30 D5
Windhill H'land 96 B3
Windhouse Shetl'd 113 D7
Windlehurst Gtr Man 50 D1
Windlesham Surrey 21 E7
Windley Derbys 40 A5
Windmill Hill E Sussex 13 D10
Windmill Hill Som'set 8 C5
Windrush Glos 30 G3
Windsor Berks 21 D7
Windsor N Lincs 58 G3
Windsor Castle Berks 21 D7
Windsoredge Glos 18 A5
Windygates Fife 84 D5
Windyknowe W Loth 83 H10
Windywalls Scot Borders 78 D2
Wineham W Sussex 13 C6
Winestead E Riding Yorks 59 F8
Winewall Lancs 56 D4
Winfarthing Norfolk 44 G5
Winford I of Wight 11 F8
Winford N Som'set 18 E2
Winforton Heref/Worcs 28 D3
Winfrith Newburgh Dorset 9 F10
Wing Bucks 32 F1
Wing Rutl'd 42 E1
Wingate Durham 71 G9
Wingates Gtr Man 49 B7
Wingates Northum 79 H6
Wingerworth Derbys 50 F5
Wingfield Beds 32 F2
Wingfield Suffolk 45 H6
Wingfield Wilts 18 F5
Wingham Kent 15 C7
Wingmore Kent 15 D6
Wingrave Bucks 32 G1
Winkburn Notts 51 G9
Winkfield Berks 21 D7
Winkfield Row Berks 21 D6
Winkhill Staffs 50 G2
Winklebury Hants 20 F4
Winkleigh Devon 7 F7
Winksley N Yorks 63 G7
Winkton Dorset 10 E4
Winlaton Tyne/Wear 71 D6
Winless H'land 111 D8
Winmarleigh Lancs 55 D4
Winnal Heref/Worcs 28 E5
Winnall Hants 11 B7
Winnersh Berks 20 D5
Winscales Cumb 60 B3
Winscombe N Som'set 17 F9
Winsford Ches 49 F7
Winsford Som'set 7 C10
Winsham Som'set 8 D5
Winshill Staffs 40 C4
Winskill Cumb 69 G8
Winslade Hants 20 G4
Winsley Wilts 18 E5
Winslow Bucks 31 F9
Winson Glos 30 H2
Winson Grn. W Midlands 40 G2
Winsor Hants 11 C6
Winster Cumb 61 E7
Winster Derbys 50 F4
Winston Durham 63 C6
Winston Suffolk 34 B5
Winston Green Suffolk 34 B5
Winstone Glos 30 H1
Winswell Devon 6 E5
Winter Gardens Essex 23 C7
Winterborne S Gloucs 18 C3
Winterborne Abbas Dorset 9 E8
Winterborne Bassett Wilts 19 D8
Winterborne Clenston Dorset 9 D10
Winterborne Herringston Dorset 9 F8
Winterborne Houghton Dorset 9 D10
Winterborne Kingston Dorset 10 E1
Winterborne Monkton Dorset 9 F8
Winterborne Monkton Wilts 19 D8
Winterborne Steepleton Dorset 9 F8
Winterborne Stickland Dorset 9 D10
Winterborne Whitechurch Dorset 9 D10
Winterborne Zelston Dorset 10 E1
Winterbourne Berks 20 D2
Winterbourne Dauntsey Wilts 10 A4
Winterbourne Down S Gloucs 18 D3
Winterbourne Earls Wilts 10 A4
Winterbourne Gunner Wilts 19 H8
Winterbourne Stoke Wilts 19 G7
Winterburn N Yorks 56 C4
Winteringham N Lincs 58 F5
Winterley Ches 49 G8
Wintersett W Yorks 57 G8
Wintershill Hants 11 C8
Winterton N Lincs 58 G5
Winterton-on-Sea Norfolk 45 D8
Winthorpe Lincs 53 F8
Winthorpe Notts 51 G10
Winton Bournem'th 10 E3
Winton Cumb 62 C2
Winton N Yorks 63 E9
Wintringham N Yorks 65 G6
Winwick Cambs 42 G4
Winwick Ches 49 C7
Winwick Northants 31 A8
Wirksworth Derbys 50 G4
Wirksworth Moor Derbys 50 G5
Wirswall Ches 39 A6
Wisbech Cambs 43 E7
Wisbech St. Mary Cambs 43 E7
Wisborough Green W Sussex 12 C4
Wiseton Notts 51 D9
Wishaw N Lanarks 75 B9
Wishaw Warwick 40 F3
Wisley Surrey 21 F8
Wispington Lincs 52 E5
Wissenden Kent 14 D4
Wissett Suffolk 45 H7
Wistanstow Shrops 38 G5
Wistanswick Shrops 39 C7
Wistaston Ches 49 G7
Wistaston Green Ches 49 G7
Wiston Pembs 24 E5
Wiston S Lanarks 76 D2
Wiston W Sussex 12 D5
Wistow Cambs 42 G5
Wistow N Yorks 58 E1
Wiswell Lancs 56 E2
Witcham Cambs 43 G7
Witchampton Dorset 10 D2
Witchford Cambs 43 H8
Witham Essex 34 G2
Witham Friary Som'set 18 G4
Witham on the Hill Lincs 42 D3
Withcall Lincs 52 D5
Withdean Brighton/Hove 13 E7
Witherenden Hill E Sussex 13 C10
Witheridge Devon 7 E9
Witherley Leics 40 F5
Withern Lincs 53 D7
Withernsea E Riding Yorks 59 F9
Withernwick E Riding Yorks 59 D7
Withersdale Street Suffolk 45 G6
Withersfield Suffolk 33 D9
Witherslack Cumb 61 F7
Withiel Cornw'l 3 C8
Withiel Florey Som'set 8 A1
Withington Glos 30 G2
Withington Gtr Man 49 C9
Withington Heref/Worcs 29 D6
Withington Shrops 39 D6
Withington Staffs 40 B2
Withington Green Ches 49 E9
Withleigh Devon 7 E10
Withnell Lancs 56 F1
Withybrook Warwick 41 G6
Withycombe Som'set 16 G5
Withycombe Raleigh Devon 8 F2
Withyham E Sussex 13 B8
Withypool Som'set 7 C9
Witley Surrey 12 B3
Witnesham Suffolk 34 C5
Witney Oxon 30 G5
Wittering Cambs 42 E3
Wittersham Kent 14 F3
Witton Angus 91 D6
Witton Heref/Worcs 29 B9
Witton Bridge Norfolk 45 B7
Witton Gilbert Durham 71 F7
Witton-le-Wear Durham 71 G6
Witton Park Durham 71 G6
Wiveliscombe Som'set 8 B2
Wivelrod Hants 20 H4
Wivelsfield E Sussex 13 C7
Wivelsfield Green E Sussex 13 C7
Wivenhoe Essex 34 F4
Wivenhoe Cross Essex 34 F4
Wiveton Norfolk 44 A4
Wix Essex 34 F5
Wixford Warwick 30 C2
Wixhill Shrops 39 C6
Wixoe Suffolk 33 D10
Woburn Beds 32 E2
Woburn Abbey, Woburn Beds 32 E2
Woburn Sands M/Keynes 32 E2
Woburn Wild Animal Kingdom Beds 32 E2
Wokefield Park Berks 20 E4
Woking Surrey 21 F8
Wokingham Berks 21 E6
Wolborough Devon 5 C9
Wold Newton E Riding Yorks 65 G8
Wold Newton NE Lincs 52 C5
Woldingham Surrey 22 F3
Wolfclyde S Lanarks 76 D3
Wolferton Norfolk 43 C9
Wolfhill Perth/Kinr 84 A3
Wolf's Castle Pembs 24 D4
Wolfsdale Pembs 24 D4
Woll Scot Borders 77 E7
Wollaston Northants 32 B2
Wollaston Shrops 38 D4
Wollaton Notts 41 B7
Wollaton Hall, Nottingham Notts 41 B7
Wollerton Shrops 39 B7
Wollescote W Midlands 39 G10
Wolsingham Durham 70 G5
Wolstanton Staffs 49 H9
Wolston Warwick 41 H6
Wolvercote Oxon 31 H6
Wolverhampton W Midlands 39 F10
Wolverley Heref/Worcs 39 H9
Wolverley Shrops 38 B5
Wolverton Hants 20 F3
Wolverton M/Keynes 31 D10
Wolverton Warwick 30 B4
Wolverton Common Hants 20 F3
Wolvesnewton Monmouths 17 B9
Wolvey Warwick 41 G6
Wolviston Stockton 63 B9
Wombleton N Yorks 64 F4
Wombourne Staffs 39 F9
Wombwell S Yorks 50 B5
Womenswold Kent 15 C7
Womersley N Yorks 57 G10
Wonastow Monmouths 28 G5
Wonersh Surrey 21 G8
Wonson Devon 5 B7
Wonston Hants 20 H2
Wooburn Bucks 21 C7
Wooburn Green Bucks 21 C7
Wood Dalling Norfolk 44 C4
Wood End Herts 33 F6
Wood End Warwick 30 A3
Wood End Warwick 40 F4
Wood Enderby Lincs 52 F5
Wood Field Surrey 21 F9
Wood Green Gtr Lon 22 B3
Wood Green Animal Shelter, Godmanchester Cambs 32 B5
Wood Hayes W Midlands 39 E10
Wood Lanes Ches 49 D10
Wood Norton Norfolk 44 C4
Wood Street Norfolk 45 C7
Wood Street Surrey 21 F7
Wood Walton Cambs 42 G5
Woodacott Devon 6 F4
Woodale N Yorks 62 G5
Woodbank Arg/Bute 73 F6
Woodbastwick Norfolk 45 D7
Woodbeck Notts 51 E9
Woodborough Notts 51 H8
Woodborough Wilts 19 F8
Woodbridge Dorset 9 C9
Woodbridge Suffolk 35 D6
Woodbury Devon 8 F2
Woodbury Salterton Devon 8 F2
Woodchester Glos 18 A5
Woodchurch Kent 14 E4
Woodchurch Mersey 48 D3
Woodcombe Som'set 16 G4
Woodcote Oxon 20 C4
Woodcott Hants 20 F2
Woodcroft Glos 18 B2
Woodcutts Dorset 10 C2
Woodditton Cambs 33 C9
Woodeaton Oxon 31 G7
Woodend Cumb 60 E4
Woodend Northants 31 D8
Woodend W Sussex 12 E2
Woodend Green Northants 31 D8
Woodfalls Wilts 10 B4
Woodfield Oxon 31 F7
Woodfield S Ayrs 74 E5
Woodford Cornw'l 6 E3
Woodford Devon 5 E8
Woodford Glos 18 B3
Woodford Gtr Lon 22 B4
Woodford Gtr Man 49 D9
Woodford Northants 42 H2
Woodford Bri. Gtr Lon 22 B4
Woodford Halse Northants 31 C7
Woodgate Heref/Worcs 30 B1
Woodgate Norfolk 44 D4
Woodgate W Midlands 40 G1
Woodgate W Sussex 12 E3
Woodgreen Hants 10 C4
Woodhall Herts 32 G5
Woodhall Invercl 82 G4
Woodhall N Yorks 62 E4
Woodhall Spa Lincs 52 F4
Woodham Surrey 21 E8
Woodham Ferrers Essex 23 B7
Woodham Mortimer Essex 23 A8
Woodham Walter Essex 34 H2
Woodhaven Fife 84 B6
Woodhead Aberds 99 E7
Woodhey Gtr Man 56 G2
Woodhill Shrops 39 G8
Woodhorn Northum 71 B7
Woodhouse Leics 41 D7
Woodhouse N Lincs 51 B9
Woodhouse S Yorks 51 D6
Woodhouse W Yorks 57 E7
Woodhouse W Yorks 57 F8
Woodhouse Eaves Leics 41 D7
Woodhouse Park Gtr Man 49 D9
Woodhouselee Midloth 76 A5
Woodhouselees Dumf/Gal 69 C6
Woodhouses Staffs 40 D3
Woodhurst Cambs 43 H6
Woodingdean Brighton/Hove 13 E7
Woodkirk W Yorks 57 F7
Woodland Devon 5 D8
Woodland Durham 62 B5
Woodlands Aberds 91 B8
Woodlands Dorset 10 D3
Woodlands Hants 11 C6
Woodlands N Yorks 57 C8
Woodlands S Yorks 51 B7
Woodlands Leisure Park, Dartmouth Devon 5 E9
Woodlands Park Berks 21 D6
Woodlands St. Mary Berks 19 D10
Woodlane Staffs 40 C3
Woodleigh Devon 5 F8
Woodlesford W Yorks 57 F8
Woodley Berks 20 D5
Woodley Gtr Man 49 C10
Woodmancote Glos 18 B4
Woodmancote Glos 30 H2
Woodmancote Glos 30 F1
Woodmancote W Sussex 12 E1
Woodmancote W Sussex 13 D6
Woodmancott Hants 20 G3
Woodmansey E Riding Yorks 59 E6
Woodmansterne Surrey 22 F2
Woodminton Wilts 10 B3
Woodnesborough Kent 15 C8
Woodnewton Northants 42 F3
Woodplumpton Lancs 55 E5
Woodrising Norfolk 44 E3
Wood's Green E Sussex 13 B10
Woodseaves Shrops 39 B7
Woodseaves Staffs 39 C8
Woodsend Wilts 19 D9
Woodsetts S Yorks 51 D7
Woodsford Dorset 9 E9
Woodside Aberd C 99 H9
Woodside Aberds 99 D10
Woodside Berks 21 D7
Woodside Fife 84 D6
Woodside Hants 11 E6
Woodside Herts 32 H5
Woodside Perth/Kinr 90 H3
Woodside Farm and Wildfowl Park, Luton Beds 32 G3
Woodside of Arbeadie Aberds 91 B8
Woodstock Oxon 31 G6
Woodstock Pembs 24 D5
Woodthorpe Derbys 51 E6
Woodthorpe Leics 41 D7
Woodthorpe Lincs 53 D7
Woodthorpe C of York 58 D1
Woodton Norfolk 45 F6
Woodtown Devon 6 D5
Woodtown Devon 6 D5
Woodvale Mersey 55 G3
Woodville Derbys 40 D5
Woodyates Dorset 10 C3
Woofferton Shrops 29 B6
Wookey Som'set 18 G2
Wookey Hole Som'set 18 G2
Wookey Hole Caves & Papermill, Wells Som'set 18 G2
Wool Dorset 9 F10
Woolacombe Devon 6 B5
Woolage Green Kent 15 D7
Woolaston Glos 18 B2
Woolavington Som'set 17 G8
Woolbeding W Sussex 12 C2
Wooldale W Yorks 50 B3
Wooler Northum 78 E4
Woolfardisworthy Devon 6 D4
Woolfardisworthy Devon 7 F9
Woolfords Cottages S Lanarks 76 B3
Woolhampton Berks 20 E3
Woolhope Heref/Worcs 29 E7
Woolhope Cockshoot Heref/Worcs 29 E7
Woolland Dorset 9 D9
Woollaton Devon 6 E5
Woolley Bath/NE Som'set 18 E4
Woolley Cambs 32 A4
Woolley Cornw'l 6 E3
Woolley Derbys 50 F5
Woolley W Yorks 57 G8
Woolmer Green Herts 32 G5
Woolmere Green Heref/Worcs 30 B1
Woolpit Suffolk 34 B3
Woolscott Warwick 31 B6
Woolsington Tyne/Wear 71 D6
Woolstanwood Ches 49 G7
Woolstaston Shrops 38 F5
Woolsthorpe Lincs 41 B10
Woolsthorpe Lincs 42 C2
Woolston Ches 49 D7
Woolston Devon 5 F8
Woolston Shrops 38 G5
Woolston Shrops 38 C4
Woolston S'thampton 11 C7
Woolstone M/Keynes 32 E1
Woolstone Oxon 19 C9
Woolton Mersey 48 D5
Woolton Hill Hants 20 E2
Woolverstone Suffolk 34 E5
Woolverton Som'set 18 F4
Woolwich Gtr Lon 22 D4
Woonton Heref/Worcs 28 C4
Wooperton Northum 78 E5
Woore Shrops 39 A8
Wootton Beds 32 D3
Wootton Hants 10 E5
Wootton Heref/Worcs 28 C4
Wootton Kent 15 D7
Wootton N Lincs 59 G6
Wootton Northants 31 C9
Wootton Oxon 31 G6
Wootton Oxon 20 A2
Wootton Shrops 38 H5
Wootton Shrops 38 C4
Wootton Staffs 39 C9
Wootton Staffs 50 H3
Wootton Surrey 21 G9
Wootton Bassett Wilts 19 C7
Wootton Bridge I of Wight 11 E8
Wootton Common I of Wight 11 E8
Wootton Courtenay Som'set 7 B10
Wootton Fitzpaine Dorset 8 E5
Wootton Green Suffolk 35 A6
Wootton Rivers Wilts 19 E8
Wootton St. Lawrence Hants 20 F3
Wootton Wawen Warwick 30 B3
Worcester Heref/Worcs 29 C9
Worcester Cathedral Heref/Worcs 29 C9
Worcester Park Gtr Lon 22 E2
Wordsley W Midlands 39 G9
Worfield Shrops 39 F8
Work Orkney 112 G5
Workington Cumb 60 B2
Worksop Notts 51 E7
Worlaby N Lincs 59 G6
World's End Berks 20 D2
Worle N Som'set 17 E8
Worleston Ches 49 G7
Worlingham Suffolk 45 G8
Worlington Suffolk 33 A9
Worlingworth Suffolk 35 B6
Wormald Green N Yorks 57 B8
Wormbridge Heref/Worcs 28 E5
Wormegay Norfolk 43 D9
Wormelow Tump Heref/Worcs 28 E5
Wormhill Derbys 50 E3
Wormiehills Angus 91 H7
Wormingford Essex 34 E3
Worminghall Bucks 31 H8
Wormington Glos 30 E2
Worminster Som'set 18 G2
Wormit Fife 84 B5
Wormleighton Warwick 31 C6
Wormley Herts 33 H6
Wormley Surrey 12 B3
Wormley West End Herts 33 H6
Wormshill Kent 14 C3
Wormsley Heref/Worcs 28 D5
Worplesdon Surrey 21 F7
Worrall S Yorks 50 C5
Worsbrough S Yorks 50 B5
Worsbrough Common S Yorks 50 B5
Worsley Gtr Man 49 B8
Worstead Norfolk 45 C7
Worsthorne Lancs 56 E3
Worston Lancs 56 D2
Worswell Devon 5 F6
Worth Kent 15 C8
Worth W Sussex 13 B7
Worth Matravers Dorset 10 G2
Wortham Suffolk 44 H4
Worthen Shrops 38 E4
Worthenbury Wrex 48 H5
Worthing Norfolk 44 D3
Worthing W Sussex 12 E5
Worthington Leics 41 C6
Worting Hants 20 F4
Wortley S Yorks 50 C5
Wortley W Yorks 57 E7
Worton N Yorks 62 E4
Worton Wilts 19 F6
Wortwell Norfolk 45 G6
Wotherton Shrops 38 E3
Wotter Devon 5 D6
Wotton-under-Edge Glos 18 B4
Wotton Underwood Bucks 31 G8
Woughton on the Green M/Keynes 32 E1
Wouldham Kent 14 B2
Wrabness Essex 34 E5
Wrafton Devon 6 C5
Wragby Lincs 52 E4
Wragby W Yorks 57 G9
Wragholme Lincs 53 C6
Wramplingham Norfolk 44 E5
Wrangbrook W Yorks 57 G9
Wrangham Aberds 98 E6
Wrangle Lincs 53 G7
Wrangle Bank Lincs 53 G7
Wrangle Lowgate Lincs 53 G7
Wrangway Som'set 8 C3
Wrantage Som'set 8 B5
Wrawby N Lincs 52 B3
Wraxall Dorset 9 D7
Wraxall N Som'set 17 D9
Wraxall Som'set 18 H3
Wray Lancs 55 B6
Wraysbury Berks 21 D8
Wrayton Lancs 61 G9
Wrea Green Lancs 55 E3
Wreay Cumb 61 B7
Wreay Cumb 69 F7
Wrecclesham Surrey 21 G6
Wrekenton Tyne/Wear 71 E7
Wrelton N Yorks 64 F5
Wrenbury Ches 49 H6
Wrench Green N Yorks 65 F7
Wreningham Norfolk 44 F5
Wrentham Suffolk 45 G8
Wrenthorpe W Yorks 57 F8
Wrentnall Shrops 38 E5
Wressle E Riding Yorks 58 E3
Wressle N Lincs 52 B2
Wrestlingworth Beds 32 D5
Wretham Norfolk 44 G3
Wretton Norfolk 43 F9
Wrexham Wrex 48 G4
Wrexham Industrial Estate Wrex 48 H4
Wribbenhall Heref/Worcs 39 H8
Wrightington Bar Lancs 55 G5
Wrinehill Staffs 49 H8
Wrington N Som'set 17 E9
Writhlington Bath/NE Som'set 18 F4
Writtle Essex 33 H9
Wrockwardine Shrops 39 D7
Wroot N Lincs 51 B9
Wrotham Kent 23 F6
Wrotham Heath Kent 23 F6
Wroughton Thamesd'n 19 C8
Wroxall I of Wight 11 G8
Wroxall Warwick 30 A4
Wroxeter Shrops 39 E6
Wroxham Norfolk 45 D7
Wroxham Barns, Hoveton Norfolk 45 C7
Wroxton Oxon 31 D6
Wyaston Derbys 40 A3
Wyberton Lincs 43 A6
Wyboston Beds 32 C4
Wych Cross E Sussex 13 B8
Wychbold Heref/Worcs 29 B10
Wyck Hants 12 B1
Wyck Rissington Glos 30 F3
Wycoller Lancs 56 E4
Wycomb Leics 41 C9
Wycombe Marsh Bucks 21 B6
Wyddial Herts 33 E6
Wye Kent 14 D5
Wyesham Monmouths 29 G6
Wyfordby Leics 41 D9
Wyke Dorset 9 B9
Wyke Shrops 39 E7
Wyke Surrey 21 F7
Wyke W Yorks 57 F6
Wyke Regis Dorset 9 G8
Wykeham N Yorks 65 F7
Wykeham N Yorks 65 G6
Wyken W Midlands 40 G5
Wykey Shrops 38 C4
Wylam Northum 71 D6
Wyld Court Gardens Berks 20 D3
Wylde Green W Midlands 40 F3
Wyllie Caerph 17 B6
Wylye Wilts 19 H7
Wymering Portsm'th 11 D9
Wymeswold Leics 41 C8
Wymington Beds 32 B2
Wymondham Leics 42 D1
Wymondham Norfolk 44 E5
Wynbunbury Ches 49 H8
Wyndham Bridg 16 B4
Wynford Eagle Dorset 9 E7
Wyre Piddle Heref/Worcs 30 D1
Wysall Notts 41 C8
Wythall Heref/Worcs 40 H2
Wytham Oxon 31 H6
Wythburn Cumb 61 C6
Wythenshawe Gtr Man 49 D9
Wythop Mill Cumb 60 B4
Wyton Cambs 32 A5
Wyverstone Suffolk 34 B4
Wyverstone Street Suffolk 34 B4
Wyville Lincs 42 C1
Wyvis Lodge H'land 104 E3

Y

Y-Ffrith Denbs 47 D10
Yaddlethorpe N Lincs 52 B1
Yafford I of Wight 11 F7
Yafforth N Yorks 63 E8
Yalding Kent 14 C1
Yanworth Glos 30 G2
Yapham E Riding Yorks 58 C3
Yapton W Sussex 12 E3
Yarburgh Lincs 53 C6
Yarcombe Devon 8 D4
Yard Som'set 16 H5
Yardley W Midlands 40 G3
Yardley Gobion Northants 31 D9
Yardley Hastings Northants 32 C1
Yardro Powys 28 C3
Yarkhill Heref/Worcs 29 D7
Yarlet Staffs 39 C10
Yarlington Som'set 9 B8
Yarlside Cumb 55 B2
Yarm Stockton 63 C9
Yarmouth I of Wight 11 F6
Yarnbrook Wilts 18 F5
Yarnfield Staffs 39 B9
Yarnscombe Devon 7 D6
Yarnton Oxon 31 G6
Yarpole Heref/Worcs 28 B5
Yarrow Scot Borders 77 E6
Yarrow Feus Scot Borders 77 E6
Yarsop Heref/Worcs 28 D5
Yarwell Northants 42 F3
Yate S Gloucs 18 C4
Yateley Hants 21 E6
Yatesbury Wilts 19 D7
Yattendon Berks 20 D3
Yatton Heref/Worcs 28 B5
Yatton Heref/Worcs 29 E7
Yatton N Som'set 17 E9
Yatton Keynall Wilts 18 D5
Yaverland I of Wight 11 F9
Yaxham Norfolk 44 D4
Yaxley Cambs 42 F4
Yaxley Suffolk 34 A5
Yazor Heref/Worcs 28 D5
Yeading Gtr Lon 21 C9
Yeadon W Yorks 57 D7
Yealand Conyers Lancs 61 G8
Yealand Redmayne Lancs 61 G8
Yealmpton Devon 5 E6
Yearby Redcar/Clevel'd 64 B4
Yearsley N Yorks 64 G3
Yeaton Shrops 38 D5
Yeaveley Derbys 40 A3
Yedingham N Yorks 65 G6
Yelford Oxon 20 A1
Yelland Devon 6 C5
Yelling Cambs 32 B5
Yelvertoft Northants 41 H7
Yelverton Devon 5 D6
Yelverton Norfolk 45 E6
Yenston Som'set 9 B9
Yeo Mill Devon 7 D9
Yeoford Devon 7 G8
Yeolmbridge Cornw'l 4 B4
Yeovil Som'set 9 C7
Yeovil Marsh Som'set 9 C7
Yeovilton Som'set 9 B7
Yerbeston Pembs 24 F5
Yesnaby Orkney 112 G3
Yetlington Northum 78 G5
Yetminster Dorset 9 C7
Yettington Devon 8 F2
Yetts o'Muckhart Clack 84 D2
Yielden Beds 32 B3
Yieldshields S Lanarks 76 B1
Yiewsley Gtr Lon 21 C8
Ynys-boeth Rh Cyn Taff 16 B5
Ynys-ddu Caerph 17 B6
Ynys-meudwy Neath P Talb 27 H7
Ynysgyfflog Gwyn 37 D6
Ynyshir Rh Cyn Taff 16 B5
Ynyslas Ceredig'n 37 F6
Ynystawe Swan 16 A1
Ynysybwl Rh Cyn Taff 16 B5
Yockenthwaite N Yorks 62 G4
Yockleton Shrops 38 D4
Yokefleet E Riding Yorks 58 F4
Yoker C of Glasg 83 H6
Yonder Bognie Aberds 98 D5
York C of York 58 C1
York Minster C of York 58 C2
York Town Surrey 21 E6
Yorkletts Kent 14 B5
Yorkley Glos 29 H7
Yorkshire Museum C of York 58 C1
Yorkshire Sculpture Park, Wakefield W Yorks 57 G7
Yorton Shrops 39 C6
Youlgreave Derbys 50 F4
Youlstone Devon 6 E3
Youlthorpe E Riding Yorks 58 C3
Youlton N Yorks 57 B9
Young Wood Lincs 52 E4
Young's End Essex 33 G10
Yoxall Staffs 40 D3
Yoxford Suffolk 35 B7
Ysbyty-Cynfyn Ceredig'n 37 H7
Ysbyty Ifan Conwy 47 H8
Ysbyty Ystwyth Ceredig'n 27 A7
Ysceifiog Flints 48 E2
Yspitty Carms 25 G10
Ystalyfera Neath P Talb 27 H7
Ystrad Rh Cyn Taff 16 B4
Ystrad Aeron Ceredig'n 26 C5
Ystrad-mynach Caerph 17 B6
Ystradfellte Powys 27 G9
Ystradffin Carms 27 D7
Ystradgynlais Powys 27 G7
Ystradmeurig Ceredig'n 27 B7
Ystradowen Carms 27 G7
Ystradowen V of Glam 16 D5
Ystumtuen Ceredig'n 37 H7
Ythanbank Aberds 99 E9
Ythanwells Aberds 98 E6
Ythsie Aberds 99 E8

Z

Zeal Monachorum Devon 7 F8
Zeals Wilts 9 A9
Zelah Cornw'l 3 D7
Zennor Cornw'l 2 F3